Kairaba

Kairaba

Dawda K Jawara

Alhaji Sir Dawda K Jawara

First published in Great Britain in 2009 by
Alhaji Sir Dawda Kairaba Jawara, 77 Gordon Road,
Haywards Heath,
West Sussex, RH16 1EL, United Kingdom

Copyright © 2009 by Dawda Kairaba Jawara

The moral rights of the author have been asserted.

All rights reserved.
No part of this book may be reproduced, stored in a retrieval system,
or transmitted, in any form or by any means, electronic,
mechanical, photocopying, recording, or otherwise,
without the prior permission in writing of the publisher, nor be
otherwise circulated in any form of binding or cover other than that
in which it is published and without a similar condition including this
condition being imposed on the subsequent purchaser.

British Library Cataloguing-in-Publication Data
A catalogue record for this book is available from the British Library.

ISBN: 978-0-9563968-0-8

Printed and bound in Great Britain by
domtom publishing Ltd, Burgess Hill, West Sussex

I dedicate this book to my parents Mawdo Almamy and Mama, my guardian Ebrima Jallow (Pa Yoma) and my teacher M D Salla.

Contents

Acknowledgements ix

1. Kairo 1
2. The bells of the brave saints 21
3. My father's heart is troubled 27
4. A safe but hungry season 39
5. Galloping my horse 50
6. After Bathurst, when do we get to Banjul? 61
7. Influential men in my life 71
8. Master Salla keeps me in school 86
9. The future belongs to us 101
10. Charles Dickens and World War II 114
11. Peace at last 129
12. Labouring and waiting 136
13. Achimota, Glasgow and Edinburgh 148
14. Abuko 169
15. Treks and a fateful reconnection 178
16. The people bring me a message 185
17. In the throes of politics 197
18. Making haste slowly 219
19. Independence 237
20. International relations 248
21. Forging ahead to greater things 271
22. Grappling with development 284
23. Relations with Senegal 298

24	30 July 1981: assault on democracy 308
25	Restructuring and recovery 327
26	The rise and fall of the Senegambia confederation 341
27	The early 1990s 359
28	Democracy overturned 379
29	Campaign for the restoration of democracy 389
30	15 Birchen Lane 406
31	The new millennium 418
32	Reconciliation and homecoming 429
33	40 Atlantic Boulevard: Retirement 439

Appendix I: The Independence Manifesto of the
  People's Progressive Party   455

Appendix II: Declaration of the People's Progressive Party
  (PPP) on the Transition back to Democracy   458

Appendix III: Former Presidents (Office, Allowances and other
  Benefits) Act 2006   474

Index 481

Acknowledgements

Having been at the service of the Gambian people for over forty-one years, as a veterinary officer, chief veterinary officer, minister of education, premier, prime minister and president, I feel obliged to put on record the defining moments of those years – as well as the formative years that shaped me as a person.

Writing this book has not been an easy task. All the same, I have tried as much as possible to put together those momentous events that surely must have been exercising the minds of Gambians for quite some time now.

With the assistance of family, friends and dedicated professionals I was able to complete my autobiography.

I am grateful to Nana Grey-Johnson for his enthusiasm and research. I am also grateful to my editorial panel consisting of Fodeh Baldeh, Swaebou Conateh and Momodou F Singhateh. They all deserve commendation for devoting their time to help me complete the book. Their input was invaluable.

The support of my family has, of course, been overwhelming. My daughter Nema, provided me with many documents and photographs which have added colour to the book. My son Ebrima oversaw the business aspects of the book diligently and provided some final editorial input, which went a long way towards the success of the publication of this book.

Finally, I wish to thank my wives Chilel, Njaimeh and Augusta of blessed memory, and all my children for their unfailing love and support.

1
Kairo

I have been an early riser all my life. At a tender age I perfected the practice of rising every morning for the early morning prayers and follow hard behind the heels of my father towards our village mosque. With early habits why then did I wait until my eighty-second year of life to begin to tell the story, the whole story of a life in large part spent thinking of how to better direct the lives and fortunes of my people and country?

I often ran to catch up with him. I could hear him recite in Arabic, with long groan-like utterances of prayers in Mandinka, as I trailed him. I was a healthy boy, bright eyed and of average build and able to keep up, even though once in a while I had to run to keep pace, especially when the hoarse voice of the caller was fading with the last notes of the *athan* (call to prayer) from the steps of the mosque.

We were never alone. People – men in white robes, older boys still in yesterday's clothes and women – came from every corner of the darkness. We all went in the same direction and that common mission held a certain excitement for me every morning. I was assured that as long as my father was doing it, I was also doing the right thing – giving up my sleep for prayers.

As I look back over the years, there is perhaps some fortune in waiting this long to tell the story of my life and times. First, there is more to tell and, second, the extra time might translate into the wisdom to judge if my life has made any difference at all.

Perhaps it is proper that I start telling my beginnings by going back to 16 May 1924[1] when I was born in the *musu bungo* – the house my father built for his wives and all their children in the family compound in the bucolic, dusty but serene setting of Barajaly in Niani District. Niani was one of seven districts that made up the MacCarthy Island Province, one of the six administrative divisions of the Protectorate. Like the colony which was the seat of government, the British had official title since 1884 and 1889 when the European powers partitioned Africa according to agreements arrived at in Berlin and Paris.

---

[1] This is the best estimate of my date of birth.

Georgetown on MacCarthy Island, the capital town of the Province, dominated this section of the River Gambia, yet small villages thrived as important trading posts (*tenda* in Mandinka) or as administrative centres for government business. Barajaly where I came from was situated on the north bank of the river and Walikunda on its south bank.

Barajaly was the bedroom community and Walikunda, across the river, was the typical provincial trading post where European firms had set up shops and their agents had large compounds fenced off into what we called *secco* for the collection of groundnuts during the bustling trade season. From early May through June and July, farmers were busy weeding and clearing their farms ready for the first rains. From August to October, they were nursing the plants and watching their farms turn from dusty brown to green. In November, they dug up the harvest and the floodgate of traders, buyers, agents, donkey drivers, shopkeepers and head carriers would descend on the village. From that time until April, the trade season was on – selling, buying, bartering and hauling groundnuts. Pyramids of groundnuts grew everywhere and the long columns of head carriers soon filled the river cutters with groundnuts.

Agriculture was the mainstay of all the families in the area and while one or two farmers attempted varying the cropping of their land with cotton, sorghum and millet, groundnuts remained the single most important cash crop in the MacCarthy Island Province. The area had seen the face of the white man for nearly four hundred years following the penetration and exploration by Europeans who engaged in trade with cowries, gold, beeswax, palm oil, livestock and, most callously of all, human beings during the Transatlantic slave trade. The trade in slaves to this day remains the most hideous and dehumanising ever conceived by human beings.

I may have trained as a scientist but history never ceased to intrigue me. I read with relish the accounts by the Gambian historian Florence Mahoney who I first knew as a young girl at the Methodist Girls High School in the early 1940s in Bathurst. Florence wrote about Portuguese sailors like Diego Gomez, who rode sail cloth caravelles up the River Gambia as early as 1458, around the same time Alvise Cadamosto[2] reached The Gambia. The famed Scottish doctor, Mungo Park, set up camp at Pisania in Sami district. An obelisk at Karantaba marks the starting point to his journey to find the source of the River Niger. All that long ago, through travel and contact between the peoples, the world had begun shrinking into the village that it is today with swift worldwide air links, internet technology and a touch button global information system.

---

[2] Italian explorer in the service of Henry the Navigator.

Walikunda where he had fenced off a small clearing with palm fronds and bamboo sticks that really was the groundnut *secco* next to his shop. I spent many thrilling hours beside my father in that shop and behind that fenced depot. Our groundnut pyramid rose right opposite the shop and *secco* of the LCA trading firm. The trader at the LCA shop was a Bathurst man named Ebrima Jallow who everyone called Pa Yoma. He and my father had become great friends and as fate would have it, he would become an important figure in my own life.

My father quickly mastered the retailing and purchasing of the main cash crop, groundnuts. I was seven, nearly eight, years old when I first began appreciating the skill and dexterity which my father had developed in his dealings with so many sellers and buyers at the same time. He had quickly learnt to handle the new paper money issued by the Currency Board. He spent whole days haggling and negotiating and weighing groundnuts. Doing all of that with good cheer and accommodation of the strings of people who came and went in the balmy 32° Centigrade heat inside the shop demanded some endurance.

There was a constant flow of people in and out of the shop. The shoppers gave my father money and took away cutlasses, fertilisers, fabrics, tobacco, nails, oil, tinned foodstuffs, soaps and cloth from the array of goods that filled the shelves behind a long wooden counter. It was amazing how he managed the charm that welcomed all those people so that they could come again. No wonder when the strain of it all began to tell on him, he quickly resorted to the services of two shop clerks, men from Bathurst who came every trade season to help him keep his stock and cash books in order. One of the men I remember very well was Pa Abdou Karim John.

A mix of my father's physical energy and the thoughts that spun inside his head always resulted in interesting new things. His courage was bigger than his small build. He stood no taller than five feet and six inches off the ground and his fair skin always the same shade no matter how long he spent under the burning sun or sweated carrying out his business. As hard work paid off he acquired more land and married more wives. When he married Sira Sukoh, his eighth wife, he housed her in the *musu bungo* at Barajaly where she joined Mama Fatty, Nna Jarai and Maa Nii. The land he had acquired was now more than twenty acres and he busied himself clearing it and ploughing and planting it with the help of hired hands. The land became known as *Almamy Leh* – meaning Almamy's valley.

The land was truly his, which ownership was upheld in a test case in December 2002, following the erroneous allocation of a portion of Almamy

Leh by the district chief to one Momodou Lamin Yafa of Walikunda. Fura Jawara, the *alkalo* (village headman) of Barajaly, and the whole Jawara *kabilo* rose to contest the allocation to the satisfaction of the District Tribunal sitting in Sare Ngai village. The tribunal under the presidency of Alhaji Fallai Baldeh passed judgement pronouncing the illegality of the encroachment of a portion of Almamy Leh.

My father's good nature as a keen negotiator with a fair and gentle spirit won him many friends. His agency work with Blain and Madi had brought him prosperity. His farms produced rice and groundnuts and his shops and seed depots were full. He did well and his family prospered. There was plenty for his family and there was peace in his home.

I was born at the height of that growth and prosperity. Mandinka tradition believes that every child comes into a household with his or her own helping of good luck. Perhaps to give thanks for the privilege and blessing, my father named me by one name only, Kairaba – the great blessing; the big peace; the peace bringer! I was given no other name and that made both me and the name special in the family.

However, while in Barajaly the name Kairaba was a revered one, it would be a bane in Bathurst a few years later. In the Colony capital, I became the butt of a great deal of teasing from the boys in the Half Die quarter where I went to live in the household of Pa Yoma Jallow. The street boys teased me to frustration by distorting my beautiful name, Kairaba, to sound like *kairabe,* which in the Mandinka tongue means 'How are you?' As if that was not enough, some more terrible boys added the response *"Kaira dorong"* – "I am all right". I wished they had stopped there but they went on mischievously and provocatively adding *"Sumo le?"* – "How are all at home?" and *"Ibi je!"* – "All are well!"

Thankfully, the teasing was only verbal and no one actually touched, jostled or hit me. However, the frustration of it all kept me from mingling with my fellow pupils. In fact, I had no knowledge of the languages in Bathurst when I first arrived. I spoke only Mandinka. It was excruciating because the taunting went on and on and soon began to wear down my self-perception as a provincial boy among townspeople. I kept to myself. I blamed my troubles squarely on condescension of the Bathurst people with those of us from the Protectorate. It was a form of intolerance I knew was just wrong. It was discrimination that was not being taken for what it really was. I could see no reason why someone's *bona fide* name or his mother tongue should become a source of molestation and discomfort for him.

I did not complain to anyone, not even Pa Yoma Jallow. I did not want the old man or anyone else to think I was a push-over. To avoid harassment from the boys on Buckle Street, I would go about my business as quickly as I could and duck back into the house. The incidents became fewer the more I kept on my side of the street away from those boys, some of whom, with the endless hours they spent out there, seemed to live on the streets. I waited patiently for my elder brother, Basadi, who soon arrived from Barajaly and was spending a few days in town.

Basadi was immediately perceptive of a major drawback on my side. I needed language to fit in. How true! My protection and survival were evidently compromised by the fact that I knew nothing of the language of the environment. I immediately took it on to get to grips with the town language – Wollof. I had to learn the *lingua franca* of Banjul the hard way having never spoken anything else but Mandinka in Barajaly and, as a matter of fact, knowing no other language in which to communicate within my new surroundings.

From then on, every moment became one for education, even the tormenting ones. But necessity being the mother of invention, I forced the Wollof words out of my mouth mastering, naturally of course, the swear words well before the good and clean sentences that more suited my nature. It was a survival plan any stranger in a hostile new place would learn. That way, Wollof came to me faster than Pa Yoma Jallow or his wife Ya Fatou Jobarteh had imagined possible for me to pick up. As the Wollof say, *Ku buga deh wehu.*[5] I realised that the street boys were warm and friendly people who simply went about having fun their own way. After a long season of talking and laughing and cursing with them and, like them, I was tacitly passed as fit to be a one of the Half Die boys. I had worked through the rites of passage to fit my surroundings.

I asked Basadi if he remembered my father giving me any other name. He should know. He was at least eight years older than I was. He confirmed that Father had given me only one name - Kairaba. However, he advised that if the name was becoming a problem for me I should add other names. He suggested that I take the name Saihou from our father's close friend, the great marabout, Karang Sekou Alkali of Kunting. I knew of Karang Sekou and knew he and my father were indeed very close friends. Basadi thought that I should also take our father's name, Almamy. He said that both men would be proud to hear that I had on my own decided to take

---
[5] Roughly translated to mean: facing death, one would fight for survival

on their names. He said they would consider it highly, indeed, that in my sojourn in the white man's town, I had done them such a great honour.

After I arrived in Bathurst, Pa Yoma wasted no time in making arrangements for me to go to school. I found myself already registered at Mohammedan School where I entered at the Sub-Standard class in 1932, even though a third of the school year had gone. Mohammedan School was slightly different from the *daara* I had started at home at 37 Wellington Street. They had a register and we had to give our names to the teacher. Although Pa Yoma had no objection to my additional names, he continued to call me Kairaba anyway. My first days at Mohammedan were unforgettable. Pa Yoma had walked me down Buckle Street the first day and handed me over to a female teacher. After that I came on my own and on registration day in class I stood in line with four or five other boys who were joining late as I was.

I walked to school marching in the middle of the sandy roadway and sort of feeling with the majesty of the giant silk cotton trees lining the street. I had took on a burst of courage. Buckle Street was cut off from the main section of the Half Die quarter by a virtual forest of those giant trees. The paths underneath the sprawling canopy were shaded with a cool and gentle breeze always graciously bathing my face until I emerged into the shock of the heat of the searing sun on the other end.

There were sixteen or so boys in my class, mostly of my age or a little older. Two or three were dressed like boys from the Protectorate. The rest were town boys, Wollofs mainly, though one or two spoke very good Mandinka. Our class was one of the four, with Standards 1 to 3, ranged along a long open hall with each class separated from the other by large, wooden screens as dividers. It was not an easy walk into a classroom of boys screaming and shouting in a language I did not understand. It was English, another town language, that completely left me baffled. Then suddenly the attention of the class was drawn to the teacher's table in front.

"Good morning, Class," the woman said.

"Good morning, Teacher," everyone else yelled back.

"Class, this morning we are going to welcome four new boys to Mohammedan School Sub-Standard Class for the 1932 school year," the teacher said pointing to us.

"You are welcome to Mohammedan School," they screeched back.

We stood bewildered hoping it was not anything terrible we had done already. She asked us to sit down. The short and rounded motherly figure of a teacher came round to take down our names.

"What is your name?" she asked when she reached me with her note pad and violet pencil in hand.

I stood up and stared blankly at her. I did not understand the first sentence of English words spoken to me in school. Somehow when she whetted the tip of the violet pencil on her lips I had figured she wanted to write something down and it was probably my name she wanted. Eager eyes from all over the room glared at me as the class waited for my answer. She repeated herself with signs as if she was helping a deaf and dumb person to grasp what she was asking.

"*Itondi?*"[6] one of the older boys prompted softly from behind in Mandinka.

"Saihou Almamy Jawara," I replied very loudly and confidently from where I stood squashed between a bench and the low table.

There was a hush disrupted only by a single short-lived snicker from the back among some bigger boys. The teacher who later became known to us as Mrs Riley enunciated my name aloud emphasising the syllables one after the other – SAI-HOU AL-MA-MY JA-WA-RA as she wrote it down in a way to assure that she spelt my names correctly. When she finished writing and went on to the next boy, a wind of relief rushed into my lungs. I deeply appreciated someone who accepted my name without making any mockery of it. While the other boys gave their names, I was feeling that finally I had found names that fitted the moment, the place and the time; and that would help me become part of the crowd rather than to stick out like a sore thumb. Even warmer was the fact that those were names of people of great meaning in my life. Bathurst began not to seem so bad after all.

I remember the classroom being muggy. It smelt a little sweaty from the number of bodies so close together in the heat within the thick walls of the room. Not all the clothes the boys came in were clean clothes. Ya Fatou Jobarteh, my new mother in Bathurst, kept me well dressed and I was satisfied with my grey flannel over shirt. She 'greased' my face, hands and feet with cooking oil from the bottles in her kitchen at home. We went to school barefooted and did not care a wink at all. In fact, I saw only one boy in Standard 1 who came to school in rubber sandals. Someone told me later that he was the son of a prosperous Wollof trader. Otherwise, under every table many bare ankles and toes blanched with dust lay flat on the cement floor.

That week, Basadi came by after a couple of days and I could not wait to tell him how I did it. One thing was certain: I was not going to change

---

[6] "What is your name?" in Mandinka.

my name again. But I have lived long enough to take back those words of oath when the challenge of the absolute need to change my name again played itself out in my life. Two more times I would change my name from Saihou Almamy to David Kwesi and again to Dawda Kairaba.

At school, I learnt the English alphabet and began a fascination with spelling and reading. I learnt to identify numbers, and putting them together to make large complex numbers was fun. Subtracting them or adding them up and making them bigger by multiplication was even greater fun. My place in the class began to be defined as I started to memorise and retain things. I answered questions in class and asked questions as well; and that curiosity, which I must have got from my father, began to help define my place in the class. In my behaviour, I copied what I saw around me at home allowing the quiet discipline to speak for me and avoiding wherever there was noise and unnecessary disagreement. I began to speak in connected and coherent sentences, first, in Wollof and then in English. By the end of the 1932 class and half way through Standard 1 in 1933, I was already helping one or two boys with class exercises and homework.

Whatever the town boys thought of my protectorate origins began to change. I had quietly asserted my place among them without ever being involved in a scuffle. I had never had to fight to make myself understood. My way to shrug off the one or two teasers that persisted was not to answer back but to love school even more. The wisdom of that patient and forbearing manner was amply rewarded when those who once bothered me soon changed their attitude when they realised my gentler ways asked for their respectful engagement. Many of my tormentors turned to be my friends.

Pa Yoma said that children took on the character and nature of the person or object they were named after. If that was true, then the value of quiet and peaceful things began to appeal to me. Kairaba was, indeed, the great peace and it seemed my nature and demeanour was living up to the name. My results in school improved and Pa Yoma took them with him upcountry every year to interpret them to my father. As time went on, I found I had the choice to keep my original name. So, I did not shed Kairaba altogether. Rather when I went back on holiday in Barajaly and Walikunda I loudly and proudly became Kairaba. But as soon as the open Bedford lorry rolled back from holidays down Clifton Road at the north entrance to Bathurst, I was Saihou Almamy again.

The peace of mind it brought me could not be compared to anything else. It allowed me room to concentrate in school and to diligently pursue what I wished to accomplish. I began living the peace my father had intended when he gave me a name, Kairaba, the bringer of peace and of blessing.

I made friends down my street and around the neighbourhood. Mam Laity Secka and I became close buddies and we took walks and chatted for hours when I found the time. His brother, the ever popular Kuru Boy Secka, had a deft hand in bicycle repairs and made a living by that trade. Mam Laity and I had a whistle between us and he invented it as his fond caricature of the sounds he said the bedridden Qur'anic master, Sering Mahtarr John, made when he wanted to call me to his side. There were other younger boys who stood out in the neighbourhood. I remember a tall Catholic youth named Tanor Senghore living with his mother Ya Fatou Njie Peew in the same compound as Mam Laity.

I made friends with Jikiba Manneh, the old shopkeeper at the CFAO store at 34 Wellington Street. His watchman, Pa Miguel, was a foul-mouthed old man from Guinea Bissau. He was a joker and a funny man and Jikiba told him that there was a *sanaw-ya* relationship between the Mannehs and the Jawaras. *Sanaw-ya* is the special social relationship between individuals and between *kabilo* families known as 'the joking relationship' in which ancient rival clans now long reconciled express their ancient rivalries instead in jocular taunts and name calling. There was never the intention to hurt; just to create fun.

People would demand clothes and trinkets from each other as payment for favours a great father had done someone else's grandfather. The great grandfather on one line could have given a place of shelter to the great grandfather who had arrived freshly on the caravan trails. It was always great fun when the grandchildren argued whose ancestors had arrived first. They would trade caste jokes that would normally not be tolerated from anyone outside that circle.

Although Pa Miguel was not a Manneh, he worked for a Manneh and, therefore, decided he would cross the line of custom and, in spite of our age difference, play *sanaw-ya* with me. Every time I passed by he would throw one terrible curse at me – an extremely rude aspersion on my ancestry. But because of his age I was too young to give him one back. The fact was I did not know where in his lineage to dig from what he left behind in Guinea Bissau. So, I would respectfully shrug him off by saying: ('Oh, quiet, you ugly, old and foolish man!') He loved that; he would crack up with laughter and would clown around with me as I went in to greet Jikiba. I guessed Pa Miguel was just fond of me.

It was understandably highly emotional for me when nearly five decades later I came to own 34 Wellington Street.[7] I went to inspect it and stood exactly on the spot where Pa Miguel used to sit in his chair outside the shop. I wondered what he would have said then if he knew that the little boy who used to exchange jokes with him now owned his store. My thoughts raced back that far again with equal emotion when, in 1992, I appointed Dr Momodou Manneh into my cabinet as Minister of Economic Planning and Industrial Development after the people returned the PPP to office for the seventh five-year term time since 1962. He was Jikiba Manneh's son.

As I moved up the junior classes and entered the senior stream at Form 4, the challenges grew and I with them. My father came on visits to Bathurst a few times and I went to see him at the home of his friend Pa Ousman Semega Janneh at 15 Hagan Street. Once or twice he refused to look me in the eye, muttering something about some big changes that had happened to me. I did not know how different I looked; I was enjoying going to school and winning the hearts of the teachers by doing well in their subjects. Those were exciting times in a new world that was opening up to me; it was all so fast and so stimulating.

Meanwhile, my sister, Nacesay, the firstborn of my mother, was going through the rigours of training under the watchful eye of Mama Fatty. Nacesay paid artful attention to the fascinating teachings my mother instilled because, according to her, a girl must learn how to hold her family together through thick and thin. She had to have a strong back on which to carry all of the siblings that not one of them proved too heavy to carry, no matter what the circumstances.

We, her younger siblings, were brought up to respect and revere her authority and to understand her automatic succession to the elevated place of Mama Fatty the moment our mother would be no more. It would be her duty to hold all family things together and to be ready to share her time between her own family of the future and the greater *kabilo*. The boys had similar rules about duty to the family, though admittedly slightly looser than the girls had. We listened for what new rules my father would lay down. I in particular was always eager to be by his side even if just to observe everything he did and to note the meticulous way in which he handled himself and his business.

I guess it was evident already to the neighbours and many of his friends and business acquaintances that I had become a favourite child. However, the Jawara *kabilo* was a close-knit family. We grew up well and made it

---

[7] I bought the property from its French owners with a bank loan.

into the world, except for Bouba, who sadly died while very young. The fact that he died when I left home to go to school in Bathurst has remained painfully with me to this day. Basadi went into business as did Nacesay. Jarai married Abdoulahi Alami, a Moroccan businessman; she became the first to settle in Brikama. Nacesay married and later retired in Brikama with her husband and family, long before I brought my mother to live there after my father passed away.

Jarai was my favourite sister. I could imagine how she sometimes forbearingly thought to herself that I fussed and played big brother too much. She had a vivacious, hearty gusto for life and was blessed with a broad mind that understood many things. While Nacesay expressed concern over my conversion to Christianity in 1955, Jarai was there with me all the way understanding the whys and the wherefores and being open and tolerant of decisions that had to be taken the way they were taken. We became very close and I was devasted when she sadly died of childbirth after helping out so busily in the campaign that got me elected in 1962. All her children became my children. I will confess my great sense of heightened vulnerability to family pressures after she died; one so close and so liberal and who gave good counsel.

My mother was not intimidated by the apprehensions of raising a new family with my father in Barajaly away from her own native village of Dankunku. It took a brave girl in those days to leave home and move so far away and to be surrounded by strangers and in-laws. She calmly absorbed the strangeness of her new village in the most rustic of all corners in The Gambia. She soon adapted to the idiosyncrasies of the Jawara lineage.

She gave birth to me in the *musu bungo*, a block house built out of the same bricks of dug-out clay reinforced with straw. The house was well laid out with several rooms. The walls were high allowing a great deal of air to circulate and cool the rooms. The roof was made of corrugated iron sheets, which at the time were a novelty in the rural areas. In those days, the zinc sheets that shone so brilliantly in the hot sun were hardly ever seen outside Bathurst. Although my father never talked about it, I always thought that his European friends had something to do with the ideas that went into the design of the house.

On the morning of the eighth day, in the presence of a large gathering, the Imam of Barajaly, Fa Kemo Ceesay, officiated my naming ceremony. He cut off strands of my hair with a razor blade and whispered my name *Kairaba* into both of my ears, the right one first and then the left. He told the griot what the name was and the minstrel then said it aloud for all to hear. The crowd mumbled in a wave of whisper, asking what kind of name Kairaba was. The griot again announced it more loudly for all to hear.

It was a good name and great, the elders said. Almamy wanted to give thanks to Allah for the blessings and prosperity He was showing him in goods and money and in his wives and his children. Then the drumming and dancing began. And no group, not even the cousins or the in-laws or the neighbours, outdid the group of *kanyaleng* women who danced passionately in their rags and beat their totem drumsticks on their beaded calabashes. They were called *kanyaleng* because they had lost so many babies, more than they could care to count. They chanted, clowned about and made noise to scare the spirits of death and evil away from their homes. They sang a song and they danced to it:

Mung dong bi jang?
Kairaba kolaa kun nding!

After the trading season ended, the hungry season began in the middle of May. But my father was ready for my arrival. He had enough grain stacked in his store. There was enough in that store to last us throughout the season; and enough food to spare for the festivities that lasted all evening with singing and dancing.

2

The bells of the brave saints

My father's small shop found a prominent place among the big trading firms that had set up along the waterfront in Walikunda. He was so preoccupied with farming and trading that it was not clear which he was – a farmer or a businessman. He seemed to me, however, to be so very good at managing the two roles. Each in its own way gave him the command, popularity, authority and respect which he seemed to carry about without much awareness of the weight of them on his shoulders in addition to the responsibility of already fathering perhaps the fastest growing family in Barajaly.

His prosperity grew and so did his family. My father took his fourth wife, Jarai Kijerah, from Sukuta in Niani district. Nna Jarai came to the *musu bungo* at Barajaly and in quiet reverence and with great regard for my mother played her part in keeping the household to which she added six children of her own. As time went by and business was good, he married for the seventh time. Mamanding Jienna, whom we endearingly called Maa Nii, came to live with us. He soon followed her with his eighth wife, Sira Sukoh, who became the youngest of my stepmothers.

Although he married eight women, there were no more than four in his household at any given time. After the death of his first two wives, he married his third and then his fourth, Mama Fatty and Nna Jarai. The fifth wife did not stay long because they were soon divorced and the sixth unfortunately fell ill and died. I was not there for the first two and I was too young to remember the two after Nna Jarai. In my time growing up, my mother was the senior spouse. She, with Nna Jarai, Maa Nii and Sira Sukoh, lived with my father until he passed away in May 1961 when he was 79 years old.

The people of Barajaly and the surrounding villages continued to look to him when they needed goods and seeds and the occasional aid in cash for one occasion or another, mostly naming ceremonies, weddings and funerals. There were frequent outbreaks of smallpox and chickenpox. Many of those who died were children in their infancy. Many women too died giving birth to their babies.

We have seen how my father was invariably involved in whatever it was that took place in the village. He was either giving his much sought-after advice, paying for one thing or another, serving as a go-between with the villagers and their suppliers or between two parties needing to sit and make peace. But no matter how busy he was, he found some time to spend with the Fula herdsmen who came to him for a fair exchange of their ghee – *ninsi tulo*, and sour milk for goods in his shop. Those cattle herders, scores of them, came every year to Barajaly, and they would take away valued items back to their country in the drier northern and eastern areas of Senegal and even as far away as Sudan and Niger.

My father lived in the main house he built of clay bricks reinforced with straw the same as he did with the *musu bungo*, the common house where his wives lived with their children, which he had constructed with large and airy rooms as a man would who had envisaged a very large family.

If the *musu bungo* sounds overcrowded, it was a credit to my father's resourcefulness that it really was not. The house was well planned with beds arranged against the walls around the room, each with a mosquito bednet hanging above it. Each woman slept in her private room with the youngest of her children and the toddlers and other older ones living in the large dormitory, lined with beds. At night, the *musu bungo* was a quiet place of sleep and restfulness. In the mornings and early evenings, it was a beehive with everyone knowing what their roles were and how to go about them. With daylight, the Jawara household broke into activity. As if by an unwritten constitution, people set themselves to chores of tending a handful of sheep fattening for the next occasion, to the washing of clothes, sweeping the forecourt, pounding grain, stoking the fireplaces or serving up the *mono*[8] breakfast hot and steaming. Some of the older women would have set off early to the rice fields leaving the younger ones to chase down screaming siblings, doing their stubborn best to avoid the cold water baths set out in the large bowls.

I would have been up and gone anyway with my father long before the break of dawn, first to the mosque for the early prayer and down the tracks to the riverside. He and I would have already had our breakfast of *mono*. I wasted no time with the morning staple. I would lap up mine with great gusto from my bowl made out of calabash gourd. My father would sit on his mat and take his time bringing every spoonful to his lips with such contemplative rhythm that I did not speak for fear that I would interrupt his very deepest thoughts. I had the grand appetite of a boy and I must say

---

[8] Porridge made from sorghum flour.

I enjoyed licking up the last dabs of porridge from the spoon. I would eat quite fast because I never ever wanted to be found unready when my father was all set to leave for the riverside. By full light every morning we would have been across the river. Occasionally, one of my brothers would come along pulling a goat my father would slaughter for the midday meal. It was a short walk from the river to his shop and *secco* at Walikunda.

I did not like being absent from my father's canoe trips. I would hobble along even on days when I would feel a little feverish and my mother thought I should not go. Occasionally, when my father left an exhausted boy to sleep late, I would run to the river and join the passengers on the canoe and cross over to join him at Walikunda. The river was an important part of our life; it was always there and going across had become a passion for me. I loved the sensation of pulling away from the rickety wharf in a canoe sometimes overfilled with anxious men, women and children patiently sharing the available space in the dugout with a sheep or a goat or two. The passengers were careful to keep their eyes glued to the water. No one ever dangled a hand over the side because the arrow points cutting just below the surface of the water and causing ripples along the sides were the snouts of the grey crocodile.

I loved the river and I would gladly have made one hundred crossings every day just to see the water creatures slither and splash in the peace and splendour of their own kingdom. But essentially, I crossed over every day to be with my father. I did not idle about, whether in Barajaly or in Walikunda. I might have played a lot with the other children but I was picking up tips on weighing, pricing as well as directing the loaded donkeys towards my father's shop. There were hundreds of animals that lumbered in daily, bringing the groundnut harvest from the outer villages all the way down to the buying stations in Walikunda.

In time, three or four other private dealers joined my father and set up stations to buy groundnuts. It was business and there was bound to be competition but not of any sort that was inimical. Everyone traded quietly and waited for what came one's way. Across the street from our shop, the Barthes (LCA) company had their shop and groundnut *secco*. Down the same street, UAC, Vezia and Maurel & Prom companies also had agents trading for them. Everyone used their haggling skills and put their smiles to work to win over the donkey owners whose prerogative it was to choose the trader to whom they would sell their nuts. Many traders came to show the flag and to shore up business for their agents. That was how I got to set eyes for the first time on a white man when Henry Madi of S Madi Ltd stood up on the deck of his splendid yacht, the *Tina,* moored at the wharf at Walikunda.

In those days, many years before heavy motor transport rendered them obsolete, donkeys were very important in the movement of the groundnut crop from the farms to the buying stations. In addition to the heavy sacks hanging on either side of them, the donkeys, guided by their drivers, carried two bells around their necks. The sound of those bells from those sturdy animals trampling in from the villages in the hinterland is unforgettable. The cloud of dust they raised and the frenzy of the *secco* agents to draw them while they scurried to reach their favourite agents were electric moments; memories of those scenes have stayed with me forever.

The bells always fascinated me. I recognised their sound from a long way. It was the sound that brought everyone scurrying out when the animals trailed into the village. The donkeys and their chime formed part of the chorale of the opening trade season and heralded the one long mood of festivity and celebration that took over the village. They were the signal that the 'hungry season' was over and there would be money and goods flowing again. I was always among the first to dash outside to meet them. It was the beginning of a playful time for us children and a fretful one for the traders. While we tried to see who among us was brave enough to go up and touch a donkey's massive ears, the traders were worried about which animals would stop and sell at their *secco.*

My father and his shop clerks would inspect the heavy bags loaded on the donkeys. I would be more interested in looking into the large forbearing eyes of those animals, those quiet brave saints whose patient endurance meant so much to the trade that drew hundreds of people to mingle during the eclectic season. The weight of the burden they carried had set the standard for the pricing of groundnuts which came to be measured in British pound sterling (and Gambian *dalasi* in due course) per *mbam,* the Wollof word for a donkey. Two sacks of groundnuts, one hanging down either side of those robust creatures, were equal to one *mbam* – two hundredweight measures of groundnuts.

It took years of reading until I discovered the true reasons for the sometimes quarrelsome outbreaks between the traders and the sellers. They quarrelled often over the new system of weighing by moving the metal blocks of weight along a bar on a bascule. In the middle 1920s and just before the changeover from the demonetised five franc piece and the change to pounds, shillings and pence, the system of weighing the groundnuts also changed. Rather than measuring by the bushel, the ancient and standard measure the farmers understood, the Chamber of Commerce brought on the scales that weighed in pounds and hundredweights as fractions of a ton measure. It turned out that the avoirdupois weights and the fractional calculations they entailed confounded the farmers and, true to the evidence, there were some traders – European, Syrian, Lebanese as well as African – who regularly left a good number of unhappy and confused farmers feeling cheated at the weighing stations.

The farmers had lost control of the simple cash per donkey load exchanged at two shillings and six pence per bushel. The colonial government's new pricing at £10 per ton for the groundnut needed some calculation and arriving at answers could be quite taxing. The farmers complained bitterly of being short-changed. The cash breakdown of the lower factors was difficult for them to understand. But no matter how hard they protested they could not get the government to go back to the bushel measurement.

The farmers' suspicions of cheating were proved. In 1917, the Wesleyan Mission in Bathurst sent a Bathurst man, Edward Francis Small, as a missionary to Ballanghar, the chief trading post in the Central River Province, not far from Walikunda. Small sympathised with the difficulties of the farmers. He brought them together in an organisation he called the Gambia Farmers' Cooperative and Marketing Association (GFCMA). The farmers were happy to have someone educated on their side to help them with the problems of weights and measures and to demand better prices for their crops. They rallied behind Small to fight against the cheating firms and traders.

It was a big challenge for the Europeans who before long got the government behind them against Small and had him removed from Ballanghar where every foreign firm in the country had opened a station. Small was committed to fighting for the rights and welfare of the ordinary person. I would later marry his niece.

Although I loved the sound of the bells around their necks I did not envy the life of donkeys. As an eight-year-old in Walikunda, I never ceased to admire them. They seemed so saintly and patient, rows and rows of them, their eyes obedient, and their mouths quietly frothing. They complained to no one and held up, with a brave calm, the regular bite of the switch that flew in the hands of the drivers who whipped them. The only time they would have their say was when they brayed and heaved with all the power in their lungs, so that their cry was heard all over the village and beyond.

I wonder what I would have done if it had been my chore to carry such heavy loads. What was certain was that the donkeys were soon gone and the mountainous heaps of groundnuts on the ground behind the fences of the *secco* also soon disappeared on to the groundnut boats that sailed down river. Who it was or what it was behind that great bend in the river that consumed all those tons of nuts was never clear to me. But in time I found out. It was the Gambia Oilseeds Marketing Board (GOMB) at Kaur and at Denton Bridge that ordered all those groundnuts.

The end of a trade season was always an emotional climax to nearly five months of rush and activity. The "strange" farmers – those who came from outside the borders of The Gambia for the farming season – were ready to go back to their homes. They would buy many things from the shops to take back with them. As business wound down, each man accounted for what he had earned during the season. The men had yard taxes to settle back home; there were new clothes to be bought for their wives. Loans had to be repaid. Many would use what was left to take new brides, many of whom had already been betrothed and waiting to go home to their husbands. The young men in the villages were waiting to be circumcised. With extra money in hand the men would stock up on food grains for the next hungry season. All of those activities cost money.

As evening came, all too quickly on the last day of the season, the sound of the bells of the brave saints tinkled in the distance as the last of them left Walikunda. The shops' kerosene lamps were out. The dust had settled and the voices hushed. The fever of trade was over. An eerie silence fell with the night over the village. The quiet of the late hours would be broken by intermittent waves of distant singing and drumming. Familiar sounds drifting from nearby Wellingara village or even beyond. Occasionally, the night would be rent by the chilling laugh of the scavenging hyena. I would curl up on my mat, pull my blanket over me and lie dead still in the dark until sleep took over.

3

My father's heart is troubled

My father's shop and *secco* in Walikunda were exact replicas of all the others. The shops were an admixture of hardware and convenience stores; at times they even looked like grain stores. Certain items sold well. Mourners streamed in almost daily to buy the white shirting for funeral. My father's brother Barrsa, who put in a lifetime of work as the Barajaly village tailor, would attest to the volume of work involved. Scythes also sold well and so did hoes and cutlasses. For the older men, sugar and tobacco leaf were their favourite purchases.

Those little parcels of fenced-off areas in which each trader carried on his business of buying and selling nuts could change from deadly quiet places to frenzied bazaars in a matter of moments. It all depended on where the owners drove their animal trains to as the donkey drivers and owners had the choice of which of the six or seven buyers and agents to trade with, a lot more went into attracting them to a depot than just opening up a shop and fencing off an area.

Each trader did the best he could to draw attention to his depot. The efforts turned out to be a lively competition and brought sparkles into the life of an otherwise sleepy village. From November to March, sometimes well into April, the bartering and haggling would become quite animated. There were very astute buyers and sellers to deal with, among them a special breed of Bathurst women who came all the way from the colony with dried and smoked fish, dried oysters, salted and dried fish and palm oil. They exchanged those delicacies for rice, millet and sorghum and other cereals and hauled bags of them onboard the river steamers back to Bathurst. They did a wonderfully brisk trade all over the provincial wharf towns. One Wollof woman, Ya Fatou Kess, in particular, came every year to do business in Walikunda and ended up fairly well off.

The salt water fish from the coast were a delicacy in upriver places. They were a tasty improvement on the bland local fresh water fish we had at Walikunda. Perhaps we got to know the difference when we grew up. But when we were children, we spent hours fishing the small and slender *balantango*[9] under the shadow of the groundnut cutters. I was good at shaping pins into hooks and tying them up at the end of long strings. The *balantango* would grow fat very fast during the trade season because they lived off the abundant supply of groundnuts that fell into the river during hauling into the groundnut cutters. We would bait our pin hooks and whisk the fish out of the water on to blazing grass and twig fires ready to roast them. A cousin of mine, Lamin Kijerah, would fish all day and so consumed was he by his fishing that we nicknamed him Lamin Balantango. Sometimes we ate so much *balantango* at the riverside that we found no use for our meals at home.

While all the adults haggled and exchanged goods, the children played the day out. Sometimes at the peak of our playful exhilaration, the shrill voice of a holler would cut through the stiffness of the heat to announce that lunch was ready. We would troop off to wherever the invitation was coming from. Sometimes we went to our house; my father had built a smaller replica of the house in Barajaly and spent the night there when things got too busy to leave on time. When he stayed over, it gave me more time with the dozen or more children I played with, boys and girls.

Pa Yoma was the agent for one of the big French companies, Messrs Barthes et Lesieur, known more popularly as Barthes. His shop stood exactly opposite my father's. That gave me ample opportunity all day to either play in the street way between the shops, go over to Pa Yoma to talk to him or help my father with errands.

When I went about helping my father in his shop, I did it in a rather diligent fashion. I caught up quickly with the art of chatting animatedly with the donkey drivers while I guided them towards my father's shop. I even tried my hand at weighing groundnuts and taking exact readings on the bascule. One of the Sarahule donkey drivers - Khorsa Kebbeh – became an influential member of his community and served the People's Progressive Party as an enthusiastic party member and campaigner.

However, not all of the men were in the mood to banter all the time. It occurred to me that sometimes no matter how courteously my father tried to hold conversations, some otherwise good days with all the chit-chat and the hum of the talkative sellers were on occasion marred by serious or quarrelsome exchanges. My father sometimes had it out with some difficult client who argued a lot about change or some delay in the service or about one fault or another in the goods. Pa Yoma experienced similar troubles too in his shop.

---

[9] Type of freshwater fish

On occasion, the grumbling would be someone wishing to see the return to the bushel measurements and to the five franc piece. Those, some clients claimed, were such easier days for them. A disgruntled farmer would complain and mill around with his donkeys until finally he sold off to one shop because he would discover all the shops offered the same prices all down the waterfront, no matter where he went to sell his nuts. The agents had nothing to do with the drastic changes the Chamber of Commerce had laid down. My father and Pa Yoma were only agents of their companies.

At other times, the complaints came from all the farmers who said they felt they were rushed with such short notice to exchange their five franc pieces and to adjust to the new weights at the bascule. The six-week notice was too short and the withdrawal of the coins ruined their business. So year after year they gradually lost the enthusiasm to travel long distances to get to Walikunda to sell their nuts. It badly affected trade in Walikunda. Pa Yoma always took the time to discuss things with my father and helped him with the background to the currency and weights and measures problems. It was he who confirmed the rumour to my father that indeed for quite some time since 1921 the colonial administration in Bathurst and the Queen's big office in London had been thinking hard to have the five franc coins withdrawn. London had already stopped the use of the coins in Sierra Leone. Businesspeople in Freetown had resorted to shipping loads of their holdings to Bathurst where their friends, relatives and agents were quickly buying goods at the fairer exchange rates. To stop the deluge in that currency movement, the British government ordered The Gambia to stop the use of the coins as well.

For me a seven-year-old boy and surely for all the other children, a little game of hide and seek or racing the other children to a dry tree stump and back proved easier to cope with than the tough subjects that preoccupied the elders. We had done our work during the growing season. We had shooed the birds from the coos fields and scared off the grey vervet and colobus monkeys from the groundnut fields. The harvest was dried, threshed, winnowed and bagged. Our work was done. All we could do was play. The heat of the day meant nothing to us when we pranced and shouted outside the shops, even when we got all tangled among the crowd and got in their way sometimes. We would run into people who would shout back angrily at us for being badly brought up or for rudely obstructing the busy street. But we knew how to dive about their legs and to get away on time. It was great fun. Our dusty heels, our blackened hands and sweaty bodies meant nothing as long as we enjoyed ourselves.

Each day, as the sun began to set and the shops were closing, my father and I joined the usually small number of people walking back to the river for the canoe trip home where Mama Fatty would be waiting anxiously for our return.

One evening, after spending a moment with Pa Yoma in his shop before we left for home, my father became quite sombre. He did not talk much during the walk to the canoe. He said even less when we boarded it. It looked like he was thinking deeply of something, possibly about the things that had happened at the shop during the day that might have bothered him. There were furrows on the fair skin on his forehead; just as there would be during breakfast when there was something heavy on his mind.

A man sitting next to him said something to him about the new money. He only muttered back that it was the subject on everyone's lips. I asked him what would happen if they took away the new money as well. The question did not change his mood. I never liked it, not even a little bit, when my father did not look pleased.

But instead of answering my question, he began to talk to a Manjago man who had been steadfastly guarding a small parcel of Irish potatoes. The man was in the company of a red bearded white man sporting a khaki safari jacket. I heard him say the two of them were crossing over to go to Kuntaur Fula Kunda on the north bank and that they would be going back from there to Georgetown. The Manjago escort explained that the European was a government official on an inspection tour of the new school in Georgetown.

My father knew that indeed the government had started a school there four years before, in 1927. Some had told him the children there studied Arabic. He waved lamely to the white man who smiled very warmly back at him. I looked away; his eyes were two shiny blue pebbles in the dying sunlight. I just had never seen eyes like that before, beady blue but soft in a harmless way. He was the second white person I had seen and so soon after the first I had seen on the yacht only a few weeks before. He continued to smile genially and asked my father through the Manjago interpreter if I were his son. When my father proudly affirmed and rubbed my head, the European told him that schools were the answer to all the country's problems. He said sending children to school would help the country to grow rapidly. He also explained that the reason why the government had opened a school in Georgetown was to enable the sons of the chiefs and important farmers to send their children there. The European asked my father to promise him that he would enrol me in the school.

My father's face only twitched. He interrupted the Manjago man and told him he would rather talk about the shortage of groundnuts and how badly the trade season was faring. He said the *seccolu* were virtually empty and many donkey-loads short of the volume of harvest for that time of year. Thousands of tons of the produce were going across the border into the French territories, my father complained. Growing groundnuts, he concluded, was no longer worth the trouble. He sounded so despondent.

The Manjago man said that it was because the price the government was offering for the groundnuts was low. He said the French were always ready to offer more per ton than the English. My father conceded but added that there were other things he could do other than grow groundnuts. He said he could grow fewer groundnuts and increase his acreage on food crops like sorghum, millet, corn and beans. The Manjago man confirmed that the intercropping was good for the soil and quipped: *Soso kana nyo faa; nyo kana susso fa.* My father was surprised that the man spoke such good Mandinka. Indeed, my father concurred, breaking a smile for the first time all evening, that farmers must always make room for beans and corn to grow together. He said he had always toyed with the idea of doing a whole year of growing nothing other than *soso* and corn.

We arrived at the other side of the river. The Manjago man was eager to continue the conversation with my father even when we set on the walk to the road. One of them brought up the old subject of the crunch of demonetisation. The Manjago man finally introduced himself to my father as Bissenti Mendy. He recounted stories of people he knew some five or eight years before who had to rush to dig up money they had buried away in secret places and in jars behind their sacred shrines to meet the six-week deadline to have the coins exchanged. He said he remembered the districts in the Foni where the five franc piece had been the favourite tender for the Jola and Manjago people who had been worst hit. One man, he said, ended his misery by throwing himself into a well. Others who could no longer pay the dowry, buy cloth or cattle, or even add new thatch to their leaking roofs threatened to do the same.

I heard him and my father joking and laughing. My father said he had acted quickly at the time and survived the crisis without having to throw himself over the side of the low canoe while crossing the swollen river. The man said he could imagine the shock on a businessman who woke up in the morning only to discover he was worth only half of the fortune with which he had gone to bed. My father, in mirthful response, assured him that during the crisis he had found ways to keep away from doing desperate things. Even if things had gone worse than they had, my father said to him showing off his prayer beads wrapped around his wrist, he only would have turned to prayer instead of throwing himself into a well.

We came to the end of the laterite road. Bissenti and the European said goodbye to us. My father and I, together with three other men talking to each other on the other side of the road, continued to walk. Ours was a short one now down the path towards our home. The old man was not as talkative any more with me. Even at that tender age, I had already begun looking like a carbon copy of him. We walked together, he quiet and seemingly heavy at heart, and I glowingly at the peak of my day walking home behind him at the end of his day's labours.

In Mandinka, and indeed, in African tradition, neighbours very quickly become relatives. In fact, some people receive more care from their neighbours than they do from their blood relations. Although Almamy was ten years older than Pa Yoma, they became great friends. They talked and exchanged news like peers and they respected each other's views. Even though they were nearly opposites in physical size and temperament, they found common ground in their abiding mutual regard and friendship. My father was of average build, light skinned, soft-spoken, a workaholic, an active go-getter ready to bargain and negotiate. On the other hand, Pa Yoma was big and brawny; he carried an imposing presence. His temper sat on a short fuse. He was completely intolerant of indiscipline.

One day while Pa Yoma was back in his home at Wellington Street, a popular young hoodlum in the Half Die area called Kebbeh Mer strayed into the compound and began making a nuisance of himself, raising pandemonium in the quiet surroundings. Pa Yoma strode out of the house and without any warning picked Kebbeh Mer off the ground by his neck and by the belt of his trousers. He carried the stunned hoodlum across the forecourt, kicked the gate open and threw the man bodily back out on to the street. Kebbeh Mer picked himself out of the dust and walked away cursing the foulest he knew. Everyone rushed out of their rooms in shock to watch the old man panting to catch his breath. It was not funny at all. He might have been everyone's hero of the day but his wives were worried that he had exhausted himself in a very bad way. Pa Yoma soon recovered and Kebbeh Mer never again disturbed the peace at 37 Wellington Street or anywhere near.

The fact that both Almamy and Pa Yoma depended on the same clients for the groundnuts they bought, and, that they sold exactly the same goods in their shops, was not enough to affect the good feeling they had for each other. Their common belief in goodness, hard work, determination and their large and generous hearts were more rewarding to them than what clients brought or took away from the shops.

One evening in 1931, when the trade season was drawing to a close, my mother arrived back at the *musu bungo* from my father's house looking a bit withdrawn. This was only a week after my father had also appeared withdrawn while we made our way home in the canoe from Walikunda. Mama Fatty seemed to have lost the lustre I had always seen in her eyes. She avoided me. When I ran to her and wrapped myself around her, she squeezed me in such a sympathetic way that I could not help feeling she was battling with something that had to do with me. The moon was out. She knew my father would soon leave the compound to air himself out among his friends and relatives in the neighbourhood. As soon as my father strolled out into the moonlit evening, my mother began to speak without restraint to my stepmother, Nna Jarai. They were both nursing their babies who had become the two latest additions to the household.

Although Mandinka society was historically matriarchal, women had long lost the authority of decision-making to their husbands, brothers and male siblings. Whether I would go away to Bathurst or not was a decision that would normally rest with my father. In modern times many programmes, legislation and policy changes were put in place during my time in government to empower women again. The Gambia signed and ratified various major international instruments, prime among them the Convention for the Elimination of All Forms of Discrimination Against Women (CEDAW). All these modern treaties are meant to help restore some of the fundamental rights that women had lost by attrition and acquiescence over the centuries.

Almamy's quiet, pensive ways gave him the enviable aura of a responsible patriarch who commanded respect and obedience without much noise. But he had decided in this case that he would leave my mother to have her way over the matter. In fact, when Pa Yoma heard that my mother was not at all keen on the issue, he respectfully stopped asking about it.

On two occasions in the last weeks of the trade season in 1931, my mother had a pressing cause to go to Walikunda. She had stopped on both occasions by Pa Yoma's shop to exchange greetings. Pa Yoma had never let her go without a gift of some kind, no matter how small, from his shop. But he never raised the matter. If he must hear my mother's opinion he must do so through my father. My mother could not discuss such important family matters with another man over my father's head. However, she counted it a great sign of respect that both my father and Pa Yoma were accepting her decision that she did not have any male child to throw away to *toubabdu* (white man's country).

Nna Jarai was suckling her baby Nna Isata, and Mama Fatty was suckling Bouba.

From the bedroom door I could hear her speak half complaining to Nna Jarai and half talking to herself. I listened and it was only then that I knew what had been eating at my mother's heart.

"I will not leave my child to go to Banjul," she complained. "Pa Yoma wants to take Kairaba to the white man's town."

"But it could be good for him," said Nna Jarai, a wonderful stepmother who herself in time had blessed the *musu bungo* with five children of her own – Mba, Dobally, Mariama, Ebrima and Nna Isata. "You never know what Allah has in store for the children."

"He is not going," my mother insisted lowering her voice as I approached them. Her voice was full of sadness. "Look at him; he is so little."

"There's Basadi, there's Alieu," Nna Jarai said. "Can't Pa Yoma take one of them if you don't want Kairaba to go?"

"The truth is, I don't have that many male children to give away to anyone," Mama Fatty said emphatically and became silent.

"Have faith; Allah never abandons His poor ones," my stepmother pleaded. "Let Kairaba go. It is not everybody that the language and customs of the white man will corrupt."

"Mawdo says our children who grow up with the white people in the town become different people," my mother said. "They come back different, if they come back at all."

Business picked up quite handsomely for my father. He and a few other traders got into ventures that soon began to prove that groundnuts were not the only thing in the world. I remember the whole movement of international economic advisers from Washington proposing diversification as the answer to solve our economic problems. I remember the sometimes self-serving manner of their presentation as the theory of diversification away from the groundnut monoculture was a new and revolutionary thought they were bringing to us. Almamy Jawara was leading the move already in the 1930s getting farmers like him to look at other ways of increasing their earnings. He made up for the downturn in groundnut collection with increased transactions in cutlasses, kola nuts, hoes, rakes, rice, calico and other consumer wares in his shop. He put some acres of land to cotton and more corn as he had told the man in the canoe he would.

Harder times for my father meant harder work and even when the village people came to open lines of credit he was able to oblige. How could he refuse anyone from Barajaly, the village his own father built out of the strength of his own hands? He could not turn down the pleas of the needy from Walikunda where he was making his own fortune and feeding his family. While debt strangulated the ordinary farmer and left many empty-handed and hungry, Almamy devised methods to keep himself buoyant and Pa Yoma admired the ways which he adopted to keep away from debt.

Everyone else, it seemed, got deeper into debt. The country itself was in debt. The government was strenuously running the Colony and the Protectorate at a deficit which by the time I drafted the Independence Manifesto in October 1960 had risen to nearly £500,000 within a recurrent expenditure package of £2 million. Debt was going to be the single stranglehold that stood to thwart every resolve of our people to become fully independent. It was one of the intractable conditions that could make a caricature of our political independence. It was the one card that some international partners used to great effect in plying our vote one way or the other. It weakened many respectable steps we had taken as a developing country to move forward.

That year, the trade season ended with the close of April. The groundnuts had been sold off and nearly 25,000 'strange' farmers from Senegal and beyond were nearly all gone away again. The once lofty pyramids of nuts had turned to mere mounds on the grounds of the *secco*. From the attitude of the trading agents, one could tell who had had a successful season or who had just broken even or had suffered a disaster. Rumours had already begun flying around MacCarthy Island Province and all the way through Niani to Niamina districts about traders who had made severe losses and were bound to lose the title deeds to their properties which they had put up as collateral to the big companies that had given them credit to trade. Those properties would be sold off to make up for the debts to the European firms. There were many such distressing stories at the end of each trade season. Thankfully, Pa Yoma must have rendered good account of the year; there he was in very high spirits, packing his lorry and ready to go back home with his family.

Out in the fields, groundnut hay had been gathered and heaped out in the fields waiting for the donkey carts to remove them into the villages to feed the livestock. The air was slowly infusing once again with moisture. Among the vegetation on the river's edge, the thorny creepers rotted and smelt again and the brown river was flowing carelessly past in humid, lazy churns. Although the grey rain clouds would not begin drifting across until the end of May or early June, there was dampness on the sweaty skin that mosquitoes and tsetse flies liked to bite with much vengeance even in the day time.

Soon, Pa Yoma was ready to leave. His devoted driver, Nfansu, was already in his seat, revving the engine and letting it idle for a long while. Ya Fatou and her two boys Dodou and Bouba had already clambered on to the back of the lorry. I had run with a posse of children to the edge of the village where I stood and waited to wave Pa Yoma away. We all cheered when the lorry sped by and disappeared with Pa Yoma waving back inside a cloud of dust.

When I returned I found my father standing at his compound gate. He was not particularly waiting for my return; rather he had just finished speaking with some people from Brikamaba who had come to see him.

"Pa Yoma is a good man and he means well," he said as we walked together into the compound. "But I had told him myself that I did not want my son to learn *nassarano*."

"What is *nassarano*?" I asked my father.

"*Nassarano* is the ways and language of the white man," he answered. "Our children will get lost when they learn them. They will not come back and when they do they will talk through their noses like the white man. They will abandon their mats and sit in high chairs and cross their legs like them. That cannot work for us in this village."

I was stunned for words. I could hardly understand what the old man was saying or what he wanted me to do with that complex thought.

"Has Pa Yoma left now?" my father asked when he realised I had no answer.

"His lorry got lost in the dust and I never saw it again," I replied. "Some day we should put a good road in Walikunda so that the dust won't bother Pa Yoma so much."

"The road won't appear on its own," my father answered. "It is hard work. Honest labour and serious, serious hard work that will build a road all the way to Banjul that will have no dust to bother Pa Yoma's lorry."

My father patted my head. There was a knowing smile on his face and we left it at that. The large mountain of groundnuts in his *secco* was now a tiny heap. It, however, signalled only a fair season; there had been bigger mountains in former years. One of the men asked him, evidently only out of the courtesy of a common greeting, how the season had gone. But my father seemed as if he had been waiting for someone to push the button and give him cause. He said for a small man playing against the giants like the CFAO and the LCA, he would not complain. He reminded his captive audience that every other trader in Walikunda was an agent for any one of the big companies that had Europeans and much money behind them. He said there was no one to thank for the great blessing but Allah the Almighty for seeing him through another season in spite of all the difficulties.

The story of Almamy Leh must have gone far and wide. My father said he had cleared the land and was ready to put as much of it at the disposal of any farmer, strange or local, as long as he wished to bend his back and work. He was ready with open arms to embrace any man who worked hard and did his best to help others. The men beamed with happiness at such a welcome.

The men and women who heard him chorused in agreement. The old man with an ending like that had redeemed himself from what had started out sounding like boastful air but which ended up in a deep prayer of thanksgiving. In the mouth of a less careful person, it could have ended uncharacteristically and miserably boastfully. The men from Brikamaba crouching under the fruit trees listened, obviously convinced that the faith, largesse and enterprise they had heard of him was true. They had waited patiently for audience with Almamy on various common matters, from land palavers or sickness in the village chickens to family strife, troubled homes or disputes over inheritance.

The quiet atmosphere in Walikunda had rubbed off on Barajaly Tenda. It was the turn of the groundnut cutters to cart away all the nuts while the men went away to their families, test new oxen and inspect new fields. The groundnuts had obediently followed the bends down river and had disappeared to close the season.

My father invited the men to assemble for the evening prayers and gave the honour of leading the prayers to a visiting marabout among them from Niamina. I sat right behind my father and when prayers were ended I heard him congratulating the marabout. His style of recitations, he commented, must have come from some respectable *madrassa*. He continued to talk with the visitors outside. As for me, I made my way with his praying mat back to his house. Incidentally, I had bowed and stood up and bent over as the others did but I would not say for certain that I had prayed. Indeed, I did not remember a single word. My heart and thoughts were far away, somewhere on the dusty roads beyond Walikunda, on the lorry that left the village only a little while before.

All night long, I thought of Pa Yoma. I began missing him immediately that lorry left the village. I could see a prominent black mould stuck on the right side of his face. That mould never ceased to intrigue me. I had taken so much to Pa Yoma; his aura was so compelling. I was consumed by his generosity with sugar candies and lemonade. I always looked at the mould on his cheek and once, completely unable to resist any more, I mustered enough courage to touch it and to ask him: "Does this thing hurt?"

Pa Yoma leaned back with such chiefly dignity in his deck chair outside his shop. He fingered the mould, smiled and answered something. I was too thrilled to remember what he answered about his mould. What will never fade, though no matter how old I may be, was the genial smile that lit his face and the fatherly glint in his eye that told my young heart that the old man was greatly amused by my curiosity.

That had always been his attitude to the children as we played our hearts out in the busy lanes between the two shops – my father's and his. I would take breaks of my own and go over to Pa Yoma. I was glad when I stood by him and he quietly sat patting my head as we waited for customers. There was always something he found amusing in the way we played. Maybe we reminded him of the carefree sweetness of a childhood he once enjoyed under the watchful eye of doting parents.

Many times, I was not able to rejoin the boisterous racing but I had seen the fistful of sweets he had ready to give us a treat. I would not give up on the soothing head patting for the world. I was glad for a moment to become a spectator. I watched the others play for a change. Lellie, my best pal and my exact age mate, was calling; so was Fura Jawara. I ignored their calls for me to come out and play. Sadly, Lellie died suddenly after we both turned eleven years old. It hurt me so deeply for being away in Bathurst when my friend died. Fura lived long and well and went on to become the *alkalo* of Barajaly. He was eighty-two years old when he died in 2005.

4

A safe but hungry season

Apart from the occasional fierce rainstorms, Barajaly had an uneventful rainy season. The planters overall had taken to the fields as soon as the clouds emptied the first downpour on the village. They had cleared every arable acre in the uplands. Nacesay, now a big girl of seventeen years old, nursed Bouba and an age-mate of hers helped her with Nna Isata to allow both Mama Fatty and Nna Jarai to join the other women in the swamps. The women had asked them to remain at home and watch their babies. But Mama Fatty had decided she would show them solidarity by going out at least for two days. Nna Jarai also thought it was a good idea. In the morning, they went to plant the rice seedlings behind the red dykes that had held in the muddy waters.

Nacesay took her day watch over the household seriously, sometimes too seriously. But she did not have to boss me around too much because I was soon gone far away from her to the fields where my father spent most of the rainy months supervising the preparation of Almamy Leh. The strange farmers had begun returning in large numbers; men with reputable family names from the adjacent districts in Fulladu, in Sandu Kantora and in Saloum. The new ones from Brikamaba were already trying out their new fields and working hard already to prove to my father that they would not let him down for giving them such a great opportunity. They all settled down side by side and it did not matter to my father if they were taking the land for a short season only or were going to stay on for generations, as some of them did, eventually.

My father also had friends who were cattle grazers. Some of the nomads who were late going back were caught in the rainstorms and would decide to stay on in the fields of Barajaly. It was safer for their animals than the risks of the hazardous journeys across swollen and rushing rivers along the long and dangerous tracks on the hillsides of Kindia in the Futa Jallon or across the swamps of the Portuguese enclaves in the area of the Rio Pongas. The nomads with their ghee and milk had always found refuge and plentiful grazing in the fields near Almamy Leh.

Everyone clearly knew that the poor takings in trade the year before called for harder work. My father told his wives that one of his farmer friends aptly described the year as a break-even season; nothing so much as lost, but not much gained either. In any case, the food stores in Barajaly had started dwindling fast. In the *musu bungo*, there were many more mouths to feed. Apart from my father's own children, my mother had brought in two or three more wards, daughters of relatives and indigent neighbours, to come and live in our household. With tenants filling Almamy Leh, the number of people under my father's domain had increased tremendously.

We held several ceremonies in the village, especially naming ceremonies and weddings. Because of the lean times, however, many men had to 'borrow' his bride while looking forward to a good season when he would be able to make enough money to hold a proper wedding ceremony. Those were obligations that severely and quickly ate into the food reserves because each time there was a wedding and each time a child received a name, the families would have to take from their herds of sheep and goats and their grain. Sometimes those ceremonial offerings of rice, oil, sorghum, sugar and other essentials would be unnecessarily lavish. In careless homes, the food stores would soon be empty and the children would suffer most throughout the six or seven hungry months, from May to November, until the next harvest.

My father endeavoured never to allow that in his household. He planned for each month and kept a strict count of the stocks in his *buntungo* - his grain store. The third of the three structures of mortar bricks in the compound, after his house and the *musu bungo*, was a very important place. From there, my father supplied the daily needs of the household. He gave his wives – my mother, Nna Jarai, Maa Nii and Nna Sira – each in her turn in the kitchen, all the provisions they needed. The women helped him manage his provisions well. That way, the fireplace between the stones that held up the pots in our kitchen kept going every day. Smoke rising from the fireplace was the sign to the village that there was food in the household. Every morning and evening, the pestles pounded grain and the sieves did their shaking, separating the flour from the chaff. And we, the children, were fed.

But all was not well for many households and that worried the elders of the village. It was impossible for my father to give away any more without starving his own household. So, late in August 1931, my father attended a meeting of the village elders and came back with the decision. With disease raging havoc among the cattle and with most of the sheep and goats earmarked for consumption already used up during the ceremonies, the village council decided that the Barajaly traditional hunter known as a danno must be called upon to go into the forest. They were going back to the ancient custom reserved for times when food supply was critically low. They called upon the official village hunter whose role and character were deeply spiritual in Barajaly. It was his traditional duty to go into the forest to hunt down meat for the people to eat whenever elders in their wisdom felt the need.

The elders assigned the task went to the hunter's hut and gave him the message. The hunter rose to the call. He was a wise man who had tremendous knowledge of the forest and guarded the secrets of its exciting but dangerous paths. It was he who put his skills and knowledge of the forest to the benefit of his fellows. At the appointed time, the hunter dressed himself in his breeches and donned his amulets. When he felt fully protected by the jujus he had inherited from his father and his grandfather, he would set out for the forest. There were gunshots as singers chanted the hunter's past; his brave exploits in his younger days when he had dragged an antelope and a duiker and some other bigger bush meat to the marketplace and upon which bounty many families fed for a couple of days, together.

The griots sang of the bravery of the hunter of past years and of other brave Somono tribesmen who played their part to feed the people when they were hungry. The Somono were a race of divers who lived by the river. Just as the hunter went into the forest, so they dived under the river in search of meat for the people to survive. There were songs among the griots celebrating those awesome swimmers who would dive for long spells and would resurface wrestling with a crocodile seized from its underwater sanctuary. The reptile, at times as much as seven feet in length, would end up on the butcher's stall at the marketplace, its white belly up and its powerful jaws agape with every prey-mauling razor-like tooth glistening in the sunlight. Each time there was a free harvest of meat out of the waters or out of the forests, the people made long queues with calabash trays and metal basins leading to the steps of the butcher's table.

Of course, a hunter fulfilled his task at great risk to himself. His mission to bring meat meant stalking his game in the territory of lion and leopard. The griots said that although mishaps had been rare the grandfathers had told stories of the finding of the mauled bodies of hunters or what was left of them. The roaming wildcats, driven closer to the villages by the dryness and the desperate search for watering holes, would have stalked the brave hunters and turned them to quarry instead of the other way round. The gri-gri and juju medicines in such unfortunate circumstances would have failed and the reputation of the family of medicine men that had prepared them would have disintegrated miserably with them.

The forays of the hunter were not only to provide food. His call-up was also an occasion for prayer to the spirits and a celebration of their providence. That link with the past and with the spirit world did not affect or take away from the people's common faith in Islam. While the tower of strength and faith in Barajaly remained unflinchingly Allah and, Allah alone, the hunter had his work to do, as did the *kankurango*, the guardian father of all spirits of the clan that danced at the initiation ceremonies. The *kankurango* danced to the sound of drums and songs from village maidens. That way it protected the souls of initiates at the *jujuwo* during the rites of passage into manhood. MacCarthy Island Province had the most celebrated of all *kankurango* spirit masks. The revered *Fang Bondi*, with a mask of green leaves and red tree bark, a cutlass in each hand, came out at night and could lift itself into the air and fly from rooftop to rooftop. When in sudden frenzy it would sing *Jalimu!* its entranced followers would answer: '*A'fa, Conteh*' – Kill! Conteh, kill at will! And it would clash its cutlasses violently together, and sparks would emit and people would run for cover.

Much of our culture and traditions were tied to the forest. Therefore, if some of those traditions would endure, there had to be forests in which to carry them out. It was therefore a singular source of honour for me many years later when as president and a man deeply concerned about environmental degradation, I signed The Banjul Declaration in 1977 – to complement legislation to protect our flora and fauna. I was doing so perhaps many decades too late to save the lion and leopard whose numbers had been so dangerously depleted to virtual non-existence. The remaining dozens of them roam the protected ranges of the Nykolokoba in Senegal, as they used to do a century ago in upper Gambia. Our last elephant in Kantora was shot dead in 1900 by a European travelling commissioner.

The whole subject of the continuing damage to the environment has always left me with a particular ambivalence in the sense that while we designed programmes and policies for development, much of the growth especially in urbanisation and road construction and settlement, threatened the environment. They terribly depleted our forest heritage and animal resources. The disappearance of our virgin forests would also mean the disappearance of our social and cultural civilisation and predict the doom of our continued existence as human beings. For one thing, our traditions of the rites of passage to manhood are tied to the mysteries of the forest. For another thing, our nutrition and our medicines still depend on the forests. Nay, our meat in the hungry season is to be found in the thickness of our forests, the repository of our irreplaceable body of knowledge of culture as well as of medicine.

A government claiming to be committed to arresting the decline should be seen to be acting to protect the environmental heritage. In 1992, my government, fully aware of the need for concrete action, established the Ministry of the Environment to coordinate the national agenda for the conservation of the little we had left and for the propagation of flora through national tree planting exercises. Each time we succeeded in bringing the land and the forest under our domination, we drove the animals further away, took up the breeding grounds of the reptiles and burnt the branches among which the birds should nest. Since it was evident that development entailed the felling of trees and scattering of birdlife, the clearing of vast tracts for agriculture and settlement and the degradation of the landscape, my government embarked on programmes that took cognisance of the fact and accordingly accepted only those projects from international partnerships and assistance that aided protection and regeneration of our environment.

My father divided his time among many other projects, the two most engaging ones being the work at Barajaly taken periodically at the village mosque and supervising the new arrivals in Almamy Leh.

My father helped repair the leaky roof of the mosque in his time. In my time I was blessed to have spearheaded the construction of a new modern mosque for the village. In 1983, a Senegalese tycoon Djilly Mbaye invited me to visit him in his birthplace of Louga, a nice, neat town in northern Senegal. That town had blessings of its own in not only having produced many well-known, rich and influential entrepreneurs in Senegal's industry, transportation, and import-export and retailing businesses but also was the birthplace of the country's former President Abdou Diouf.

Djilly Mbaye entertained me, Njaimeh and my party in his palatial home, resplendent with gold-headed faucets and door knobs. Prominent among several glittering edifices and facilities reminiscent of décor from the Arabian Nights was his private mosque where his family and invited guests worshipped. I was impressed by the fairy tale magnificence of the surroundings and I could not help but let him know how pleased we were to be his guests. At the end of the visit, Djilly announced a surprise parting gift. He offered to build a replica of that mosque in my birthplace so that I could have one just as he did in his home. It was indeed a pleasant surprise.

Within weeks, Djilly Mbaye did send a team of surveyors to the site. He selected a reputable local Gambian contractor, Mustapha Bittaye, and work soon started. After five years of construction, the project was in its finishing stages and, though by no means complete, the cheques stopped coming. Anyway, we had a structure of a mosque in place. All it needed to be completed were a roof and the finishing touches. The people of Barajaly took up the challenge. We all decided that it was not going to be left unfinished. We set up the Barajaly Mosque Completion Fund (BMCF) under the leadership of Imam Talibo Ceesay and my brother, Tasili, who drew up the list of all eligible Barajaly natives for a mosque levy.

Wherever they were in the country or abroad, natives of Barajaly made contributions to the project. It worked wonderfully. Money flowed in. With volunteered labour from community groups, we kept costs down and the contractor was able to hand the mosque over to the village in 1991. It is a magnificent edifice complete with a beautiful Roman column minaret tower, a low white wall and grille iron fence, a resplendent white dome, electrical fittings, water supply, all powered by solar energy. There are toilet and bathroom facilities and a floor space for several hundred worshippers.

Well, in his day during the growing season, my father busied himself, if not seeing to mosque affairs, supervising Almamy Leh. He went around ensuring that the enthusiasm of the planters did not spill over into quarrels over encroachment on each other's plots of land he had allocated them. He intervened on several occasions to draw the lines between some local farmers who wanted to exercise the right of the native over the privilege of the 'strange' farmer. My father would settle the matter by preaching that the land was Allah's and we were simply keepers who had a duty to tend it and to ensure that every living soul had a piece from which to make his living and feed his family. He said that was the duty of all humans and then one day to die peacefully and leave everything to others to carry on with. He taught that otherwise there would be no peace among people for that wonderful life to be realised.

The tenants were ready to till; they all waited like the rest of the village and would not spring into action until the first rains. The rice and groundnut seedlings looked healthy because despite the poor returns, many farmers had had the sense of keeping the very best seeds for planting when the new season would begin in 1932. My father looked upon the valley as a trust that Allah put in his care; it was not surprising when the district tribunal sitting at the village of Sare Ngai in 2002 gave judgment in favour of the Jawara family. The local chief had allocated a large tract of land in Almamy Leh to a family that did not belong there. It was phenomenal during the proceedings that a host of ageing witnesses, as well as younger ones whose parents had fortunately handed down the correct history, told the tribunal about the exact boundaries of Almamy Jawara's land in Lower Fulladu.

Some of them testified with lucid memory and a still grateful heart that Almamy Jawara was the kind one who had allowed them, in some cases their migrant parents, to farm on his land in Almamy Leh. They spoke of how he had left them to build a life of peace and prosperity and had even found them wives to marry.

No matter how faint my recollection may be of my toddler days, I remember the back-breaking work my father had done on those farms where I spent the days of my boyhood digging earth, building hedges and raising mud dykes with my own little hands. That I did when my cousins and I were not shooing monkeys off the groundnut patches or chasing the sound of the bells around the necks of the donkeys when they brought the harvest down those dusty lanes to my father's *secco*. I remember the tender care he took watching over the welfare of the tenants to whom he gave land in Almamy Leh.

After my father passed away in 1961 and I had become a strong figure in the family, we decided the legacy of Almamy Leh and the tradition of sharing and caring for the descendants of my father's wards and tenants must continue. My brothers, Alhaji Kawsu and Saikounding and the other relatives who continued to live and work on the land, carried on Almamy Jawara's legacy and gave out seeds and farming tools every year to keep those families farming and productive.

Scores of nomadic herders came every year to exchange their milk and ghee for goods to take back home with them. It was an important part of their business with my father; and amazingly, they would have walked a hundred or more miles with their animals to come to Barajaly. As time went by, a great number of the settlers at Barajaly were seasonal cattle grazers, Fula-speaking nomads who came into MacCarthy Island Province from as far away as the upper arm of the Volta River in search of grazing.

Some of them stayed on and intermarried and became the forebears of those who today live in Kuntaur Fula Kunda, a small settlement of Fula people wedged along the main road between Kuntaur and Barajaly. The more adventurous moved even further south across the river and stayed in Fulladu and have remained there for longer than one hundred years. They showed their gratitude and respect to my father and always called him *Mawdo*! The name they gave him became more widely used than his own name, Almamy. Even his wives called him Mawdo. One of my brothers, Kawsu, himself one of the veterinary assistants in the department during my time there as veterinary officer, named his eldest son Mawdo in honour of the old man.

My father kept diligent records of what he gave away to the tenants, what they gave back from their harvest or what they sold. The books were ruled in standard columns of accounting, thanks to the two bookkeepers from Bathurst, Pa Abdou Karim John, and another man, a Roman Catholic gentleman, whose name I have now sadly forgotten. Indeed, later on my father did not have to go to Bathurst to engage clerks; he soon found one called Kebba Jaiteh, from Georgetown. They kept the books well and accounted for the stocks and sales in the shop at Walikunda. The respect with which my father dealt with them amply showed his gratitude. Together with his clerks Almamy guided his investments and worked to expand his trade and influence.

Whether as a businessman or a farmer, Almamy made those under him feel happy that he was their host, although there was the occasional complaint that he probably drove them too hard. If he did, it was more out of his love for work and his tendency to be a workaholic than being a taskmaster. All lived freely – locals, relatives, his own children, as well as the good number of strange farmers who had decided to stay on after the trade season. Those among them who came from Senegal would keep the places warm, as it were, for their colleagues who returned home to spend the money they had made; some to make new clothes or marry new wives, others to pay for ceremonies, name their new babies that had been born to their wives while they had been away farming in The Gambia.

My mother spent many rainy seasons worrying about sickness hurting her household. When I was four or five, the medical teams came round to our village and spoke of the smallpox scare. It was a near stampede to Kuntaur or Kaur or to Georgetown for vaccinations. It was, however, impossible to escape the group of strange men who appeared in long narrow khaki trousers, about six of them in white knee-length coats. We were chased half-naked and caught and taken to line up before them. The men in the white coats dabbed our upper arms with wet cotton swabs before planting long needles in our flesh. We screamed and cried and made a rebellious racket. I even remember boys and girls my age and older rolling in the sand before anyone could hold them down to take the injections.

My mother always insisted that we got the injections. She was scared of smallpox and any disease for that matter. She personally supervised the wailing queue of everyone else in the *musu bungo* lining up for inoculation at the makeshift centre set up by the medical teams that alighted from the river boats. Keeping everyone well in her household had become a well-nigh obsession for her. The sound of vomiting, even when it was from morning sickness in one of the pregnant neighbours, the slightest wheezing in the chest of the infants, sent panic red lights all over the house. Malaria was the dreaded disease with mosquitoes whining wickedly every night. But thanks to the bednets and smoke from the *santang* that scared the mosquitoes away malaria did not bother us too much.

She was right in her fear of malaria and smallpox. At the close of the 1920s MacCarthy Island Province recorded four hundred and fifty-one deaths among every one thousand children born there. This was high even though it was lower than in the wetter districts of the country like Baddibu and Foni. The number of women who died during delivery was also high and pregnancies had become as much a burden of joyful anticipation as they were of fear and death. Many women died while giving birth; a few went stark raving mad after delivering their babies. When mysterious things like that happened, no one knew how to explain them and everyone, almost without exception, pointed to witchcraft or to evil spirits roaming about in the night breeze.

All the same, the population of the Province continued to rise steadily over all, from births as well as from settlement. There was very little emigration since there was from the evidence of the people that thronged into the Province a more manageable standard of life there than further east where it was drier or further west where there were stricter land tenure systems and a more conservative traditional culture. Many places welcomed strange farmers but very few had their doors as open and as receptive to them as MacCarthy Island Province.

Years later, under my administration, The Gambia was able to forge ahead and even become a leader in maternal and child health delivery. The launch of the Five Year Health Development project for 1981/82 to 1986/87 was a testimony to my government's commitment to developing a comprehensive and dependable health delivery system. The project estimated at $20 million was jointly financed by the Republic of Italy, the Kingdom of the Netherlands, the United Kingdom, the World Bank and the Gambia government. It was of utmost importance to us as a government and as a people in the way it involved an intensive restructuring of the health services since 1972. In particular, it promoted the change of the Royal Victoria Hospital (RVH) in the capital and Bansang Hospital in the provinces from semi to fully autonomous institutions able to manage themselves and to recover costs in medical service delivery. By 1987, we had completed major works refurbishing and upgrading the facilities in the Children's Wing at the RVH, Banjul Polyclinic, the Brikama Health

Centre and Bansang Hospital. We also approved plans to construct health centres in Kaur, Essau and Fajikunda.

By 1989 we were able to show a firm national commitment to a Primary Health Care (PHC) approach at the highest political level. Government provided 90 per cent of the total healthcare budget with the complementary contribution being provided by the UK-based Medical Research Council (MRC), private and traditional practitioners and medical missions mostly in the form of governmental or other charitable organisations. People's participation also contributed to the health service extension through which village development committees over time had become increasingly involved in the organisation of their own health system. Regional health teams coordinated inter-disciplinary interventions at the field levels through units such as divisional development committees and joint committees set up for specialised areas such as water and sanitation. Life expectancy increased tremendously in the provinces in that time, a vast improvement on life there in the early 1930s.

Back then, throughout the rains, it would appear all that my father and the other elders did, apart from farming, weeding and waiting, was to attend funerals. There was great worry for my younger sister, Jarai, and my younger brother, Bouba, who were born quite close to each other and who my mother had been watching like a hawk for the slightest sign of smallpox or malaria. My mother fussed every day to make sure that there was not a single gap between the mosquito netting and the mattresses. She would fume in the *musu bungo* if anyone was so careless as to break the tuck line along the mattresses where a single mosquito could have entered the net. She fussed over all the bednets around the house – hers, her children's – as much as she did over those of my father's other wives and their children. Apparently, she must have been showing signs quite early that she did not have enough children to throw away; not to disease, and certainly as she would pronounce later, not to Europe.

By and large, thanks to her untiring efforts our home was a safe place throughout the rainy season. Apart from a serious cold that clogged Bouba's nostrils making his tiny pink chest heave and his ribs pound against his weak sides, all went well. Jarai's tender skin developed a scary red rash that my mother quickly attended to with some herbs and plant oil. Sometimes we suffered from whooping cough but she would see us through that as well. The old man showed more robust health than the rest of the household because, not only did he work late in Walikunda, sometimes crossing the treacherously swollen river at night to get home, but he also kept his sisters and cousins and, indeed, the whole Jawara *kabilo* busy with the regular ritual of naming the string of new babies adding to his household.

Naming ceremonies in the Jawara compound had become such a common occurrence that people teased us behind my father's back that for every dozen naming ceremonies in the Province there were at least two in our home. It was only a tease even though it was true that by the time the trade season opened again in 1932, and I had gone to Bathurst, the count in Almamy's compound was one husband and head of household, four wives and seventeen children. Two decades later, when my father was retiring, the tally from the first time he had married until then was one husband and head of household, eight wives and twenty-eight children.

5

Galloping my horse

The trade season ended in early April of 1932. The rains had come and watered the fields and soon robust coos stalks were waving in the wind and the green and yellow flowering groundnut plants covered vast tracts of the land. The heat from below the ground warmed our feet as armies of us children trudged through the furrows ripping out the tares that had grown too close to the good plants. We pulled up the parasite striga plants. In spite of the ravishing beauty of their bright pink petals, they were a treacherous menace on the farms.

When harvesting began, a great thrill seized Barajaly. It was as if the whole village had gone to the farms. Indeed, everyone had something to pull down or dig up. The change in the rhythm of life was exciting. The coos stalks, already almost of the height of the tallest man in the village, bowed their pollen powdered heads to the eager hands of the croppers. The harvest was good; we the children had done a good job shooing off the birds. As the groundnut heaps rose higher in the fields, the men praised us for our hard work, chasing the monkeys all season off the fields.

I wish we had known much earlier about building the silent men we came to know as scarecrows. We made simple crosses from dried sticks and hung old muslin or cotton wrappers and headscarves that easily fluttered in the wind. However, they were not as effective as the scarecrows which took some skill to construct. Even so, the enthusiasm and fracas of us children running and shooing and stoning the bird pests away knew no bounds. I found an old felt hat Pa Abdou Karim had thrown and I put it on the head of the scarecrow on one of my uncle's farms.

It was amazing that the next time I saw anything looking like those scarecrows was in Bathurst. The Christians there celebrated the Good Friday in which they sewed up grass figures. Pa Jones, one of Pa Yoma's friends, explained that the dummies were of Judas the man who betrayed Jesus to the Romans. That was why the children dragged his effigy through the town and flogged it to shreds with stems of mangrove wood. Once I joined in the flogging at Half Die but when it proved a dangerous enterprise of flying wood and breathless chasing I took to the quieter recess of my veranda and watched the Serer fishermen bring in the catch. Until that experience and Pa Jones's explanation, I had always wondered why the people in Bathurst made scarecrows because they did not have farms as we had at Barajaly.

Back at Barajaly, because the rains were good, the farmers had gathered a good harvest and the new trade season that began at the end of the year took off with great promise. The donkeys arrived and the riverside at Walikunda was busy and noisy once again. The cutters swallowed the mounds of groundnuts that were carried on board on the heads and shoulders of hundreds of bare-backed carriers. The sun shone brightly and spread its golden warmth every day. When it shut out occasionally and grey clouds drifted past, the farmers did not like the signs. Dark clouds worried them seriously because freak downpours would ruin the crop that would rot out in the fields.

Groundnut farming was men's work, so they threshed away and winnowed. The women joined in the winnowing to speed up the work and constantly, the donkey trains and their chiming bells filed in again bringing the harvest. The street way between Pa Yoma's and Almamy's shops was perhaps the busiest section. Pa Yoma had returned and opened up again. The goods on the shelves in my father's shop were going fast. He had to re-stock quite often. The sun set and rose again. We closed shop and opened up again and each day brought its own fun and its own story. I must have been the happiest among all the people who travelled across the river every morning and evening in that canoe.

Time went fast when the going was good. Before we knew it, the mountains of groundnuts on the *secco* floors were gone; the number of donkeys coming in had run down to a trickle and the agents were counting their profits at the end of another season. It was a great season. I could tell by the more relaxed and accommodating way the agents carried on. By the end of March, Pa Yoma had made a quick crossing on the river canoe to Barajaly. What was unusual though was that he had asked to see both my parents together. He had not gone visiting empty handed. Before stating his business, he opened his travelling bag and offered my mother gifts of a set of expensive cloth of soft brushed cotton. He also gave her a shawl - known locally as *kaala*. He gave my father a string of brown prayer beads with lovely black tassels. He told them he had gone to Sierra Leone on leave after the season closed the year before and had thought of buying and sharing with them some of what he found interesting in the shops in Freetown.

My parents were deeply appreciative and my mother thanked Pa Yoma for his kindness in bringing them such wonderful gifts. My father asked for a short word of prayer and thanksgiving over the gifts. The three elders rubbed their hands together and muttered *Amin! Amin! Amin!* My father kept watching for any sign of a motive for this unexpected kindness. In any case, I noticed that my father's face twitched.

Pa Yoma brought up the subject of my schooling. He said he was daring to do so again because I had grown one more year and the more delayed it got the more difficult it would be to learn all the things that there was to learn both at the *daara* and at the regular school. He was calm and spoke in low persuasive tones. My mother sat silently and pensively followed the conversation which had shifted to all intents and purposes to a very serious discussion between the two men. Pa Yoma said there were no schools in Barajaly, not even a Koranic school for the young children to learn to exercise their minds. In those modern days, he said, a country would only go forward if its citizens were educated. Barajaly would grow to become a different place with modern schools, a bigger mosque, hospitals and a big village marketplace when its children went to school and brought development back to the village. He was very blunt with his idea that my father should not allow all of his children to go without learning English and writing and counting like those children already doing so at Armitage School in Georgetown.

"Whatever happens," Pa Yoma said, "you must not deny Kairaba the opportunity. There is so much that school can bring out in that little boy."

My father heard him out and was hesitant in his reply. He and my mother had given the subject a lot of thought since Pa Yoma had suggested it the year before. They knew it was going to come up again. However, they were still not convinced that they should allow any of their children to go to Bathurst to go to school.

"I do not want my son to learn the ways of the white man," my father said. "*Nassarano* will not bring anything good to him."

"My stepfather is sick in bed right now but his assistants continue to run his Koranic school," Pa Yoma said. "Kairaba will begin there and he will learn the Koran in my own home from the teachings of Sering Mahtarr John."

"I want him to learn that and to learn it well," Almamy answered. His eye caught my mother's rather shocked reaction to the statement which seemed to show my father sounded like changing his song.

"Some visitors of mine told me last week that there was a new Koranic teacher in Dankunku," Mama Fatty said to offset my father's shift.

"Then he will study the Qur'an to a higher level in Mohammedan School, only a few hundred yards from my home and there Muslim scholars and good teachers of English will teach him," Pa Yoma said rather assertively, refusing to allow the idea of Dankunku to linger. "The school is just like the one in Georgetown. They teach the children to read and write Arabic and they also teach them English to do business and to buy and sell. If you have a literate son in your shop you need not bring clerks all the way from Bathurst any more. Imagine how much money you would save and how safe your business would be in the hands of your own child who will take over after you. Besides, the school will give him a choice of what he will do in life. But he would have been well versed in the Qur'an to help guide his choices."

After a good lunch, Pa Yoma left Almamy and Mama Fatty to think things over. Over the next few days, my father seemed to have softened up considerably. My mother, however, still remained unconvinced. It was my father's work now to convince her it was a chance they ought to take. He soon decided that the campaign slogan, as it were, to get my mother thawing was to emphasise that I would master the writing and reading of Arabic and that I would be versed in the study of the Qur'an; and to point out to her that nothing else would work, otherwise.

"Not all the children would be farmers," my father pleaded with her. "Alieu is already trying his hand out in the fields. Basadi seems to like buying and selling. Nacesay and Jarai are growing well under your care and Allah knows what the baby, Bouba, will grow up to be. I say, we should leave at least one to go and see what the world has in store for him."

My mother was not happy to see her strongest support flailing off in that manner. The next three nights were vigils of deep pondering for her; but, finally, she gave in. She had gone into near mourning because my father had granted permission for me to leave with Pa Yoma whenever he was ready to return to Bathurst. I felt it for her so deeply when I saw tears in Mother's eyes yet deep down inside me I was ecstatic. In all my life with her, I had only seen her cry twice. The first would be when I packed my luggage to go away with Pa Yoma and the second time would be in 1947 when I returned home from Achimota in Ghana to take leave of her before my departure to study veterinary medicine at Glasgow. It would sadden me terribly that both times would be about her saying goodbye to me.

As usual, everybody was in high spirits ready to go away. Now that she seemed to have lost the struggle, my mother told my father that she was leaving everything to him, Pa Yoma and to Allah. But she warned my father never to forget that letting me go did not mean that she had male children to throw away.

Pa Yoma got his possessions packed in the vehicle. The Bedford lorry was ready to leave Walikunda. I was going to Bathurst with my father's friend. He was going to take me away to the big town where I would go to school. I am not going to pretend now that I knew what going to school was all about. My vague idea of it was from what I had heard from the conversation my father had in the canoe with the red-headed European and his escort, Bissenti Mendy. But even that was many months before and there was not much I could have retained. I was more thrilled about going away with Pa Yoma than I was about school. I was thinking that wherever it was that he and Ya Fatou and their two children, Bouba and Dodou, came from and went back to every year could not be all that bad a place. I was eager to go with them.

I watched my mother and my sister, Nacesay, pack me a bundle; a kaftan or two, neatly folded, one on top of the other, a couple of short trousers that some of my older cousins had ruffled up from their belongings. My father had packed some foodstuffs from the shop. I was bursting with excitement. But my secret itch, I thought, was that finally I would get to see that thing that swallowed all those bushels and pyramids of groundnuts the cutters took down river from Walikunda. I wanted to see for myself the size of its pot and the length of its serving spoon and what a dish of its *domoda* would look like.

One of my tearful aunts who must have been the frisky one who had lost her headscarf when she went announcing my birth on that Friday afternoon back in 1924 had wrapped some *dempetengo* for me. The steamed and pressed rice cereal with a little sugar made an excellent snack, especially on long journeys. The whole family had crossed over to Walikunda. My playmates came around as well; Fura Jawara and Lellie and the others. They stared from a distance saying nothing. Finally, Pa Yoma gave the signal for everyone to get on the lorry. My excitement was now uncontrollable.

My father failed utterly in his pleas to get my mother to stop weeping. A couple of Mama Fatty's friends had come with her and they too tried by cajoling her, being hard on her and finally pretending to be angry with her. She only stood a short distance from the lorry, her shawl about her saddened face and wept. Ya Fatou Jobarteh consoled her and promised her that she would take good care of me. She told her it was not as if I was going away with strangers. She promised her that she was going to be a good mother to me, and Pa Yoma, who she said was already an adopted son of Walikunda; and who would be a good father to me.

"Will you come and see us often?" she managed to ask me.

"I will come and see you often," I answered.

Perhaps that helped my mother calm down a little. She dried her eyes with her *kaala*. She told me to behave well and never forget that I had people back in Barajaly praying for me. Nfansu, the driver, hoisted me aboard the back of the lorry. Like a small monkey testing the tree branches, I clambered over luggage, beds, mattresses, chairs, bags of charcoal, few sacks of peeled groundnuts, baobab fruit, bags of coos and sorghum, bales of cloth and rolls of hurricane lamp wick, until I found myself a safe and anchored place, close to Ya Fatou. I riveted myself in and I was ready. I could feel my smile stretch from one ear to the other. When Pa Yoma finished his own goodbyes, he climbed into the front cabin. Nfansu fired the engine; I could hardly contain my excitement when the lorry began to move.

Although I had always envisaged travelling out of Walikunda in one of Pa Yoma's cutters, I was fascinated enough by being in the open carriage of his Bedford lorry with his wife Ya Fatou and the boys, Bouba and Dodou. Pa Yoma at the time owned two big groundnut cutters, the first he named the *Fatou Jobarteh* and the second he named the *Nancy*. Those boats plied regularly transporting thousands of tons of groundnuts from trading posts along the river to Kaur and Bathurst. He spent his money wisely and bought property in Bathurst. He bought 21 Leman Street, which everyone called *Bakamon*. He also bought No 1 Cotton Street. His brother Omar owned the property next door; it seemed the two brothers always bought property next to each other.

I would have loved to sail in one of those wooden boats around the bend on the river that disappeared behind the thick green creepers out of Walikunda but I figured a lorry was as good as anything as long as it was going to Bathurst. I stopped my daydreaming about sailing as soon as the lorry started to move because something very strange began to happen. The trees along the roadside were moving backwards. The houses were moving too; gently at first then at a high speed. My stomach heaved. I held on to some luggage. My mother, the crowd of men and women, the other children and my pal, Lellie, waved frantically. They began to recede and soon they were little, blurry images in the distance. In a quick moment, they were no longer visible. It was just us in the lorry and the trees, the occasional bystanders near firewood stacks along the road, all speeding past. Behind us, everything was blanketed by clouds of brown dust churning in a giant whirlwind chase after the groaning lorry.

There could not have been anyone else more excited than I was on board that lorry. Ya Fatou looked sombre. Her face was marked with some prescience. Like the dedicated wife she was, she had come through another year travelling the uncharted and treacherous paths of the provinces to be faithfully by her husband and to be part of his labours. I could only compare her steadfastness to that of my mother who even on hot or cold days would go with the women into the rice fields and would wade knee-deep into those lowland swamps to plant the rice seedlings and then throughout the season, tend them daily until they ripened for the harvest.

Bouba and Dodou seemed to know every bump and every turn of the way. Bouba was older than Dodou by two years and was at least four, if not five years, older than I was. It seemed they knew the road enough to even anticipate certain jolts and to flow with the shocks when they hit. They were returning for perhaps the third time since I first met them in their father's shop in Walikunda. I was happy to be travelling with them to join their household. I was sure we would become brothers. I was eager to reach Banjul, the only name I knew at the time for the big town from where they came every year. I knew nothing of what a hazardous journey we had embarked upon.

The driver, Nfansu, of course, I quickly realised, was master of the tracks. He moved that lorry along over what I was not sure I could call a road because what I saw laid out in front of us and behind us was just one continuous track running among the trees and over the low hills. The potholes were so large that there was no way of getting the lorry to drive around them. Nfansu knew how to bounce in and out or over them. He did so with such great skill and I might say to the satisfaction of Pa Yoma who bounced next to him inside the front cabin in his blue kaftan and his red fez.

As soon as the journey had started, the bumps on the road caused their own special thrill for me. In my innocence, I took each with a rush of boyish excitement and I felt such fun bouncing up and down. The lorry threw us violently about and with great fillip I shouted in Mandinka: *Mbe nna suwo borilla! Mbe nna suwo borilla*! (I'm, galloping my horse! I'm galloping my horse!)

Ya Fatou was so vexed by my indiscretion that she shushed me by pinching me back to my senses in one sweep of an admonishing hand. The pain of her pinch seared through the flesh of my thigh. I sank back into my place. When the lorry steadied, the accusing looks on the faces of the two boys told me that there was something I was missing.

"People are breaking their bodies on the bumps and you are galloping horses?" Ya Fatou irately scolded.

My thigh burnt so much that an involuntary wetness came over my eyeballs. I muttered an apology and sank back into my cave among the luggage. I clutched my small bundle of clothing. For a moment it represented my mother and by wrapping myself around it I found comfort away from the sad look of reproach and disappointment on the woman's face.

For many miles after, I sat quietly shaking with everyone else over the kinder bumps. As we travelled I discerned the true interpretations in Ya Fatou's eyes of whatever it was that was going on with the lorry. When she gathered the skin on her forehead, I read the going was about to get rough. When the lorry went quietly over the hill and the going was fair again, I saw the relief of it in her brightened eyes. How many times had I seen that face smile in Pa Yoma's shop; seen it in the *secco* and in the outdoor kitchen in Walikunda? I had seen Ya Fatou throw up her hands to her ears in prayer, those hands that were decorated in exotic geometric motifs from henna. I had seen her clean her teeth all day with *ratt* and it fascinated me how she would periodically spew an arcing streak of fluid between her teeth into the distance. Although modern public health would frown upon it, *sereti* in the old days was fashionable among elegant Wollof women. What I had never seen until that day was that stern look on her face. I also never knew those delicate fingers could pinch that badly until a lorry named *Ndey Kumba* rattled Ya Fatou's body and I made a silly remark.

It finally dawned on me that there was some real danger involved in having a heavily laden lorry smashing against rocks on the road and swaying from side to side. While it was the sensation of a galloping horse I experienced over the potholes, others were thinking of death and their bodies that were shaken to exhaustion. Then again, I did not know what length of journey we had embarked upon. Nor did I know the rigour and ever-present dangers of road travel that lay ahead in a journey that would take all of four days to cover nearly one hundred and sixty miles of dirt tracks over hills and ferries across rushing reptile-infested tributaries not to speak of the treacherous bends in the road, all the way to our destination.

After an hour and a half of rough riding, we arrived at Brikamaba. Nfansu was there again to hoist me out of the lorry and set me down on my trembling limbs. It took a good minute or two for me to regain equilibrium. Bouba and Dodou had jumped down by themselves and were helping their mother climb down the sides with all the maternal and elderly decorum the woman could muster.

Pa Yoma alighted and a crowd gathered almost instantly. We were all covered in dust. I could hardly recognise Bouba. No wonder water was the first thing people brought with them as they swarmed around the lorry. Water to drink; water to wash off the grime; more and more water. I observed very quickly that the water was not just for us humans. I stood in amazement to see the driver lift the huge green bonnet of the lorry and pour nearly half a gallon of water down a pipe in the front.

"The lorry drinks water too?" I could not help asking Nfansu.

"Not only water, it drinks oil and it drinks gas oil," Nfansu replied, his big muscles glistening with perspiration in the evening sunlight.

He proceeded without paying any further attention to me. He seemed serious about his business. I watched him pour some dark oil into different places in the engine, different from the front where he had poured the water. He then jerked up a huge quarter drum and blew into a piece of pipe through which the petrol started to rush into a huge metal tank hanging just outside the underbelly of the lorry's carriage. *Ndey Kumba* seemed to have had more refreshment than any of us humans on that first stop. In fact, it got to enjoy that special treatment at all the stops on the way.

Even as short as the stop was, many of my father's relatives came out to greet us. There were cousins of his and their children from Nanko kunda who came out to welcome us. They served the coolest, most refreshing water I had drunk in a long time. I don't know how they managed to keep the water so cool. I drank to my stomach's fill and so did Pa Yoma, Ya Fatou and the boys. I must say however that no one among us could have drunk more water than *Ndey Kumba* did.

Many of Pa Yoma's clients came to see him and to greet him. They were loyal to him and would travel all the way to Walikunda to do business with him. I would learn how that kind of allegiance worked when during my early days in politics I came to count on the loyalty of people. Loyalty to the cause would of course be the backbone behind some of the tremendous waves of support the PPP pulled off while we were consolidating the identity of the party and convincing people with the principles it stood for – principles of nationality, inclusion in the mainstream of national life, the people's guarantee of freedom and dignity after nearly three hundred years of European domination. Faith in that kind of loyalty did take into consideration that in politics there was loyalty and there was treachery. Because upon closer study it would seem quite natural that our world was run by both.

Those loyal clients asked Pa Yoma about the trade season and said they hoped it had gone well. Pa Yoma assured them that Allah had been good to him and he had no complaints and was even already looking forward to returning the following year. One of the men cried out: *Insha'Allah!*

Ya Fatou climbed back aboard having changed her gown and resumed her old place. Dodou and Bouba exchanged places. I decidedly went back to mine because I had come to fit rather snugly in what had become my burrow among the luggage. I tried as best I could to keep my thighs away from Ya Fatou's reach. Somehow, the surroundings, mostly mattresses, cushioned me somewhat from the bumps. We waved goodbye to Brikamaba, a village to which I would return many times on animal health campaigns when I became a veterinary officer and during political campaigns across the country to sell the agenda of the PPP to the people. I also spent many pleasant nights there during the stopovers with Tasli, a younger brother of mine, who had settled and raised his family there. Every time I came by, he would give me and my team a warm welcome; and it was a pleasure every time to see him, sometimes after my very long spells in Bathurst.

Not even the many prayers we had to send us off changed the bumps on the road. The road was still undefined. The grass grew where it wished and rocks stood challengingly in spaced outcrops. We drove through Sukur, Medina and Jahally – important villages of the Sarahule people. After we had left Jahally it became obvious that we were climbing a steep hill. The engine groaned louder and louder as it inched forward along the infamously dangerous rise in the land, so steep and perilous that a British commissioner, N M Ashetton, had named it *Koro Wuleng* (Mandinka for "Red Disaster"). The hill got its name from the uncountable number of accidents that had occurred there. A number of relics of failed crossings strewed the hillside with twisted and rusting metal of lorries that did not make it over the hill. Those always brought memories of many traders and drivers who lost their lives there where the land rose unusually from the general flatness along the length and breadth of The Gambia, which the geography books I would read later on at the Methodist Boys' High School said did not rise higher at any point than two hundred feet above sea level.

Nfansu and Pa Yoma in the front cabin had their heads up ahead of us on the hill. The sound of the engine changed to a struggling and sustained drone. No one spoke; and I who had learnt the hard way kept my eyes glued to Ya Fatou. I could feel the strain she was going through; the skin on her forehead gathered in anxious ridges as the lorry heaved upward on the hill.

It was all over in a short while. We were soon over the hill and riding much easier down the side, one huge danger past. We relaxed, but for Nfansu it was still his business to continue negotiating which turns to take and where to plant the lorry's giant wheels. The thatched huts and the trees never stopped speeding by; they sped past as if they were all in a mad hurry to get somewhere. The bumps never stopped bumping either. Many times in the thick of the engine noise I heard the Brikamaba water make funny globular sounds inside my stomach. The dust started up again and Ya Fatou drew her shawl over her face. Bouba and Dodou were indifferent; they sank in where they were among some bales of cloth and pulled the edges of their woollen caps down around their ears. I pried into my bundle and pulled out the woollen cap my mother had packed for me. I did what I had seen Bouba and Dodou do with theirs; and I dug into my burrow again.

After only a few miles, all of those precautions against the dust were in vain. Our ears were clogged. So were our throats and nostrils with fine brown powder of road dust. Some caught in my eyelashes like the pollen on ripe coos cobs.

6

After Bathurst, when do we get to Banjul?

There was silence for miles after *Koro Wuleng*; a silence I took to be part of the rules of road travel over the area. People fell silent when danger lurked. I have experienced similar rituals of people falling into silence at dangerous points of a journey. I remember vividly the kind of electrifying silence that descended on passengers on board the steamer in which I was travelling across the Bay of Biscay in 1947. In rough seas no one spoke a word. People simply disappeared into their cabins while the ship bobbed defencelessly against two storey-high waves that rolled in from the far distance and rocked the ship like a matchbox in the ocean. In the tens of thousands of the frequent flyer miles I have chalked up in my time travelling by air across the globe, I have never ceased to wonder why talkative, high-spirited passengers always fall into a sudden deadly silence as soon as the aircraft flies into some horrific turbulence. What the silence does to affect the outcome has always mildly amused me. Death can come whether we are quiet or noisy!

Words formed on everyone's lips as soon as danger was over when we arrived at Kudang and the lorry eased to a stop in the main village of the chiefdom of Niamina East. The sleepy village was to feature prominently in many ways in my personal and official affairs as the years went by. It would be the birthplace of Sheriff Sekouba Sisay, who was born there in 1935. He was the chief's son who would serve with me in a ministerial portfolio in the first coalition government in 1960 and in the PPP cabinet that began directing the affairs of state after the PPP swept the polls and formed a government in 1962. Kudang would also produce Lamin Marenah, an expert in the science of agriculture, who, as a student in 1944, had come to live at 37 Wellington Street. He had joined Pa Yoma's household in Bathurst for the same reason I was living there – to go to school.

Nfansu had pushed the lorry hard all afternoon. Pa Yoma agreed to his suggestion of a night stop in Kudang. Seyfo Sekouba Sisay had extended such unforgettable hospitality with comfortable sleeping quarters in his compound with lots of good food to eat. The chief spared no comfort to make sure we passed a good night as guests in his compound. I have indelible recollections of the animals and rows of low hanging fruit on the trees in the yard. Early the next morning, we were up and on our way but not before an early crowd had surrounded the lorry to watch us board and to say goodbye. The bush was thick and green through the Niamina district and we soon drove into Dankunku, my mother's birthplace.

In the mêlée of greetings and salutations, somehow word went round that the little boy travelling in the company of Pa Yoma and his family was, indeed, Mama Fatty's son, Kairaba. Women popped in and out of the compound gate at Fatty kunda. I was brought out to meet my mother's closest relations for the first time. I had only heard of Dankunku from her stories. It was a much bigger village than she had described, certainly much bigger than Barajaly with just a dozen or more compounds.

The welcome was tremendous and generous. We were feted. The Fatty *kabilo* came out with fresh and roast groundnuts with drinks. Someone got us some lemonade from one of the corner shops in the village. I did not realise that I had so many cousins. Everyone wanted to touch me or carry me or talk to me. They brought me goodies. Pa Yoma was able at last to convince them that there was a long trip ahead of us and I needed to rest.

While we rested in my grandfather's compound, Pa Yoma went out to pay a courtesy call on Seyfo Bora Mboge and the imam and to offer greetings to the *alkalo* and other village elders. Tired as I was, I did not fail to notice that *Ndey Kumba*, of course, did not fail to get its full treatment about the engine area and even though the ritual was happening for the fourth time since we left Walikunda, it did not cease to amaze me that a lorry would drink water, just like people did.

We retired early for the night and sleep quickly drew me away. I returned to reality at the crack of dawn when I heard Pa Yoma bumping a kettle of water on his way out to the veranda of compacted earth to say his *fajar* prayers. I cannot remember if I followed him out to pray but I definitely remember my poor body racked with pain from the bumps. To think of what lay ahead could have dissuaded me from even rising from my mat on the floor. I probably fell asleep again.

Before the sun cleared the height of the trees we were off and away from Dankunku. Although we had not stayed long enough to make any formal acquaintances, it was a great feeling being among my mother's people for a change. Until then I had known very little of my mother's relatives; well, except perhaps for those young cousins of mine who had come to look for accommodation, to work in Almamy Leh.

The cool breeze of the April morning struggled failingly against the sun which opened up fiercely. It was going to be hotter than the day before. And we had better be ready for it. We were well on our way by the time the sun stood with shattering brightness up in the sky. It burnt down severely and there was no cloud in between to lessen its burden. Bouba tried to open a large black umbrella; but the strong wind frustrated his effort and after a futile struggle, he gave up.

My throat was parching; and I was wondering where all that refreshment we had in Dankunku had gone so quickly. Dodou thoughtfully passed a kettle of water to me. I thirstily wrapped my lips around the snout while expertly letting the bumps shake the water into my mouth. It worked beautifully; I had mastered a new skill – the art of drinking and bumping without spilling a drop or breaking my teeth on the snout of the metal pot. After a long spell on the road with the engine noise as the only reference, we at last arrived at Bintang Bolong - the large tributary of the Gambia river that divides Kiang from Foni.

The ferry was a large iron pontoon with side railings. We alighted and crossed over with all the other passengers we found waiting at the crossing. There was a rope curving outwards in the water from one bank to the other. The strong men on the pontoon pulled on it and the pontoon began to move across to the other side. Bouba and Dodou helped them. Ya Fatou covered her head in her shawl and stood in the middle with me. The sensation of bobbing over the water was wonderful.

There were familiar lazy bubbles rising to the surface of the water. When I saw the familiar arrow heads cutting just below the surface of the water, I knew the submariners lurked down there just like they did at Walikunda. The crocodiles cruised without a care in the world while the pontoon inched over. Once we set our feet safely on firm ground again, we gave way to a crowd that got on the pontoon, on its way back to the other side where Nfansu and Pa Yoma waited with the lorry to cross over. Getting the lorry to roll on to the pontoon was quite tricky but Nfansu and the men of the Marine Department who operated it made an easy job of it; and the lorry was soon pulling over to our side. We watched with concentration as Nfansu guided our lorry off the metal ferry; and we were happy to jump aboard again for the short drive to Kalagi.

Thankfully, *Ndey Kumba* was sturdy. Its wheels were well taken care of and its engines fired beautifully. A group of women selling vegetables and fruit in large baskets welcomed us to Kalagi. The village stood at a crossroads, at one end of the main artery road driving west into lower Gambia and a dirt road winding south into the Casamance region of Senegal that shared ninety miles of common borders with the Foni Districts all the way to the village of Bulock at the other end. It was an important junction for human and commercial traffic.

At Kalagi, Nfansu decided the lorry needed to stock up again on the usual fluids. Dodou and Bouba thought they had seen some foodstuffs they had fancied at the roadside tables. I went along with them to busy-body over their purchases and I made sure I got some of whatever it was they had bought, a yellow sugar cake – *lamarsess*. I was biting into my sugar cake when a towering figure of a policeman came walking up to Nfansu. I overheard their conversation about the rest of our journey. I heard the policeman ask Nfansu where we were going. The driver muttered a strange answer.

"Bathurst," he said.

"Ah, Bathurst!" the police officer exclaimed. "The road from Kalagi is in reasonably good condition. You should arrive in Bathurst in very good time."

As soon as the policeman ambled off, I ran over to Nfansu who was checking the oil by dipping a thin metal rod over and over again into the engine and wiping off the dripping oil in a dirty black cloth in his hand.

I asked him. "Nfansu, when we reach Bathurst, how long will it take us to get to Banjul?"

Nfansu intended to laugh but he croaked instead. I was serious about my question. I wished badly that he would answer. I really wanted to know after we got to Bathurst how long it would take us to get to Banjul.

"It is the same place," he answered cleaning the metal rod again in a dirty oily mop. He jumped off the lorry. "Bathurst is the white man's name for Banjul. That's where we are going, to Bathurst."

The road was indeed better. I kept that name printed in my head – Bathurst! I was so eager I could burst. However, I trusted the policeman's predictions that we would get there very soon. The road was clear of grass and the driver was more at ease the way he moved the lorry forward with less trouble over the potholes. We completed the few miles to Bwiam and stopped for the night there. The next day, we took off early again to cover as many miles as we could in the relatively cool weather of the morning hours. It was an uneventful ride; less dust though and greener with rice swamps stretching for miles on either side of the road. I had fallen asleep among the luggage until Bouba shook me and announced that we had arrived in the Kombo district. What difference did that make to an eight-year old that we had left Foni and were now in Kombo? For me all of it was heat, dust, bumps and more bumps. I went back to sleep.

When I woke up again, we were driving through the biggest village I had seen on the trip. Dodou said it was called Brikama and that there was a very big chief living there. He should know, I guessed because he must have been back and forth across that village so many times in the years since he started accompanying his father to Walikunda. I looked out over the side of the lorry and saw it was indeed a busy place we were driving through. The bushes along the roadside were green and grew very high up almost to the height of our lorry. The green vegetation in places always seemed to capture my attention, especially with the large number of sheep that ate the grass quietly below the tall overgrowth. I heard the people speak in Mandinka. But they were really no different from the people in Barajaly and I understood everything they said. Their clothes were the same. The young people seemed very carefree and one or two of them jumped about too close to the lorry. They meant no harm, though; they were just excited to see Nfansu.

After Brikama, there were more and more lorries on the road. The rushing sound the engines made when one passed by captivated me and I waited long moments to hear it when a vehicle went by. After a long while of travelling, our lorry came to a stop at the gaping mouth of a massive waterway. This was larger than the stretch at Bintang. I looked quickly out on the beach. There was no pontoon ferry there – only a bridge. Our lorry had to wait for the car that was standing on the other side to come gently across over to our side. There was a policeman there waving to it and guiding it until it came safely across. Only one vehicle at a time from either side was allowed to cross. Eventually, it was our turn to go.

"Here's my promise from last November," Pa Yoma said once we reached the platform near the edge of the bridge. Pa Yoma drew up the ample sleeves of his blue kaftan and put his hand out of the window. He dropped several brown two shilling coins into the cupped hands of the police officer.

"You never fail your word, Pa Ebrima," the policeman laughed and waved Nfansu on. "Welcome to the Denton Bridge, Nfansu."

"A promise is a promise," Pa Yoma answered. He told us later that what he had given the policeman was nearly half the man's monthly salary.

Bouba seemed so fascinated by the massive steel girders and braces and the nearly one million bolts that held the pieces of the bridge in place. While the bridge held his attention, the more gripping sight for me was the great blue sea that spread large and sparkling in the late afternoon sunlight to the left of us. We got off the bridge on the other side. Nfansu drove with more ease now as he moved the vehicle steadily through a large expanse of green level ground straddling the road. I had never before that day seen grass so green, that covered the ground so evenly all the way.

I came to know much later that we had been driving through the Bathurst Golf Course where important traders such as Henry Madi, the white man I had seen a year earlier in 1931 on his yacht, the *Tina*, at Walikunda, and Charles L Page of V Q Petersen Co Ltd were members. Mr Page and Mr Petersen were chairman and deputy, respectively at the prestigious Bathurst Club. It was in that same year when I first saw Henry Madi in Walikunda that his club applied for and got the lease to lay a golf course across the north and south stretches from the water mark. The course lay over a stretch of 34 acres, measuring 23 acres on the south side of the road and nearly 11 on the north side adjoining the Forster estate to the north-east.

I could be taking a first here as a Gambian golf historian to put on record the beginning of golf in The Gambia. My interest in attempting so is obvious. I love golf. The landowners of the Forster section of the grounds, Sir Samuel John Forster and his wife, Lady Comfort Love Forster, of 5 Wellington Street, Bathurst, had rented it for a monthly sum of £4 3 shillings and 4 pence to the War Department of the UK whose officers in turn sublet the land on a long lease to the Bathurst Golf Club. Naturally the golf course became useful to the military officers for recreation.

Obviously, the remote Colony of The Gambia was not expecting that the Hitler menace was going to be as protracted and widespread as it did. In the heat of the war in 1944, the area was taken over by the Air Ministry for the use of the Royal Air Force that needed to plan air strikes against the Vichy Government in control of Dakar, in Senegal. That of itself entailed some fresh negotiations with the Forster estate.

On the Bathurst side, the golf course was on the right side of the road and the police guard post exactly where it is standing today. Sir Sam Forster died in 1940 leaving executorial powers to his wife, Comfort, and the respected journalist and social commentator in his time, Thomas Hamilton Joiner. However, all over the world the conflict of interest between naturalists and industrialists is well known. The V Q Petersen company on 14 March 1940 put in an application to government for permission to instal an oil mill for the purpose of decorticating and pressing groundnuts, palm kernels and other oil seeds to supply the local market and to export the residue pressed into hard cake as animal feed.

Because the golf club had fallen into hard times and could not continue to justify the holding of such prime land, government considered the proposal of the industrialists. Henry Madi fought tooth and nail to keep it though. In fact, in 1948, when he had become chairman of the Bathurst Club, he re-christened the land and the facilities with a new name, the

Denton Bridge Club. But government insisted on taking it over and repaid the Bathurst Club £800 to surrender by July 1948 the lease and building and everything on the land, by the end of the four years remaining on the lease to enable the application of V Q Petersen to proceed. While it continued to use the facilities as a club house Madi and his fellows were charged a yearly rent of one shilling, payable every first day of the year.

However, the plans to convert such a beautiful open recreational space did not go down well with everybody in the government and strings began to pull in different directions. We could consider this one of our first environmental test cases between industrial developers and conservationists. In the end, Governor Andrew Wright put a moratorium on the V Q Petersen plans while some people put forward arguments about preserving the environment. But the governor had to go away on leave to England in 1948 and while he was away, some confusion occurred in the administration. Someone apparently misunderstood the standing orders of the governor about keeping the area as a natural green belt and gave the green light to the V Q Petersen company that immediately began constructing the oil and cake pressing plants on the site.

By the time the governor returned and called up the files on the subject the project had gone too far to be stopped. Muscles flexed in the meeting rooms at the Chamber of Commerce. Only money and influence, it would appear, talked. Suffice it to say, the groundnut pressing plant went ahead and took over the grounds of The Gambia's first golf course.

As a child, I had always wanted to know what swallowed all those sacks of groundnuts my father put on those cutters that came to Walikunda. When it became my business to run government, I found the facilities opened there and later run by GOMB were such a crucial sector of the economy I managed. I am tempted now as even then to conclude that the economy was more important than golf. But when I think of my stand on the environment and our dire need for green spaces and recreation and my passion for golf, I fall back on the need for us to work towards holding a balance between growth and the threatened life of our planet with the disappearance of rain forests and cover vegetation in the name of development.

I find it a good piece of history that is relevant to my story with a game to which I was introduced some time in 1962, thanks to the persistence of J P Bray, the last British holder of the post of superintendent of police. I have never stopped playing since. Bray took me golfing at the Fajara Golf Course where the club moved after the Denton Bridge site became a groundnut collection depot. He flattered me that I had a marvellous grip of the putter and a decent swing to go with it. I found the game an excellent subject for casual conversation and a very relaxing pastime especially after the massive weight of a day's politics and the running of government on one's shoulders. Besides, the fact that I did bring a few trophies home from highly competitive evenings proved that I had finally found one sport after dinghy sailing in which I could respectfully hold my own.

Beyond the stretch of the Denton Bridge Golf Course the sea crashed massive waves on white beach that stretched satin white between the majestic baobab trees all the way down that road. Next we passed some solemn looking white stones I would later discover were gravestones standing in the town cemetery. Nfansu slowed the lorry down as we drove into a wide street. Bouba and Dodou were wide awake now and they sat up. I could tell when they removed their *sumbuya* and stashed them away that we had arrived at an important place. We drove through the main street over hard and firm roadway. There were no bumps and the blackened earth screeched underneath the wheels of the lorry as we passed the rows along the street lined with houses. Nfansu gave a playful toot of his piercing horn as if to announce we had arrived.

"Banjul!" Bouba shouted across to me.

He need not have. I had figured that out myself by the sudden change of activity. The road was smooth and black and *Ndey Kumba* did not jump as it had done all the way there. The buildings of different shapes and sizes looked strong with corrugated iron roofs just like the shiny ones that covered Almamy Jawara's house and the *musu bungo* in Barajaly. Many smaller streets ran in straight order and joined the main street along which stood electric poles with decorated lampshades. I raised myself against the side to take a good look at most definitely the straightest street I had ever seen. Bathurst appeared to be a very large and organised village, larger than I had ever thought it would be. The streets were filled with people. Some of the white-painted houses built out of wood and stone stood along the edge of the streets but others were enclosed by *kirinting* fences.

As we drove further into town the rows of high block houses stood more neatly with their verandas overhanging the streets below. People were busy going in and out of the many shops in the town. It would be difficult for me to imagine what else in my experience could match the way I felt in April 1932, driving through those tall houses along Clifton Road and Hagan and Buckle streets. At last Nfansu brought the lorry to a final stop at 37 Wellington Street. The noise of chattering children took over as soon as Nfansu shut off the groan of the engine. An indescribable sensation gripped me as the driver helped me out of the lorry and set me on my feet as he had done at all the preceding stops.

It was a wonderful welcome. As soon as Pa Yoma got out of the front cabin it seemed like the small fish market on the beachfront broke into a near stampede to reach him. While we stretched our legs a crowd mobbed the old man. It had been four days since we left Walikunda and Nfansu was the star of that story; he and his machine, *Ndey Kumba*. He had admirers, too; a noisy crowd of children swarmed around him pulling him this way and that.

The gate burst open and a choir of children, most of them my age and older, rushed up chanting *Papa Yoma niouw na! Papa Yoma niouw na!* I hadn't a clue that the clamouring was Wollof for saying, "Papa Yoma has come! Papa Yoma has come!" Bouba, Dodou and I found very little to do. Volunteers clambered up the lorry and began carrying things inside the compound. Ya Amie Gaye, Pa Yoma's stepmother, got stuck among the children and had to be helped through with the cup of water she was carrying to welcome Pa Yoma and Ya Fatou.

It was such a joyous scene. Anyway, she was more successful at the ritual of welcome when two weeks later she, in like manner, received Pa Yoma's younger brother, Pa Omar, when he arrived from his trading post at Fatoto. It took a longer while for Pa Omar to get home because he was coming from Fatoto, the farthest trading post on the circuit, on the eastern tip of the country.

I had always thought that Almamy Jawara's compound at Barajaly was full of people but what I found at 37 Wellington Street was hardly any different. That compound was home to the Jallow family – the two trader brothers and their wives and children and the numerous wards and other members of the extended family. It was open to people who only wandered in search of some food or a cup of water to quench their thirst or simply a place to rest from the heat of the day. No passer-by who was hungry was ever turned away. There was a row of houses at the back of the compound where some Serer fishermen who came seasonally to fish and trade lived. Next to theirs was the room of the famous Qur'anic teacher Pa Yoma had talked about with my father. In my excitement I peeped inside the room and I saw Sering Matarr John; he was bedridden and communicating only in monosyllables.

But we had a huge welcome to attend to and I followed Bouba back to the main house where his father was already seated and receiving people who had come out to greet him. It was impossible to count the number of pairs of shoes at the door. Men and women, old and young, arrived, took off their hats and shoes and went in to shake hands with Pa Yoma and to bid him welcome.

The volunteers soon cleared the luggage out of the lorry. It was nearly a whole shop that that lorry had carried and all was now safely removed to the stores at the back of the yard. However much I enjoyed running back and forth among those bigger porters who came to help, I must say I enjoyed more the rich smell of good cooking that was constantly drifting from the back of the compound. There I soon discovered the secret of the huge cauldrons of food sitting on raging fireplaces and where a few young women fussed about as they prepared a sumptuous feast to welcome the man of the house.

The fish was a treat. Every day I watched the Serer fishermen, mostly from the villages of Dionewar and Niodior in Senegal, bargaining their wares on the beach in front of our house. Standing on a bed in our living room, I would watch them through the window overlooking *Marché Mussanté*, the marketplace incomparable to any in Bathurst for good and tasty fish. Anyhow, that lively market has long disappeared and in its place now stands some of the facilities of the multi-million dollar Gambia Port Authority which my government started in 1970.

7

Influential men in my life

In all my time in politics in or out of office, my preferred role has been to influence my surroundings with the principles of equity and to encourage due consideration of divergent views. Difficult as the actual practice of fairness, thoughtfulness and tolerance were, they were central to the focus and conduct of the convicted democrat. Every conflict in the field of human endeavour needs the benefit of hearing the other side. If it is true that every face tells a story, then listening to the other side becomes paramount in the search for peaceful solutions. Dialogue is crucial towards the objective of human reconciliation when bonds have been broken. Many have dismissed this as naïve pacifism, idealist at best. But in this world of distorted heroism, it is democracy that will provide the true sense of balance that will ever be able to control our animal and spiritual urges to ever consider the views of anyone else.

I have heard people argue that democracy is not a natural human pattern of behaviour. They say human beings having been hunter-gatherers have been solely keen to provide for themselves and their immediate circles, and, therefore, are by nature selfish. While the selfishness of the gatherer might have some validity over a certain period of his species' development, I would argue that democracy has come out of people's civilised awareness of community. That belonging had long demanded higher standards of behaviour and order that would curb, control or generally manage instincts of selfishness, greed and the unbridled law of the strong over the weak.

It is so easy to hide behind the argument that attributes selfish behaviour to our nature a position that deprives men of the responsibility to recognise and provide for standards that uphold that all men and women are created equal and have inalienable rights to preserve and protect their traits of conviction and diversity. The contention between those who would have society ordered democratically has through history been challenged by the attempts of those whose conduct, prosperity and fulfilment have rested in disorder and chaos, domination and enslavement, denial and restriction. Throughout history, society has preserved recognition for the few that have sued for peace, has never let go of the olive branch and who have searched for the fairer and more equitable ways out of human misunderstanding.

There are well-known prizes, awards and incentives to encourage the promotion of peace and democracy in the world.

Democracy and goodness are universal values. At some point Mahatma Gandhi must have thought that his ascetic and pacifist morals were meant to influence political and social order in India alone. Martin Luther King Jr must have been thinking that he was striving to bring rights to America's bigoted society alone. These two great icons of the 20th century were in fact setting the whole of humanity standards of decency inherent in the human character. Nelson Mandela must have soon realised that he was not alone in that maximum security jail cell on Robben Island. He was actually sitting there with the spirit of a whole universe of people of truth, peace and justice imprisoned in there with him; people whose moral conscience and personal dignity spent all twenty-seven of his years behind bars with him.

My basic political worldview has in the main been influenced primarily by the moral codes of natural justice that have driven those men and women who have placed the dignity of human beings and their inalienable rights above all considerations. I found those the cornerstones of my nurturing in my home with my mother Mama Fatty teaching us to look to upright things and hold on to faith and consider other people's voices. My father would give to people in need before he even thought of retaining what he needed himself. He taught his children from early childhood that discipline and uprightness of spirit and of character imbued in people the strength of quiet endurance, openness to challenge and a will to be the best they could be.

My father's teachings were reinforced by many people along the way. Two of those people remain significant to this day since they made a lasting impression on me very early in my life. When I arrived at Wellington Street in 1932, I found Sering Matarr John, the renowned teacher of his day, bedridden and paralysed from a massive stroke. I learnt his teachings through one of his senior students Abdoulie Jaye who continued to run the school while he lay sick. I soon went to Mohammedan School where I met a teacher, a holy man named Sering Habib Jobe. People called him by his nickname, Ngak. His teachings and personal example of faith would shape my religious attitude and philosophy for a lifetime.

I arrived in Bathurst a few weeks before my eighth birthday, now that I can talk about marking birthdays. I felt immediately at home in the Qur'anic school I found there in Pa Yoma's home. Pa Yoma had immediately fulfilled the first of all his promises to my father. I enrolled in the *daara* under the trees in the forecourt under the hovering presence of a very sick Qur'anic master. I had taken to that ailing man almost immediately. I picked up my first *aaluwa* and reed pen at his school under the supervision of Abdoulie Jaye.

In a matter of only a few days, writing came easily to me. Abdoulie Jaye started with me on the basics of the Arabic alphabet *(Ijja)* – *Ba, Siin, Meemara, Aleef,* and *Laam!* This helped later in spellings and forming sentences. Now and again that moment comes back to me with such a touching resonance that there I was taking my first steps into a world of writing, education, knowledge and awakening. It seemed nothing then when I wrote for the first time. At the time it was, of course, not immediately apparent what a giant step that was for anyone to take. While I struggled with the Arabic alphabet one could have easily asked of what use that knowledge would be to any one of the dozen or so boys who came to the *daara*. But for some strange reason it seemed to me to be exactly what I wanted to be doing and since Pa Yoma seemed happy that I was doing it, there could not have been anything wrong in learning to write. Gradually, I began to feel a whole new world opening up for me when for the first time in my life I was using my fingers to write.

Abdoulie Jaye taught us exactly what he said he had learnt at the feet of the master in the days not so long before when the teacher sat in his deck chair and taught them. Sometimes when overtaken by emotion, Abdoulie would weep bitterly for seeing his master immobile in bed and unable to utter a word of the scripture he knew so well. I understood perfectly that it was the shell of the disciplinarian I had found and a drooling old man whose mouth I regularly mopped to keep it dry.

While I learnt to recite, I bonded with Sering Matarr even in his grave illness. I became involved in looking after him. The stroke had badly affected his speech and he could only manage sounds. I gradually mastered those grunts quite well. When the others wanted help with figuring out what the master wanted, they called me in. I was able to understand his wishes and interpret the little signs he made with the fingers on his unaffected right hand but more particularly the expression in his eyes.

A wonderful relationship developed between Sering Matarr and me. The master left me with impressions that were to give me a deeper understanding of the greatness of the human soul and the weakness of the human body through which it manifested its powers. Our souls had interconnected, as it were, and in a short time I could interpret his needs, taking cues from his monosyllabic utterances, but more particularly by the expressions in his eyes. By intuition I was able to decipher his instructions and it was through me that he was able to communicate again with the world around him. I got the best out of Sering Matarr's crippled world. I learnt the alphabet from the older pupils and I also learnt directly from the courage and dignity with which he bore his illness. But the old master's condition worsened.

However, I saw clearly that the illness did not take away the lively expressiveness in Sering Matarr's eyes. It seemed every other part of him was sick except his eyes. In them I discerned a man of great compassion and dignity. My association with him at his bedside taught me things that set me thinking about human nature; how life could bring people from heights of the kind of learning that everyone said Sering Matarr had attained to a weak, paralysed man lying on a bed unable even to put into words the simple things he wanted to say.

Sering Matarr died just before the rains in 1933. Our relationship affected me with a deep sense of compassion. I found myself wanting to be able to help sick people regain their strength and get out of bed. I began to feel a little sad that I had been unable to do anything to restore Sering Matarr so that I could have drawn from the fountain of knowledge everyone else so passionately attributed to him. His passing was a very deep sadness for me; I felt as if I had been with him for a lifetime. When I reached the senior classes at the Methodist Boys' High School and heard of science, I began to wish I could study human medicine so that I could help the sick, like Sering Matarr.

If a man who lay dying had moved me as much, imagine what he would have done for me had I found him in full and able motion. Sadder for me still, the school could not carry on without its master. It was closed down and the one dozen odd students scattered about. We had become quite close to each other, even for a latecomer such as I was. Abdoulaye left. Foday Manneh left. So did the others. I was transferred with Bouba and Dodou to another *daara* in the middle of the town at number 2, Anglesea Street where Sering Modou Sillah was the master. My grounding in Islam was set to broaden under Sering Modou, whose daughter Ya Awa Sillah lived in Wellington Street. She was Pa Yoma's second wife.

We spent wonderful years at school under Sering Modou. I made new friends there: Amara Batchilly, who later became a well-known figure in the airline industry and Ebou Touray (whom we called ET), who worked with me at the Royal Victoria Hospital and became a lifelong friend of mine. There were many others. We refined our alphabet and recited and competed in reading chunks of literature from memory. The racket we made in the neighbourhood during classes was alarming. But any excessive behaviour on our part was soon punished with the flash of a switch the older prefects had about the place. Stubborn boys got the switch regularly on the back, neck and shoulders to keep them on track. Sering Modou's *daara* was a bigger school and we must have numbered nearly forty students.

During the long school holidays of July and August 1934, when I turned 10, Sering Modou decided that we should be circumcised. The teacher could see no reason for postponing the ceremony any longer. He appointed a day on which about seventeen of us in the school lined up and one by one we went into a room in the compound. When it was my turn, I walked in and a man led me to a mortar and sat me down on it. The circumciser was ready with a big, gleaming knife. I was petrified but was held down on the mortar. In a flash, it was done. I was wrapped up in bandages and led out of the room by another door. There was not much crying or screaming among the boys. Every effort was made not to cry; because one of the attributes of a boy going through the rites of passage successfully would be to show courage as a man should. We changed into long white cotton frocks with capes. We filed out into the yard and the school compound was transformed into one camp of gowned *njuli* boys, circumcised and housed for the duration of the rainy season holidays.

Those older boys taught us the *passin* – riddles that taught survival, behaviour in society and relationships – respectful ways in which to treat our parents and our elders and how important it was to help people in difficulty. We were punished by lashes from a switch when we failed to answer correctly or misbehaved. I avoided both categories of misdemeanour as much as I could. We trooped out to *Tann Ba,* the salt flats outside Half Die. We would pass the whole day out there in the outdoors among the tall grass learning all kinds of survival techniques – how to conserve water, how to endure hunger, how to find one's way out of a forest. We learnt parables and proverbs that built character and manhood. The bush school was over and done with in about six weeks. Our wounds had healed and we returned to the *daara* and Mohammedan School, where I resumed classes at Standard 2.

It was a very busy and exciting time for me since I had arrived in Bathurst. Pa Yoma had taken me straight to the primary school where I enrolled in Sub-Standard, almost halfway through the school year. We were promoted to Standard 1 in January 1933 and to Standard 2 in January 1934. When Pa Yoma went to Walikunda, I was left in the care of Ya Amie Gaye and any one of his wives, Ya Fatou or Ya Awa, whichever one did not accompany the old man to the provinces. Pa Yoma, indeed, fulfilled his promise to my father that the primary school on Buckle Street would also teach Arabic and the Qur'an. Every school day was a joy for me to take the fifteen-minute walk straight down the street from my home under the sprawling silk cotton trees that dotted the roadside from Wellington Street to the school. Schoolwork took up so much of the week that our *daara* lessons at Sering Modou's had to be reduced to attendance at weekends.

Mohammedan School was an exciting place. The combination of and the balance between religious and secular teaching was a great blessing. It offered me the opportunity for a choice of direction, depending on which disciplines a student would find more interesting. If a child was cut out for religious studies, the best teachers of religion were there. If he was cut out for academic subjects, the best teachers were there as well ready to impart knowledge with missionary dedication. The school was a fine example of religious and cultural interface. Although it was supposed to be a Muslim school, its headmaster was a Christian from Sierra Leone called Master J D O Wilson. Many in the senior staff have been Christians – former headteachers Master Robert A Frazer, Master Wilson himself and Master J E Williams before the first Gambian Muslim headteacher, Master Tamassa Jarra, was appointed.

This was characteristic of the pattern of transition The Gambia had experienced in many fields where pioneer church missions had founded schools and opened a window of opportunity for Gambians - both Christian and non-Christian – to have access to education. For many years, The Gambia depended personnel on Sierra Leone, the Gold Coast and Nigeria for technical support in its educational and administrative institutions. They filled the gap for many years until the local Muslims could qualify to take up the new roles in teaching and directing their own affairs. It was gratifying to learn that the school was the product of a colonial government policy that sought to teach Muslim children within an environment that was better suited to their Muslim and Islamic traditions. The government endorsed the recommendation in 1903 that the Muslim community needed a formal school tailored to their specific needs so that the local people would be encouraged to send their children to school.

The success of the policy in Bathurst was extended to the Protectorate; in 1927 Armitage School was opened with the prime objective of getting provincial people to send their children to school. They encouraged chiefs to send their children with the notion that if chiefs supported education, the rest of the populace would easily follow suit. Education Officer W T Hamlyn negotiated with the Roman Catholic Mission for the use of the buildings of their school in Georgetown, which the Mission had closed down in 1926. The government took over the structures and after refurbishing them opened Armitage School as a provincial replica of

Mohammedan School in Bathurst. Both schools then were set with the logic that if the study of the Arabic language and instruction in Qur'anic studies were introduced, it would be a great incentive for Muslim children to also learn English, geography, history, reading, writing and nature study and hygiene as in regular institutions in the colonial school system.

I have already described the trauma of self-redefinition that pushed me to announce my new name at registration at the school as Saihou Almamy Jawara to Mrs Riley and the other female teachers at the nursery. It was a good thing that names and origins did not matter to them. They impartially encouraged every pupil that they felt was making progress in their classes and in general schoolwork. School was also a great place to make new friends. Some of those friendships have lasted all my life. We may all be octogenarians now and mostly house bound, but thanks to the miracle of the science of the telephone, their friendship and contacts are still enriching. A great example of such enduring relations is in my friend Ebrima M Touray, my mate at Sering Modou's school in 1934 and also a year my junior both at Mohammedan School through the 1930s and at the Methodist Boys' High School when he enrolled there in 1941.

It was a friendship that grew and blossomed over those many years. In 2003 while I lived in exile in England after the military overthrow of my government ET asked me to stand in his place to give away his daughter Fatou Kess in marriage to Capt Momodou Kassama. It was such an honour giving away Kess who was not only my friend's daughter but was also living in my household in Sussex at the time and was being given away in marriage to my former presidential aide-de-camp, a young man who had served me loyally in the final days of my government.

It was a deep joy for me to stand as father in the shoes of ET. We had been together through the rigours of Qur'anic school, late hours of study at high school and through the hard days of working in government at the Victoria Hospital on a monthly salary of £4. 3. 4d. ET was there through the many nights of campaigning for the PPP to win the trust of the Gambian electorate in the first general elections in 1960. I could not forget the support of another old schoolmate, Ousman Kaliba Joof, who became a master tailor after school and made all the khaki safari suits I wore during the tough countrywide campaigns that launched the PPP into the centre stage of national politics.

Many such friendships have endured while a great many as well have faded with the end of school and otherwise with the passage of time. I remember with fondness some from the Qur'anic School and others from the formal school. I remember Dembo Jagana, a Sarahule provincial boy, who had come to Bathurst and pulled his weight in business in later life. I remember Foday Manneh, Eliman Bah, Amara Batchilly, Mam Sulay Khan, Mam Malick Jobe, some of them still alive and reminiscing on some of our pranks and escapades. I am sure Amara Batchilly would not forget when he walked away with the prize at a social event we had attended in our brash late teens. Niumi Samba was the prettiest girl ever to have come out of Kuntaur. We all wished to be friends with the startlingly beautiful young girl but none of us had found the gift of the gab or had the handsome sway of the tall and debonair Amara.

At the height of my serenading of that pretty lady, Amara appeared. Niumi abruptly ended our conversation: *Saihou, dukareh fatama!* Saihou, she said, please leave me alone! I knew I had lost. Although I might have lost her socially in the early 1940s, the PPP won her over in the political arena of the 1960s. Niumi became an influential woman and a dedicated organiser for the party under my leadership. She helped us carry the message of our fledgling party to all corners of the Kuntaur area and throughout Niani district. We became very close during her dedicated work for the party and it was great working together as grown-ups. What I, the pubescent hothead, did not realise in the chase twenty years before, was that Niumi was the granddaughter of Mba Jawara, Almamy Jawarah's elder sister. It was Kaddy Kijerah, her mother, and Mustapha Kijerah, her uncle, who made my passage on foot through Kuntaur so memorable. The fact that we were relatives made our political campaigns all the more successful. Niumi and a friend of hers, Mariatou Joof, who later married Seyfo Dodou Ndow of Niani, became active members of the PPP.

Hard work at Mohammedan School turned into results of satisfaction to all around me. We finished school in 1939 after taking the national Standard 7 Examination. The Photo was the coveted prize for coming out first among the competing primary schools. It was a mounted picture of the namesake city of Bathurst in the Australian state of New South Wales. Bathurst, The Gambia and Bathurst, Australia were named after the same person, the British Colonial Secretary Lord Bathurst. At about the same time that the town was being named in Australia, Brigadier General Charles MacCarthy, Commander-in-Chief of the British West Africa settlements, had chosen St Mary's Island on the mouth of the River Gambia in 1816 as a lookout post against poaching slave traders. He named the settlement, Bathurst.

The people of Bathurst in Australia had given the Photo as a souvenir to the governor of The Gambia, most probably Sir Cecil Armitage, who was commander-in-chief of the Colony from 1922 to 1927. It was meant for display on the wall at Government House but the governor turned it over to the Department of Education as a trophy to be awarded to the best student of every Standard 7 year in The Gambia Colony. There were two parts to the prize – the Photo and a full scholarship to the secondary school of the student's choice. Passing well at Standard 7 opened new vistas for my education. After I had won the Photo I chose to attend the MBHS and there I made new friends, faced new challenges and found new teachers – all these destined to change my life forever.

One of the unforgettable teachers called S G Mules, who laid comical emphasis on my friend, Mustapha Fye's, first name, called him '*Must*-tapha'! "*Must*-tapha must have a name," Mules would tease him. Indeed, Mustapha Fye made a name for himself with the scholarship he won to the MBHS. He came second in the same national examinations. Not only that, he later passed with flying colours in high school and went to study at Fourah Bay College in Sierra Leone. He returned home to serve the government as a provincial commissioner. I was away in Edinburgh when he sadly died from malarial complications. We found Mules one of the more memorable comical diversions at an otherwise straight-jacketed study-oriented school. There were lots of cricket, drama, football and athletics but since those did not constitute much distraction for us provincials, we tended to concentrate on our books and to read every scrap of notes that came our way.

I also remember Njiin Jallow of 36 Wellington Street; although he was much older than we were, he opened his house to us youngsters to talk and read and argue all day long. His room was in effect our rendezvous. The brothers, Dodou Wally and Nene Wally, and Foday Manneh and many other boys from the immediate neighbourhood came there. We read Islamic religious tracts and debated topical points we would have heard in the sermons during Friday prayers. It was in Njiin's room that I once picked up a book by Clifford Powell to read and was awestruck by a wonderful line I came across in it: *The great thing in life is not so much to win the game as to play a bad hand well.* Therein I found a personal motto and have never shrunk from its inspiration to guide many choices I have made in life. I was about 18 years old when I read that line.

My friend Dodou Wally Mbye became Deputy Accountant General but unfortunately died tragically in 1965 in the prime of his life in a car accident. Many others in our class have passed on. But longevity has its drawback in that it leaves those who stay alive in the melancholy of lonely recall, having none around to understand the whistles, cat calls, anecdotes and the vignettes of the times together as friends. I feel lucky though to have a few with whom I journey along and keep reasonably informed on each other. ET, for example, retired from government service in 1976 to his home at Sukuta surrounded by photographs of us in various family and political and social situations. His compound is full of mango trees including the *Bakary Ceesay* variety I had introduced to him from my Tesito Farms many years ago. Apart from granting me the honour of giving away his daughter in marriage, he has extended many friendly considerations to me.

We first met in 1934 at the *daara* Sering Modou Sillah at Anglesea Street. He had been transferred there because his school in Niumi across the river on the north bank had closed for exactly the same reason mine had closed down. His Qur'anic master had died. He and another mate, Papa O Njie, brought their great sense of humour to the school and we shared moments of great fun and laughter. ET showed me great respect during the *lhel* processions to the bush which I led under the watchful eye of two older boys, Njai Boye and Arona Paa, who were the senior *selbe* and chief acolytes of Sering Modou. During the rigorous training after circumcision, those two taught us the songs and riddles and punished us when we transgressed.

The moments of growth and transformation in that period of early acquaintance are too numerous to mention in one breath. Suffice it to say there was great advantage to my bent on a resolute attack on languages – English in class and Wollof on the playground. I practised constantly at understanding other people and being understood by them. Significant moments also stood out; I remember how the school's deputy head, Master J E Williams, even though he did not teach me in class, would seek me out amid the playful maelstrom that break time was in the school compound. While everyone else gorged into helpings of the delicious *nyambee nyeebe* or bread and liver sauce which women sold at the school, Master Williams always wanted his special bread from the corner shop down Buckle Street.

"Saihou, browned one," he would instruct in a baritone voice.

"Browned one, sir," I would reply, and would be off like a shot with his money to get him a browned loaf.

Master Williams for some reason quite unknown to me trusted me with his lunch bread. He was a regular fellow in his shirt and necktie inside a jacket. He was stern-faced by choice, I guessed, to create distance and instil respect but he was happy to let me in on his love for browned bread. He was from Sierra Leone as were a great many of those in the teaching profession in Bathurst of those days. For all those years between 1865 and 1900, The Gambia was administered from Freetown where all the colonial officials in Sierra Leone also enjoyed jurisdiction in Bathurst and the Protectorate. The Governor, the Colonial Magistrate, the Colonial Surgeon, even the Bishop in Freetown came twice or three times a year to preside over matters pertaining to their offices. It was for the government departments to post teachers, telegraph workers, printers and health workers, prison staff from the overflow in Sierra Leone to The Gambia.

The fact was that Sierra Leone, the Gold Coast and Nigeria had long established a tradition in education, a key to rapid development and economic expansion. That was the exact principle I tried to apply even as early as 1960 as Minister of Education in the Coalition Government under Governor Edward Windley. Sierra Leone had boasted a teachers' college since the 1840s that grew into the famous Fourah Bay College. The founding in Georgetown in 1949 of our own Teacher Training College was cause for much hope in our case. It was relocated to Yundum and renamed Yundum College. It became Gambia College later, before it moved to its present location at Brikama. Over the years it has trained thousands of teachers who have gone out to fill the ever-demanding slots in our school system as well as providing health and agricultural training.

The non-Gambian teachers, mainly Krio men, were smart in white shirts and black neckties and suits, sometimes with felt hat to match. The local staff also turned up in neat kaftans with neck buttons and in British made shoes. Master M D Salla, Master Abdoulie Njie, Master A B Sallah and Master Garba Jahumpa when they were not in kaftan also came in suits. By the time we finished Standard 7, Master Wilson had left and Master Williams had taken over the school. After him, Master Tamassa Jarra, always in his well-ironed kaftan, broke the mould when he became the first Gambian to head the school. Increased training in education and teaching has been able to help us provide headmasters from among our citizens. Among the fourteen heads who came after Tamassa Jarra, three were female – Mrs Joanna Mbye (1966–1973), Mrs Rohey Samba (1982–1983) and Mrs Awa Njie who took over in 2000. Known today as Mohammedan Lower Basic School, it celebrated its centenary in a most fitting way in 2003.

Master Williams was not the only memorable distraction I had at Mohammedan School. Many of the boys went into adult life quoting our energetic and erudite teacher in Standard Six, Master Salla. One day, our teacher whom everyone called Master Salla, stood in his usual ramrod posture to deliver on English history. In a moment of transportation, Master Salla bellowed with such inspired force – *Dum spiro spero*, a famous quotation from William the Conqueror that the whole hall of the upper school was left spell-bound. While I live, I hope! Standards 4, 5 and 7 stopped to listen to a teacher in his elements on a subject he had always loved. They were stunned by the outpouring but were full of admiration of Master Salla. Our Standard 6 broke into clapping for him. We were glad we had a teacher who was so committed to imparting such excellence to us.

Master Salla regained himself. The seniors returned to their individual lessons. It was indeed always a miracle that each class was able to concentrate at all on the different subjects that went on at the same time. The senior section was perhaps more in control of itself because of the fear already instilled by the strict masters. In the junior section of the school – from Sub-Standard to Standard 3 – blameless children shouted recitations in sometimes piercing levels of falsetto. The task of getting them to keep their voices down, I was sure, equalled that of just teaching the subjects. But somehow there was real learning going on. The school's performances in nationwide examinations in which it took the lead in 1922 and in 1939 were eloquent testimonies to that.

Indeed, Master Salla etched in all of our young minds that hope sprung eternal in the human breast. In fact, I owe him a world of personal debt for his foresight and diligence. Without his intervention, school would have ended for me after that term, a semi-literate at Standard 6. Master Salla sent messages to my father at Barajaly twice, pleading with him to allow me to return to Bathurst from holidays I had taken in Barajaly in 1938. He succeeded.

As was common in primary school, one teacher taught all the subjects to his or her class. But at Mohammedan, religion and physical education were two specialised subjects and we needed specially trained teachers to come in to handle them. It was in the Islamic religious knowledge class that I met one of the people whose character and spirit would mould my religious faith in such formidable ways. Sering Habib Jobe was the *oustass*. Upon seeing that man walk into the room for his very first lesson, I felt his aura, a mist of his piety, fill the room.

However, he was such an ordinary man, a man who loved roasted peanuts. I quickly add this humble trait of his love of roasted peanuts so that I do not spin a confusion of him as a saint or prophet or anything like that. I simply could never have estimated the extent to which that man was about to change my views of life and how he would imbue me with trust in the human condition, replacing the fire of any rebelliousness in my belly with charity while teaching me to repose absolute faith in the omniscient providence of Allah.

Listening to Sering Habib teach and interpret and watching his confident poise and calm and venerable disposition, I was uplifted spiritually. His classes were inspiring and he sought to guide us to newer and educated ways of pronunciation and diction.

His pronunciation differed greatly from the common forms that were in use in at the time. He taught the refined form of the language as close to the authentic Arabic pronunciation as possible. Sounds were of great importance to him. For example, '*da*' for him made a world of an incorrect difference where the correct sound ought to have been '*tha*'. Those were just some of the finer elements that separated the wheat from the chaff for Sering Habib.

Under him I found a clearer understanding of good things about life and about people, which I was sensing but perhaps too young and inexperienced to figure out. Some of those feelings I had got rudimentarily from my father and from Sering Matarr. But with Sering Habib, I began to sense a deeper meaning to all of it so coherently that it seemed whatever knowledge of things I had craved in the dying eyes of Sering Matarr I found streaming and playing out in the person and demeanour of Sering Habib.

I made extra efforts to present good homework when he set us some. I began reciting with more confidence building quickly on some of the rudimentary material I had picked up at Sering Matarr's *daara*. Sering Habib's class produced some promising young students who later served in senior religious circles in society. Dodou Jallow grew from that learning environment and went on to higher learning in Mauritania where he became a great *marabout*. Another student was Eliman Bah, a friend I met at Mohammedan School and who became a close disciple under Sering Habib. Little surprise that when he grew up, Eliman went into Islamic jurisprudence and served as Cadi of Bathurst.

Eliman and I were both enthusiastic about Sering Habib's teaching and we made it a point of visiting him at home and sitting in for extra lessons. We soon mastered the *Salaatan Tunnajina Bih'aa* and it must have pleased the master that we recited it flawlessly, paying great attention to the inflections and the poetic pauses. During those visits, in which the master would munch away quietly at a parcel of roasted peanuts, he taught us ethics and standards of moral and religious behaviour. He also taught us from the *Lahtharyiou*, a compendium of Islamic acts of worship.

One morning, Sering Habib arrived in class and gave me the surprise of my life. Out of the blue he announced that he was appointing me prefect of the class and asked me to lead the class in recitations. Of course, my heart missed a beat. Sering Habib might have forced between my teeth a morsel too large for me to chew. What if I stumbled on the scripts or failed to intone correctly in the presence of older boys who had years of instruction before me? Then it hit me as quickly as a flash that the last thing I wanted at that moment was to abuse such high trust in the presence of all those pupils of his. Or to let myself down that I was not able to rise to the honour the master had given me. I stepped forward and the class fell deadly silent. I felt inside me like the tiny tot of an *oustass* that I had suddenly become and intoned the prayer he had taught us.

The muttered responses behind me in response to my recitation told me the whole class was hinged on. With every motion and every phrase from there on I sensed my confidence surging. Half way through the prayer I already knew Sering Habib was responding with the satisfaction of an elated instructor touched by the maiden effort of his young student with promise in the subject. I knew it from the way he responded to each of my incantations.

Every lesson with Sering Habib was a new seam of gold struck from the rock of that human being's bottomless mine of knowledge. I picked up great principles from him of the way people should deal in fairness and equity with their fellows. It was there that the loveliness of life and the need for its preservation and the guarding of its beauty came to be an important part of my personal beliefs. Most of what my father had taught us at home was by example rather than by precept and by counselling rather than by punishing. He grounded us with the sense of equity in our everyday dealing at home, on the farm, in the shop or at the *secco*, all of which I found redefined in deeper religious tones in Sering Habib.

When we had the opportunity to meet on occasion in the very busy schedules that life put before us as adults, Eliman Bah never failed to remind me of the time when I accompanied Sering Habib on a trip he made in 1939 to visit his own teacher in Niumi Kerr Mass Kah. It was my final year in the school and Sering Habib had asked me to go with him on that trip. As soon as the school broke up for the long rainy season holidays I was ready. We crossed over by canoe to Barra and set out on the twenty-five mile journey on foot to Kerr Mass Kah. Like his real disciple that I was, I cradled his *tassalo* with his praying mat firmly under my armpit and walked one step behind him. Walking was the least of my problems. During my holidays in 1938 I walked one hundred and sixty-seven miles from Brikama to Barajaly to see my mother. Walking to Kerr Mass Kah was nothing compared to that.

We sojourned there for a few days until his business was done with his own Qur'anic master before we set on the road back to Barra. The trip back across the channel by canoe proved to be more hazardous than the long walk to and from the village. The passenger canoe struggled against some unusual high water and very strong currents. But I had been so drawn to Sering Habib that the quiet calm with which he sat in the boat gave me the fullest confidence. The way that experience of a journey by sea and on foot with the teacher to whom I had become so drawn influenced my view of the world. My visit with him to Kerr Mass Kah was for me an unforgettable spiritual experience.

The legacy of Sering Habib lingered on for ages in the hearts of his former students. I went on to high school and we lost track of each other most probably because he left the school. But Mohammedan School continued to be blessed with a crop of religious instructors. Sering Habib was replaced by another learned soul, the tall and wispy Momodou Lamin Bah. Sering Momodou Lamin was the son of Imam Waka Bah who was the son of Sait Matty Bah who had sought refuge in The Gambia after his defeat in the jihad in 1887 against the Kingdom of Sine in Senegal. The governor in The Gambia offered him and his followers sanctuary in Bakau where he later died.

However, he left a religious legacy that his children kept alive as leaders in religion in The Gambia and Senegal. Sering Momodou Lamin Bah became the Imam Ratib of Banjul from 1953 until his death in 1983. The mantle then passed on to Imam Abdoulie Jobe whose high school education made him the only imam up to that time with Western education. During the twenty-one years of his imamship, which ended when he died in 2004, he wrote extensively on Islamic religious issues in essays, serials and books in both English and Arabic. His successor, the Imam Ratib of Banjul, Alhaji Cherno Mass Kah, hails from Kerr Mass Kah, the village Sering Habib and I visited in 1939.

8

Master Salla keeps me in school

The Easter holidays in March and April of 1938 could not have come at a more opportune time. I badly needed a break to go and see my mother and to reconnect with Barajaly. I had almost turned fourteen. My father had come down to Brikama and to Bathurst on business maybe three times in that time but I had not seen my mother in six years. I was hopelessly homesick. I had no money of my own. And since I was not going to place the burden on anyone to pay for my holidays, I hitched a ride on a lorry to Brikama. I thought it would be easy in that busy town to get on vehicles going out into the provinces. But it was not to be. The track ran cold very quickly at Brikama. I had only gone twenty-two of the one hundred and sixty-seven miles I needed to cover to reach Barajaly. After a whole day of waiting for a chance to hitch further, I resorted to the surest means of transportation nature had given me: my feet.

I discovered in Brikama that many people in the provinces did not wait for lorries and cars to go about their business. Road transport was available but lorries left after long intervals, sometimes up to three days in a row, and cars were indeed an even more rare sight. I joined a group of a dozen or so people who were leaving Brikama to various destinations along the beaten roadway. I did not know that by choosing to walk, I was preparing myself for the future when it would become my job as a veterinary officer to reach the afflicted herds during mass rinderpest eradication campaigns I led in the 1950s. It was a good thing I had learnt to walk when I put all my stakes into politics in the 1960s and embarked on political campaigns that demanded ruggedness and knowledge of the terrain to meet the people and to reach their hearts and get their votes. In some forty years of touring – walking, driving or sailing – I can safely say that there is no square foot of Gambian soil that I have not trampled on as a vet or as a politician.

We walked and stopped and refreshed and walked again. Ours was not the only group. There would be one behind us and another well ahead of us. Along the way, one or two people would branch off when they reached their destination; two or three others would join in. There were head carriers and women, many with babies on their backs. There were people, by the gay colours of whose clothes, it was easy to tell, were going to next the village for some ceremony. There were traders with sacks and leather bags taking their wares to their customers. There were others like me who were going on a long journey. We needed to draw strength for the journey from walking with others. People shared things as they went along. Someone gave me some of their water to drink; I gave others some of my *mbudake;* I had wrapped plenty from home. The sugared snack of coos and groundnut butter was the favourite of travellers. Three or four cakes of this delicacy with a bottle of water could keep one going a whole day.

After only three brief rest stops, I hardly realised we had covered the thirty-eight miles to Bwiam. There, I let the group carry on. My sister, Nacesay, would not let me go. She and her husband, Sidi, had settled into business there and my brother, Alieu, was also living with them and working as Sidi's shop assistant. They were surprised but ever so happy to see me. I spent two days with them after which I was ready to set off again. I accepted a couple of tins of sardines and replenished my stock of *mbudake*. My short kaftan was ready to wear; my sister had washed it and hung it out overnight to dry. I got in my khaki shorts and my well-worn canvass shoes looked like they would hold out well in the heat and rubble. I was now on my way.

I got into a new group that left Bwiam at the crack of dawn. We walked briskly through the morning but the mounting heat of the afternoon slowed us down considerably. We stopped many times and waited under shady trees until we could go again. Foni Sintet was only eighteen miles from where we left off but we only got there very late in the afternoon. Cherno Ceesay, from Bathurst, took us in. He was a kind shopkeeper; he fed us – six complete strangers – gave us water to drink and prepared a large room where we all slept soundly on soft Madeira reed mats on a cleanly swept floor. In the morning, a grateful company prayed profusely for his prosperity and long life before everyone scattered again into other groups towards their different destinations.

It took a day and half to reach Dankunku in Niamina district. It was impossible to avoid the entire *kabilo* at Fatty Kunda. I could not wrest myself away from my mother's relatives but I insisted I would stay only one night.

I seized the great opportunity of an overcast weather and fine breezy morning to set off again from Fatty Kunda. The group was much more my age now. We walked the extra miles with more energy while the overcast lasted. But as soon as the mid-morning sun began to peep and to dry up the air above us the road under our feet began to heat up. We slowed down at times and stopped a few times and on one occasion we sat out a long moment in the village *bantaba* to rest our feet and refresh ourselves. One Mauritanian carried a goatskin bag of water from which he allowed everyone in our small party to have a mouthful.

The walk had become more leisurely through the villages until we got to Kudang, a distance of eighteen miles or so. There were corner shops and people were able to buy fizzy drinks and biscuits. Seyfo Sekouba Sisay could not believe I was the boy who passed by on Pa Yoma's lorry six years before. He was amazed at how much I had grown and he insisted that I should spend the night as his guest in his compound. I thought I recognised a landmark or two in Kudang from scenes racing back to me from my first passage through in 1932. The chief's compound certainly left me with an exciting feeling that it was a place I had seen before. In the morning, as we got ready to leave we became the subjects of curiosity for a large gathering of wonder-lust toddlers and young children in the chief's compound. The children watched us suspiciously from afar.

I left the pack at Yidda, some distance from Kudang. I took to the short crossing in a dugout canoe. From Kuntaur *tenda* it was a short walk to the compound of Mba Jawara, my aunt. They were taken completely by surprise to see me arrive unannounced. All the same, they welcomed me warmly; Niumi Samba and my other young nieces, nephews and cousins crowded around and were overjoyed to see me. Niumi had lost her father quite early; she was shy and remarkably pretty. Everyone in the family kept on exclaiming how I had changed and how they were really surprised that Bathurst had grown me up so fast.

At this point, there was no hurry for me. I spent the entire day with them and I enjoyed the way they spoilt me. I got a change of footwear; a brand new pair of brown canvass shoes this time and fitting very comfortably. My aunt and others virtually force-fed me and made sure I drank more water and fizzy lemonade. I thought of Pa Yoma's lorry; but not even *Ndey Kumba* would have drunk that much. I was, however, so grateful. I thought it was really nice that my own people were fussing over me. I rose quite early. Mba and Niumi were already in the kitchen and before long I had swallowed a good bowl of steaming *tia kere churoo*. I thought after six years I would have lost touch with slurping porridge from the *kalaama*. But I was still master of the technique, not to allow a drop to drip off the spoon back into the bowl. I was still good at it.

I was ready for the final leg of my journey. It was another steady two-hour walk into Barajaly. I arrived there in the mid-morning. The sun was just beginning to heat up. Only one street into the village, I chanced on a noisy posse of boys chasing white feathered cattle egrets and shooting at them with catapults. They asked me who I was and I told them I was the son of a man in the village called Mawdo Jawara. One of them, not more than nine years old, jumped at me and volunteered to lead me by the hand to his grandfather's house not far away. He said he knew Mawdo had gone there for a meeting that morning. Indeed, the young man was right. My father had been to see his grandfather but had returned to Walikunda. His grandfather informed me that with the rains only two months away, Mawdo had come to discuss with him what to do about the leaky roof of the village mosque.

While talking with the boy's grandfather the news of my arrival reached my mother in her kitchen. I was not the least surprised that she heard about it before I reached home. That young volunteer guide of mine had disappeared too quickly from his grandfather's house. I found Mama Fatty anxiously waiting for me. Jarai came running breathlessly to embrace me.

"Is it true that you walked all the way from Banjul?" she asked. "The boy who took you to his grandfather told us so."

Jarai was beautiful and looked a couple of years older than her ten years. I recognised her immediately because she looked exactly what Bouba and Dodou had told me when they came back home with their father after the trade season. It was a terrific welcome. Many young ones I had never met came out of the *musu bungo* when they heard the women's cries of welcome. It struck me sadly that Bouba Jawara would not be among them. Maa Nii and Nna Jarai covered their gaping mouths exclaiming how much I had grown. My mother was so thrilled to see me that she could hardly speak.

"And your father just left here this morning for Walikunda," she said with disbelief.

She could hardly say anything else. However, she immediately turned her typical self complaining that she was not happy with my crazy adventurism and all that walking from Bathurst. She said she kept asking herself what would have become of her if some wild animal had eaten up Kairaba in the bush. She warned me never to do a thing like that again, walking with strange people through strange places over such a long distance.

"You should go straightaway and see your father and hear what he has to say when he learns that you walked to Barajaly," my mother said.

"I hope he can wait," I replied with a warm embrace of her. "I will go and see him after I have had enough of your company."

"Stay with me as long as you want, Kairaba," she said. "But I want to hear what your father thinks of your walking. Just imagine your walking all the way from Banjul. You want to kill me, Kairaba, that's all."

I rested all day in a bed all to myself in the hall of the *musu bungo*. That was how long it took for me to feel ready to leave my mother's side after such a long time away from her. All the while she kept stealing glances at me as if there were things on my face about which she had to remind herself that it was really me. I caught her a few times at it, and we laughed together.

The following day, I went to Walikunda. My father could not believe that I had walked from Kombo Brikama. He looked stunned for the minute or two he spent studying my face to see if there were any signs of mental distraction or distress that had led me to do such a crazy thing. When he realised from my own irrepressible delight in making it home to see them, he accepted all was well and began to relax a little. I spent a day at Walikunda. My father arranged for his clerk to take care of business while he attended to his unexpected guest.

Pa Yoma, brimming with good health and a prosperous outlook, did not complain about my adventure. He only enquired whether Ya Amie Gaye knew I was going to be absent from home. It took deep thinking for me to understand that his question would only come from the mind of a wise and experienced one. He had asked because he had noticed that even after two days I had not presented anything, however small, as *silafando* from his home – some gift or token any of his wives would have given me to bring to him. It was probably a sign that I had left without the knowledge of the women at Wellington Street. It could have been a simple fruit, a simple token – a message of greeting to say he was being missed at home.

Fortunately, I had that courtesy well covered. I said to him Ya Amie had found no trouble with me wanting to see my mother and sent her prayers for all at Barajaly and Walikunda with assurances that everything was going well at 37 Wellington Street. No one had gone hungry or thirsty or without clothes. I admitted though that Ya Amie naturally expected that I would make the trip by mechanised transport and not on foot. All the same, my father could hardly hide his disappointment with my idea of walking all the way from Bathurst to Barajaly.

Although the trade season had closed, Walikunda was still busy. The brave saints still filed in each carrying more than its own weight in groundnuts and their bells tinkling with the sounds I knew so well. My days were spent weighing groundnuts, selling goods and issuing receipts. Mr Sarkis Madi, a Kuntaur-based merchant, for whom my father was a buying agent, always insisted on receipts. These signed pieces of paper were very helpful to Pa Abdou Karim when he rendered the accounts. Pa Yoma himself asked that I write receipts when I received monies for his rents I collected from his tenants in Bathurst. He also insisted that I should bring receipts home for the tuppence a term he paid as my fees at Mohammedan School. He said a person's reputation could hang on just a tiny bit of paper with ink scribbling on it that the lawyers called a receipt. Without it a trader's whole world could go up in a cloud of groundnut dust.

At the end of a long working day, my father and I returned to Barajaly. The three-mile crossing seemed shorter now than when I was a boy. Then the canoe seemed to zoom along the banks with Almamy Leh lying along almost all of the distance it took to row the canoe east on the south bank to Walikunda. My father had three guests lodging at his house; they had been out enjoying the fresh air outside in the compound and were talking together when we got home. My father invited them to join us for dinner during which I heard them take leave of him. They would be leaving after the morning prayers to continue their journey to Sami.

During our walk home, I could not help notice that I walked side by side with my father and that he was now probably only a half inch taller than I was. He also realised that I was no longer the chubby-faced baby he used to know. I had become a youthful and trim teenager and I had just walked from Brikama to Walikunda on my own to take my holidays. He might have disagreed with the idea but I did not think it ever took away from his ultimate acceptance of the manliness of the venture. I had also returned with a reasonable knowledge of arithmetic and English and some deftness in calculating weights and measures enough to move business quickly and briskly in his *secco*. My father's second weighing clerk, the Roman Catholic man (sadly, I cannot remember his name now), was sitting in for Pa Abdou Karim who had returned to Bathurst to take care of an emergency in his family.

The old man told my father he was amazed at the skill at which I weighed the nuts and arrived at a fair charge. Speed with accuracy, he said, meant more customers, more buying and more profits. He should not have said that to my father whose attention he had drawn to me by that recommendation. From that time onwards, my father kept a close watch on whatever I did and how I dealt with customers. He was obviously nursing other thoughts. The glint in his eyes told me he had made up his mind about something he would not discuss with me until we were safely lodged for the night.

"My prayers have been answered," he said after we had finished evening prayers and were waiting for our dinner.

"Yes, your prayers have always been answered, Mawdo," I innocently replied. "Business has been good today. Allah is good to you."

"I thank Him for His mercy," he said. "Now, I need not spend all that money employing two clerks from Banjul to help me with the business. What more can a man ask for when his own son can read and write and keep account in his shop?"

I heard him correctly but still proceeded to ask for clarification. Dinner arrived but so did the three guests who had returned from a short walk in the village. I shelved my question. We all sat around the bowl and we ate a wonderful meal. My mother had quickly set aside the dinner of coos porridge with sour milk she had planned to go with the more elaborate *futoo* she served with goat meat stew. My father had sent word back to the house for a goat to be slaughtered to welcome me home and to show some extra hospitality to his three guests.

The food was good. The *futoo* was firm just as I liked it and the meat sauce sat on top of it in the dish. It did not sink to the bottom in oily mix with water as it would have done with less careful cooking. My father joked that I should come home more often so that he would be better fed. He only wanted me to feel that the dinner was specially prepared for me and I appreciated that. My father and I enjoyed eating together; I suppose the guests also did.

"What did you mean, Mawdo? Which one of your sons?" I asked as soon as the strangers had gone back to the house and I was alone with my father again. "You said something about your own son reading and writing?"

"Do you see any other son I have who reads and writes the white man's tongue?" he asked in a rather off-handed tone. "Why would I need to pay two shop clerks if my son can read and write?"

"But I am still at school in Banjul," I answered. "I am only here on holiday."

"You have now finished with school, Kairaba," Mawdo said with finality. "You now work in your father's shop as his clerk."

"But Pa Yoma will be angry if I do not go back," I stammered.

"He has Bouba and Dodou," my father said coldly. "Why does he not put them in school but brings them here every year?"

"I don't know why," I answered. "What I do know is that he will ask what all his work had come to if I did not finish Standard 7. I must go back, Mawdo."

"Go back to what?" my father cut in. He was sounding rather serious. "I thank Ebrima Yoma Jallow for taking you away for a while and to give you exactly what you need to make our shop grow. He did say that school was to make you useful to your family. Your family needs you now. If he can keep his two boys to learn his trade what is wrong with me asking my own son to help me in my own shop?"

My father was so deeply convinced that I felt it would sound disrespectful to argue any further. Although a great deal of water had flowed under the bridge since I left home six years before, I did not think that it had flowed enough for me to begin going against my father's wishes. We talked some more and he sounded like someone absolutely needing my services to help him turn the business the way he wanted. We talked about the religion and I told him stories about Sering Matarr and Sering Modou. I recited to him the *Salaatan tunnajina bihaa* prayer Sering Habib taught us and he was impressed. He said he was convinced that I could rise to be the reincarnation of his father, Foday Sheriffo, and return religious scholarship to the forefront of the Jawara family. He went into a sentimental recall of his father who, he said, had built a name for himself beyond the borders of MacCarthy Island Province well into Senegal and Mali.

He was obviously already seeing me in a role totally different from what was raging to come out from inside me – a young man who was beginning to see the world through radically different spectacles from his. I loved the faith but there was nothing of a cleric anywhere in me. The misunderstanding was beginning to turn my wonderful holidays a bit sour, although I dared not show it.

The thought of not going back to Bathurst was painful. After a few days, my homesickness kicked into reverse for Wellington Street and E T and Mam Laity, Mustapha Fye, Alieu Ceesay, Kaliba Joof and others. I was really missing my friend Arona Jallow, whom we called Battling Siki after the great wrestler. I would miss the company of the boys at our second rendezvous in his house at the Jows at 76 Hagan Street. Who would go and get the browned loaf for Master Williams? What on earth would become of Fatou Sarr Aret, the young lady on Wellington Street? I had the biggest, most secret crush on her.

But how could I do something as disrespectful of my father as disobeying his instructions and wishes? By morning, Bathurst had begun to recede into history; something that happened once upon a time in my life. I took the decision to remain in Barajaly and to work next to my father as his shop clerk. I accepted that six years of primary education was enough. If that was what would please my father, I was ready to give him what he wanted. I was ready to do what he expected of me to make his business grow.

The two-week Easter break was soon over. Schools in Bathurst had reopened for the second term. Pa Yoma called me over to his shop and asked why I had not gone back to school. I told him I felt happy being home. I thanked him for the hospitality in his home in Bathurst and indeed for everything he had done for me. I told him I was not going back as I was now fully engaged as a clerk under my father. If Pa Yoma was shocked or distressed he never showed it although I must say I did see his mould twitch once or twice.

As the day's business went on, I could see his mood had changed. Although he was fuming inside, he would never let my father notice it. He waited for the right moment. One evening, he came over to the shop. He told my father it was a bad decision to have me employed as his clerk. He spoke very calmly. My father put on his usual stagecraft of profound age and religion and tried to explain why he needed me in his business.

The matter was not getting anywhere. As usual, Pa Yoma let go, at least for two more days, maybe three. At home, my mother was beginning to glow again when she heard I was not going back to Bathurst. She must have prayed some more that I had come home finally and become a clerk under her Mawdo.

A week passed. Business was trickling down now in the closing weeks of the trade season. I was weighing the bags that drifted in and was counting the cash and nothing else in the world seemed to matter. One day I was shooing off the last of perhaps fifteen donkeys I had received when a messenger arrived at my father's shop. He brought a letter from Mohammedan School addressed to my father. It was a note from my Standard 6 teacher, Master Salla, telling my father that the new term had started and yet there was no sign of Kairaba at the school. My father began to stammer and to insist that the school had given me what I went there to look for. When Pa Yoma intervened on the matter my father told him that I was already at work putting the gift of learning to good use in his shop.

The month of May burst on Barajaly with the most glorious fury. The donkey trains were slackening off and the agents were counting good money for it. A second message reached Walikunda. Master Salla issued a final warning to my father through Pa Yoma instructing him to: "release the boy post haste and effect his immediate departure for Bathurst". It was not an easy message to pass on but Pa Yoma added his diplomatic weight to Master Salla's message explaining to Mawdo that Standard 6 was just one year away from finishing school. Finishing, he told him, would see me off to a good start in life with perhaps a good job in the trading firms like Barthes or UAC. He told Mawdo I could earn a salary so large that it would make him a proud father some day. That money would be bigger than anything I would ever make in a *secco* at Walikunda.

My father brooded and took his own good time thinking about it. It took him another couple of days but finally, he baulked. He said I could go. He, however, sent me off with the strictest instruction that I should return to Walikunda as soon as I had finished with Mohammedan School. Whatever big money there was to be made, he said, could be made at Walikunda. He said there was Almamy Leh, large and ever abounding with land of our own, ready for anything I might wish to grow or raise there. And all of that, he threatened subtly, was if I really meant to make him a proud father.

A groundnut cutter, the *Aduna,* was leaving Walikunda that morning. I boarded it with very little ceremony. It arrived back in Bathurst and landed me right opposite my gate where it was scheduled to be beached for repairs. Only royalty could have claimed better door-to-door service than that anywhere in the world. Everyone was delighted I had come back. Master Salla swelled around the chest with satisfaction that he had shaken my father out of a disturbing decision.

Then it was the proverbial burning of the midnight oil for me to catch up on weeks of backlog of schoolwork. I spent afternoons and nights copying the notes I had missed and catching up on vocabulary and grammar bits that had gone by without me. Fortunately, I was able to get away from the distractions such as running errands and fussy housemates at home. I climbed into the empty boats beached across the street; they were the quietest place to read in the evenings. The market had closed and the Serer fishermen had gone out to sea for the night. The haggling fishmongers and the women with their broad trays of fish had gone home. Seagulls fluttered, cawing and lifting fish entrails from the lapping water's edge. There was peace to read my books as long as the daylight lasted. Not so long afterwards, I was writing homework inside one of the boats and only realised it was my birthday when I put the date at the top right-hand corner of the page as the masters had taught us. It was my fourteenth. I did not know what to do with birthdays; so I simply read until darkness fell and I went back home. I read some more by hurricane lamp well into the night. Invariably, I would be the last one to go to bed in the house.

By the amount of reading I had to do, I felt as if I had been away a whole term. But catching up I had to do and catch up I did. At the end of the year, we finished Standard 6 and broke up for the Christmas holidays.

Although we had looked forward eagerly to the new term in January 1939, it began with very disturbing news we heard our teachers discussing in school. We heard Master Williams and Master Salla discussing some trouble that was taking place in Germany. They said those were troubles brewing between Poland and Germany that could get the world into a very big mess.

The facts were that Adolf Hitler, the German Reich Chancellor, had made public plans that he had hatched since October 1938 to foment serious social unrest in Danzig and during the ensuing disturbances German troops could then launch the surprise attack on Danzig and complete the total occupation of Poland. But that was exactly the recipe for conflict in Europe and Master Williams was very worried about the repercussions if Britain or some other powerful country would rise up and go to war against Germany. That, he said, was a very big possibility; and if Britain should go to war, the consequences would be very serious for small countries like The Gambia, for as a British colony, we would also be at war with Germany.

All of that, however, seemed very remote to us students in Standard 7. What was immediate and hot in our hands were the practice questions for the public examinations awaiting us school leavers beginning our last lap in school. It was a rigorous year of learning and homework. Master Jahumpa left no stone unturned in drilling us. We read and wrote a lot. Before we knew it, December was upon us and the dreaded day came. Although Master Ibrahim Jahumpa prepared us well, we were not taking any chances. We knew what the Wesleyan, Anglican and Catholic schools were capable of achieving. Mohammedan School had massacred them once before in 1922 with an almost 75 percent pass ahead of the other schools but they had fought back and held their ground over the years. We were not raising any bets but we went to the examinations with self-confidence.

On the appointed Saturday morning, we in Standard 7 arrived at the school compound and took our places behind the desks. It was less dramatic than we thought it would be. We had always thought that school leaving examinations would be crushing. We quietly took the examination and hoped for the best. Out in the compound again, we realised that that would be the end of the road for many old friends. The boys were now men who would soon be going out into the real world in search of jobs. It was sad to say goodbye. That morning, we walked out of the school gates together for the last time as schoolmates. Once out on Buckle Street we scattered, going our separate ways to wait for the results.

While we were schoolboys we thronged Njin Jallow's room in the evenings. Now that we had finished school, the boys came around in the morning. Chattering and arguing became a whole day's affair and no one would like to be outdone, not on the rumblings of the war that had just broken out between Britain and Germany and not on the bleak future that lay ahead of us. We talked about everything – work, marriage, family. Some wondered which teacher would give them good testimonials or whether eight years of the toil we had just come through was worth anything at all.

I sometimes wondered how the venerable Imam Omar Sowe was able to concentrate on reading his holy books and preparing his sermon with the racket we made. He lived in the main house just a stone's throw from Njin's room. He and his wife Ya Mariam Jallow, a cousin of Pa Yoma's, did not seem to mind our noise at all. However, Ya Mariam was strict over one rule: if any of the five prayer hours found us there, we must stop our argument to pray. Thereafter, we could carry on our noise to our hearts' content. Her two lovely daughters Pol and Sainabou were there also – our ever-willing couriers on our endless errands for bread, biscuits, lemonade and all the odds and ends the boys wanted to buy from the street corner shop. The two girls would bring us large trays of lunch that would come from any one of the households in 36 and 37 Wellington Street. They always made sure we had water to wash our hands with and to drink. They cleared away the empty trays and swept the floor after us and they would leave us to continue to talk our throats hoarse. They did not seem to mind our noise, either.

Saikou Jobarteh, a boy my age from Barajaly Su Ba, came to see me often. His elder brother, Aboubacarr, lived as a ward of the famous Rev Wallace Cole. He went to the Methodist Boys' High School, joined the Methodist Church and took on the name Alexander. He became a well-known building contractor and was one of the founders of the Gambia National Party in 1958. The Jobarteh family were very well known to my family in Barajaly and Saikou and I became even closer in Bathurst. Like me, he had the bug for adventure. It was he who put in my head the idea that we should go and see what it would be like travelling by train. We had no trains in The Gambia. For that experience we would have to go to Senegal. With time in my hands after school, one day Saikou thought it was a good time for us to do it. My adventure bug at once started to itch all over. But for the examination results, which we were told would be out any time from then, I would have taken off with him the same day.

I proposed that we should postpone it for a later date. That time did not come until later while I was already in high school.

In 1942, Saikou and I met again by chance in Barajaly where I had gone for a short holiday from high school. Since we were both only staying a short while and returning to Bathurst, we thought it was an opportunity to fulfil our promised adventure of travelling by train. So, we hitched a ride on a lorry from Kuntaur across the border into Senegal. We travelled through a small village called Sali and on to Koungheul. With not much food or drink or money in our pockets, we waited for the goods and passenger train. It was a long anxious wait. We knew nobody and we did not know what we would do if there were no trains at all. Wide eyed and hopeful and getting hungrier by the hour, we waited. At last, after many hours a train arrived from its long journey from Kayes in Mali, through Tambacounda. We hopped on the dusty wagons and had the time of our lives rolling through the countryside at thirty miles an hour on the seventy miles of tracks that went west through Guinguineo to the regional capital, Kaolack.

We puttered around the busy Kaolack market and found ourselves something to eat. We had charcoal roasted goat meat, I think it was, before we hopped on a cattle lorry that bumped and shook our bones all the way to Sokone. There was not a single vehicle there with room to take us further. We walked to the next big stop at Toubakouta where we found a lorry belonging to a Syrian businessman who had packed all his belongings and was ready to leave. He said he was going across the border to Barra in Niumi where he had shops. Barra! That was a God-send.

The potholes in the road did not scare me the least. In fact, I dismissed some of the jolts wondering why they were not as severe as those on the road in Fulladu and Niamina. I teased the driver saying that I once knew a sturdier lorry called *Ndey Kumba* and that he should ask Nfansu the driver what potholes really were. We reached Barra and gratefully accepted some money the shopkeeper offered us to pay for the crossing to Bathurst. There were many pirogues beached at Barra, ready at any time of the day to cross over to Half Die. Saikou and I disembarked in Bathurst and walked across the road to Njin's room at 36 Wellington Street. We found the boys there arguing, as usual.

One afternoon, in mid-January 1940, we were in the middle of an argument about the war when one of the boys arrived with the news that the results had been announced. By the time I got to Master Williams' office the boys had filled the place from all corners of Bathurst. It was so good seeing each other again. Master Williams was full of emotion when he announced to the eager crowd that the school had broken the record and had taken the first two places in the nationwide examination.

"First in The Gambia," Master Williams announced, "Saihou Almamy Jawara, Mohammedan School! Second in The Gambia, Mustapha Fye, Mohammedan School!"

The boys cheered and screamed. They hugged Mustapha Fye and me and carried us shoulder high around the school compound in one mighty explosion of jubilation. Master Williams said he would post the list on the notice board for the others to see how they fared. He invited me back later that week to present to me the trophy prize for coming out first in the examination. I dressed up in a long white kaftan, and a new pair of Marrakech shoes. I donned a black pillbox hat which Pa Yoma had earlier given me as a *Koriteh* gift. Our proud deputy headmaster proposed a group photograph of the staff with some senior boys who were around. I held up the prize, the mounted Photo of Bathurst, New South Wales, Australia.

As we posed for the group photograph to be taken, I could not help but think how much the prize really also belonged to Master Salla who had so much to do with it all. Although he was not there when the group photograph was taken, I deeply appreciated his concern that brought me back to school. Indeed, if he had not cared so much for me, there would not have been a prize with which to pose. It all served to confirm my gratitude for his teaching. Besides, I now understand how and why he got carried away in class with *Dum spiro, spero!* Indeed, hope springs eternal in the human breast! That quotation of his which had brought the whole school to a standstill one hot and muggy afternoon in Standard 6 was worth every decibel.

I have always prayed ever since that our school system would be filled with dedicated teachers who would support the hopes and dreams of students that would inspire them towards the building of a better life for all citizens. Master Salla did just that and proclaimed so in poetic Latin in a fitful moment of inspired emotion and catharsis that while we live we all must hope and in hope endeavour to reach our dreams.

The news reached Pa Yoma in Walikunda. He wasted no time in relaying it to my parents and the people of Barajaly. He expressed to them his great pleasure in my achievements. He explained that not only did it mean I had carried the trophy every primary school student wanted to win but that it also meant I had won a government scholarship to go to high school. After high school, Pa Yoma explained to them, it would be time for Kairaba to work and make a living and help the family in Barajaly. I suppose my father was convinced. However, he did not ask that I should return to his shop as he had laid down firmly only a year before.

My friend, Mustapha Fye, was also celebrating. By coming second, he too had won a scholarship. He and I must have talked about it endlessly. We changed our minds a hundred times which of the two boys' schools we would choose – St Augustine's Secondary School (SASS) in Hagan Street or the Methodist Boys' High School (MBHS) in Dobson Street. We were still undecided at Christmas. But when the new term started, Mustapha and I were off to a start in Form 1 at the prestigious MBHS, barely two blocks away from Mustapha's father's compound on the same street.

The war that Master Williams had feared and talked about for so long had come upon the world. Europe was under the crushing weight of the German war machine. It was yet not fully known what disaster lay in store by the rise to power of the German Reich Chancellor Adolf Hitler. However, Britain's declaration of war on Germany had already started sending ripples all the way to The Gambia, the tiny British enclave in West Africa. We were indeed at war with Germany as all British citizens and subjects were all around the world.

On the first day of term on a Monday morning in mid-January 1940 Mustapha and I walked through the school gates and up those famous steps at the MBHS. High school was at first intimidating. The solemnity of the atmosphere seemed dismissive and prompted one's feelings of inadequacy or un-readiness for the challenge. The people who buzzed around looked too smart, too neat and left me wondering if I would ever fit into such a circle.

However, the moment we settled in and classes began, Mustapha and I realised life could adjust so wonderfully well. After a few weeks, the issues changed dramatically away from our self-consciousness. They were no longer about us or high school for that matter. They were about the all-engaging subject of the war. Although it was only four months since the declaration of hostilities, military and naval movements had started to increase in Bathurst in what was only the beginning of six years of a horrendous war with rationing, blackouts and emergency sirens that, in fact, lasted from 1939 to 1945 – our entire time at the MBHS.

9

The future belongs to us

All through August and early September 1939, we listened to radio broadcasts from London of news about the war. A school headmaster, Master John Bolingbroke Fowlis, owned a radio receiver at his home at 9 Louvel Square in Bathurst. His was one of the popular rallying points in town for listeners to the BBC. At 6 o'clock every evening our eager group of students joined other people standing in the street outside the headmaster's window to listen to reports on the peace treaties being discussed between the Western Allies (especially Great Britain and France) and Germany. The news only got worse by the day. Hopes were dashed when the radio announced that Warsaw, the Polish capital, had been bombed by German warplanes.

Many important towns in the industrial heartland of Poland had been hit in the blitzkrieg and word was awaited to see if Hitler's apparently marauding forces would finally attack Danzig. Even if that had been Hitler's plan, the world might have been saved an all-out war; and the stupidity of his actions would have been discussed politically and diplomatically afterwards. Apparently, Britain and France were taking no chances and were not ready to wait for the eventuality of the continued and final destruction of Poland. The decision was already being formulated in Paris and London, namely that war against Germany was inevitable.

It became quite clear that Hitler was horribly deceiving British Prime Minister Neville Chamberlain who had been left junketing back and forth from London to Berlin and Munich carrying a briefcase of failed promises of German readiness for a secured peace. Hitler had arrogantly designed and dished out a number of tricks and delaying tactics to the British prime minister. The Germans constantly shifted the goalpost, as it were, after every agreement. Every time this happened, Chamberlain's government came under severe pressure to call Hitler's bluff and to declare war.

On a Sunday evening, 3 September 1939, I was sitting at my study desk on the veranda at home reading. Though it was her day of worship, Augusta Mahoney hopped over quickly from her home at 40 Buckle Street, barely two hundred metres away, to have me help her with some mathematical problem in homework she had to present in school the following morning.

She was impressed by my new study desk. I was glad she noticed it and I was proud to tell her that Modou Joof, a shipwright friend of mine, had made it for me out of scraps of wood lying about in his workshop. I agreed entirely with her that it was perhaps the most important gift a shipwright could give to a student. Indeed, Modou Joof was always kind to me and treated me like his younger brother.

We spent perhaps an hour over her sums. She told me that her father said during the Sunday lunch that Britain had formally declared war on Germany. Her father had heard the news from some people who had stopped outside the house of Uncle Petersen Riley and his wife, Aunty Sophie, living in the Catholic Mission property at the corner of Anglesea and Leman streets and had heard the declaration of war from London. Someone else who had heard it from Pa Cecil Richards' home on Russell Street also confirmed it. There were a few radio sets in homes around Bathurst and people found them very useful for such vital information.

The school compound was noisy on Monday morning with argument about the declaration of war. In the early evening, every doubting Thomas filed quickly away to Louvel Street to listen to the BBC over Master Fowlis' radio set. Some of the boys, like Tom King, John Roberts and Christian Davies, preferred it out there to stroll around and seize the occasion to stop and talk with the pretty girls going about their home errands in the New Town neighbourhood. I was content to listen from the remote background as most of us provincials did in that environment, and to learn with the most formidable tool available to us – observation. Some of the bookworms among them were already quoting from the note the British Prncipal Secretary of State for Foreign Affairs had sent to the German Foreign Secretary:

"Although this communication was made more than twenty-four hours ago, no reply has been received but German attacks upon Poland have been continued and intensified. I have accordingly the honour to inform you that, unless not later than 11 A.M., British Summer Time, today 3rd September, satisfactory assurances to the above effect have been given by the German Government and have reached His Majesty's Government in London, a state of war will exist between the two countries as from that hour."

Those simple words were loaded with far-reaching consequences. The Second World War had begun. In the last week of January 1940, we took our places in Form 1 in the shadow of that declaration. I woke up early and was already dressed by 7.30 am. I whistled up Mustapha Fye who was already waiting outside his gate. We arrived at the school and found the front entrance undergoing the final touches of repair work. The principal, Mr J J Baker, was standing out there on the dug-up balcony outside the front doors of the school welcoming students and watching them file in. The men were working on the concrete flooring and as a result the hollow space beneath the floor was completely filled in with sand and rubble, and a new surface laid.

The great debaters in the school could not wait for classes to begin before digging into each other's opinions on the pros and cons of the war. They argued over it in-between classes and carried on during the break period - in brilliant style I might add. No wonder many of them ended up on the bar and bench in life after school. The late Sam H A George was one of them. He rose in his time to be acting attorney general before going on to a longer career in private practice. There were the quieter ones like C I Jagne, Matthias Charles George and Sam J O Sarr. There were the more vocal students such as Albert Andrews, Ernest Bidwell and Reuel Andrews, who must have their say. Everyone found the war a curious subject of analysis and debate. Frankly, although we would be arguing the subject all through the school day, there was yet very little to go on to fully understand what was unfolding in Europe. From observation, the senior fellows and girls in Form 4 also had their own discussions going. Sammy Palmer, Louise Mahoney, Samuel H M Jones, Marion Fowlis, Andrew Njie and others carried on their own exchanges along the way. In a school population that in certain lean years had numbered between 35 and 40 students, it was easy to notice the outstanding characters.

The full picture of the real threat Hitler posed came rather gradually as the war progressed. By the end of 1941 and the beginning of 1942, mobilisation of personnel, collection of war contributions, recruitment and conscription took on in earnest in the colony and the protectorate. The war became real, the more so when young men we once knew, often fathers and brothers of our friends and neighbours, started trooping off to fight. Soon, there was news coming back of either their deaths or of their valour in the battlefield. Dispatches from the warfront came through Accra and the Information Office in Bathurst under a maverick Englishman called Capt George Peters, who set up loudspeakers over the clock tower at MacCarthy Square to give war news to people who did not have access to the few radio sets in town.

The town suffered greatly from shortages on account of the war and so did the school. There was the constant fear of bombing raids and on many occasions we were asked to run home when the shrill and fearful blasts of the sirens warned of a threatening bomb attack on Bathurst by

Vichy forces in control of ports and maritime facilities in Dakar, Senegal. Studying at night was made difficult because of the prolonged blackouts during which citizens were not allowed to light candles or hurricane lamps for fear of giving away the location of any settlement.

Bathurst had become a virtual troop yard with Free French bases and military barracks opened inside the town. 21 Leman Street had become known as *Bakamon*, possibly a corruption of the French name for the officers' quarters that was there. It was the place where General Charles de Gaulle stayed when he visited the forces during the war. This particular compound would some day be of great importance in my affairs after it became the property of my guardian, Pa Yoma, who later sold it to the PPP through me. At the time the party had not yet appointed a board of trustees. When the PPP eventually appointed one, and raised a loan to pay for the property, it was duly transferred to the party which continued to utilise it as its national bureau.

The town also became a base for British warships that berthed regularly at the Admiralty Wharf quite near my home. The Sunderland Flying boats carried on the mail, cargo and passenger services with their BOAC markings. The waterfront was immensely busy with landings and take-offs. Accidents were rare but there was one terrible one in particular that was a cause of much distress among the Europeans in Bathurst when a flying boat named the *Clare* caught fire midair around the Cape Verde Islands and crashed into the sea killing all twenty passengers and crew. The aircraft had taken off successfully from the Bathurst waterfront at Half Die but soon sent a distress signal that an engine had caught fire. The charred bodies of some of the passengers which were retrieved from the water were returned to Bathurst for burial at the cemetery for Europeans at the end of Clifton Road. Ships that travelled down the coast from Bathurst had to be escorted out by the British Royal Navy to protect them from the German U-boats.

With the closeness of the beach to my home I could not help taking up swimming as a pastime. Every boy in Half Die could swim. I did not check the statistics on the number of Barajaly citizens who could swim but I would not be wrong to say it was very small indeed. The presence of crocodiles in the river at Barajaly made swimming foolhardy. Swimming relaxed me and I took to it, sometimes just to wash off the terrible heat from my body, at other times just for exercise. I had no formal training in swimming. Hardly anyone else did in Half Die. The sea was part of daily life for *ndongo* boys and, like any one of them, I waded into the water and after several choking splashes soon became a fish – well, almost a fish. It was as simple as that. And I was lucky I waded in myself; most beginners got pushed in and left to swim. They would not drown; the boys would not leave anyone to drown. It was just for the ritual of it; a kind of initiation.

I swam nearly every day with the boys under the armpits of the T-shaped wharf in the great shadow of the warships. We held on to the mooring ropes and grappled up along them as far out towards the ships as we could go before plunging back into the water and swimming back to the beach. We talked and made friends with the sailors and officers who came on shore. I was satisfied with simply talking to them and asking about their country and the progress of the war. Some of the more streetwise boys showed the marines around the bars in the town. They brought back money with them that they spent freely or gambled away at card games under the silk cotton trees.

Pa Yoma who was also a shipwright found extra work cut out for him. He was still trading as an agent for the Barthes company but had moved from Walikunda to Fatoto. Now Nfansu did not have to drive all the way there. Instead, Pa Yoma paid for cabins on the river steamer, the *Lady Denham,* and got off at Basse before Nfansu could take over and drive the family over the 40 odd miles it took to the trading station. The government hired Pa Yoma's cutters. There were communication stations, bomb shelters and jetties to be constructed at several important locations up-river at Kaur, Kuntaur, Georgetown and Basse. They needed cement, rhun palm beams, cockle shells, pierced iron runways for light plane landings and laterite stones to carry out the sudden surge in public works that the war had brought about. The metal rods, poles and light vehicles had to be moved to help the builders and engineers accomplish their various tasks.

With four cutters to his name, Pa Yoma was a successful shipwright. When the war was over, the vessels went back to the transportation of groundnuts, the mainstay of the country's economy. One of Pa Yoma's sons, Ousainou, born in 1938, grew up to love commerce. He took over the groundnut delivery business after his father and did well. However, when the development of trunk roads began in earnest in the 1960s and 1970s the cutters could not withstand the competition of transportation by road of the national cash crop and soon went out of business. I was glad in the 1990s when the National Museum on Independence Drive, in consideration of the preservation of our national heritage, refurbished one of Pa Yoma's cutters and set it up as an exhibit.

The MBHS held its Speech Day in May 1940 and Governor Sir Thomas Southern, the chief guest of honour, distributed the prizes. I remember Sam Jones, reputed to be one of the cleverest boys in the school, being called up the stage to receive the Richard Cooper prize for excellence in religious knowledge. His prize was the revised edition of the Bible, the version the Methodist Mission in The Gambia used at the time. There was great cheering for him. Sam made such excellent scores in the Standard 7 examinations that he was placed straight in Form 4. In fact, he had done so well that the European Director of Education asked him how he knew so many things about international affairs. The shy schoolboy, perhaps too tall for his age, replied that he had drawn a great deal of information from reading widely. Sam's father, Pa Horton Jones, one of Pa Yoma's business acquaintances, was making his boy read papers like *The Times* of London since he was only nine years old.

I took inspiration from the cheers that went up for Sam. I felt perhaps if I worked hard I would one day be invited to receive a prize from the governor. I did win a book prize in 1941, but on account of the war there was no speech day that year. The MGHS did not have one either. The staff numbers at both schools had been affected because teachers could not travel out of Britain. Books and teaching aids were held up as well. I remember Mrs Ethel Baker, the principal's wife, was not able to be at the ceremony because her ship could not break through the blockade. It was not safe sailing the Atlantic seaboard because "The Battle of the Atlantic", as Prime Minister Winston Churchill called it, was raging.

In 1942, the school authorities decided to bring the girls' and boys' schools together to celebrate a joint Speech Day. That was going to be a special treat for me. It had been announced that I would receive the Richard Cooper prize. It was a great honour to receive my Bible prize at the hands of Governor Sir Hilary Rupert Blood. It opened the way for other Muslim students to win the prize over the years and have their names etched on the board of honour mounted in the school hall to celebrate the prize. Mustapha B Wadda, I understand, won the prize at a later date as did a few other Muslim students. It was not only a great feeling walking up to receive a prize; it was also great that the girls of the MGHS were watching. Every high schoolboy cherished that opportunity.

Governor Blood had only recently arrived in the Colony and that was one of his first big public engagements. The speech he gave was a landmark for education in The Gambia. The programmes he proposed opened up new vistas for education. It was by his urging that science subjects were introduced in the school curriculum and opened the way for the number of doctors, engineers and science teachers who received training within the very first decade of the speech he gave in 1942. The governor was impressed by the wonderful entertainment of songs and plays the schools put on for parents, guardians and important government officials. The students performed brilliantly in the play entitled *Dr Jenner* and the governor remarked that he enjoyed it tremendously. A good thing about that play was that the schools repeated it later in the year as their contribution to the awareness-raising campaign in connection with the celebration of Health Week.

When the principal, J J Baker, brought his imposing bearing on the podium, I found his words so uplifting that I resolved to work even harder. He disclosed the details of a new Colonial Development Scheme by which there would be many opportunities for women and men to rise to responsible posts and for boys and girls to gain scholarships in order to obtain the training necessary to equip them for those posts. The thunderous applause of the sixty boys and nearly fifty-five girls who assembled before him in the school compound was enough to tell the principal of our delight at such good news. But Mr Baker said those opportunities and privileges would come only to those who had a thorough general education – education beyond the Junior Cambridge Certificate. He said the Junior standard was by no means satisfactory and criticised those parents who far too soon whisked away their children after the Junior Cambridge Examination into the job market.

The principal urged parents to aim at keeping their children at school until they had obtained the School Certificate. He left them with a slogan: *Keep Them at School and Give Them Time to Do Their Work. The Future Belongs to Them!* As far as I could see that slogan should still be fresh and relevant today in our first-in first-out attrition rates in school, especially for girls in the rural communities.

For a brief second after the principal had reminded us that the future belonged to us, the children, the leaders of tomorrow, I wondered whether he and Pa Yoma had consulted with each other. Those were essentially the same words my guardian said to my father when he passed on the message that I had won a scholarship to high school and that he should not cling too strongly to his request to have me return to work at Walikunda as his clerk. My father had still argued that the money he was paying to people outside would be better given to a responsible family member, especially his own son. But Pa Yoma knew differently. He knew that if I finished high school I would go further than many of the Europeans who came out to work in the firms. Many Europeans who came to the colony to trade and to be soldiers or other had only little education. Some were straight off sheep farms and were aghast to discover when they came that Africans could think, count, speak and be humorous; that they also had feelings.

Obviously, gauging from what Governor Blood had said during his opening remarks, it was not likely that my father would ever succeed in getting me to return to work as a weighing clerk in his groundnut business. The governor said that he was very disturbed about the extremely bookish nature of secondary education in the colony. He emphasised that he quite understood the predominance of the classical tradition he had gone through himself but the education and high school authorities must look to the modern trend that offered biology, chemistry, physics, and subjects of that nature. After the war, he went on to say, the children must look out to a modern, practical side of secondary education.

There was not a single student who did not applaud. Maybe that proposed policy statement was the signal to spur the mission authorities to introduce science classes to the two schools so that students could study engineering and medicine later on at the university. Becoming doctors was, in fact, the singular aspiration of the class of people who dominated the school. Every parent sitting there wanted to hear that; every student sitting there – Aku, Fula, Mandinka, Sarahule or Wollof, especially the Aku – had their mind and spirit engrossed in the desire for their children to become doctors or lawyers. The large number of qualified people returning home with legal training showed that at the time law was a logical conclusion to the kind of classical education the governor was talking about.

Many of us left that Speech Day ceremony inspired and fortified. I felt far removed from anything that had to do with weighing groundnuts. With that kind of society around me, I had begun to soak into a culture I had hardly realised was so surreptitiously taking possession of my personality, intellect and spirit. It was by no means a negative takeover; far from it. The more exposed I became to facts and behavioural patterns of Western civilisation, history and culture, the more defined the transition that improved my personality and fixed my place in the scheme of modern things. As I therefore gradually attained them, soon many aspects of modern living did not seem to belong solely to a specific kind of colony people to the complete exclusion of protectorate people. They seemed to belong to all people – human beings. Knowledge was there to be explored and its boundaries knew no limits. More fascinatingly, it had no smell or taste, no colour or age. It had no caste or tribe, no race or religion.

It was the beginning of the term. The director of education came to show us talking films at the school. I had never seen a talking film before and I felt privileged to be in that distinguished audience. Augusta was there too and, together, we watched moving pictorial images making intelligible sounds on a piece of white canvas screen. It was overwhelming, to say the least. The novelty of it all was naturally the subject of our conversation for weeks. Did it occur to me to ask myself when I would be able to watch a reel of talking films in Barajaly? Yes, it did. And it was not only the people in Barajaly who had not seen talking films.

When I told the household at Wellington Street that I had been watching talking films it was evident that I was reporting something only Europeans would know to talk about. After only a few years of schooling I was already a different person in my household. I was a few steps ahead in the information spiral of the people who had brought me to Bathurst. School was giving me the edge and the opportunity to fulfil Pa Yoma's promise to my father that school would do exactly that. No doubt the new culture I was imbibing would play out in my future affairs in religion and politics and in my own desire to be my own person – independent, accommodating and democratic.

One more thing about the Speech Day: Miss Norah Senior, the principal of the MGHS, was in no way outdone by the two male speakers before her. She spoke eloquently, even if with frustration, of the difficulties of keeping the girls in school, let alone getting them to excel. She lamented the dropout rate in which, for example, eighty-five pupils on the roll in 1940 had by the end of the 1941 Christmas holidays dwindled to sixty-nine. Reduced attendance, she reported, was due to withdrawal from school of those students who were either too old to profit by the education given or were unable to pay their school fees. Again, the numbers hit rock bottom in 1942 with only fifty-four students, mainly due to evacuation by parents of their children to the Protectorate for fear of enemy invasion or air bombardment by the Vichy forces occupying Dakar. When parents took their children away, the girls went from school for as long as three to six months. That kind of disruption was not good for the rhythm of the school or for the planning and execution of effective teaching and learning.

There is a good reason why I dwell on these details even if sentimentally. They helped me understand all the more why I insisted on instituting the principles and policies I did as minister of education, prime minister or president. In all of my exhortations to children in my *'Boys and Girls'* speeches during their march past on ceremonial occasions, I spoke with similar understanding of the role of our children as the future leaders of our country and the need for the education system not to fail them. I concede that not all the policies turned out as planned. The policy in the early 1970s of the delayed entrance of children into school at age eight was one that backfired terribly. The burden it caused on parents and the late graduation of students imposed a heavier burden on the system than was anticipated.

Parents were not to blame for wanting their children to begin formal schooling earlier than the policy allowed. They were willing to meet the extra burden on the family budget. The government itself became stuck with the knock-on effects of late graduation, which caused a jam at the tail end of the tunnel. The job market and tertiary training institutions were also unprepared for the mass of fully grown primary school leavers.

Miss Senior also lamented the rate of attrition of teachers and the difficulty in recruiting them. She was however happy to report that in September 1940 the school made two permanent African appointments in the persons of Miss Mary Owens and Mrs Mary Cole. Another young woman, Miss Cecilia Rendall, a Junior Cambridge Certificate holder who returned from abroad as a trained teacher, was appointed in January 1942. Miss Rendall was among the first Gambian girls ever to obtain the Senior Cambridge Certificate. She became Mrs Cecilia M R Cole in 1952. Her career would span nearly half a century of dedicated service to education. Born in 1921, she passed away in July 2006. She was a veritable leader in the church and in civic associations. In 1998 she became Deputy Speaker of the National Assembly, a position from which she retired in 2002.

The significance of the examples of these three legends in teaching – Miss Mary Owens, Mrs Mary Cole and Mrs Cecilia Cole – will be found everywhere in my personal campaign for grooming our own, training and retaining local human resources. Miss Senior's recruitment headaches were solved in Miss Rendall's case by a national who committed her whole life to bringing up others – men and women. Quantifying the value of the contributions to development made by the hundreds of dedicated teachers throughout the years would lend credence to our belief that our future as a country is in our own hands. The human resources that have to drive our political, governmental, civil, military, commercial and all other services must be moulded by people – preferably our own. We cannot do it if all our trained human resources look for better jobs outside the country. I reflected on the same sentiments in my speech at The Gambia's independence in 1965. It was never lost to my government in designing economic and other policies that only *Tesito* – hard work and self-reliance – would ever make sense of our independence. Foreigners will not do it for us, strangers will not come and till our soil for us.

Over the years, more women have become outstanding in their contributions to education and raising an enlightened citizenry. Louise Antoinette Njie, whose name featured in Miss Senior's speech as having been awarded a scholarship to pursue a course in education at Achimota in 1941, had been a stalwart both in classroom teaching and leading- education policy and administration. I nominated her to parliament in 1971 and appointed her the country's first female cabinet minister in 1979. Harriet Njie, better known today as Mrs Ndow, also trained at Achimota and, after a long spell of teaching, established nine educational institutions, from day care and nursery to junior, upper basic and senior secondary schools. I decorated Harriet with the national medal MRG in February 1985 in recognition of her pioneering work in education and social development for girls. Among many of the social and volunteer caps she has worn, she was the country's Girl Guides commissioner for many years.

These stories and many others will always be proof of the guiding principle of the importance of the training and empowerment of women. With women making up 51 per cent of our country's population, speedy legislation or policy to improve, enhance and empower half the total human natural resources was necessary and compelling. That was the drive behind my policies on girls' education and the reason for the cohesion and continuity that I emphasised by approving the setting up of the Women's Bureau in 1980 for the advancement of women's interests. Many prominent women came to serve the bureau as executive secretaries, including Ralphina de Almeida, Saffiatou Singhateh and Isatou Njie, until the post-1994 dispensation when Siga Fatma Jagne was appointed executive director. Isatou Njie later became better known as Isatou Njie-Saidy, and she is currently the Vice President of The Gambia.

Norah Senior said education at the MGHS and the MBHS was education of hand, body, mind and character. That, she concluded, was what the schools were out to give. Did I honestly get an education of hand, body, mind and character at MBHS? That I will answer by simple illustration. My time at the school was a treat. It was a treat that could best be described in a nutshell by the enculturation I was going through as characterised by the programme during Speech Day in 1942.

A host of provincial boys including me not only received prizes and the applause of our Bathurst peers but also established our genuine claim to new frontiers made possible through education. It was part of a new civilisation that we exerted as part of the drive towards equity and their acceptance of it as a necessary objective for a fuller and more representative national identity. It was the necessary process to reduce the sharpness of the 'we' and the 'they' dichotomy towards a more cohesive national centre. Within that learning process, I sat and watched Scottish country dances put up by the girls of Forms 1 and 2 of the two schools with the boys performing brilliantly in a wonderful adaptation of great scenes from the tricking of Malvolio in William Shakespeare's *Twelfth Night*. Ernest Bidwell acted superbly as Malvolio. The girls did wonderful turns in singing the great old tunes: *Put on the Smock on Monday*, *The Old Mole*, *Mage and Cree*, *Picking Up Sticks* and *If the World were Paper.*

Since one could never pinpoint that moment in time when that transition was made, it would be necessary to stop and think about what transformation one's mind and character were going through. Was I breaking down cultural barriers and tasting the sweetness of the subtler entrapments of a sophisticated culture? Was I finding that truly there was a whole new world outside Barajaly and the tinkering bells of braying donkeys and a dusty groundnut *secco*? Was I constantly in the company of a young and effervescent town girl named Augusta Mahoney whose father was a company accountant and a legislator and her mother one of the first women to have risen to the position of secretary in the Colonial Secretary's Office? Was I the envy of many town boys at the MBHS who would have given an eyeball for the privilege? Was I beginning to enjoy it all? Yes, I was. Very much, indeed.

Although the war affected supplies of materials that were vital to school operations such as chalk, books and teachers, it would be wrong to give the impression that nothing else preoccupied us. There was enough to do to keep us busy. Apart from watching the family purse strings at home and weighted also with the responsibility in Pa Yoma's absence to give the women the daily housekeeping allowance, I had the added duty of collecting Pa Yoma's rents and made sure I deposited every penny with Pa Arthur Johnson at the corner of Anglesea and Hagan streets in Dingareh. Pa Arthur was Pa Yoma's best friend and reputedly the strictest Aku disciplinarian alive then. I always found it a pleasure to go and see him either to take money there or to bring him a leg of mutton from the ram slaughtered as sacrifice at *Eid ul Adha* that Pa Yoma sent him and his wife, Aunty Mary, as a gift. I was always moved by the churchlike quietness in the Johnson home. The younger Arthur and his sisters, Esther and Elizabeth, were there, quietly and busily going about the house. Elizabeth, like Augusta, was one of the students whom I helped with maths lessons. It was great how a small society soon made family of everyone.

Significantly, here we all were from two different homes, not even of the same religious persuasion, yet the discipline of upbringing and domestic conduct seemed so similar! No wonder Pa Yoma and Pa Arthur were such trusted friends. Young Arthur and Esther would bring Pa Yoma bowls of *nan-mburu* that Christians distribute to neighbours and Muslim friends on Good Friday. Bouba, Dodou and I would hurry back to Pa Arthur's house to return the bowls, towels and trays. Maybe I should also add that the lozenges and cabin biscuits Pa Arthur gave us from his shop were great incentives for us to go there.

Apart from this disciplined circle of influences at home, at school and with Pa Yoma's associates, I spent the greater part of my time reading. The study desk out on the veranda became a most prized piece of furniture. Augusta and I spent hours at that desk. I had very few social distractions. Occasionally, Wollof drumming would break the monotony of the evenings at Half Die. From time to time there were dancers from Senegal - very athletic artistes who performed at these street celebrations. But even though I enjoyed the entertainment I endeavoured to keep my sorties to a minimum so that they did not interfere with my books. I had to live with thrift. I paid close attention to what things cost. I carefully rationed and frugally attended to the use of the little money that ever came my way.

With that strict regimen, school was the predominant interest. It was also the most vital point of contact with Bathurst society. It may have been of itself a protective mechanism, a kind of insulation while I searched for what I could become. Therefore, it was a simple life for me as long as I kept to the details of respect and courtesy with my guardians, did my own part of the domestic chores, kept myself clean, arrived early at school, studied hard and passed my exams. Other social distractions did not seem to be of any priority at all.

10

Charles Dickens and World War II

I made friends at the MBHS. Some of them were great sportsmen. They played in the school teams and brought us many trophies. On one or two occasions I did try to kick a football or throw a cricket ball. I could never claim the quality of ball sense that was apparent in the Bathurst boys. I realised very early that, even with the most artful of intentions, I tended to try to kick the ball with both feet at the same time. So, I decided that my best bet was to keep away from ball games. But school friends like Ernest Bidwell would put me through hell to get me to bat like a pro. He insisted that I should play even when I told him that stardom at cricket was impossible for me.

As a provincial boy, I perceived the game at firsthand as ridiculous. It actually turned out to be a dangerous game for me. Bidwell, the fast bowler that he was, threw that red leather ball at such tremendous speed that it destroyed many opposing batsmen's confidence and thus secured many victories for the MBHS side. But why an ace like him would always insist on bowling whenever Mustapha Fye or I was at the crease was not quite clear to me. Perhaps it gave him the only civilised excuse to intimidate us and to have cause to tease us for our crudeness. One day our class was out in MacCarthy Square for games and, although it was not his turn to bowl, he insisted he would. He threw an illegal fast one at me. But instead of me joining bat to ball, I missed entirely, leaving the hurtling missile to slam on the right side of my forehead. The pain was excruciating and even now, many decades later, the dent is visible.

When it happened, I could not help but chase Ernest around the field with my cricket bat raised above my head. He very wisely escaped out of the Square running towards the Tower Clock in the Secretariat. True to my intentions, however, I did not pursue to hit him. It was a known rule of the jungle then that if one wanted to survive among *ndongo* boys one had to make a point occasionally. I would certainly not have hit him with the bat and, indeed, I stopped chasing him when I felt my point had been made. I swore then not to go near a cricket pitch ever again.

However, my opinion of the game improved tremendously over the years. With better acquaintance with the game I was able to watch club matches and also the national side carrying on admirably against visiting teams during thrilling encounters in MacCarthy Square. In 1973 I gladly accepted the honour the Gambia Cricket Association bestowed on me when they appointed me their chief patron.

Thanks to a scholarship award, Bidwell went on to train in medicine and served at the Royal Victoria Hospital and at Bansang Hospital before representing the WHO at four stations in Africa and in Geneva, culminating in his retirement as Assistant Director General in 1986. I might as well make the connection that I finally found out why I was unable to assess the speed or trajectory of Ernest's cricket ball. It was not until I arrived to study the sciences at Achimota College in Ghana in 1947 that it was discovered during a routine eye test – my very first – that I had the worst eyesight ever all along.

The eye specialist wondered how I ever carried on with school and other activities without ever feeling any inconvenience. The diagnosis showed I was long sighted in my right eye and short sighted in my left. My vision was so bad that there was nearly nothing of a left eye of which to speak. Together, they distorted images in front of me and gave me a false sense of distances. The specialist recommended wearing thick glasses immediately after that test. The major eye-opener, if the pun could be excused, came after a series of complicated cataract operations at the Queen Victoria Hospital, East Grinstead in 2002 that restored my ability to see well and to distinguish colours. Now I only use glasses for reading. After wearing bifocal glasses since my early thirties and got so dangerously close to cataract blindness, I have always said my recovery has been nothing short of a miracle.

Most things at the MBHS fulfilled the dream that it took to get there. I mingled enough among my student peers in Bathurst to sum up the serious competition to get scholarships to places into any one of St Augustine's Secondary School, Methodist Boys' High School, St Joseph's Secondary School and the Methodist Girls' High School. Those who went there must either earn scholarships or come from families that could afford to pay the school fees.

In the girls' school European etiquette and high social manners were the order of the day. The staff at both the MBHS and the MGHS were European – Mr and Mrs Jenkinson, Miss Helen Forward, Mr S G Mules, Mr Jarret, the principal, Mr J J Baker and his wife, Ethel, Rev and Mrs Treleaven and others. Well, except maybe for Mr Pattersen – Charles Luther Pattersen; he was only a shade European. He was from the West Indies via the University of Liverpool. He spoke impeccable French and served as both a bookkeeper and the librarian at the two-bookshelf library we had. An interesting endnote on our former French and Latin teacher was that he later worked as an aide to President Kwame Nkrumah of Ghana and then to President Leopold Sedar Senghor of Senegal before he finally retired from public life.

The material for our lessons at school was in English and about England, obviously meant for the cultural climate and lifestyle that upheld Anglo-Saxon values. Not that there was anything wrong with it; a student of protectorate extraction would need to adjust to some extent to fit in. Besides, as is simply human nature, personality changes and belief alterations happen unconsciously as one thrives and grows in a more sophisticated environment. I willingly let my environment take me where it was going to take me to make me the best I could be within it.

I was however not alone in that new world. There was a handful of students from Muslim and provincial backgrounds. During assembly before classes we all sang the hymn *New Every Morning is Thy Love*, a moving celebration and tribute to the creative genius of God and His ever-abounding love for us. At the end of the school day, we sang *Now the day is over; Night is drawing nigh; Shadows of the evening; Steal across the sky*. We sang those hymns with gusto and evidently with much poetic licence welcoming the night even though it would be under the brightness of a searing tropical sun when we closed for the day at 2 pm.

One other prominent provincial student who also basked in that experience was Lamin Marenah, who came in 1944 to live at 37 Wellington Street where Pa Yoma had offered to host him while he went to the MBHS on a scholarship he had won from Armitage School. Lamin was born in Kudang but had lost his father early. He went to Georgetown to be brought up by his uncle who was at the time the senior badge messenger of the chief of Georgetown, Seyfo Moriba Krubally.

Lamin arrived in Bathurst in the company of Nfally Krubally, the son of Seyfo Moriba Krubally. Nfally and Lamin were on scholarships and Pa Yoma agreed with the Education Department to take the two boys in. Pa Yoma was out trading when they arrived, so I welcomed them to 37 Wellington Street. Those two boys could not have differed more in temperament. It was not surprising that while the calm and soft-spoken Lamin blended effortlessly into the noiseless discipline of 37 Wellington Street, Nfally soon fell out with the unyielding Pa Yoma. He left school and joined the police force where he rose to the rank of sergeant. Lamin stayed on and finished high school. He was among the first batch of students who learnt their science subjects in Bathurst. That was a thrilling time; Governor Blood's recommendations were bearing fruit. A science teacher soon arrived and since he opened the single-storey Science School on Dobson Street, students did not have to travel to the Prince of Wales School in Freetown as Bidwell did or to Achimota as a host of us did to study science.

Lamin's quiet and unflappable temperament made him a winner already, apart from his brilliance. We shared great and cherished moments together in 1957 at Edinburgh where he came to stay with me and Augusta after he finished from Kirkley Hall Farm Institute not far from Newcastle where he had gone to study in 1952. He went back to attend the University of Newcastle in 1961 under a Commonwealth scholarship and charted a career in agricultural science. He became Assistant Director of Agriculture in 1964 and Director in 1967. In 1966 he earned himself a doctorate degree from the Imperial College of Agriculture in Trinidad, West Indies and broke new ground with his thesis on *The Carrier Types of Cyto-Genetics,* a study of the chromosomes that bear the genetics of the plant, *avena sativa,* which is known to the uninitiated simply as oats. Now in retirement, he continues to regard me as his elder brother and says he would never forget how the bicycle he inherited from me saved a great deal of transportation woes while he studied for his master's degree at Cambridge.

The MBHS was a big change from the two large classrooms we had at Mohammedan School. There were classrooms; a hall, the principal's office and staff room downstairs and there were the living quarters of the principal and his wife upstairs. There was one teacher for each subject and each took pains to inculcate good manners, courteous behaviour and good speech. Students were groomed in the performing arts – acting, singing, miming and piano playing. Baker was a gifted actor and his wife, Ethel, a fine pianist. They regularly organized plays and singing festivals for which the school became famous.

It was an engaging time throughout the school day with hymns to sing and lines of verse and sonnet stanzas to memorise from the European classics. There were games to play and teams to cheer on. There was an incentive for every endeavour – book prizes and gift certificates, something for excellence in class work and self- application. These spurred us on to meet the objects of the school motto exhorting us in Latin – *Age Quod Agis,* meaning whatever you do, do it well. That drive must have gone over with me into the political arena where my hand found much to do and which I did with all my might.

The war raged on and we made do with the little supplies the school could get. Governor Blood was struggling along with his executive and legislative councils to keep up morale in the colony towards the defeat of the Nazi dictatorship that gripped Germany and then the world. The main struggle was to keep the lid on a disgruntled Bathurst press that felt gagged with the wartime press regulations. The government was also concerned to keep the people's morale high enough to ensure their willingness to send their men to join the ranks of the fighting forces. Recruitment was not all voluntary; there was conscription and many men in the colony and the protectorate had to be conscripted for duty. It was a difficult time already even without the threats by Marshal Henri-Phillippe Petain to bomb Bathurst and to cripple the colony and thereby score a hit against the Allies. With Petain's forces ranged just next door in the Senegalese capital, Dakar, and loyal to the pro-Nazi government occupying France at Vichy from 1940 to 1944, that threat was always real.

Bathurst was the base for the Free French government of de Gaulle. The British had also opened a naval base and made Bathurst the main centre of the campaign against the pro-Nazis in Dakar. At the height of the war, a royal navy ship stopped by at Bathurst while on a tour of the West African coast. Perhaps it was the *HMS Gambia*. Anyway, if it was not, it had to be one very close to the visit of that great ship to Bathurst. Frankly, it would have passed off as a visit from just one other ship had Mr Baker not arranged for our class to visit the British warship berthed at the Admiralty Wharf. We lined up early in neat and orderly fashion in our white shirt tops and blue drill shorts ready to go on board the ship. The smartly dressed crew and other officers lined up the gangway for our special welcome. I wore the first pair of leather shoes I had ever owned. It was one I bought at a jumble sale held in the school grounds by one of the girls' associations – perhaps the Busy Bees.

Now that I think of that pair of shoes, I recall all the used clothing that became big business in our warehouses and on our street pavements in Bathurst of the 1970s. That was what the jumble sale looked like – a bazaar of used clothing, hats, belts, underwear and shoes that provided the poor and the needy with apparel they could not afford to purchase in the shops.

Off the ship and back in class, J J Baker set us essay writing homework on our experience during the visit and our impressions of the war machine and its staff. We competed for book prizes. The boys wrote really beautiful essays. Master Baker picked my essay as the winning effort and I must quickly add, I probably edged out the second boy by only a few marks. It was a competition keenly contested and ours was a good class of writers. The principal gave out prizes to the best three. Mine was the popular classic *Great Expectations* by the celebrated English author Charles Dickens. I received my prize and was ambling off rather shyly in my sweet contentment when Tom King caught up with me after class and raised the subject that Baker might have meant to make a symbolic statement to me with that book prize.

"And what statement could that be?" I asked.

"Well, think about it," Tom laughed. "Pip left the countryside with the help of a great benefactor who had once enjoyed a good turn at the boy's hands and wanted to pay him back. Pip took up his offer of sending him away for polishing in London and seized every opportunity to make himself a gentleman," he said.

When I got the gist of what he was getting at I commended him for his very astute sense of literary analysis but asked that he should allow me some time to read the book and get back to him with answers. The following week after I had finished reading the book, I thought I would set the record straight with Tom. Whereas in Pip's case his benefactor was an ex-convict, mine was a gentleman and a businessman who excelled in his agency work and cut a respectable life for himself in the Bathurst community. I thought any comparison with Pip would have ended there. Or did it really?

When I bumped into Tom again, I jovially challenged the analogy he had drawn at the time when he considered Pip meeting Estella at the mansion home of the jilted aristocrat, Mrs Havisham, as similar to my meeting Augusta, the daughter of a prominent Bathurst family I had become well acquainted with. True, Augusta came from a privileged home and my association with her in part would shape a great deal of my dealings in the future with the Aku people who were the educated elite of Bathurst society of the 1940s. But the Mahoney home was far from being Mrs Havisham's cob-webbed castle. Unlike Estella, Augusta was a bright and beautiful girl full of life and was making a star pupil of herself at the MGHS. With her sharp literary wit, a grand soul and an open mind to face challenges and take risks, Augusta was miles the opposite of the selfish and conceited Estella.

Her parents, John and Hannah Mahoney, had opened their home to me, first, as the ward of Pa Yoma, their long-time neighbour and, second, as a schoolmate of Augusta's – schoolmates in the sense that the MGHS and the MBHS were twin schools. Frequently, the girls would join us at our school for certain subjects, especially when there was a shortage of teachers for some of our common subject areas. The almost co-educational arrangement was productive for both boys and girls as far as socialisation was concerned. That was how I got to start helping Augusta with her mathematics homework.

Holding short classes to help some of my schoolmates with mathematics or general homework would come in handy when I finished school and I was waiting for the results of my London Matriculation Examinations. There was plenty of idle time which I quickly turned to earning some pocket money. Dr Arthur E Carrol, home after qualifying in 1937 from the University of Liverpool, and a medical officer at the Victoria Hospital, had this great idea that I could help his niece, Pet Carrol, with extra lessons. We held classes at the doctor's residence at *Edina House,* 78 Hagan Street in Bathurst where she went to live after her father, a popular barrister and legislator, Wilfred Davidson Carrol, died suddenly in 1941. I received ten shillings a month for my services. That seemed quite enough to keep me in steady funds.

Pet, I was glad to learn, grew up and went into medicine, like her uncle and became Mrs Wolfe, a medical doctor married to an English dentist but whose services we shamefully lost after they both tried quite unsuccessfully to have the medical authorities allow them both to work together in the medical services in Bathurst. While I was enjoying the monthly fruits of my labour at *Edina House,* the word went round fast. I was soon helping out at Pa Arthur Johnson's home in Anglesea Street with his daughter, Elizabeth, another bright-eyed and outgoing girl, who later married my MBHS senior, Sam H M Jones.

By the end of the war in 1945, a major development was unfolding in which collaboration between the Anglican and Methodist missions led to the setting up of a science school in The Gambia. The first and founding bishop of the Anglican Diocese of Gambia and Rio Pongas, John Sydney Daly, successfully negotiated with the Anglican Young People's Association in England to acquire the services of a scientist, Vidal Joseph Sanger-Davies, and his wife, Nancy. Mr Sanger-Davies arrived in October 1946 and set himself immediately to transforming a little wooden house owned by the Methodist Mission in Dobson Street into a classroom laboratory.

At last I found a great way to end my idle waiting. I was one of the volunteers who came to help him set up his equipment. But it was amazing how the money I earned coaching the young women in home studies disappeared so fast. Constantly empty pockets for a young man done with school were not what I called good times. I had to take up work. I had to search for testimonials to blow my own trumpet to employers. I needed one from my primary school and another from my high school. I raced back to my old teacher at Standard 7. But strangely, no matter how many times I went back, I was unable to get one from the teacher who had seen me through to the winning of the Bathurst Photo trophy. I turned to Master Salla, who immediately wrote one for me. I put his together with that from Master Baker; and following the principal's advice, I applied for a job at the Victoria Hospital.

It was not a long wait at all for me to begin work as a nurse-in-training at the hospital. From a ten-shillings-a-month mathematics coach, I shot up to a monthly salary of £4 6 shillings and 8 pence. Working in a medical set-up and helping Mr Sanger-Davies in his laboratory served quite easily to hone my interests. I had always wanted to help sick people like Sering Matarr John to get well again. I made up my mind that I would study medicine. The idea of the Science School was first mooted by Governor Blood at the joint Speech Day in 1942 when he made that resounding call for a change in the school's classical tradition to the modern trend of biology, physics and chemistry.

I was not in any way a wild spender, and thrift with Pa Yoma's housekeeping allowance helped me to take care of my own money. But I was failing gradually to resist the temptation of acquiring the beautiful and tasteful things on sale at the shops. I bought shoes, socks, shirts, combs and neck ties and donned habits that made me look a perfect town boy. I also made the time to visit Augusta at home to see if her homework was going well. Whenever I went there I thought about Charles Dickens but I certainly found no cobwebs or yearning or anger or vengeance in the makeup of that home at 40 Buckle Street. Instead, I found a tight ship of discipline and learning and a respectful feel of gracious openness. Mr Mahoney was a member of the Legislative Council in the colonial government. He was a legislator long before the country dreamt of setting up the House of Representatives in 1960. In 1961, constitutional reforms opened the way for his rise to become the first Speaker of the Parliament and to be knighted.

I was just walking into politics with the fickle finger of fate having pointed at me to be leader of the inchoate People's Progressive Party in 1959 when Mr Mahoney's long and sterling services were being crowned with the accolade of knighthood from Queen Elizabeth II of Great Britain. I had the great fortune of being part of the family celebration of that wonderful attainment of honour by both Sir John and Lady Hannah. I had become their son-in-law four years before, in 1955, and had already given them two lovely grandchildren, David, born in Edinburgh in September 1957 and Nema, born at Abuko in August 1958.

Augusta, endearingly known as 'Darling' to her parents, would return my visits and would often come in the company of a good-looking Oku Marabout girl called Alafia who was a ward of the Mahoneys. We talked about school and books. Augusta and I were born the same year and, although she was one class my junior in school, we got on very well. We would sit at my writing desk and do sums; we would read to each other or go out to the beach across the street. Sometimes we would sit there and just watch the sea.

Her immediate elder brother, James, and I became friends and exchanged visits as well as talked about many things together. Some of his advice helped me focus on my 'mission' in life, which was simply to be the best person I could be and to help others along the way. He suggested I should join one of the social clubs around so that I could meet the 'right' kind of people who would in the long run be important in my future professional life. He was a sharp brain, a real society man who left favourable impressions on me even from our first meeting. He became a formidable figure in law in Sierra Leone, a country he later adopted as his own by marriage.

The elder sister before James was Louise Antoinette, named after the wife of the manager of Maurel & Prom, where her father worked as an accountant. She was a teacher for many years before I launched her career into politics by nominating her to parliament in 1971. She joined my cabinet in 1979 and held various ministerial positions until she retired in 1992. Aunty Lou's forthright deliveries in her authoritative boldness of voice will long be remembered by colleagues who crossed her either in parliament or at the ministry.

The two eldest children of the Mahoneys, Priscilla and John, I did not know too closely. Priscilla, I do know, married Mr Louis Valentine, one of the first Gambian college graduates to have been employed in the Colonial Civil Service and whom we were glad to appoint as our first high commissioner to the UK on our attainment of independence. John went away to study and I only heard little of him. Reserved in his ways as he might have been, he made a world class doctor of himself, serving his country from 1951 as a medical officer at the Victoria and Bansang hospitals before taking up international directorships with the WHO. He retired and returned home from his last stint in Geneva. His wife, Florence, whom I knew quite well during school days as Asi Peters, went to the School of Oriental and African Studies, University of London, and in 1963 earned a doctorate degree in history.

The MBHS in 1940 led to my association with well-placed people in the colony. It also led to a place at Achimota College in Ghana in 1947 and, finally, to a course in veterinary science at the University of Glasgow in 1948. Those years, until I qualified as a veterinary surgeon in 1953, constituted time in the crucible long enough to have broadened my direction and dimension outwardly and inwardly. The education I acquired was indeed meeting what great expectation I had. It was undeniable that I was already galloping a different horse from the one on which I had left Barajaly some two decades earlier.

I was only using what I had gathered by way of studious self-comportment and the best book prizes that came with it to equip and transform myself into being the person I could be. Indeed, coming to Bathurst had become as fascinating as Pip's journey was to London. It broke the country mould and set me up as a new townsman with a new character and a new personality that otherwise would have remained undiscovered in a remote rural setting. Education proved, indeed, the most arming of all opportunities. It was the key to a world of privilege and of service to oneself, one's family, one's people and country.

Recently, I got sentimental while in London and bought a copy of *Great Expectations* to replace my MBHS prize copy that went missing along with many of my heirloom photographs, books and mementoes after the 1994 coup. I took advantage of a BBC Big Read book sale that advertised the 100 best in English literature and that Dickens true classic was on the list. There must have been a special reason why of all the things I had lost I took the decision to replace that book. I wish I could as easily as that replace the 54 volumes of The Great Books of the Western World under the Britannica Great Books series. Only one, Vol 43, *The American State Papers,* featuring studies on *The Federalists* by Alexander Hamilton, James Madison and John Jay and on *Liberty, Representative Government* and *Utilitarianism* by John Stuart Mill, was saved. I must have taken it to Atlantic Boulevard as part of my weekend reading. The rest of the volumes covering works from Homer, Plato and Herodotus Thucydides to Shakespeare, Hegel, Dostoevsky, Freud and Cervantes were not so lucky. I learnt with great delight that a collection of those great books exists in the home library of one of my former schoolmates, Sam H M Jones.

In addition to that wide body of general knowledge, the reasonable advances I made in Islamic education from my Qur'anic schools gave me that balance to properly discover my environment which was also discovering me. Together, we seemed to be doing the right things for each other. Pa Yoma's constant approval and seeming satisfaction with my personal progress and development were reinforcing. His opinion was easy to figure out. He stressed a point and raised his voice when he was unhappy. I came to learn that that was his way, quite different from Mawdo who groomed by example and admonished by quiet action. Whipping or bodily chastisement was a rarity in our home in Barajaly. My mother's voice would be heard but not my father's. It was Mawdo's aura and body language that guided us to understand what he wanted. That was the way, by quiet practice, that he instilled religion and piety in his children. Our sense of common standards he demanded seeped through to us in the way he did things. Mawdo hardly ever instructed.

When adapting got really rough upon my arrival in Bathurst, my brother, Basadi, though prone to occasional effusion, was right when he recommended that I should endeavour to speak Wollof so that I could communicate effectively with others within my environment. He was teaching me to adapt to my new life and to use what there was around me to make a gentleman of myself. I did not know he was also preparing me with a vital language tool to address the thousands of Wollof-speaking voters who heard my numerous party political broadcasts in their own language. It was the same teaching, to have Pip adapt when he learnt from his London roommate, Herbert Pockett, what words were decent for the use of young society gentlemen or how not to speak at the dinner table with his mouth full or whether it was the fork that was held in the left hand and the knife in the right or whether it was the mouth that went down to meet the spoon or it was the spoon that came up to meet the mouth.

The MBHS helped me lay solid foundations which I found useful in my professional, social and political life. I must have become a gentleman, judging from people's reaction of respectful regard and civility towards me, quite different from the time when I was the butt of teasing and ridicule among the *ndongo* boys in Buckle Street. I do not know how my father felt when I sat in a high chair and crossed my legs or whether after years away I spoke through my nose. I wish I had asked him before he passed away.

However, a most touching message for me lay in the situation of the boys in our street who were now grown up into youthful men but were still in the street. Over the years, the change in their attitude towards me was remarkable. They had become aware that the school uniform and piles of books under my arms were changing the little country boy. In their eyes I had somehow moved on from *Kairabe! Kaira Dorong!* to Saihou Jawara or Mr Jawara as some of them resorted to addressing me while they still only sat out their pubescence in the same street where we used to play. They must have noted that education was causing that subtle but crucial transformation. Perhaps they had no one to guide them or they did not bother to look for themselves for that life raft of the opportunity of education to grab to make it out of the tedium and waste of just sitting under the silk cotton trees in Buckle Street.

Today, as it was in 1937, education is the surest way for young people to make a change for the better. Spending hours drinking China green tea as things are today and waiting to flee to Europe are no answers for them, especially when that continent is closing its doors on them. Where the academic roots have not been properly watered, vocational and technical education still stands as beneficial outlets for young people in a country where 43 per cent of the population is under 25 years of age but where good plumbers, electricians, bricklayers and welders are hard to come by.

My government paid keen attention to this. Indeed, it was the reason behind the policy of basic education and the establishment of secondary technical schools. Sessional paper No 8 of 1966 on the Development Programme for Education in The Gambia (1965 to 1975) is an instructive document for reference purposes. The Vocational Training Centre, formerly the Bathurst Technical School, offered courses for the upgrading of craft workers already in employment. The school was organised by an expert from UNESCO. It did very well, considering the limited resources at its disposal, and made a realistic assessment of the needs and opportunities of trade training. It devised practical and effective procedures resulting in a high level of skill among its trainees.

From modest beginnings with sixty students it grew over the years with approximately one half of the intakes going into carpentry and joinery. The rest were in mechanical engineering, craft practice, telecommunications, auto-electricity, motor mechanics, gas and arc welding, and some of those at the level of City and Guilds. We also founded the Clerical School which operated within the Department of Education and had as early as March 1965 begun receiving assistance from the International Labour Office. My government could not have functioned effectively without the immense input from workers who came from the Clerical School after one-year full time secretarial studies for people with the General Certificate of Education, in-service courses in shorthand and from six-months in typewriting for clerks in government or in private employment.

My personal experiences coupled with my mental evolution heightened my awareness of the isolation of the thousands of Gambians who lived in the protectorate from those who lived in the colony. Their issues and daily challenges were hardly central to the political or cultural programmes of the educated cream living in and administering the provinces from the colony. It became quite clear that perhaps there were two Gambias – the colony and the protectorate.

Everything that happened thereafter drew my attention daily to the disparities and led to questions about them. The government in the colony ran on revenue from the groundnut, corn, sorghum, coos and millet crops that were produced on land and by the labour of the protectorate. When the war effort needed recruits, the government naturally turned to the thousands of men mainly from the ordinary ranks of the population. While some protectorate people volunteered, others were conscripted and forced into uniform. In the provinces, Gambians as well as strange farmers were drafted. It did not matter to the chiefs or the village head men. When the commissioner said he wanted soldiers, the chiefs chose able-bodied young men who ended up in Burma particularly its Kaladan valley. Yet three quarters of all the revenue was spent on projects and facilities within the colony while the villages of the producers went without electricity, pipe-borne water and good medical programmes. There was very little by way of programmes and projects the colonial government was directing towards equating the opportunities and standards between the colony and the protectorate. Those contradictions were stark.

Lest the critic jump immediately with charges that my government in its turn did not provide electricity and pipe-borne water for every provincial village we have examples to show the effort we put in that were a great improvement on what the situation was during the colonial period. My government made it a policy to take many programmes in water, road, telephony, telegraphy and electricity as far as they were possible under the constrained national budgets. Rural water supply always commanded a high priority for the provision of potable water. Major advances in this area were made in 1986 and 1987 with the UNDP, the UNCD, the Federal Republic of Germany and the Kingdom of Saudi Arabia making major contributions to our rural water supply effort. Meanwhile, the Gambia River Basin Development Programme diligently pursued the most effective method of controlling saline intrusion to protect our current and future irrigation investments.

It did not take much for any provincial coming to the colony to see the difference between the two standards of living. Although at the outset, the divergences did not immediately become central to my concerns, they were notions that began to form after I returned from training in Glasgow and started work as a veterinary officer. The job took me on many tours of the provinces. I immediately appreciated the importance of livestock to the existence and cultural cohesion of the people up country. My business was to tackle rinderpest and other cattle diseases that were poised to decimate cattle herds in The Gambia and ruin the lives of many herders. When I arrived at the Veterinary Department at Abuko in 1954, there was no other campaign more pressing to me than to rid the country of rinderpest and contagious bovine pleuro-pneumonia. Politics was not even the last thing on my mind; it simply was not there.

Those tours, officially known as treks in government circles, gave me the opportunity to learn more about my own people. It became evident that the decisions taken in Bathurst had direct connections to the condition of the people and their animals in the provinces. Therefore, the state of awareness of the decision-makers and the administrative forces in Bathurst was crucial to action being taken on those people's behalf.

The presence of the PPS attracted my attention and I attended some of their meetings and contributed money and ideas upon my sincere conviction to align the common interests of the protectorate people with those of the colony towards national consensus. I saw an opportunity for building up a national platform for our people's common development. It made good sense to use the already active groups to kickstart the organisation.

These were the mid-1950s. The old political parties had been on the scene in the colony area for at least six years and seemed to have concentrated in the colony while a whole country sat mute and unchallenged. The Rev J C Faye and Ibrahim Garba Jahumpa led the Gambia Democratic Party (GDP) since its inception in 1951. Jahumpa founded the Gambia Muslim Congress in 1952 after he had broken away from Faye. Towards the end of the decade, philanthropist and entrepreneur, John Bidwell Bright, bankrolled the Gambia National Party in 1957 with Alexander Jobarteh, Melville Benoni Jones, Edrissa Samba and Kebba Foon as the leaders.

The Wyn-Harris Constitution of 1957 pumped a great deal of energy into political life across the country. Universal adult suffrage was now the law and every citizen who was twenty-one years and over could vote and be voted for. The amendments to the 1947 Backworth Wright Constitution, which had for the first time introduced an official elected African majority in the Legislative Council (instead of being nominated by the Governor), increased the number of elected members in the Legislative Council and introduced the ministerial system with a minority of elected African unofficial members in the Executive Council. It also provided for provincial chiefs to be represented by four of their peers.

The provincial people living in Bathurst were using their societies to address their years of being idle spectators and were gravitating towards leaders and forerunners who would bring forward their political and economic concerns. My approach was giving them support by raising the level of awareness among decision-makers I worked with in Bathurst and doing everything I could to get more protectorate students into the reputable institutions such as the MBHS and the MGHS or more desirably still to raise the status of Armitage School to the ranking of a grammar school, which was really the type of education that the MBHS was offering. More graduates would mean increased engagement with the decision-making structures and consequently more attention to provincial issues within the corridors of power.

If Charles Dickens could pass as a euphemism for school and education, this is where it cross-pollinated with the opportunities brought about by the post-war reconstitution of the law, government and society. Between the end of the war in 1945 and the coming of the Wyn-Harris Constitution the field was opened up for provincials to make their mark on the national stage with dramatic political developments in the offing. It offered great opportunities for provincial people to finally play at the centre stage. Provincials saw the sense of using those opportunities for their fullest engagement in the daily life of the country.

The number of provincials who had come out of high school or who had been to university had increased. Many of us already in the civil service or in private firms became the human resource base the emergent Protectorate People's Party counted on to influence the scene. Naturally, the charitable societies were rudimentary as far as political organisation was concerned. It was natural therefore that apart from the positions of the chairman and his deputy, key positions on the executive committee went to people who had had educational qualifications.

When the PPS evolved at the mature stage of becoming the People's Progressive Party, and the chief organisers of the new political organisation wanted a leader, they turned again to educated ones within their set-up to help them craft the relationship between them and the colonial government. Sheriff Sekouba Sisay, only two years out of Armitage School, became secretary general. When they finally found a leader in me, the dedicated grassroots people put in my hands the instruments of a legally constituted national movement that would bring respectable competition to bear on the traditional political leadership structure in The Gambia.

11

Peace at last

Although VE Day – Victory in Europe – was declared on 8 May 1945, the real peace did not begin to return until nearly a month later. For many of the older people who cared to discuss the war in Bathurst, there was no peace as long as Adolf Hitler had not given up completely. However, there were celebrations with huge bonfires at *Tann Ba*. People thronged the place to hear the soldiers, scouts and girl guides sing songs around the raging bonfires. Wollof traditional singers and dancers entertained the public and the festivals went on well into the wee hours to mark the end of the war.

The more studious students, those who had missed the 1 o'clock news at the Tower Clock, gathered promptly at 6 o'clock at Master Fowlis' window or in Russell Street, outside Pa Cecil Richards' house. On one of those occasions, the BBC newsreel reported a vivid description of the advancing Russian army fighting its way through the city of Berlin to Hitler's bunker. Some returnee ex-servicemen and marine reservists were listening in. One of them said that he would not be convinced of the end of the war as long as Hitler was alive. He was apparently drawing attention to the saying that a beast cannot be considered dead unless its head is crushed.

Today, the impressive buildings of our Supreme Court stand on the site on Clifton Road that was a field of tents camping the soldiers and officers of the Royal West Africa Frontier Force (RWAFF) and of the Royal Air Force (RAF) during the war. At Half Die on the other side of my home, the War Office built giant hangars of solid steel beams and plates inside the Public Utilities Department yard where they kept warplanes. Many young men and daily paid hands had found work during the construction of the hangar and the massive conversion of the slipway. About three hundred metres away the government had demolished houses and relocated the occupants elsewhere to make way for the proposed fuel storage depot. Many small streets disappeared from the map of Bathurst to create space for the massive shiny metal barrels of the diesel, kerosene and petrol tanks that soon rose above the low houses at Half Die.

The state of war remained and it took close to another month before the old soldiers in Bathurst heard what seemed to them like the real end of the war. I took advantage of the mood in the senior class at school that anticipated the rainy season and the forthcoming long holidays with some unusual aloofness. Much of our time was spent mostly revising for the Senior Cambridge Examinations. If the Junior Cambridge Examinations in Form 4 were anything to go by, there was a lot of ground to cover and aloofness was therefore the last thing I could afford.

Mustapha Fye and I slipped away, probably unnoticed, and went in search of copies of the *Daily News Bulletin*. Like everyone else, we were avid readers of the snippets of the BBC news the bulletin carried. Although the news was mostly tailored propaganda from the Colonial Office in London, it carried important reports of the war. We found the day's supply already bought up by the news-hungry crowds. In fact, we also arrived a little late for the broadcast in English. Mr Badou Lowe, a nephew of Ya Fatou Jobarteh, was translating the news into Wollof. During the war Lowe and his boss at the Information Office, a hardy Englishman named Capt George Peters, had become quite famous in town for their reading of the daily news to the public.

Every day there were large crowds scattered about. People stood around or sat on the hard ground on the edge of MacCarthy Square and listened to Lowe's translation of the reports Capt Peters would read out in English. Lowe made a fashion of it when he announced in picturesque Wollof – *Yengu yengu yi cha toli xhareh ba!* – inviting the mostly illiterate crowd to imagine the earth-shaking events taking place far away in the field of battle. We enjoyed that expression so much that we nicknamed him *Yengu Yengu*.

Mustapha knew Lowe very well while the broadcaster doubled up right throughout the war as a distributor of government food aid rations to needy homes. Because of his public relations skills Lowe was selected to be part of the Social Welfare distribution team that gave out tons of food aid – cracked wheat, corned beef and sardines – to people during the difficult days of the war. The government distributed cracked wheat to replace the rice staple that went scarce while the Asian suppliers of rice – Vietnam, Burma and Thailand – were in the grip of fighting. The firms and even the government had great difficulty importing adequate quantities of rice into the country.

The government engaged public speakers and animators like Lowe and invited Mustapha's father, Sheikh Omar Fye, to convince people that the cracked wheat was a good and tasty substitute for the rice staple. Sheikh

Omar, already a prosperous trader and legislator, included the campaign in his Friday homilies to convince Bathurst citizens to eat the wheat meals. Mustapha's own mother helped the old man in his campaigns by cooking promotional dishes of cracked wheat. What I tasted of the cracked wheat *benachin* Mustapha's mother made was so good that I could not see why it needed much persuasion for people to like it. It was indeed tasty and nutritious. I ate it heartily any time it was served.

The old cleric would tell his congregations that the main supplier of the rice staple, Burma, was steeped in bombs and blood and even Gambian soldiers were dying in its jungles. He told them that up until the war ended people would have to adapt to the taste of the cracked wheat. Evidently at that time Lowe broadcast the war news as enthusiastically as he distributed the food aid. In the process he became quite prosperous and made a name for himself. Local legend has it that he lived it off in the grandest style and lost all his fortune before too long.

At that particular news broadcast of *Yengu yengu yi cha toli xhareh ba!* Lowe announced that there was good news, which, he said, remained unconfirmed, namely that the German Reich Chancellor, Adolf Hitler, had died the day before. People broke into loud applause; it was such an animated applause that it was almost impossible to hear the rest of what I considered was excellent news.

More subdued as my own reaction was to the news of Adolf Hitler's death, I was quietly jubilant for no other reason than that it would mean our return to school at the close of the rainy season to a new term with the long and troublesome war behind us. That boded well for us as seniors at the MBHS. The shipping lanes would open up again; school supplies would arrive. It also meant renewed concentration on reading for the Senior Cambridge Examinations.

A few days later, it was confirmed that Hitler had, indeed, committed suicide together with Frau Eva Braun, his wife of only a few hours on 30 April 1945. Their bodies had been incinerated by petrol fire in a trench in the Chancellery yard by Heinz Linge (Hitler's valet) and members of his personal SS bodyguards. They were burning their leader's body amid massive bombardment in the city from the advancing forces of the Russian Red Army.

I find stories of World War II fascinating. It was well worth it when I spent part of my annual leave in 1977 in Munich reading the last of the six volumes in my collection of British Prime Minister Winston Churchill's *The Second World War*. Munich's Berchtesgaden was a favourite haunt of Adolf Hitler when he was in power. When I visited it I saw why Hitler had fallen in love with the place. For me it was like tying up the loose ends of a very trying period I had lived through as a young student. Getting to know the full story of Hitler and Hess and the cast of characters that shaped the world of those days left a clear lesson that diplomacy could have easily averted this catastrophe and global conflagration. It seemed that looking back at World War I the world had learnt nothing. For me visiting Munich to speak at the Peutinger Collegium sharpened my faith in the correctness of my personal mission that completely believes that leaders, governments and people must do everything in their power to make sure that peace is the first option and peace the ultimate.

Churchill captures those last moments of Hitler's with such simple but captivating imagery that I find so gripping no matter how many times I read it over that in the early hours of 29 April Hitler made his will. Churchill wrote in the sixth volume he titled *Triumph and Tragedy*:

> The day opened with the normal routine of work in the air raid shelter under the Chancellery. News arrived of Mussolini's end. The timing was grimly appropriate. On the 30th Hitler lunched quietly ... in his suite, and at the end of the meal shook hands with those present and retired to his private room. At half-past three a shot was heard and members of his personal staff entered the room to find him lying on the sofa with a revolver by his side. He had shot himself through the mouth. Eva Braun, whom he had married secretly during these last days, lay dead beside him. She had taken poison. The bodies were burnt in the courtyard, and Hitler's funeral pyre, with the din of the Russian guns growing ever louder, made a lurid end to the Third Reich.

Churchill describes vividly the final hours of the Reich and indeed succeeds through the mastery of the craft of language to make extremely horrid images at least palatable for his readers. I find myself still drawn to this passage and it leaves me as fascinated by human nature as I was as a student listening to the radio reporting on the closing events of the Reich on 30 April 1945:

> That evening a telegram reached Admiral Doenitz at his headquarters in Holstein:

In place of the former Reichs-Marshal Goering the Fuehrer appoints you, Herr Grand Admiral, as his successor. Written authority is on its way. You will immediately take all such measures as the situation requires. BORMAN

Chaos descended. Doenitz had been in touch with Himmler, who, he assumed, would be nominated as Hitler's successor if Berlin fell, and now supreme responsibility was suddenly thrust upon him without warning and he faced the task of organising the surrender.

Many events stand out in my mind from the war years. I will never forget how the Sunderland flying boats fascinated us young people, landing as they did on the surface of the water and speeding away and up in the air again. In 2003 I was a happy interviewee when my 10-year-old granddaughter, Nadua, sat me down to ask questions about the flying boats for a school project on eyewitness accounts of World War II. The presence of those flying ships was as comforting as it was for us to hear Winston Churchill in 1943 vow to retaliate with vengeance on Vichy inside France if any French bombs fell on Bathurst.

It was heart-warming that Churchill stood up again for our colonial capital against the ungracious comments made of Bathurst by the US President, Franklin Roosevelt, in one of the scores of letters he wrote to his war ally. In the note to the prime minister in 1943, Roosevelt said: "I had picked up sleeping sickness, or Gambia fever or some kindred bug in that hell hole of yours called Bathurst". Churchill, who used to sign off his letters to Roosevelt as "Former Naval Person", must have felt the same sense of outrage Gambians felt about the low esteem in which the American visitor held our capital town after just a half day's stop-over.

With the relief in Bathurst of the news of the death of Hitler one was suddenly struck by the sad and tragic waste of millions of lives lost including those of Gambians that perished in the jungles of Burma and at the hands of the heartless Japanese army. It was at Kaladan that the Gambian contingent recorded a significant effort in frustrating the enemy. I must have been drawing from these sentiments when, as prime minister and then president of the Republic, I paid particular attention to ensuring that the ceremony of the laying of the wreath at the Cenotaph to mark Armistice Day was given its proper role in my official annual schedule every second Sunday in November

One thing that never ceased to touch me was that the number of ex-servicemen who came to a small reception at State House after the parade would diminish as old soldiers passed on year after year. Alhaji Yusupha Nyabally, a decorated World War II veteran from Kantora, became a close friend of mine. It was with pleasure in 1981 that I decorated a veteran, Sgt Major Ousman Jallow, with the national insignia of ORG. Jallow came out of retirement to help senior police officers hold out against Kukoi Samba Sanyang's rebels when they attacked the police headquarters during the events of July 1981. His assistance to the police chief and the loyalists around him was significant in helping to defend my government. He answered the call on his patriotism and rekindled his skills at marksmanship that had lain dormant since 1945 when I was a high school senior.

To me it was a sad war considering the extent of its devastation and whose rationale was founded only in the unbridled ambitions of a group of men whose skewed vision of domination of one race over others tried to make falsehood triumph over truth. These were ambitions totally antithetical to the teaching that had raised me from my modest God-fearing family in Barajaly, the humanity I sensed in Sering Matarr John and the moral discipline in the home of Pa Yoma. It was from that personal level that I understood and approved of the applause of the crowd at the news broadcast when it was announced that Hitler had died.

As Mustapha Fye and I walked back to the school, it seemed quite assuring to us that the world would finally begin to enjoy peace again. I personally felt, even though I had hardly said this to Mustapha, that the experience of the previous five years was a kind of confirmation of the teachings of Sering Habib – of the need for everyone to realise that a nation's peace, a continent's peace, the world's peace must take source from the peace in the individual. When we finally read his life story, *Mein Kampf*, it became clear that Hitler's mind was totally devoid of peace.

It is only when people are at peace with themselves that they can share it with their neighbours. One can certainly not give what one doesn't have. One has to have peace to be able to give peace. One has to have a democratic spirit in order to live democracy. This lesson would come in handy in many of my political encounters. Not only was it necessary with opponents but also with supporters and close collaborators in my own party and government. We had to teach each other to adhere to the principles of democracy in designing our policies and programmes. I had tense moments when I had to put my foot down against undemocratic interests in my party in favour of the upholding of democracy in the national character and outlook.

I can never claim it was easy to sow democracy. People criticised me for being too democratic, too soft and too ready to listen to the other side and to weigh their stories and their concerns. They castigated me, saying that a leader ought to be decisive. They expected leaders to be autocratic in wielding power and authority. The chief has the last say. I insisted that power must be guided by law and society must be governed by conscience. Democracy is a culture that has to be learnt. The life and times of Hitler were in effect a study of absolute power and its destructive energy unless it is governed by democratic principles.

From listening to the debates at school and from the eager consumption of the printed word we read in foreign newspapers, the dissection of Hitler's mental state indicated a man completely possessed by a lust for power that fuelled his ambitions towards hate and utter corruption of his faculties to understand the limits of human strength. The war and the story of Hitler were important for me as a background against which to test all the values of respect for the human being, openness to the views of others, tolerance of their views and opinions while being faithful to the principles of natural justice and the laws that govern society. From very early on in my life, these principles had found a place in my heart. Perhaps these were the sources of inspiration that helped me govern when destiny propelled me from the simple duties of a relatively inconspicuous veterinary officer to the public glare of a prime minister and, ultimately, president of my country.

Peace, as befits the name my father gave me, Kairaba, was my first lesson towards the motive of ensuring that the peace of all humankind was the ultimate in all the themes and policies I proposed. If the policy would breach the peace it was probably not a good policy and had therefore to be revisited. But I hasten to add that indeed to err is human; to forgive, divine. I certainly did not always achieve the ideal but the state of mind set on the object was beneficial to society and to family. And it is against that belief that I would like history to judge my every action, private as well as public. When my cabinet considered the motto for our independent nation, we made sure that the concept of peace was paramount – Peace, Progress and Prosperity – and etched it on the nation's coat of arms. It is enshrined in the national anthem in which we pray that all Gambians may live in unity, freedom and peace each day.

This, however, is not calling for the understanding of a naïve adherence to peace only in its most basic meaning of the absence of war or strife. Rather, it means that people must be guided towards a deeper and bolder understanding of the wars to be fought, spiritually and intellectually, for true peace to prevail.

12

Labouring and waiting

The months immediately after the war were strenuous times for the government in Bathurst. The people were worse hit. While a few enterprising ones made a fortune in the kola nut, palm oil and textile and other war-fed trades, not excluding the emergency food aid distribution, the general populace endured deprivation, notably in losses in employment and income. Recruitment stopped; the army was disbanding troops, unemployed ex-servicemen were roaming the streets of the town.

By Christmas 1945, contingents from the West African countries began leaving. Gold Coasters and Nigerians, some Angolans and Congolese marched on board army troop ships going home. Gambian soldiers were also coming home from Burma and elsewhere. Five years before that, they had left to go and fight. I remember a guitar player, Ebrima Jallow. Everyone called him Ebrima Gougou. He was a dockworker who lived not too far from us and used to play beautiful wartime songs on his guitar. He loved to sing: *Gaal gang chi raat bi; Eleg chi suba teel, di naa dem Congo!* It was the song of a Gambian fusilier going away and leaving behind a forlorn lover with the assurance that it would be very difficult for her to find someone else to love her as much as he did. Indeed, some lovers waited for their men to return from war; many others did not. It was a popular song during the war.

As the days and months passed, the remainder of the African soldiers also left Bathurst to go back home. The camps of the West Africa Frontier Force and those of the Royal Air Force and West Africa Air Corps were gradually pulled down. But while the war lasted the over-concentration of the wartime budgets on military and security ordinances meant that other vital areas received reduced funding. Unscrupulous traders increased prices on local commodities and imported goods, making life extremely hard for many people. The few who opened shops or found money enough to trade from loans guaranteed by the bank or the foreign trading companies made huge profits and consolidated the position of the cream of Bathurst society. Down the rungs, spending power suddenly evaporated and mounting debts led to depression; that became a major cause for concern.

Court files burgeoned with debt recovery and bankruptcy cases. Family breadwinners were scraping the bottom of the barrel. The low producer price of groundnuts did not help the situation either. The French government in Dakar continued to subsidise the groundnut and cereal farmers in Senegal and surrounding French territories. The British government on the other hand left the hapless Gambian farmer to his own devices with not a single subsidy, no matter how much the legislators cried for help. The policy was not without reason. The British Colonial Office discouraged any policy that would give the country any semblance of continuity. London had from time to time nursed the desire for the Gambia Colony to merge with Senegal.

I fought tooth and nail against that notion, making it clear during the London Independence Conference at Marlborough House in 1964. I told the British government through Colonial Secretary Duncan Sandys that The Gambia was thinking in sovereign terms. While it would cooperate with neighbours in vital economic, diplomatic and military areas, for it independence was the goal and not what Paris and London had proposed and envisaged for our country since 1886. It was even more irksome when our neighbours during our interstate sporting events taunted our country as being the *'huitième région'* – the fallacious diminution that considered The Gambia as the eighth region of Senegal instead of the sovereign entity that it was.

Gladly, I was not the first to have carried this banner of our right to self-determination and sovereign existence. Earlier patriots, Providence Juff, Charles Pignard, Sam John Forster, William Reffles and Harry Finden and others - dug in their heels in the Bathurst mud from 1871 onwards against French and British ploys to hand over the Gambia enclave to France for the convenience of European diplomacy rather than for any measure of good calculated for the benefit of the citizens of the Gambia colony.

The liberated Africans living in the colony in union with the peoples from the surrounding countryside who had settled and founded the community of citizens loyal to their cause as Gambians were not ready to be used as pawns in the game of European diplomacy. Gambians resorted to training their first lawyer, Joseph Fox Reffles. He was the son of William Reffles, the watchmaker and wine merchant. After two years of law studies in London, he returned to join his father to lead the fight for his country to remain British and, ultimately, a sovereign entity. Somewhere remotely in that stance and argument was the vision of an independent Gambia in commonwealth with Britain.

The precariousness of life after school had begun to show itself long before the results of the Senior Cambridge School Certificate Examination were announced. Until I was able to find a job at the hospital or until Dr Carrol invited me to teach his niece, I woke up to lazy mornings in Half Die. I spent balmy hours among the boats where I used to study and think of what Providence would bring my way and when.

I studied hard through high school, not resting on any of the laurels of book prizes or citations. I always took extra care not to fall short of doing creditably well at the School Certificate or the London Matriculation Examination because that would mean that there would be no scholarships forthcoming. And without a scholarship, a student might as well say goodbye to dreams of studying medicine, unless, of course, one's parents had the means to pay for one's private education. If some of the students at the MBHS - sons of doctors, lawyers and others among the business classes - had a claim to the comfort of such financial support, I certainly could not make the same claim. My father's business at that time simply did not bring him that kind of money.

Nonetheless I took the School Certificate Examination with less trepidation than I had expected. My keen interest in all the subjects on offer was my assurance of a reasonable performance that might find favour with the scholarship committee. Although time at high school did away with my initial feeling of being provincial, after six years they came rushing back with the final examinations. At that point all my thoughts turned to scholarships to study abroad. There were too few scholarships and too many who wanted them. I could not help but feel that I might be at a disadvantage in the hands of townspeople on the committee.

When the results finally arrived, word about them went round quickly. By the time I reached the school noticeboard, there was already overcrowding around it. There was not much chance of me forcing my way through those big fellows but when I stood on my toes, the first thing I glanced was my name on the list. Then I heard someone in front of me say: "Jawara has done it!" When I made it to the front to read the board myself, some of the boys were jubilant. They patted my head and shook me around the shoulders while I struggled to confirm for myself what grades I had made. My grades turned out very good in all the subjects; good enough for me to hope for a scholarship.

I badly needed a scholarship. Mawdo might once have helped a whole village cope through a terrible and exacting hungry season, but business had not been as rosy since. My father was just getting by on what he made at his shop in Walikunda. He was no longer as rich as he used to be when he was younger. Only a scholarship could get me away to study.

I collected my results and went back to Wellington Street. Mustapha Fye came with me but not before we had rushed down the street to his home, where he announced his results to his father, Sheikh Omar. The old cleric, who had come for a short while to Bathurst to see to some business in connection with the Legislative Council, broke into prayer in the middle of the courtyard at Dobson Street and raised a song of praise. This amazed the little ones and the women who came crowding around to find out what had so pleased Sheikh Omar that he would burst into such cheerful thanksgiving out in the scorching sun.

The days that followed were bitter-sweet. I was glad to be a man at last but the decision that could happily end my idleness was going to be taken in London, miles away at the Colonial Office.

I carried on, keenly aware of all the attendant evils that people warned us could happen to young men and women after school; they were soon stuck to a paying job, the girls would have been married off, half for love and half to assuage economic hardship. Others would have given up on school or gone off to whatever it was that would result in making school irrelevant after all. I decided I would keep on the straight and narrow path and the success of that, I realised, lay all that distance away in London where the scholarships were decided.

Indeed, London had all the say over the future of all those who waited for the results of the London Matriculation, the placement examination for universities in Britain. Passing them was one thing and getting one of the places the Colonial Office offered was another. The repercussions of the war were still affecting the amount of money available for scholarships. The Colonial Office, therefore, was constrained to allocate only ten places to the British colonies and dependencies as a whole. That was a disheartening thought for anxious students in tiny Gambia. I weighed my chances among all the applicants from all the British colonies and dependencies in the world, multiplied by the number of certificate holders; there were easily thousands of qualified candidates. To think of my chances against Nigeria, Gold Coast and Sierra Leone alone was overwhelming. I was particularly intimidated by what I had heard of bright brains from those English-speaking West African countries, which enjoyed the added advantage of well-known institutions of learning, especially of science, for nearly one hundred years.

Pa Yoma was calmer than I was; not that I showed any more excitement than my usual quiet nature. I just thought it was rather anticlimactic the way we struggled to the line only to be told that one's chances were so slim. My father had no money to even begin discussing coming through with it if I failed to obtain a scholarship. There was plenty of time on my hands. One morning, I went out to the Marché Mussanté to wander among the fishmongers. I sat out on the beachfront right by the shoulder of the Admiralty Wharf and watched the tide come in. The water was chilling cold at that time of the year but I got in my trunks and took a long refreshing dip.

Then I overheard the men talking; one of the cutters was ready to go up country in the next hour. The chandlers were dragging supplies up the gangplank and a wood painter was just finishing going over the name of the cutter, the *Ndey Kendak Sarr*. The Manjago sailors were scrambling and screaming and harnessing the ropes and hoisting the sails. The river was there, open and ready as always with its blue estuary that just stretched interminably into the mangroves that separated it from the white sky beyond. The whole scenery began tickling me with thoughts of adventure.

While I swam around, I was thinking, in another couple of days, that cutter would be berthing alongside the wharf at Kuntaur. That thought threw me straight into wishing to see my mother. Indeed, I said to myself, if there was nothing for me to do in Bathurst, I might as well go and see my mother. Under the other armpit of the wharf, little naked boys chased each other in the water. If the chaser caught up with one and touched his head it would be his turn to chase the others. When we were younger, we would swim and chase each other for hours.

I remember Dodou Jobe back then at the Qur'anic school in Wellington Street. He was big and strong and he used to love to chase; because when he caught up with a boy he wished to bully he would keep his head under water until he panicked. He was not particularly bright with schoolwork but he was such a great swimmer that we teased him mercilessly and called him *pippa daara* – 'the school's dolphin' – good in the water but dull on land! Dodou did not like that at all and he would wait until we went swimming again, then he would take it out on us. Once he grabbed me under the water and swam far out with me and then mockingly continued to swim right next to me while I, terrified, fought back to the safety of the beach on my own. That taught me to leave Dodou Jobe alone.

I popped up from a moment's dive underneath and ended my thoughtful and therapeutic swim. I waded out heading straight across the beach market and across the street back to my house. As usual, the market people haggled over fish and salt. I was out again in half an hour, refreshed from a great cleansing rinse of tap water. I carried a small bag of clothing, a handkerchief full of roast groundnuts and a bottle of lemonade. I ran up the gangplank into the groundnut cutter where my good friend, Najum, the cook, waved me on board. He and the galley boy, Oumpa, were happy to see me and wondered how hungry I was. When I said I was very hungry, Najum pulled up a sack full of groundnuts and said that the faster I was at shelling the sooner we would eat some *domoda* he was preparing with offal – tripe, intestines and bits of bone, lungs and liver. I got to work immediately and the cutter pulled away from the wharf. I got cracking and shelling and putting the clean nuts in a great big washing bowl. Then Oumpa said I could eat as big a lunch as I wanted as long as I also scrubbed a pan or two in which he would serve the food.

By evening that day, the *Ndey Kendak Sarr* was slicing the surface of the channel at Tendaba, the big village that sat on the right bank in Kiang. We had sailed a good part of the day and docked at Kuntaur. The rest was easy on foot to Barajaly. The news that I had come by cutter was happily received; I would have hurt my mother if she had heard anything about me walking home again.

People were doing exactly what they were doing when I first left. Little had changed except for the remarkable thing that many of the boys looked much older than me. One of them, my birthday mate, a 21-year-old like me, and who used to enjoy helping me in my father's weighing station, was already married. I was glad to find many of them alive and well. I caught up with news on the latest additions to the families in nearly all the compounds in the village. I asked about all those who had recently died and I went to their homes and offered condolences to the bereaved. They told me of two young men who died in the war in Europe. It was the travelling commissioner who came with messages from the War Office in a cablegram addressed from Accra in the Gold Coast. Both men were killed in brave action against the enemy. I wish I had recorded the details on them then. Anyway, they were from a small village just before Georgetown but had lived in Barajaly for some time before their conscription.

The following day Pa Yoma came over to my father's shop for a discussion between what he called three grown men. Before he took his seat, my father remarked to him that I had sat and crossed my leg over my knee like the travelling commissioner did. Pa Yoma laughed when he remembered that, indeed, my father had said that when people went away to Bathurst and learnt the ways of the white man, the first things they did were to sit in high chairs, cross their legs and then talk through their noses. At once I uncrossed my legs. However, even though I had crossed my legs

I was speaking perfect Mandinka through my mouth and not through my nose, and in my homebred Barajaly accent.

As soon as the pleasantries were over, Pa Yoma asked me a direct question. He wanted to know what I would study if I ever had the opportunity to go to England. I answered that I was thinking of becoming a doctor. He asked me to give reasons why I wanted to study medicine. I said if I had been a doctor I would have been of greater help to Sering Matarr John in his illness. I also said that I thought with all the illness around us it would be a very good idea to be able to help people get well again. Pa Yoma laughed, scratched his head and butted in again before my father could put in a word.

"Make sure you come back home quickly so that you look at our aching knees and joints that are cracking up with old age," he said.

My father laughed too but said nothing. It sounded as if Pa Yoma was working through an agenda without any rehearsals with me. It seemed he did not want my father to speak.

"Well, to be a doctor you must begin where doctors work," Pa Yoma said. "And that is at the ...?"

"The hospital?" I added.

"Exactly," he concurred. "Make sure you rest very well. And when you get back to Bathurst go to Mr Baker at your former school. Tell him to speak with the people at the Health Department and they should be able to get you a place at the hospital. With this big certificate you have won, getting work at the hospital will not be any trouble. And that's where you will show them that you really want to become a doctor."

My father's silence seemed to indicate that he had been drawn into the meaning of the conversation that he had left to Pa Yoma and me. His attitude was positive and he did not seem lost to what Pa Yoma really wanted. When my father got back to his work, I walked across the street with Pa Yoma to his shop. He sat again in his beloved deck chair. I sat beside him in a straight wooden chair he reserved for important visitors. Then he let me into his secret. The fast talking and all of that was simply to stop my father raising the old demand for me to keep my promise to return and work in his shop. Now that we had passed that chance of him ever asking, it would be wise for me to return to Bathurst and wait out there for word on the scholarship. Pa Yoma advised that if I wanted to speed things up and to keep going I needed to be within the hub of things in Bathurst, not in Barajaly, which was too far away for anybody to pay attention to me.

I returned to Bathurst on a cutter that left Walikunda early the next morning. In the quiet time by myself, I began to better appreciate Pa Yoma's strategy to out-speak my father and keep him from any thoughts of asking me again to be his clerk. That would have been like giving away a lifetime of work, as Pa Yoma had put it earlier. If my father had been allowed to raise the matter, it would have meant fresh rounds of negotiations with the old man, and I always kept in mind that Pa Yoma was mindful of the age difference. My father was at least eight years older than him.

The short visit was over. I returned to my usual chores in Wellington Street, collected the rent and went over the daily housekeeping allowance account with Amie Badjan. I took care of other errands Pa Yoma had asked me to do. I handed the gift to Ya Amie Gaye. There was something for their youngest brother, Abdoulie Jallow, whom we all fondly called Mbeh. He was a great friend of mine and looked out for me in every caring way like the big brother he was to me. He took personal care of a coconut sapling I had planted in the backyard in the 1940s. When I became president and the sapling had become a tree, Mbeh was happily watering it and harvesting coconuts he gave me whenever I visited Wellington Street. Once he told my orderly to leave the coconuts to me to carry to the car myself. "They are *his* coconuts," he told the bewildered policeman.

Pa Yoma asked me to deliver the message to Ya Amie Gaye, stressing that we should not listen too much to the rumours of a poor trade season. He wanted his household to know that although the returns of the season had been less than expected, there was no cause for alarm. He would make ends meet from the earnings of his cutters which were engaged in the clearing up after the war. Allah was always gracious!

Ya Amie Gaye said that Pa Yoma really needed not to worry. She said a reply had to be sent by the next groundnut cutter to Pa Yoma, that the family was doing fine and the household was happy. Her son, Pa Omar Jallow, was going through the same difficulties at his trading station at Fatoto and that he too had sent a word of thankfulness that despite the shortfalls there was enough to keep body and soul together.

Lamin Marenah certainly seemed happy to receive his little gift from Pa Yoma. He smiled appreciatively and returned stealthily to his books. He too was doing very well at the MBHS chalking up excellent results not only with books but also in athletics where his speed in the 220-yard, 440-yard and the team relay races brought trophies to the school at the annual Empire Day sports on 24 May. He excelled in biology and pure mathematics and proceeded on a scholarship to study agricultural science at Durham University in 1953. We had spent three years together at Wellington Street before I left for Achimota.

The school holidays ended and Lamin was ready to go back to his classes. I walked down with him on the first day of term. A group of new students chattered away under the palm tree outside the school gate waiting to walk into the grounds for the first time. Only six years before I had looked everything they did at that moment – shaking with anticipation and ready to step into such an intimidating presence that those looming stone buildings were. It was the feel of seriousness that made it look so fearful. I remember my first morning feeling that if I but kicked as little as a stone out of place someone might turn me out of the school; or that the slightest false step I took would send the world crashing on my head. And indeed when the boys standing under the palm nut tree decided to walk into the school, they were watching their every step.

Busy as he was on the first day of term, J J Baker was quite pleased to talk with me. It felt like old times again under the arches of the staircases looping left and right into the living quarters upstairs. From where we stood the wide open doors led to a hallway and across to a back veranda, giving it the look of a raised concert stage with steps rising up to it from the front entrance and falling away again behind it into a vast yard beyond. Mr Baker was in khaki shorts, a white shirt and a brown tie. The cold harmattan wind was biting and Mr Baker seemed to be taking it much better than me in my woollen sweater. Even though it was already January, there was still that chilly feel of Christmas in the morning breeze.

Mr Baker was quite happy with my interest in studying medicine. He was quick to remind me, of course, that it would mean two years somewhere along the West African coast to catch up on my science subjects. He told me he was hopeful that those new students filing by would not have to leave Bathurst to study chemistry, physics, botany or biology if the plans worked out for a science school that could begin before the end of the year, provided a good science teacher could be found in the UK.

I had to find some work to while away the time. With Mr Baker's help I was employed at the Victoria Hospital where I would spend two years working as a nurse in training. My old school friend, ET, had also joined the nursing staff. It seemed nothing would separate us, not even in the world of work. I worked in various sections of the hospital – the operating theatre, the laboratories, the Wards and the European Ward. The colour bar was an ugly thing but it was real at the hospital. The European Ward was strictly for Europeans, even to the exclusion of the most senior Africans, be they civil servants or businesspeople. We were aware of the colour bar in the civil service but at the hospital it was even more manifest.

The work was generally tough; hence we welcomed the relatively calmer pace of the laboratories under our section head, Mr Johnny V Wollay Coker. The tall, dark and smiling Aku gentleman had an admirable way of gently mixing very serious work with light humour all through the day. This made very hard work pass relatively easily. We tested blood and urine samples and we incubated specimens of all kinds in bottles, tubes and Petri dishes sent from the medical and surgical sections of the hospital.

It was there that I made my first proper acquaintance with Sammy J Palmer who had joined the laboratories while he waited for word on the second leg of his scholarship. Sammy was two years my senior at the MBHS. He had returned from the first leg of the scholarship at Achimota. The hospital was the ideal place to labour while he waited for word from England. With large rimmed glasses, a warm fixed smile that had become his trademark and an elegant centre part in his hair, he looked every part a doctor already even before he finally left to study at Bristol University.

It was a long nail-biting two-year wait but I took great consolation in the experience the hospital was providing me. I found good reason to continue to labour and to wait. At last, in 1947, news arrived on my scholarship. Under the chairmanship of Dr Sam H O Jones, the scholarship committee offered me an 'open' award. It hit me like a bolt. My heart fell. My father had no means of coming up with the rest of what I would need to study at university abroad. There was another bigger twist to the story. The Gambia had been offered three medical scholarships: two for studies in human medicine and one in veterinary medicine.

While the news of my award was thrilling to Mr Baker, I was desperate to send messages to Walikunda to say an offer was made to me but that I would need a great deal of help to make it work. Pa Yoma was thinking fast. He called my brothers, Basadi and Kawsu, and my father to discuss the situation. He told them he knew it was true that business had yet to pick up so soon after the war but urged my family to do everything in their power to help raise the cost of my boarding and lodging as this was not covered by the open scholarship.

Pa Yoma suggested an amount of money he would give as his contribution towards the bill. Basadi, who was already doing reasonably well in his business, also did likewise. Kawsu, our eldest brother, suggested his contribution. Although business was tough for him at Bansang where he ran a shop, he said he saw the importance and privilege of it all for a member of the family to train as a doctor.

My father was moved but remained cautious. He felt it would be a great strain on everybody and asked whether it did not make more sense for me to start working in Bathurst and bring money to the family. Pa Yoma, who was not given to too much argument, was resolute about the importance of the scholarship offer. He told my father in a calm but emphatic way that he thought I should accept the scholarship. Although the amount we needed to raise was large, and the offer of a scholarship was coming as it did during a very poor season, it was not too large to deny a promising young man the pride of a medical degree. It was that statement that Pa Yoma made in 1946 that came straight back to my mind when in later days I first came across the truism: 'If you think education is expensive, try ignorance!' Education was and still is the best investment any parent could make in their children.

"*Doktoro!*" Kawsukebba Jawara reiterated to my father to make it sink what I would become.

"Mawdo, remember how you praised those doctors for their good work when they came in their white coats to inoculate the children during the big fever," he told his father.

"Or those at the big hospital in Bathurst," Pa Yoma added to seal the argument. "You have been to Bathurst many times and you have seen them. That is what Kairaba will be when he comes back. A doctor. A big and important man."

"*Allahu akhbarr!*" That was what my father said, after a long-drawn-out thought. He concluded his thoughts and said with a deep breath: *"Bismillah,"* indicating his agreement.

The following day, my father returned to Walikunda with a bundle he had retrieved from his safe in his house in Barajaly. He loosened the knots holding the ends of the cloth wrapping and laid it out on the counter in Pa Yoma's shop. There were French notes, English pounds and West African Currency Board notes. Basadi was there with them; and they counted the money – if I remember correctly – a hundred and fifty pounds or more.

I heard the whole story when Pa Yoma came back to Bathurst. He narrated his meetings with Basadi and how they succeeded in convincing Mawdo that this was not giving more money away to the white man but rather a way of taking back from him in the form of the education our children needed to build the country. Pa Yoma said that my father was finally convinced when he considered that after qualifying I would be paid enough to recover all that the white man had taken away from the village.

He told the whole story of how it happened the next day when he closed the shop in the evening with Mawdo and Basadi inside and how the three crowded around the light to count the money. He described how the hurricane light threw large looming shadows of them on the walls making them look no different from robbers counting their loot after a night's haul. My father thanked God when he found out that there was enough to cover the amount. He wrapped it up and with open palms the three of them recited the *fatiha*. That sealed it for Mawdo. Then he told Pa Yoma it would be money well spent. He also agreed that I deserved it and he was happy to give it, after all. Pa Yoma said it was at that point that he felt that my father was really speaking from the bottom of his heart. Basadi thought so too.

I gave Pa Yoma the contribution my elder brother, Kawsunding, offered me when he came to Wellington Street. Kawsunding had come to tell me how glad he was to hear that the people at Walikunda and Bansang had come up with their contribution. I deeply appreciated his concern and brotherly gesture. He was at the time living in Bathurst with the family of another of my father's great friends, Pa Ousman Semega-Janneh, at 15 Hagan Street where my father stayed during his short business trips to Bathurst.

After Pa Yoma's narration, I told him and Ya Amie Gaye and the other women in the house how grateful I was to everyone for their financial contributions towards my scholarship. However, I wished to make it clear to all who had contributed to my education that I would pay them back after I qualified and found work.

"*Insha' Allah,*" the women in the house chorused.

At that moment I said to myself how right Henry Wadsworth Longfellow is, in his poem, *The Psalm of Life*, that we should learn to labour and to wait. If I might add to this, I would say 'and to forbear' – unless, of course, that the meaning of Longfellow's *wait* includes forbearance; for whereas we can safely assume patience to be implicit in waiting, forbearance is not necessarily so. Forbearance is one thing I have managed to learn, too.

13

Achimota, Glasgow and Edinburgh

When I appeared before the scholarship committee for an interview in 1945, I discovered the Colonial Office made only three science awards available to The Gambia: two for studies in human medicine and one for veterinary medicine. The interview went very well and half way through I was almost sure of a place. The question remained – would I get the award I wanted? The committee then informed me that the first two places for human medicine had already been filled. They said that if I wished to have the third award I would have to study veterinary medicine. And what is more, whereas the two scholarships for human medicine were full scholarships the one for veterinary medicine was an open scholarship.

Let me explain. A British closed scholarship meant that the student was fully covered, from tuition to travel fares, to meals and even warm clothing. However, under this arrangement, the student was under a bond to be posted wherever the colonial office decided their services were needed. An open scholarship on the other hand meant that the colonial office was only responsible for tuition and the student had to provide the rest of what it would take to cover boarding and lodging. Although it meant students were free after qualifying to work anywhere they chose, this difficult option placed a burden on many families who sometimes could not afford to pay. In that unfortunate situation, many deserving students missed out on training and corresponding professional careers.

As if putting together the money for college was not traumatic enough, the discovery that there was no place for me for the course I wished to pursue was initially disheartening. But I refused to feel downhearted. I bounced back immediately. I was determined to seize the opportunity to go out to study. I could have gone on thinking about it but it seemed to me that the committee wanted a decision – and I gave them one. I would take whatever they offered me. We shook hands and I walked away exhorting myself to rise to the occasion and endeavour to turn a minus into a plus – to play a bad hand well!

In fact, by the time I made it out into the street the moment had become electric for me. There was nothing more important than having been confirmed in a scholarship slot. At last I found the analogy for that act of fate when I finally arrived in the UK and saw how a whole train moved from one track to another by the simple switch of a track lever. I saw the scholarship committee as the railway engineers, who, with one decision, had switched my train from destinations in London, Bristol or Newcastle medical schools to Glasgow. The consolation was that, as far as I was concerned, whatever tracks my train was on, my engine was unstoppable. There I was again trusting in my quiet boldness to face a challenge that destiny was placing on my shoulders. As usual, I summoned enough courage to rise to the call.

From then on the countdown had begun for my training in an area whose purpose began to show forth when work as a veterinary officer would practically take me on trek to every corner of the country. As a vet, I went out into the provinces to meet the people and to help save their animals from disease. As a politician, a decade later, I went out again to meet them, in the numerous tours I had to make in some thirty-five years of political campaigning.

A qualification in human medicine would, indeed, have given me the comfort of a doctor's quarters in Bathurst or at Bansang, where medical officers cut their teeth in rural medical administration and delivery. But destiny began laying down its plans in the scholarship committee room in 1946 for fulfilment in 1965. Only the fickle finger of fate was capable of such a design. I was at every turn in my life appreciative of how education was widening the horizon for me. I, in all modesty, considered myself a living testimony of what hundreds of protectorate children could become if given the opportunities for an education. These thoughts contributed to shaping my policies that sought to bring education to the doorstep of every Gambian. My government's subsequent Education for All (EFA) policy was fuelled from that standpoint.

After high school, I had continued, especially at weekends and time away from my work at the hospital, to help Mr Sanger-Davies set up his equipment at the new Science School. Mr Davies was a dedicated science teacher. As I packed my bags to leave for the Gold Coast, I was quite happy The Gambia had recruited him. We were the last batch of students who had to go abroad to get an education in the sciences. The opening of the Science School in Bathurst meant it would be much easier for students to study science at home from then on. It cost the colonial office much less than sending scholarship holders abroad for two years.

I bought a travelling bag from the French company, CFAO. I filled it with trousers and shirts and odd clothing I thought I would need away at Achimota. It was an exciting feeling getting ready to travel by aeroplane and I looked forward to that novel experience. I could not answer some of the questions the children at Wellington Street asked about flying. Not many people in Bathurst at that time had ever been in an aeroplane.

Pa Yoma invited his friend, Abdou Wally Mbye, the legislator, to come with him to see me off at the airport. I sat at the back of the car with my luggage. I had a large suitcase and a handbag filled with the gifts my friends had brought me. Arona Jallow, whom we nicknamed Battling Siki after the world famous light heavyweight boxer, came to bid me farewell; so did Alafia and Marie Sarr and Dodou Wally and his brother, Nene Wally. I felt a sudden pang for having to miss them all as I drove away from the excitement that had gripped all the people at 36, 37 and 38 Wellington Street and 40 Buckle Street.

It was a bumpy flight to Accra. The propeller plane often dipped into some air pockets with drops that left my stomach heaving. At one jolt the aircraft must have fallen a few feet before regaining its balance; most of it was indeed scary. We finally arrived in Accra where I was received by officials from the Colonial Secretary's Office. They drove me in a comfortable car to the school, eighteen or more miles outside Accra, the capital.

There, I found a warm community of Gambians, the majority of them in the School of Education. Apparently, the students I found there were following in the footsteps of a number of predecessors who had built a pleasant and respectable reputation of Gambian kindness and calm respectfulness. At all events it made my fitting into Achimota much easier than I had anticipated. It was quite an honour being so well treated on account of the pioneering endeavours of decent people.

I blended well in Achimota, an institution which I found in many ways reflected the grammar school moods and styles of the MBHS. The Gold Coast at the time was a country in the news. Apart from its powerful institutions of learning, its politics was in a flux. The local party leaders such as J B Danquah and others in his United Gold Coast Convention (UGCC) were priming the country towards political and economic advancement. In the background, a young vocal member of the youth wing of the UGCC, Kwame Nkrumah, had returned home after storming the lecture circuits in London and talking politics. I was amazed at his clarity of argument when he came to address the Students' Union at Achimota. He struck me as a very good speaker and I was impressed by his enthusiasm and eloquence.

Although his ideas were soon to cause a rift between him and the old guard in his party, the youth loved him. Before long the colonial government sent him to prison for precipitating a windstorm for African self-determination and independence. That wind steadily gathered momentum over the years and when it blew strongly enough the political landscape of West Africa began to change; that wind was to blow over the whole continent of Africa. I had no idea then that in a little more than a decade that political wind would blow over my own country and sweep me along in its wake.

I settled in to work and looked forward to a good two years ahead. I soon met and befriended a young and budding scientist named Kwesi. My attraction to his friendship was his fair-minded and kindly personality that paid great attention to his studies. There was no sign in his scholarly carriage that said his would be a very short life. I stayed only for a year at Achimota and he helped me enjoy every minute of my stay there. I left and upon my arrival in Bathurst I learnt to my utter dismay that he had died. I felt I was paying him a fraternal tribute when, seven years later, I borrowed his name when an interesting twist in my life led me to search for a suitable one for me in my conversion to the Christian faith.

I have said before that the story of my names is an intriguing one and this would become even clearer as we get closer to the telling of the events that led me, a third generation Muslim, to the altar of the Anglican chapel of St Cuthbert's at Basse in the Upper River Division on one sunny Sunday morning in February 1955 when Augusta Mahoney, a devout Methodist, became my wife.

My year at Achimota went fast. I settled down well and took to the spicy food and the gay lively music of the Ghanaians. I ate platefuls of *dodoche*, the fried plantain treat that the college kitchen served at weekends. I enjoyed plantain as an alternative to the sour *kenke*y, the staple served with fish and *shito*. I needed the starch to help fill out my skinny body. Otherwise, I would keep to my own version of 'home cooking', which was fried eggs and corned beef or some other tinned food. When that was not fitting the budget of a student on an open colonial office scholarship, I settled for my favourite porridge. It was not the same as Mama Fatty's porridge in Barajaly but I could ravage bowls of it with much contentment; and perhaps the reader knows by now that I could eat porridge, especially oats porridge, every day of the year.

If any memory of the Gold Coast endured for me like that of my friend Kwesi or of Nkrumah's fiery addresses on the meaning of a new and vibrant African way of thinking and how that must lead us towards fuller emancipation through independence, it would have to be the close encounter I had when I walked into a riot in the centre of Accra. On what began as a quiet Saturday morning in 1948, I fed well on a delicious breakfast of *dodoche* and went sight-seeing in Accra. I was enjoying a pleasant stroll around the city and soaking in the sights and sounds that advertised the promise that the Gold Coast was already becoming. I was leisurely turning corners and window shopping when, as I approached the post office, I realised that the people had become frightfully agitated. Down the street, police and a crowd were clashing and whatever it was soon deteriorated into a riot. In the twinkling of an eye, the police descended on protesters with batons and battle riot shields and soon all hell broke loose. I was caught in the middle of the fray and nothing was of concern to me than finding the fastest way out of the line of crackling gunfire which I thought I heard. I quickly found my way out of the city and was soon on the road to Achimota.

The riot spread fast and there was rampant looting. Traffic on the roads came to a halt. It was becoming very unsafe. Public transport stopped operations. There was nothing left for me to do but to set out on foot back to college. It was about a two-hour walk back to Achimota. For a young man who had once braved walking one hundred and sixty-five miles to go and see his mother and without the urging of police batons and riot shields, the distance to campus was child's play. My worry was not the distance but the fear that I might again run into rioters or armed police reinforcements coming into the city. I made it in one breathless piece back to campus and went to my room where I quietly wrapped myself around a book and prayed that the tensions soon die down.

I did not fully grasp the political reality of what was happening that day until many months later after I arrived in Glasgow and in my conversations with Ghanaians, some of whom happened to have lost property or whose relatives were affected in some way by the unrest. I realised there was a connection; it was part of the knock on effect of the ideas and feelings that came out of the Fifth Pan-African Congress held in Manchester in 1945 that was manifesting itself on the streets of Accra. Among the people who attended that meeting in 1945 were Edward Francis Small, Ibrahim Garba Jahumpa and Kwame Nkrumah. Politics was in full thrust and the colonies were clamouring for independence.

I had escaped on foot to campus back then but it was significant to me when I became a politician that I was in that vicinity when people came out to make their voices heard. That exercise of civic expression was for me a respectable part of the democratic process that began to set the tone of Ghanaian national consciousness. Those bold challenges to the colonial government were sending a message to the younger elements of the UGCC that it was time Gold Coasters thought in terms of self-government according to the resolutions of the Pan-African Congress. The next nine years were to be decisive with younger cadres breaking away from the old guard of the UGCC to join the Convention People's Party of Nkrumah.

I had just begun postgraduate studies for the Diploma in Tropical Veterinary Medicine (DTVM) at Edinburgh when Ghana became independent from Britain on 6 March 1957. I put in my two bits when we the African students in Scotland celebrated it with the Ghanaian community. I had begun liking ballroom dancing, and I still have fond memories of the wonderful time we had when we marked the occasion of the first declaration of independence in Black Africa.

It was amazing that only three years after Ghana's attainment of independence, I would also be thrown fully into the centre of The Gambia's quest for its own independence. This was the last thing on my mind when I listened to the broadcast of Nkrumah's memorable speech in the Black Star Square that the independence of Ghana was meaningless unless it was linked to the total liberation of the whole African continent. I would be straddled with the duty of negotiating with the British government the terms and conditions of The Gambia's own independence just as Nkrumah planned to do with Ghana's when he spoke to us at Achimota.

When the school authorities at Achimota announced to me the colonial office's decision of my successful placement at Glasgow University, they asked that I should proceed immediately to Scotland from Accra. I insisted that I could not go directly to the UK without seeing my people at home. I felt I owed it to all my family to return home and take leave of them. I had been away for a whole year and I missed my mother very badly. To proceed to Europe for five more years without her blessing was inconceivable to me.

For the second time in my life I was seeing my mother cry. The touching thing for me was that both occasions for this rare event had to do with my going away. It did not seem honourable or fair on my part that my mother was trying at all costs to keep me near her and all I was doing was bidding her farewell with eagerness to get away. It was torture for her. Even the explanation to her of how great it would be when I became a doctor was not enough to mitigate the pain she was going through.

Mama Fatty pronounced in a deep voice with soreness in her heart that she would let me go but again pleaded with the world that she did not have male children to throw away. She pleaded with the world to be careful not to hurt her child. She asked the world to be kind to her child and if at any time it decided it did not want her son any more to send him back to her. She would pick up whatever the world had left of him, and she would embrace him and take him back in her bosom.

The poetry of her Mandinka was solemn and transfixing. Water gathered in the corners of my eyes. My older relatives led my mother back to the house. I took leave of them and told them I would take the vehicle to Kuntaur and board a groundnut cutter back to Bathurst. I would go to the UK by a *kulun tiila* just like I had done when I went to Achimota. The older ones were sad and ecstatic at the same time. The children with loud screams chased the Land Rover pickup all the way down the dirt track until the driver and I could no longer hear them.

Back in Bathurst, I found Cherno Jagne, one of my old classmates, beyond himself with excitement. His joy was about his acceptance to a college in Aberystwyth in Wales to study administration and, besides, he and I were scheduled to travel on the same steamship to Europe. Mustapha Fye also had great news to share; he would soon be off to Fourah Bay College in Sierra Leone to study commerce. That was what he had wanted and, the sharp brain he was, a BCom degree would indeed be an easy walkover for him and it would be a good enough degree since Fourah Bay was already an affiliate of Durham University in the UK.

There was good news everywhere for us boys. Cricket fast bowler Ernest Bidwell had returned from the Prince of Wales School in Freetown and was one of the two Bathurst boys who had picked up the medical scholarships and was looking forward to leaving any time for the University of Newcastle. Cherno, Mustapha and I took to the town in our own way of celebrating our success. We must have strolled around to give ourselves some kind of send-off. I started mimicking the typical Pall Mall gentleman in a dark suit swinging a slim umbrella and doffing a bowler hat. Cherno imitated Europeans walking down the streets of London. He said he wondered how differently the pavements of England would sound compared to the sounds on our own sandy streets. He said he could not wait to hear the heels of the ladies on the sidewalks, the kind of precise and purposeful 'clop clop' of the steps of the European teachers on the wood and cement passageways at the MBHS.

Mustapha, who always admired the soft percussion in Mrs Jenkinson's footsteps, said he could even, with his eyes closed, tell whether it was a European or an African teacher approaching by the way they walked. I warned him that he could be misled by the tap of the well-sprung heels of Aku girls at the MGHS when they walked. He must have seen Marion Fowlis, Louise Mahoney, the King sisters, Blanche and Ivy, the young Annie Mensah, or teacher, Hettie Forster, from the junior school, walk. Cherno, a great observer of people, agreed that the new 'London' steps of the new models at the MGHS and the MBHS could indeed trick him in a place or two.

The two Bathurst boys who had won the medical scholarships left for England by air. Cherno and I got bookings on a cargo ship. We thought we could have been treated more fairly and given a chance to fly out to England considering I had bragged when I took leave of my people in Barajaly that I would be flying to England. Human nature being what it is, it was not unreasonable for Cherno and me to feel jealous and disappointed that we were not going to the UK by air after all. I was sinking in disillusionment when better sense got a hold of me reminding me that I had flown in an aeroplane before when I went to Achimota. With that consolation, I was able to look on the bright side and to convince Cherno that perhaps the reason for our booking on a steamship was that our open scholarships were not big enough to cover the cost of flights. We left matters at that.

The excitement of travel and the preparations were too overwhelming for banal or self-pitying thoughts. I faced my hardest moment when I had to say goodbye to Marie Sarr, the young lady next door at 36 Wellington Street, who, to my mind, was the most beautiful girl I had ever set eyes on. I had such a crush on Marie right through my years on that street and I always damned the fact that her parents did not send her to school. Her beauty and carriage would have outmatched those of the girls at MGHS or St Joseph's if she had had the good fortune to don any one of those uniforms. I would watch Marie fetch water from the public tap or walk back to her house with baskets of live fish from the nearby market. She moved with an air of almost sinful contentment going about her business.

One late afternoon, she rushed into our compound but was forced to break her speed when she saw me standing on a prayer mat under the trees just opening my late afternoon prayer. She tip-toed past towards Ya Fatou's kitchen where she gathered some live embers for her mother's incense pot. The coolness of the dimming sunlight played on her chocolate dark skin. She provocatively swayed past but, this time, too close by and therefore accorded me the honour of touching the ground with the vessel. It was the tradition that when a woman carrying any vessel of fire or heat walked by a man she should touch the ground with it. She then ran off in an almost bird-like mating giggle.

Pa Yoma had been getting more and more excited since my preparation began in earnest for the trip. Government Wharf, where the boat was berthed, was a straight walk about half a mile down Wellington Street from our house. Pa Yoma apparently had planned a special send-off. He told Ya Sai Njie that there was going to be a brand new car to drive me to the wharf; she thought he was exaggerating but said she knew the old man too well for that. And true to his word, there was a new car from CFAO waiting outside the gate. Amie Badjan, a good and kind girl who was a ward in the household, was extremely good at packing and did a fantastic job with my luggage.

Cherno Jagne was already waiting at the quay when we drove in. His father was with him. We went straight to the ticket office to get through the boarding procedures. After about an hour of milling around, the loading ended and grease-covered sailors cranked the mighty hatches close. The ship's horn sounded. We hugged and shook hands with relatives before we set off for the shaky walk up the gangway. We waved again when we got safely behind the railings. The ship blasted a long haunting horn again with thick black smoke spewing with every blast. A fellow in some responsible looking uniform led us away to the ship.

It was a fine morning in September 1948. The magnificent ship weighed anchor and began to sail out to sea. We were soon out again because we did not want to miss anything outside; marvellous sights we had never seen before. It was a terrific blue up in the sky and I could tell we were moving by the way the wispy clouds raced past the funnel of the ship. Barra was receding on one side and Bathurst was doing the same on the other side. For the first time I pictured in my mind what the first European explorers could have seen – the whitened beaches of the island, the swaying palms and the huge trees looming over its vast swamp. Although there was not much else to see from the ship, at least I was able to point out to Cherno the white stone buildings of Government House sneaking past behind the thick foliage on the waterfront.

The *McGregor Laird* steamed on its own like a beast of burden out into the Atlantic Ocean. There was nothing now except more blue sky and a huge cauldron of surf churning in its wake with white foam trailing for miles behind it. It was a rugged cargo boat. Passenger accommodation was limited and until I saw a few more people I wondered if there were any more passengers other than Cherno and me. The food was good, especially the bread; so oven browned that I wondered what else Master Williams (were he with us) would have done other than to live in the ship's galley. The bread was indeed browned. We ate lovely fruit; avocado pears, grapes and apples. I enjoyed the vegetables and sometimes breakfast was served with baked beans. I ate well, as Ya Fatou had advised that I should, to build some fat around my bones. She said someone told her I would need the fat against the cold European weather.

There was not much trouble as the ship made its way northwards, steaming fairly well. After two days of travelling, the waves began to get bigger and the boat started to rock harder. One of the deck hands asked us if we had travelled before and we said it was our first experience. He exploded with laughter. "Get ready to roll, boys," he said. "Here comes the Bay of Biscay. I warn that if you can't take it, you could always run down to your cabin and stay in there until we get over the crossing."

That scared us especially when the ocean began to swell and the boat started to rock mercilessly. Alone I would have gone down below to the cabin. Cherno and I braved the rocking a little longer. We stayed on and held on as we saw the sailors do. Someone else said there was worse to come and tried to give us a fair understanding of the strength of the wind which he said would sometimes reach gale force. Even though we had never experienced gales, we felt that anything above the branch-breaking winds of September in Bathurst would indeed be dangerous.

Some people went back to their cabins; they could not stand the sight of the mighty waves curling from the distance and crashing under the ship. We, on the other hand, found it quite a spectacle and we thought the ship was taking it all well. The *Laird* steamed on gallantly, taking us out of the swells. It was rough but we must have been spared considering the way the hands on board got busy as if preparing for an emergency. It seemed crossing the bay was indeed a dangerous affair.

As we entered the English Channel the winds moderated. The surf shone and the mid-sea waves foamed at the head. There were ships of all sizes travelling along with us or coming from the opposite direction. They were cargo boats mostly. We passed some bigger ships with bunting strewn along the sides. Their high decks were as beautiful as those of the passenger liners *Accra, Aureol* and *Apapa* which used to call at Bathurst. At night when the rows of decks were all lit up the boats looked exactly like the *fanal* we made at Half Die at Christmas.

The number of ships increased greatly as we got closer to the United Kingdom. The *Laird* slowed down because there were so many ships in that part of the English Channel. The ship coursed its way through the traffic and suddenly in the distant horizon we had our first glimpse of the famous white cliffs of Dover. But it seemed an age before we got any closer. We had read so much about those white cliffs at school that I had to concentrate to take it all in that those places did exist after all. As the ship cruised closer, the cliffs rose higher and higher until we steamed into Dover port. I could see smaller boats moored in the distance bouncing with the surges. My attention was entirely swallowed up by other exciting new sights.

The excitement of stepping off the steamer and seeing all those naval and merchant seamen was suddenly interrupted by a rush of emotions. I was elated to have arrived and it was suddenly unreal that it was indeed the soil of England I was treading on under my shoes. I was in the UK at last. I could not quite figure out what was racing in Cherno's head but his wide open eyes told me that he must have been feeling no differently. The sentiments were short lived, to say the least. A light cold rain fell intermittently which left me feeling chilly.

There were white faces all around – porters and loaders and cleaners and people doing all kinds of odd jobs around the quay. The station guards were smartly dressed. Two porters arrived promptly and took our bags and led us through the mêlée. We handed them a small tip from the change with which Pa Yoma had armed me and they went away. In the hour or two we spent in Dover I kept hoping to see a black face to relate to; it felt like the sight of just one would have reassured me. By the time my train pulled into the station it was very cold. Everyone else seemed so normal while I had begun shivering inside my light overcoat.

Almost all the men who boarded the train with us at Dover had a newspaper. As soon as they were seated they all turned to the pages of their papers. The train whistled and with the smoothest roll took off. The platform began rushing by as much as the trees and the people did when *Ndey Kumba* groaned out of Walikunda back in 1932; only that it was faster and quieter. With fifteen or more people in the train cabin, not once did anyone say anything to the other. It was strange. It did not take long for me to notice that some people left their papers behind on their seats when they got off at their station. That was how I got my first British newspaper. I picked one at random. It happened to be *The Telegraph*. At least I found something where I could bury my nose instead of just sitting there and staring at a whole race of people who sat so close together but without saying a word to each other. I could not help imagining the unrepressed congregation and electric din it would have been in this cabin had this train been running from Basse through Walikunda to Bathurst!

It was not until we had arrived at a train station in London that we saw a number of non-whites – Africans and Asians – getting in and out of other trains. Just like the English people they also looked straight ahead and mutely rushed about their business. No greetings and no handshakes here, Cherno rightly observed. It was a shame for a black person to pass another without a greeting. That was an absolute shame. So we also kept our mouths shut. From London he would be going westward to Wales and I northward to Scotland. However, despite our trepidation we kept looking out for anyone who looked like us or any that would talk to us. There was none.

Cherno and I parted company in London, wishing each other well. We promised to write to each other after we had settled down. Alone now, I started reading my paper while keeping my eyes open for dark faces. The Africans I saw increased in number as my train stopped off at stations inside London and there, at last, I bumped into some Gambians. We talked. When they dropped off somewhere in the Midlands, dark faces became fewer and fewer again the further north I travelled towards Glasgow.

The temperature kept dropping badly. When we arrived in Glasgow I was almost insane with cold. I was met by an official of the university and I was glad he had come in a car to fetch me. The car was warm but the bigger blessing awaited me when I got into a well-heated room at the hostel. I cheered up immediately and I settled down quickly in my room. I took a good hot shower and had a hot meal and took my first chance to look around inside the buildings. The following day, on my way to registration, my curiosity got the better part of me and as soon as I finished the process of getting my classes and timetable sorted out, I went to the Veterinary School and looked around. The school showed great age. History glared at me from the grey mildewed walls and the glum arches bespoke of a link with ancient spirits that lingered in spaces in the quiet corridors.

Classes had started ten days before my arrival. A number of my mates were young ex-servicemen and women who were being trained for re-absorption into professional careers in veterinary medicine. Breaking into life in Glasgow was made easy for me when I ran into Christian Davies, a Gambian who had arrived there two years earlier. Christian knew the place well, and showed me through the town and shops where I could buy good things for much less money than in the big shops. He was very kind to me and I appreciated his help in making me feel welcome in such a faraway place from home. Strangely though, in about a year after we met Christian suddenly fell off my radar screen and I heard nothing of him until I got news that he had died in 2006 in Leeds, where he had probably lived all those years.

I met Othman Shariff at the hostel where we turned out to be the only two of a kind. We both came from Africa and we shared a common background as Muslims. He came from Zanzibar in the Indian Ocean and I from the bulge of West Africa on the Atlantic Ocean. It was easy, almost natural, for us to strike up a friendship, especially when we discovered kindred interests in ballroom dancing and the sounds of the Big Band. We enjoyed great moments of leisure away from studies listening to great big bands like the Joe Loss Orchestra.

During the first year of school we took private lessons and refined our ballroom dance steps. We made lots of friends. I also took up Scottish dancing and learnt the traditional musical styles of the highland tribes. At Yuletide in 1949, I went to hear the Royal Scottish National Orchestra play at Kelvin Hall. It was an evening of musical transportation. Even though this was my first encounter with Western classical music, I sat through the entire oratorio, *Messiah*, by George Frideric Handel. I heard the *Hallelujah Chorus* for the first time and I was enraptured forever by it and the genius of the composer. In all the five years of my stay in Glasgow I never missed the annual event. I always looked forward to that moment of ritual when the hall rose to the rendition of the *Chorus* similar to a tribute the king and gentry paid to the composer who first performed *Messiah* in 1742 and annually afterwards in London in support of the Foundling Hospital.

Concerts given by the Royal National Scottish Orchestra were a treat and it was a tremendous fulfilment for me that at every performance I found deeper reason to celebrate the profundity of the human artistry and spiritual expression. Suffice it to say that I was so captivated by it all that not only did I become a member of the support group to the orchestra, but I also registered for classes in classical music at the Scottish Academy of Music. When that got me nowhere, I decided to have a private tutor for the fiddle.

I was drawn forever to classical music. As I write, I am making do with a miniature cassette recorder on my library desk giving me the best it could manage of a ten-minute rendition of the *Andante* from Mozart's Symphony No 29 in A Major. There is also *The Magic Flute* and *Marriage of Figaro* recorded on the B-side, among some great overtures from Mendelssohn, Strauss, Rossini and Beethoven among others.

I could have chosen and perhaps should have chosen a much easier instrument to learn but why the violin won my heart I could not quite clearly say. I found a violin teacher, Mr Clucas, who had retired from the *Royal Scottish National Orchestra* which was at the time under the baton of the world famous conductor, Walter Suskind. The respected institution was founded in 1891 and Mr Clucas had played there for more than twenty years.

I could no longer afford to stay in the hostel on my open scholarship. So I moved to some digs not too far from the university at Maryhill. This fine teacher agreed to come to my digs to teach me and was happy with the fee a poor African student was able to offer him, probably a third of what he would have charged normally. Then he took me around many shops to look for an instrument. He firmly believed that to learn well a student must own an instrument. When I finally found one, the shopkeeper was straight and honest about his product. It was a sleek looking, second-hand copy of the Stradivarius, the famous brand of fiddle that could cost thousands of pounds. I parted with £15 for the copy, a whopping amount for a student on an open scholarship.

It was a very difficult instrument but I had great fun learning to play it. I was late in starting to learn an instrument which the maestros normally begin learning at age three or four years or even earlier. At 25, it looked every ounce a lost cause. The violin was indeed a challenge; but Mr Clucas thought I had a chance. As usual, I asked myself, why not? I went for it! I wish I were as gifted as William Tsitsiwu, a student from the Gold Coast, a consummate musician, an outright genius on the piano whose prolific talent amazed the professors at Glasgow. William was totally reserved, strange some might say, and was completely absorbed in his music. My amateur lessons proved productive and my fingers were not doing too badly spreading over the fret board. After a while of practice I began to play pieces – simple ones such as the opening bars of Hayden's *Surprise Symphony* and the piece which the German National Anthem is based.

The academic course was as tough as the pastimes were relaxing. We had good professors who not only taught the subjects but were personally concerned with animal welfare and husbandry. Professors Smith, Russell, Pride, Thomson, Ballard – these were some of the fine directors who helped me through the tough coursework towards my qualification for which a whole family at Barajaly had had to empty their wallets and give up their savings to help me achieve.

As would have been expected, I was homesick a great deal of the time. At times I felt in so much of a hurry to qualify and to start paying back the debt I owed to my family. I prayed and plodded on. In time, everything would fall into place. All I had to do then was to labour with my books and to wait – for time to run its course. While I studied I was steeped in whatever the Scottish landscape and culture had to offer.

I loved the annual *Doon de River* excursions down the River Clyde in motorised vessels. Our group of students would spend the whole afternoon eating and drinking and enjoying ourselves. To battle the wintry weather down in the Scottish mountain gorges and on the Isle of Arran, I puffed experimentally on a cigarette to keep myself warm. I gave up and I have kept away from cigarettes to this day.

Othman Shariff, ordinarily the epitome of a ladies' man, smooth and suave, had become very political in his preoccupations. He was reading for a degree in agricultural economics. Naturally drawn to politics, he read and wrote papers on how politics related to agriculture and the realities of farming and the survival of peasant communities in Africa. He was particularly interested in stories about my days as a boy in my father's *secco* in Walikunda and how my father got on by letting strange farmers on his land and buying groundnuts as a trader. He was a pleasant fellow and very precise about his political views and the way forward for African agriculture and the African way of life, especially for farmers, growers and producers. He was two years older than me and we enjoyed the speciality of being the two Africans among the students in our otherwise all-white hostel.

He liked attending meetings with a political slant. I went along and ended up being grateful to him for the exposure I had to international issues. Cheddi Jagan, the Prime Minister of Guyana, and his Minister of Education, Forbes Burnham's visit to the University raised a lot of the issues facing the nations emerging from years of dependency on Britain. They were bringing forward the burning issues affecting Africa with its emancipation as the central focus. The news reaching us through the student newsletters and magazines was highlighting a young prominent Gold Coaster named Kwame Nkrumah, leading an African political vanguard and making waves at speaking engagements about African self-determination. Othman found a great deal of interest in the young Nkrumah, who would later become a great ally and source of inspiration when it became my lot to spearhead the quest for independence for my own country.

We had many sessions during our time in Glasgow and Mr and Mrs Arthur Young enjoyed our conversations over tea at their house. The Youngs took great interest in us and always wanted to know how we were getting on. They regularly invited us over to tea. I loved tea with scones filled with raisins and served with a spread of butter. I first watched television in their home on Coronation Day in June 1953. Othman and I watched the colourful ceremony of the crowning of Queen Elizabeth II. I remember the excitement we shared with the crowds on seeing the Queen of Tonga, who, like her subjects, would be at least twice the size of the average Gambian. This created a pleasant stir when she arrived at the ceremony. What a thrill it was to see the Gambian delegate, Mr John Andrew Mahoney and his wife, Hannah, walk up to greet the new queen. Incidentally, I might add, I did not then have the faintest idea that in about two years John and Hannah would become my parents-in-law.

The Youngs were from Perth, fifty miles north of Edinburgh, as the crow flies. They were to play more important roles in my affairs, especially when they gave so much assistance to my wife Augusta when she was hospitalised at the Royal Infirmary in Edinburgh in 1957 to give birth to our first child David. Mr Young worked as a bank official in Glasgow and he and his wife were very kind and hospitable to us.

It was with great distress that I learnt of Othman's mysterious disappearance while he advocated the issues on his home turf in Zanzibar in the 1960s.

The Isle of Arran, only a stone's throw from the bustling city of Glasgow, was a place I found in its extreme bucolic nature to be the Scottish answer to Barajaly. It was just the place for student vets. It was going to be a long summer and I was quite happy to join a bunch of students who had suggested that we should acquire practical experience in the real setting with farms and animals that abounded around us. We visited and spent time at an agricultural outfit. Then we went off to a sheep farm in the Highlands. My adventure bug as usual got the better of me and I was off on my own to study on a sheep farm in the north of Scotland in Oban – from there I could see the Isle of Mull across the Firth of Lorne. I spent three weeks in this remote and sparsely populated paradise, face to face with rugged nature and the raw cold. The experience did a great deal for my spirit and made me more aware of who I was.

It was in that pleasant relaxed atmosphere of study and adventure that I completed my course in Glasgow. Four years before I arrived, the Veterinary School had been absorbed into the University of Glasgow and plans had been afoot to phase out the Member of the Royal College of Veterinary Surgeons (MRCVS)[10] course to the more modern BSc degree. While I was there the college was in the process of moving from the dismal old building someone had dubbed the 'Satanic School' to the more pleasant area outside the city called Garscube, the more modern facilities that housed the veterinary college.

I worked hard, which reminded me so much of Achimota where my personal keenness, I guess, coupled with my desperate sense of urgency, pushed me day and night on the books. That way, exactly a year to the month in September after I arrived at Achimota, I received news that I had satisfied the entrance requirements and had therefore been accepted at the University of Glasgow. It was the same concentration on class work that I took with me to Glasgow that encouraged a classmate of mine, James A Gibb, to nickname me 'Zoo' because I constantly came out first in zoology. I am glad the name did not stick lest more cruel minds rushed to racist undertones James never intended. I still doff my hat to the teachers I found

---

[10] I would be admitted a Fellow of the Royal College of Veterinary Surgeons (FRCVS) in 1987.

there for physics, chemistry, zoology and biology. They taught the lessons and I in turn did not disappoint them.

We had our graduation dinner much earlier than usual. Some adjustments had to be made in the school calendar to accommodate the transition. We ate our dinner on Friday 24 April 1953 and those of us who enrolled in 1948 were allowed to carry on with our coursework until our final papers in December 1953. The dinner was a festive celebration at Central Hotel, Glasgow's premier hotel, where we all gathered for the banquet. It was a black tie affair. With Sir Hector Hetherington, the Principal of Glasgow University, presiding, all forty-three members of the graduating Class of 1953 were at table as was Prof W L Weipers, the Director of Studies, and all members of staff. The dinner was also graced by Prof G M Wisehart, Dean of the Faculty of Veterinary Science.

We raised our glasses to wonderful toasts beginning with that to Queen Elizabeth II, to the students and staff and to the profession of veterinary medicine. There was wining and dining and we showed off as the latest proud addition to the roll of Member of the Royal College of Veterinary Surgeons. The party continued in the digs. We celebrated until the wee hours with friends and ladies we knew we were going to miss very dearly. I could not believe that I had at last earned my laurels even though I would be staying on to finish certain requirements to the degree. When I finally did on 5 December 1953 and officially graduated, I found nothing more to ask for. I had a job. London had already appointed me veterinary officer, second in command to a European at the Veterinary Department of The Gambia. I was 29 years old.

One day while I was out visiting historic sites in London, I bumped into Foday Saidy; he was from Barajaly Su Ba and had stowed away to London and found his way into the rags business. He was raking a reasonable fortune selling second-hand clothing. He did well and married an English girl and cut out a good life for himself. I would have known him back in the village if I had not gone away to school in Bathurst. I enjoyed Foday's company and appreciated his suggestions that I stay and see what life I could make out for myself in London. Incidentally, another person I met in London was Jikiba Saidy, also a native of Barajaly Su Ba.

At that moment Bathurst was the only place I would rather be. I wanted to be home again after five years away in the wintry climes of Scotland.

I left England about 16 January. The comfortable cabin on board the *MV Aureol* was super luxury compared to the *McGregor Laird*. I travelled in the company of senior government officials – European and Gambian – who were bound for Bathurst with many stories of success either in their appointments or after training. One JV Lister, an administrative officer, his wife and two children were good company. So were B A Hughes, rural water supervisor, J A Austin, agriculture officer, and his wife, and Nigerian national, J A George, who was the government printer in Bathurst. Marion Lloyd-Evans travelled with us; I remembered her as Marion Fowlis, one of the bright girls at the MGHS; she was coming back from a course in teaching.

The six days on board gave me plenty of time to think and to ask questions about the civil service. I remembered civil servants I knew were generally dressed in drab grey trousers, white shirts and black ties. I knew it did not have to be that sombre a uniform but civil servants hardly ever got any more elegant than that.

The civil service was every schoolboy's ambition. The only other serious employers were the commercial firms, but strict parents preferred their children to go up the slow, lowly paid civil service ladder which guaranteed a pension and a gratuity. They had seen too many young men who rushed up the higher paid jobs in the commercial firms where indiscretion encouraged lifestyles and appetites that often led to trouble.

Returning home seemed the right thing to do. Even as I sailed away from the coast of England I looked back with fond memories at the vast openings and the experience of student life at Glasgow. I was a member of the African Students' Union – a small but significant number of students who made its influence felt in the university and highlighted its concern for developments in Africa. I became the group's secretary and before too long its president. Together with George Tomson I became a member of the Forward Group of the Labour Party and canvassed door-to-door during elections. George later became one of the Labour leaders, and at one time Secretary of State for Commonwealth Affairs in Harold Wilson's government. He was later raised to the peerage.

Tomson and I became friends and we enjoyed hours of talking politics in the company of his girlfriend who accompanied us on our campaigns and whom he later married. We explored liberalism within its socialist context that shaped political thought within the parameters of a democratic middle. It was the political doctrine that saw no room or need for extremism or fanaticism. Life was to be conducted within the laws of natural justice entrenched in the rules of democratic human rights weighing in with the Magna Carta, the UN Charter and the Universal Declaration of Human Rights.

The *Aureol* docked close to midday on 22 January 1954. In five years I had not been in weather steaming nearly 70F and close to 53% humidity. I flung my jacket over my arm as I walked down the gangway in long sleeves and a tie. The sweat was already running down my back. There were indeed some drastic adjustments to make back to tropical weather straight out of wintry Scotland. Pa Yoma was there on the quay at Government Wharf with his son Ousainou who had grown so quickly to a pebbly-eyed 16-year-old. The old man and his son had come for me in a car but they found some competition. A government Land Rover was already waiting to pick me up. I decided to drive in Pa Yoma's car and to have the official Land Rover follow to 37 Wellington Street. There we said a word of prayer and had a family get-together. It was a wonderful welcome back home.

Almost everyone was there, including my friend, Mbeh. Ya Amie Gaye brought me some water to drink and obviously there were many questions to answer from all my curious onlookers. The first thing my brother Basaadi asked was whether I said my five daily prayers when I was in England. I realised I had missed his tendency to melodrama. Thankfully, a dozen other questions crosscut his and so I did not have to answer.

One cold day in December 1956 Augusta and I arrived, ready for me to take on the Diploma course in Tropical Veterinary Medicine (DTVM). That story, in fact, goes as far back as 11 April 1950 when the Secretary of State for the Colonies circulated a telegram announcing the decision to revive the diploma designed especially for newly appointed veterinary officers before proceeding to take up their duties and for young serving VOs after their first tour of service.

The Colonial Office had sold the idea of the course to the colonies as a much improved version on that which obtained before the war and placed more emphasis on practical problems of stock improvement. It was also decided to conduct the course in conjunction with the provision of facilities for research into tropical disease problems. They placed it in the capable hands of professors at the Royal (Dick) Veterinary College in Edinburgh under its new name, the Royal Dick School of Veterinary Studies, Edinburgh University. There was provision for a dozen officers who would come and study with support provided by the Colonial Development Welfare Fund.

I was the obvious choice for The Gambia but the staffing situation at the department was so bad that we had to ignore the course. In 1956 when the subject surfaced again, my head of department, Mr Walshe, said it was impossible to release me, even though there was a sign in the air that the course was going to be withdrawn after the 1957 session. I applied anyway and on 13 August 1956 the Colonial Office wrote to announce my admission. There were problems from all angles. Staff position was difficult already and with the principal veterinary officer in poor health and ready to leave the jurisdiction or to retire, there were moments when it seemed a lost cause. But it appeared there was a 'guardian angel' in the Colonial Secretary's Office looking over my application. The office wrote to London in June to nominate *'D K Jawara who will appear in your records as S A Jawara'* for the course. No doubt you will remember my troubles with my many names.

Precious documents now read with such interesting hindsight into the movements and actors behind the scenes in the colonial bureaucracy and it never ceases to fascinate me to read the details of the absorbing discussion that went on before my wife and I could travel to Scotland. To catch the start of the course which was scheduled for 8 January 1957 and to last until June 1957, I should have left Bathurst not later than 15 December 1956 according to the guardian angel in the Colonial Secretary's Office. Initially one official wrote that there was to be one booking for a staff student on study leave. Another official wrote pointing out that that member of staff on study leave had become a married man back in 1955, arguing that the government could not be so heartless as to send a young man to the winters of Scotland without his wife.

But where was the money going to come from for the second booking? On the face of it, the administration was quite reluctant to pick up such a heavy tab and would rather just drop the whole project and blame it on shortage of staff and the lack of money to have two people travel on one scholarship. The guardian angel however insisted that government pick up the tab for Mrs Jawara's passage as the wife of an officer on leave. That guardian angel turned out to be the Establishment and Training Officer - a gentleman by the name of A C Spooner.

At one point of the heated exchanges, one pedantic officer was ready to refer the whole matter to the Executive Council for a decision. Spooner interevened again showing how well versed he was in General Orders and Financial Instructions. He wrote back to say that my course fell under departmental training and need not be decided upon by the Executive Council. He drew every foot dragger's attention to the fact that time was precious if the veterinary officer must arrive in Edinburgh on time for the course. Mr Spooner's firmness seemed to have held and the cost of our travel was calculated and presented to the Standing Finance Committee. It was approved on 27 December 1956 with no further argument. The £240 was itemised as £25 for tuition fees; £2. 12. 6d for matriculation fees; £3. 3. 0d for exam fees; £148 for the passage cost return; £20 for travelling expenses and incidentals, making a grand total of £238. 15. 6d.

But strangely, in the end I only received £226.18. 6d voted for the total expenditure of the course. Thankfully, my salary would continue to be paid by my department. The letter sent to me was signed on 30 November 1956 by Francis A J Savage, an administrator who would become very useful to me six years later when I became prime minister and needing his experience and commitment to a civil service badly short of able Gambian hands in a now self-governing administration.

This thus resolved, Augusta and I travelled onboard the *MV Sekondi* that left Bathurst on 7 December 1956. It was a wintry passage and most of it we spent in the company of hot cocoa in the pantry or cuddled up in our cabin. We finally arrived in England in blustery cold weather and the Home Office was prompt in furnishing my subsistence allowance of 25/- per night for the first twenty-eight nights and 15/- per night thereafter. I was given papers to sign on to a medical insurance plan not otherwise covered by the National Health Service in the UK.

Someone had deleted my warm clothing allowance in the calculation of my incidentals. Someone else promptly stepped in and I won't be surprised if it were Spooner again, to say that the item had to be put back because: *"It would be a shame if Mr Jawara is unable to take this course through contracting pneumonia after his arrival in the UK in winter."* I arrived in London to teeth-rattling weather but well clad with a thick woollen neck scarf and winter gloves to match with my wife well wrapped up and warm right by my side. We travelled up to Edinburgh and I began the course along with eleven other veterinarians from the Gold Coast and Nigeria.

14

Abuko

Now and again I think how my being alive to become a vet and getting my life on a reasonable course towards happiness and well-being were a direct result of some administrative and humanitarian decision taken to inoculate the vulnerable rural community in which I lived. That responsible act by people in government at the time left me with a desire to emulate them and save lives, if I could. The health of livestock was of paramount importance to the rural economy and to the health and well-being of the people, and if I did not have my first desire to save human lives, I was happy saving livestock that kept the human body, soul and society together.

It was obvious when I walked into the vet camp at Abuko, a village twelve miles from Brikama, that Principal Veterinary Officer Sam L H Walshe was successfully laying the foundations of the new base camp for veterinary work in The Gambia. The Abuko camp was coming on well in the footsteps of others he had set up at Basse and Yerroberi Kunda in the Fulladu district and at Brikama in the Kombo Central district. Mr Walshe welcomed me with open arms and was by all indications overjoyed to have a qualified vet to assist him.

There was plenty to do and I got on straight to it. I packed a few belongings into the staff bungalow in which I felt immediately at home. I sank myself into my work, ready to launch my mission to rid my country of the plague of rinderpest. It was a small department of two veterinary officers, six vet assistants and sixteen inspectors. We made up a fine team even though our number was woefully inadequate to cope with the work, if any of the diseases especially rinderpest would resume in any epidemic proportions. The department was now ready to put the professional and ancillary staff to real work. Mr Walshe had built up a comprehensive portfolio for field campaigns to begin; he was only waiting for the human resources.

A great deal of time went into shaping up the Abuko bungalow which would become my home for the next six years. In that time, it grew from a veritable bachelor's pad to a properly furnished home for a family of four. It was a spacious old colonial two-bedroom bungalow with an overhang of lush green fruiting and decorative trees. There was great space all around and the evenings were pleasant with the refreshing breezes playing among the foliage and giving the lungs that bracing feeling of clean freshness. I used some of the space to do gardeing which became a great hobby of mine.

I would spend very pleasant evenings tending my garden. But well before I entered politics my gardening had been regularly interrupted by the challenges of rinderpest and contagious bovine pleuro-pneumonia infection among the livestock. There were also recurrent outbreaks of rabies killing farm dogs in remote villages and that began to be of serious concern to me. I opened files immediately and worked closely with Mr Walshe. I was ready to tour the countryside to see what could be done.

I was pleased with the excellent vegetables and flowers I produced for my kitchen table or as gifts to friends and colleagues. Even after I resigned and lost occupancy of the house which was reputed to be one of the best in the entire colony, I still continued to do gardening. Indeed, after winning a seat in the first general elections in 1960 and joining the Executive Council as minister of education, I was gardening one evening at No 3 Staff Site, Yundum, an abandoned house where I had moved the family, when Governor and Lady Windley gave me the most pleasant surprise when they dropped in to see me. They said they had been out on a drive and, since the bungalow stood quite close to the main road, they thought it would be nice to come and say hello.

I washed my hands and cleaned my soggy garden shoes. I welcomed them away from the beds because it would have been embarrassing if I accidentally splashed dirt on the dainty white casual shoes on her ladyship's feet or on her cheery floral dress. Her wide genial smile approved of the unannounced visit. The governor also smiled warmly and joked. He said he was impressed by my gardening and thought that with the good job I was doing of it I probably got the wrong portfolio in the cabinet and joked that I would have made a great agriculture minister. We talked about gardening and Mrs Windley remarked how much their predecessors, Governor Percy and Lady Wyn-Harris, had done for horticulture and home gardening. Indeed, under Governor Wyn-Harris the annual Horticultural Show became very popular. In fact, I was the proud winner on one occasion of the coveted Banksian Medal for the best show of fruits and vegetables from a home garden.

We discussed politics casually as I accompanied them back to their car. The governor mentioned that the new team of senior government officials were all settling in beautifully. They all seemed to come from former positions in East Africa. Director of Agriculture C B Garnet, Senior Commissioner G Humphrey-Smith, like the governor himself, had been sent in from service in Kenya. A handful of others arrived from positions in India, Pakistan, Egypt and Borneo.

I enjoyed their visit and for some time I assumed that I could count on other gestures of friendliness from the Windleys. But there was a shock awaiting this assumption when a few months later I published my party's Independence Manifesto that would write my name indelibly in the bad books of the governor.

To understand the difficulty involved in taking on a mission to eradicate or control animal disease, the conditions of the people must be put in proper perspective. Bad weather and poor soil management practices had rendered the 1955 cropping season a failure. The loss of our crops to more competitive prices across in Senegal increased uncontrollably. With the rosette disease having affected the main groundnut crop, the rest was easy to bring down production by nearly 6,000 tons from the already low 46,585 tons traded in 1954.

The Gambia Oilseeds Marketing Board was struggling to give farmers unsustainable subsidies on the price of their groundnuts resulting in a heavy dependence on the Colonial Development and Welfare Grant and the Farmers' Fund to cover the losses. The government was still reeling from the record deficit of 1953 in which it spent £99,000 in excess of the £1 million colony revenue. It was a troubled economy with the production of groundnuts steadily going down since 1952.

Not only did it cause squeezes in every sector of the administration, it also forced the government to prioritise. And if social services were being cut and reduced under health, education, nutrition and other key areas, one might easily see how difficult it would be to make arguments for the health and welfare of animals. But there was no stopping it. The country's livestock and those who contributed to the economy by their general husbandry had to be factored into the administrative decisions.

There was already an active proposal on the table when I first arrived at Abuko to merge the Veterinary Department with the larger Agriculture Department. The administration gave copious budgetary reasons for desiring such a move. I resisted the proposal with all the muscle I could muster on the grounds that there should be no line drawn between animal husbandry and animal health. The two went on together and programmes designed with an agricultural outlook still had a distinct line of support that emanated from the medical aspects of animal husbandry.

I was concerned that a merger would also wipe out any administrative clout the Veterinary Department had sown and tended with university-trained personnel in advanced animal medical science leading it. It would be a waste to dump all of that as a sub office under a directorate at agriculture. It was also an honest attempt on my part not only to keep the department but to make salaries and positions attractive to the larger pool of qualified veterinary scientists already graduating and returning home to other parts of West Africa, especially Ghana and Nigeria.

I further suggested that if the government decided to override my proposals and merge the two departments it should consider increasing the emoluments of the principal veterinary officer and recruiting two more qualified vets to handle the volume of work in the department. I wrote to government emphasising the need to recognise the importance of the Veterinary Department to the economy. This turned out to be a most misunderstood petition. Some senior officials in the administration saw this as being a ploy by me to upgrade my status and level of earning. With the coincidence that Mr Walshe, the PVO, was waiting for reassignment outside the colonial jurisdiction, it was easy for some people to construe that I was feathering my nest to begin serving in his place.

V E Davies, the assistant secretary at the Office of the Financial Secretary, disagreed in his minutes to his superiors on 4 July 1957 averring that there was no earthly reason why the Gambian head of Veterinary Services should ask for a salary equivalent to the Nigerian incumbent of a similar post in his country. He further argued that The Gambia must resist the temptation to pay more than it could afford. While that sounded quite a catchy response and logical on its face value, the real fears of the financial secretary's office lay in the fact that neither it nor the Public Service Commission had drawn up a comprehensive plan on human resources, salary scales, allowances and upward mobility that would evenly absorb the influx of university graduates returning home and occupying senior positions. The civil service was expanding but the structures were stuck and obviously waiting for a shake-up. It seemed my petition had provoked just that kind of rethinking.

Evidently, Davies was worried about the repercussions of changes in the salary structure to the rest of the civil service. He reckoned that an increase in the benefits of the head at the Veterinary Department with medical qualifications would also draw similar demands from officers in the same category across the service who would want an equivalent pay. And if the medical and dental surgeons, the engineers, and others at that level put on a similar pressure it would mean a mass movement of heads of department and all rising to par in emoluments with the traditional senior service cadre of comptroller of customs, post master general and the accountant general.

I could have withdrawn my petition with the understanding that under the circumstances of the already strenuous national deficit, an increase on the £1,980 annual salary of the veterinary officer and more for the other senior servants would have meant a serious fiscal headache for the colonial government. But because I was convinced of the need for such a transformation in the Veterinary Department and across the civil service, I asked my ever challenging question: Why not?

On 12 January 1959, while the staff prepared for the presentation it would make at the *mansa bengo* in Basse three weeks later, I sent in my letter of resignation. The government would not accept it and instead called me in for discussions and reconsideration. Although my letter was already filed and numbered 2E/184, I withdrew it. The threat eased the unfair and unnecessary pressure certain hawkish quarters of the administration were putting on me. We went to Basse and as a department won the governor's praise for ridding the Central River Division of cattle disease. On the sidelines of the conference the members of the Protectorate People's Society decided on advances that would change the political landscape forever.

A year later, on 4 February 1960 I sent a second letter resigning my appointment. Some of the hawks continued to connect it to my possible frustration with the government's rejection of my proposals. We will soon find out how wrong they were. I was deep into the rinderpest campaign and trekking for weeks on end and had returned from a resoundingly successful presentation of the Veterinary Department at the Basse *mansa bengo* when a higher call to serve my country landed on my doorstep and led me to agree to stand as a candidate in the general elections in 1960. I resigned from being an overworked but contented veterinarian to become the leader of a political party that was soon to take me into the Executive Council as minister of education.

Frustration was certainly not the case, since I still continued with my missions up country as ardently as ever. Reaching the thousands of animals we vaccinated meant rigorous trekking into the nooks and crannies of the countryside. It also meant months on the road generating the vaccine on the spot with the hundreds of rabbits we took with us in several hutches. We injected the rabbits with the Lapinised Rinderpest Virus (LRV) – what we called *passaging*. The vaccine would then be harvested at the appropriate time. This increased the number of cattle that could be vaccinated with the LRV available and also reduced the need for refrigeration. In addition, we taught villagers and spread awareness among herders on best practices and methods of disease prevention. The Gambia being surrounded on the north, east and south by Senegal posed a problem. The cattle in those parts of Senegal had not yet been vaccinated in accordance with the FAO rinderpest control programme such as those in The Gambia had and re-infection of our animals was an acute and added burden.

I had a plateful to deal with. There had already been ten outbreaks of rinderpest, twenty-eight of blackquarter, two of anthrax and forty-eight of haemorrhagic septicaemia. The latter disease was making its first appearance in epidemic form and had caused much trouble already before the department was able to bring it under control. The department kept a close watch on contagious bovine pleuro-pneumonia which was recurring on account of the open borders with Senegal. Our neighbours had not as yet developed a programme against this scourge, even though the FAO had launched extensive campaigns with modules that countries as far away as Ethiopia and Sudan were already using.

Rinderpest also known ass cattle plague was a far more serious threat to herds. This disease has been destroying livestock since it was identified as a distinct plague around AD 376. For more than 1,500 years, it has caused unimaginable economic losses to herders and set off great distress of famine and even war in communities. This fragile virus is spread by contact and is nearly always fatal to cattle and hoofed animals. In Western Europe alone it killed nearly 200 million head, triggering investigations that led to the founding of veterinary science and the opening of the first Veterinary School in 1762 at Lyon in France. The disease spread quickly through international trade in the 19th century and soon reached all the five continents. It was said to have entered Africa at the Red Sea port of Massawa unleashing an outbreak in N E Africa in 1887 before spreading west to the Atlantic Ocean and all the way south to the Cape. In its wake it killed millions of buffalo, kedu, eland, swine, cattle and game animals.

In Europe as in Africa, the economies of many herding communities were so damaged that it was necessary to recognise the disease and to find ways of controlling it. I draw this worthy information from the citation honouring Dr Walter Plowright when he received the prestigious World Food Prize in 1999. I do so by way of paying tribute to a great scientist who led his team in his laboratories to produce the vaccines that were very helpful to us in The Gambia.

The poor conditions of our long dry season and poor foraging fields that forced close herding of the animals were a recipe for catastrophe. The dearth of wide open grounds to allow ample space for grazing could be seen as a direct consequence of Britain's apparent lack of foresight in mapping the shape and size of the country. A world power wanted a long navigable river into the interior of Africa and it got it. Nothing else in the area seemed as important to Britain at the Berlin Conference towards the end of the 19th century.

One of the numerous treks I had to make with my team was to Baddibu Nokunda in the north bank where we launched a successful vaccination campaign. We were going back to see what we had achieved on the ground. Follow-ups like that were expensive on the department's budget but were necessary to keep the tabs on animal movements and human understanding of the problems. It was comforting and distressing at the same time to see the stark difference our efforts had achieved. The animals on the Gambian side were robust and healthy while across the frontier, the land was strewn with carcasses of animals – the striking difference between the herds that had been vaccinated and those that had not. Dead animals on the other side were signs that the FAO regional vaccination programme had not yet reached that area of Senegal and this remained a threat to our work.

We attended to animals and demonstrated to the owners practical examples of how re-infection was the ever-present threat to our achievements. Just one severe outbreak of rinderpest could nullify all our efforts, even after our most tiring sorties vaccinating nearly seven hundred head a day, camp to camp, over a twenty-mile radius, trudging with teams of men, equipment, ice boxes and hutches of rabbits and producing the vaccine ourselves as we went along.

At some point in our campaign we suffered troubles of our own making over poor preservation of the vaccines. There were also occasions of fault in the technique and administration of the vaccine. We quickly arrested those flaws out in the field and plodded on. We appreciated the help we received from the laboratories in Vom, Nigeria and the Veterinary Research Laboratory in Kabete, Kenya, that sent us the dried modules of the LRV vaccine which started arriving in the middle of 1955. At the time we had nothing more than the Formalised Spleen Vaccine (FSV) to fight our own rinderpest wars in The Gambia. So, we gladly took what they sent.

An English veterinarian from Lincolnshire, Dr Walter Plowright, had worked tirelessly on research into the LRV vaccine that replaced the FSV, the preparation of which was rough, involving the injection of the rinderpest virus into two-year-old calves, slaughtering them and using the animal's spleen treated with formalin to weaken the virus. The extract was then used to inject cattle. This crude method though effective killed about five per cent of the animals.

From Vom, Dr Plowright moved to Kenya in 1956 where, as senior principal scientific officer at the East African Veterinary Research Organisation and as head of the Department of Pathology at Muguga, he diligently researched into the tissue cultures that would change history. Here he developed what became known as the TCRV (tissue culture rinderpest vaccine) that helped us so much in our campaign in The Gambia because with it animals of any age or breed and cattle in varying conditions of health, including pregnant cows, could be inoculated. The TCRV was a breakthrough that saved millions of economic animals from cattle plague across Africa.

I was in Haywards Heath in 1999 when I received an invitation to the ceremony marking the award of the World Food Prize to Plowright. As much as I would have liked to attend the London event the invitation reached me too late. However, I sent fitting felicitations to him for winning the prize, the foremost international award recognising the achievements of individuals who had advanced human development by improving the quality, quantity or availability of food in the world. It was most deserving of Plowright who had given so much of himself since he had opted out of lecturing at the Royal Veterinary College, London, his *alma mater*, to enter the Colonial Veterinary Service in 1950.

From Muguga in Kenya to Vom in Nigeria and back to Muguga he committed himself to research that developed the TCRV which saved livestock and livelihoods and improved life by preserving both food and income activities for hundreds of thousands, if not millions, of pastoral people. Added benefits were the stemming of famine caused by catastrophic cattle losses in rinderpest epidemics and the reduction of socio-political upheavals that could result from impoverishment of prime food resources.

We worked hard in the fields with the vaccines we received from East Africa. We were totally committed to our mission to stem the disease so that the financial benefits of its control could be realised in terms of the value of the reduction in mortality in cattle that would exponentially mean an additional production of milk, meat and hides. This in itself would translate into stability in society and improvements in the quality of life among the people.

By the end of 1955, we had vaccinated 41, 606 animals, a little lower than the 45,102 we had done the previous year. And it was not just cattle that got our attention. We had to deal with diseases affecting other animals such as the Newcastle disease which attacked poultry. Here we depended greatly on the Lederles Wingweb Newscastle disease vaccine to curb the dangerous spread among the free-range poultry that every family kept for the occasional social ceremony or the honoured visitor at their doorsteps.

There was also fowl pox to deal with. There was, indeed, never a moment to spare.

It was with equal drive to arrest epidemic trends that I went to Kanikunda, a village in Upper Baddibu where the Hon Seyfo Tamba Jammeh had reported a highly fatal disease among dogs there. The chief had first suspected rabies and, on 11 August 1955, I visited three villages in the Kanikunda vicinity and carried out a thorough investigation. According to the head men and dog owners of these villages, half of their dogs had died of the condition in the previous four or five weeks. They reported that all the affected dogs showed similar symptoms of depression, loss of appetite, discharge from the eyes and nostrils, coughing and sometimes fits. The dogs simply wasted away, emaciating and lying weak before they died.

My investigation showed that it was not rabies when the villagers further reported that there was never any aggression in the animals and that no one had reported ever having been attacked or bitten by one. There was also no paralysis, not even in the terminal stages before the animals died days after the symptoms had appeared. Since I was able to rule out rabies, I put an extension team on watch in the area to study further outbreaks and to see if an animal in throes could be found for further study. However, the investigation came to a halt because we could not find any diseased dogs in the villages for clinical or post-mortem examination.

15

Treks and a fateful reconnection

Were I able today to document all the mileage my vet team had covered in five years of touring the countryside, I am sure we would have covered The Gambia many times over. Treks over trackless country took their toll on me but I have learnt from them, and the fitness and ground knowledge I gained as a result would serve me so well in later life during political campaigns and in my annual *Meet the Farmers Tour*, which became an important feature of my presidency. Those tours served my government and party to reach out to the prime producers in our country, to hear their stories and work with them to reach the goals of developing our nation.

The Upper River Division was an important region for livestock and the reports of devastating outbreaks of cattle plague were not very good news for the Veterinary Department. The statistics collected in 1954 from Basse and Yerroberikunda indicated that the URD was a virtual disaster area, especially with the appearance of outbreaks of bovine pleuro-pneumonia as well.

Before Christmas in 1954, my team and I returned to the Basse camp from a gruelling two weeks of vaccination out in the impassable tracts in Sandu district, in places where floods out of season had left many herds isolated. Ferrying across a swollen, hissing stream or waiting for the kit car with a noisily crackling left shaft to be pulled out of a mud patch was hardly my idea of a pleasant day out. But nature itself is a strange phenomenon. While parts of Sandu and Wuli suffered from flash floods, farming communities in the Baddibu and Kiang districts were so dry that they were left with no choice but to offer prayers and charity for rain.

The team had done the best it could to produce as much of the lapinised vaccines we used in batches that would last three or four days at a time. Once during the rinderpest campaign in Wuli district we had to cut short a busy outing and return to base because we had run out of cooling agents for the leftover vaccines. In fact, the speedy deterioration of the blood vials had begun testing our skills in appropriate technology. It had become impossible to keep the vials cool from the searing sultry heat; something had broken down in the refrigeration system.

We were at our wits' end and I reluctantly refused the suggestion of a well-meaning villager to wrap the vials in plastic raincoats and to bury them in a sand patch by the river bank to keep them cool. I must admit I refused only because it went against my most scientific intuitions. While I understood such rudimentary ways of cooling, it would hardly have matched the high standards of the veterinary profession. A single microgram of contamination would have done colossal harm. Rather than risk the catastrophe of killing the animals I was meant to save, I ordered the team back to base at Basse until our refrigerator was repaired. We camped and waited and after a few days we were back over the hazardous terrain and, in the end, we successfully vaccinated many head of cattle, at times in excess of six hundred in a day.

One hot evening, late in 1954, I was in the rest house in Basse, thinking of what I might have for supper. I had just finished scrubbing my weary body and although the harmattan winds blew softly early in the morning and in the late evening, the daylight hours were hot. It was so hot that I needed very little effort to dry myself with my bath towel; the water drops disappeared, sucked up by the sultry atmosphere. I had some water heating up in a white basin over the WW II army kerosene stove the rest house provided for the use of its guests. I was yet undecided how exactly to prepare the four headless sardines I had plopped from the tin on to a plate in the pantry – to eat the sardines with some onions, vinegar and pepper or to make paté out of them. A cup of local tea with sandwiches would not be bad at all for the evening, I thought.

I was listening to the boiling tune beginning to rise in the white basin over the fire when there came a rapping on my front door. A Fula house boy offered me copious greetings and delivered a message that the sister-in-charge was sending me greetings from the Sister's Quarters at the medical camp.

I was surprised. My information was that Sister Augusta Mahoney had gone to Bathurst for a few days. I did not have the faintest idea she was in town. If the boy had not come I would have picked up my cranky refrigerator and would have gone into the bush again. The house boy confirmed that Sister Mahoney had indeed travelled out but had returned early the evening before. It was she who had sent him to say that if I needed dinner and could not cook up some of my own, she had some dinner she could whip up.

I immediately shut off my kerosene stove and abandoned the four sardines lying so pathetically side by side in the plate. Why not? The idea of properly cooked food was too good an offer to let pass. I had not eaten cooked food for several days. I chuckled at the house boy's comical struggle to pronounce Sister Mahoney's name as I sent him off with a reply that I was starving on sardines and dry bread. I said that I would be over at the Sister's Quarters in a jiffy. I threw a khaki tunic over my shoulders. The cotton shirt was more suitable for the sultry evening weather.

Augusta, only ten days younger than me, had arrived back from England in June 1953 in the company of her parents. She had just become a State Certified Midwife (SCM) from the prestigious Guys Hospital, London, to add to the earlier certificate she had earned as a State Registered Nurse (SRN). She had been immediately absorbed into the Colonial Medical Service and appointed sister-in-charge of the Basse Health Centre. It was government policy that medical personnel in the service of the Crown would also cover beats in provincial locations. While doctors mainly went to Bansang Hospital (and for a while to Bwiam Hospital until that project was closed), qualified nurses served their turns in the main health centres opening up in the provinces and the Kombos.

It was a wonderful reunion after our high school days. There was plenty to talk about and to catch up on the many things that had happened in our lives since I first left Bathurst in 1947 for Achimota. It turned out that she too had had a wonderful life, training in London and earning enviable certificates there. Within the first few spoons of our sumptuous meal, I was able to sense that although she had not lost any of the depth of her caring and courageous personality, there was remoteness in her eyes, a look that seemed to spell some quiet but brave endurance. Part of her face spoke to me; but part of it also always spoke beyond me. It was a face assailed by a charge of decision; a spirit looking for a discharge of a painful past, perhaps. It could have been about anything – love, future, work or family or being at home instead of in England!

We both knew clearly from the first evening that that dinner was not going to be our last. She was in as much of a hurry for me to return the following evening as I was getting there. No sooner had the team returned to Basse than I ran to the Sister's Quarters where I took a long cool shower and ate good home-cooked food. One or two of the older boys in the team teased me that it must be wonderful for a Bathurst bachelor to have found such goodness in the remoteness of the Basse bush. I kept my cards close to my chest. Augusta and I had not addressed any specifics up to that point and so I defended myself to them that it was simply a reconnection of old neighbours and schoolmates.

We had indeed been very fond of each other at Wellington and Buckle streets and we were so often in each other's company that many of her

Aku peers at school were frustrated by the amount of attention she gave to our friendship. There we were in 1954, finding ourselves again in the outpost of Basse, she living in a comfortable Sister's Quarters and I living in the spartan conditions of a rest house. It was not surprising that I soon gravitated to the quarters and was very well received. I even thought I was foolish to have doubted why the platonic friendship of long ago so quickly burst into a fully blown love relationship.

The team finished the tour and we left Basse. But I was back in two weeks. I had an overwhleming reason to look for the smallest excuse to convince Walshe that with the state of affairs with the outbreak of bovine pleuro-pneumonia, I absolutely needed to be back up-country to clean up certain pockets I might have missed. I soon returned with a smaller team trailing along this time. As soon as the New Year public holiday was over I was back as usual at the Sister's Quarters. I realised that I wanted to marry her. She said she would love to be my wife and for me to be the father of her children. But there was a major obstacle: religion! Augusta was an uncompromising Methodist and would hear nothing of converting to Islam.

There I was uncontrollably in love, needing to take very quick decisions to convince my department head of the need for an extended stay in the division for more official work. I needed more time to stay with Augusta, a young woman who had bonded with me as a sister, a neighbour, a schoolmate and, above all, a trusted friend.

Did it really matter what religion I espoused in the expression of my deep faith in God? There was our world of two people helplessly in love with each other but which was being shattered even before it started by the circumstances of religion. Augusta said how much she loved me but feared that religion was a gulf between us.

To my mind, everything would fall in place if only I were to convert to Christianity. Nothing really mattered to me at the time. Augusta and I were even deeper in love and I wished very badly to marry her. I was a veterinary surgeon, 30 years old and earned an enviable annual salary of £858 with some decent savings already put away, even after just one year on the job. I could keep a wife and give her a reasonable standard of life no less than what she had always known. We discussed my predisposition and she introduced me to a straight-laced English priest called Fr Alan Herbert Grainge.

We had at least a whole month to work on the arrangements for my conversion. Of the three or four names Fr Grainge had suggested, David sounded more resolute and from the short stories he told about the young king with all his human foibles but still God's chosen, I settled for my new Christian name. My real name Kairaba would have sufficed, I thought, but I quickly decided on honouring my Ghanaian friend from our Achimota days and that way stopped the priest's prolonged difficulty of finding a church equivalent translatable of a 'K' name acceptable to me. And so I also became Kwesi.

Fr Grainge had recommended and organised two very speedy ceremonies of baptism and confirmation. For the ceremony of conversion I could only now depend on the account of it in a Bathurst newspaper that located it at St John's Church, Kristi Kunda. Confirmation took place on a weekday in St Mary's Church on Clifton Road where Bishop Roderick Coote received three of us adults into the church at a weekday ceremony at which a couple of little curious altar boys served. The wedding took place on a Sunday morning at St Cuthbert's Church, Basse, on 20 February 1955.

The marriage was solemnised according to the rites of the Church of England after banns. That meant that Fr Grainge had announced to a congregation three Sundays in succession that I, David Kwesi Jawara, bachelor of St Cuthbert's Parish, Basse, intended to marry Augusta Hannah Mahoney, spinster of Wesley Methodist Circuit, Bathurst. I understood later from Augusta that that was the opportunity for the public to state if they knew of any just cause or impediment why *these two may not be joined together in Holy Matrimony* and may declare it there and then or forever hold their peace.

There should have been a thousand objections. I had only brushwork Catechism; all the Bible scripture I knew was what it had taken to win the Richard Cooper Prize at the MBHS. My personal beliefs must have gone through a revolution of their own with all the new cultural exposures my mind had gone through from the first day I walked into Mohammedan School in 1932 and the MBHS in 1940. My worldview had reorganised and reworked religion in my mind which, though it firmly believed in God, had relegated and understood religious expression in its most liberal of terms, perhaps too broad and too contaminated to please any of my former Qur'anic associates or even members of my family.

There is no point asking if any of my relatives was at the service. None of them knew I was getting married and no matter how fast the word of mouth was, I did not think it was fast enough to beat the speed of the wedding arrangements. There was none of Augusta's family members there either. One or two of the veterinary staff from Basse stood among the curious crowd outside the crammed church. It was and still is a tiny church on the main road to Basse Santa Su. Sompo Ceesay was there, of course.

Despite his strongest objections to my youthful exuberance, he arranged for a ring from Bathurst. We needed only one because in those days the woman did not give the man a ring, Sompo told me. He knew much about local Christian affairs, acquainted as he was with the culture from the solid grounding he had at two mission educational institutions - St Mary's School at the corner of Leman Street, Bathurst and the MBHS. Mr Mungo Lusack, a veterinary assistant, was there to help us with valuable tips on the conduct of an Aku wedding ceremony.

Today, I could only depend on the account of the occasion as set out in the pages of *The Gambia Echo* newspaper of March 1955 which wrote: "This was the first wedding that had ever taken place in St Cuthbert's Church as a fully licensed church for marriages. A large congregation of well-wishers and friends had assembled to witness the ceremony and the small building was severely taxed for accommodation when the bride arrived, and there was a large crowd outside the building.

"The bride who was given away by Mr W Haythornwaite, MBE, dispensary superintendent of the Anglican Mission, was attired in a costume of mustard coloured material with a matching straw hat. The bridegroom was attended by Mr A Lumley Frank of GOMB as best man and the service was conducted by the Rev A H Grainge, priest-in-charge of St Mary's Pro-Cathedral, Bathurst, who was taking charge of the mission in the Upper River Division while the permanent priest, the Rev PFC Lamb, was on local leave in Bathurst."

The newspaper went on to list the hymns that were sung during the service, ending with the hymn *Now Thank We All Our God* as the happy couple left the church after signing the register. The musical part of me retained some of the tunes at the wedding that I thought were wonderfully brilliant in their composition. However, others did fall flat in my estimation for monotony of note and form, especially with too many logical progressions. I remember thinking Mr Lucas, my fiddle instructor at Glasgow, would have frowned on some of those notations as probably musically boring.

The *Echo* wrote on the advice Fr Grainge gave us in ... "a very stirring and memorable address on the sanctity and indissolubility of Christian marriage. After the service a reception was held at the house of the commissioner and his wife, Mr J Howe, and a large number of friends were present to toast the bride and bridegroom whose health was proposed by Mr Frank and the bridegroom responded in a very well -chosen speech. Mr Jawara disclosed that he and his bride had been in school together and claimed to have done her homework for her even then. After Mr

Haythornwaite had said a few words, the bride added her thanks to all who had helped to make the occasion so memorable and happy. Afterwards photographs were taken and the happy couple departed for their home amid the good wishes of friends."

Immediately after the wedding, I came back to Bathurst, relieved that Augusta could now take the quiet time to figure out how to pass the news to the rest of her family. The changes had been dramatic, almost surreal, the way they had unfolded in the life of a bachelor plodding his weary way through the mud and filth of the cattle fields in the URD, officially out to rid the infected cattle of disease but ended up falling head over heels in love in a very fateful reconnection.

I found I was much calmer and my thoughts more collected after arriving at Abuko. I wasted no time on the way back to pass by Barajaly and to have a word with my mother who received the news about my marriage with muted incomprehension and consternation. My sister Nacesay was stunned with disbelief. I might as well have announced my own death. I assured my mother that my faith in Allah was as strong as it had ever been. At the end of the long time she took to adjust to it all, she said she would take refuge in her own faith and belief in the power of prayer.

My father was getting on in years and was not as strong as he used to be; nevertheless he was hurt by it all. But he seemed to have taken it much better than the women did. In Bathurst, Pa Yoma, though visibly shaken, showed no other estranged feeling towards me, which was a relief, I can tell today. However, he decided he would leave it to deep daily prayers, that it was just flitting exuberance and that I would soon be back calling the *athan* as I had done during my days at high school at the Half Die Mosque. His second wife, Bajen Awa Sillah, quietly confided in me that Pa Yoma was calm with me on the outside but was particularly broken inside, especially when he recalled my father's insistence on never wanting his son to study *nassarano*. Pa Yoma, she said, was feeling that he had failed my father and was bitterly blaming himself for encouraging me on so far and that my father would actually live through his worst fears.

16

The people bring me a message

The societies that came together to form the PPS were to become more prominent with radical changes in the Wyn-Harris Constitution of 1957 that began to recognise their increasing vitality and relevance. Membership of these societies grew mainly around the leaders of the Kombo Niumi Lillahi Wa Rasuli Society under the influence of Sanjally Bojang, a labour contractor in the groundnut business, the Fangkanta and Kambeng Kafo, led by his rival, Ebrima Njie, and another, Janjangbureh Kafo, led by Musa Keita. The leaders, however, soon began aligning themselves with the colony political parties only to find themselves mere pawns in the hands of the older, more seasoned political guard. Sanjally Bojang threw his weight behind J C Faye and Jahumpa in the Democratic Congress Alliance and Ebrima Njie sided with P S Njie's United Party.

Only a week or two before the end of 1958, I had convinced Sanjally Bojang to mend fences with the PPS and to join the ranks of the organisation. He was the older man and his experience and drive would be of great value to the PPS, especially when the younger people were willing to receive him. Once Sanjally was convinced of the need for reconciliation, he and his chief associates, Farba Fatty, Bakary Manneh and Lang Saho, came in a small delegation with me and Lamin Marenah to the reconciliation meeting of the PPS that was being held in the Nissen hut within the precincts of the Bathurst Town Council headquarters. Sanjally calculated and enjoyed the advantage of striding into the meeting with Marenah and me, two senior civil servants. And the truth was that the younger factions were happy to have Sanjally join them. The discussion went well and I listened to the tempo of the meeting and realised that the rivalry between the leaders was the only trivial issue that was hampering the gelling of a dynamic movement.

When I was given the floor, I suggested that the groups should unify under a single banner and further consolidate towards becoming a political party. The idea set off a wave of approval. When it finally caught the attention of everyone, it simply wiped away the petty bickering between the factions led by Sanjally and by Ebrima Njie. With the damaging attacks that the Committee of Gentlemen was already launching against the PPS, the factions quickly realised that they needed to unite to survive.

From then on, the dynamics changed in an unbelievable way. People were fired up and, at the end of a reorganised agenda an executive committee was elected to lead the renewed organisation. Sanjally was elected president and Mamadi Sagnia, a long-time devotee to the PPS, was elected vice president. Sheriff Sekouba Sisay became the secretary general. Sheriff had only arrived in Bathurst two years before to work at the Education Department as a third grade clerk. He had been showing deep political awareness and his growing militancy within the ranks of the PPS was already causing him some difficulty in his workplace.

It was that unified PPS that went to the Brikama conference in 1959 to struggle for official recognition as a bona fide political society and, furthermore, to request the government to consider more serious issues towards constitutional development. The 1959 Basse meeting came out with far-reaching decisions about political representation. A group of chiefs led by Seyfo Mama Tamba Jammeh of Upper Baddibu and Seyfo Jewru Krubally of Fulladu East argued strongly for provincial constituencies to be represented by their own people instead of by colony people. On the sidelines we the civil servants who were in sympathy with them followed the political debate with keen interest, ensuring that the assembly paid attention to those issues that were important to protectorate people. Although I was concerned with selling my department's programmes to the local chiefs for a change of attitude that would bring new awareness in disease prevention in livestock, I considered it a welcome development that while they were receptive to our proposals to eradicate rinderpest and other cattle plagues, they were also eager about altering the way protectorate people saw themselves in the equation of national development.

Despite the conservative and sometimes parochial language in which the chiefs put some of their arguments, the bottom line of the message was that provincials were calling for more involvement in national development and to interpret their own interests through their own representatives. To my mind, these were fundamental changes in political thinking. On the sidelines, the PPS was selling a similar programme to the political establishment to recognise it and to bring provincial issues into the mainstream. The call by the chiefs was so strong that its effects were almost immediate. Henry Madi stood up there and then and announced that he would not be running for re-election to the Legislative Council in the Kombo district seat which he had held since 1951. He was convinced that it was time that a Kombo-born person represented the district.

It was my privilege to help modify the chiefs' enthusiasm on the issue of representation to make it more democratic and even more representative. It would become my position that while the call for district representatives to be natives was fair, it needed some more progressive redefinition away from narrow regional interpretations. They also had to understand that the decisions arrived at during the conference were recommendations and were not binding on government or any political party. Therefore, for proper balance to be achieved, the choice must be left open to parties to field candidates anywhere in the country.

This was also to further guide the understanding of the chiefs of what the colonial government meant when the governor said it was time that *"your sons"* took over their own representation. It was a generic call to local participation urging local people to come up and take their rightful places in the nation's leadership. It was not the specific granting of a licence to the sons of chiefs to become political heirs or to straightjacket districts to select only from among them.

The PPP, when it came to be, made it clear that when a chief's son was qualified our party would put him up as a candidate and anywhere in the country for that matter. We rejected outright the narrow concept of the special privilege for the chiefs and in favour of the broader interpretation of "sons" to include everyone rather than the sons of the chiefs alone.

In the first ever general elections held in The Gambia in 1960 in which the PPP challenged the older parties, namely the United Party, the Gambia Democratic Party and the Gambia National Party, we fielded candidates in all the constituencies, except four out of the five in Bathurst. To begin with, my party put me up as a candidate in the Kombos, miles away from my native Niani district. Over the years, we fielded a Bathurst-born candidate, Howsoon Semega-Janneh, in Kiang. For ready examples of how we broadened the call for indigenous representation, we put up A M Drameh from the colony in Jokadu, Alieu Badara Njie from Bathurst in Kombo North and Baba Touray from Niani in Upper Baddibu. It was good to have the principle in place and it was even better to leave its practice to democratic choice. We opposed that parochial interpretation as a matter of party policy that one had to be born in a place to represent it. The other parties shared the same views and fielded candidates in constituencies other than their places of birth.

The chiefs' conference of 1959 came up with many breakthrough decisions. It was resolved to appoint more teachers and more nurses and that midwives would be put on the job where they were needed. A VHF radio would be established and lateral and feeder roads would be constructed.

The river steamer service would be re-introduced and wharves would be rebuilt to accommodate the revival of the services.

Although I was there as a government official, I played my little part all the same in the corridors, pitching the issues in private briefings with the chiefs and elders. The groundwork yielded fast results in helping to present the case for the recognition of the PPS as a viable political organ that was representative of a large body of protectorate opinion. The PPS had innovative programmes to suggest to the conference. These needed a fair hearing. Although at the time the PPS's constitution was only in the drafting stages, the advance party of spokesmen to the conference, Jombo Bojang, Saja Mboge and others, had adequately sensitised the chiefs and their advisers. In fact, the response of the chiefs and people was so encouraging that it was of great advantage to push for the launch of the party there and then. At the end of the conference, on 14 February 1959, the Protectorate People's Party (PPP) was born.

My personal notes from the *mansa bengo* lay untouched on my desk for nearly two weeks. I was still toying with the exciting ideas that came out of the 16th annual chiefs' conference and local headmen which took place in Basse from 10 to 14 February. I was also feeling quite satisfied that my team had covered important elements of animal husbandry and disease prevention during the hour-long demonstration we gave. The time in Basse was well spent and I was satisfied that the show put on by my laboratory assistant, G W Fergusson Mahoney, had caught the attention of the governor and his officials. The aim of the practical demonstration of our work was to urge the government to allocate more money and staff to help the department meet its objectives.

It was a good conference for the department. We gave our work the much-needed exposure and succeeded in having some of our recommendations accepted. Our proposal was approved to have a livestock improvement officer and a cattle marketing officer begin talks with the authorities for a mixed farming system to commence and for the main slaughtering centres to begin programmes in the drying of hides. Governor Windley had given us full recognition in his opening address when he said that the department had been rewarded by the virtual absence of epidemics among cattle in the previous year. The 1959 Disease of Animals Ordinance declared that the MacCarthy Island Division, an infected area since 1958, was now clean.

"It is a small department," the governor said during his speech, "but I congratulate their small staff for the good work they have done."

When I finally got round to discussing the conference with my wife, two decisions pleased her tremendously. She fully endorsed the proposed increase in the number of women teachers and the call to fill the demands for nurses and midwives at all the health and first-aid centres in the country. It was Saturday morning. I was fondly dandling David on my knees and trying to be a good father and thinking what I might do with myself that morning in my garden. Then Augusta parted the window drapes and called my attention to some visitors approaching the house along the gravel walkway. Indeed, coming up the path in flowing gowns was a single file of three elders striding with purpose towards my door.

Amid loud salutations and pronouncements of blessings of peace to the house I welcomed Sanjally Bojang, Bukari Fofana and Madiba Janneh, elders in the PPP. I introduced my wife and our two little children to them. Augusta also welcomed them, showed them to seats around the living room and offered each a glass of water. Then, true to a townswoman willing to accord customary respects to local elders of tradition, she went about her chores and left the men to state the business of their visit.

As soon as she left the room, another volley of greetings rekindled. My traditional roots understood the courtesies and prayers and more blessings outpouring from many voices muttering greetings all at the same time. I had missed this customary treat for many years and I felt rather special in that it was the first time I had received such a distinguished group of visitors in my house in the five years since I returned from Glasgow.

They were thrilled that the *mansa bengo* went as well as it did. They said they had been discussing the matter since they came back from the conference and that they had a few ideas to share with people like me who had the interest of the new party at heart. They needed all the able hands they could find to help the protectorate people take their rightful place in the future development of their country.

I gave them my impressions of Governor Windley's speech at the conference. I told them that from what he said he sounded like a man who was willing to work with our people and bring development to the rural areas. We discussed a few of those impressions but it appeared that I might have been straying a little from what they had in mind. I said finally that I hoped the governor would pay more attention to the Veterinary Services, because a great deal of the nutritional health of the nation depended on good and healthy herds that produce beef, milk and hides. I stopped when I sensed that I had strayed too much for the comfort of the visitors, especially when they looked quite eager to discuss something else.

Sanjally was eager to get to the point. He spoke flamboyantly and said that the party needed someone to lead it. He said they believed that I was that person and they were there to ask me to be their leader. I swallowed a lump of nothing that stubbornly stuck in my throat. My glasses fogged up. I cleaned the corners of my eyes; I could see the three men staring at me. The visitors seemed to have come to the edges of their seats as if they would pry an answer out of me or disappear again into the morning air from which they had materialised. It would be a cliché if I say that a thousand things went reeling in my head. There was very little I could say.

I tried to explain that although I had attended PPS meetings and given support where and when I could, the message needed time to find its answer. It was not a small request and it was not a request for just me to answer. I was one person in a family and one person in a government job where I was head of a whole department. I told them that I would need some time to give them an answer. My visitors agreed.

The days following were full of thrill and I had sleepless nights. I spoke with colleagues at the office, with neighbours and older people whose judgement I respected. As it turned out, the PPP leaders had been working down a list of possible people they thought would be suitable. I learnt later that they had spoken to Lamin Marenah through Seyfo Karamo Kabba Sanneh of Kaiaf in Kiang East and also through his uncle, Landing Marenah. Lamin did not want to be considered. He described himself as serving happily and diligently as agricultural officer at Yerroberikunda and was not the least interested in politics.

Ya Fatou Jobarteh, the chief matriarch at 37 Wellington Street, told me categorically not to go into politics. One man I held in high regard was Landing Kotoring Janneh, a trusted straight-talking elder and a large and warm-hearted man. He warned me with candour to be watchful. He worried desperately about my job and my young family. People, he said, were fickle and in particular he warned me that the ones who come to lift you up would be the very ones who would pull you down.

I took everybody's opinion into consideration and I shared each with my wife when I got home. She gave Landing Kotoring's wisdom a biblical edge saying that those who cried *Hosanna* would be the same who would later shout *Crucify Him!* In less than two years, in the heat of confusion and betrayal within the senior ranks of the PPP, Landing Kotoring's prophecy came to pass in the most dramatic way.

I dug back into my school past and called on one or two of the old boys. Ernest Bidwell was living in flat No 8 on the Marina and comfortably on the salary of a medical officer after returning home from the University of Newcastle in the UK. He was frank with me. My former classmate advised that I think thoroughly through it. He agreed it was not an easy decision to take when one's own people came asking one to lead them.

But whatever I decided had to be well tested against my job as well as the young family I had. All that weighed against the uncertainties of politics. Ernest reminded me that if I finally decided to run for election and failed, I needed to understand that there was no coming back to the civil service, not to speak of my job at Abuko. The decision really was mine, he said, and he wished me good luck as he accompanied me to my car.

That was one thoughtful drive back to the Kombos, if I ever had taken one in my black Morris Minor, registration number G941. For one moment I would see the future with me leading a strong popular party and riding on the crest of a wave and fulfilling all the memorable things Nkrumah had envisaged in the quality of leadership that must be in the Africa that he envisioned with us at Achimota. Then in another moment I saw myself sorrowing, let down, abandoned and jobless; my family scattered and I, just as a flash in the pan, forgotten by the crowds that would all have evaporated.

I replayed in my mind everything I had heard from people. There were those who rather thoughtlessly patronised me that I was born for the party while others were practical and spontaneously urged me to press on and take the bull by the horns. There were also some who told me in no uncertain terms never to walk into that perilous arena of African politics. They said what they were hearing about Ghana, Guinea, Mali, the Belgian Congo and what they had read about Kenya and the Mau Mau had already scared them. There was also the daring voice reminding me of William Shakespeare and my teacher, Master Salla, who quoted the bard regularly to bring home to us the fact that, indeed, there are tides in the affairs of men, which, if taken at the flood, will lead on to fortune.

I got home with what I could safely describe as an open mind. I consulted further with my wife. Perhaps she still needed more time to think matters over. She was not readily dismissive of politics and, in fact, thought it could be exciting. The future was not made bleak by the proposal, she said, but there was a great deal of it that had to be carefully assessed for a proper answer to be given. We did not have a house of our own; she was out of work; the family was growing with a toddling boy and his baby sister! What choices were we about to make for them?

Apart from thoughts about the family, it was a worrying thing to think that stepping into the political arena was going to pitch me against household names such as J C Faye, I M Garba Jahumpa and P S Njie, older and more seasoned men, albeit within the tight circle of Bathurst and Kombo St Mary politics. The PPP, it appeared, would do reasonably well in the provinces but the task of selling it to the colony voters would be a mammoth one.

I went to bed resolved to take the challenge in spite of many people's concern about my career and my young family. This great opportunity to serve my people in such a capacity had found the ready and latent will I had nursed from the early years of lectures I attended at Achimota and my membership in the students' movement at Glasgow. I was ready to serve faithfully and diligently in any situation I found myself. By Governor Wyn-Harris's own confirmation, I had performed creditably well in the pledge to which my training had called me to fight against cattle plagues and to bring them under control. It could not be different now when my people were urging that I should lead them in their struggle to achieve self-realisation and, later, nationhood.

I used the following busy weeks to round off my private consultations with friends and well-wishers. Some were still asking me to leave room for that last-minute change of heart considering the brightness of the future ahead of me in the civil service – after just five years of work I was already head of a government department and earning a European-scale salary! Others were surprised that I was sacrificing the sweets of such high office to answer the call of my people. I clearly understood all the views and concerns and I was even more grateful that people could be as open and honest in expressing such deep feelings for my family's and for my own welfare.

Having spent a few months on consultations and planning for such a major move in my life, I finally wrote a letter on 4 February 1960, resigning my appointment which was to take effect on 14 March 1960. I argued that if The Gambia was to take full advantage of the opportunities offered by the constitution outlined in Sessional Paper No 4 of 1959 there must be considerable preparation before elections by way of a sound political organisation of the people. It was with the hope that I might be able to play my part, however humbly, in that difficult and important work that I had taken this by no means easy decision to resign from a job which I loved and enjoyed so much during those six years.

The staff gave a small farewell party in my honour in my office. Until I had told them I was leaving the department, I had not realised how strong the bonds were that we had forged as colleagues. I shocked my own brother, Kawsunding, who had been a veterinary assistant long before I arrived there. Some members of my staff were in tears parting company with me after the miles we had done together out in the field, learning from each other on the job, looking out and covering for each other over the five years we worked together. My laboratory superintendent, Fergusson

Mahoney, was devastated and in a short speech made me realise what a jolt my resignation was to the department.

I explained the rules as set many years before in the Colonial Secretary Circular of 18 April 1950 prohibiting senior civil servants from holding office in any political organisation. In addition, the rules as then laid down by the Executive Council clearly stated that civil servants were not permitted to accept office, paid or unpaid, permanent or temporary, in any political party or organisation. Civil servants were not to indicate publicly their support for any party, candidate or policy; or to make speeches or to join in demonstrations. Laughter lifted the sadness a little in the room when I said that those rules were exactly what I was opting to follow with the choice I had made.

Slowly, some of them came out of shock and agreed that I should go if my people were calling me and theirs was a voice I had chosen to answer. Life is full of decisions and people must make them and move on. I promised them that I was ready to face the challenge with the same resolute spirit and faith with which I had faced other calls to duty in my younger years. All I needed was their support and prayers.

The initial doubts I had felt when the party elders asked me to lead them were nearly the same as I felt many years before when in 1935 Sering Modou Sillah, in an unexpected reshuffle of the pecking order in the *lhell* of circumcised boys at 2 Anglesea Street, pulled me out and placed me to lead the school processions to the bush and back. I was a minuscule, noiseless ordinary member of the pack and the *lhell* master had done that for no reason apparent to me. With much confusion I did no more than muster courage and rise to the occasion.

It must have hurt Abdoulie Senghore, the traditional procession leader in the school, that the master had done that. For him to have all so suddenly lost such a coveted position must have been disheartening to him. I was embarrassed for him by my elevation but I soon came to respect him profoundly. Not once, even in jest, throughout the two months of the gruelling rites of passage and through the grand *samba sohho* that marked our release from the circumcision school did Abdoulie show me any vindictiveness or disrespect on account of the master's decision. He was obedient to the teacher and respectful of the new procession order; and that debt I owe him to this day. He, like all the other eighteen initiates in our bush school, trusted completely in the wisdom of Sering Modou.

Similarly, I had shaken on my bare feet but had risen to the call of Sering Habib when in 1937 the great teacher picked me out of the blue to be prefect and to lead his class prayers at Mohammedan School. I also remember how my heart raced and I struggled on one cold dew-drenched morning in 1940 when the elders pulled me, a simple worshipper in the congregation, to perform the *athan* for the *fajr* prayers at the Half Die Mosque where the revered man of great learning, Tafsir Demba Mbye, was the Imam.

With some officials in the government, my decision to quit was received with deep suspicion. They thought that my departure was a protest over the administration's baulking over my proposals to upgrade the emoluments of the veterinary officer and principal veterinary officer positions and for the engagement of more professional staff. The proof of that perverse attitude could be found in the minutes of one of the assistants to the colonial secretary who, as late in the day as on 4 August 1960 even when I was already steeped in work as minister of education, wrote to tell the governor that perhaps the results of a salaries revision which government was setting up would help me change my mind to come back to the job. Obviously, this was one man who was completely sold to the notion that my resignation might have been connected with my want of a bigger pay. Mine was a much nobler cause.

Well before I packed my personal effects out of the office and handed back my camp bed and my mosquito net, the administration was already running cablegrams to the Colonial Office and scouting for a replacement from Accra and Lagos. The search through the list of qualified veterinarians on the Colonial Veterinary Service list sent enquiries as far away as India and Ceylon. I was already leading the government as premier when negotiations with Prime Minister Kwame Nkrumah of Ghana soon made available the services of a Ghanaian national on secondment for a year. Sidney Quartey, a fine veterinarian and an avid sportsman, came to The Gambia in 1963.

This response by Nkrumah was more than just filling a vacancy in The Gambia. It was a demonstration of African self-reliance that he was teaching was possible with Ghana's independence. The sterling service Sidney offered crowned our faith in our claim to pan-Africanism whereby each would take upon itself the responsibility to attend to each other's needs. We were privileged to see Sidney return to serve The Gambia again for a much longer period as a consultant for the UNDP and the FAO.

Sadly, Sidney passed away in March 2007 after a full life of service. I sent a note of condolence through Dr Sammy Palmer, a mutual golfing colleague, to his wife Alberta, in Accra, in appreciation of the life and service of a man who had touched us Gambians in very special ways in veterinary medicine as well as in international golf and cricket. Many will remember Sidney's brilliant and gentlemanly contributions to The Gambia's performance during the West African inter-territorial cricket matches played in Bathurst. I wrote my message with a great deal of satisfaction with fond memories of Achimota when Nkrumah, then a young political activist, talked to us students about African self-reliance which theory then we gratefully had seen fulfilled in practice in our time.

At last it was all done and accepted. I had resigned my office as principal veterinary officer. Augusta and I and our children faced the most painful of all the goodbyes. Leaving our bungalow at Abuko was the toughest part of the parting. I dare say our bungalow was one of the most commodious and relaxing of places as far as government housing was concerned. Augusta and I had come to love the quiet and spacious surroundings into which we had really settled. She had given our place a homely décor that had a feel of a cross between European and African. That took some doing to dismantle and to wrap up.

Down the main road, a few miles from Abuko, I bought a place in Banjulinding. Staff Site No 3 belonged to government but had been left derelict. I bought it from government. I scraped a reasonable bit from my savings to bring it to a habitable state and was not disappointed with the results when the masons and carpenters presented me with the keys. I was not one to be bothered about spartan facilities because if one cared to name it, I had slept in it – from raffia mats, grass mattresses and sheepskin to *tara* couches and scout camp beds – from Barajaly and Walikunda to 37 Wellington Street or provincial rest houses, I had seen it all. Therefore, anything above those was a blessing and a luxury.

When Augusta expressed satisfaction with our new dwelling, I breathed a sigh of relief. She began with self-assured diligence to set up beds and cots and tried her best to create something reasonably. Nothing would have worked if Augusta had had any reservations about the new place that was clearly no match, not even close, for what we vacated at Abuko. But satisfied as I might have been with the situation, the fact that I was not going to receive a salary at the end of the month left me with a queasy feeling indeed.

I sent out an application as fast I could to the offices of British Petroleum to start an outlet for their products. BP surveyed the place and approved the setting up of a filling station outside my house at Staff Site No 3. We also opened a small shop on the side. Thus, a veterinarian and his SRN and SCM wife became petrol pump attendants and shopkeepers to make ends meet. I was grateful to God that the family found some means to cover its expenses from the commission we received on the BP sales and the little we made from selling candles and matches in the shop.

The year 1959 was a watershed in many aspects of my personal life and that of the country. In February, the former charitable societies had merged into the Protectorate People's Party (with emphasis on protectorate). In March, elders came to my doorstep and offered me to lead the party. In May I celebrated my 35th birthday and with my wife pregnant with our third child I was going through the anguish of deciding to choose between the stable life of a family man and senior government official and the rough and tumble of politics.

17

In the throes of politics

The year 1959 ended with the good news that Jombo and Famara Wassa were sending back from their tours on bicycle, into towns and villages of central and eastern Kombo. They were spreading the good news of the founding of the Protectorate People's Party. These two indefatigable pioneers were well on their way to launching across the Bintang Bolong into the lower river regions, working diligently and setting up PPP branches in towns, villages and hamlets as they went. They were nailing down the principles and beliefs that the constituent power of the new movement was the people. They were relentless in their scouring of the niches and before long they had covered the whole country. In Kantora in the Upper River Division, a joining patron was so delighted with the energy and determination of the two men that he arranged the marriage of his daughter to Jombo. There could not have been a happier ending to a tough mission to introduce our party to the people.

When 1960 rolled in, the pulse of the people was already beating with the excitement of that great achievement of a party forged and ready to get into action. What was even more thrilling was that the first-ever general elections with full universal adult suffrage for both the colony and protectorate were already planned for May. Jombo and Famara Wassa had thus laid the groundwork in the protectorate and when Sanjally Bojang thought up an even more flamboyant campaign tour, it was an idea borne out of its own necessity. Sanjally gathered masses of the new breed of party supporters and set off in lorries for a countrywide tour to ask an already eager and receptive electorate to vote for the PPP.

However, it was not an uneventful tour. When the campaign reached the Upper River Division, where tribal, chieftaincy and other family issues divided the supporters, things turned ugly. The reception almost turned violent in places where our presence was resisted with a passion. Kantora and Basse were particularly hostile to the PPP and it would take us a number of years of committed work at the grassroots to turn the tide in our favour in those areas.

In 1960 the British government announced that it was considering introducing a bill that would be enacted as early as January 1960 to extend the loans for colonial development programmes. It was a good enough promise to encourage Governor Windley to set up a committee to consider the areas that the increment in development funds would go to. He appointed the financial secretary to chair the committee. He also appointed Henry Madi, J L Mahoney, Seyfo Karamo Kaba Sanneh and Seyfo Landing Sali Sonko to assist him in examining proposals and to submit recommendations for improving government departments and expanding public services. The committee also invited ideas from the public to be considered for the 1960-1965 development programme.

For the members of the Protectorate People's Party all development efforts by the colonial government were of course welcome. Although for obvious reasons I restricted my participation to clandestine meetings, I followed the outcomes of the more public gatherings of the party whether at Brikama or at the Ritz Cinema or at 4 Jones Street in the capital where the party often met. Whatever suggestions were submitted to the development committee improvement of facilities and conditions in the protectorate was a central issue. There was also new thinking brewing which was coming straight out of what the more radical elements within the PPP were reading in the daily bulletins of British Prime Minister Harold Macmillan's positive comments about Nigeria's "year of destiny" during his rousing visit to Lagos on 12 January 1959. That was perhaps the most public declaration of London's readiness to consider independence for Nigeria. If there could be a year of destiny for Nigeria, why not one for The Gambia?

The annual chiefs' conference was scheduled for Basse that year and the Veterinary Department busied itself all month long preparing demonstration kits. My colleague Fergusson Mahoney was busy putting together a presentation to draw attention to our work at Abuko. It was important to us, especially as it was connected to the new designs for mixed farming and livestock improvement proposals the agriculture and veterinary departments had collaborated on. We waited anxiously for the return of Governor Windley from Kenya where he had gone to give evidence in the trial of Rawson Macharia whom the colonial government in Nairobi had charged with making false declarations in the evidence he gave in 1952 during the trial of Jomo Kenyatta and the Mau Mau.

The governor returned from his former colony and shortly afterwards presided over the Basse conference. On that Saturday morning on 14 February 1959, the PPP came away finally recognised as a bona fide political entity and accorded its rightful place alongside the old parties from the colony. We boarded the *Lady Wright* that morning with bridled enthusiasm. Among us civil servants the discussions about the new phenomenon, the

PPP, were muted in contrast with the animated discussions among the rest of the passengers.

There were other important matters raised and resolved in Basse, eg feeder road construction and the introduction of VHF Radio. There was also the quest for district authorities to continue giving grants to mission schools and that the livestock improvement officer and the cattle marketing officer get together with district authorities to discuss a mixed farming system and demonstrate improved methods of hides drying at the main slaughtering centres around the country. There were also important decisions taken on education and health. Until we arrived at Bathurst on Monday, the topic of discussion on board was more about the future of this new movement than it was about government or the far-reaching recommendations that came out of the conference.

It will be helpful to paint the picture of the political background in the country in which I had been working already for five years, happily trekking and inoculating livestock and making the Veterinary Department a household name in the rural communities.

In 1958 the governor formed an All Party Committee comprising chiefs, elected members of the Legislative Council and the leading lights of the political parties. The committee was chaired by Henry Madi with Kebba W Foon as secretary, and charged with the formulation of ideas to amend the constitution to reflect social and political developments in the colony. They were to report in 18 months. On 2 June 1959, Secretary of State for the Colonies Allan Lennox-Boyd arrived here from Sierra Leone to attend an official meeting to which he had been invited to study proposals for constitutional change which the All Party Committee had submitted.

At the meeting with the secretary of state on 3 June 1959 the All Party Committee was informed that the British government had rejected nearly seventy-five per cent of the recommendations. Some frontline party people were not happy with that situation. At the official reception at Government House grounds in honour of Mr Lennox-Boyd and his entourage some members of the committee announced that they would hold a mass rally the following day to draw up a plea for redress that they would put before the distinguished visitor.

On 4 June 1959 the Gambia Democratic Party took the initiative by inviting the other parties to a meeting at Albion Place, a venue that would become very important in the political life of the colony and the pre-independence movement that would soon emerge. Of the three party leaders, only Rev J C Faye (leader of the GDP) attended and addressed the rally after which the organisers asked him to go home and leave the rest of the evening's activities to them. The crowds began to chant: *We Want Rights and Justice!* as the organisers led them towards Government House. Soon the chanting crowds added the now famous lines: *We Want Bread and Butter!* This gave the name Bread and Butter Demonstrations to the event that has become a historic one in the political development of The Gambia.

Police Superintendent John Patrick Bray was on hand and announced from the balcony of Government House that the secretary of state was out on official engagements and asked the demonstrators to select six representatives to meet with Lennox-Boyd the following day. The organisers insisted they would wait no matter how long it took to meet with the secretary of state. Bray read the riot act and warned that on the third reading, if the crowd was still there, orders would be given to disperse them by force. The crowd did not budge and true to the superintendent's words, the Force units charged.

The crowds threw stones. There were ugly scenes and before the police gained control of the situation many people had been injured. In the morning, the leaders of the demonstration, Crispin Grey-Johnson and A E Cham Joof of the Democratic Party and Melville Benoni Jones of the National Party, came out again circulating leaflets calling for another mass meeting at the same venue. At this point the police arrested and charged them with incitement.

In the background, the unfortunate fracture between the old parties over the demonstrations played into the hands of the Windley government. We will see P S Njie and Governor Windley becoming close allies against the other parties so that the UP would not take part in anything to challenge any programmes of the Windley government. The UP would later on take along the GNP as its satellite party. The Muslim Congress as usual sat on the fence. The Protectorate People's Party was too new to influence that confusing scenario. Besides, it appeared to us that the new ideas being suggested for constitutional change well accorded with our objects of enfranchising the people of the protectorate and of bringing them into the mainstream of the political life of the country. The PPP continued to address some of those issues at district and town meetings and kept a regular assessment of the fall-out of the demonstration.

A close friend of mine at the time, the youthful and fiery advocate, A S Bamba Saho, took up the case as defence counsel and soon got Grey-Johnson, Cham Joof and Benoni Jones out on bail. Later, he successfully argued in court for a quashing of the case against them on the grounds that the political leaders were expressing their constitutional and human rights when they peacefully marched to see the secretary of state at Government House. The men were freed. The tension that had gripped the town since the arrests blew over while word was anxiously awaited from London as to the way forward.

Finally, an answer came in September 1959. The British government had decided on measures contained in the governor's dispatch No 366/59 of 15 June setting out the recommendations which arose out of a conference of the All Party Committee held in March 1959. The governor, on his leave of absence to London, had taken away with him those proposals and the recommendations he made on them for discussion with the Foreign Office.

The PPP was thrilled by the salient points finally approved in London, which Governor Windley reported to the Legislative Council. Every citizen over the age of twenty-one years had the right to vote. The Legislative Council would become the House of Representatives, whose membership would increase from twenty-one to thirty-four. Five members would come, one from each ward from Bathurst, two from the Kombo St Mary's districts and three would be nominated. Of the twenty representing the protectorate, eight would be chiefs or their representatives.

Governor Windley announced to the legislature the far-reaching decisions on the future of our country. He emphasised that with these developments there was a great need for all Gambians to think cautiously on the steps in their political development for the future so that those should be in the interest of the country and not influenced by sectarian interest or personal ambition. He said the constitution must be allowed to develop flexibility and such a development must be along the lines of greater self-government.

The governor was using language that the PPP was slowly writing into its own body of rules and regulations. It was not clear in the minds of some of the members what self-government would entail but it certainly was becoming obvious what possibilities and responsibilities lay ahead. Meanwhile, the music to our ears was the consideration being given to the measures which were necessary to enact the new Electoral Ordinance for the colony and the protectorate. Registration of voters was expected to begin before the end of the year and from the governor's own words elections would take place in May 1960.

It was a good thing that the new law, while it required two passport-size photographs for colony voters, did not ask that of protectorate voters. The technology of passport photography had not reached the provinces and the demand would have posed huge problems for villagers and virtually nullified the advances of the new and welcome franchise. It is necessary to highlight this because when the tables would turn in favour of the PPP, the UP limping out of office would ignore the origin of this long-standing order, as central to the hollow petition charging us with vote rigging in the 1962 elections.

With such fundamental new regulations coming from the governor there was nothing more to do than to increase the frequency of our party meetings and invite people with the gift of the gab to come along on tours with us through the Kombos. While the party leaders scoured the countryside, I kept my nose on my job and helped my wife to cope with bathing and feeding our two infants. On 12 December, Sheikh Omar Fye, the revered Muslim scholar and father of my old schoolmate, Mustapha, died. The successful trader and Muslim scholar was already eight years into his retirement from the Legislative Council. It was the biggest funeral I had seen in Bathurst.

For most of 1958 and until I left the department in 1960, I was defying the rules barring civil servants from political activity. Under cover of night, I would accompany Jombo Bojang and Famara Wassa Touray and other stalwarts in the PPS to meetings. I had felt that my financial contributions to the society would have gone a long way towards covering some expenses. But they were certainly not enough considering the work at hand that needed some personal attention. We visited people at the *bantaba* and homes alike and I assured many compound owners and heads of *kabilo* that the future of our country was bright; it was one that would bring provincial people once and for all into the centre stage of national development.

Many of the initial support cells that grew up to be branches of the consolidated People's Progressive Party (with emphasis on people's) in later years started off this way. When the change of name to an all-inclusive national party was agreed to in 1960, Jombo and Famara Wassa had already known the path their bicycles would take to bring in the expectant harvest of members. We were in fact setting the tone for standards and attitudes that would later give character to our party constitution similar to that which the government and old parties were busy constructing at the national level with the Constitutional Conference that was held from 6 to 11 March 1959.

In retrospect, the March All Party Conference established some advanced features that pointed to an already growing democratic atmosphere in the country. It would be appropriate at this point to pay tribute to members of the commission for coming up with advanced proposals that significantly improved upon the 1958 Wyn-Harris Constitution. With the colonial secretary presiding and aided by the attorney general, the conference was attended by nine *seyfolu* – Karamo Sanneh, Landing Sonko, Muhammadou Krubally, Koba Leigh, Moriba Krubally, Matarr Sise, Tamba Jammeh, Yugo Kasseh Drammeh and Fabakary Sanyang. Henry Madi and James L Mahoney sat as Independents, while Rene A Blain and J E Mahoney represented the UP, Henry J Joof and Kebba W Foon, the GNP, Sulayman Beran Gaye and I M Garba Jahumpa, the GMC and Crispin Grey-Johnson and J C Faye, the GDP.

The commission's recommendations which were adopted included universal suffrage for all Gambian citizens who had reached the age of twenty-one years. They created the residency clauses and set up the electoral units of Bathurst with five one-member constituencies – the Kombo St Mary with two and the protectorate with twelve. They set the rules for eight chiefs to represent their peers and those for the disqualification of candidates. They confirmed English as the language of legislative business, established the positions of speaker and deputy speaker and named the assembly the House of Representatives. They determined the composition, powers and duties of the Executive Council. They proposed seven ministerial portfolios but got six approved in addition to four ex-officio members.

But, first things, first. The party had to be sold to the constituents countrywide. The masses declaring their support had to be taught the unfamiliar and truly daunting new territory of voting by the casting of marbles. As Governor Windley himself put it to Her Majesty's Government in London, we were a rural electorate "new to the mysteries of the ballot box". The introduction of the marble system by the attorney-general was acceptable to us; it was an easily manageable method of elections which so wonderfully suited the largely illiterate, calm temperament and small size of the country's population.

While we seemed assured of scoring big points in the protectorate, there was something intrinsically bothersome about the nature of our party that was inhibiting our access to the homes and hearts in the colony. It was the Protectorate People's Party, ironically restrictive in name, but with national intentions. The country, having reached a crossroads, it was with a great sense of urgency that I mounted the platform at a mass meeting the party had called at Albion Place in Bathurst to justify the need for a very important change in the name of the party.

I explained that events had overtaken the original name that now lingered with a limiting feature about it. The Protectorate People's Party carried a parochial aftertaste and presented a politically incorrect image which needed immediate correction to avoid disaffection within an urban public whose sympathies we absolutely could not afford to do without. It was a blessing that the tradition of democratic consensus was already bearing fruit. Thankfully, the party was built on principles that derived authority from no other source than the people.

The meeting quickly saw the need for a name that properly reflected the national character of the party, and accepted my suggestion to retain the already recognisable abbreviation PPP – which would henceforth stand for People's Progressive Party. This opened doors to the hundreds of people who joined enthusiastically in Bathurst. A number of faithful people spring to mind as I write and it means no disregard for the hundreds of others who came to sign up in the party. Abel Samuel Charles Able-Thomas, the old headmaster, immediately accepted to stand as the party's candidate in New Town West. Sister Julia Williams, Louis Chery, an accountant with the CFAO, Joseph Francis Cole, a GPMB executive, Mrs Hannah Forster, a businesswoman and her daughter, Mrs Catherine Collier, a radiographer, and others flood my memory now – ordinary as well as distinguished folk who shared our mission and vision and joined in unreservedly.

Dr Reynold Carrol and his wife, Delphine, became members. Reynold, who later became my dentist, reminded me recently that he and his wife were Members No 10 and No 11 in the PPP register in Bathurst in 1960. He said his argument for joining was that it was right and democratic for the majority people of the country's populace to take their rightful place in national politics away from the monopolistic features of the colony parties which were simply duplicates of each other. Such detail of memory and the fondness with which he recalled them was indicative of how much some of the influential Aku people in the capital came to embrace the party very early.

We also campaigned vigorously in Bathurst. Augusta offered to speak at public meetings and in fact proved to be a very convincing public speaker. She and her caucus groups made house-to-house visits and spoke to women's groups. Through the Gambia Women's Contemporary Society which she founded and did great work for girls' education, she was able to build the necessary consensus that drew many supporters to her and naturally to the party.

Augusta's public presence would not go unmarked at social events and the occasional sporting gatherings such as the Female Athletic Meeting organised by the Gambia Athletic Association. On 19 November 1962, I accompanied Augusta to Dakar where she was attending a seminar on the advancement of women in Africa. The Senegalese government in collaboration with UNESCO recognised her interest and work in adult female education and invited her to represent The Gambia. Apart from having blazed the trail of standing in parliamentary elections, she was already well known for her work in the advancement of women. Under the pen name of Ramatoulie Kinteh she would publish a popular play, *Rebellion,* supportive of women's reproductive health and education. Her other literary works and her fiery political speeches had already written her into the annals of political activism.

As Assistant Secretary and Treasurer of the Gambia Women's Contemporary Society, Social Secretary of the Gambia Women's Federation, Organiser of the *Banta Sunkutu Kafo*, a rural young women's association with a membership of some nine hundred young women in Bakau, Brikama and Faraba Banta, she led these organisations with education in all its forms as the basic emphasis for the members. After the Dakar seminar, Augusta broadcast a report on it on Radio Gambia on 4 and 5 April 1963 enumerating the gains women particularly in The Gambia and Africa in general were making.

The registration of voters ended in early April and the electoral registers were compiled towards the end of April. There were 114,724 voters. The PPP had become a force to be reckoned with and took its place side by side with the more seasoned competitors of the UP, GDP and the GMC, who now, suddenly feeling the threat that woke them up to the potential of our party under the new universal suffrage, coalesced in their desperation and became known as the (Gambia) Democratic Congress Alliance (DCA). The two ministers and heads of the two parties, the Rev J C Faye and I M Garba Jahumpa, were forced to mend the fences they had broken back in 1952 when the latter defected from the GDP, which they had co-founded, to form the GMC.

All of a sudden, they needed each other to take on the challenge posed by our new party. The constitution had now given the franchise to all citizens, 21 years and over, to vote and be voted for. We made campaign promises that we would increase workers' wages. We called for more radical amendments to the loopholes that still remained in the 1958 Constitution.

While we fought tooth and nail to win support in the colony, Sanjally Bojang was making waves in the provinces on his countrywide tour. Undaunted by the hostile reception in the URD and energised by the continued increase in the following from district to district, he turned the march, already in a carnival atmosphere, back westwards along the north bank. The tour and the speaking stops could only be likened to the famous post-war whistle-stop campaigns made by American politicians on board trains and buses decorated with their party flags and bunting. Sanjally had neither trains nor buses. He had lorries that were filled with merrymaking party militants, hangers-on and busybodies, with *sikko* band music into the bargain that took the message to the people about the new lease on the political and social life of the country.

We came out with the solid understanding of the sacredness of the cause of the PPP to bring all the peoples of the protectorate into the mainstream of life in the country, involving them hand in hand with the people of the colony in building a truly united nation. This would ultimately bring development to the doorsteps of every Gambian. Nearly five years later, in 1964, when I was premier, the message was still consistent when, on the insistence of critics, I expounded on what type of government we were running. I pointed to the litany of experimental ideologies that were bubbling around in Africa's newest states. I argued against the dogmas of socialism and communism and explained that we were building a socially responsible system that was based on self-reliance.

Through self-reliance, we could, for example, look forward to a time when government would be able to guarantee advances from the banks to enable cooperative societies to purchase more and more of the farmers' produce. This would be distributed by their own organisations leaving room for radical changes in the function and preoccupations of the Gambia Oilseeds Marketing Board. This was resonant in my campaigns, be they at the annual dinner of the Chamber of Commerce in 1963 or at District Council meetings. What came to be rounded off as the battle cry for self-reliance, I called *Tesito* – a philosophy morally consonant and demanding of all citizens to play their part honestly, diligently and transparently in national development.

Sanjally's march went well as the throngs progressed on the north bank through Darsilami, Kuntaur, Kaur, Farafenni, Nja Kunda, Kerewan and at stops in between, and all the way down to Barra. When Sanjally and his supporters arrived back in Bathurst on the ferry from Barra, he finally abandoned the lorries and decided on what some people vividly remembered as 'the Blue March' – so called from the sea of blue flags and uniforms, the colour the party had adopted. From the ferry terminal at Half Die, through the busy Hagan Street and Clifton Road, the teeming masses walked behind the party executive to a rousing reception outside Sanjally's residence, which had become the *de facto* PPP headquarters. No witness to that march through the town was left indifferent to the presence of the PPP.

We closed our campaign and the country went to the polls in May 1960. The PPP took 50 per cent of the votes. I won the seat in the Kombo constituency where I stood unopposed. The PPP won nine of the twelve seats in the protectorate but promptly lost one to defection when Michael Baldeh, for reasons best known to him, switched immediately after he won to join the UP where we had long suspected his allegiance to be. Andrew Camara, the independent candidate, won the Kantora seat in the Upper River Division. The United Party won seven seats, including two seats in Saloum and Niumi.

Our performance in the colony was not as dismal as had been expected. We won handsomely in Bakau. The UP gained all five of its traditional seats, bringing its national total to seven. The co-leaders of the DCA, J C Faye and I M Garba Jahumpa, both lost their seats in Bathurst where Alieu Badara Njie won DCA's only seat in Jollof and Portuguese Town constituency. The PPP had more seats than any other party. Governor Windley at this point held on and did not announce his intention of forming the government. He did not announce the appointment of a chief minister either. We were keen to see what he would do and, accordingly, waited on his pleasure.

Meanwhile our party rejoiced over our inroads into the capital - once the domain of the old parties. In Bathurst, Augusta ran on the PPP ticket for the seat in Soldier Town constituency. She polled 232 votes and lost to Bathurst stalwart Melville Senami Benoni Jones of the GNP who won the seat with 644 votes. Augusta's performance was nonetheless encouraging for a campaign of only a couple of weeks. Putting it in a larger perspective, it told us of great possibilities for the PPP among the more conservative voters in the capital when compared with the combined total of nearly one thousand votes the people of Bathurst cast for the PPP.

Not only did the PPP show signs of placing a significant foothold in the formerly parochial niches of Bathurst, it was also winning a first by putting up a woman candidate to run for public office. *The Gambia Echo* of 6 June 1960 graciously welcomed Augusta's participation in the elections and even dedicated an editorial paying tribute to the pioneering spirit of both the party and the candidate: "We take off our hats to Mrs Jawara who has demonstrated that all intelligent and decent persons in the community can contest elections in spite of the terrible barrage of abuses aimed at opponents by some political parties."

That reference to 'the barrage of abuses', in my view, was putting it too lightly. It was one filthy and disturbing element of the campaign as far as I was concerned. The UP, GNP and DCA held nothing back in abuse and utter slander of their opponents during street 'broadcast talks'. I urged all the PPP candidates that issues and policies were what the people wanted to hear, and not abuse. Throughout the campaign, unnecessary vilification and abusive language was used to ruin the decorum expected of people who wanted to take up seats in government. This was most worrisome to me. Speakers would set aside the real issues and speak disparagingly of their opponents' parentage and blood line. They vilified those with caste labels about them, especially those of the *gewel* caste or the *oudeh* or the *tegga* caste as not fit for leadership in government. I simply treated such puerile notions with disdain and always wondered what caste had to do with one's ability to serve one's nation.

Even when I moved into the Prime Minister's Residence at Number 1 Marina, I could hear slander directed at us through the loudspeakers screaming through the night from three hundred metres away at Sam Jack Terrace or a little further away at Albion Place. Most of it was fallacious diatribe about my being of the lineage of leather smiths and too low in social rank to run government. It was also the irrational cause of arrogance among certain elements within the PPP who saw their chiefly lineage as their right to office and leadership in the party, no matter how crude their vision or unlearned their methods. The PPP was far from being an ethnic party. It was a national party and could not be ruled by such unacceptable standards that considered people inferior on account of the caste into which they were born.

I find it a negative concept that is destroying the lives of millions of people in places such as India. I had very sound reasons for not addressing it at all in my time in government. I deliberately ignored it and insisted on its futility, convinced as I was and still am that it has no place in modern society. It is therefore of great satisfaction to me that the new millennium generations are damning the concept and marrying across castes all over The Gambia and most effectively ridding our civilisation of one of its most despicable social scars.

My father grew up as a farmer and through his own enterprising nature opened up business opportunities for himself. He became rich though he later lost most of his wealth along the way. He lived the great life of a philanthropist and aged gracefully as a respected man until he passed away in 1961. I remember his death coming at a time when I was deep in the struggle in the political wilderness for the adoption of the 1961 Constitution. His prayers were answered because it was those changes we had struggled for that brought the PPP into power in 1962 with a resounding majority that established a sound and democratic government and made me premier.

The people in a culture that would rain insults on someone on account of the kinds of labour skills that a great grandfather used honestly and creatively to keep his family alive must be a group of people that disrespected honest labour and the expression of latent skills. Provocation had to have its limits. Before long the idea of revenge brewed within our party ranks. When party marketing and public relations thinkers and strategists came up with a platform to reply to the abuses, our musicians found work cut out for them. The idea of the campaign band Sanjally had used for his tour and on the Blue March became the answer. *Sikko Gambia*, as the folk band became known, came complete with singers, clappers, metal shakers and a big bass drum. The music boomed under the frenzied direction of energetic young men and women who staged public displays and musical extravaganza at popular locations in the towns and villages. Their compositions included scathing jibes at opposition characters.

Sikko music was used to set the scene at our political rallies. At times, the band played all night with spontaneous lyrics that lampooned opponents of the PPP. Any social scandal the singers knew about them would be made into a dance song. A famous venue for the street carnivals in Bathurst that competed with those in Serekunda and Bakau-Katchikali was 48 Grant Street, the house of Farimang Singhateh, where our headquarters had moved after we had broken up with Sanjally Bojang and left his Jones Street residence. Singhateh was rewarded for his services to the party when he became our country's first and only indigenous governor general in 1966. He always enjoyed the unfailing support of his wife, Lady Fanta Basse, who had been a keen PPS member in the early days of our movement.

At last, on 20 June 1960, nearly a whole month after the general elections, Governor Windley announced appointments to the Executive Council. Of six ministers, two were from the PPP. I was offered the portfolio of education and social welfare and Sheriff Sisay was appointed minister without portfolio. Omar Mbakeh, the head chief member of the council, and Andrew Camara, an independent, were also ministers without portfolio. Howsoon O Semega-Janneh, another independent candidate, who later switched his sympathies to the UP, became minister of agriculture. Alieu Badara Njie of the DCA was minister of communication.

P S Njie, the leader of the UP, promptly refused his appointment as minister without portfolio. He queried the decisions and, at one meeting of the Legislative Council, led a walkout with his supporters. What we waited for with bated breath and which did not seem forthcoming up to that point was the appointment of a chief minister to lead government business.

The governor ignored the approved details in the 1959 Constitution on the delicate appointment procedures that clearly stipulated that "... the governor, when the election results were known, be required to ascertain whether any member of the House of Representatives commanded an effective majority. If there was a person with such a majority, that person should be designated chief minister and should advise the governor on the selection of members to fill ministerial posts and the allocation of ministerial portfolios among them".

We may not have had "an effective majority" to form a majority government with our nine seats to UP's seven but that situation had the benefit of tradition to fall back on. An unbiased governor would have been guided by tradition that the leader of the party with the largest number of seats, democratically, even by a majority of one seat, should have been invited to begin negotiations with the other parties for a coalition government or propose the means by which his party would govern. It was not the right of the governor to tamper with the constitution to satisfy a personal reservation he had nursed and which was blown out to full force against me and the PPP when we proposed more constitutional development that included our quest for self- government, which must lead to ultimate independence.

As recently as 3 May 2007, the protocol and tradition we expected was exactly as unfolded when the Scottish National Party (SNP), with only a narrow majority, time in its history outvoted the Labour, Liberal and other parties in Scottish Parliamentary Elections. The SNP leader, Alex Elliot Salmond, was sworn in as first minister in albeit a minority government. The SNP won by the smallest of margins (47 seats, 1 more than the Scottish Labour Party). But on 16 May Salmond was nominated to head a minority SNP administration. As far as the British system is concerned the party that wins by a majority, however slight, is given priority. Governor Windley ought to have known this tradition but decided to do otherwise in 1961.

In the months ahead we would define and redefine our policies choosing the more patriotic line of sovereign independence. Jahumpa supported the Malta Solution by which The Gambia, like the Mediterranean island of Malta, would elect and send delegates to parliament in the UK. It was a system well known in the French territories where delegates from the colonies served as deputies in the French parliament. Blaise Diagne and Leopold Sedar Senghor after him had been deputies in Paris for Senegal as had been Houphouet Boigny for the Ivory Coast.

The Malta Solution was far from our party's stated policy of full independence. Nor was the full merger with Senegal an option. There was little point in even considering the other hair-brained proposals that contrived to have The Gambia function as part of Nigeria to be administered from the distance of Lagos just as West and East Pakistan were before the declaration of Bangladesh independence in 1971. We came into the political limelight with a firm resolution to go all out for national sovereignty. We knew that the way towards establishing the foundations for it was to ensure victory in the general election.

As was to be expected, the young party was immediately faced with the challenge of being complete strangers in the colony, that is, in Bathurst and Kombo St Mary. If it should win the forthcoming elections, all those social and political hurdles would need to be cleared. To do that the party would have to have a foundation in the capital and a following large enough to capture such important seats as were being held by the indigenous big names on the opposing party tickets. It seemed a daunting task but we knew that only robust policies and exemplary showcasing would make our party a household name in Bathurst within the few weeks left until the elections. Those policies must include making our party an even more inclusive movement, reducing the parochial connotations of provincialism, enhancing the local economy, improving the living standards of the people and guiding the direction The Gambia would take to independence – not a merger with Senegal as was apparent in the hedging behaviour of the colonial government and in the agenda of some of the politicians in Bathurst.

The sad spectre of this tendency to give away our nation to a merger was picking up steam at a time when developments around us in West Africa had seen Ghana become master of its destiny in 1957, a country that was already working on building up its own national shipping and air lines and launching its own national currency. Guinea Conakry had also become independent under Sekou Touré demonstrating clearly that national will and determination could overcome that country's horrific abandonment by France.

There were other great examples that made union with Senegal a very important matter to get into gently and soberly; not with any parochial search for ethnic sympathies as envisioned by some politicians but with coherent, historical, equitable and well-thought-out considerations on the table.

On 1 October 1960, Nigeria became independent. I was selected to represent The Gambia at the celebrations. While I packed my bags to leave, I had the draft of a document, entitled *The Independence Manifesto,* in which were spelt out the details of a programme towards independence for The Gambia. Although I took the original document with me, I was surprised to discover that while I was in Lagos, details of the document had leaked in Bathurst. Nevertheless I printed a few hundred copies of it and brought them back home with me. I went straight into serious private discussions with key leaders and militants in the party and shared with them my consideration of the need to force the governor's hand on the issues we considered important.

The party organised an extraordinary meeting at Albion Place where, for the first time, I publicly addressed the issue of independence. I drove home the urgent need for the government and administration to work on the finer points of the proposal for the Gambian people to become masters of their own destiny. The party secretariat staff distributed hundreds of copies reproduced for the purpose. In a short while the crowd had taken up all the copies. Many who could not wait to sink their teeth into the document left the meeting to go and read it. The document poured fuel into Windley's raging fire and that of Civil Secretary Kenneth G Smith.

That document was the blueprint for the achievement of self-determination by the Gambian people. It opened with the boldest declaration that The Gambia could not afford to remain much longer in the backwaters of African political advance. While the whole continent moved to its destiny of freedom and self-determination, the right place for The Gambia, it said, was the mainstream of that movement side by side with Senegal, Mauritania, Sudan, Sierra Leone, Somaliland, Ghana, Gabon, Guinea, Nigeria, Madagascar and others.

The People's Progressive Party, I wrote, had pledged the achievement of The Gambia of self-government by 1961 and the means to fulfil that pledge by constitutional means if possible. The people of The Gambia had an undisputable right to freedom and self-determination. They should be free to negotiate in freedom and equality with Britain, Senegal or any other country matters which affect the economy and social, cultural, military and political destiny of their country. The argument was not valid that because of its small size and its lack of natural resources The Gambia dared not claim its freedom. All peoples, rich or poor, were entitled to freedom and no right-minded person in the 20th century would deny the Gambian people their claim to fundamental human rights.

Gambians could not be denied the same freedoms that their sisters and brothers were already enjoying across the border in Senegal where independence had been granted a few months before, in June 1960. It was unnatural and unjust, and sooner rather than later, that denial would be resisted. The manifesto was explicit in its presentation of the PPP's consideration of the urgency that The Gambia talked with neighbouring African states in the spirit of brotherhood and equality to determine their common future. It was therefore imperative that independence for the country should not be delayed any longer than the time required to prepare for the physical transfer of power to the Gambian people. It called for internal self-government based on the party system and that should be followed by the fulfilment of the destiny of The Gambia as a people and a nation – and that was independence!

The people adopted the manifesto immediately while the governor and his aides found in it exactly the kind of excuse they were looking for to brand the PPP as brigands and as unworthy of leadership. I was no longer that great gardener and host the governor and his wife had visited at Yundum. I had become a rabble-rouser despite all the democratic processes I followed in presenting the document to the party executive and to a public meeting for discussion.

I cannot agree more with *The Voice of the People – The Story of the PPP* in its description of the situation that existed and which the government was ready to use to paint the PPP as the *bête noire* and to frustrate its every plan:

To achieve the sinister design, they concluded that it was necessary to isolate the troublesome party. In that regard, the UP, which always saw in the PPP the only threat to their dominance and their ambition for power, could readily be counted upon. The DCA was easily written off as enjoying too little influence to matter much. Of greater significance in that sense were the chiefs, the only other influential bloc. It must be remembered here that, in terms of attitude to the PPP, the 36 chiefs had different leanings depending on the levels of their political sophistication and on personalities. At one end, the educated chiefs appeared anxious to preserve their elite positions and to secure an enhanced role for chiefs at the national level. The more ambitious among them even saw themselves as naturally destined to play second fiddle only to white masters and to no one else. However, the majority of chiefs had no formal western education and some of them only feared the PPP because of the perceived destabilising influence of some of our ways.

I returned from the independence celebrations in Nigeria only to find the party in turmoil on account of a plan to have it merge with the other parties in what its architects called the Gambia Solidarity Party (GSP). The idea appeared most hurriedly thrown together under the lamest pretext of being a common front to put forward demands of national import to the colonial authorities. I found the GSP ready to launch and with the decision to involve the PPP taken apparently by one man, Sanjally Bojang. He had not even tabled the subject for a decision by the party's executive. I was devastated. Sanjally was deep in collusion with leaders of the DCA to undo all the work we had so painstakingly achieved since our grassroots work began in 1958.

It was clear that apart from Windley's destabilising work among the chiefs, the majority of whom were now convinced that the PPP was set to destroy their influence and privileges, the DCA had also been at work behind the scenes roping in Sanjally, the PPP kingpin, into an unholy common front that would destroy our party forever.

We discovered that money had changed hands. They promptly rejected the offer. The old-guard leaders of the DCA seduced our national standard-bearer to refute the political direction enunciated in our manifesto. The authorities were deeply disturbed by our manifesto. The same governor who had paid me a visit at my modest home at Staff Site No 3, Yundum, was now working on a common agenda with the old-guard politicians whom he had previously considered dangerous. But now preferring their slower and accommodating policies and interest more palatable than the PPP's firm stand on independence, he changed his mind about the provincial novices he had erroneously thought would be more pliable. It was his way of choosing the lesser of two evils.

Independence and national sovereignty sent the two propelling concepts that sent the government scurrying back to the colony parties. London did not want to encourage national sovereignty; total unification with Senegal was the preferred development and J C Faye and I M Garba Jahumpa had long swallowed the bait. Now they needed to break our resolve and the way to do that was to rope in our standard-bearer into an unholy alliance. It was a great pity that Sanjally was game to such treachery after all the work he had done to set the party on its feet. From all sides, there was a willingness to subvert the party with bribery and ideological contamination, targeting, most of all, its national president.

P S Njie rebuffed the hair-brained proposition for the UP to join the GSP. That left Sanjally squarely in the company of Faye and Jahumpa who promptly went with him on a broadcast tour of Bathurst by Land Rover. They spoke in turns, broadcasting their message through a megaphone. Sanjally, speaking in Mandinka, announced to his bewildered hearers: *PPP teh ta!* – PPP is broken to bits! He likened the party to an egg in the middle of his palm and all he had to do was to let go and the PPP would be finished – smashed on the pavement! On that day as I passed by the Albert Market, I was more sad than angry to see these three gentlemen – Sanjally, Faye and Jahumpa – passing the microphone among them betraying their open treachery against their colleagues.

To call the bluff and counter the treachery, I had to move very quickly to launch a vigorous damage-limitation exercise and to effect immediate repairs to the fabric of our young party. There was the man who had marched through the same streets in a sea of blue back from his successful tour of the country to sell the party to the people! There he was again, barely twelve months later, driving through the same streets, offering our opponents the rewards of our hard work. Naturally, Sanjally did not understand the issues of independence if all he had on that account was from Faye and Jahumpa. As soon as I had gone to Nigeria on an official mission, he showed his true colours. He deluded himself into believing that his rank as national president was powerful enough to lord it over the people who made up the party.

My immediate reaction was to save our party and to protect social and political cohesion. Sanjally's message of a broken PPP reaching the people in the provinces would have confused them. He must have missed the mood since the *mansa bengo* in Basse – to have allowed Faye and Jahumpa to convince him that the GSP was a better alternative to the PPP.

I had to take the risk of bringing the charismatic and popular president of our party to book. I called for a public meeting at Brikama. The party assembled with urgency a couple of miles down the road from Sanjally's village home in Kembuje. In putting the case forward, I did not mince my words. I explained the threat to the cohesion and, in fact, the whole life of the fledgling party the actions that Sanjally and his cohorts had undertaken. I called for the firmest commitment of the members to the central idea that set us off in 1959 and whose gains we were already reaping with seats in the heart of government, especially in our noble quest for independence. Sanjally's treachery was set to reverse those gains that would be countered only by one decisive act – to expel him from the party. That act, I was convinced, would deal a decisive blow against the scheming triumvirate.

The house broke down, so to speak. Although I strenuously argued for his expulsion, a thorough and prolonged debate was to follow. There was no better way to practise the seeding of the democratic culture of discourse within the rank and file of the party than this occasion. We discussed all sides of the issue. At the end of a flurry of diatribe, tempers cooled and the house resorted to the democratic showing of popular opinion. The people voted to expel him. It was a bitter experience for all. But when the sun broke again above those ominous clouds and the party began to sail again in calmer and more directed waters, many of the former sceptics were thankful for the firmness and resolution of the leadership. Nothing more was heard of the GSP.

By the end of 1960, the mind of the ordinary Gambian had been well oiled for self-government. Independence was only one constitutional step away. Although the word itself had become common usage, it was the PPP's policy to walk democratically up every step so that the importance we attached to it would be realised. Attaining it would have been worth our toil to give tangible meaning to our freedom.

We came into a new year, 1961, already a pariah party for publishing the Independence Manifesto and for insisting that the governor take responsible democratic decisions. After the storm of Sanjally's expulsion had blown over, we went back to work, thankful to have escaped the terrible damage that the near-disaster could have caused us. Just out of professional interest, I kept my eyes on the Veterinary Department reports on the immunisation against rinderpest and I was glad to learn that things there were proceeding well with the exception of minor outbreaks. Otherwise I spent the greater part of my working day concentrating on running the Education Ministry, patiently waiting for Windley to make an announcement on his selection of chief minister.

While he dragged his feet, courtesy demanded that we commiserate with him when he had to rush home from his leave in England to be at his wife's bedside. Lady Windley had taken a fall in January 1961 and suffered spinal injury. She was flown to Dakar to connect to London where she was admitted at Guy's Hospital. We extended our wishes for her speedy recovery. Just at this time, the news broke that Patrice Lumumba, the Prime Minister of the Belgian Congo, had been killed. For us trying to make sense of politics and government in The Gambia, the news was disturbing.

We certainly were not going to go the way of the Belgian Congo, where foreign interference and internal betrayal had led to the fall of the government in December 1960 and the assassination of Lumumba and his companions, Joseph Okito, the deputy president of the senate, and Maurice Mpolo, the information minister.

The death a few months later, in September 1961, of UN Secretary General Dag Hammarskjold in a mysterious plane crash only five days after his visit to Leopoldville (Kinshasa) was deemed not unconnected with the seething crisis that forced Kwame Nkrumah to insist on keeping Ghanaian forces in the Belgian Congo to police what he called 'European vandalism' of the politics in that vast and resource-rich country.

But The Gambia was part of the fabric of that bigger picture. Therefore the complexity of the political developments in the Belgian Congo with its size and economic potential and measured against those of The Gambia did not make the struggle of the two countries any different. Respect and dignity and the sanctity of sovereignty were common issues for both. Perhaps the only difference was that, while dialogue had broken down and guns were speaking in place of the human voice in the Belgian Congo, in The Gambia the parties and the colonial administration were engaged around a table and talking, as we did in May and July 1961, to unravel the political impasse that arose from the governor's appointment of a chief minister.

We were in the middle of praying for peace in Congo Kinshasa and stability in our countries for growth to be realised when within our own backyard the Gambia Workers' Union called a general strike at the peak of the trade season. In a matter of forty-eight hours, M E Jallow and the GWU had turned the streets of Bathurst into a battlefield. The news of the unrest and economic disruption baffled the colonial office.

On 16 February 1961, it was my pleasure as minister of education to assist Windley when he cut the ribbon to open the new buildings at Armitage High School in Georgetown. Sixty new pupils were admitted, thanks to the new and improved facilities. The upgrading of the protectorate school was of tremendous importance to me and my ministry in its fulfilment of a long dream for a secondary school in the provinces. When the school celebrated its thirty-fourth anniversary, it was a sentimental and quite fulfilling honour for me that my home division, the MacCarthy Island Division, could now boast a secondary school. In my address I emphasised the dawn of a new era for the protectorate people in particular and the nation at large. I called on parents and guardians to endeavour to send their girl children to school. The education of girls was crucial to our development. So, we had better make it our duty to educate them if we did not want to be found wanting in neglecting 50 per cent of our collective national talent and energy.

I returned from the provinces to find a *note verbale* on my desk. Windley had convened a meeting of the Executive Council for 4 March 1961. It had already been ten long months since the elections. At the meeting the governor explained that after careful consideration he had reached a decision on who to appoint as chief minister. He announced to the council that he was pleased to appoint P S Njie as Chief Minister of The Gambia.

At that point, I reached into my jacket pocket and laid an envelope before the governor. It contained my resignation as minister of education. The next day, Sheriff Sisay, my PPP colleague, resigned. A week later, Alieu Badara Njie of the DCA also resigned. The governor quickly filled the vacancies with independents and UP members to complete his government. He had, in fact, by this singular act created a deep political crisis that constituted his biggest error ever in his three short years of service in The Gambia.

My resignation sent me into the opposition side of the House; it was the boldest stand for me to take to drive home the fact that democracy and constitutional tradition had been transgressed. The administration was tottering on the brink of political explosion through April. Striking the iron while it was hot, we called an all-party meeting in Bathurst in May 1961.

In July 1961, we went to London for the Constitutional Talks. In a bid to get to the bottom of the crisis, the Colonial Secretary Iain McLeod called Windley and me to a private meeting with him. I seized the opportunity to have my say. I narrated the true details of how the governor had subverted the age-old Westminster traditions just to suit his own grudges against me and my party for daring to publish our independence manifesto. I went into the details of his machinations in the background to have the old-guard parties break down the PPP. I literally went to town with Windley. At one point in my tirade the fully blushing and agitated governor shot up to his feet as one who had been badgered enough: "Sir," he screamed, "Mr Jawara is accusing me of ..." The secretary of state did not allow him to finish and asked him to sit down and allow me to finish what I was saying. I was deeply consoled and pacified by the opportunity to tell it all in the presence of his boss.

While the constitutional crisis persisted in Banjul, the PPP withdrew from the limelight to set its house in order. Sheriff Sisay and I retreated from government into full engagement with party colleagues in consolidating our gains. Our principled act of resigning from government gained the PPP popularity and great respect.

We used the time wisely and waited; it did take all of ten months before the general elections. We used the intervening period to strengthen the party structures. We set up branches in new and vital corners of our support base and consolidated executive and administrative mechanisms to ensure a well-governed political movement. The party's fullest authority continued to derive from the people with each party member solidly linked with the Central Committee and the National Executive Committee through branches that elected delegates at divisional, district, ward and village levels.

I walked away vindicated from that private protest consultation in London and from the more public Constitutional Talks with a winning decision in my briefcase. That was a bigger scoop for us than any which the opposition was able to imagine. We went to the polls in May 1962. The PPP surged into power and was poised to change the face of politics in The Gambia for the next thirty-two years.

18

Making haste slowly

Cutting my teeth in government for ten months as a cabinet minister from May 1960 to March 1961 and for another fourteen as opposition leader in the legislature had prepared me for my return to mature politics in 1962. While the team at the Premier's Office and I straightened out the infrastructure of the civil service, I deeply wanted to speed up the 'Gambianisation' of all senior political and administrative positions.

The guiding vision of our journey in our country's constitutional development was that which kept us ever aware of the sacredness of our pledge to transform the country we had inherited into the new nation we were forging. Up until 1821, Britain had administered The Gambia through a series of charters given to trading companies to oversee British interests in places where they carried out their trade. However, those powers were soon transferred to the British Crown. Under special arrangements, The Gambia had functioned on and off as a British dependency governed from Sierra Leone until 1888 when it finally established its own Legislative Council and consolidated an identity of its own.

At first, this body consisted entirely of Europeans representing government and commercial interests. It was only much later on that prominent Gambians (or African immigrants) began to find places in it. Indeed, that situation remained in place until 1947 when a significant change was made in which the council drew up a constitution that provided for the appointment of more Gambians than Europeans to sit on the executive body and Gambians to elect their representatives to the council.

More development was to take place later, around 1951, when political parties were formed after the laws had been improved upon, providing for voting rights to yard owners and other responsible adults in the colony area. The constitution also introduced a system enabling the governor to appoint elected Gambians as ministers in the government. We are familiar with the struggle in 1958 and 1959 when demands made by chiefs and other Gambians led to the 1960 Constitution, which for the first time introduced universal adult suffrage to include people of the protectorate and to all Gambians twenty-one years of age or older. Those changes led to the elections in 1960 after which six ministers and a chief minister were appointed. Those were remarkable achievements indeed but still fell short of the real aspirations of Gambians who preferred self-determination and independence.

In January 1961, the Joint Industrial Council (JIC) was acting on recommendations of the Panda Lewis Commission to upgrade salaries and wages when the Gambia Workers' Union (GWU) assumed an intractable stance demanding a 90 percent blanket increase. It put an ultimatum on the table for a general strike if the proposal was not accepted. During the negotiations, M E Jallow, the GWU leader, walked his delegation out of the JIC meeting thereby setting the scene for a rather difficult outcome. It is important to note that the union leader, generally known by his sobriquet "Jallow Jallow", was wielding influence at this time that did not end with labourers and workers only. He was an articulate speaker and a charismatic leader whose ideas were taking a rapid foothold among civil servants and the youths.

A great deal of tension grew out of the GWU's action when work stoppage began at important economic centres in the provinces. On 20 January labourers in Kuntaur and Georgetown stopped work. In Bathurst, the police authorities refused the union's application for a permit for a procession of striking workers to go ahead. Defying the refusal, M E Jallow summoned a mass union meeting on 24 January. When the men began to gather and the police moved in to enforce the law, the situation quickly deteriorated. Bathurst was thrown into pandemonium, and there were ugly scenes between the demonstrators and the police. M E Jallow was arrested and charged with inciting the crowd. The government had to resort to calling in reinforcements of police units from Sierra Leone to help calm the unrest. It was a very tense two weeks.

Naturally, as a state minister, I found personal interest in these developments but especially so when the conflagration that had begun to die down after five days of unrest suddenly sparked up again. This time the unrest had reached the corridors of government where the Senior Civil Servants' Association (CSA) convened a meeting in Bathurst to which they invited the participation of members of the Junior Civil Servants' Association. They sent a letter of protest to the government presenting their grievances against the police. They called for a commission of inquiry into the conduct of the security forces during the strike that had just ended.

This development was to have immediate and far-reaching effects on the political situation. The wrath of Civil Secretary Kenneth G Smith was unleashed on the leading figures in the CSA such as Secretary General Mohammadou Lamin Saho who was at the time an administrative officer at the Secretariat and members, Sam Daniel Goddard, Chief Storekeeper at the Public Works Department, Charles Louis Carayol, Commissioner of Income Tax and Sam H A George, Solicitor General and Legal Secretary. In the absence of Windley on leave in England, Smith took on the full reins of power and said that he was brooking none of the 'extravagant language' and the 'undisciplined manner of the presentation' of the letter of protest. The civil secretary who was also doubling as Acting Governor debunked the charges against the police and even those of the protest note against the contingent of forces ferried in from Sierra Leone to deal with the violence.

Smith asked for apologies in writing. Saho refused and was dismissed from the civil service. He went to the UK to read law and returned home a few years later to serve as attorney general in my government. The others were reprimanded after their letters of apology in demeaning fashion and allowed to continue work.

Nevertheless, I was perturbed by the highhandedness of the civil secretary's response that raised red signals to me of a need to move faster forward from the weaknesses of the constitutional arrangements that vested such massive power in one government official. Windley returned post haste to Bathurst and promptly endorsed every action of Smith's. `

Talks opened in Bathurst on 4 May 1961 with the purpose of sounding out the various political parties and the chiefs on issues of constitutional reform. The draft proposal already envisaged a fully representative and responsible government. Other issues addressed included the size and composition of the legislature, the role of chiefs, self-government, independence, relations with Senegal, the size and composition of the Executive Council and its eventual transformation into a cabinet. Each of the main parties was represented by a delegation of three. There were three chiefs representing their peers with M E Jallow, Rachel Palmer and Henry Madi attending as independents.

Sheriff Sisay, Paul Baldeh and I represented the PPP. Sheriff was our party's General Secretary and Paul had just returned home from studies in Ireland. It turned out to be an amicable meeting which largely decided the agenda we agreed to present at the follow-up talks which took place from 24 to 27 July 1961 in London. The colonial secretary McLeod presided over the meeting and in his opening statement set the tone, as far as I was concerned, when he said he understood that the clear purpose of our being there was "to consider the next stage of the constitutional advance against the background of the special circumstances of The Gambia with which we are all familiar."

We understood what constitutional advance we needed in The Gambia and I called for a definite date for independence and proposed January 1963. P S Njie on the other hand felt that a date for independence should not be fixed at that conference. Instead he wanted the issue to be left to the next government that would emerge to negotiate. J C Faye and Jahumpa supported those views. Seyfo Omar Mbakeh, Rachel Palmer and Henry Madi considered that though the ultimate aim should be independence the present conference should not look further than to the creation of full internal self- government. However, M E Jallow supported our position that The Gambia was capable of running its own affairs and he urged that a date for independence should be fixed.

I could not understand the reason for the foot-dragging among some of the delegates about the urgency of independence and for the fixing of a date for such an important event in our political advancement. Faye, back in April at the first PPP/DCA annual conference in Bathurst, had suggested 7 November 1963 for our independence. Although he later withdrew it, at least it was a sign that he was committed to a date and at one time had actually favoured immediate independence. The shift in tune in so short a time seemed to have occurred when it became apparent to him that we had done our homework and were ready for independence. Perhaps the fact that the PPP was the likely party to take the country to independence did not go down well with him. I was pleased with the stance of M E Jallow who saw the issue from our perspective and wanted a definite date.

Admittedly, it was not all the crossing of swords with P S Njie, Faye and Jahumpa at the meeting. At least they agreed with me that relations with neighbouring countries should be left to a new independent government in Bathurst, even though P S Njie stated that the question of association should not be linked to the question of independence. All said and done, the essentials were agreed. There would be a House of Representatives and no second chamber. There would be a minister of finance; the attorney general would be a member of the House but without a vote; the number of elected members would be thirty-six – with twenty-five from the protectorate, seven from the colony, and the remaining four given to the chiefs who would have the same voting rights as other members of the House. Most profound of all under the circumstances and that which the PPP supporters back home were eager to hear was the confirmation that elections under the new constitution would be held by May 1962.

There were far-reaching provisions affecting the Executive Council, the governor's special responsibilities and reserve powers, the legislature and the public service. We concluded with general discussions of the financial and economic problems of the country. The secretary of state took note of the general desire of the delegates that the form of the administration of the grants-in-aid should be modified. He undertook to review the arrangements and it was agreed that the budget for 1962 would be negotiated with the Gambia government rather than decided unilaterally by London. It was a good thing that Sheriff Sisay was there; he would be minister of finance after we swept the polls in 1962 and it would be his business to negotiate our British grants-in-aid and handle our budget in the future.

We breathed a sigh of relief. There was the framework of a workable constitution in place and my party went to work accordingly to prepare for May. There was not a moment wasted after I resigned my ministerial position. I kept fully engaged with party militants and elders on campaigns throughout the protectorate preparing for the eventuality of a revised constitution that London had approved. The people were woken up to the truth of those working for them and those who had worked against them in the past. The party secretariat issued membership cards to better identify our members in addition to organising programmes to raise funds for the party. At home and abroad, the response was overwhelming.

I kept one eye on the family and the other on politics as well as on happenings around the world; in fact, on anything and everything that had the potential of becoming an issue for government after the elections. On 9 December 1961, I applauded Tanzania for joining the family of the twelve Commonwealth members, eight of which had achieved independence since the close of the Second World War – India (1947), Pakistan (1947), Ghana (1957), Malaya (1957), Ceylon (1948), Cyprus (1960), Nigeria (1960) and Sierra Leone (1961). With some balance between sentiment and pragmatism, my thoughts were daily centred on when The Gambia would join such an august rank in the comity of nations.

Incidentally, the US had failed in its attempt to invade Cuba on 17 April 1961. Nearly a year later, the two countries broke off diplomatic relations, straining international relations all over the globe. Emerging African nations were hardest hit with decisions as to which camp would make better sense of their allegiances after independence. The US charged the Cuban leader, Fidel Castro, with making his country a bridgehead for Soviet imperialism in the Western hemisphere. The intense sabre-rattling left many countries restless even though US Secretary of State Dean Rusk had said that the US would protect its interests but without the use of force.

Her Majesty Queen Elizabeth of Great Britain paid an official visit to The Gambia on 3 December 1961. But contrary to democratic practice, the opposition PPP was left out of the official programme of welcome for the Queen. We decided, nonetheless, to put up our own show of welcome in our unique way. We paraded our colours and our party supporters along the roadside at Yundum for Her Majesty to see us as she drove by. Not only did we do that to demonstrate our goodwill to the British monarch but also to show our desire to participate in events of national import and also to point a finger at the poor quality of democratic leadership of Governor Windley, Civil Secretary K G Smith and Chief Minister P S Njie who would not invite the bona fide opposition party in the Legislative Council to the official welcome of the Queen, the country's head of state, or to the reception given in her honour at Government House.

Not to be put off by the omissions of the government, the PPP busied itself campaigning countrywide. In addition to the demonstrations of the PPP in Bathurst supporters turned out in large numbers in their party colours when she stopped at Foni Bintang Karanai. We were stomping the electoral grounds and building the trust of the domain when it came to us as a great relief that the colonial office had reassigned Windley to some other post. So suddenly, his tour of duty would come to a close.

On 28 February 1962, Windley, in the company of his wife, and their young daughter, Fiona, left The Gambia. He was replaced by Sir John Warburton Paul.

The British government was anxious to have the errors of Windley blow over and for the government in Bathurst to begin conducting its affairs with less controversy than there had been in 1960 and 1961. Our prudence in waiting quietly out of the limelight proved fruitful from the outcome of the elections of 1962. Soon after Governor Paul's arrival the electoral system went into full gear to prepare for the May elections. Under the new constitution the position of civil secretary was suppressed and the new role given to a Deputy Governor. Former Civil Secretary Smith retired on 18 May 1962 handing over to Paul Gore who assumed the position of Deputy Governor.

Under the new governor, people went to the polls on 31 May 1962. That same night Radio Gambia broadcast the results. We were breaking new horizons with the launch of the national radio station that went on the air for the first time on 1 April 1962. Listeners were now able to sit at home and receive the election results on the airwaves. The PPP won eighteen seats against the UP's thirteen, with one seat going to the DCA. The results refuted every argument and action of our former governor and his chief minister, and laid out the true aspirations of the Gambian people for all to see.

In June 1962, I was sworn in as premier. I was seriously considering the overtures of the DCA to form a loose merger with us. It seemed the right thing to do drawing from our experiences collaborating in council against some of the deficiencies in the provisions of the 1959 Constitution. The way had already been paved for this collaboration with the DCA delegates riding closely with us during the Constitutional Talks. That goodwill helped to fire our imagination to accept a merger as of great advantage.

It would take much work to get the 1962 House of Representatives ready for the inauguration of its new mandate. We assembled for its first meeting on 5 July 1962, a kind of dress rehearsal for the official opening ceremony which took place the following day. It was a touching and splendid turn-out indeed. Governor Paul in his speech from the throne touched on the vital values which our legislators must uphold to keep the tenets of democracy, fair play and the rule of law towards an improved standard of living for the average person. It was a people's government and its lawmakers must never lose sight of that objective and duty.

In my best judgement I selected my first cabinet in which the government kept two expatriates carried over from the colonial service in the persons of Winton Lane as Secretary to the Premier and Philip Bridges as Attorney General. Yusupha Samba became Minister of Labour and Social Welfare, Andrew David Camara, Minister of Education, Amang Kanyi, Minister of Works and Communication, J L B Daffeh, Minister of Health, Sheriff Mustapha Dibba, Minister for Local Government and Lands, Sheriff Sekouba Sisay, Minister of Finance, and Alieu Badara Njie, Minister of External Affairs. We had one man out of the small crop of graduate civil servants - Hatib Semega-Janneh – serve as Deputy Secretary to the Cabinet.

The technology of radio was proving a blessing to the government and to the nation at large. I was able to make frequent broadcasts and to hear vital information on government activities covered in daily news broadcasts. The immediacy of its delivery was rewarding, much as it was able to dilate on domestic and foreign policy, albeit from the rudimentary studio facilities set up in a disused kitchen of Messrs Cable & Wireless Co Ltd where broadcasting in our country was born.

We were thrilled when, on 16 and 17 July 1962, we received our first foreign visitors, a delegation of the Senegalese government. It comprised Mamadou Dia, President of the Council of Ministers of Senegal, Foreign Minister Doudou Thiam, Minister of State Ibou Diallo, and Vice President of the National Assembly, Ibou Diouf. We listened to their hearty message of congratulations from President Leopold Sedar Senghor, after which we went into bilateral talks. We discussed many issues of common interest. It was helpful that on both sides there was eagerness for cooperation and mutual understanding of the interdependence of the two countries. The visit whetted the appetite of the External Affairs Ministry already placed in the hands of an experienced former civil servant, Alieu Badara Njie. His and the Premier's Office were already bracing themselves to engage Senegal and our overseas partners. Incidentally, there was no shortage of challenges, judging from the list of foreign appointments already on schedule.

Everyone in the new government was swept up by the thrill of events. In particular, the young people in the cabinet were over the moon, as it were, with the new things that came with prestigious office. While a poorly paid civil service and a struggling farming community looked on, I insisted on modest and inexpensive lifestyles for government officials. We approved new *Zephyr 4* cars for ministers; and, for his official duties the premier was allocated a standard Jaguar sedan, that a *New York Time*s correspondent reported would hardly attract a glance in any other African capital. For my family's private use I got a Hillman *Minx* in which Augusta drove the children to school every morning. Modest means of transport that should vindicate our consciousness of our coat vis-à-vis our cloth. After all, the premier's salary was $8,400 a year and he lived with his family in a three-bedroom house. No one had to remind us we were Africa's smallest and poorest nation, the *Times* had reported me as saying. Therefore, everything we did would have to be a question of pounds, shillings and pence.

As a government we soon realised that settling down would have to be done while fighting massive litigation into which the UP had drawn us with their petition to the courts for the annulment of the entire elections. We were ill-prepared for combat. They put together a team of lawyers – E D Njie and Sheriff Njie, brothers of the party leader, and some other local associates led by a Sierra Leonean, Berthan Macauley QC. The party leader, P S Njie, who had, as of May 1961, while he headed the government as chief minister, been debarred from the practice of law, now had to make do with pulling the strings from the background. We had had no legal representation of which to speak until Ghana's Prime Minister Kwame Nkrumah made available to us his own Attorney General Kaw Swanzy, ably aided by another senior Ghanaian counsel, Alex da Costa, to defend us.

It was significant and much appreciated that Nkrumah would send us his attorney general to lead our case over weeks and months away from his national duties at home. It is worth noting that self-reliance and sub-regional cooperation were at this time close to the Ghanaian prime minister's continental agenda. Apart from sending us the defence team, he also seconded Sidney Quartey to serve as principal veterinary officer while also generously meeting the cost of his salary and allowances. In addition to helping us fill this vacancy that had been caused by my departure into politics, Ghana offered scholarships to three members of our veterinary staff on a three-year training course at the Ghana Veterinary Assistants School.

While Kaw Swanzy and da Costa fought our cases, we carried on with consolidating government and ensuring that at both party executive and cabinet levels we understood what each of our roles was and what it meant to hold ministerial and parliamentary positions and the oath that went with the assumption of such high office. Most of the team had to learn from scratch and were novices to whatever portfolios they held. Accordingly, we posed no pretensions to having all the answers or had all the right people in the right jobs. Anyway, however bad a hand it might have been, it was our determination to play it well.

The court hearings took a great deal of the energy we had reserved to set up government. It was difficult, to say the least, that key people in the new government had to abandon their desks to appear in court to give testimony. However, in a short time, eight of the petitions were soon heard and thrown out. Trouble was to begin when the court upheld the petition against one of our candidates, Yusupha Samba, Member for Sabach Sanjal constituency (Samba regained his seat in a bye election the following year).

The UP's lawyers thought they had found the peg they were looking for. Pouncing on that case they put forth the argument that what was true in that case was also true for all the others. They demanded the nullification of all the results, including mine, even with the undisputable majority I polled in the Kombo East constituency.

The governor intervened by invoking the rarely used constitutional instrument of the Queen's Order-in-Council. This validated the electoral registers and more or less closed the issue. There were unconfirmed reports that the UP was having difficulty settling their huge £30,000 legal fees.

At last we were able to get round that ugly moment and turn to the business of making sense of the running of the government that was now our responsibility and duty as duly elected leaders. We turned our concerns to the urgent matters such as how and what to do to raise funds to add to the insufficient grants-in-aid we were receiving from the UK. We began by planning our national budget and setting up the necessary programmes for development. We worked diligently on a three-year programme we called The Gambia Government Development Programme 1964 – 1967, which was strictly an expenditure sheet on projects we were going to pay for from our Development Fund. With nearly £4.5 million budgeted for development, The Gambia was set to spend amounts never dreamt of before. The outlay was intended to refurbish public assets and rescue certain rundown facilities in the health and education services. Road infrastructure received the biggest slice of that budget in line with our philosophy of bridging that gap which the colonial period so badly neglected, not opening up this vital means for the inclusion of the protectorate.

We embarked on the inspection of agricultural and health projects; I needed to familiarise myself with the field. There was once again some 'trekking' for me to do up country, only this time it was not going to be on foot or in Bedford kit cars but in the appreciable comfort of the official government launch, the *HMCS Mansa Kila Kuta*. Augusta came with me on Friday 24 August 1962 and we made official stops at Kemoto, Keneba, Tendaba, Barrokunda and Katamina. I inspected ongoing work on several government sites and heath facilities. It was a great opportunity to have face-to-face explanations and to give pep talks on the new directions government was taking. What was more, the tour provided me with the opportunity to inculcate new attitudes to work, especially as regards our keen sense of self-reliance – doing things ourselves!

On the family level, realising that Augusta had still not been formally introduced to the Niamina section of my family, I thought it was an opportune time for her to meet the Fatty *kabilo* and my mother's village people. The stop-over in Dankunku was great. Augusta and I spent five hours there and left some very impressed folks in Dankunku before we sailed back after lunch. The relaxation helped relieve me from a bothersome fever. I was feeling so poorly that at Kemoto I had to ask someone in my delegation to address the people on my behalf.

We were ready for our first official visits abroad on 10 September 1962 when I led a delegation on a tour of Commonwealth West African countries. It was necessary for me to become familiar with the leadership and political and social trends in the sub-region and to discuss my government's plans with our neighbours. Generally, ours was an ambitious but highly feasible development programme for which we hoped to receive aid from overseas countries, particularly the United Kingdom, the USA and West Germany. But we considered that West African countries with longer experience in those matters might be able to assist us. In this connection, we also planned the possibility of Gambian civil servants going over for brief visits to familiarise themselves with the manner in which our neighbours in West Africa were tackling the problems of self-determination and development.

In Freetown, we held discussions with Prime Minister Sir Albert Margai. We traced our long association and explored every avenue for the use of experienced Sierra Leoneans to fill vacancies in the establishment back home. We were grateful that Sierra Leoneans came to join our judiciary and in other technical areas where we badly needed personnel. Indeed, even after our independence, the records show we still had openings in senior positions in the public service.

In Lagos we met with Nigerian Prime Minister, Alhaji Sir Abubakar Tafawa Balewa. We learnt important facts about Nigeria and the common market issues that were being discussed in connection with the African Groundnut Council, a matter that had been under negotiation with other groundnut producing countries at the time. This was a pertinent subject since Nigeria at this time was a bigger producer of groundnuts than Senegal and The Gambia put together. Before the circumstances of his sad demise in a coup d'état in January 1966, I would meet the Prime Minister again when I visited Nigeria after we attained independence in 1965. I would thank him and the people of Nigeria for making available to us the services of a magistrate, and informed him that we envisaged putting part of Nigeria's generous independence gift of £10,000 to starting a Public Records Section.

A memorable part of that tour of Nigeria was our visit to the Northern Region where the Premier and Sardauna of Sokoto, Sir Ahmadu Bello, warmly received us in Kaduna. It was a red carpet welcome he accorded my delegation. We had a lot to see and learn from the modern techniques Nigeria was putting into the production of groundnuts and other agricultural produce. We left convinced that Nigeria would undoubtedly be a major partner in development and our vision was that it would step in decisively in training our agricultural personnel. Then, as much as we did in 1962, we welcomed whatever technical support Nigeria could offer. The fact that we did not approach any other West African government for that kind of financial assistance showed how importantly we considered the scope of our relations with Nigeria.

From Lagos we went to Accra. Meeting again with Prime Minister Kwame Nkrumah was both reminiscent and forward-looking. We were now both leaders in our respective countries, I having just assumed the reins of government and he having led Ghana already to independence eight years before. We talked about the inchoate OAU that African leaders had formed in Addis Ababa, Ethiopia, in 1963. We revisited the original pan-African vision he had spelt out while I was a student at Achimota and we tried to see how that energy was linked to the ultimate birth of the OAU. He was a man with a grand soul and he carried so much feeling for Africa. We shared our awareness of the great need for African unity and we lamented the sad situation of the deep divisions between rival liberation movements seeking to promote the independence of the Portuguese territories in West Africa.

We discussed possible ways of intervention in the form of reconciliation efforts so that those countries under colonial rule would forge a common front towards total independence. The struggles on the continent, we agreed, were even worsened by the recent troublesome position taken by French-speaking West Africa not to hold the next OAU meeting in Accra. Something was amiss again with foreign interests in the background to the Francophone and Anglophone disagreements. It was evident that while African countries were rejecting their fellows, the African vanguard would weaken and African dignity and independence would be compromised. Such divisions would have to be solved if we were ever going to make head way with African unity. We agreed that it was an awesome task leading our individual countries and being genuinely concerned at the same time about Africa, its independence and its united future.

During my visit to Ghana I was to learn at first-hand the wonder of God when I flew in a glider piloted by a former Luftwaffe pilot - Hanna Reitsch.[11] My hosts had arranged for a visit to the Afienya Gliding School near Accra, where a handful of former German World War II pilots had set up a training facility. The offer was made and it was up to me to fly. I felt brave and took up the challenge. Why not? I said to myself.

I sat behind Hanna as we were catapulted into the air in a tiny winged craft with no engines, powered by nothing more than thrust, lift and air currents and, of course, the flying skills of an experienced German woman flyer. I viewed the world below as we flew through the rushing silence of space. I experienced a profound sense of the power of God. I love sailing; and, as it were, spiritually touched the hems of God's garments many times out at sea even to the point of nearly losing my life in 1973. But I found the brief gliding encounter far more exhilarating than sailing, flowing as we did at a speed with the weight sensation of a feather and taking a view of the world only eagles were allowed to take. When at last I set my feet back on terra firma, I came away with lessons that left me with the same teaching I would find in all monotheistic religions, for me to be a humbler servant of God, of my people and of my country.

---

[11] Hanna Reitsch was once Adolf Hitler's personal pilot, and was the first woman to fly a helicopter, rocket plane and jet fighter amongst other remarkable achievements.

Local government administration also needed our attention. There was much sore feeling between some chiefs and their people who had voted overwhelmingly for the PPP. During our campaigns we received reports from people on how heavy-handedly their chiefs treated them because they were PPP supporters. The state of ferment resulting from the acrimonious elections was indeed compounded by the various acts of heavy-handedness of some of the chiefs that alienated significant sections of their communities to the extent of compromising their positions as respected and important traditional rulers.

We walked into a hostile local government environment. New rules and conditions had to be designed and implemented to restore confidence in chiefs and people alike that the new political dispensation had, as its central principle, a high standard of democratic governance and the interest of *all* Gambians at heart. None of these preoccupations however detracted us from the central mission of our government, which was to deliver to the people the promises we made during the election campaigns to improve the well-being of the people and to take the country to full independence.

We were steaming full ahead with our target in mind when in December 1962 I raised the issue again with the governor. We were fortunate in many ways to have had at the helm of affairs, this time round, Governor Paul, a man of candid speech and an encouraging disposition. He showed a sincere desire to work with us. He worked diligently to calm the excitement and in a candid written reply gave us his views on the immense work that needed to be done to the fabric of government and the infrastructure for independence to make sense. The work at hand needed us to make haste slowly.

But after only a year in government, we were ready to receive the full reins to move on to internal self-government. We felt ready to put into action this particular provision which had been agreed at the Constitutional Talks in London in 1961. In July 1963, an Order-in-Council provided for the leader of the party with the majority in the House of Representatives to become prime minister and for a cabinet of six ministers drawn from the House.

Those constitutional changes prepared the way for my declaration on Friday 4 October 1963 that The Gambia had attained full internal self-government. Many sections of society took on a festive mood. I had raised the sense of attainment in speeches I gave at various gatherings including a dinner I attended in Bathurst given by the Bathurst Reform Club in honour of the occasion. However, before the dinner at The Gambia's oldest private club which was founded in 1911, and of which I became a member, I recorded a speech that was aired the following day on our VHF radio station. In it I gave the Gambian people the good news for our country, explaining how the British parliament discussed and approved this last milestone on our road to freedom and independence.

We had a lot to be thankful for as we had reached this situation in peace, unity and concord. This enviable record of orderly progress was not achieved without the exercise of tolerance, patience, self-sacrifice and good sense on the people's part; and for this I congratulated everyone. I told them that the first step towards the fullest benefit of this great leap forward was the adherence to law and order. I emphasised that people had their freedoms and rights and I called on them to embrace democracy that recognised those rights. I asked the Gambian people for the support that the new government would need to raise the standard of living we all needed. Everyone must put their shoulders to the wheel and work hard. The text of my declaration on 4 October 1963 was as follows:

> Today as we inaugurate a new climax in this constitutional evolution we should remember those veteran political leaders, statesmen, patriots, both men and women, past and present, who played their invaluable part in bringing our goal of Independence within sight. When I look back on the record of the past, we can all be justly proud of the way in which genuine democracy has evolved in this country in a most happy and orderly manner. The elected government, which I have the honour to lead, will continue to follow genuine democratic principles. To this end the new amendments to the constitution introduced, among other things, clauses for the protection of the fundamental rights and freedoms of the individual. We shall work for the development of this country and try to raise the living standards.
>
> All these are worthy goals, but let us not imagine that we can go anywhere near realising them without the wholehearted cooperation of all men and women. For example, genuine democratic principles cannot be long maintained unless every citizen continues to pay due regard to law and order and to observe the rule of democracy. The fundamental rights and freedoms of the individual cannot be long protected unless every individual respects the rights of others, according to the law of the land. We cannot improve the economy and raise living standards

unless we all put our shoulders to the wheel and work hard to our benefit and to that of the country as a whole. Finally, we shall work for early Independence of The Gambia, and wherever we have the influence, we shall work for the Unity of the African people.

While we reserved high commendations for the entire party and government for the hard work in formulating the ideas and quality of the substance that went into the preparation for self-government and the final draft of the 1961 Constitution, no one could ignore the vital role Governor Paul played in wisely putting our case most favourably to Her Majesty's Government.

I recall with fondness the pleasure I had of receiving and acting upon the minutes and personal and confidential notes the governor sent to the Prime Minister's Office. Governor Paul sent me sincere suggestions taming our urge that even though he was aware we wanted to 'Gambianise', he warned that we had to be systematic and to do so by all means quickly but not hastily. Upon his advice I proceeded gingerly in my approach because as much as I was eager to fill the senior cadre of the civil service with Gambians, I realised that qualified locals were not returning at the same rate as they were needed to take up the new roles. Governor Paul was always in his natural element of candour. He called the attention of the Public Service Commission to what he thought was an apparent lowering of recruitment standards just to serve Gambianisation. The commission took heed and adjusted their recruitment style.

His note to the administration, only three days before I declared the country fully self-governed in October 1964, warned that "the value and significance (of our record) of Gambianisation will be lost and standards will suffer if the policy is to be pursued irrespective of the qualifications and suitability of the candidates concerned". His arguments were at once fair and from the heart, as when he pleaded that we should renew the services of good Europeans until suitable replacements could be found. We could see he was working for our advantage when, for example, in arguing out the case for the retention of Financial Secretary Williams, he advised in his petition that preparations for the 1965/1966 budget and all the problems attendant to the attainment of our independence were going to tax our limited staff severely. Mr Williams' experience and knowledge, the governor said, not to mention his astounding capacity for work, would be invaluable during this very testing period. If there was an obvious

Gambian officer ready to take over from Mr Williams in September he would have advised quite differently – but as he saw it there was none.

We took heed and had a closer look at postings and the indigenous personnel available to us. We had to slow down to scout out qualified people to replace the expatriates, if we did not wish to grind the civil service to a halt with mediocre servants. He gave me the professional and collegiate support I needed to take over the ship of state.

I spoke highly of Governor Paul in the House of Representatives on 31 January 1966 when I responded to his valedictory. During the many constitutional changes and the certainly attendant socio-economic advancement of those four years, Sir John applied his wisdom, knowledge and experience to the needs of The Gambia. He proved himself singularly well adapted to the demands of our changing times.

No wonder when Sir John took formal leave of the House as Governor General in 1966, I was very sincere when I said that while we were proud that a Gambian would henceforth take up the office, we would not be human if we did not feel real sadness in seeing him and Lady Paul leave our shores. In offering them, on behalf of the House, our sincere good wishes for their health, happiness and prosperity, I was reminded of words from Milton's *Paradise Lost* — 'For solitude sometimes is best society; And short retirement urges sweet return'. Sir John enjoyed that firm promise of a sweet welcome back to The Gambia when he returned to celebrate with us our silver jubilee of independence in 1990.

Since self-government and 'Gambianisation' demanded a trained and qualified local workforce, we needed Gambians who were committed to the goals and aspirations of our young nation. I continued to be uneasy about key positions still being in the hands of expatriates and that we as a country still continued to be under a monarchical constitution. Deputy Governor Gore realised this streak in my attitude and he did not fail to share with Governor Paul his sense of my urgency to put Gambians in charge. The governor had always been sympathetic with my plans and one of his landmark contributions and one that raised him highly in the estimation of my government was that he was a stabilising factor and had a head for good counsel.

Until he left on 10 February 1966, he worked amicably with me and my colleagues who found in him a warm and genuine man who did all he could to help us take off, especially in the structuring of a good and apolitical civil service.

Typically, even letting officers go away on earned leave at times left the system severely handicapped. We had only a tiny crop of young administrators to choose from. S M Sissoho was the most senior Gambian in the administration as Assistant Secretary under the Establishment Secretary, C G Dixon. M D Njie was a Higher Executive Officer and Frederick E Grante was an Executive Officer. We had about a dozen trainee executive officers, three of whom were away in Ghana and the UK. The Prime Minister's Office was clearly still the domain of Europeans with K J W Lane serving in a dual capacity as Secretary to the Cabinet and Secretary to the Prime Minister. There was the Principal Assistant Secretary R K M White and Economic Adviser D A Percival. The Gambian staff comprised Francis A J Savage, Assistant Secretary and Hatib B Semega-Janneh, Assistant Secretary who also carried the duties of Deputy Secretary to Cabinet and Clerk of the House of Representatives.

There were people in the civil service – some of them Europeans – at the rank of Senior Assistant Secretary and in the staff grade posts who were on the verge of retiring or were making other arrangements now that The Gambia had gained independence and obviously eager to handle its own affairs. Some of them were retained on contract. We trained as many of them as our budget could sustain and as much as friendly countries were willing to award us places in their institutions of further training.

Of course, we endeavoured to train our human resources in the priority areas. Agriculture was the backbone of our young economy and as far as our government was concerned we attached great importance to the role of cooperative societies to invigorate agriculture. While the administration flexed its new muscle with new brains and faces, we realised that there were many parts of our agriculture-dependent economy that were still without these societies. One of the first acts of government therefore was to send four or five members of the Cooperative Department abroad for training while many more were being trained locally to take up junior positions that would ensure countrywide coverage beginning in the 1964/1965 trade season.

These cooperative officers and their assistants were vital to the well-being of the farmers in securing incomes and earnings that would increase their capacity to produce. We laid great emphasis on agricultural production. For only with higher production of food and cash crops could we hope to raise the living standard of the people. It was the only way for the unskilled labour force to enjoy the higher wages and the better standard of living which they deserved.

The need for sound and seasoned administrators was there when Sir John was governor. It was still there when he returned twenty-five years later, even if with a tiny technical difference. In 1965, the qualified Gambian workforce was simply not there. An unofficial count in 1990 showed a very high percentage of trained and qualified Gambians continuing to live abroad after completing their studies in Europe. It had formed part of the gravy-train – the mass emigration giving to Europe the vital technical and intellectual capital we needed at home. The brain drain continues to be perhaps the most serious subject for modern Africa after grinding poverty, war and disease. Many believe that the current sociological and political conditions at play on the continent have a direct correlation to the continued exile of such vital human resources.

On every trip I made out of the country, my itinerary would be incomplete if I did not share with Gambian students my thoughts of them coming home and taking their rightful place in our development. My colleagues in government were also aware of this dire need and plugged the message wherever they went. Two things were always high on the agenda of our foreign visits – scholarships and training opportunities for Gambians. Gambian students had gone away to the United Kingdom, the United States, France, Ghana, Nigeria, Malaysia and many other countries under various scholarship schemes.

In 1966, when Eric Christensen arrived on the scene as Principal Assistant Secretary at the Prime Minister's Office and Secretary to the Cabinet, we knew immediately that some rare energy had kicked into our toddling limbs. Until 1965 he had been Counsellor at the Senegalese Consulate General and acted as Consul General on several occasions. His hard work and competence soon helped him rise to be the first Gambian Secretary General and Head of the Civil Service in 1967, a position from which he retired in 1978.

Indeed, by 1969, the human resource picture had improved a great deal. Gambians who worked at the core of the civil service had completed their training and returned home. They were taking over at very senior levels of the administration which we had worked so diligently to improve upon from what we inherited from the colonial era. We succeeded in raising a highly qualified and efficient professional cadre of administrators and technicians. At the risk of missing out some of them, and as a tribute to all of them, I would like to mention M M Sosseh, Francis A J Mboge, Hatib Semega-Janneh, Ebou M Taal, Demba A Ndow, T G G Senghore, S M Sissoho, Salieu M Cham and, latterly, Dr Jabez Ayo Langley and Abdou Sara Janha. By 1970 when we became a republic, the cream of the civil service had been formed. Gradually, our indigenisation programme matured and progressed while we did our very best as politicians to make policies and enact laws that would be attractive to Gambian graduates abroad to bring them back home.

19

Independence

In March 1963, after only ten months in office, we again requested Governor Paul to address the council on the necessary constitutional amendments that would set us on the way to internal self-government. The governor showed great accommodation by telling me confidentially beforehand his thoughts and discussions with the Colonial Office on the biggest issue we had on our agenda. Movement in that direction hinged on four issues, prime among them, changing the nomenclature of Executive Council to the Cabinet and from the nomenclature of Premier to Prime Minister.

When Governor Paul addressed the council he spelt out the important issues we would have to deal with as a matter of urgency. The new government would need to cover pensions and gratuities for public servants, especially the large number of expatriates who would continue in the service of The Gambia under the new dispensation. The portfolios of Defence and Internal Security, the governor said, would have to remain under the purview of Her Majesty's Government but should be handed over to a minister with the governor retaining overriding control. Her Majesty's Government would not surrender entirely its ultimate responsibility in this field until independence. However, in the interim, a degree of delegation was negotiable. The new laws would give the Public Service Commission an executive mandate.

The leader of the DCA, the Rev J C Faye, addressed long handwritten treatises to me on 9 July 1963 on his fear and according to him, that of the backbenchers in the House that 'self-government' was the colonialists' tactic to delay independence. I wrote back to say that I did not perceive that difference in the attitude in the House and that there was really nothing to fear. Self-government, I assured the Rev Faye, was a sign that the colonial government was actively thinking our way, and that I believed self-government would take us a step further towards independence.

We refrained from putting the challenge the DCA was urging us to put to the governor; instead, we slowed down according to the governor's advice and waited. I promised, as the governor had advised, to keep it confidential up until London made up its mind. There were stumbling blocks, however. Not everyone was convinced, least of all Deputy

Governor Paul Gore, who, during the governor's short absence from the jurisdiction, was worried that it was only comparatively recently that the 1962 Constitution conferred a substantial measure of autonomy on The Gambia. He wrote to the secretary of state on 29 July 1963 wondering if we were not being too hasty about internal self-government, which he said was the final stage to independence and consequently the steady reduction of our financial dependence on Britain.

We would, nonetheless, press on with our demand, confident that the issue of financial support was never going to be a stumbling block to our independence. We were already set in our attitude as we expressed clearly in London in 1961 and would do so again in 1964 at the Independence Talks that The Gambia intended to remain in the Commonwealth, to keep Britain as its prime partner in our development and to open our country up to friendships and collaboration with every other country that would be disposed to befriend us. Union with Senegal for us was not an option; and, as many times as it came up in colonial insinuation or direct policy suggestion, we nipped it in the bud. Independence was our goal and our relations with our neighbour would be studied more closely, preferably by independent international experts.

In the background, P S Njie, leader of the opposition, was deliberately absenting himself from meetings of the Legislative Council that addressed anything that sounded like internal self-government. I was however determined to see to it that such a momentous advance in the life of our country should be one that was achieved by a general consensus. Accordingly, I sent letters to the leader of the opposition inviting him to form with us a common front to consider the draft instruments for a proposed Order-in-Council to be presented to Her Majesty's Government. P S Njie, for reasons best known to him, refused outright to be part of that consultation.

His brother, E D Njie, sent us a reply on 25 July 1963 stating that the opposition could not meet with us on 29 July as we proposed because the party leader was away in London. E D Njie was deputy party leader and we therefore saw no reason why with the opportunity of such profound political development he could not have stepped in. H R Monday, the clerk of council, issued a reply under my instruction that the opposition should appreciate that some urgency should be attached to completing the legal drafting and discussions necessary to implement the proposed constitutional changes. Monday was then instructed to write back stating that since the all-party discussions were stalled due to the opposition's failure to attend, I was still willing to postpone the meeting for a few days.

E D Njie still made an excuse of his brother's absence in his letter of 31 July 1963, which Gore described as friendly but procrastinating. The fact was that he was clinging to the same query his brother had raised in London in 1961 that there should be another general election before the achievement of full internal self-government. The clerk of council, under my instruction, sent another terse reply that there was no indication anywhere of any agreement to hold elections before the tabling of the issue of internal self-government. We also asked them to indicate whether or not they agreed that the multi-party consultations should take place. We could see that it had nothing to do with his brother's absence. It was their party's policy not to talk about independence under the aegis of the PPP government.

In accordance with the agreements reached with the United Kingdom, The Gambia attained full internal self-government on Friday 4 October 1963. It was the first indication to the Gambian people that we were indeed on our way to fulfilling the promise of self-determination. We declared the day a public holiday. I addressed the nation on Radio Gambia and took the salute at a march past of uniformed and voluntary units in front of the Government Wharf in Wellington Street.

It was during that talk to the nation that I most fully appreciated how absolutely essential the improved services of radio were in reaching the people. From then on I frequented the airwaves to remind my compatriots of the fact that we should take into account that many problems lay ahead, but with tolerance, understanding and a country united in the national interest behind its freely elected government, I was convinced we would be able to progress steadily towards our ultimate goal of independence. I found it always important to keep the focus on the spiritual as well as physical journey that brought us to the point of asking Britain to grant us our fullest rights as an independent nation. I had every reason to broadcast those messages because of the many and varied shades of understanding and interest in the groups that made up the government.

In forwarding self-reliance as our watchword, I realised that there would be basic difficulties with the unwritten rules of engagement. It would be prone to many interpretations. Democracy and what it meant and how it was to be executed often fell prey to malpractice. I had on many occasions found myself having to dig my feet in to ensure that there was no misuse of it, no matter how easy the short cuts or how inconvenient it was for the individual or for the party. This insistence on democratic principles did not endear me to many people inside and outside the PPP or within the government itself. Some people thought too much democracy in the face of political exigencies was utter luxury. Often I had to insist on curbing some undemocratic tendencies some individuals would want us to perpetrate in the name of the party or of the government.

Much of our self-reliance was, however, undermined, not by falling short of democratic principles or practices but by the state of the economy. We would continue to seek from the British government between one quarter and one third of the funds we needed to pay for our normal recurrent expenditure in 1962. In looking at internal correction to the economy I thought it was undesirable that our retail trade would be entirely in the hands of non-Gambians. I also did not feel comfortable with the trade that was seasonal, with certain essential goods being scarce for months at a time. As always, the key to our activity had lain in the fate of our groundnut crop. Thus, through drastic reductions in export duty, GOMB was able to restore the balance of the Farmers' Fund to its original purpose, namely price stabilisation, which enabled government to offer farmers a price of £27 per ton with reasonable safety. Since this was the equivalent of prices in Senegal the economy was well stimulated, especially with a satisfactory improvement in the world price for the crop going into 1962.

It was my view that although GOMB was operating well in buying groundnuts, as a government we wished it gradually to have its services taken over by the farmers themselves in cooperative societies. When we could get GOMB away from buying then there would be money saved to invest in new enterprises such as housing, construction, roads, mechanical garages, tyre rethreading and fish, meat and vegetable packing. There was the hotel and catering industry too. In a speech to the Chamber of Commerce, I reminded them of the statement by the British public figure, Sir Hugh Foot, who once said: "One hotel is a risk, two hotels are a resort; three hotels a Riviera". With only one hotel – the Atlantic Hotel – operating in The Gambia at the time, I challenged them to growth and expansion, especially with the possibilities of a tourism industry. We should seek to become at once a resort and a Riviera within a few years.

But first, the party in government had to take stock of what we had in human and natural resources to successfully handle such growth and expansion. The PPP soon needed to examine its own reality. In April 1963, we gathered at the Crab Island School hall for the first National Party Congress of the PPP, chaired by my former teacher, M D Salla, whose personal touch gave the event a heightened significance. There, in the presence of invited high-powered delegates from the ruling Parti Socialiste of Senegal and representatives of the Democratic Congress Alliance with whom we had forged a closeness towards national unity, we reviewed the achievements of the four-year-old party and hammered our programmes and objectives for the future.

Not only was there a need to share that understanding with the people, there was also a great need to step outside the confines of our borders to reach friends sympathetic with and supportive of our becoming a nation. Senegal got our prime attention. In fact, as soon as we were ready to take stock of our progress at our first party congress, we received a high-ranking PS delegation from Senegal. Their head of delegation, Harr N'dofen Diouf, delivered a special message from President Leopold Sedar Senghor.

Addressing the congress on Friday 5 April 1963, I set the tone for the importance in contemporary Gambia of the four years since the PPP was founded. The party, I said, had pioneered developments which any African national movement could be proud of. It was time to take stock of our past activities, determine our future targets and discuss important matters of policy. Needless to say, the goals we had set ourselves were highly complicated and, therefore, could not be achieved all at once. I outlined the goals as being, first, our desire for independence, a demand which was clearly in evidence in the numerous resolutions submitted by the constituencies on the issue. Second, there was our desire also to develop our country by improving agricultural methods and increasing the production of food and cash crops. Third, we were convinced that this country had the potential for the development of tourism and we promised to do everything possible to stimulate it. Fourth, we would like to have an economy stimulated by industry and by improved communications.

I recognised the generous help that the United Kingdom was giving us, exemplified by an outright grant to The Gambia only a few days before of £146, 000 to enable us to start work on Yundum Airport whose completion was estimated to be July the same year. Although I could not disclose details of the government's development programme which was still on the drawing board, I hinted at an unprecedented size of the development expenditure and expressed the hope that a large share of it would go to agriculture and communications. This was important to break down the barriers between the colony and the protectorate. It was our dream to build one country; it was a campaign promise.

These were to remain our central preoccupation at the domestic and external levels for the rest of 1963 and into 1964 – putting our future in perspective and talking to Britain about how to go about creating the requisite political dispensation and ensuring the financial support that would help achieve our objectives. Those objectives included our foreign policy engagements which meant we would have to have not only a strong and dedicated team at home, but also the requisite foreign policy initiatives that would lead to the right circle of friends. It was important how we chose our friends; because we would have to share with them the ideas we set out in the 1964-1966 Development Plan.

On 23 July 1964, representatives of government, political parties, chiefs and members of civil society assembled at Marlborough House, London, for The Gambia's Independence Conference. I sat across the table from Secretary of State for the Colonies - The Right Honourable Duncan Sandys and negotiated the terms and conditions of independence for my country.

In his address of welcome, Sandys harped on the country's need for financial assistance in which the crucial support of Britain was envisaged. He, to my satisfaction, said that we all realised that independence was not all about money. It was also a question of hard work, careful planning and the development of a sense of unity and common purpose in our country. That, he said, was the special challenge faced not only by our government but also by all our people.

I had to remind him of a few salient points about his country creating the difficult geography that now reduced our capacity to function anywhere beyond the north and south riverbanks, with no land for serious agriculture and no land either for serious grazing of our cattle and other ruminants. Small and close herding hurt animals and lowered their resistance to disease. The lack of land was one direct result of the bad choices the British negotiated with the French in setting the borders of The Gambia.

I argued that as things had turned out, the peculiar position of our boundaries had impeded the natural flow of trade and prevented the full use of our one great natural asset – the River Gambia. Our small size and the narrow basis of our agriculture, based as it was entirely on one cash crop – groundnuts – severely limited our ability to become self-supporting at a reasonable level of services.

I made it clear that there was going to be no dumping of our country, not after three hundred years and a shape that left no choice but to work with partners and friends all over the world if we must survive. We were ready to take our governance in our own hands and we were ready to do so within the Commonwealth. There was no giving in to a surreptitious merger with Senegal, without our proper exercise of self-determination.

I assured the British government of our readiness to face with confidence the challenges the secretary of state had outlined. I underlined that with hard work and the help of those nations which believed in the right of people to self-determination and independence, we would make our independence a reality.

While insinuating pessimism saying he hoped independence would not interrupt the Gambian way of life, P S Njie requested a referendum before independence was granted. I emphasised that The Gambia's reputation as a peaceful, friendly and law-abiding country was well known and that I was proud of the political stability the country enjoyed. I promised our continuance of the practice of democratic principles that Britain had bequeathed to us and that had made the country a shining example of democracy. In the end, the opposition had its say and the government had its way.

I represented the government and was accompanied by Sheriff Sekouba Sisay, Sheriff Mustapha Dibba, Alieu Badara Njie, Amang Kanyi, Seyfo Omar Mbakeh, Kalilou Singhateh, Famara Wassa Touray and Paul L Baldeh. P S Njie led the opposition side and with him were I A S Burang John Kebba W Foon and I M Garba Jahumpa of the GMC. The Gambia government officials were Philip R Bridges, FDC Williams, K J W Lane and the Rev J C Faye whom our government had already posted to London as our liaison officer. Governor Paul was also in attendance. The working sessions opened under the general chairmanship of the Marquess of Lansdowne with the rest of the UK representation of Sir John Martin, J M Kirsch, H Steel, and R G Pettitt. With a professional secretariat provided by the UK government, the talks proceeded through ten sessions stretching until 30 July.

We heard all sides on all the issues that were laid on the table. Eventually, we reached important agreements among which were The Gambia Independence Constitution, the structure of the civil service, appointments to senior positions and to the Public Service Commission, citizenship, constituency boundaries, the overseas aid scheme, the monarchy and membership of the Commonwealth and future relations with Senegal. Above all, we agreed on a date for independence.

On 30 July, we held the last session of the meeting to conclude business. The Rt Hon Duncan Sandys was in the chair. He said he had an important announcement to make before the end of the conference. The United Kingdom was going to grant independence to The Gambia. It was however sad, as I recall, that on the side of the opposition, only I M Garba Jahumpa remained in session there to hear such a historic announcement. Where were the others? They had obviously betaken themselves to other pursuits around London. Our government team, the UK representatives and Governor Paul stayed the course to hear the secretary of state for the colonies confirm that the country would become independent on 18 February 1965. He also announced that The Gambia would, on attaining independence, seek membership of the Commonwealth and that Her Majesty the Queen would become Queen of The Gambia.

In my closing remarks I lauded our very long association with Britain and expressed the hope that the granting of independence to The Gambia would mark not only the end of a phase of that association, but also the beginning of a new, close and friendly one in many fields. Jahumpa, in his closing statement, apologised for his late arrival at the conference. He praised the British government for the excellent arrangements but said he wished to make a last-minute observation that whatever happened between then and the next general elections, no major step should be taken in connection with our association with Senegal without a referendum. He associated himself with my remarks of the conference being a historic event that marked the end of one and the beginning of a new phase between Britain and The Gambia. That done, the four of us – the Rt Hon Duncan Sandys, Lord Lansdowne, Sheriff Sisay and I – proceeded to sign the document sealing the future of The Gambia.

Back home after the conference in London, Governor Paul, in his address to the House of Representatives, made the official announcement of Her Majesty the Queen's assent on 17 December 1964 to The Gambia Independence Act 1964. The House received the announcement with tremendous approval. Governor Paul also announced Her Majesty's approval of my recommendation for him to serve as the first Governor General under the new constitution under which he would not in any way be responsible to Her Majesty or to any minister of her government but to the government in Bathurst. Only a few years later, in 1970, a close reading of this rubric would have helped Sir Farimang Singhateh, our second governor general, to avoid the acrimony and misunderstanding of where the authority of his office derived. It would have helped him and his closest advisers to better understand our quest for republicanism and probably would not have publicly opposed it as he did, seeing it as a threat to his office.

The British government promised support to both our capital and recurrent needs while we were committed to continuing our efforts to decrease our dependence on assistance from Britain. The Queen's statement emphasised our commitment to improving the economy and ensuring the government's total subscription to the rule of law. In furtherance of the welfare of the people there was entrenched in the new constitution embodying the supreme law of the land, the protection of the fundamental rights and freedoms, including the right to personal liberty, freedom of expression, freedom of association, freedom of movement and freedom from any form of discrimination.

I fully endorsed Queen Elizabeth's sentiment that The Gambia's ability to achieve independence by peaceful and constitutional means must be attributed, in no small measure, to the devotion to duty of the country's civil servants, both overseas and Gambian, and, above all, to the good sense and restraint of all its people. This, she said, was a matter of profound satisfaction to Her Majesty's Government.

During my broadcast to the nation on the eve of independence, a few hours before we entered what can be described as a new era in the constitutional history of The Gambia, I paid tribute to all who had contributed to our country's evolution and development – all those political leaders who had preceded us, some of whom were no longer with us. I did not forget the missionaries, who, over a century before, had laid down the foundation of our education system. I paid tribute to the public servants, both Gambian and overseas, who had given their best to lay down a sound foundation for our civil service and to those who had given unstintingly of their time and energy in voluntary service to their country and their fellows. The biggest tribute was however reserved for the Gambian people in all walks of life. Without them all the efforts would have been to no avail – if they had not recognised their birthright to freedom and independence and pursued their goal, not only with determination, but also with patience, tolerance and understanding.

At a solemn ceremony in MacCarthy Square, in the early hours of a chilly and dew-drenched morning, on 18 February 1965, the final curtain on the colonial era fell with the lowering of the British Union Jack for the last time. In its place was unfurled the red, blue, green and white colours of the Gambian flag. That momentous occasion was the final act closing more than three hundred years of our colonial experience. It was a moving moment, a moment I would cherish forever. The weeklong celebrations, which had begun three days before Independence Day, were fitting and were marked with fireworks, beautiful lantern parades, drumming, dancing and wrestling. I hosted our chief guests, HRH the Duke of Kent and his graceful consort, HRH the Duchess of Kent, the government and a cross section of the Gambian business and civic communities to a garden party on the Government House grounds.

I had already received the constitutional instruments from His Royal Highness and requested that he convey our gratefulness to Her Majesty the Queen. I reassured Her Majesty that we were a nation who liked to think that the orderly nature of our people could contribute something to the peace and stability of our continent. For that reason we intended not only to concern ourselves solely with our domestic affairs but also to align ourselves on the side of the world's peaceful forces, particularly with our friends in Senegal, and to contribute, in every way possible, to the establishment of peace among peoples.

During the march past of schoolchildren and voluntary and uniformed contingents, I reminded the country's future leaders of their responsibility to build on the foundations that were being laid for them. I gave my constant word of caution, namely that in the process of building the country we envisaged we must understand that independence would not turn our groundnuts into diamonds. It required a great deal of hard work. It was in that determination that lay the success of what we would make of our independence. I am proud to state that I had a cabinet of responsible and determined ministers assisted by a corps of senior civil servants made up of Gambians and those expatriates who had decided they would stay on. We had the good fortune to have a dedicated person to assume the office of Governor General.

From 1960 to 1965, the country's economy was running at the 30 percent deficit between what we produced and what we needed to function as a government. Our total revenue of £9 million continued to need the support from British grants of some £5 million to meet our recurrent and development expenditure. As long as that relationship persisted, there were doubts about our ability to sustain our governance and meet the responsibilities of an independent nation. There were many sceptics, one of them Berkeley Rice, the American author of the book *Enter Gambia: The Birth of an Improbable Nation,* who doubted our chances of surviving as an independent nation.

On the contrary, convinced that we could improve markedly on the status quo, we concentrated our energies on areas that would show signs of our growth with agriculture on the top of our priorities. The increase in food and cash crops was an underpinning factor in the welfare of the people. Only a strong, healthy and well-fed people could find the energy and the will to contribute to nation-building. A way forward was the development of policies and the wherewithal to diversify the economy away from groundnuts and thus increase our export potential. The commercial and industrial sectors also came into focus; and prime among them was the tourism industry, potentially a major foreign exchange earner.

Along with that, we listed river transport, roads, wharves and ports, the narrowing of the income differential between rural and urban workers and ensuring that we kept prices within the reach of the ordinary citizen.

My mother, Aja Mama Fatty

My stepmother, Aja Jarai Kijera

My stepmother
Aja Mamanding Giyena

My guardian Ebrima Jallow (Pa Yoma)

With my stepmother Sira Sukoh, during
a visit to Barajaly in 1992

Augusta with l-r: Nacesay, Dawda, Kawsu, Almami and Nema

Augusta chatting with President L S Senghor of Senegal

My sister Fatou Kess

Back row l-r: Foday, Mustapha, Ebrima and Momodou
Front row l-r: Mariam, Baby Njaimeh and Fatoumata

My sister Na Isata

My sister Sainabou

My brothers - Alagie (left) and Abdoulie

On a sailing boat with Mariam (sitting beside me),
Fatoumata (with the doll) and Foday (looking up)

l-r: Chilel, Momodou and Njaimeh

Nema, the family archivist

Foday, in dress uniform of the British Army, 2008

l-r: Foday, Mustapha, Ebrima, their friend Pa Malick Kinteh and Scout Master Sam Sarr, 1985

Back row l-r: Foday, Momodou, Almami, Ebrima, Housainou and Dawda
Front row l-r: Ramatoulie, Baby Chilel, Kawsu, Baby Njaimeh, Njaimeh
Taken during Baby Njaimeh's wedding to Richard Asamoah-Owusu, 1998

Housainou and Baby Chilel in the
drawing room at 40 Atlantic Blvd, 2004

Ramatoulie, 2004

My brother Basadi

My brother Kawsu Nding

My brother Saikounding

My brother Tasili

My brother Sheriffo

My brother Kawsu Kebba

My sister Marie

My sister Nacesay

My sister Turunding

My sister Jarai

My sister Nano Nding

With Governor Sir Edward Windley, 1963

In London with the Secretary of State for the Colonies - Duncan Sandys

United Party Leader P S Njie, I M Garba Jahumpa and M B Jones in London

In London with Governor Sir John Paul

PPP /DCA alliance, l-r: A S C Able Thomas, Alh I M Garba Jahumpa, Sheriff Sisay, Rev J C Faye, me and Pochi Samba

Standing l-r: Alh Sir Alieu S Jack, Sheriff Sisay, Sheriff M Dibba, J L B Daffeh, Fansu Demba, Sabilo Secka, Yaya Ceesay, Bashiru Jagne, S B Foon. Sitting l-r: K N Leigh, me, I M Garba Jahumpa, A B Njie and Famara Wassa Touray

With HRH the Duke of Kent meeting schoolchildren on Independence Day, 1965

Sir Farimang Singhateh (first indigenous Governor General of The Gambia) and his wife Lady Singhateh (Aja Fanta Basse)

Jombo Bojang, a stalwart of the PPP

Famara Wasa Touray, a former PPP National President

Sanjally Bojang (left), former PPP National President and Fabala Kanuteh, a PPP militant

Bakary Marong, a PPP militant

At the inauguration of President Yahya A J J Jammeh at the
Independence Stadium in Bakau in January 2007
L-r: Aja Ashombi Bojang (President Jammeh's mother), me,
President Jammeh and Njaimeh

With President Jammeh during celebrations
marking The Gambia's 41st Independence Anniversary at the
July 22nd Square, February 2006

Addessing the United Nations General Assembly in New York, 1966

Received on arrival in Dakar by Senegalese Prime Minister Mamadou Dia (middle) and General Fall, far left

Sharing a joke with Ghana's President Hilla Limann and Tanzania's Julius Nyerere, 1980

At 10 Downing Street with British Prime Minister Harold Wilson

With Kwame Nkrumah of Ghana in Accra for OAU Summit, 1965

With Chilel during our first meeting with Chairman Mao of
The Peoples Republic of China

At an OAU summit having a side
meeting with Libyan leader
Muammar Gaddafi

With President Olusegun
Obassanjo of Nigeria

Showing Senegalese President L S
Senghor the PPP symbols

At the 1978 OAU Summit with Presidents Moussa Traore of Mali, Omar Bongo of Gabon, Gnassingbe Eyadema of Togo and Kenneth Kaunda of Zambia.

At the Oval Office with U S President George H W Bush

Posing (I am in the front row, 2nd from the left) with members of the Africa Forum in South Africa, 2006

1987 Commonwealth Heads of Government Meeting held in Vancouver
(I am sitting in the front row, second from the left)

Discussion with Ghana's President Jerry J Rawlings in Banjul, 1994

Sitting with British Prime Minister Margaret Thatcher during 1989 CHOGM in Malaysia. Commonwealth Secretary General Sir Shridath Surendranath Ramphal sitting with arms folded

With Senegalese President Abdou Diouf on board Lady Chilel during the signing of the Kaur Declaration, 1982.

At the UN HQ in New York with UN Secretary General Boutros Boutros-Ghali, 1995

In Morocco during the King Hassan II Trophy with HRH Crown Prince Sidi Mohammed (now King Mohammed VI) and Njaimeh, 1985

With Chilel and HRH the Duke of Edinburgh on board HMS Britannia in Banjul

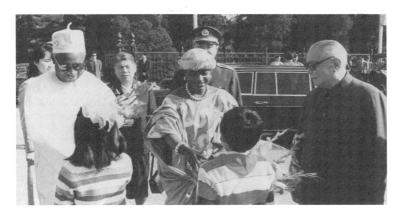

With Chilel on our 3rd visit to the Peoples Republic of China

With Njaimeh and HRH the Princess Royal at a State House reception, during our 20th independence Anniversary celebrations.

With Alh Sir Alieu S Jack (Standing), Cheikh Ibrahim Abdoulah Niass and "Pochi" Samba

PGA Tour Pro Lee Trevino (far right) and British TV personality Bruce Forsythe (second from right) at British Caledonian sponsored pro-am golf tournament

Opening the Banjul-Barra Ferry Terminal during the 13th Independence Anniversary celebrations

Flanked by Minister of Finance Sheriff Sisay during opening of Central Bank Building

PPP Minister of Education Alieu E W F Badjie

Kukoi Samba Sanyang and some of his co-conspirators
Left to right: Kukoi Samba Sanyang, Dembo Manneh, Baba Joof, Unknown, Abdou Mbuka Sarr, Alagy Jammeh, Momodou Sambou, Sub-Inspector Fansu Camara, Corporal Metta Camara and Field Force driver Momodou Ceesay, 1981

Taking the Salute at the Independence Stadium during Army Day.

Being received by Speaker Alh Sir Alieu S Jack during a State Opening of Parliament

Once again a veterinarian, inoculating cattle during the 1968 rinderpest campaign

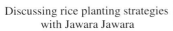

Discussing rice planting strategies with Jawara Jawara

On the campaign trail in 1992

Being awarded the Diploma of Fellowship of the Royal College
of Veterinary Surgeons (FRCVS)

Sitting (Teachers) l-r: B S O Jeng, A B Sallah, Tamasa Jarra, Master Williams, I M Garba Jahumpa, Ousainou Jobe and Abdoulie A Njie.
Standing (students) l-r: Mbye John, Assan Senghore, Amara Batchilly, me (holding the prized standard seven photo for coming first in the Gambia in the 1939 Standard 7 examinations), Kaba Gaye and Liety Njie

Sering Modou Sillah

Receiving an honorary degree of Doctor of Laws
Honoris Causa from the University of Ife, Nigeria, 1978

Frisky, 2008

On board Sir Adam Thomson's yacht off
Minorca, Spain

With nursing staff of the Royal Victoria Hospital

With laboratory staff of the
Royal Victoria Hospital

My cherished Morris Minor

Chatting with then Gambian Honorary Consul to Germany – Englebert Eichner at a reception in State House during an Independence day celebration

At Loro Parque with l-r: Wolfgang Kiessling, Thai Ambassador, MomodouBobb and Momodou L Kassama

Everything we did or would do in the future would therefore have to be directed at reducing our dependence on grants-in-aid. We could not forget that that was the single factor everyone pointed to as the determinant of our independence. But at the same time we kept our focus on the fact that independence was not all about money. The expansion of social services to improve on the basic conditions of the people was crucial to our mission. In the background to all these measures we strove for the fullest indigenisation of our administrative machinery in order to ensure loyalty and patriotism that would also reduce our dependence on expatriate capacity. Only then would our independence have any real meaning.

20

International relations

The first thing we learnt after independence was the absolute need for interdependence with our neighbours. The build-up to independence was exciting; the celebration of it went on with a great deal of exuberance and expectation. All of that of course died down as we got on with the real work in government. So I did not fail to make the point that the reality of it was that independence would have to be backed by selfless hard work on the part of everyone for the realisation of its promises.

The job of any African leader would have been much easier had independence meant managing domestic issues and ruling one's people in pristine isolation from the rest of the world. Although life may have been much the same externally, independence was preparing us to make our voice heard in the international sphere. Because of that interdependence, no one would or could grow in isolation.

We set out with a firm conviction that The Gambia must take its place beside the rich and powerful and its message needed to be taken and presented. We strongly believed that the peaceful and friendly nature of our people was a gift we could bring to the African continent and to the world to show that our people's brand of tolerance and understanding had something to teach and that was what we had to offer by aligning ourselves with the world's peaceful forces.

Our country's application to join the United Nations had been sponsored by the United Kingdom, Malaysia, Jordan and the Ivory Coast and the Security Council had prepared a recommendation to be put forward to the General Assembly at its meeting slated for September 1965. Indeed, after we were admitted, I addressed the UN General Assembly on 21 September 1965 at its 20th Session and spoke of our becoming one of the smallest countries to have acceded to international sovereignty and explained the deep sense of pride and humility with which The Gambia had taken its rightful place in the family of nations.

We began initially by setting up a mail box at UN headquarters and asked a Gambian national, Pa Puye Njie, a long-time resident in the New York area, to deal with correspondence in a private capacity. That arrangement went on until February 1979 when we sent Hassum Ceesay in our foreign service as Counsellor-in-Charge to open the diplomatic mission in Washington, and, a month later, in New York. We then sent Ousman Sallah to Washington DC as Ambassador with the added portfolio of Permanent Representative to the UN. This way, we established a small presence, with Ceesay as Counsellor and Galandou Gorée-Ndiaye as Mission Secretary, which was all we needed at the time.

Senegal had sponsored our membership of the OAU at the Meeting of Foreign Ministers held in Nairobi in February 1965. We recognised the OAU as the main forum where Africans could together examine their common problems in search of unity, solidarity and peace. We were also aware that we were being accepted into the continental body at a time when it was going through a crisis brought about by the divergent attitudes of member countries on a number of problems, particularly the Congo.

I had since those early days viewed with concern the developments both in the Congo and in Rhodesia. Those two countries were still matters of high priority in my agenda when I addressed the 4th Session of the OAU in Kinshasa from 11 to 14 September 1967 in which I highlighted the situations in the two countries as threats to the very foundation of our sovereignty and unity. I said the perpetrators were bent on violating the territorial integrity and sovereignty of those countries.

I raised decolonisation as a major issue confronting Africa and a deciding factor on how fast we moved towards achieving unity. The situation with the liberation movements needed our urgent attention. The sad aspect of them was the disunity that was manifest between rival factions. It had to be understood that the accelerated development of the colonial territories depended on their ability to present a united front. I remembered President Joseph Mobutu of the Congo describing the OAU summit of 1966 as the 'summit of wisdom'; I prayed that the 1967 summit would be characterised as the 'summit of realism'. It would have to take realism to solve the problems of the consolidation of independence, not only politically but also economically.

It was of great satisfaction to me that before we left Kinshasa the OAU was firmly resolved to work for the defence of the independence of the Congo, for the crushing of the white-led rebellion in Rhodesia and for the introduction of majority rule in that country towards the full independence of Zimbabwe. The same was to be accorded to resistance movements in Angola, Guinea Bissau, Cape Verde and Mozambique that were under oppression from Portugal.

Given The Gambia's good reputation as a democratic, peaceful and stable country, it was no surprise that in 1987 the OAU decided to locate the African Commission on Human and Peoples' Rights (ACHPR) in Banjul. Consequently, in line with Article 25 of the OAU Charter enjoining countries to educate their citizens on their rights, privileges and obligations, my government created a national human rights institution that in 1989 became the continental civil society flagship, the African Centre for Democracy and Human Rights Studies.

We were proud of the consistency of our message and the sincerity with which we presented it to the world. It was the same when we first came out after independence to attend the Commonwealth Prime Ministers' Conference, which was held in London in early July 1965. We seized this opportunity to build bridges with the eighteen countries that welcomed The Gambia to the body of former British colonies and dependencies. Alieu Badara Njie (then Minister of External Affairs) and I joined the four other national delegations from Africa. It was a pleasant welcome. We fortified our historic links with the host, Britain, and then drove in the pylons for sound and fruitful bridges with the other new friends.

In mid-1966, it was with great honour and pride that I received my knighthood from Queen Elizabeth II, at Buckingham Palace.

Later that year in November, I accepted the invitation of the editors, G P Gooch and Dominic Le Foe, to place my thoughts in the centenary year edition of the *Contemporary Review* to spell out a future for the Commonwealth. Then the troubles within the Commonwealth family were so tense and so racially and regionally divisive that the Australian Prime Minister, Harold Holt, in the same edition, admitted his doubts as to whether the new and mixed interest within the Commonwealth was not a threat to its survival. He explored the key elements of expansion that needed to be addressed if the family body was to remain relevant.

The significance of the Commonwealth as an international body would have been lost had growth been arrested at the five-member stage. The Commonwealth would in effect have consisted largely of Britain and the extension overseas of people of British descent. With its membership of 23 it embraced people of almost all races and religions scattered all over the globe. It included big states and small states, some of them highly developed and others developing, or frankly, underdeveloped. A miniature UN, one might say, but with a difference; it had only one-fifth of the membership of the world organisation and was therefore a little cosier. It had only one official working language and since, like most institutions of British origin, it had no constitution or set of rules, it was less formal. With the Queen as head, the free association of the member nations was warmly personified.

Holt's basic question of whether the Commonwealth could survive gave rise, first of all, to another question: Has it sufficient continuing value to its members to justify the efforts needed to ensure survival? Members of the "old" Commonwealth, looking for a basis for unity to emerge, might feel that they would look in vain. The newer members, perhaps somewhat less concerned with unity, might nevertheless conclude that they perceived too many policy differences of a fundamental kind. Holt's view was crucial to the entire structure and cohesiveness of the body, considering the major issues facing the various members of the group. Britain was busy with all kinds of measures aimed at strengthening the pound sterling, measures which did not exclude reduction in assistance to emerging member states with economies as dependent as The Gambia's was.

In my short and frank submission, I spilled from the heart that at the September meeting of Commonwealth Prime Ministers, the overriding feeling about the Commonwealth was one of crisis. The prevalent view, widely expressed, was that the organisation might face the possibility of a large-scale withdrawal of members over the intractable problem of Rhodesia, because of what was described as a 'crisis of confidence' in Britain's handling of the Rhodesian rebellion. For us and the other African members, our relationship with the Commonwealth was discoloured by tacit influences on the continued rebellion of the white minority regime in Salisbury of the complacent "white" old Commonwealth. In addition, British Prime Minister Harold Wilson's unfortunate over-optimistic assessment in Lagos of the effect of sanctions in bringing about political change in Salisbury in only a matter of weeks only increased the sense of disappointment and frustration in African members.

I did not wish to imply by what I just said that it was only the African, Asian and Caribbean members who felt strongly about the attempt by Rhodesia to consolidate a minority racist regime in a British colony. As far as I could discern, there was unanimity among all members about objectives, namely an early ending of the rebellion and the establishment of a democratic and just society in which all sections of Rhodesian society would enjoy equal rights and equal opportunities. Owing to the complex nature of the situation, however, views about how to achieve such a solution were bound to differ considerably. In view of the wide publicity which had been accorded to Rhodesia it was unnecessary to enter here into a discussion of the various remedies suggested.

If anyone had asked for my view of the future of the Commonwealth I would have answered that I was hopeful for continuity judging by the easy way in which the members instinctively drew closer together even when the arguments over Rhodesia got hotter. The unexpressed verdict seemed to have been that it was worth keeping it going as something of value in its own right. The Commonwealth had passed at that meeting a severe test of its capacity to survive – "It has been tested in the heat of the flames" as Mr Wilson put it – but of course the real test lay ahead and was bound up with what actually would happen in Rhodesia. As long as Rhodesia remained unresolved, it would continue to pose a serious threat to the unity and cohesion of the Commonwealth.

However, if the Rhodesian issue were resolved satisfactorily in a few weeks, I could see the Commonwealth coming properly into its own. With the help of the newly established Secretariat, it could come to grips with problems of the century other than the racial one. There were questions such as under-development and the related problems of the worsening terms of world trade against poorer nations, inadequate food production coupled with a rapid increase of population, all of which tended to widen the gap between the standard of living of the rich and that of the poorer nations.

With such a gloomy, unpromising start, it was interesting and gratifying to see the Commonwealth emerge, after nine days of frank discussion, a much stronger organisation than it seemed only two weeks before. Of course, lots of things were said about the Commonwealth in the press, on the radio and television and, no doubt, by large sections of the British public, which showed some misunderstanding of the nature of the modern Commonwealth. Some openly lamented the passing away of the old, small 'white' Commonwealth of Britain, Canada, Australia, New Zealand and South Africa representing people of largely Anglo-Saxon origin, with similar traditions, who had overcome the problem of underdevelopment. One could not imagine the cohesion of such a homogeneous 'club' being shaken to its foundations by a problem such as we faced in Rhodesia. For one thing, one of its members, South Africa, had already successfully imposed a white racist minority government on its twelve million African inhabitants and made the latter citizens without rights.

The evolution of the former British Empire into the modern Commonwealth was one of the most imaginative international happenings of our era. While it derived its strength from such a diversity of races, of cultures, of regions, it also derived its cohesion from certain unifying forces. Language, I wrote, was possibly one of the most important factors keeping the Commonwealth together. It was of great significance that at any Commonwealth gathering, language was never a problem since whatever might be the native tongues of the delegates, be they Gaelic or Mandinka or Yoruba, English served as a *lingua franca* among the educated class, thus making direct personal communication possible and translation, simultaneous or otherwise, unnecessary.

Taking a longer-term view, one possible threat to the continued existence of the Commonwealth in that form was the inevitable development in its member states of regional interests which might conflict with or transcend Commonwealth membership. In Africa, for example, the division of the newly independent states into English-speaking, French-speaking and Portuguese-speaking states was too artificial to last for ever. Already we had seen in the formation of the OAU the first sign of the desire of African leaders to redress the 'balkanisation' of the continent inherited from the colonial period. Though any elimination of colonial frontiers between states to create larger viable units was likely to start at the functional level such as the creation of common markets and common services, it was likely in some areas to reach its logical conclusion of organic union.

If such a process involved a Commonwealth member it was bound to raise a question of definition of membership, but more likely than not, because of its resilience and flexibility a way would have been found around this. After all, the Commonwealth got round the problem of the continued membership of India when the latter became a republic in 1949 and posed what was then quite a knotty problem; in 1961 it survived the expulsion of South Africa; and took in its stride Britain's probable entry into the European Economic Community which was bound to affect considerably the structure of the traditional pattern of Commonwealth trade.

Today, four decades later, the Commonwealth remains vibrant. The activities of the Commonwealth Secretariat in the international affairs seem more coordinated and formalised. Some may still argue about its relevance but to my mind one can say on the whole it has stood the test of time.

It was significant to us that our minister of agriculture was in Rome towards the close of 1965 to attend meetings at which The Gambia became a member of the FAO. The minister of health had taken part in a Commonwealth Medical Conference in Edinburgh and the minister of works and communication had come with me on a visit to Lebanon. The Commonwealth Conference in Lagos from 11 to 12 January 1966 was significant in that The Gambia took its place among its peers to discuss the rebellion in Rhodesia. I lent my voice to those other prime ministers underlining the fact that any political system based on racial discrimination was intolerable, and that the future goal and progress of Rhodesia should be the establishment of a just society based on equality. The meeting ended with a communiqué calling for an end to Ian Smith's Unilateral Declaration of Independence.

We warmed up to the Organisation of Non-Aligned States after the Lusaka meeting of 1970. Although we did not attend that meeting, we were greatly impressed that the Non-Aligned Movement was beginning to make a head way with a dramatic change from the anti-Western dogma that marred the rhetoric of previous resolutions at the Belgrade meeting in 1961 and in Cairo in 1964. We became fully engaged with its bold actions in line with the OAU and the UN against Portuguese aggression in Africa and apartheid in South Africa.

Together with other continental and world bodies, we all called for an increase in support to the freedom fighters in southern Africa. We imposed sanctions against the sale and import of Portuguese arms and armaments to Africa and placed a ban on their handling by African seaports and airports. The Lusaka meeting appointed President Kenneth Kaunda as chairman and charged him with the mandate as spokesman of the Third World to contact, in the most appropriate manner, North Atlantic Treaty Organisation (NATO) countries and, in particular, the US, Great Britain, France, West Germany, Italy, Switzerland, Brazil and Japan to put an immediate end to their assistance which directly or indirectly strengthened white racist oppression in Africa.

We travelled to Tokyo in September 1970 where I was guest of honour at a reception given by the Confederation of Japanese Industries. I held talks with Foreign Minister Aichi and visited Expo 70 in Osaka. There was so much to do and so little time in which to do it. In fact, the delegation had to take the wise decision of splitting up into two to enable us to meet our bridge-building engagements. While I proceeded to Honolulu, Hawaii, External Affairs Minister Andrew Camara and Secretary General Eric Christensen went to North Korea where they finalised discussions on that country's offer to us of large consignments of drugs we badly needed in our health delivery system.

If we were asking the rest of the world for standards, we had to be seen to have the moral authority to do so. It was therefore with a great sense of soberness that the House of Representatives ratified the Treaty on the Non-Proliferation of Nuclear Weapons on 22 October 1970. I happily assented to that bill sent to me by our legislators as it pronounced to the world our stand on peaceful co-existence. I was proud to say we were at peace with all. I pronounced later on at the 25th Meeting of the General Assembly of the United Nations: "We believe in good neighbourliness and friendly cooperation among countries for the common good and I am sure our record in this field will stand the closest scrutiny. We believe in non-interference in the internal affairs of sovereign states. We hold these views and we pursue these policies because we sincerely believe that only in this way can we attain universal peace, without which there can be no true happiness." I reiterated Africa's stand on the situation in southern Africa and the responsibility of the world's major powers to curb the sale of arms to the racist and minority regimes that waged war on the African people. I drew attention to the difficulties of terms of international trade that left some of our developing economies fully stretched. We left New York and headed for Lagos where we were guests at the 1 October celebrations of Nigeria's tenth independence anniversary.

Njaimeh was with me on this successful tour of Africa, Asia and the Pacific and she and I arrived back home to be greeted with the good news of Chilel's delivery of a baby girl on 3 October 1970 at the Royal Victoria Hospital. Chilel had come through very well indeed. We named the child Fatoumata, which celebrated my mother, Mama Fatty's, other name.

On the official front too there was more good news that increased my sense that The Gambia was gaining more friends on the world stage. The government of Cambodia and its leader, Prince Norodom Sihanouk, had been toppled in March 1970 in a coup and the prince had sent a four-man delegation led by a royal envoy, Phan Buoy Hak, to Bathurst. The Cambodian envoy saw Vice President Sheriff Dibba to canvass our support as a member of the Non-Aligned States to uphold the integrity of Cambodia.

Our relations with Mauritania warmed up with the state visit to Bathurst of President Mouktar Ould Daddah in March 1967. I reciprocated the visit a short while later during which I continued to actively pursue the preliminary consultations on a sub-regional economic grouping. We abolished visas between the two countries and Gambian students received scholarships to the Institute of Higher Islamic Studies in Nouakchott. Teachers of Arabic were sent to teach in Gambian schools.

A regular feature in the weekly schedule of the Governor General in the earlier days, and which I took over after April 1970, was to receive letters of commission or credence from diplomats accredited to us confirming our country's decision to work with them. Many of them operated from Dakar; but a number opened up chanceries in Bathurst. Britain was the first, followed by Senegal and the USA, before the influx that brought Guinea, Nigeria, Sierra Leone, North Korea, Libya, and Taiwan. By agreement, Senegal continued to hold brief for us in the countries where we did not open missions.

Early in the life of my administration, we opened two key missions abroad (in London and Dakar) and as contacts matured we expanded with six more in Brussels (covering the EEC), Freetown, Jeddah, Lagos, Tripoli and Washington with representatives being duly accredited to several countries within their respective geographical jurisdictions. Meanwhile, we also opened our doors to important agencies of the EEC and those of the UN such as the FAO and the World Food Programme. By 1994, a myriad of non-governmental organisations and civil society groups had also arrived to set up offices – all within the democratic dispensation - to give technical or professional advice to the government and people of the country. Theirs were vital contributions to our development.

I recall the many interventions I made over the years at the OIC in which I held positions on the executive committee. Every time I spoke the basic principles of peace, tolerance, human rights, oneness of human purpose and a world free of racism and war were paramount. At the OIC Conference held in Taif, Saudi Arabia, from 25 to 28 January 1981, we adopted the Mecca Declaration. For me, the Declaration from the meeting we called the Palestine and Jerusalem Session served all that the Muslim *Ummah* could ever pray for. It contains the noblest principles and values of Islam, whose application and practice stand to change the world for Muslims and for the rest of humankind from one of conflict to peace, from division to unity and harmony. It emphasises the unity of the *Ummah* and commitment to the respect of the sanctity and inviolability of human rights. It rejects racial discrimination and racism and affirms the right of peoples to self-determination and independence and calls for economic cooperation among Islamic states as an eloquent expression of the supreme Islamic values of equality and social justice.

Yet there were daunting issues on the agenda of the OIC. It was a privilege serving on the Islamic Peace Committee and with the added honour of succeeding President Sekou Touré of Guinea to the chairmanship in 1974. That elevation gave The Gambia an even greater responsibility, especially when war broke out between two Muslim states, Iran and Iraq. Well into 1986 when I chaired the Ninth Session of the Peace Committee, the conflict worsened. The rift was typical of those that compromised the true spirit of Islamic unity. There could be neither victor nor vanquished; if anything, it was common enemies of Islam who would benefit. For as long as the *Ummah* was divided instead of closing ranks in a solid alliance it would be difficult, if not impossible, to realise a major objective, that is, the liberation of Palestine!

In my address to colleagues in Taif I reminded the meeting that this was not the first of its kind. In 1924, King Abdul Aziz, founder of the Kingdom of Saudi Arabia, organised an Islamic congress in Mecca. Like the summits of the OIC later, it enabled Muslims throughout the world to discuss and consider matters of common interest. It was important that the *Ummah* met to look for answers to the varied religious, political, cultural, social and economic problems facing the Muslim of today. There was a need for the revitalisation of the fundamental principles of Islam with a view to setting up new perspectives and guidelines for the resolution of the problems in the Muslim world.

I asked for immediate help to cover our food deficit and the means to strengthen the capacity of our members to achieve our cherished goal of food self-sufficiency. More importantly we needed urgent financial assistance to harness the vast surface and underground water resources of our region, especially through the construction of dams to enable us to develop a more reliable form of agricultural production through the wide-scale introduction of irrigation agriculture, and to wrest our agricultural economies from complete dependence on rainfall. I did not spare the conference the evidence that the situation had become critical and that concerted action needed to be taken before it was too late.

But while I appealed for peace and unity and urged that relations among OIC members ought to be determined by Islamic principles which called for unity and solidarity, I seized the occasion to zero in on a domestic situation that was badly affecting stability in my own country at the hands of a fellow-Islamic state. Libya was training subversives and rogue elements to destabilise countries in West Africa, including The Gambia. It was incomprehensible that any member of our *Ummah* should choose to indulge in a policy of destabilisation of another member country. That we were united under Islam required the mutuality of respect, assistance and understanding and excluded subversion, sabotage and interference in the internal affairs of each other's country.

I always looked to the many fair-minded partners in the OIC who had made support available to The Gambia when we needed it most to deal with drought and economic difficulty. Support from the OIC rose to an overall high in 1984 when I reported to Parliament that through the Committee of Islamic Solidarity, the organisation had solicited pledges of US$120 million for an Emergency Food Aid Programme and rural water supply projects for the Sahelian countries. It was in appreciation of such successful relations that I pleaded constantly for the intensification of Afro-Arab cooperation among all Third World countries in order to transform our peripheral and dependent status into one of collective self-reliance and South-South cooperation.

Over the years however we had to sever links with countries whose governments propagated instability among our peace-loving people. We uncovered Libya's involvement in the training and financing of Kukoi Samba Sanyang and his cohorts who, in July 1981, attempted to unseat the legitimate government of my country.

In March 1970, there was a prolonged scarcity of fertiliser that had become a real threat in our farming communities. Fortunately through the active intervention of Rudolf Junges, the West German Ambassador to The Gambia, 2,000 tons of fertiliser promptly arrived to see us through that patch of difficulty. Valued at about £40,000, the fertiliser went straight to the badly-hit farming communities. Over time, the Germans provided some more valuable assistance, especially their gift of a motor launch, the *Mansa Kila Kuta III*, for the Prime Minister's official river travels. In addition, apart from a mission of community development experts that was posted to the URD, they gave three more scholarships for Gambians to study in their country.

Soon after independence, The Netherlands gave us £200. I must hasten to add that this was not a paltry sum. Indeed, it enabled us to acquire the services of the legendary Dutchman, Mr Van der Plas, who worked without a salary, to kick-start a community development programme for The Gambia. Nigeria, fulfilling its promise, sent us a few members of its agricultural staff and other technical assistance, over and above the gift of £10,000 at independence.

Those results certainly accrued from formal and informal contacts in discussions along corridors, at dinners and banquets. Some were finalised on the golf course or at flower shows. These social outlays, the cushions and pillows between which real politics was conducted would be replicated and expanded as 'the game' became more sophisticated as it spread into northern Europe, into the Soviet Union and the Balkans, the Middle and Near East, to China and Japan and on to Latin America, the Caribbean and out into Oceania and Australia. It was important to keep those contacts in our one-world village.

It is impossible to list all the benefits from our missions abroad without mentioning my visit to the UK in October 1967 to attend a conference of the World Veterinary Association. Once again, it was refreshing to be in familiar company with some of the old boys from my days at veterinary school in Glasgow. We shared the latest breakthroughs into veterinary medicine and learnt of new projects being researched for answers to the challenges to animal health worldwide. We looked to the future with much confidence that underdeveloped countries such as The Gambia might well find lasting answers to bovine diseases that continued to ravage so many of their pastoral communities.

We discussed the important projects we had developed and consulted with qualified people who could possibly come and help us run them in the absence of our own qualified personnel to do so immediately. One such contact led me back to W I M McIntyre who was a member of the academic staff at Glasgow when I was a student there. The news of his death on 20 March 2008 at the age of eighty-eight sent my thoughts back to the time in 1963, when he and a couple of other researchers were setting up a veterinary faculty at the University of East Africa, in Nairobi, Kenya, which culminated in his interest in research on bovine trypanosomiasis. At my invitation, he made short visits to Banjul in 1973 and 1974 to assess the traits in our local *ndama* breed and its possible use in the search for a vaccine against trypanosomiasis.[12]

Tests at the Medical Research Council in The Gambia confirmed that our animals showed traits of resistance, which triggered a huge interest among veterinarians in this field of study. McIntrye began work at the International Trypanotolerance Centre (ITC) in 1984. The ITC was established in 1982 by an Act of Parliament. It is an independent research institution that is not for profit. Today, it is one of the leading research units in animal science in Africa and runs a multi-million dollar annual budget. Its research and development agenda is consistent with and pertinent to the current policies of the governments of West Africa. Over the years the Centre has worked closely with its main partners, the National Agricultural Research Institute (NARI) and with reputable institutes in the EU, and individual countries such as Belgium, Italy and Switzerland.

Exchange visits between Dakar and Banjul were regular both at the ministerial and executive levels – a regular in and out-flow of missions attending to the urgent demands of cooperation. There was constant interaction at the more dynamic people-to-people level. For very obvious reasons, we exchanged a great number of missions spanning politics, sports, religion, family and a host of other collaborative disciplines. Our sporting and cultural contingents were proud participants at the first World Festival of Negro Arts in Dakar in 1966. Even with the occasional border tensions flaring up menacingly such as in 1969, 1971 and 1974, it seemed nothing could break up our relations.

Between 1962 and 1981 when he voluntarily retired, President Senghor visited six or more times and I was in Dakar many more times as it took these personal contacts to work out the details of our political and economic future. A uniquely African and courteous recognition existed between us as part of the politico-cultural motif. There was a cultural

---

[12] Trypanosomiasis is an infection carried by the tsetse fly that affects both humans and cattle.

understanding brought about by our homogeneity and the cementing culture that recognised this fact and found its place in the manner of negotiation and concession.

At the sub-regional level, The Gambia was irrevocably committed to bigger issues. Despite the occasional border troubles, both sides in the main respected the various agreements and treaties they had signed. The Gambia, in particular, used the spirit of its collaboration as a living model of what could and must be done in West Africa and across the continent as a whole. As far back as 1968, seven years before ECOWAS was born, I had already formed some solid thoughts on sub-regional integration and on issues pertinent to trade and economic collaboration that I saw as essential to Africa's re-emergence. I laid out that formula in April that year at the OAU summit in Monrovia, namely that regional unity must be speeded up towards the higher goal of continental unity. We used the example of Senegal and The Gambia to encourage other West African countries towards similar agreements with their neighbours.

When ECOWAS became a reality in 1975, the fact of the huge disparities and unfair practices of Western nations against our best interests was glaring. The persistent deterioration of the terms of trade of primary products made it imperative and urgent for us to take concerted action, not only to arrest the adverse trend, but also to consolidate the economies of West African countries into more viable units.

I was deeply concerned that the national per capita income was low and that markets were restricted, in addition to the unacceptable anomaly that the volume of trade between West African countries was small in relation to their trade with the rest of the world. I made a strong case for an urgent need for trade liberalisation with the ultimate goal of complete integration of the economies of West African countries. I told my colleagues that the first step was to develop transport and communications among the group so as to facilitate the free movement of goods and people.

The importance of these international consultations could clearly be seen when one considers how ideas and motions deliberated and agreed at these meetings ultimately filtered down to influencing the domestic scene through the ratification of the protocols by our individual parliaments heralding our compliance with the details of the agreements as partners. It was from ideas like these from ECOWAS heads of state that we derived the elements that went into the protocols of the free movement of persons, inter-country trade, the Brown Card insurance system, etc.

I had long accorded high priority to our foreign affairs outreach to other African states as well. The organisation and what it stood for and the need for Africa's ultimate unification demanded that keen attention be paid to its deliberations. That interest saw me or my ministers on the one hand leading important delegations on business, friendly and peace-building visits to many countries on the continent and, on the other hand, receiving the heads of state and their delegates from a great number. A number of them came only once but others such as Mauritania, Nigeria and Sierra Leone visited more often. One-day visits and airport stopovers, short as they were, came in useful. Indeed, any occasion to exchange notes and update views was very useful in keeping alive the links between us and other African countries.

On many occasions, civil conflicts ravaged the sub-region, thereby reducing all the advantages we could have gained as individual countries. Of all the troubles, however, none would match the loss of life and property as the Biafra War that shook the sovereignty and unity of Nigeria in particular and West Africa as a whole. Even though the war raged from 1967 to 1970, it laid out the negative climate that spurred us towards the formation of a strong sub-regional body, dynamic enough to be a building block towards continental unity.

It was in 1964 that I began my first of many trips to the USA, bringing The Gambia to the attention of the big players in the international arena. During that first visit to Washington as head of government, I had talks over lunch with Under-Secretary of State for Political Affairs, W Averell Harriman. I asked for technical and financial support of the US government to help us make headway with our internally self-governing country waiting to be independent. It was important that we should begin laying the firm foundations for the bridge over which Americans and Gambians would have to walk for the most effective and mutually beneficial exchanges.

I had talks in Washington with US Secretary of State Dean Rusk and shared with him the vision of this small West African country that was launching out into nationhood. I discussed with him ways in which the US could help bring our dreams to fruition.

As the years went by, I met more Americans in the executive and legislative branches. I got on well with President George H W Bush. In 1989 I led a delegation to crucial meetings with the World Bank and took time to meet with him in the Oval Office towards the close of his term as president. He was receptive of The Gambia and commended our attitude to the IMF, whose demanding economic recovery and structural adjustment programmes we had taken on with some success and which he pointed out had drawn fair comments from the Fund. Bush casually remarked that we were the first African or Third World country for that matter that he knew that had anything positive to say about the IMF and the World Bank. I hope that was a compliment, considering what my country had gone through with its structural adjustment programme.

We struck a friendship. A few months later, in February 1990, he delegated his son, Governor of Texas, George Walker Bush, and his wife, Laura, to represent him in Banjul when we celebrated the 25th anniversary of our independence. We rolled out the red carpet and provided tight security headed by a young officer, Lt Yahya Jammeh.

I was deeply touched by a handwritten note from President Bush. I shared the warm sentiments it carried with our Ambassador to the US, Ousman Sallah. The president was wishing me well with the celebration of our country's silver jubilee and was praying for more years of peace and prosperity. He wanted me to know that he was busy preparing for some critical elections ahead and if things went well in November and he was re-elected he was thinking I should come again to the US, this time on an official visit. I was delighted by his kind thoughts and expressions of friendship. My prompt reply to him expressed our thanks for the distinguished delegation he sent, a gesture that would go a long way towards further strengthening the ties of friendship and mutual regard that existed between our two countries and peoples.

I was confident he would do well in the elections and indeed I wished him success in the campaign. I was willing and ready any time to make that official visit. However, the proposed state visit never took place. The November elections came and the Democratic candidate, William Jefferson Clinton, won. Bush ended his one-term tenure in the presidency.

My message to the Americans on our independence and how the bridges could be forged to make them work was the same I took with me to Europe. We kept regular consultations with France, where a large number of Gambian students had graduated from universities such as Besançon, Grenoble, Lille, Lyons, Paris and the Sorbonne. My government was already reaping the benefit of that partnership with trained technicians teaching in Gambian secondary schools, working in the Foreign Service or elsewhere in important translation and interpretation roles in the public and private sectors as well as in the international arena.

French culture and civilisation was rubbing off and was captivating many young students who opted to study French. Among them was Bakary Bunja Dabo, who took a Bachelor of Arts degree in French at the University of Ibadan in Nigeria and later became vice president in my government.

Further visits and discussions in France under President François Mitterrand led to assistance that set up the Gambia Telecommunications

Company (Gamtel). We were fortunate to have an astute and sound technical mind in Bakary Njie in our Telecommunication Department. He played a vital role in the discussions with the French on the communication system that best suited our needs. Bakary later became the Managing Director at Gamtel and, with the support of Caisse Central in Paris, raised it to earn the reputation of being a leading telecommunication company in Africa, second only to that of South Africa.

Over the years, I met with Chancellor Helmut Schmidt and Chancellor Helmut Kohl on separate occasions. More technical assistance came in the form of fleets of MAN buses for the Gambia Public Transport Corporation. I made friends in Munich and I enjoyed many visits with them in Germany's lush Bavarian countryside. One such acquaintanceship that developed into a lasting friendship was that with Engelbert Eichner, whom we fondly called Eich. He proved a true friend of The Gambia and I was glad to approve him as our Consul General in Germany. Eich invited me out on several private visits during one of which I had the opportunity of addressing the Peutinger Collegium in Munich on 14 January 1978. I was installed as Honorary Procurator for Afro-European Dialogue.

I appreciated the honour and devoted my speech to opening friendly contacts between Europe and Africa, emphasising the benefits of friendship between the peoples of the two continents. I dwelt on the principles of democracy and human rights underscoring the importance of world peace, the equality of all human beings and the commonness of our destinies. It was always a pleasure to expound on Afro-European friendship in front of the august gathering of private and professional people of like mind and social orientations. It was a heartfelt honour for me when, in January 1979, the Collegium decorated me with the Peutinger Gold Medal.

Those initial international exposures were good practice which we would fall back on later in the 1980s in having our party forge links with other politically active European organisations such as the Frederich Ebert Foundation. The German foundation specialised in political education and spent quite large sums of money in support of political parties in Africa that had democracy as a central theme and policy. Such a link developed into a partnership with the political bureau of the PPP, which, by our constitution, manifesto and, of course, our general international outlook, was the right make-up for collaboration. Together, we conducted many seminars and workshops in Banjul in which we developed and propagated the tenets of democratic governance.

Increasingly, our relations with Europe were also raising our country's profile as a competitive tourist destination. We worked hard at developing our hotel bed infrastructure from only the Atlantic Hotel in the early 1960s to a chain of city hotels – the Adonis, Palm Grove, Wadner Beach to the more exotic beach resorts of the Sunwing, Fajara, Senegambia, Kairaba and Kombo Beach Novotel that drew the budget sun and sand seekers of Scandinavia, the UK and Germany to the "Smiling Coast." We took the bull by the horns by initially opening offices in Frankfurt and London which raised the number of visitors from the trickling tens in 1967 when the industry began to annual figures running into double digit thousands between the 1980s and 1990s. Quite respectable growth considering the fact that it was only in 1967 that a Scandinavian tour operator, Bertil Harding, brought over the first planeload of Swedish tourists to kick-start the industry.

Today, The Gambia enjoys on- and off-season tourism which has now expanded into the new-wave eco-tourism. My government responded with eagerness and set up the ministry of tourism and constructed improved airport and hotel bed facilities to cater for the influx. The late African-American writer, Alex Haley, published a book entitled *Roots*. The book was about the life of Kunta Kinteh, a village boy who was snatched from the Gambian village of Juffureh in the 1700s and shipped to the United States. *Roots* has opened up opportunities that still await The Gambia's fullest exploitation of the American and Caribbean markets.

In the 1960s we had good relations with Israel. The Israelis had opened up their institutions of higher learning to train Gambian technical students. On one visit to Israel, I attended a conference on comprehensive planning of agriculture at the Weismann Institute of Science at Rehoboth. It was a conference to stimulate agricultural production in newly independent states. It was a gathering of important government officials with the Vice President of Togo, twelve ministers of cabinet rank, scientists, journalists and agriculturists. I was chosen to present the greetings of the African delegates. I spoke of how wonderful, timely and important it was for politicians and scientists to meet at economic roundtables. I said the balance was of great value because the two disciplines had to inform each other for any venture in agriculture to succeed.

Our delegation brought home many tips and contacts that the Agriculture Department would use in subsequent years to draw up programmes and shape policy towards the replication of projects we had seen in Israel. The fruitful contacts led to mutual full diplomatic relations and the extension of the Israeli ambassador's accreditation to Bathurst from his official base in Dakar. Israel offered to train Gambians in agriculture, education and journalism. Later on, when we established the Ministry of Economic

Planning and Industrial Development, we promptly despatched a ministerial delegation to Tel-Aviv for consultations on technical cooperation.

We kept a keen eye on the Middle East, especially the unfortunate tensions that suddenly aggravated after 1966. I was in Lebanon in 1966 where I was decorated with the Grand Cross: National Order of Cedar of Lebanon.

The Arab-Israeli conflict presented a particularly difficult dilemma for us in that it was a situation where on the one hand we wanted to side with justice in the Palestinian quest for independence and freedom from occupation, and on the other hand to live up to our admiration for Israel as a shining example of a country whose determination turned a virtual desert into a booming agricultural economy in less than thirty years.

The build-up exploded destructively in 1967 into what became known as the Six Day War. Israel's pre-emptive strike wiped out the Egyptian air force on the ground and pretty much settled a great deal of the war in one day and took another five days to finish off the other Arab fortifications occupying the Egyptian Sinai, the Golan Heights, parts of the West Bank and Arab East Jerusalem. Sinai was later returned to Egypt after President Anwar Sadat reconciled with Israel, but the other captured territories still remain occupied in a tussle gravely compounded by the intransigent and illegal building of Jewish settlements on traditionally Arab lands in Gaza, the West Bank and East Jerusalem.

In solidarity with Egypt and under the banner of the OAU, The Gambia was of course keen on Afro-Arab solidarity. We seized every occasion to bond with Egypt and Arab issues and to empathise with the people in their struggles. I was away in New York when the news of the death of President Nasser on 28 September 1970 reached me. I immediately relayed instructions to Vice President Sheriff Dibba to represent The Gambia at the funeral, which took place in Cairo on 3 October 1970. Our delegation fittingly demonstrated our long-standing respect for a president whose passing away at the age of only fifty-two years had robbed Africa in particular and the Arab world in general of one of its outstanding leaders.

In this way, my official travel clock must have clicked up the thousands of miles it took to build new bridges and to repair shaky ones. Whether on behalf of the PPP or of government, we consulted with the world family and spread our goodwill to others. We made our presence felt and we heard the points of view of interlocutors as we worked out a system for a coherent foreign policy. The trend was the same, whether in Germany, in France or in the USA.

Through those meetings, friendships could be forged or lines drawn. This arena was a school of its own and well did we learn as we went along.

In the field of international relations, friends are made or lost depending on national interests. Our relation with the two Chinas provides an interesting example of how indeed friends are made or lost.

However experience quickly taught us that the two Chinas were completely polarised on the issue and it was useless even considering a two-China policy. Gradually, the logic of keeping nearly a quarter of the world's population out of the UN soon became no longer tenable and we conceded and voted with the majority and recognised Beijing. Opponents of the resolution such as the USA had to give way to the majority voice of the General Assembly. The PRC was thus recognised and admitted.

Our foreign policy interests guided our action to establish relations with the PRC, which automatically resulted in the break-off of our relations with Taiwan. We based our actions on our convictions and in compliance with the UN Resolution that recognised the PRC's accession to a seat in the Security Council. True to our sense of impartiality and flexibility, we stressed at the 26th Session of the General Assembly in December 1969 that there was room in the UN for two Chinas and that we would consider voting for the admission of the PRC if it applied. We expressed our policy that the admission of the PRC would not be at the expense of the ROC.

The Gambia was fully engaged with the PRC, ending diplomatic relations between Bathurst and Taipei that had lasted since 1968. The ROC had since then left the UN and embarked on a driving campaign to have the world recognise its sovereignty as an independent republic and not as a renegade territory, as the PRC would claim.

After Rhodesia's Unilateral Declaration of Independence, we supported and cooperated in the application of selective mandatory sanctions and along with the majority of members of the OAU we did not consider that Britain, as the colonial power, should rule out the use of force should the situation so determine. With regard to South West Africa, the Gambia government fully supported the decision of the UN to withdraw South Africa's mandate over the territory and to set up an administering authority under UN auspices. The Gambia considered apartheid inhumane and was ready support to any rationally organised move aimed at preventing its perpetuation.

On Vietnam our position on the pursuit of a peace settlement was consistent. While the war with the US persisted, The Gambia did not consider that there was any useful purpose to be served by branding one side or the other as the aggressor. What was essential was to bring the Americans and Vietnamese to the conference table in order to bring about a speedy end to the unnecessary waste of human life.

As much as we welcomed the assistance from partners in the wider world, we never lost sight of what we could do for ourselves as Africans. Our call had long gone out for the continued strengthening and promotion of human rights as the basis for the socio-economic development of our peoples. Our policy of a staunch commitment to the pursuance of human rights and dignity always had as its focal point the right of each individual to basics such as food. As far as the unmitigated destruction of food and agriculture resources was concerned, African countries ravaged by drought in the mid-1970s took the bold step of coming together to look for common solutions in the fight against drought. Using our relations with Senegal as reference, we published the exemplary endurance of the many years of fruitful and dynamic cooperation in the mutual interests of the two peoples.

The ideal was always embodied in our determination to pave the path to greater intra-African cooperation for development. Our support for this ideal was seen at the sub-regional level with the high degree of interest we always reserved in our support for ECOWAS and for groupings such as the Permanent Inter-State Committee to Combat Drought in the Sahel (CILSS). In December 1977, The Gambia played host to its other members, Cape Verde, Chad, Mali, Mauritania, Niger, Senegal and Upper Volta, during which I assumed the chairmanship for two years.

These countries were coming together against great odds with inadequate financial resources to meet national recurrent expenditures. As its new chairman, I was undaunted as I went on extensive travels, sparing no effort to search for support to meet the two biggest challenges in CILSS – finances and effective cooperation. The founding of CILSS gave the affected countries the all-important equipment of a fully operational secretariat in Ouagadougou, Upper Volta, to handle the large amounts of bilateral, multilateral and private sources of financial aid we were able to acquire for the fight against drought. The Gambia has since maintained a full and effective role in CILSS, guided always by the practical and realistic consideration of our intra-African relations.

While we met at that level on the one hand, all was not well on the other with the continued distraction of the rancour that had pitched the Ivory Coast's President Houphouet Boigny and Guinea's President Sekou Touré against President Leopold Sedar Senghor of Senegal. I was glad we were able to finally resolve those quarrels in the African traditional way of mediation, dialogue and reconciliation. I was privileged to be part of the mediation in Monrovia in 1977 that brought meaningful peace between the parties. It was in that same spirit that I extended an invitation to President

Touré to visit Banjul the same year and requested Guinea to join the Gambia River Basin Project (OMVG), a bilateral scheme I chaired from 1987 to 1988 and which later evolved into a multilateral development programme in which Guinea Conakry and, later, Guinea Bissau, became members.

Upon every opportunity, we intensified our ties outside West Africa; we built on relations with countries of the Maghreb and it was to this end that I made state visits to Algeria and Tunisia. We received high level missions from Libya and Morocco, and it was my government's policy to maintain and strengthen cordial and mutually beneficial relations that existed between The Gambia and the North African countries. We patiently waited for the opportunity to spread solidarity further to eastern Africa where the names of African independence champions had become liberation champions against white supremacy in Africa. Although we had interacted at Commonwealth and OAU gatherings, we were still eager to put our cases directly to one another.

On our way to Addis Ababa for the 6th OAU Assembly of Heads of State and Government taking place there from 6 to 10 September 1969, my delegation killed two birds with one stone, as it were, which our short purse strings suggested we should on foreign trips. On 28 August 1969, we reciprocated Zambia's President Kenneth Kaunda's visit to Bathurst earlier in June. It had always been our desire to visit the frontline state and to declare among the Zambian people our solidarity with them against Ian Smith's odious UDI regime in Rhodesia. It was a good time as well to meet with Mwalimu Julius Nyerere in Tanzania, and to hear at firsthand what actions were being taken by the frontline state against the racist regime of South Africa and Rhodesia. We were satisfied with the staying power of the Zimbabwe African National Union (ZANU).

Although it took a long while after our visit to the frontline states, at last, on 18 April 1980, the sovereign state of Zimbabwe was born after a hard and bitter struggle. I sent a note of felicitation to Prime Minister Robert Mugabe. The Gambia hailed the valiant people of Zimbabwe for their gallant victory and for the display of magnanimity in being prepared to share with the former white oppressors even in their hour of glory. That historic triumph of African nationalism and the continued support of the OAU provided immense inspiration for the people of Namibia and South Africa that increased the pressure towards freeing them from the yoke of apartheid.

Travelling on many occasions left me jetlagged. In the summer of 1964, I was away in Europe and visiting Bordeaux in France when the rigour of the travel caught up with me. My body was paying for the stress my enthusiasm was putting it through. The hectic official engagements had caught up with me. I took a short leave and we returned to Bathurst. I arrived so badly under the weather that I had to miss the weekly cabinet sessions. I left the presiding to Acting Premier Sheriff Sisay while I rested. Then there were the long hours of work and travel away from home. Many times I had had to make up for lost quality time with my family by travelling with them on every opportunity. I also had to plan some of my leave time around the children's school holidays where possible.

I always apprised my cabinet of developments that came out of the tours and also invited the national press corps to State House to a press conference after every visit. I spelt out the purposes, conduct and results of my visits. In the earlier days I gave a radio broadcast every time I returned. I realised that despite my reports on the visits some of the press and also critics from the opposition were unconvinced that the returns were worth the cost of the trips. Some described the missions as junkets and money-wasting sprees and a drain on our foreign exchange reserves.

I felt deeply disturbed on reading the opinion of the AFPRC government in its White Paper put out on the Akoto-Bamfo commission of inquiry ordering that I pay back to the state D9.8 million in respect of private overseas trips, improperly utilised imprests along with per diem allowances. I went back to the glossy catalogues of American and European model executive aircraft that expatriate economic advisers had suggested to me in the 1980s as economical to the state. I remember the colossal figures of more than $9 million, excluding running costs, per diem and hotel accommodation for staff, family, protocols, security and hospitality whenever I would use the aeroplane. I turned my back on this and on every other temptation, always declining with a courteous reply that our treasury could not afford it.

Although there was a relatively large bill to pay, the country's role in world affairs could not be left unattended only on account of the cost of air tickets and allowances paid to the servants who went to take the message across. Prudence, of course, was paramount as to which meetings we attended and which we declined.

I did not fail to point out to my government as early as 1965 that the costs of taking responsibility as a nation were high. I was forthright in disclosing to the House the financial burden that came with our independence. I brought to their notice, for instance, that at the meeting of the Committee of Supply, my office had sought supplementary appropriation, in other words additional provision of £3,000 to cover attendance at conferences outside The Gambia. The contributions which we were required to pay to the UN, the OAU and to the specialised agencies of the UN had already reached figures which caused me considerable concern. We were seriously obliged to consider whether we could afford to join such agencies of the UN, which, although desirable in themselves, might well be beyond our financial capability.

There was every advantage in building bridges. Overseas bilateral aid, much of which came from international contacts, grew quickly after 1965. It was our largest income portfolio financing government development projects. Foreign Direct Investment, novel programmes and fresh initiatives blossomed almost every time a mission returned from abroad. Not all might have been visible at first glance but each mission brought back a building block that went into the construction of the solid bridges over which Gambian youth walked to scholarships and training abroad, or over which partners brought us new techniques in agriculture or goods to fill the shops and market stalls, or brought us fuel and modern amenities at rates and charges our people could afford. Acquiring those gains was not automatic; a great deal of them had to be negotiated and this could hardly have been done by staying at home.

This summarised *tour d'horizon* of The Gambia's stand on the necessary entrenchment of brotherliness, peace and unity at home and abroad shows clearly that our country was always ready to pursue realistic policies of non-alignment while firmly pinning on the UN our hopes for world peace and on the OAU and other sub-regional bodies for Africa's attainment of unity and economic development. This means developing countries themselves had to be left to make free choices of partnerships and not swallowed into global Cold War politics. So whether at meetings of the UN, the OAU, the Non-Aligned Movement or the OIC, my stand did not change.

21

Forging ahead to greater things

On 13 May 1969, the National Executive of the PPP responded decisively to the constant enquiry of the mass of people who desired that the government should raise the issue again for a republican form of government. It had been almost four years since the defeat of the first proposal and time enough to have recovered with newer insights from lessons we learnt from November 1965. The committee passed a resolution urging the government to consider, as a matter of priority, the holding of a referendum before the next general election. The cabinet worked diligently and refined the resolution into a paper ready for the sitting of the House of Representatives. On 18 June, I made a statement in the House presenting the case for the introduction of a Republican Constitution that would provide for a president.

The House was apprised of the details of the constitutional proposals and the debate was animated as was to be expected. The opposition parties tried to portray a bleak future of a republican Gambia with an executive president. They flung all wild accusations at us trying to instil the fear that republicanism was the prelude to our declaration of a one-party state. That however was not our chosen system of government.

Undaunted, we prepared the ground over the intervening months. In October 1969 during a visit to the Baddibus, I addressed a crowd that had given me and my visiting group an enthusiastic welcome at the village of Saba. I expressed my surprise that opposition to a republican form of government was gravitating around party affiliations. I told them that ought not to be so. The issue was a national one. "My government is not seeking power;" I told the cheering crowds, "rather it is the completion of The Gambia's political evolution and independence. If it was just power there would have been no need to proceed from self-government to independence. All along, our party had sought to liberate this country politically and to improve its economic situation." The women of Saba assured me that they would campaign vigorously to ensure the success of the republican issue.

When the House met in December 1969, we were ready for the closing debates. The details to amend the constitution were finalised reflecting as they did the desired advancement of The Gambia to republican status.

The amendment bill was laid before the House and was passed by an overwhelming majority of 27 votes to 5. The early months in 1970 went by very quickly. We had covered all the ground and the campaign teams hit the trail and combed the towns and countryside with fervour. When the House closed its sessions, our party seized every opportunity to continue to make the case to the people. In my Kombo constituency I drove the message home to the people that a one-party state was the antithesis of democracy, and to establish such a thing would be courting the sort of troubles that existed in certain other states. I told them: "In this country, democracy is the watchword!"

Back at party headquarters we analysed every bit of information we could gather. Before long it became apparent to us that the United Party and its allies did not stand a chance of winning a No vote. If anything, we kept receiving reports of disagreements and rancour between the party leader and his lieutenants. Nevertheless we were not taking anything for granted. The light winds of April brought some jitters; naturally, we left no stone unturned because failure of the referendum a second time round would spell disaster for the PPP.

With faith in our programme we covered all the ground we possibly could and on the eve of polling day we took to the airwaves. There was very little else I could add to Attorney General Momodou Lamin Saho's prior broadcast to the nation on Radio Gambia. He explained that the constitution proposed an ultra-democratic system of which all Gambians could be proud. It guaranteed primarily the protection of the dignity of the Gambian citizen and upheld his or her human and civic rights. It planted the country firmly within the Commonwealth tradition with a national document worthy of the pride of all Gambians.

The draft constitution guaranteed the citizens fundamental human rights – freedom of worship, freedom of association, freedom of movement and freedom of expression. Discipline and promotion in the public service would be left to an independent Judicial Service Commission and the Public Service Commission respectively. We provided for separation of powers between the three arms of government – the Executive, the Judiciary and the Legislature – so that each, within its own sphere of influence, would operate independently.

It provided checks and balances so that none of those bodies could abuse its powers with impunity. The executive branch was finally answerable to Parliament and to the courts. Parliament could remove judges for misconduct and if Parliament itself operated outside the constitution its action could be tested in the courts. The president reserved the right to dissolve it and send its members back to the electorate. Similarly if the president abused the constitution or was guilty of misconduct, impeachment proceedings could be invoked.

The country's finances were controlled in such a way that no one, however powerful, could dip their hands into the public coffers and get away with it. The constitution also ensured that power was not concentrated in the hands of any one person. It enshrined the supremacy of the rule of law so that citizens could go about their business confident that as free people they could say and do openly exactly what their conscience dictated without fear. It guaranteed the peacefulness and maturity that entitled each Gambian to freely breathe God's air and to give expression to their thoughts. Power ultimately rested with the people.

I appealed in my broadcast to everyone for an orderly conduct of the nationwide consultation so that the smooth running of the polls would not be marred by clashes and conflicts with other people who thought differently. I urged everyone to remain cool and calm, and conduct themselves in such a way as to maintain the well-earned reputation of the country for peace and orderliness. I enjoined Gambians to once again prove to the world, whose eyes were focused upon us as we voted, that we could do it as we had done in the past.

It was the second time we were asking and so we put all our forces out in the field, taking all the lessons we had learnt from the first failed attempt. We virtually took the issues to the people. For three and half months we spoke with them at different places including their homes, workplaces and village meeting grounds.

The task was not only to drive home the benefits of republicanism to our people but also to dismiss from their minds the myth that the opposition was spreading, namely equating republicanism with dictatorship. I remember some outspoken opponents in the senior ranks of the legal profession in Bathurst opposing the measure because they were convinced that republicanism concentrated too much power in the hands of two people – the president and the attorney general.

We also needed to save the image and reputation of the party while we asked for a fresh round of votes. We received our first major sign of victory when we welcomed to the PPP perhaps the most formidable opponent of republicanism after P S Njie. UP Secretary General Ibrahim A S Burang John had carried out the ultimatum he had given his party leader that considering that the UP was in no fit shape countrywide to change the country's readiness for republican status, he would resign if the UP opposed the bill. When P S Njie repeated his 'No' campaign again,

Burang John not only resigned as party secretary, but applied straightaway for membership of the PPP.

It was a major uplift for us and a mighty blow to the UP which had become a sinking ship. An avalanche of defections began that brought over to us key names such as Momodou C Jallow, Momodou Cadi Cham, Andrew David Camara and others from the UP camp. The UP was indeed floundering. I remember sitting in my office one day when Seyfo Abu Khan of Kuntaya marched into my office in the company of a young man he introduced to me as M C Cham. The elder had brought the young fellow to me to 'become' a member of the PPP and that was that. The chief said Cham was deeply interested in politics but was wasting his time in the wrong camp. The apparently tongue-tied M C Cham seemed well under instruction to obey the old man who there and then brought one new member to the party. Thus began the turning-point in the young man's political life. He contested and won the seat in Tumana and much later became a cabinet minister.

Two years before, in 1968, perhaps the most devastating for P S Njie was the switching to our side of Momodou Musa Njie, for years the main bankroller of the UP. Momodou Musa had not only joined ranks with us, but had also become my father-in-law. Other signs of rebuilding were seen with the return of Sanjally Bojang to the fold. He was not the only one making peace with the party. Lamin Bora Mboge would also mend fences after his expulsion, just as Sheriff Sisay, after his resignation from the party to form his own - the People's Progressive Alliance. The PPP had also had the added advantage of a merger with the Gambia Congress Party in 1968 which also earned the party leader, Jahumpa, a place in the cabinet as minister of health. The final touch to our journey of national self-fulfilment was only a few days away.

The long nights and the endless tours paid off. The people were awakened to a new drum roll and endorsed the call to be masters of their own destiny. The results of the referendum showed 84,968 votes in favour of republican status with 35,638 against; a resounding endorsement. The 60, 000 abstainers in 1965 dropped to only 13,181 in 1970. The bill was laid before parliament to enact the people's decision into law. On 24 April 1970, Chief Justice Philip Bridges declared The Gambia a sovereign republic and I took the oath of office as the first president of the Republic of The Gambia.

A tumultuous crowd thronged MacCarthy Square. It was for me the crowning point of a political journey which started with my response, despite initial trepidation, but finally enthusiastically to lead a people in

1959. I addressed the nation with a deep sense of pride and privilege in a new and different capacity – that of the first president of the new republic. I thanked the Gambian people for bestowing such an honour on me. There we were witnessing the final stage in the political evolution of our country. Political independence, achieved a little over five years before, was just one of the important stages in the evolutionary process, but the harmonising of our country's overall constitutional framework with our local needs, heritage and true aspirations was another step forward, no less important though, which we had now taken.

At my swearing-in, Senegal's Foreign Minister Ababacar Ndiaye sent me felicitations put in words I will never forget. Ndiaye wrote:

> In the battles which you will necessarily have to wage to put the young republic of The Gambia in the proper rails of the future, we shall be by your side ... We will not spare any effort to bring our respective governments to greater solidarity and greater cooperation as your qualities of heart and spirit impel us all to those efforts and in doing so we shall be contributing to a better future for the whole of humanity.

Some time later, I was happy to receive Ndiaye's letters of commission accrediting him as his country's high commissioner to The Gambia. I was glad too that he stayed long enough to become the dean of the diplomatic corps.

I explained in general terms that a republican system of government meant for us more than the formal acknowledgement of the supremacy of the voice of the people in the body politic through their chosen representatives. While we had a democratically elected parliament and government since independence, formal power was still vested outside those institutions in a distant monarch with a representative in the person of the governor general. After independence in 1965, it was expedient that the constitutional set-up with which an independent Gambia was ruled was made more realistic and reflective of our true Gambian heritage. That was not possible under the old arrangement which, stemming from a foreign concept, naturally tended to confuse the minds of many people.

I assured my listeners that the policies of the new government both in the fields of external and domestic affairs would remain the same. We would continue to be a member of the Commonwealth. We would remain a member of the UN and the OAU. I firmly pledged my government's belief in the principles and ideals of those organisations. Our relations with neighbouring states would remain guided by those same principles and ideals. On the domestic front, I pledged my government's commitment to policies of economic development within the country, guided, of course, by sound fiscal and financial traditions. I committed my government to striving, to its utmost, and within the financial resources available, to improve the social services and amenities in the country. I nailed down the specifics of the rights and responsibilities as the bedrock of the future environment without which all the high-sounding pledges would be unworkable. I cannot do better than share with you the deep feelings as they moved me:

> Much has been made of the fundamental liberties and freedoms which have been guaranteed to all citizens under the monarchical system of government and fears expressed that these might be eroded away under a Republican Constitution. Let me make it crystal clear here and now that all those fears are groundless. The fundamental liberties and freedoms of all citizens are the cornerstone of the present constitution as indeed they were in the old constitution. From my government's past record you will all bear witness to our scrupulous respect for the fundamental freedoms and liberties of the individual. This is the rock on which the stability of my government is built and I give my earnest pledge that as long as the present Constitution is operated by my government, things will remain this way. At the same time, I expect all well-meaning Gambians to realise and to live up to their obligations and responsibilities under democratic society. Peace, Progress and Prosperity are still the goals for which my government will strive; Peace not only at home but throughout the world; Progress through hard work and cooperation, so that we shall all enjoy some measure of prosperity. Long Live the Republic of The Gambia.

There was absolute justification for going republican since the day-to-day running of the country and our constitutional monarchy presented many inconveniences that made the need for such a change imperative. Such internal administrative inconveniences while not being unique to The Gambia, having played out the same way in Ghana, Nigeria, Kenya and

Sierra Leone, left us in a peculiar situation that encouraged the persistence of practical problems. Traditionally, and in the collective experience of our people, the ceremonial and the real aspects of power and authority were inseparable. Both aspects had always been represented in the self-same king, chief or governor. To vest such power in a local head of state improved the perception and the respect accorded the office and, consequently, the people's own self-perception and relevance.

On 30 June 1970 I addressed parliament. There was a pervading sense of occasion. The House was filled to capacity and blazed with colour, from the speaker's tasselled tricorn hat, the ceremonial guards, the judges in their ceremonial gowns down to the parliamentarians, government officials and the sea of expectant faces thronging the seats in the public gallery. My flowing traditional robes of embroidered hand-woven cotton befitting such a high national privilege blended well with the surroundings. Long before that, I was resolved to grace all national ceremonial occasions in national dress for its cultural appropriateness.

In my bid to clear up all misconceptions and ill-informed campaigns, I told the House that there was going to be no departure from the pattern of foreign policy hitherto pursued by the government. As a matter of fact, with the constitutional change it was my government's resolution to stand even more firmly on the principal pillars of this policy to cooperate with other nations for mutual benefit and the pursuit of peace and harmony throughout the world. They had already heard much of it accentuated in my inaugural speech a month before.

I was left with nothing but candid exhortation of my party, my government and my compatriots on what really that final step to political independence must mean in practical terms for all of us. The struggle for independence had passed and we must all now find the common ground upon which to forge ahead to greater things. Indeed, the Gambian people had heaped an overwhelming vote of confidence in us. I had emphasised the same message during the campaign across the country that independence must be marked with hard work and unity of purpose. In Georgetown, I cited the Taiwan rice growing programme as a good example of the kind of hard work that must go with independence. The kind of industry that would make an acre of soil yield twofold in one season should bring many answers to the problems of a nation solely dependent on agriculture.

The people's confidence in voting the country into a republic had raised the profile of The Gambia internationally. The country would therefore have to take its rightful place on the international stage. And the world heard us, indeed, in September 1970 when I addressed the OAU for the first time as President of the newest republic on its list of members at the 7th Assembly of Heads of State and Government. I reaffirmed my government's confidence in and support of the continental body and gave it the accolade of being the best institution created that far for the unity of our continent. Once again, I condemned the odious system forcibly imposed in South Africa. I emphasised my government's association with all the international standards, chief among them being the inalienable rights of the individual in any society and the collective rights of any people to decide their own fate.

When I addressed the 25th Session of the UN General Assembly in New York later that year, I reiterated to the world how we felt about the unfair disparities in international trade and spoke of the urgency of changing the existing economic order for better service to humanity. With the turn of the 1970s, the developing countries had begun to feel the pinch of a gathering world recession. The only answer to peace in our time was for the world to take a fresh look at the way international trade and its benefits are patterned. I described the UN as the world's greatest hope and the most effective instrument for the maintenance of peace. I pointed out that it was as a matter of gratification that it remained unflinching in its striving to attain social justice despite the difficulties in finding solutions to some of the most perplexing issues that faced humankind. Although economic considerations continued to limit the scope of our participation, we would continue to take a keen interest in the work of the organisation and its allied agencies.

From then on it was a deluge of engagements and obligations to meet and share with colleagues and partners where I or members of my government would speak or make presentations that would further etch the entity called The Gambia on the map of the world.

We reiterated our commitment to cooperation with Senegal. We worked hard at it fully aware of the inextricable nature of our contiguity, spelling out many things we ought to do together for mutual optimum results. At the wider regional level, my government had at all times underscored its willingness to cooperate with other West African states in matters of mutual concern. Again, I raised the hope that the following year would see the resuscitation of the idea of the creation of a West African economic grouping waiting since 1968 for translation into concrete results. That had been of particular interest to me since the Conference of West African Heads of State in Monrovia on 22 April 1968 where I cited our relations with Senegal as an example the rest of West Africa could follow towards a strong and unified sub-region.

Now that our people, by casting their ballots, had decided on an executive presidential system, I laid out my government's plans for robust domestic policies with emphasis on agriculture and social development. Poor attention to production and low productivity, for example, could stifle economic growth. And certainly poor health conditions would negate every plan, if the people were not well enough to work in the fields to produce for the nation's breadbasket. As a developing nation, the country's development policies and programmes ought, of necessity, to take into account the welfare of the bulk of the people.

Thus, I endorsed the policy in the Ministry of Agriculture in its drive to intensify extension programmes for more impact on a greater number of farmers. To that end, I committed all efforts to attract the best brains into agriculture by improving the conditions of service of agricultural workers and by intensifying the training provided at the Yundum Agricultural Centre. As it happened at that time Dr Lamin Marenah was the director.

In order to increase groundnut production the government decided to create credit facilities to allow farmers to purchase agricultural inputs. We were gratified by the strides towards self-sufficiency in rice production and since the Taiwanese rice mission had shown proof since their arrival in 1966 that we could produce two crops per season, we readily put an extra five hundred acres of land under cultivation, ten times the acreage in 1969. The project was yielding about £36,000 annually in foreign exchange savings.

Education was also a high priority for my government. We put forward the Development Programme in Education for The Gambia 1965-1975 prepared under the aegis of a UNESCO Educational Planning Mission. The Ministry of Education worked with Dr D F Sleight in a survey with a view to providing information that would serve to raise standards, especially towards the attainment of the Addis Ababa target for universal primary education. The programme included the construction of schools and the provision of school furniture. It advocated particular attention to education in the rural areas.

At the secondary and post-secondary levels, there was provision for the upgrading of existing institutions and the establishment of rural vocational schools which should make a great impact on provincial communities. It also covered the whole gamut of teacher training, the education of women and girls, adult education and employment opportunities. It spelt out the financial implications of the programme that called for an initial outlay of nearly £1 million. In August 1966, my cabinet endorsed the programme wholeheartedly. Government was thus poised to develop more dynamic education policies and programmes as new challenges emerged into the 1980s and 1990s.

The USA sent us Peace Corps volunteers to strengthen our teaching corps in science and mathematics; the British government, volunteers from their VSO scheme and from Canada we had technical and vocational assistance. This is not to suggest that we had not already laid down a solid foundation for education by our own efforts. I announced the adoption of an education policy aimed at the consolidation of education at the primary level and further expansion at the secondary level.

On other matters of state, I spelt out the inventory of the government's policies and programmes for the legislative year covering communications, tourism, health, local government and all the vital sectors that holistically would go into determining our well-being as a nation. I outlined my government's financial policies as being steadfastly based on stringent financial control, which was necessary if our country was to continue to be self-reliant and progressive in financing our recurrent budget and a larger proportion of our capital expenditure. I reminded the government, legislators and the nation at large that if we wished to be able to finance our development, we should then look to the very difficult but necessary policy of the careful husbandry of our resources and the stringent control of our finances. Although foreign assistance was welcome, it was desirable that we, by our own efforts, ensured the viability of our economy.

A positive external image of our government grew steadily. We earned international respectability and, soon, richer, more powerful nations were courting our votes in international forums. Our key interests invariably determined whom we voted for. Also the justice of the cause had a great deal to do with which side we supported. It was my responsibility to weigh every vote my country would cast to ensure that the development of the people I represented was the major underlining consideration driving those decisions. That is not to say that there were no pressures; nor does it mean that we did not concede to a few of them. Our tussle in the 1980s with IMF-imposed structural adjustment measures is just one such case.

Every day we learnt new lessons with which we tackled our foreign policy portfolio. We tried with diligence to tailor our objectives to our national interests. However, some of the time, cross-cutting issues could make decisions difficult to justify. For example, just after the outbreak of hostilities between Israel and the Arabs in 1967, I had to clarify to some concerned Muslim elders who wanted to find out from me the moral reasoning why The Gambia, a predominantly Muslim country, was voting in the UN in favour of Israel. I explained the subtle differences between the Israeli government, the ideology of Zionism and the people of Israel. As a country we had diplomatic obligations to the Israeli government. While we differed with the government we could not abandon the people with whom we shared a common humanity.

In fact, our best proposal would have been to mediate between Jews and Arabs and to bring lasting peace between them. That was our stand. I itemised all the agricultural, medical, technical and educational aid Israel was giving to us in support of our national development, amounting to thousands of dollars and yet they did not see us as a Muslim-dominant country when they helped us. They saw us as a developing country needing assistance. There were also criteria for engagement or disengagement with a development partner that went beyond just the surface issues of solidarity on account of a shared religion.

Almost a year later, following the Six Day War, we complied with the OAU resolutions which took a stand against the occupying forces, asking member states to sever diplomatic relations with Israel. The same Muslim elders were later satisfied with the value of our argument when The Gambia, without any shadow of restraint, condemned Israeli aggression against the Palestinian people and supported the call by the OAU for a return to the pre-1967 borders as the first essential step towards peace in the Middle East. The crisis polarised the world. It became ironically the yardstick for many international engagements. The world's attention was focused on the Cold War struggles of the big powers in that theatre – with the North Atlantic Treaty Organisation (NATO) firmly behind Israel and the defeated Arab countries looking up to the Soviet Union for support.

I had the privilege of addressing the UN General Assembly once again at its 33rd Session in September 1978. My language was as direct as it was thirteen years before when I addressed its Sixth Special Session upon our admission. I spoke of the dire economic state of my country that was battered by the economic storm which had been shaking the suddenly discovered their interdependence in the face of a universal economic threat that was triggered primarily by an unprecedented increase in the prices of the indispensable international trade commodities. I told the world body that the gravity of that situation was accentuated by the total un-preparedness of the international community, which, in the preceding decade, had failed to recognise the urgency of changing the existing economic order in a manner that was fair, just and equitable to the majority of humanity.

Paradoxically, I said, the great progress made in international politics in the same period, which significantly coincided with the first decade of the OAU, was not matched in the sphere of economic relations between nations. On the one hand, Africa had emerged from colonial domination and was approaching total liberation at a pace that could be neither slowed down nor halted; on the other hand, international relations, hitherto characterised by superpower politics and conflicts operating within a dangerous framework of bipolar interest blocs, were evolving into a system of general horizontal cooperation in the developed world.

It was, indeed, that worsening economic crisis, rooted in the unsatisfied basic needs of the vast majority of humankind, that constituted the greatest threat to world peace. In the Sahel, those conditions had led to the loss of thousands of human lives, a severe decimation of the livestock population and a drastic drop in the level of production of food crops. The destruction of the fragile ecosystem had been further accelerated by the relentless advance of the desert. Inequitable international trade practices, ignoring as they do the basic principles of free enterprise, have been the root cause of the continuing deterioration of the terms of trade of the Third World and the ever-widening gap between rich and poor nations.

On security as an ultimate global goal, I drew the attention of the UN to the urgent need for a review of the violation in practice of the basic principles of democracy under Article 2 of the voting procedures designed to uphold the principle of sovereign equality. That tenet in reality was contradicted in the demonstrated predominance of the five permanent members of the Security Council, whose powers of veto negated the principle of one man, one vote, and, by extension, one country, one vote.

Between then and July 1980 when I addressed the 17th Session of the OAU Assembly of Heads of State and Government in Freetown, Sierra Leone, tremendous changes had taken place in Africa. The racist government in Rhodesia had given way to liberation and the country had become the free and independent state of Zimbabwe. We all drew inspiration and strength from this development. I proposed to my African colleagues to intensify the struggle in the rest of southern Africa, first, to ensure the independence of Namibia as a short-term objective and, second, and to liberate South Africa. For as long as one square inch of Africa remained under foreign or racist domination and occupation, the independence of the rest of the continent was incomplete and insecure.

Earlier, in April, the Lagos Summit had adopted the all-important Plan of Action for the Implementation of the Monrovia Strategy for the Economic Development of Africa. The Plan was set to bring about the economic emancipation and transformation of our continent into one of the most developed and powerful in the world. However by all counts we were far from achieving those objectives which had been set for the year 2000.

Our markets still remained un-integrated. We registered more successes however at our sub-regional level when the sixteen countries of West Africa formed ECOWAS in 1975. Rather than sustained action the continent continued with perennial political problems and internecine conflicts that shattered every attempt at building the foundations at the expense of the suffering masses and to the detriment of our development targets.

22

Grappling with development

There is a story behind the period of steady growth that preceded the first development programme we ever designed. After the PPP was firmly established in government, there were more national issues to attend to than purely party matters. We left the party's executive committee to design programmes to further consolidate our gains while the government concentrated on shaping the civil service and to think up a cohesive national development plan. There needed to be a succinct programme of development and a committed robust civil service to ensure its implementation. I was also firmly resolved to developing the potential and the energy of the private sector.

I keenly looked forward to a time when government, for example, would begin guaranteeing advances from the banks to enable cooperative societies to purchase more of the farmers' produce which would be distributed by their own selling organisations, thus bringing radical changes to the function of GOMB, which could then concentrate on expansion into other innovative directions.

We had recognised privatisation as the answer nearly two decades before it became a popular concept in foreign technical advice. As soon as I became premier, I seized the opportunity to address the Chamber of Commerce at a gala dinner where I stated that we desired to retain the freedom of enterprise, the liberal trading arrangements and the high standards of commercial dealings. Government would give its support to the role of the private sector.

We put forward our first ideas for such advancement in 1964 in which we outlined the three phases of the National Development Programme 1964-1974, concentrating on key public sector projects. Fifty per cent of the budget was allocated to infrastructural development in communication and internal security such as the south bank trunk road, water and electricity installations, river wharves, coastal defences and barracks and offices for the police. Education and health were also on our priority list.

Agriculture, education and communication therefore formed the central theme in my address to the first party congress on 5 April 1964. With our allies, the Democratic Congress Alliance, we reviewed our recent past and projected our future. I proposed plans to improve agricultural methods, increase food and cash crop production, stimulate tourism and put more children in school.

Only a few days before the congress we received a generous grant of £146,000 from the British government for work that had already begun on Yundum Airport. We started at long last to remedy the lack of a proper airfield in The Gambia where airport facilities before our time at Yundum and at Jeshwang were mere runways of pierced metal plates placed flat on the ground. We were optimistic about the follow-up projects under which, in subsequent phases, the terminal buildings were constructed and the dilapidated control tower was repaired.

We encouraged the establishment of industries. In the past, private investment in The Gambia had been largely restricted to the trade in groundnuts and imported retail goods. We were aiming at the expansion of private enterprise, both by Gambians and by overseas concerns, in housing, transport, manufacturing, fisheries and several other fields. As a government, we realised those were key duties: to provide the facilities and to create the conditions in which private enterprise could flourish. We also planned to modernise the Bathurst Harbour to take more and deeper ocean-going vessels, the reconstruction of the slipway at the Marine Dockyard, the improvement of the ferry services and, of course, the continuation of the road building programme.

However, development, whether by government or by private enterprise, was not simply a matter of finding the money, it was also a matter of organisation and skill. Construction works would have to be done preferably by skilled Gambians, quickly and efficiently.

The National Development Programme provided the country's first coherent, coordinated and comprehensive plan. Steadily, our successes continued to prove the prophets of doom wrong. Indeed, for an independent nation to be launching a development programme on the proceeds of a groundnut export crop was a daunting proposal. Nevertheless, our eyes were set on the goal and we continued to forge ahead with our main annual economic activity.

Naturally, we had to diversify the income base and look for more productive sources of revenue. The first attempt at any industrialisation in The Gambia was a poultry experiment in the early 1950s by the Commonwealth Development Corporation which soon collapsed, leaving its grounds and huts to form the nucleus of the campus for the Yundum Teacher Training College. One other attempt was a short-lived venture of the extraction of ilmenite in the early 1950s by the Gambia Minerals

Ltd. One other project was the attempt in groundnut processing and oil extraction first begun by the Viggio Quistgaard Petersen Company Ltd (V Q Petersen) in the late 1930s at the Denton Bridge oil mills and which was later taken over by GOMB.

A British firm, Cable & Wireless, handled telecommunications and it was the skeleton of what we found of it that we transformed many years later into the highly successful Gambia Telecommunications Ltd (Gamtel). In 1964, Radio Gambia increased its transmission time to three and a half hours daily.

With our foreign reserves greatly improved from what my government inherited in 1962, we set sail after independence with a treasury worth £4.4 million, made up of £1.6 million representing 41% contribution from the Recurrent Budget. The British Development and Welfare Grants contributed £1.8 million covering 46%, and from reimbursements and other receipts from the Development Fund we put in £280,000 or 7% of the total outlay, into the national treasury. The colonial government could boast only twenty-two miles of tarred road from Bathurst to Brikama. Trade and social interaction were carried out along dirt roads and potholed stretches, some even worse than the ones over which I bumped on my first trip out of Walikunda in an open lorry some thirty years before.

We addressed desperate issues in the health sector, where the impact of services hardly went beyond the reaches of Bathurst. We started up mobile clinics, and medical equipment arrived resulting in major improvements in the quality of service delivery, especially in the provinces. At the end of the year we had spent £3.7 million. The sum of £1.5 million was allocated for the construction and upgrading of roads and river wharves and the purchasing of river vessels in line with the political and social agenda of opening up the country. The sum of £920,000 went to agriculture representing 18% of the budget with 19.9% going to administration, 10.9% to social services and 9.8% to utilities.

The Public Works Department (PWD) report summarised the development period from 1964 to 1974 in which it declared that out of a total of one hundred and thirty-five construction projects of various sizes, seventy-six were located in what became known as the Greater Banjul Area, embracing the island and the urban network that made up the conurbation that stretched from Jeshwang to Yundum Airport. Fifty-nine of those major construction projects included staff and project structures at the mixed farming centres, other radio and public buildings that were opening up and expanding new facilities in provincial centres in fulfilment of years of policy objectives to include the majority of the people in the rural areas and to have them participate in national development.

The PPP government's initial promise to close the disparities between incomes and access between the urban and the rural communities had not wavered through three decades. That narrowing of the colony/protectorate gap was absolutely necessary to make for a more cohesive national picture. Not only did we improve on the price per ton of groundnuts for the farmer and provided fertiliser through donor aid as well as new techniques in farming, we also opened up service facilities in communication, primary health care, primary school and secondary technical education and water supplies. Thus, with civil engineering projects, mainly roads, boreholes, storage tanks, ferry ramps and wharves, soon there was a shortening of the disparity between colony as distinct from the protectorate. We had gone a long way towards forging one Gambia.

The urban areas enjoyed improved water supply and major rural capitals also saw great improvements in their supplies with boreholes sunk in Basse, Mansakonko, Bansang and Georgetown during that period. The colony and, later, certain growth centres in the provinces had telephones. A great deal of homework had gone into identifying and selecting what projects went where with the rationale for their execution based entirely on the sole objective of development that would make our independence real. It was inevitable in the early stages to pay much attention to buildings and structures but the bottom line was the well-being of the people, which should best be counted in the quality of food they ate; the standard of housing they enjoyed; the level of education and health care at their disposal; and, above all, the scope of the peace and freedoms they enjoyed.

Two years into the second phase of the Development Programme (1967-1971), the Barra-Karang road linking Bathurst and Dakar was upgraded. The Brumen-Soma road linking Bathurst with the provinces was also nearing completion. Many gravel-covered roads connected to the main stretch, bringing once far-flung villages and towns such as Farafenni, Kaur, Kuntaur and Laminkoto into the communication grid. Other landmark development projects proudly marked our evolution and spelt out our march towards well-managed development.

By the start of the third phase of the ten-year economic programme, we were aware of a serious lack of skilled human resources to carry out some of the objectives of development similar to the teething troubles we had with personnel in 1962 when we were advised to make haste slowly. The PWD did not have the requisite capacity, for example, to take on the contracts and to deliver professionally on the huge road and infrastructural construction projects. We then concentrated on diversifying the base for economic activities and financing the carry-over programmes of the Port of Banjul and Yundum Airport.

With no way of knowing the terror of the gathering economic storm the decade would bring, we celebrated the fifth independence anniversary in February 1970 with great hopes for the future. I told the more than one thousand schoolchildren who marched past at MacCarthy Square of the deep sense of pride they must have for what we had been able to achieve together after only five years of independence. I reminded them of the fact that we had been able to balance our recurrent budget without recourse to outside aid.

We maintained a stable and democratic government without which we could not have achieved anything worthwhile. In an atmosphere of peace and stability, we had within the means at our disposal endeavoured to improve the lot of the average Gambian. I told them how we sought to achieve this by improving communication – road, river, radio, and telephony; by expanding social services and amenities – education, health, water supply and electricity; by encouraging and stimulating increased agricultural production both through the introduction of modern techniques and by ensuring that the farmers received a reasonable price for their produce.

Indeed we had done so by encouraging agricultural diversification and promoting the introduction of new industries and commercial activities such as tourism and fisheries. I referred to some of the setbacks to those landmark advances. The common attitude of unrestrained desire for and consumption of imported items, especially non-essentials, was an example. We needed to be in a proactive state of mind with a keen sense of industry that would aid us in the sustenance of our creative efforts to expand and diversify exports while increasing the utilisation of local resources particularly in the output of food that would help reduce our huge imports.

We built institutional structures and human resource capacity to convey our development trends. Our investments in agriculture improved upon our extension services and we expanded into cooperatives to ensure the introduction of new methods to farmers and to work towards the increased production of groundnuts. Improvements in our export portfolio brought in the much-needed foreign earnings into our national reserves. Naturally, with an old vet at the helm, we paid great attention to livestock development and expansion into hides and skins from which, in five years, we opened our first hide drying facility at Abuko.

In March 1970, while we campaigned to transform to a republican state, the Minister of Finance, Sheriff Dibba, was off to Washington to negotiate our first major loan with the IDA. He and the other members of his delegation, Chairman of the Currency Board, Horace R Monday Jr, Attorney General M L Saho and Chief Marine Officer, Capt B M Sallah, were soon back in Bathurst with $2.1 million to cover the foreign exchange costs of our port development programme. This money was going to cover the cost of overhauling the port facilities in Bathurst.

We had fifty years in which to repay the IDA loan; we had a little bit of stretching to do to pay the $328,000 matching funds. We launched phase one of the three phases of the port development project, deepened the harbour waters at the Admiralty Wharf to 30 feet and extended it 400 feet to handle general cargo ships and petroleum tankers. We used the money to construct transit sheds and to rehabilitate Government Wharf with new moorings and dolphins.

I had the privilege of visiting the site to see ongoing dredging works around the spots where, as a boy, I used to read my books on the Admiralty Wharf and from where I watched the magnificent Sunderland flying boats during the war land and take off on the sea outside my old home at 37 Wellington Street. To be presiding over the rise of such an important economic object out of the relic of the old wharf where I used to do some of my homework after school filled me with some feeling of achievement and purpose in life.

While the country struggled to emerge from the backwaters of colonial neglect and now had to borrow large amounts of money to pay for its development programme, its relevance in the world also hinged on it taking the right positions – to play our part both nationally and internationally.

All over the globe, the abdication of responsibility of the developed nations was reaching such a crisis that it seemed impossible that the voices of the poor would ever be heard. Protectionism in the developed countries was soundly defeating the South's attempts at economic growth and even the gains in North-South trade were being grossly reduced. The promise of the transfer of technology to the developing world was not as uniform as many people envisaged. While some countries such as the Asian Tigers were able to transform their economies using technology and commercial know-how from the North, for most countries, particularly in Africa, the transfer did not take place.

We closely monitored the worsening weather conditions and the sharp decline in groundnut production from 123,000 tons in the 1968/1969 trade season to 112,000 tons in 1970/71. At that time a great deal of planning went into the change of the national currency. I opened an exhibition of The Gambia's new coins and paper money in November 1970 in preparation for the launch on Dalasi Day - 1 July 1971. On 1 May 1971, I cut the ribbon to inaugurate the Central Bank of The Gambia which took over from the colonial West African Currency Board. The dalasi and butut replaced the British pound, shillings and pence, which the country had used since its introduction in 1922. Fortunately, the national currency fared well, considering the risk it was for a small country like ours to take on an independent currency.

By 1972, having established the National Order of the Republic of The Gambia the first awards were made to the following people for outstanding service to the nation:

The Order of Grand Commander of the National Order of the Republic of The Gambia (GCRG) was conferred upon: Hon Sheriff Mustapha Dibba and the Hon Sir Alieu S Jack.

The Grand Officer of the National Order of the Republic of The Gambia (GORG) was conferred upon: the Hon Andrew David Camara, Mr Eric Herbert Christensen and the Hon Alh M L Saho.

The Commander of the National Order of the Republic of The Gambia (CRG) was conferred upon the Hon Alh Yaya Ceesay, Mr Harry Lloyd-Evans, Dr S H O Jones and the Hon Alh A B Njie.

The Officer of the National Order of the Republic of The Gambia (ORG) was conferred upon: Imam Momodou Lamin Bah, Alh A B Gaye, Seyfo Koba N Leigh, Dr Peter J Ndow, Mr Yusupha M Ngum and the Hon Alh Famara Wassa Touray.

The Member of the National Order of the Republic of The Gambia (MRG) was conferred upon Alh Kebba Conteh, Mr B E Fye, Mr Providence H Lloyd, Mr B Nian, Mrs Rachel Palmer, Mr A S C Able-Thomas, Mr T K Bittaye, Mr L K Bojang, Ajaratou O Ceesay, Mrs T Jaiteh, Alh B Kora, Mr E Njie, Mr SA Njie and Mr S Rahman.

On 24 April 1973, to further consolidate our independent outlook, parliament adopted the local name Banjul for our capital city.

By the end of the third phase of the National Development Programme in 1975, we had broadened the agricultural base, sufficiently reorganised the public utilities and increased public sector capacity for development. We had put three quarters of development funds to natural resource sectors in poultry development, forestry plantations, fisheries development, tractor ploughing, rice development, seed multiplication, water conservation and agricultural credit. The rest went into buildings that were badly needed to support the mixed farming centres, cooperative stations, agricultural stations and veterinary treatment centres. But a new dimension that would add to our financial woes was debt servicing. Where grants did not meet the shortfall in revenue and expenditure, we had to take out loans to bridge the gap.

As we dealt with our new economic situation, there was a heightened sense of urgency in our need for a strong planning organisation to handle the intricacies of international loan management. In 1974, the Ministry of Economic Planning and Industrial Development (MEPID) was created. It had the mandate to scrutinise and endorse all fiscal proposals, even before they became the subject of cabinet papers. There was good reason for this concentration of oversight. We needed an engine for strict adherence to planning and the fulfilment of the conditions attached to aid.

The new ministry gave a sense of maturity to our worldview and the directness of purpose with which we were intending to change the economic downturn from drought, the high cost of imported fuel and the ample evidence of a looming world recession. We brought Sheriff Dibba home from Brussels and reappointed him into the cabinet to be Minister responsible for MEPID. After a hard slug the ministry put the finishing touches to the last of the capital expenditure programmes and prepared for the launch of the First Five-Year Plan for Economic and Social Development 1975-1980.

On 28 June 1974 I was appointed an honorary Knight Grand Cross of the Most Distinguished Order of St Michael and St George (GCMG) by Queen Elizabeth II. The GCMG is the sixth most senior in the British honours system.

On 12 August 1975, Njaimeh who had been admitted at a hospital in Tenerife, Canary Islands, gave birth to a boy. I named him Ebrima, after Ebrima Yoma Jallow - my dad's great friend and one of the most important people in my life.

In late August 1975, Sheriff Dibba set up his party - the National Convention Party (NCP) – at a gathering in Busumbala. Consequently by the time parliament met to consider the Plan on Wednesday 28 January 1976, Sheriff had long since been replaced by Lamin Bora Mboge. The Plan was adopted and, in it, my government put forward measures to reduce the disparity between rural and urban incomes through greater concentration of resources in the rural sector. By the end of 1975 just before the plan was implemented we had official exchange reserves of D72 million, representing 10 months import cover. It was a good start.

Up until 1975, about 80% cent of our foreign exchange came from grants-in-aid from Britain. An economy dependent on grants-in-aid could not succeed in taking independence forward. Unless we looked beyond grants-in-aid our political independence would be meaningless and we would still continue as a semi-autonomous colony. We had to diversify our funding resources. Our reputation as a stable country, with liberal and progressive policies coupled with my official travels building bridges, attracted more development partners. We received more support from the People's Republic of China, the Federal Republic of Germany, OECD, Nigeria, BADEA, Islamic Solidarity Fund, Islamic Development Bank, etc. Total bilateral and multilateral support was D409 million in the first five-year plan.

However, encouraged by some of the strides we had made over the period of the implementation of the National Development Programme, my government put in motion its policy of privatisation. I had advocated this idea as far back as the 1960s. We were putting it into practice only in the 1970s and 1980s at a time when personnel were still untried and investments too risky for total severance of responsibility. Therefore government held on to shares and supervision until such a time as the companies were able to go on their own. Thus the idea of the quasi-government commercial enterprise – the parastatal – was adopted.

As it turned out, right through the life of the first five-year plan the returns from some of the parastatals left a lot to be desired. There was an apparent inability to earn the expected contributions to government towards the development budget, since the contributions were meant to serve as a catalyst to business establishments in banking, road transport, insurance, merchandising and agricultural cooperation, as well as enable us to make more investments in river transport, fishing and tourism, and set the general pace for appreciable returns to the national coffers. And we did not just create them and leave them to fend for themselves within the difficult economic arena we knew they were being born into. We continued to restructure and reorganise management whenever it was feasible to do so.

We transformed the old GOMB into the GPMB – the Gambia Produce Marketing Board – after we had launched diversification projects in agriculture away from the groundnuts with the introduction of cotton, sesame and other cereals. The creation of the Agricultural Development Bank, the Limes Commercialisation Enterprise, the National Trading Corporation, the Gambia National Insurance Corporation, the Gambia Public Transport Corporation rising out of the ashes of the Gambia – Libya Public Transport Company and the Gambia Telecommunications Company Ltd and other significant investments were meant to ensure more independent budgeting and financing of development projects without recourse to grants-in-aid or loans from development partners.

We established the Gambia Commercial and Development Bank, the Gambia Cooperative Union and a chain of others right across the energy and agriculture sectors buttressed by village credit systems, whereby the village development committees get fully involved in the decision-making process. The thinking in community development strategies had changed from the traditional top-down delivery system to the grassroots system of the bottoms-up, informing the programmes and decisions at the top. The drive was geared to fulfil our strongest conviction that certain services were better suited to the private sector. We appreciated the importance of electricity supply and regular power to attract the necessary investment and to energise industry; so we set up the Gambia Utilities Corporation. However when it was realised that it was not solving our serious power crisis, we took measures to remedy the situation. It was replaced by the Utilities Holding Company under a contract with the Management Services Gambia Ltd.

We allowed some of those parastatals to invest further in joint ventures that resulted in the creation of other specialised service sector operations such as the Gambia River Transport Company and the Gambia National Insurance Corporation. We also founded the National Investment Board (NIB) and mandated it to facilitate and monitor the operations of those financial houses. Its first managing director was Horace R Monday Jr, a civil servant with long-standing experience.

The NIB was expected to bring about reinforcement to the capital structure of those organisations in the areas of investment, skills and management with great attention paid to the training and grooming of local human resources and the scouting for experts, nationally and internationally. Up until 1994, the NIB was responsible for streamlining the parastatals, charged with a programme to properly organise the divestiture of government from public operations which might become ready for transfer to private domestic ownership and management as soon as they attained maturity.

In May 1977, I declared *Operation Tesito*, calling on every citizen to gird up their loins for work. *Tesito,* simply put, was a tenet we needed to adopt if we had any intention of being serious about dealing with an issue as complex as national development. Early in the life of the PPP, I explained the concept of people's participation in development in partnership with government as best expressed in the concept of *Tesito* or self-reliance. By *Tesito* we meant not only full and enthusiastic participation by government and the people of this country in national reconstruction, we also meant less dependence on outside resources, and the ability of our people to improve themselves and their surroundings without excessive dependence on central government.

The young nation responded well to the call which is a concept common to all Gambian ethnic groups to get to work. Everyone had to be ready and willing to put in something as much as possible, be it by brain or by brawn, if the country had to develop. Gambians must put in the effort that would make the country more likely to succeed. The logic was unavoidable, especially for a developing country. There had to be personal and public commitment to good financial and moral behaviour. Communal society, where individuality took but second place to community interest, was the first building block in *Tesito*.

We were in a situation in which we had so much to do and with so little to do it with. We could not afford luxuries; neither could we afford waste and fiscal intemperance. And with more than a quarter of the national budget coming from our own resources we were determined to show our development partners that we were ready to help ourselves, so that whatever additional assistance we got from outside, it could take us the full distance.

In inculcating *Tesito,* we seized every opportunity to condemn the dependent attitude that made people expect everything to come from government. We taught that the people were the government and the government was the people. There was so much government could do for the individual or for the community. More had to come from individual endeavours to maximise domestic resources, particularly the mobilisation of our greatest resources – the people, the land and the river. *Tesito* became the national slogan and dovetailed perfectly into our traditional systems of mutual aid and collective work. It was admirably suited to a common work mentality that transcended ethnic and regional divides.

As a democratic government, we endeavoured to separate political issues from governmental ones, thereby giving full cognisance to the separation of powers. We encouraged a well-trained workforce in an apolitical civil service.

However, it was not lost to us that *Tesito* would have to have different ways of applications for different people. Grassroots society, for example, responded differently to the call from the way the urban population saw it. Many local communities seriously took up the construction of roads, causeways, bunds and dykes around their farms, all on a self-help basis. Without waiting for government, they took full responsibility of their immediate needs and funded most of them with help from their area councils or communities. Villagers built causeways across creeks, facilitating trade and contact with neighbouring villages. In other places, they cleared farmland, where suitable, for rice cultivation and opened up new pastures for cattle grazing.

In the urban areas, where dykes and causeways were not part of the environment, *Tesito* was sacrificing time and talent in the workplace or in the community in the spirit that offered itself to working for the common good.

However, the public service was at times fraught with a tendency to make one's office a place for personal enrichment instead of one for contribution towards national development. But wherever it manifested itself in the public service, I would seek to put brakes on indiscretion. I appealed to lawyers, magistrates and judges to think deeply of what they owed to their country and how they could best repay some of the great debt in service to the nation by arbitrating fairly and speedily. I said they ought to realise that *Tesito* was meant as much for them as for the poorer and less privileged members of our society. I specifically mentioned the legal profession but the appeal for *Tesito* was also meant for other professional groups – doctors, accountants, engineers, administrators, nurses, veterinarians, police, revenue collectors etc.

The little strides made in the communities that adhered to *Tesito* in the building of dykes might appear too small to count on as any victory. Indeed, in contrast to the bigger and more compelling issues of health care, child mortality, balance of payments, national security and integrity and keeping the state viable and stable, they would not tip the scale as any sign of major progress. However, to my mind, they were the little pieces that could connect in the larger jigsaw of development and were immediate enough for villagers to see that there had been a change in their lives because of their own effort in the spirit of *Tesito*.

There were rice farmers whose fields produced a surplus crop because the agricultural extension services had shown them and their families the techniques for harvesting up to three crops of rice in a single season. Businesspeople from the area immediately turned to rice cultivation and one Sarahule man in particular, Jawara Jawara, became such a successful rice grower and a role model. Every season, he produced three crops on his land and made much money in the process. That success story said something positive about the entrepreneurship of our people.

After a while, we realised that we might have been too ambitious in starting some of those projects, considering the level of sophistication of the personnel and the state of readiness of our infrastructure to handle such delicate and high-risk investments. The NTC and the ADB were clear examples of ventures meant to boost the economy. While the NTC was divested, the bank was closed because it could not find the requisite investment power in the farmers for whom it was established. Just as was the case with this bank, many of our administrative and managerial operators in our parastatals were inexperienced and smarting under sheer incompetence in managing such important institutions.

The temptation is always there to easily attribute the collapse of the majority of the parastatals to corruption. But even with honest people at the top, things can go wrong. Of course, where there is corruption that naturally compounds the deficit. My government however recognised that these institutions needed guidance to direct their attitudes to managing financial and commercial institutions within such delicate circumstances.

Where charges had been preferred against officers in the public service and where they had been found wanting, punishment was meted out to them in the form of dismissal, retirement and even jail sentences. Due process was ever the backbone of our juridical system. For example, when it became obvious that the GCDB was being run with managerial and administrative ineptitude, the government took action. In 1988, my government invited Robert R Nathan Associates Inc, an international economic consulting firm in the United States, to conduct a diagnostic study of the bank and present a report.

The report revealed a lack of direction that permeated the GCDB, describing the board of directors as lacking authority and somnolent. The board's minutes indicated that its meetings were infrequent, and its agendas basically devoid of all matters of substance. The study succinctly described the ineptitude and sheer incompetence of the managing director, his entrepreneurial attempts to build a viable organisation using considerable trial and error and a high degree of concentration in the decision-making process which failed. The study concluded that he must personally assume the responsibility for the chaotic status of the bank which was also weakened by the services of a deputy managing director who demonstrated no grasp of the fundamentals of accounting, finance or business management.

The general malaise of such incompetence was compounded by other human resource deficiencies. For example, the Development Department which had loans running into millions of dalasi (much of which turned out to be unsecured or interest free), was run by a staff of five consisting of a manager, three project officers and an accounts clerk – with every decision dictated by the managing director. This was most unacceptable and along with other revelations was an indictment of all the people and institutions concerned with monitoring and evaluating the bank (the IMF advisers, the NIB, the Central Bank and Ministry of Finance). It was their responsibility to know that the lack of duality at the GCDB was contrary to normal banking practice. It appeared that the GCDB was the fiefdom of its managing director and his board of directors.

The managing director, his deputy and some senior bank managers were dismissed and the board dissolved. To enable us to recover debts owed to the bank, we set up the Assets Management and Recovery Corporation (AMRC) and, after a long tussle in the appellate court, finally settled down to retrieve properties illegally acquired by public servants or those private entrepreneurs owing the GCDB large amounts of money, which, as of 31 March 1988, stood at D216 million. The sum of D103.7 million was owed by just twelve customers. This extremely high loan concentration represented 48% of the total outstanding loans, 82% of the total customers' deposits and 377% of the share capital and reserves of the bank.

The bank's long list of borrowers included Gambia Airways, Gambia Utilities Corporation, Saihou Ceesay, O B Conateh and the Gambia Cooperative Union (GCU), the leading purchaser of groundnuts. GCU was responsible for as much as 80% of the supplies to the GPMB. Despite earlier comprehensive restructuring, sustained credit facilities with the GCDB and large injections of grants of D5.9 million from the EEC Stabilisation Fund for Exports (STABEX) and £91,500 from the Royal Norwegian Society Emergency AID Fund, the GCU was mired in a credit crisis. It was owed D32.6 million in unrecoverable loans it had disbursed to buying agents, and owed the GCDB D3.7 million. The study further concluded that the fortunes of the GCDB and the GCU were so closely related that any attempt to solve the problems of one entity without solving those of the other would fail.

My government effected the cleaning up of the board and management of the GCDB and the AMRC was in action to recover bad debts owed to the bank.

I swore in members of the commission of inquiry into the GCU on 8 June 1994. It was chaired by a Sierra Leonean judge, the Hon Mrs Patricia Macauley. Ironically it was the AFPRC government that received and acted upon its findings.

23

Relations with Senegal

I took pains at the 20th Mansa Bengo held in Basse at the end of January 1963, and again at the Constitutional Talks in London in June 1964 to revisit the history of our association with Britain since 1587 when English merchants first sailed up the River Gambia. I felt duty-bound to trace the deep connections because they would have so much to do with future choices we would make in the life of our people and country. The English used the river both for trade and for further exploration of the continent of Africa. England was not alone in this search. Hot on the heels of the English were the French who arrived and claimed the lower parts of the Gambia basin and fought the English over James Island for possession and title of the land and waterway.

The English and the French were working on information the Portuguese had collected when they explored the coast as early as 1455, searching for gold. Not much of the precious metal was found lying on the river banks, as myth had it. The new explorers carried on trading in other commodities and in 1652 started trading in human beings. The importance of the Transatlantic Slave Trade lies in the international, political and cultural attitudes that grew out of this new hideous commercial phenomenon; and how those made an impact on the mission to free ourselves from slavery and colonialism, the twin systems that directed the lives and purses of many Africans, Europeans and people in the Americas, for over three centuries.

Incidentally, when Robert T Hennemeyer was US Ambassador to Banjul in the 1980s, he shared with me a copy of a thesis written by Eva Seligson, a young American who was a West African Studies major at Mount Holyoke College in the US. Seligson had written a convincing senior thesis that showed that the Latvians colonised The Gambia from 1651 to 1661. The Duke of Courland, a fellow named Jacob Kettler, had embarked on an ambitious plan in which he traded Baltic manufactured goods for gold and other raw materials in Barra and Kombo. He was successful enough to claim land for his duchy and established his colonial headquarters in a fort he built on St Andrew's Island, which the Portuguese had so named nearly a century before. Fate, the young researcher wrote in her thesis, dealt Kettler a devastating blow when an Englishman called

Major Robert Holmes extinguished the Duke's dreams by ousting him from his island base which the English thereafter renamed James Island. The English later built Fort James there.

The French arrived and, in a bid to remove the English, bombarded Fort James with destructive results. The island changed hands several times before the English settled in finally. Bathurst, established in 1816, closer to the mouth of the River Gambia, assumed greater importance in that regard. In 1884, the contending powers met in Berlin to decide who owned what in Africa. At a meeting on 10 August 1889, the French and English agreed on how much of our land each owned. In 1891, the Colonial Boundaries Commission arrived in the Senegambia area and firmly mapped out the territory. The people and the land became divided into The Gambia and Senegal, separated from their common history and heritage of thousands of years into colonial British and French entities. From then on relations between the two colonies became the business of London and Paris.

Political independence from France on 4 April 1960 put the Senegalese at the helm of government in their country, while in The Gambia political independence from Britain was attained in 1965. Peaceful co-existence between the two neighbours henceforth would depend on negotiation and collaboration. The two governments immediately began consultations on closer cooperation in all fields. As early as 1961, inter-state ministerial meetings were held. Chief Minister P S Njie made visits to Dakar to explore the ways that relations between the two countries could be formalised. The Senegalese returned the visit to Bathurst in May 1961 when Prime Minister Mamadou Dia, accompanied by his Foreign Minister Waldiodio Ndiaye and other top cabinet members, came and worked out the agreements that set up the Inter-state Committee as the second-tier point of contact after the summit meetings.

To show how brisk the contacts were P S Njie was back in Dakar in October 1961 at the second inter-state meeting. Over the three days they met, both sides nailed down plans on road communication, agriculture and other aspects of national life. The PPP was at the time the opposition in the Legislative Council and in 'shadow government' fashion we followed the issues closely. We were mindful of the possibilities that lay in our call for constitutional improvements towards a more representative government in Bathurst. It would not be long before the same chores of negotiation would fall under our purview as the party in government.

When we took over the reins of government after the 1962 General Election, we inherited the work of the Inter-state Committee. As cooperation with Senegal increased, we factored into our national budgets trade, movement of persons, currency, banking and other matters.

However, taking over from P S Njie was not as smooth as I had envisaged it would be. We had gone to Dakar with a slightly different and more defined notion of Senegalo-Gambian relations from what our predecessors might have been working out with the Senegalese.

At our first meeting with the Senegalese, we sensed that there were some among them who would rather deal with P S Njie on account of their consonance with his total union programmes. We had a programme with solid objectives. We listened attentively and moved quickly to consult closely with those of them who appeared to be more sympathetic to our views on self-determination in partnership with Senegal rather than in union with it. We found a ready and welcoming ear in the influential parliamentarian, Ibou Diallo, and his group of officials who were willing to work with us and forward our own agenda of cooperation with the Senegalese government. In fairness to all involved, this was only our perception of things; no one at any time pronounced any preferences.

With the head of government and the foreign minister of Senegal at odds with our agenda, we found our initial meetings quite difficult. However, we would not be cowed and, overtime, we began to make some head way with the concrete issues of sovereignty, independence and territorial integrity, issues that Dia struggled to diplomatically entertain even though it was clear that he was deeply intolerant of any independence agenda for The Gambia. He would rather see our country merge completely with Senegal.

Dia and P S Njie were not alone in setting their sights on total union of the two countries; it was also the tacit agenda of the British Colonial Office. In October 1961, P S Njie's visit to London for financial talks with the British government coincided with President Leopold Sedar Senghor's visit to the British capital. Whether the three parties – P S Njie, the Colonial Office and Senghor – had consulted directly is pure speculation, but certainly it was revealing that Senghor issued an official statement during that visit saying: "It would be only natural if The Gambia sought to unite with Senegal after achieving independence. We have no intention of taking other initiatives on the matter... [It] will be up to Gambians to decide what they want once they have got their independence."

Thankfully, that position coincided with the PPP policy on independence. We were fully aware of the subtle difference in intentions despite the president's accommodating statement. We continued to be discreet, courteous and forthcoming during inter-state meetings and at summits between the president and me. We stressed our desire for good neighbourliness and that we looked forward to becoming independent. We carried patriotic and clear directions to ensure that Senegalo-Gambia cooperation was achieved under a controlled and equitable platform. We were confident that Senegal would act with democratic goodwill along those lines.

Dia soon fell from grace and went to prison in circumstances surrounding a coup plot against the Senghor government. Nevertheless, no matter what the internal issues were in Senegal, that country continued to be top priority in our books and remained so throughout my time in office. It featured prominently in the resolutions that emerged from the crucial discussions at the all-party talks we had in Bathurst with the Earl of Perth in 1961 on constitutional reform. At that meeting and at the follow-up meeting in London the same year, all agreed that the future relations with Senegal were better left to the government that would emerge after the 1962 General Election. It was therefore that mandate we were so diligently executing by keeping Senegal in the forefront at all times.

Although we were capable of handling our relations with Senegal ourselves, I felt strongly that the opinion of independent experts would be helpful for an unbiased and more detailed understanding of the situation between us. I therefore requested the UN Secretary General U Thant to send a team of experts to carry out a study of what type of cooperation was possible under the circumstances. U Thant was receptive to the idea and, indeed, his response was encouraging especially when he expressed that he was gratified by the constructive approach of the two governments and shared our conviction that the decision could make an important contribution to the stability, development and prosperity of Senegal and The Gambia and to the cause of African unity.

The UN experts who arrived in October 1962 completed their study after two months. The team, led by Hubertus Van Mook, produced the report entitled *Alternatives for Association Between The Gambia and Senegal*. That document, published as Sessional Paper No 13 of 1964 and laid before the House of Representatives, presented some insightful and significant possibilities for closer forms of association between the two countries.

We showed how important communication was for us when in 1964 we allocated £180,000 of our first development budget for the resurfacing of the road from Bathurst to Brumen, the construction of the Trans-Gambia Highway and of the feeder roads to it. These networks complemented those the Senegalese were constructing to link their capital, Dakar, with the rural areas. Our positive response to update our road system opened up tremendous business opportunities for trade in and out of Senegal.

Following a conference on foreign affairs held in Dakar from 27 to 29 March 1965, we signed a joint communiqué outlining our foreign policy strategies. This first conference with Senegal since we became independent was one of the most successful of many we would have over the years.

To strengthen our economic ties we signed a Free Trade Agreement with Senegal in 1966. Some time in 1968, some two years into the Agreement, Senegal found itself unable to comply with the tariffs and other implications on account of its prior commitments to other Francophone economic blocks to which it belonged. In consideration of its own interests in those commitments, Senegal pulled out of its agreements with us. We understood perfectly and, without rancour, simply reorganised our platform of collaboration to accommodate their difficulties. They expressed the choice to withdraw from the agreement and we accepted it.

In 1967 I was honoured to receive the Grand Cross of the National Order of the Republic of Senegal.

We met regularly and alternately thereafter in Bathurst and Dakar, contacts which bore their finest fruits on 28 January 1968, when we signed an agreement to open the Senegalo-Gambian Secretariat in Banjul. By 1 February the office was fully functional. Senegalese national, Seydina Sy, took office as its first Executive Secretary.

By the time President Senghor had made his second official visit in 1969, the 1967 Treaty of Association encouraged us further in our cooperation, and we twinned our capital cities with symbolic ceremonies held in Bathurst in April and in Dakar in November.

The Gambia government engaged experts to study the hydrology and topography of the Gambia River Basin. Based on the findings in a USAID report on the state of our Senegambia transport links, we began the reconstruction of the Mandinaba – Selety road. We firmed up trade and other mutual agreements under various subjects such as the prevention of cattle rustling and the violation of our territorial waters by foreign ships. This presented a great opportunity for us to study and demarcate our own maritime boundaries. We strengthened the VHF links between our two airports at Yundum and Yoff and we tendered our application for observer status in the Organisation of the Senegal River Basin States.

There were more celebrations in 1970 apart from The Gambia's attainment of republican status or my inauguration as President in April. On 1 May, in a traditional wedding ceremony that took place after the Friday prayers at the mosque in Niamina I got married for the third time to Njaimeh Mboge, according to *sunna*. The nuptial rites were presided over by Seyfo Saja Mboge, an uncle of the bride. Njaimeh was an employee of the Medical and Health Department and a granddaughter of Ya Njaimeh Mboge, a close friend of the matriarch in the Jawara *kabilo*, Nacesay Jawara.

The governments of The Gambia and Senegal were committed to those projects that facilitated economic growth to mutual advantage. It was within that framework that I met with Senghor in Kaolack, Senegal, in late June 1978 and we agreed to set up the *Organisation pour la Mise en Valeur du Fleuve Gambie* (OMVG), one of the earliest practical results of our cooperation. Out of this emerged the important proposal of the project to build a bridge-barrage over the River Gambia the bridge – to provide a connection between north and south Senegal, would be part of the African Highway network. The barrage would harness fresh water for Gambian agriculture and irrigate an additional 24,000 hectares for rice cultivation.

The issue of a bridge across the River Gambia was one of major importance to Senegal. A bridge would not only cut travel time from Dakar to Ziguinchor considerably, it would also mean massive reduction in toll fees at ferry crossings across the River Gambia. The Bridge Convention of 1975 gave full sovereignty over the toll bridge to The Gambia and guaranteed the right of passage without hindrance permanently, day or night, to persons, goods and vehicles to and from Senegal. The bridge was never built; neither was the barrage. The crossing by ferry of Senegalese vehicles at Farafenni has always been an easy target for gripes.

Historically, the relationship had largely been harmonious given the fact of our homogeneity and pre-colonial heritage. The advent of colonialism brought about a parallel development of cultures along those of the colonising powers – the French in Senegal and the British in The Gambia.

I will risk some controversy to say that the most popular musician in the past twenty years in The Gambia has been Senegal's Youssou Ndour. It is also true that in the late 1960s and early 1970s, the most popular band in Senegal was The Gambia's Super Eagles Band. That was the way the people carried on even with the colonial separation of the economies and the consolidation of two separate countries. Many Senegalese have contributed and continue to contribute to the Gambian economy. They are actively engaged in fisheries, construction, weaving, art, bricklaying, welding, etc.

My government would point to such entrepreneurship on the part of the Senegalese to challenge the young people of The Gambia. In effect, our youth should take full advantage of the academic skills and vocational training opportunities the government was putting at their disposal. The millions of dalasi spent on skills acquisition in technical and vocational training projects was meant to prepare our youth for jobs in both the public and private sectors. It was meant to help them qualify for access to loans and credits in the lending schemes run by NGO and village credit VISACA projects and by commercial banks.

The country's economy depended to a large extent on the youth on the farms and in the workshops and offices. Improvement in their skills would help them respond with equal energy and entrepreneurship to what non-Gambians were demonstrating so that they too would make their mark in similar technical jobs either at home or abroad. The option to remain idle or to leave for Europe had always confounded our thinking; it caused great moments of frustration in my government as some of the reports to cabinet from the Ministry of Youth and Sports could verify.

Border problems were not unique to Senegal and The Gambia. Indeed, African countries with borders like ours have had their share of tense standoffs. However, every time tempers erupted the people and the two governments would use language and familial ties to talk over problems and mend fences. Over time, the two governments signed many treaties, among which the Treaty of Mutual Defence and, perhaps the most complex of them all, the Senegambia Confederation, were exemplary. The last of them was the Treaty of Friendship signed between us in 1991. Those were the first talks to mend fences since the breakdown of the Senegambia Confederation in October 1989.

Between 1965 and 1976, we signed twenty-three agreements. In 1965, on Independence Day we signed three - the Agreement on Cooperation in Foreign Policy, the Agreement on Cooperation on Matters of Security and Defence and the Agreement on the Integrated Development of the Gambia River Basin. Other important agreements include the Treaty of Association signed in 1967, the agreement for Mutual Administrative Assistance between the Customs Departments of The Gambia and Senegal in 1970 and, in 1975, the Convention Concerning the Utilisation of the Trans-Gambia Bridge.

We had always been interested in keeping the momentum through talks and treaties despite the difficulties. One of the worst moments occurred in 1969 when Senegal's Minister of Finance and Economic Affairs, Jean Colin, launched an 'anti-smuggling' offensive against The Gambia by calling so-called Gambian smuggling economic aggression. In our estimation, what he termed smuggling was no more than people plying their trade and weighing the advantages and disadvantages of tariffs across our borders. The daily activities could not have been organised smuggling *per se*. I completely agreed that the situation should be policed and regularised, but certainly not by sanctions, nor, indeed, at the expense of harmony between us.

My government was flabbergasted by the charges but disagreed entirely with our angry youths who demonstrated against President Senghor's visit to Bathurst. He came for urgent consultations on the tension resulting from the minister's statements. Led by some radical elements of a social club, the Kent Street Vous, the youths marched on State House carrying banners and placards and chanting revolutionary slogans. To show concession and respect for their democratic right to political expression, I agreed to speak with the leaders. However, when they presented their letter to me I was taken aback by the tone and content of the petition. I summoned them back immediately to register my own protest against their attitude.

I was rather disappointed when I later read the police reports on how suddenly the mood of the crowd outside the Quadrangle courtyard changed for the worse while I was addressing the leaders inside my office. The agitated crowd soon began moving out but, instead of dispersing, marched away in sections to lodge a similar protest note at the Senegalo-Gambian Secretariat where they caused minor damage. They continued their protest at the Senegalese High Commission. By this time, of course, the size of the crowd had increased and the demonstrators were getting unruly. They threw stones at the High Commission building causing some minor damage.

The police and Field Force units had to be called in to deal with the angry crowds growing in such numbers as to outstretch our security forces. But they were able, during the course of the day, to disperse the large crowd of protesters, among whom were hooligans who had taken advantage of the situation to unleash attacks on Senegalese nationals and businesses.

However, Dakar hardly showed any mood for compromise. Over the whole year, the situation did not improve; in fact, it worsened. In 1971, I was left with no option but to send a little-publicised note to the UN Secretary General expressing "serious apprehension over Senegalese intentions towards The Gambia". I asked U Thant to inform the Security Council of our complaint "in order to prepare world opinion for acts of aggression which could follow".

Senegal's reaction was uncompromising. Dakar immediately announced its intention "to construct a road around The Gambia" so that there would be an all-Senegalese trunk road linking Dakar to Ziguinchor. To our mind, such a road was unrealistic, considering the capital outlay to build a road nearly seven hundred and fifty miles long around The Gambia.

Jean Colin's charge encouraged harassment of travellers and traders at Senegalese police and customs border posts.

While we were strenuously being described as smugglers, the rug was pulled right from under our feet in 1972. Kutubo Dibba, the younger brother of Vice President and Minister of Finance Sheriff Dibba, and living with him at his official residence at No 1 Marina, was stopped at Kaolack by Senegalese customs officers. They searched the Gambia Government vehicle he was driving and discovered commercial goods he had failed to declare at the border and a huge collection of butut coins, which was in great demand for ornamentation by jewellers in Senegal. Needless to say, my government was embarrassed, the more so by the capital Senegal tried to make out of what became known as the "Butut Scandal".

On 15 September 1972, the Vice President addressed a letter to me touching on my discussions with him on 13 September of the preliminary police enquiries that the alleged contraband was actually loaded on to the vehicle at his official residence. He assured me that he stood high among all Gambians in condemning what he described as a shameful crime and that all the culprits should be brought to book. He wrote to inform me that he had no knowledge of the crime and wished to declare his innocence. He also announced his decision to resign as Vice President. I wrote back the same day congratulating him on the high sense of responsibility to the nation which prompted that difficult decision. I said I was accepting his resignation with much reluctance but offered that in consonance with his pledge of loyal support to the party and to the government, he could continue to serve as Minister of Finance. Apparently the depth of his hurt was such that he overlooked the offer for him to remain in cabinet. Dibba gave up both offices. The following day, I appointed Assan Musa Camara (formerly Andrew David Camara) Vice President and I M Garba Jahumpa Minister of Finance.

We succeeded in convincing Dakar that our acceptance of the resignation of the former vice president was a sign of our will not to compromise our good relations and not to allow anything to jeopardise the advances we had made. The year before, I had proved our commitment to promoting cordial relations when, despite the continuing tensions caused by lingering border restrictions, I honoured the invitation of President Senghor to attend the festivities of Senegal's 11th independence anniversary on 4 April 1971 in Ziguinchor. We had to rise above moments of unnecessary severe provocation and for the sake of good sense, good neighbourliness and the higher cause of working resolutely towards solutions.

The most critical challenge in our relations would come years later in 1981 when rebels announced that a Marxist Leninist group had taken over my government. We invoked the Mutual Defence Pact, a clear recognition of a need for common actions to protect each other against external aggression and internal upheaval that could pose threats to the governments or to the peoples. Senegal's direct intervention helped quell the coup attempt.

Senegal was getting ready for a major change of the guard in its executive leadership and we watched that development closely. President Senghor was about to do a first by stepping down and allowing an unprecedented political transition in Africa to take place. Consequently we began our homework sizing up the heir apparent whom he had chosen to succeed him. We congratulated Abdou Diouf and undertook to work closely with him in the interest of our two countries.

This peaceful handing over of power reminded me of statements I made at the 17th Ordinary Session of the OAU Assembly of Heads of State in Freetown, Sierra Leone, in July 1980 when I emphasised the importance of democratic transition. I exhorted my colleagues that we must strengthen the democratic institutions of our individual states to bring about smooth political transitions wherever necessary and which would be consistent with our African values.

24

30 July 1981: assault on democracy

The year 1981 started joyfully with a new addition to the family. Njaimeh gave birth to a girl, Ramatoulie (named after Njaimeh's mother), on 17 February, the eve of our 16th independence anniversary. Chilel had a boy later that year on 24 June, whom we named Housainou (after Chilel's eldest brother).

In June 1981 Njaimeh and I left for Nairobi to attend the meeting of the OAU Assembly of Heads of State and Government. The meeting was the moment for the average person in Africa. Since the creation of the OAU in May 1963, our attention had been taken up by decolonisation and how to do away with apartheid in South Africa. But while we fully endorsed the principles of the Universal Declaration of Human Rights of 1948 and wanted all African countries to be fully compliant with UN standards, the continent had no mechanism with which to police itself. The Nairobi summit discussed and adopted the draft of the African Charter on Human and Peoples' Rights. Through the efforts of various pressure groups the OAU had long been made aware of human rights abuses on the continent. Some even accused the organisation of clearly failing to condemn the human rights violations committed by some of its own members while everyone made plenty of noise against colonialism and apartheid.

There had to be a mechanism to protect human rights on the continent. From the 1961 Lagos Conference organised by the International Commission of Jurists (ICJ) to the 1979 UN-sponsored Monrovia Seminar on the Establishment of Regional Commissions on Human Rights with Special Reference to Africa, a great deal of pressure was brought to bear on the OAU and its leaders, as one commentator put it, "to uphold the spirit that motivated the struggle for political independence – to restore to the African peoples their dignity lost during slave trade and colonial eras – a cause for which they won international sympathy and support".

At their July 1979 summit meeting in Monrovia African heads of state decided to form a committee of experts to draft an African Charter on Human and Peoples' Rights and to provide the mechanisms to promote and protect the rights to be embodied in the Charter. It was that draft that came before us in Nairobi at the 18th Assembly of the OAU and which was unanimously adopted. A new dawn broke for Africa and when the Charter later came into force on 21 October 1986, the date was proudly declared "African Human Rights Day".

Upon the adoption of the African Charter, nothing could equal the pride and gratification with which I viewed The Gambia's contribution in hosting two preparatory meetings of the jurists who came to Banjul to work on the drafts of a charter. Even more gratifying to me was the accordance of the name – The Banjul Charter – to such a worthy document in the advancement of the African people.

I made a brief statement during one of the sessions in Nairobi in which I laid emphasis on the issue as I had done back on 18 February 1981, when I toasted President Hilla Limann of Ghana at the banquet celebrating our 16th independence anniversary and his state visit to The Gambia as the chief guest of honour.

After such a successful meeting I was ready to begin my annual leave. Accordingly, Njaimeh and I proceeded to England where I began a well-earned rest at my home in Birchen Lane, Haywards Heath. Britain was in the grip of a royal wedding fever. Prince Charles, heir to the British throne, and Lady Diana Spencer, were to be married. The wedding took place on Wednesday 29 July 1981. My wife and I considered it a great honour not only to have been invited to attend but also to have the royal palace accord us the use of a chauffeur-driven Rolls Royce to bring us from our home in the Sussex countryside to St Paul's Cathedral, London, where the nuptials were taking place. We immersed ourselves in the sights and sounds, glamour and pageantry of the fairytale wedding. We went back home in the quiet warmth of the early summer night and went to bed as soon as we got in.

The next day I was playing a round of golf at the Haywards Heath Golf Club when Richard Luce (now Baron Luce), then Minister of State for Foreign Affairs at the Foreign and Commonwealth Office, came with really bad news. I can't remember his exact words, but he must have said something like "Sorry to interrupt your game sir, but I regret to inform you that there is a coup in your country."

My initial thoughts went to the safety of the people back home, particularly my family. I abandoned the game and left for Birchen Lane immediately.

We tried unsuccessfully to get through to Banjul. Finally about midday on Friday 31 July I spoke to Vice President Assan Musa Camara. He reported to me his shock over what he heard on Radio Gambia in the early hours of 30 July. He said he was preparing for the day's work ahead when he heard the shrill and agitated voice of a man on the radio denouncing the Jawara regime and announcing the suspension of the constitution, the dissolution of parliament and the arrest and detention of all government ministers. The voice announced the establishment of a Marxist-Leninist government under the chairmanship of Kukoi Samba Sanyang and his 12-member Supreme Council of the Revolution.

The rebels and some civilians had broken into the armoury at the Field Force Depot in Bakau, seizing a good quantity of arms and ammunition. They then opened the prison gates at Mile 2 and armed any prisoner wishing to join them, thus strengthening their numbers. They also took over the airport and State House.

Through the telephone line I could hear the gunshots and the booming chaos through the crackling line from the police headquarters where a few ministers and a handful of other brave men were holed up and working on strengthening the resistance. The vice president said Attorney General Momodou Lamin Saho came early that morning to his residence to discuss the announcement that he had also heard on the radio. Together, they left in a taxi under pelting rain and drove to the Police Headquarters in Buckle Street. There they found Inspector General of Police Abdoulie Mboob already dug in with 17 lightly armed men on duty. They then sent for Agriculture Minister Saihou Sabally who promptly joined them there.

With weapons seized from the rebels, the loyalists were able to increase their firepower. This situation further improved considerably when a small unit of reinforcements from Farafenni led by Modou Njie turned up on the second day, after having made their way against countless odds to reach the police headquarters.

Overnight, the world was told that our claim to democracy and our socio-economic progress as a country since 1965 were nothing more than a sham. Some people agreed with Kukoi Samba Sanyang that I was the oppressive despot sitting heavily on the heads of a wretched citizenry yearning for freedom. The rest was left to the imagination of the readership of the newspapers that were ready to believe the worst about misrule and despotism in Africa.

The vice president told me that after the longest sustained rebel attack the day before when the action began and not being quite sure of how much more firepower the rebels could muster, Saho advised that the 1965 Mutual Defence Agreement with Senegal be invoked. I gave my blessing to the decision and informed him that we were also in active discussions with the Senegalese Embassy in London. I was glad that they had gone ahead and invited the First Secretary at the Senegalese High Commission to the Police Headquarters. Their discussions ended with the vice president signing the official request to President Diouf for the commitment of Senegalese troops to assist in putting down the coup.

During the course of that Friday morning, the Senegalese Ambassador in London came to Haywards Heath. We called Dakar and I spoke to President Diouf. I formalised our request for Senegalese assistance under the Mutual Defence Agreement. President Diouf confirmed his agreement and I decided to go back home as soon as possible. We discussed the absolute necessity for me to be close at hand to direct the rest of the resistance. There and then, Diouf kindly offered the use of his official aircraft, *Pointe de Sangomar*, to airlift my party to Dakar.

Before long, a cablegram from Dakar reached Banjul sealing the agreement between President Diouf and me. The vice president's next move was to give assurance to the key foreign diplomats in Banjul that Senegalese troops were on their way and that the government had not fallen.

Later that day, I gave an interview to the BBC Network Africa programme. I told them of my utter dismay at the coup because whether it succeeded or not, it had cost The Gambia the impression of an unstable country. It would be a pity indeed if the list of rebels I had received – Kukoi Samba Sanyang, Dembo Jammeh, Kartong Fatty, Junkung Saho, Jerreh Momodou Sanyang, Simon Talibo Sanneh, Kambeng Badjie, Ousainou Jawo, Apai Sonko – many of them school drop-outs and taxi drivers – were to be allowed to take over our peaceful country.

Close to midnight on 31 July, three hundred Senegalese airborne paratroopers dropped over the village of Jambur and began combing through the bush as they headed for Yundum Airport. They encountered a barrage of counter fire, but after a while of stiff fighting, they soon destroyed rebel positions. Infantry units supported by tanks entered the country through Selety and proceeded to Banjul through Brikama, Lamin and Serekunda. As soon as Serekunda was cleared, the rebels only held the road around Radio Gambia and other parts of Bakau towards the military barracks. The relatively long hours it took the Senegalese to advance over the territory was because they were under strict instructions to minimise civilian casualties and damage to property.

I learnt that the coup plotters had seized my wife Chilel and ten of my children, forcing them at gunpoint to declare their support for the coup over Radio Gambia. When I later heard the recordings, I was deeply distressed at the terror in Chilel's and my children's (Momodou, Fatoumata, Foday, Mariam, Njaimeh, Ebrima and Mustapha) voices pleading with me and the government to give in, because the rebels threatened to kill them unless we surrendered. My daughter Chilel was only 3 at the time and my two babies – Ramatoulie and Housainou - 5 months and 1 month respectively.

At one point, Kukoi seized the microphone and announced who he was – the chairman of the Supreme Council of the Revolution! He said he wanted the Senegalese, the outside world and Gambians to know that I could not frighten him and that the whole country was with him. I could not quite assess what "whole country" he was talking about. It certainly could not have been the country that gave the PPP a landside victory in the 1977 Presidential and Parliamentary Elections in an 83% turnout of voters.

Then he made the most macabre of proclamations about his childlessness and reference to his possible death. "All of Jawara's children are here," Kukoi declared, "His wife is here and I shall kill the whole lot and thereafter stand to fight against the Senegalese soldiers. I have no children and I am prepared to die. The Supreme Council of the Revolution has empowered me to kill the whole lot ... Jawara has eight children. Baby Anne is here. I have no sympathy for them if Jawara has no sympathy for his family. I am prepared to fight with the Senegalese and if I am killed, well that is that. I shall know that I died in the cause for The Gambia."

I did not have a Baby Anne among my children. Nevertheless, the misnaming of one of them added pain to the whole charade that showed me how neurotic Kukoi was. At the same time it galvanised me with the resolution to ensure that I free my family, my ministers and the other innocent hostages from the grip of a mad man. I feared seriously for the lives of my loved ones and other innocent people in Kukoi's hands. It was clear to me that this was a man desperate and armed who had reached the end of his tether.

Other hostages included my elder brother Sheriffo, Sanjally Bojang, my father-in-law Momodou Musa Njie, Momar Fall, one of the secretaries at the Senegalese High Commission, Saidou Nourou Ba, the executive secretary of the Senegalo-Gambian Secretariat, his wife and children. They threatened to kill all of them if the Senegalese troops did not withdraw.

What cowardly coercion by sick criminals who could seize the elderly, women, children and even babies at gunpoint to achieve their aims. Later, I learnt that on their way to Radio Gambia the rebels stopped at the residence of Sheriff Mustapha Dibba in Banjul, only a few metres away from the residence of the vice president, who was busy at the time coordinating the resistance.

Back in London, Richard Luce put me through to Prime Minister Margaret Thatcher, and I asked her for the British Government's assistance with resolving the hostage crisis. Two British Special Air Service (SAS) troopers – a Major Ian Crooke and a sergeant were despatched to Banjul via Dakar. Upon their arrival in Banjul they were met by Mr Clive Lee a former SAS major who was working in The Gambia at the time of the coup. I was confident that the three-man SAS team – men with considerable experience in dealing with hostage situations – would, with the help of our own loyal forces and the Senegalese, be able to free the hostages unharmed.

I gave a press conference before leaving London on Saturday 1 August, making it clear that my government had not been removed and that I was at that time more concerned with foiling the attempt than apportioning blame as to who was behind it. I expressed no fear for my own person whatsoever in returning and doing something about the situation. I reaffirmed the plurality of the system in place in The Gambia which should have made a coup unnecessary. It was a democratic government with freedom for everybody to express themselves strictly in terms of the constitution and in conformity with the respected principles of human rights.

Our flight from London to Dakar went by quickly. The five hours it took were filled with an intense review of the situation and what I would have to cover in the broadcasts and interviews I would give. When we landed in Dakar we were received by High Commissioner Bakary Dabo and senior Senegalese government officials. Dabo gave me a precise briefing of the negotiations with Diouf on the size of the contingent of troops that was already deployed in Banjul. We went straight to work, finalising those matters as well as the statements I had prepared.

The Senegalese government immediately accorded me the privilege to address the Gambian people on Radio Senegal. I did so in English, following up in Mandinka and Wollof. I announced that I had arrived close to home and that I understood my supreme duty to do everything possible to save the country from the hands of the coup leader and his collaborators. I saluted the courage of my vice president, ministers, the Inspector General of Police, his officers and others in the Field Force who stood loyally by their country and government. I paid tribute to those who lost their lives in the tragedy, and assured their grieving families that they did not die in vain.

It was clear in my mind that my supreme responsibility was towards our country and its people. I told them that apart from invoking the Defence Agreement, I had decided to come immediately to help restore law and order as quickly as possible. I assured the nation that Senegalese troops had joined forces loyal to my government and their effort was producing a marked turnaround in the rebels' standoff. The Senegalese troops had already retaken the airport and had also expelled the rebels from the Trans-Gambia Ferry at Farafenni. With the troops cleaning the Kombos, before long they would be joining up with our loyal forces in Banjul. With more Senegalese troops continuing to enter The Gambia through Casamance, I reckoned that it would only be a matter of hours before the coup would be over. I urged all citizens, wherever they were, to continue to defend their country against such lawlessness. I asked them to be calm and vigilant.

I reminded my compatriots that for the nineteen years I had been at the helm of affairs of our country, my efforts had consistently been in the direction of safeguarding the liberty of its citizens and at the same time striving to improve their living conditions. Indeed, my country was not a country flowing with milk and honey, and our economy had come through some severe times. But my government never promised the impossible. However, I was prepared to see to it that the peace and progress achieved so far was not destroyed. I promised to be home with my people shortly to continue that noble task. I urged Kukoi and his fellow insurgents to lay down their arms and stop the wanton shedding of Gambian blood.

The Supreme Revolutionary Council, it turned out, was made up of nonentities. Their leader Kukoi Samba Sanyang was a candidate for the NCP in the 1977 general election in the Eastern Foni constituency, where he polled 708 votes against 4,532 for the PPP candidate, Ismaila Jammeh. He thus updated his curriculum vitae as a failed teacher, a failed seminarian, an unsuccessful politician and now a coup plotter, directly answerable for the deaths of hundreds of people between 30 July and 4 August 1981.

It was a long-drawn-out ordeal. I prayed fervently that every one of the hostages was safe. I had meant every word I said in my stern warning to the rebels that there would be severe retribution should any of those innocent people get hurt. I was also sincere when I offered them a fair trial and possible lenient treatment if they released all the hostages unharmed.

After Senegalese troops had cleared Yundum Airport and stretches of the road through the Kombos of rebels, we flew in from Dakar. We arrived around midday on Sunday 2 August and I was received by the vice president. After a short debriefing, we were airlifted by helicopter to Banjul around the Admiralty Wharf from where we then travelled in an armoured convoy to the Senegalese High Commission.

I immediately made an Emergency Proclamation and got published the Emergency Regulations 1981 (Legal Notice No 8 of 1981) having considered it expedient that certain measures were necessary for securing public safety, the defence of The Gambia, the maintenance of public order and the suspension of mutiny, rebellion and riot and for maintaining supplies and services essential to the life of the community. The notice stipulated stiff cash fines and terms of imprisonment. It gave the presidency wide-ranging powers but which, in my own conviction, would be used with the greatest consideration and restraint.

I drove to Radio Syd, the Swedish-owned private radio station just outside Banjul. I spoke in Wollof to the terrified and besieged people who in the previous few days had no markets to attend and no shops from where to get food. It was highly reassuring and welcome to the populace that I was back and speaking to them, especially telling them that the ordeal was virtually over.

We spent the next two nights at the Senegalese High Commission. On Monday 3 August, reporters from Radio Gambia came to see me for an interview. I gave them one not only to further assure the people, but also to allay the rumour making the rounds among the people that I was not really among them in Banjul. I reiterated the messages I had broadcast from London and Dakar and thanked all those who physically and morally stood by my government and by the nation when we were faced with a most regrettable event.

As the day progressed, we were ready to move to the State House that had been safely under the command of the Senegalese forces. What was of great relief to me was the news that the SAS men had successfully freed Chilel and some of the children at the Medical Research Council without incident. The US Embassy had also furnished us with the information that the Senegalese troops had freed my other children and scores of hostages including some Europeans from the Bakau Depot. The rebels holding them fled when they realised their colleagues guarding Chilel and some of the children at the MRC had been disarmed and arrested.

Kukoi had escaped on Sunday 2 August and was broadcasting recordings of his ranting from portable transmitters. He had slipped with some of his men through the confusion and made it to Kartong, a fishing village in southern Kombo, from where he escaped to Guinea Bissau. We would express our concern to President Joao Bernardo Vieira that he was harbouring the fugitive murderer and his gang if he allowed them to stay on in his country. From Bissau, Kukoi flew to Cuba, and finally to Libya.

I was united again with my family. Chilel and the children looked tired from the ordeal they had gone through, but had held up admirably well. I cringed to think of the level of cruelty meted out to my family and the other hostages; it must have been horrendous for them. Their captors constantly barked threats at them, feeding them poor food comprising mainly of half-cooked potatoes and rice not fit for human consumption.

It was after the thorough and heart-searching review of our system of government and party operations that we realised that the first shot of the events of 30 July 1981 was actually fired on 27 October 1980 when a renegade junior member of the paramilitary Field Force, Mustapha Danso, shot and killed Field Force Deputy Commander Eku Mahoney. The cold-blooded gunning down of one Gambian by another was uncommon in our criminal record books.

The shooting of the Field Force commander was shocking and there was an air of apprehension in the country. There were no apparent complaints within the uniformed forces with which to trace such a callous murder. We invoked the 1965 Defence Agreement signed between us and Senegal for Senegalese troops to assist in the event things got out of hand while arrangements for the deputy commander's funeral and other investigative orders were being carried out.

In the period leading up to Mahoney's murder, anti-government graffiti had been written on some walls in Banjul. Our security personnel were also hard put to search for the sources of clandestine tracts that preached revolution and mayhem in our peaceful country. At all events, *Operation Foday Kabba I* went into full gear and Senegalese paratroopers, replete with helicopter air cover, arrived as an extra security measure. Mahoney's funeral service at the Wesley Methodist chapel on Dobson Street and his interment later in the evening passed off without incident.

During Danso's trial there were street protests by members of the Movement for Justice in Africa Gambia Chapter (MOJA-G). Leading members in MOJA-G rallied their members and denounced the presence of Senegalese troops as a signal of Dakar's intended annexation of The Gambia. With a bit more intelligence tipping, it was not surprising that the police began rounding up MOJA-G members for questioning and later preferred conspiracy and treasonable offence charges against them.

At the end of his trial, Danso was sentenced to death. Yet, irony beset the application of the full brunt of the law. I personally do not believe in the death penalty but I was obliged under the constitution to be advised by the Committee on the Prerogative of Mercy comprising Dr S J Palmer as Chairman, Mr Melville E Jones and Alh Bun Gaye as Members, with Attorney General M L Saho as Legal Adviser and Secretary. They were considering the case when the events of 30 July 1981 took place. Nine months into his waiting on death row, Danso was set free from jail that same morning by the rebels. He armed himself and went on a rampage murdering innocent civilians.

Consequently, the Attorney General's Chambers prepared itself to modernise the necessary provisions to take on these new dimensions weighing into the criminal justice system. Hitherto, our constitution had prescribed death only by hanging. Since the gallows were dysfunctional – they were last used in 1917 – parliament under the circumstances passed an amendment to empower the Attorney General to use his discretion on the method of execution. The Attorney General then advised the use of a firing squad in place of hanging. When Danso was caught during the events of 1981, the law took its course and he faced the firing squad on 30 September 1981.

The courts later acquitted many of the MOJA-G members who had been arrested and charged, when there was no evidence found linking them to the actions of Danso. However, as the matter went through the legal process, facts were produced that warranted the Ministry of Justice to recommend the banning of the movement, which parliament and the Executive speedily approved. That ban on MOJA-G was closely followed by our break in diplomatic relations with Libya, where it turned out some of the leaders behind the events of 30 July 1981 had been trained.

In June 1981, while we finalised our briefs before taking off for the OAU summit in Kenya, the Libyans had rushed in a request through the Attorney General for a secret meeting with my government as soon as we got to Nairobi. The Libyans had wanted to talk about restoring diplomatic links. I flatly turned down the idea of a secret meeting. I was not ready to talk with any Libyan official outside the jurisdiction of The Gambia. Any questions they had could be asked in Banjul, using normal diplomatic channels.

On Tuesday 4 August, I went to my office as did the vice president and a few ministers who were on hand. We reviewed the situation regarding the remaining hostages, and within a couple of hours, we received the good news that the rest of the hostages had all been released.

I prepared statements for the press. I called on everybody – members of the administration, commissioners, chiefs, area councillors, chairmen, men and women, youths and their organisations – to play their full part towards returning the country to normality as soon as possible. I congratulated all those who gallantly fought from the windows and verandas of the Police Headquarters in Banjul and I gave personal recognition to the twenty-three young soldiers who made their way to Banjul from their station at Farafenni and played a pivotal role in reinforcing the Inspector General's men and initially flushing rebels out of the State House at the cost of three of their men. I commended the people in the remote parts of the country. Although they might have been removed from the real action of defending their country, I said their thoughts, prayers and loyalty to the government had helped to sustain the effort.

I would travel to Dakar at the end of October to personally offer condolences to the families of the Senegalese soldiers who had lost their lives in active service on our behalf. Thirty-three Senegalese soldiers had died in the coup. I visited those of them still in hospital and held talks with the Senegalese government in which we again registered our heartfelt sorrow for their loss and our deep appreciation as a government and people of the statesmanship of President Diouf in honouring the long-standing agreement between us.

I urged people to go about their normal business. I invited shopkeepers to open up again so daily life could go on. I called on sellers at the market to return to their stalls so that people would be able to resume the buying and selling of their daily necessities. However, alongside one's daily work, all should remain vigilant against any rebels escaping justice or hiding in the villages and towns. The rebels should be captured and disarmed and anyone finding such arms should return them to our security forces.

Steadily, government resumed business. It had been too soon to expect a full cabinet in attendance but those who came immediately began a thorough assessment of the coup and set plans for the resumption of work. Senior government officials were slowly emerging and reporting at their workplaces with stories of how each weathered the storm. Although some of the stories were quite humorous, nothing took a whit away from the seriousness of the experience of the near disaster. The stories abounded with encounters of youths stupefied with alcohol dragging Kalashnikov rifles in one hand and swigging looted bottles of expensive whisky in the other.

What followed was the conscious assessment of the lessons and a steady-headed dealing with the situation with strict adherence to the rule of law. Much of that was there for all to see in the trials in 1981 in which Sheriff Dibba and the hundreds of detainees who were taken in after the coup had been foiled were arraigned in open courts. Whatever verdicts were handed down, the process and outcomes spoke volumes for the independence of our judiciary and our respect for the rule of law and the sanctity of life.

Indeed, we considered it of great credit to our government that Sheriff Dibba was able to contest the 1982 presidential election while he was still in detention. We were in effect grooming a civilised culture of governance and jurisprudence that allowed Dibba to walk out of prison a free man, after the public prosecutors failed to connect him *beyond all reasonable doubt* to aiding and abetting the coup leaders.

Many people at home and abroad assumed that government would deviate from its traditional stance on human rights in dealing with the conspirators. It was widely felt that government would abandon its strict adherence to the principles of democracy in order to consolidate itself. We confounded the sceptics. At an immense cost to the nation, arrangements were made for international jurists to deal with the cases of the detainees so as not only to ensure that justice was done, but it was also seen to be done. Most of the detainees were held for about twelve months after which they were released. At the end of that period, only three hundred were awaiting trial from the initial list of about one thousand.

We spent long hours at the PPP Bureau reviewing the situation. It was intriguing to listen to what party officials had to say. Some blamed the problems on too much political freedom that was guaranteed by the Constitution under our multi-party system. The same people thought a one-party system of governance would be better and they continued to suggest that a one-party system would guarantee better security.

Some therefore asked whether the opportune time had not presented itself for the consolidation of the powers of the State and the Executive. Fortunately, most of us believed that the system of democracy that we had chosen should prevail. There would be no dictatorship in The Gambia – not by the president, not by the government, not by the proletariat as proclaimed by Kukoi.

In the end, we did not adopt those apparently convenient but undemocratic ideas, even though at the time the majority of the independent African states were under a one-party system. We did not consider that suitable for The Gambia. We resolved to re-dedicate ourselves to the principles and ideals of parliamentary democracy. We refrained from all temptation to postpone the general and presidential elections, and we decided we would hold them on schedule in May 1982.

On Friday 14 August 1981, I hurried back home after Friday prayers where Imam Ratib Abdoulie Jobe delivered a moving sermon. He drew the minds of the faithful to the duties of the human being under the authority of Allah and how everyone must play their part in fostering and promoting law and order so that society can live in the beauty that He had planned for His creation. It was in effect a service of thanksgiving for the return of peace to the country.

My hurrying back home from the prayers had to do with the State Opening of Parliament later that afternoon. I included in my address ideas from the review sessions from all levels of the party and government.

It was heart-warming to see once again the Speaker of the House and the judges of the law courts in their splendid robes. It was good to see our security chiefs, they who stood against tyranny when it threatened our democracy. It was above all refreshing to see the MPs once again seated. The seat of the leader of the opposition NCP was conspicuously vacant. I seized this solemn occasion to thank the Speaker and MPs present for the enormous contribution they continued to make towards the development of our country. The last time I was before them was only three months before, on 26 June, at the start of a tough Budget Session, one that was coming in the wake of the fourth consecutive year of a poor harvest, a second season of erratic rains and considerable insect pest damage to our cereal crops.

The IMF congratulated us on our approach to the problems and commended us for driving a liberal system for current payments in such difficult times. In that budget, government had proposed to the House a tax packet of the magnitude of D18 million, the highest that far in the history of the government levying for additional revenue. Hard times demanded hard measures and the House understood the problem. I told them I could do little more than encourage them to continue to perform their parliamentary duties with the same degree of responsibility.

I told the House that we should be grateful that it had been possible through the grace of Allah that, so soon after the experience of July, parliament was able to meet. Thus, its session was only delayed but not abolished. Having dedicated ourselves to building our nation for nineteen years, my government was not prepared to simply hand over the authority that had been vested in us by our people, and, by the grace of God, we managed to survive the crisis.

Until the unfortunate episode of 30 July, we had an impeccable record of peace and stability and we had become a haven for people, especially those from the sub-region, in search of a life away from pain and agony.

It was indeed regrettable that a handful of criminals were able to wreak such havoc on our nation in their attempt to destroy some of the very basic things that the vast majority of Gambians cherish most. Paramount among those were the fundamental rights and freedoms of the individual. Since the achievement of internal self-government, my government had been resolutely committed to the protection of the basic rights of our people. Those were what the criminals denied the many people that they murdered while they, by wantonly destroying property, refused to respect the citizens' rights of ownership. They destroyed the homes of innocent people, commandeered cars and looted shops. And in their attempt to impose a new government and an alien political system on our people, they were denying them the fundamental right of political participation, guaranteed by our democratic system of government and our constitution.

Some called the rebellious activity a revolution, purely to glorify the whole affair. But it was merely anarchy caused by lawless, trigger-happy criminals who, because of their individual and collective inadequacies to face up to the challenges and sacrifices of independence, had abdicated their responsibility to themselves and to their country. The indiscriminate destruction that took place was not only directed at government, but also at the people and, for that matter, the nation.

Kukoi's menace did not end with his flight out of the country. In fact, he continued to be a security risk. On 31 March 1992, my office released a press statement reporting that Kukoi Samba Sanyang (now bandying an alias Dr Manneh) was poised to attack The Gambia again. Still under the patronage of Libya, he and his group were operating from their base in Ouagadougou in Burkina Faso where he ran a bar.

It was important that we shared information with Senegal. There were treaties in force between us, for shared information on security and defence. I sent my ministers post haste on briefing meetings with my colleagues in the sub-region. External Affairs Minister Omar Sey went to Dakar and Tripoli as my special envoy to President Diouf and Libyan Leader Colonel Muammar Gaddafi. Minister of the Interior Lamin Kiti Jabang visited Bissau, Conakry and Freetown on similar missions to deliver my special messages to Presidents Joao Bernardo Vieira, Lansana Conté and Joseph Saidu Momoh respectively.

Our intelligence gathering was accurately corroborated by a defector from Burkina Faso. One Ebrima Jammeh, described in despatches as one of Kukoi's chief lieutenants, returned to The Gambia to report to that effect. The revelations further disclosed that seven persons, all Gambians, identified as collaborators with Kukoi, had already infiltrated the country. They were promptly sniffed out, arrested and taken in for questioning.

Gambians were reassured that our security forces were on the alert and were more than capable of dealing with the new threat. We had also had enough to go on from the press conference held on Saturday 27 December 1981 by newly arrived Gambian nationals from Libya where they said they were undergoing training for subversion along with nationals of Burkina Faso, Senegal, Egypt, Mauritania, Cameroon and Guinea Bissau. In addition to nearly two hundred Gambians captured there in Sabha and put in military camps, fourteen had been recruited directly from Banjul.

Mawdo Badjie, Dawda Ceesay, Zakaria Conteh, Kebba Demba, Yoro Jallow, Lamin Saidy-Khan, and Assan Sowe reported having been recruited in Cotonou, Benin, by Cheikh Ahmed Niass, a Senegalese national who had initially promised them jobs in Libya. They were flown in by Libyan planes and with their passports in the hands of Libyan government agents, they were seen through airport formalities different from ordinary passengers. They were driven to a military camp where they were informed that they were to undergo training to help Niass's Islamic Party which would operate in both Senegal and The Gambia. When they refused and asked for proper jobs, they said, they were arrested and detained; some of them were treated inhumanely until they were able to find their way home.

Government took immediate steps to secure external aid in the form of food and medical supplies to alleviate the suffering that resulted from the crisis. We set up the External Aid Commission to coordinate and administer all the assistance flowing in for the purpose. We needed some 14,000 tonnes of cereals to cover three months of food relief for a target population of 300,000 in the main areas affected, namely the Western Division, Kombo St Mary and Banjul.

The response to our appeal for emergency relief was tremendous. The FAO pledged 2,481 tonnes of cereal amounting to US$862,000. It also offered an additional 3,000 tonnes equal to US$734,000 for drought-related food aid. The World Food Programme (WFP) made available 200 tonnes of sorghum, the United Nations Disaster Relief Organisation US$30,000, the WHO, medical and surgical supplies equivalent to US$25,000. The International Committee of the Red Cross gave US$12,000 in addition to funds made available to government for the procurement of food and fuel supplies. The Catholic Relief Services (CRS) gave 200 tonnes of rice, US$10 000 in cash, 90 tonnes of cooking oil and an undetermined amount of foodstuffs. The CRS also made arrangements for some US$750,000 from the US State Department that went into the purchase of vehicles and to cover their operational costs. The World Permanent International Meat Office (OPIC) and the Italian Consortium of Industrial Slaughter Houses actively took up our request to consider the protein needs of the people affected.

Friends of The Gambia at the bilateral level responded enthusiastically and generously: Saudi Arabia gave US$10 million; Germany offered 500 tonnes of cooking oil and 670 tonnes of flour; Sweden offered three tonnes of medical supplies; the People's Republic of China pledged D128,000 and Nigeria made available a large amount of medical supplies. On behalf of the Gambian people I thanked those donors for their gesture of solidarity.

That which needed special mention however and which I did not fail to highlight were the donations that came from local sources in aid of their compatriots. Companies, firms and individuals gave generously. Altogether, we received more than D30 million from local donors that went into the External Aid Fund.

There was much discussion in the country about what we as a party might have failed to do to prevent the sad events of July 1981. There were frequent meetings, rallies and consultations all over the country. Even if we did not hold regular congresses, we were in touch with our people. A Congress Planning Committee was set up and it immediately went into arranging for a national congress as soon as it was convenient. Besides, 1982 was going to be an election year - only nine months away. So the demand on the organisational skills and determination of the party stalwarts was immense.

I went on an extensive tour of the provinces to discuss the crisis and what people could do as individuals and as groups to ensure that evil did not penetrate our society the way it so recently did. The party went into designing and programming modules for public media relations that would bring the party and the people closer through more regular civic education consultation. Meanwhile, our congress organisers, led by Louise Antoinette Njie, set to work. They laid out an elaborate and well-thought-out programme that soon brought us together in March 1982 at the Atlantic Hotel in Banjul for the Third National Congress of the PPP.

It was a homecoming – a reunion of mind, body and soul of the party. The representatives from all over the country could not hide their feelings for the occasion. Many people fought back tears during their speeches. But, as was usual at our PPP gatherings, there was a wide spectrum of opinion – conservative, progressive and radical – as to what the PPP should stand for. The majority preferred inclusion in our movement that justified the name and motto the party had lived by all those years and anchored in our support countrywide. One important suggestion failed the test. Its discussion almost dogged the assembly. Strong voices rose to propose the indefinite extension of the state of emergency so that we could continue in office for some time without elections. But the point is we did not have a say over such an issue. The holding of elections every five years was prescribed by law.

I endured vilification from some quarters (fortunately only a small minority) for always sticking to democratic principles. For adhering to democracy, some people raged that my leadership had been nothing but one of compromise of the objectives of the people who had chosen me as their leader. In fact, they were mistaking adherence to the rule of law and respect for the Constitution for weakness.

When parliament was duly dissolved, we, like the other political parties in our enviable pluralist political dispensation, launched a vigorous campaign to win the hearts, minds and votes of a people who breathed much more easily under the order of the law. The 1982 general and presidential elections were held. There were a few new amendments to the law that governed them. Constitutional improvements now provided for separate elections for choosing the president and parliamentarians. The mandate of the head of state was more clearly defined if directly elected by the people. Hitherto, we had followed the British pattern that chose the leader of the majority in the House of Representatives to automatically be president. Having the people vote for a president directly was further empowerment of the people in a crucial decision that was once left to the party with the majority to make.

With presidential candidates now obliged to test the electorate directly, everyone went about campaigning despite the State of Emergency which, thanks to the calm character of the Gambian people, won through again in the successful conduct of the campaigns in a peaceful manner. Our campaign was doing very well on the ground until we decided, for reasons of speed and opportunity, to take it to the air. President Diouf was acting out of the greatest goodwill when he offered me the use of a military helicopter to tour the country. It was a novel departure from our good old lorries, jeeps and Land Rovers. A helicopter seemed so convenient to cover the long distances into the provinces in much shorter time than it would take on the roads.

On Wednesday 20 April, our party executive finished addressing a mass rally in Banjul. It was our second major gathering in the capital city since the party congress only a month before. The helicopter lifted off impressively from the cricket pitch in the middle of MacCarthy Square, amid the thunderous cheers of the crowds. We were up and away, with the wide estuary of the River Gambia sparkling brilliantly below us. While on the flawless flight all the way to Georgetown I noted the drastic signs of drought on either side of the river as we followed its winding eastwards into the countryside. I had not been in a helicopter since January 1979 – when the Chevron oil company invited me at the end of their operations to see the ongoing work onboard their ship, the *Pereli*, while prospecting for oil and gas off our shores.

After a restful night stop in our campaign, we gathered for another rally in Georgetown, where a large turnout of supporters came to welcome us. It was a rousing rally and when it ended no one was in doubt that we had underscored the essentials of reassuring the people of our commitment to their development as a government and as their party. We nailed down the need for the people's awareness of signs and symptoms of dissent or social alienation that might threaten national security. We drove home the key points highlighted in our congress resolutions that deplored extravagance in the country. We reiterated our vision whereby the number of secondary schools would be increased, especially in the rural areas, and government would take immediate and practical steps to redress the dire foreign exchange situation.

Our next stop was Brikamaba, a village growing both in size and influence in the MID. Villagers from several miles around had gathered there waiting to welcome us. We were up again, but only a few moments after take-off, we realised that the helicopter was stalling. It was not gaining any more height and the engines were roaring strenuously. Suddenly, the French-built rotor blade helicopter veered violently and spun around vehemently a few times, as if over the same spot, before it made one ferocious splutter.

We crashed into a small hut in Brikamanding, a mile away from our destination. I clambered out of the wreckage and since I did not feel too badly hurt at the time, I asked some people rushing to help me to go over to others who seemed to need more assistance. I stood under a tree to get my wits back, as it were, as rescuers struggled through mangled metal to retrieve the others, many of whom were injured. It was a terrible scene made even more devastating by the realisation that my election campaign adviser, Alieu Badara Njie, had been killed instantly. Only four weeks before he had announced his retirement from public office after nearly forty years of active service. He had spoken with such eloquence in his valedictory to the House of Representatives in which he said he was strong enough to carry on but wished to make room for the younger minds to come on board and take their place to help build the country. It was there that he offered himself to give advice to the government and party whenever and wherever possible.

That was how we had asked him to come out of his short retirement to bolster up our campaign, knowing how much we could benefit by his presence from the feel of cohesion and continuity, especially after the near-disaster of July 1981.

Some of us were rushed to the Royal Victoria Hospital where we received prompt medical attention. When I was declared free of any serious injury, the doctor sent me home with orders for a complete rest. Others were flown out to Dakar as quickly as possible. Those on board were Secretary General Dr Jabez Ayo Langley, Minister of External Affairs Lamin Kiti Jabang, Acting Inspector General of Police M Mass Jarra, Chief of Protocol Sheikh M Jeng, Minister of the Interior Abdoulie Mboob, State House Press Officer Jay Saidy and Parliamentary Secretary

Jallow Sanneh. My chief steward, Yusupha Drammeh, was very badly injured; so also was the griot kora maestro, Fabala Kanuteh, and other senior and middle-level officers in the media and civil administration. I commended the Senegalese pilot without whose skills in manoeuvring the doomed helicopter the outcome would have been much worse.

All the same, it was a terrible moment. The loss of A B, as he was fondly called, was one of the bitterest moments I have had to endure in all my time in government. Retired Secretary General Eric Christensen, a man noted for his lucid expression, put it in the most fitting in his letter of condolence to me on 6 May 1982 that it was impossible adequately to pay tribute to this extraordinary Gambian. His place in society, Eric wrote, would remain void for a long time because men like him were created singly. I could not agree more about a man I knew for hard work and fair-mindedness and one who set himself high standards in work and comportment. His quality of sportsmanship far outstripped the ordinary with his left-handed facility in cricket, tennis and, especially our mutual love, golf. His body lay in state in parliament where hundreds of grieving people filed past it. We gave him a most fitting burial. He was decorated, albeit posthumously, with GCRG.

Back home and recuperating, I was feeling clearly out of danger. President Diouf offered to have me see specialists in Dakar just to be sure that I was indeed all right. Chilel and two senior medical officers accompanied me to Dakar where I was admitted at l'Hôpital Principal. I was diagnosed with "bony damage to the spine and ribs; but no major fractures". According to my doctors all I needed was some rest.

I returned to Banjul on 30 April and was received by party and government officials at State House who came to keep me abreast of events. I learnt the campaign had been doing extremely well. As a main signatory to the party's bank account, I realised my time away for treatment had gravely handicapped the campaign's access to funds. The PPP executive in particular and the party in general were truly grateful indeed to Vice President Camara who believed enough in what we were doing to put up his own home as collateral at the bank for the loans the party took to keep it on the campaign trail.

We returned from the campaigns, albeit by the more familiar means of transport of lorries, jeeps and Land Rovers, bringing hopeful stories of the people's resolution to vote for democracy, the rule of law and continuity.

25

Restructuring and recovery

Only six months after we launched the First Five Year Development Plan in 1975, The Gambia was caught in the downturn of exacerbating conditions of drought in the Sahel and the rising prices of oil that plunged the global market into recession. Between 1981 and 1983 the prices of our primary export crop would further depress in US dollars by 18%, while imports continued to rise thus wiping out all the gains we had made over the 10 years of prudent management of the National Development Programme from 1965 to 1975.

If the per capita indicator was anything to go by, the overall rise from D293 in 1975 to D317 in 1980 would then spell an improvement despite the odds in the tightrope balancing between domestic production and population demands and, of course, the performance of government in properly managing the two. The per capita indicator in 1980 was a great sign of success of the First Five Year Development Plan conceived with the intent of taking a more systematic approach to achieve the most efficient mobilisation of resources and a self-sustained and more balanced growth, apart from the equitable spread of the benefits of development to the entire population.

In order to ensure that we achieved the targets we set out in the Second Five Year Development Plan for both food and cash crop production, a number of policies and activities were essential. Principal among them was the need to ensure that recurrent revenues were sufficient both to maintain ongoing and completed projects and to provide counterpart funds for the new ones in the agriculture sector, plus the establishment of the appropriate financial institutions such as the Agricultural Development Bank to support farmers. It needed especially to be responsive to the needs of the farming communities and to ensure especially that women farmers found access to technological packages in order to help them raise their productivity and incomes. Achieving those targets did not have to mean penalising our farmers with low producer prices and unnecessary indebtedness, especially subsistence credit.

In August 1976, we could do no more than declare The Gambia a drought stricken country. We became a member of CILSS, the organisation with a French acronym for the Inter-State Committee for the Control of Drought in the Sahel. We knew only international assistance and a rededication of our people to good conservation practices could save our country from the vicissitudes and vagaries of the weather.

In December 1977 CILSS met in Banjul and I became chairman for a two-year term. In that capacity I immediately undertook a tour of the USA, France and Italy in May 1978 not only to draw attention to the problems of the Sahel but also to mobilise the necessary financial resources for the implementation of the Sahel's medium and long-term development programme. This laid emphasis on increased food production, human resource development and that of the entire water resources of the Sahel region. I was happy to report that I was greatly encouraged by the response and reception I received throughout that tour. It was again in the context of that appeal to the international community that Mrs Lillian Carter, mother of US President Jimmy Carter, visited The Gambia and four other Sahelian countries. That visit greatly enhanced American public interest in the Sahel and further involvement of the US government in the funding of the Sahel Development Programme. I followed that mission up with visits to European countries that were members of the Club du Sahel, an association that provided a new approach in the relations between developing and developed countries.

We immediately began receiving the much-needed drought relief donations from friends and well-wishers the world over. Britain, Iraq, The Netherlands, Sierra Leone, Togo and a heart-warming list of countries sent us financial assistance that further convinced me of the resilience of the finer side of the human spirit. President Houphouet Boigny of the Ivory Coast sent us nearly half a million dalasi. The pledge by the USA in March 1978 of some $200 million to the Sahelian Development Programme uplifted our spirits and reasserted our confidence in the prime values of our human family. It provided the CILSS Secretariat with the added momentum to take on more advanced scientific methodology and more informed studies into the socio-cultural and political issues underpinning drought and desertification. It worked on research into resistant crop varieties, tree planting projects, exercises in irrigation and damming for vital water retention, attitudinal change programmes for the awareness and sensitisation of the local communities and a myriad of other timely measures.

We embarked on major tree planting and reforestation programmes. Schoolchildren memorised the words in The Banjul Charter to answer questions in their social studies lessons. The number of cases that appeared over the period before travelling magistrates and district commissioners for damage done to the environment attests to the seriousness with which we considered the situation. Our food situation was precarious and our production mechanism seemed to be at a standstill. Farmers looked miserably over dried-up stretches of baked farmland that should have been swaying with ripening crops. The World Food Programme, health organisations, international and non-governmental agencies monitored our situation and they sped to our rescue when the figures showed we had been as badly affected as some states like Burkina Faso, Niger and Chad.

While we implemented the projects at hand and waited for injections of cash, the picture in the Sahel remained dismal. Livestock perished, their carcasses dry-rotting on cracked beds of scorched countryside, perhaps reminiscent of the scenes when rinderpest killed hundreds of cattle in the 1950s and 1960s, but only worse. Prospects in many places were dim and the sparse vegetation cover in the Sahel was being vehemently attacked by human need and indiscretion. Desertification was drastically reducing forest cover and governments across West Africa, and certainly The Gambia had to put speedy budgetary subheads to cover human and material resources to arrest the life-threatening decline.

Minister of Finance M C Cham had taken on the challenge very vigorously but he soon found it an uphill task to change the local habits of centuries or curbing the business inclinations of the suppliers, no matter what the penalties were. One major loophole was that citizens ignored the ban under the pretext that the charcoal they were burning was from supplies outside The Gambia and not from our local forests. Customs and frontier police were also overwhelmed and overstretched.

The good rains that had fallen in the 1980/1981 season raised our harvest output and also our hopes for good yields and our improved export and subsistence situation in 1982, which I considered was a watershed year. There were big changes on the political, social and economic fronts. The experience of a coup attempt and bloodshed on our streets resulted in a new consciousness for those who witnessed the carnage or lost relatives or property. The economy was under great stress with shortages in foodstuffs and a nearly depleted foreign exchange account.

Apart from it being the launch year of our Second Five Year Development Plan we put other plans in motion to improve our public relations. We brought in Jay Saidy as press officer at State House in January. Jay was a good journalist who at a crucial period had edited our party newspaper *The Gambia Times*.

He was part of my delegation in the early part of 1982 when I went to Conakry with External Affairs Minister Lamin Kiti Jabang and Interior

Minister Abdoulie Mboob for a one-day working visit. We had gone to discuss with the Guinean government the critical security situation of our sub-region and the continued threat by external forces. President Toure appreciated the seriousness of the situation and the need for closer collaboration on the economic, social and security fronts.

I was gratified to learn of the increased recognition of our trypanotolerant *ndama* variety of cattle. The Livestock Marketing Board had exported 850 head to Gabon. It would also soon export to Nigeria while noting the great interest in the scheme registered by Ghana, Liberia and Sierra Leone. For inter-African trade to grow from such small beginnings to the lofty dreams of a West African common market or a continental economic powerhouse there would have to be political stability and social order. I therefore could not help being downhearted again with the news of another military takeover within the sub-region.

Flight Lieutenant Jerry Rawlings had led a coup for the second time by overthrowing the government of President Hilla Limann who had been our guest during our 16th independence anniversary celebrations only in February 1981. While my delegation had spent a full day in Conakry exploring prescriptions to rid our sub-region of military interventions and civil disorder and charting a future for our people living freely under democratic governance an elected civilian government was being negated yet again by soldiers who were making a second bid for power in Ghana after having handed over to the same civilian government just two years before, in 1979. It was troublesome that the military factor was so recurrent in the African political equation.

Every success reported in the annual returns of the divested enterprises or the parastatals contributed to the fulfilment of the PPP campaign and policy promises. Likewise, every loss reported in the financial statements meant the people had to pay more taxes and our development targets missed. My government sounded the clarion call for probity in all public servants.

But one of the major scars on the face of the economy throughout the early 1980s was the worsening foreign exchange situation. By 1982 the economy had worsened. High interest rates, the continued difficulty in servicing debts and the general decrease in official development assistance meant that the loss in external trade could not be compensated through larger resource flows from commercial loans or bilateral grants.

Following the events of July 1981, the UN approved a loan to The Gambia. On 17 March 1982, a UN envoy, Mr A A Farah, who was Under Secretary General for Political Affairs came to consult with us on a rehabilitation and reconstruction programme.

The main subjects that were to engage the government as well as our partners from then on well into 1983 were the structural imbalance in the economy whereby we imported more than we exported, clearly pointing to the need for selective import substitution. Our industrial policy demanded that we make maximum use of local products and materials. But since our economy was based on one major cash crop there had to be increased efforts to diversify and to aim at processing and manufacturing for local consumption and for export.

First, import substitution must be concentrated on basic consumer and intermediate goods with a sustained growth potential. Second, regional cooperation and trade arrangements had to open up suitable markets or economic capacity utilization and scale. Government strategy in the industry and manufacturing sector was to assign the leading role to the private sector which I urged again to take the initiative and mobilise investment funds for industrial capital formation. While the conducive legal and physical infrastructure was being considered, government was determined to carry out conservation measures to reduce consumption of both domestic and imported fuels.

In March 1982, while government looked seriously into rehabilitation and reconstruction the PPP gathered with much determination and resolution at its Third National Congress from 29 to 31 March at the Atlantic Hotel in Banjul. Again we needed to demonstrate to the people that we were paying keen attention to the development programmes that should bring them a higher standard of living.

While we were busy setting up the new government, we paid close attention to the opening of the Gambia Court of Appeal on 24 May 1982. It was the first time the justices were sitting and government was well disposed to assist in ensuring that the historic event received its due recognition. Acting President of the Appeals Court Justice Sam J Forster, assisted by Justice Olayinka Ayoola and Justice P D Anin were ready to hear among others the 35 criminal cases brought up by persons convicted by the Special Criminal Court for their part in the events of July 1981. This judicial process was very costly considering the serious strains on our coffers but we would not leave any stone unturned to ensure that the principle of justice was honoured. The whole process which lasted more than a year of trials and appeals cost in excess of D2.5 million. Due process was worth every butut of it.

On the ground some outcomes of negotiations with partners were already being implemented. The Saudis had provided $3 million to begin the construction of the project that would give the capital city a decent central mosque. We signed the contract with the ADB and the Nigerian Trust Fund to get D10 million in loans for Phase 4 of the Yundum Airport development project and for some badly needed assistance to the Livestock Marketing Board. In October we received £4.9 million to carry out the second phase of the ports project and awarded the contract to Kier International of Sandy in Bedfordshire, England, to do the new concrete jetty.

In the same sweep of projects taking off, the $16 million Jahally/Pacharr small holder rice project was launched with financing from IFAD, ADB, and the governments of the Netherlands and West Germany. We sent Sainey Darbo there from the agriculture ministry to manage the project. The importance of these injections was their statement of confidence reposed in our government by the donors and the crucial nature of those interventions as the keys to growth in a struggling economy.

We introduced price control under a unit in the ministry of finance and tried to stabilise the price of meat at D5 per kilo to make it more affordable. Several other key items were also controlled to give the consumers a better deal. Of course, the drawback of that was increased scarcity of certain items. Government subsidy of rice had to be reduced, hence we removed D25.70 on the bag of 50 kilograms, shooting the retail price to a new high of D79.45 per bag. There was much groaning around but even though it continued to be tough on many breadwinners, my government was still paying nearly 35% of the cost per bag to ensure that they were able to take a bag of rice home.

We lifted the curfew in October 1982. Radio programmes were organised that outlined the roles played by citizens in conjunction with government. One of the programmes designed and implemented was *Jakarlo*. There was also a civic education panel that discussed citizens' concerns and explained the law and the constitution in simple language.

It was a busy time indeed and I found myself playing less golf because of my busy schedule. However, I followed closely the steady progress Njaimeh was making on the golf course. In fact she had improved her skills enough to be noticed by the organisers of the Trophée Lancome International Pro-am Golf Tournament who invited her to participate in a meeting outside Versailles. She joined 54 prominent ladies from around the world who were taking part and played with a handicap 9 teaming up with the golf famous Arnold Palmer. Her performance was remarkable and the experience would spur her in both her skill and enthusiasm for the game. She has since been known to play 36 holes in one day: 18 in the morning and another 18 in the evening.

Golf aside, for many years, Njaimeh was chairperson of the SOS Kinderdorf at Bakoteh where she guided policy and administration of the welfare and education of less fortunate children. The children needed all the help they could get to prepare them for a better and more secure future.

The year drew slowly to a close with a splendid ceremony held in November of the first Legal Year celebration. The legal bar could have been taking their cue from the grand way in which the judges had opened the sittings of the Gambia Court of Appeal earlier in the year. This novel way of the legal profession making its presence felt was very encouraging to me and I looked hopefully to future celebrations. I felt we were on our way when I received during my weekly cabinet consultations a great progress report on the Independence Stadium in Bakau, the 25,000 capacity multi-purpose sporting complex on which the Peoples Republic of China was spending D32 million to build.

No matter how great the infrastructural developments were, the economy and its troubles were our daily challenge. In February 1983 we negotiated a Standby Arrangement with the International Monetary Fund. Even with the stringent rehabilitation drive the economy still required further adjustment and additional resources. We needed additional balance of payments support from the IMF in conjunction with other measures to increase productivity and domestic activity. The 1983/84 groundnut harvest was not going to do it; the total export tonnage was below average and not enough to make any appreciative impact on the balance of payments situation.

But all was not lost. We had to show there were avenues in support of our diversification policy that was underscored when the ministry of finance was confident enough to stage our first National Trade Fair to showcase our agriculture and small industry to consumers and business partners alike. It was a success beyond our expectation in its fulfilment of a grand demonstration of what we could do and could become as producers. The fair introduced Gambian-made goods and provided a novel opportunity to test markets, stimulate demand for local products and encourage general employment and earnings. Products displayed included groundnut products, cotton lint, lime juice and lime oil, fresh fruits and vegetables, cassava, hides and skins, forestry products, palm kernel, honey and cashew nuts.

There were stalls with marine products such as frozen seafood and smoked fish. Industrial items included metal beds, bed springs, doors and windows and wooden furniture. Soft drinks, mineral water, beer, stout, cosmetics, soap, confectionery, candles, suitcases, construction materials, paints, textile garments, tie and dye and batiks along with leather goods, wood carvings, musical instruments and jewellery showed the vast array of potential that Gambians could engage in to make our own home markets prosperous. Contributions to GDP from these areas were the surest way of increasing the average per capita earnings of Gambians.

The government budget was constantly coming under increasing pressure as recurrent expenditure was well ahead of the estimated figures. It was significant that in the decade during which we had been hit by drought and insect infestation, we had been hit simultaneously by the devastating effects of the vast increases in the cost of petrol and petroleum products to the extent that we were recording an annual fuel import bill of D50 million for both government and the private sector. This was equivalent to 42% of our total export earnings. We had to take steps to stabilise the economic situation.

In early 1984, we negotiated with the IMF the Economic Stabilisation Programme (ESP) designed to address two fundamental imbalances in the economy – our country's growing external indebtedness and government's increasing budgetary deficit. Among the most prominent of the measures taken under it was the devaluation of the dalasi by 25%. We had hesitated on this move for some time because of the sweeping effects it would have, but which we were nonetheless compelled to take because of the seriousness of our short-term trade deficit. Devaluation was expected to slow the domestic demand for imported goods and provide enough dalasi for export crop production. Further to that we insisted on major cuts in government spending to contain inflation and encourage domestic savings. With stabilisation we were set for economic recovery and the redirection investment to expand the productive base of the economy.

However, after the 15-month life of the ESP our economic problems continued to intensify. We identified the problems as essentially structural in nature. For that reason my government adopted a more comprehensive set of measures to restore financial equilibrium and the foundation for sustained economic recovery and growth in the form of the Economic Recovery Programme (ERP). The ERP was aimed at ensuring financial and balance-of-payments stability; maximum short-term expansion of outputs; elimination of major exchange rate and price distortions; and the creation of a conducive climate for the longer-term growth of the private sector.[13]

The ERP would help us to contain demand and encourage output and production particularly in agriculture and fisheries, reduce government consumption and expenditure particularly expenditure on salaries and wages and improve the performance of public enterprises.

To achieve those financial objectives we increased the producer price of groundnuts not only in line with the priority accorded to agriculture

---

[13] Letter of Gambia Government Policy to the World Bank, August 1986.

and the expansion of our productive capacity but also with the policy of providing greater incentives to our farmers through higher prices for their produce. This way we avoided price distortions and sustained efforts made to pursue realistic policies in the agriculture sector as well as in other sectors.

But there were difficulties beyond our scope. Whatever gains we made on the ground could be wiped out by a slump on the world market. While our producer price of groundnuts increased over the year from D1,200 to D1,800 per ton, an increase of 43% into the 1986/1987 trading season, low world market prices effaced those benefits and we could not sustain that level of support to the producers. We had the painful task of having to reduce subsidy from D83 million in 1986/87 to D50 million in 1987/1988, bringing the producer price down to D1,500. We continued to review the prices of imported items, particularly petroleum products, to the effect that prices soon began to reflect more accurately the true cost to the economy of those imported commodities.

Government completed a civil service staff audit and implemented a retrenchment exercise to cut down on the number of employees on the payroll. Notwithstanding the obviously great cost to society in the absence of a welfare system in the country, we negotiated a Structural Adjustment Credit (SAC) with the World Bank. My government made it clear that the credit carried a component that would finance employment-creation schemes so that at least some of those retrenched would be re-absorbed elsewhere in the economy.

The Indigenous Business Advisory Service (IBAS) and the NIB worked on resettling retrenched workers through employment counselling in what was called the Civil Service Resettlement Programme with D1 million from government to kick-start the service. Hundreds of beneficiaries are today fully engaged in business from the small mobilisation credit support loans that IBAS administered.

For a while since their inception until 1983 several parastatal organisations such as the National Trading Corporation, the Gambia Commercial and Development Bank, the Social Security and Housing Finance Corporation and the Central Bank of The Gambia were specifically commended for achievements despite the difficult economic conditions. However, my government was greatly concerned about the continued inefficient performance of some of the other public enterprises and the financial and other losses being incurred by them. The GPMB was an exception. Our largest and most strategic parastatal was reporting such heavy losses that government had to do something drastic to curb the decline even with the situation of the low export price of groundnuts and their by-products, cake and oil.

We engaged the services of a consultant from the Hindustan Oil Corporation to undertake a detailed study of selected parastatals and to make recommendations for the strengthening of the National Investment Board to enable it to become effective in the control and development of public enterprises. Government in due course negotiated the Public Investment Programme (PIP) with a view to reducing the portfolio to a manageable and consistent size with emphasis on the productive sectors and rehabilitation and maintenance of infrastructure. Therefore, government substantially reduced the scope of our Public Investment Programme from D776 million over a three-year period to D640 million with quick-gestation projects and rehabilitation and maintenance as points of concentration.

In due course, we found it necessary to introduce performance contracts with a number of the parastatals whereby their responsibilities to government were clearly outlined and their financial objectives and managerial accountability clarified. We initially signed up with the three main enterprises – the GPMB, the GUC, and the Gambia Ports Authority as pilot schemes. The others signed on later. Gradually there was a marked improvement in returns to central government coffers and a general upswing in the running of those vital support pillars to government and its development programmes.

But the ERP was not without its own hiccups. While it depended essentially on adequate foreign financing to allow for the grassroots measures to take hold, there were fundamental imbalances in our economy that led to a variety of financial difficulties, principally an immediate foreign exchange crisis and heavy external indebtedness. There was thus a seemingly intractable liquidity problem in our hands and the US$12 million soft loans and the additional financing of some US$7 million from the UK government were seen at the time of their negotiation as absolutely crucial.

We were however not blind to the 'conditionalities' that came with all the World Bank and IMF assistance and we set ourselves engaging in the measures that would make us qualify for credits and loans to adjust the economy. We agreed that the public investment, export promotion and the diversification of the economy were crucial in that list of conditions. At the Donors' Conference on The Gambia held in London in September 1985 we mobilised US$54 million worth of assistance which went into supporting our foreign exchange demands for a year until December 1986. The foreign exchange kitty had been empty and we had been performing as a country only with the help of the international community. The UK and the Netherlands honoured their pledges to us.

In the drive to increase agricultural production we worked on the sector's main projects – the Second Agricultural Development Project (ADP2), the Jahally/Pacharr Rice Project, the Mixed Farming Project and the Agricultural Research and Diversification Project.[14] These focused on increased production and improved quality of yield. Today, we have seen the improved techniques passed on to extension services for the benefit of the farmers as we had anticipated so many years ago.

While we continued to monitor saline intrusion, we proposed to construct a bridge/barrage at Ballingho as part of the Gambia River Basin Development Programme. I undertook a series of sensitisation missions in the sub-region and in Europe on behalf of the OMVG in my capacity as chairman of its Conference of Heads of State and Government and we were able to utilise funds from the ADB and the ECOWAS Fund which became the leading conduits for the mobilisation of funds.

These and every other measure we took hinged on the need to improve the foreign exchange situation. Without that, the tourism industry would not be feasible. River transport – ferries, barges and ferry ramps and bridges – was important to ensuring a working transport network. The completion of a four-lane Oyster Creek Bridge with funding from the UK greatly enhanced communication and made road transport to and from port facilities in Banjul better.

Naturally, the fuel shortage that characterised the tough years from 1986 onwards had devastating effects on our productive capacity. The domestic energy demand was huge and we instituted a number of projects that included oil exploration which targeted 1986 through the Integrated Energy Project with the IDA to attract oil companies. These were to intensify hydrocarbon exploration on the basis of analysis being made by consultants or available geological and geophysical data.

We introduced the flexible exchange rate for the dalasi away from the fixed rates of exchange pegged to the pound sterling. Commercial banks could now give out foreign exchange without recourse to clearance from the Central Bank. As a result, there was a steady and growing inflow of goods back into the country and an even more welcome increase of flow of foreign exchange into the banking system.

We decontrolled the price of rice and opened importation to others away from GPMB monopoly. The increased availability of the staple commodity was immediate. After the staff audit, we retrenched 2,284

---

[14] Later renamed National Agricultural Research Institute (NARI)

temporary and daily paid workers from the payroll and removed 459 established posts from the Estimates of March 1986. At the end of July, a further 340 temporary workers and 750 established posts were scrubbed, making savings to government of D3.4 million. That money was used to fund recurrent supplies and maintain the rehabilitation of government's assets which had hitherto suffered from under-funding.

For the duration of the ERP, no further government guaranteed loans were financed by the GCDB as the risks associated with continuing the scheme were great and inconsistent with the fiscal objectives of the ERP. I went on an extensive Meet the Farmers Tour and promised to increase both the subsidy to farmers and the buying price of groundnuts. The public expressed satisfaction with the substantial increase in farmers' incomes that followed in the trade season from December 1986 until March 1987.

The Danish International Development Agency (DANIDA) completed the construction of a generating plant at Kotu from a $19 million loan contracted between the Gambia government and the World Bank to rehabilitate, improve and expand electricity and water services throughout the country. There was no point putting a recovery programme in place without addressing the inadequate electricity and water supply which had hampered economic growth since the first major breakdown at the Banjul power station in late 1977. The GUC was only just breaking even since its inception in 1972 and we were looking forward to operational profit if the trends continued. It was a big relief that the suspended Banjul Sewerage and Drainage Project had recommenced and 1987 had been specified as the target date for completion.

The contractors SOBEA finished the construction of the sewage system after a six-month extension. Some 2,000 households were ready to be connected to the system. The EEC provided D3.9 million and additional funding came from the Gambia government. When I addressed parliament again in November 1987, I was glad to report also that in addition to the improvements in electricity supply the first phase of the Urban Water Supply Project for the Greater Banjul Area had secured financing for boreholes for Sukuta and Brikama and treatment plants for Serekunda and Sukuta with additional boreholes and distribution pipelines for the Banjul area. In 1985 the Rural Water Resources Division of the Ministry of Water Resources and the Environment, with assistance from UNCDF/UNDP and other UN agencies, sank more than 300 concrete-lined wells, some of which were fitted with hand pumps, in the MID. The Federal Republic of Germany also provided assistance in the execution of a water supply project to sink 200 wells in the NBD and the MID. The Saudi Sahel Rural

Water Supply Programme covered the Lower River and Western divisions with nearly 200 concrete-lined wells and eight boreholes.

For the human resources to keep the development systems running, we designed the Second Education Policy programmes with emphasis on self-reliance to reflect the basic needs of our people and development goals. There was a clear need to improve access to quality basic education. We emphasised the development of science and technical/vocational education.

The policy also gave greater attention to non-formal and adult functional education. That eventually led to the establishment of the Non-Formal Education Unit. Because even more trained human resources were needed, it was gratifying to note that our efforts in that direction bore fruit. Primary school enrolment increased from 25,000 in 1976 to 69,000 in 1986, 25,000 of them girls, showing an increase in female enrolment of 204% over a 10-year period. Enrolment for secondary technical schools increased from 4,000 in 1976 to 10,000 in 1986, representing an increase of 34 per cent. High school enrolment also increased from 2,000 in 1976 to 4, 600 in 1986. At the tertiary level we inaugurated the Gambia Technical Training Institute and continued to work on the blueprint for the Management Development Institute.

In the midst of the strain of restructuring and recovery, the National Health Development Project continued to have an impact on health delivery and management. We completed the main building of the Children's Wing at the RVH and plans were under way for a pathological laboratory. The Banjul Polyclinic, the Brikama Health Centre and major refurbishments at the Bansang Hospital and the RVH were also completed. Our health care system was already making a name in child survival and delivery and prenatal care, especially in a number of health centres that were built in different parts of the country. We were ready to implement the recommendations of the study on cost recovery in medical services, although government would maintain its subsidy to this area in the interest of equity. Cost sharing with the communities would go a long way towards lessening the burden on our scarce resources.

Throughout 1986, the dalasi stabilised reasonably well against the pound sterling. At that time devaluation had not exceeded 10% for most of the year and the differential between the official exchange rate and the rate prevailing on the parallel market continued to shrink. People, especially the business community, restored confidence in the dalasi, showing greater willingness to hold on to dalasi-denominated assets instead of foreign currency. The marked deceleration of domestic inflation as measured in the Consumer Price Index declined from 70% at the end of June 1986 to 20% at the end of June 1987. The foreign exchange flow increased, showing clearly that the reforms were working.

Thus only one year into the ERP the economy was clearly on the mend. The ERP ended in 1989 having reduced our debt burden and increased our reserves from zero in 1986 to 3 months cover by 1989. The currency continued to be stable and consumer prices were rationalised.

'The bitter pill' had almost claimed notoriety in referring to the tough conditionalities the World Bank and the IMF had laid down. Nonetheless, the Gambian people showed resilience through the difficult times and carried on with the traditional spirit of discipline.

26

The rise and fall of the Senegambia confederation

After the coup attempt in 1981, the need for more formal cooperation between The Gambia and Senegal was thought necessary by the two countries' leaders. That realisation brought about the signing of the Kaur Declaration leading to the establishment of the Senegambia confederation in 1982. The confederation was to cover the integration of our security forces, communications, a monetary and economic union, and coordination of foreign policies.

On 14 August 1981, I addressed the legislators at the State Opening of Parliament and embarked the following day on a nationwide tour to meet the people and to explain to them the July events and how Senegal's intervention was a welcome development. That tour went on until 25 October 1981 taking us to thirty-one stops throughout the country. Much of it reminded me of my daring trek on foot decades before to visit my mother in Barajaly. This time I was not just covering the journey because I wanted to see home; rather I wanted to meet the people to reassure them that we had put the coup attempt behind us and we must now forge ahead as a more security-conscious nation. The placards that welcomed us were indeed reassuring, if not outright flattering: Speed Up Senegambian Confederation; PPP For All; D K JAWARA – The Man of The Year 1981 and Victory for Democracy: Down With All Evil Forces!

People came out in large numbers to listen to us. They requested their community and party leaders to speak on their behalf. We heard from *alkalolu*, area councillors, *yai compin* and party militants. Prominent among them at Brufut was Alkalo Alhaji Kalifa Sanoh. At Sukuta, another influential *alkalo*, Alhaji Braima Cham, spoke on behalf of his village. So did Alkalo Alhaji Bakary Jaiteh of Bakau and a prominent petty trader and strong community leader, Aja Fatounding Jatta.

We rounded off the five-week tour in the Serekunda West Constituency. The constituents and their MP, Omar Jallow, the Minister of Water Resources and the Environment, welcomed us in a jubilant mood. Serekunda was indeed the ideal place to end the tour considering the fact that the sprawling congested town took much of the brunt of the rebel onslaught. The meeting there was a perfect setting for the conclusion of the programme of sensitisation.

The Gambian people were grateful that Senegal did not stand idly by while democracy and law and order were threatened. The Senegalese government said for its part it was fully conscious that legal considerations aside, it rightly felt the moral obligation to accede to our request. For this magnanimous gesture of assistance in that critical moment, I led a delegation to Dakar and expressed our grateful thanks and offered a cheque for $1 million to be used for the welfare of the sick and wounded soldiers and the bereaved families. However, we considered this amount far too small compared to the huge debt of gratitude we owed to the bereaved. I assured Senegal of our steadfastness in our pursuit of higher levels of cooperation and called on all Gambians to play their part in further cementing the Senegambian relationship.

My delegation returned from Dakar and shared some of the groundbreaking decisions with members of our government already engaged in the tremendous task of internal reconstruction and the reshaping of our foreign affairs. Senegal, naturally, loomed large in our plans.

On 12 November 1981, President Diouf accompanied by his wife, Elizabeth, arrived in Banjul at the head of a delegation of political pundits and legal draughtsmen. Diouf and I had talked at length during my visit to Dakar about even more advanced steps in cementing our cooperation, perhaps at the level of a confederation. His visit to Banjul was to take that proposal forward. Hundreds of cheering Gambians lined the route from the airport to welcome the Senegalese visitors.

Dancers, singers and schoolchildren lined the route from the airport cheering as the motorcade drove through. People waved flags of Senegal and The Gambia and our guests well read their feelings of appreciation. In Banjul, the motorcade stopped for a solemn moment of remembrance at the mass grave located in the small pathway between the Muslim and the Christian cemeteries, where the health authorities had buried scores of bodies they had removed from the city streets during the coup attempt. President Diouf and I laid wreaths there.

We drove on, cheered by even thicker crowds lining the Independence Drive all the way to State House. Alhaji Alieu Badara Njie was there to chair the meeting and in his opening statement welcomed the guests to what he called a historic meeting of two champions of peace and democracy. He said a great deal of what was going to take place during the three-day consultations was to establish the peaceful environment without which democracy and development would hardly thrive. He said he was certain that the exercise was in the hands of two peace makers who had shown their expertise in working to broker peace between others as members of the Iran-Iraq Peace Committee of the OIC.

In my statement I spoke of the intricate interrelationship between the people across the borders and highlighted the history of collaboration between the two countries at both the party and personal levels – between President Diouf and me and before him between President Senghor and me. Even more than the official channels of contact were the daily interactions across the borders between relatives and people speaking the same languages and enjoying the same traditions and customs and practising the same religions. I seized the moment to make the official announcement that during my visit to Dakar on 14 August, I had suggested to the president that we should consider the setting up of a confederation between our two countries and that both governments had already been laying down the details on paper towards that goal.

President Diouf had, indeed, arrived with a draft agreement of the proposed Senegambia Confederation. While the officials from both sides were considering the document, I led the executives on a tour of the provinces. The people came out in large numbers to show their gratitude and appreciation. It was a hectic tour in which we called on communities and their leaders, who in no uncertain terms condemned the insurrection and thanked Senegal for coming, like a true neighbour, to help put out the flames when our house was on fire.

The highlight of the three-day visit and tour of the provinces took place on board the *Lady Chilel* berthed at the wharf at Kaur. The provincial town always carried a ring of significance in my family history. That was where my grandfather, Foday Sheriffo Jawara, had first settled when he arrived with his caravans from Bundu in old Mali. There, on board the passenger vessel, President Diouf and I signed a communiqué that became known as the Kaur Declaration, celebrating the town for hosting such a historic agreement. Although it was only in draft and not binding as such, it showed our determined political will for a framework for deeper cooperation.

In the heat of technical discussions, we created much latitude so that all views were fairly aired and considered. There were expressions of fear on our side that the draft proposal as presented might make us lose some of our sovereignty to Senegal. There was the school of thought that recommended a step-by-step testing of the waters until we fully understood what Senegal really wanted. It was obvious that Senegal would rather have full political unification and monetary integration, more in line with a federation than a confederation.

Our side gave the document the serious consideration it deserved. The differences in size and sophistication of the two economies were considered. We would not allow frigid positioning on issues to ruin the bigger opportunities the agreement presented. We accepted the proposals in principle with an understanding that there would be further amendments to those areas we considered necessary. We took the issues to our parliament to look closer at the matters that we had raised in the draft. Needless to say, we could only move forward after we had reached consensus in cabinet and parliament.

Although some officials in my government did not favour the idea, I have always believed in the historic need of our two countries to come together for the mutual benefit of our peoples. With the difficult aftermath of balkanisation in which European colonialism has left us, we needed to encourage any possibility of re-unifying our peoples and economies. In theory, I was and have always been enthusiastically in favour of African unity and I genuinely believed our case with Senegal was one occasion when we could put it into practice. Putting my name to the Kaur Declaration was far from being a sell-out of my country. In the early 1960's we managed to steer clear of being merged stealthily with Senegal. In the aftermath of the coup attempt, we were again vulnerable as a country.

I understood, of course, that the vulnerability was not confined to The Gambia; any destabilisation in The Gambia could readily spill over into Senegal. That was the very reason President Senghor quickly endorsed operation *Foday Kabba 1*. During my visit to Dakar, I had sensed in the Senegalese a strong desire for a merger with The Gambia. It was clear we needed something to move the idea of cooperation further and the idea that occurred to me was a confederation – a positive move forward in our relations I thought Senegal would consider favourably. This would fit in with the ideas of African unity, in which the two countries could cooperate in many areas–economic, social and political while maintaining their sovereignty; hence my emphasis on *confederation*.

We consented to several key points, among them the setting up of the confederal army and other security forces - to which each member state would contribute troops; to look into any areas in which the two member states were mutually interested to negotiate, for example, an economic and monetary union, external relations, communications and any other joint institutions, especially in fields in which member-states might deem fit to exercise their jurisdiction jointly.

On 17 December 1981, the agreement was ratified and came into force on 1 February 1982. The two countries exchanged the Instruments of Ratification of the Protocols of the Senegambia confederation at a ceremony in Dakar.

The independence of the states was entrenched in the preamble and clauses proper resolving to establish an institutional framework. The two states would constitute the union to be known as the Senegambia confederation. Coordination was absolutely necessary for success. The Wollof put it proverbially in their saying – *Wat gal ak yegoo*! If fishermen must successfully beach their fishing boats, they all must pull in unison!

This led quickly to many new areas of cooperation. The Confederal Parliament was one of the first and biggest to be established in November 1982. Senegal's Moustapha Niasse was appointed Confederal Minister of External Affairs and Lamin Kiti Jabang was appointed Confederal Minister delegated to the Ministry; the equivalent of a deputy minister. Daouda Sow of Senegal became Confederal Minister for Security and A E W F Badjie was Confederal Minister delegated to the Ministry. Sheriff Sisay became Confederal Minister of Finance and Dr Momodou S K Manneh was appointed Confederal Minister of Economic Affairs. Eleven other Gambian MPs were appointed members of the Confederal Parliament.

The Confederal Parliament was composed of sixty members, two thirds made up of Senegalese delegates and one third of Gambians drawn from the PPP and NCP represented in the Gambian House. It was based in Senegal and the Speaker of the Gambian Parliament was appointed Speaker of the Confederal Parliament. We were committed to funding the confederal budget on the shared basis of two thirds coming from Senegal and one third from The Gambia. We rose to the occasion in proposing initiatives. While other new areas at the party levels of the PPP and PS were being explored and concretised, new partnerships were being formed. Early the following year, Dakar and Banjul were able to create a single business chamber known as the Association of Senegambia Chambers of Commerce and Industry. It comprised representatives from the Gambia Chamber of Commerce and the National Union of Senegalese Chambers of Commerce and Industry.

However, there were still some warning lights flickering. We had put forward during our parliamentary consultations following the initial signing of the Declaration for a rotation of tenure of the presidency simply for the correctness of it and for the defence of our national interests. Besides, it was practical, as has been seen in operation in the EU where the presidency rotates every six months to even very small states. Senegal, on the other hand, stood firmly by its terms on the presidency – which it would not rotate. After long debates in Kaur however we agreed to maintain the clauses as proposed by Senegal.

The Gambia settled in good faith with me as the Vice President of the Confederation, deferring all powers to the Confederal President who had full command of the Confederal Army. I remained Commander-in-Chief of the Gambia National Army, which, ironically, did not exist at the time. We had however already agreed to form such an army. Along with the Declaration we signed other specific treaties covering foreign affairs, transport, telecommunications and information.

Whereas Senegal would not broach any delay in the designing of the framework for a monetary union, our understanding was that the proposals for such a far-reaching union were premature. We would rather leave them on the table with the expectation that time would serve to bring new ideas to bear on them. However, the complexity of the subject did not seem to impress upon the Senegalese the need to take any caution in moving towards a monetary union. The objectives seemed to supersede all other considerations. It soon appeared that even the fact of our already integrated armies did not serve as a serious enough indication that we meant business.

Indeed, several elements of cooperation were already working smoothly including a Confederal Parliament, regular inter-state ministerial meetings and all the handsome results those were producing. Advanced ventures at the social and party political and at the business and grassroots levels were being undertaken. We were merging our external affairs, telecommunications and sea and road transport systems. Apparently, all these seemed inadequate and left Dakar with little impressions.

The general areas of the Agreement provided for confederal institutions consisting of the Presidency with a General Secretariat for the execution of presidential directives and the coordination of all the various ministries in the Confederation. The secretariat was headquartered in Dakar. When the staff appointments were finally announced a Senegalese was appointed Secretary General. This flew in the face of the tradition that provided that a country could not host the head office and at the same time provide the secretary general. In addition, the Deputy Secretary General was Senegalese and so were four of the five department heads. Two directors, Gambian and Senegalese, headed the Economic and Technical Affairs and Social and Cultural Affairs respectively. The research, press, legal and documentation centres were all headed by Senegalese. The only department headed by a Gambian was the Translation and Interpretation Department.

Meanwhile, Senegal vigorously pursued its pet issue of monetary integration and the merging of the two economies. This naturally posed more challenging questions and needed more time and more planning. Senegal seemed to be moving faster than the natural growth rate the concept could afford. The record on the ground in West Africa on attempts to merge economies and establish monetary unions was nothing to go by. In fact, it advised against rushed harmonisation of the two historically different fiscal and administrative systems. Generally, two or even more countries could come together in a union of sovereign states and their economies did not need to merge. The European Union (EU) was always there as a great example of what we would like to see happening in West Africa. After all, that was the prime objective of setting up ECOWAS.

Naturally, a few things would need time to iron out. For example, as regards the proposed monetary union between us, it would have to be taken into consideration that Senegal was already a leading member in WAMU, the West African Monetary Union, made up of sovereign French-speaking countries. The technicalities would have to be worked through as to whether The Gambia would join WAMU in its own right or whether it would be admitted in joint membership with Senegal. These and many other problems needed the opinion of the experts. Our conviction was that a platform for economic cooperation could have been established while the two economies functioned independently. We have already cited the EU as a working example of what arrangements we could adopt. In the end, we did not join WAMU.

To set up the Confederal Army, we had to reconstitute our national security forces. Therefore, in 1983, the Field Force was transformed into the Gambia National Gendarmerie (GNG). A Ghanaian Regimental Sergeant Major trained the first batch of Gambia National Army recruits before the arrival of the British Army Training Team (BATT). BATT consisted of Major Kenneth Wright, Sergeant Major Tim Paton and Sergeant Major Stan Allen. Senegal carried out the training of the GNG. The security and intelligence services and the law enforcement agencies were thus poised for modernisation as the training took off quickly into high gear and in just six months there was something to show for the effort.

In February 1984, the Senegalese Foreign Minister Medoun Fall and the Senegalese Army Chief of Staff Idrissa Fall arrived for security talks. The confederal forces conducted a joint military exercise on the outskirts of Banjul. Operation *Wiping Out Enemy Troops* proved highly professional and they were both satisfied with the quality of the exercises and said the men had demonstrated, on the one hand, the effective integration of the two countries' security forces and, on the other, the determination of the security forces to defend the frontiers, the security of people and property, particularly the territorial integrity of the two member states.

Meanwhile, back in Dakar, President Diouf was flexing his muscle out on the Senegalese electorate to make his mark as a politician. If ever anyone were in doubt whether he had fitted well into the mantle of his predecessor only two years before, the elections held in March 1984 spoke loudly in his favour. He faced his first personal challenge at the ballot box and was elected by an overwhelming majority against his key opponent, Abdoulaye Wade.

The developments in our new army left me and many in my government convinced that there was much to be gained from collaborating with other countries in the sub-region. As I saw it, there was nothing stopping the coming in of more countries to join the nucleus of what The Gambia and Senegal were beginning to enjoy from cooperation. A good example of the snowballing effect of collaboration could be seen in the case our collaboration on The Gambia River Basin Project that led the way for Guinea and Guinea Bissau to trust enough in our progress to join in.

I had a busy schedule both at home and abroad since the confederation in which I often suggested that other countries should be encouraged to participate. I was in Rabat, Morocco, on 27 March 1984 when I heard of the death of President Sékou Touré in the USA where he had gone for medical treatment. Through the several visits we exchanged, we built a friendly relationship.

I have fond memories of working with President Touré at the OIC, a common platform of faith where we found common ground on many subjects, from religion and social revolution to the blissful dream of a unified Africa and the Islamic *Ummah* free from war, want and disease. I succeeded him as Chairman of the Peace Committee of the OIC. I went direct from Morocco to attend his funeral. Right through the life of the Senegambia confederation I tried to keep alive the promise I made to him to minimise disagreements with Senegal and to highlight the crucial points on which we agreed.

I set off again to Dakar for a meeting, this time, to work through the details of the 1984/1985 confederal budget proposals. We decided to cut down on the CFA 4 billion budget by 25% cent and to operate within CFA 3.2 billion francs (D320 million). Those were hard times for the dalasi, which, despite the laudable measures taken by government, continued to fall. From D17 to CFA 5,000 before the coup, it fell rapidly to D45 around 1982, taking a further beating down to D100 by February 1986.

Therefore, the cuts in the confederal budget reduced our burden only slightly. We were still left with a D106 million annual obligation to the confederation. The fall in exchange rates wiped away all that we should have enjoyed from our first-ever recording of a trade surplus of D4.4 million.

I celebrated my sixtieth birthday in May 1984. It was great news also that the country recorded a trade surplus of D4 million which, unfortunately, was swallowed up at such speed by the attendant demands on the economy including the cost of the confederation. I felt none of the dramatic changes I had expected of turning sixty. I had anticipated for years that when one marks such a significant milestone as a diamond jubilee, one feels some earth-shaking difference. There were the aches and pains and perhaps a slower golf swing that were not there the year before; maybe those were the most certain changes ageing kept in store, after all.

The intervening months until November 1984 were hectic at the training depots around the country. The British Army Training Team, and the French and Senegalese technical officer corps had been busy honing the skills and endurance of our selected troops to the requisite standards of a professional armed forces. On 8 November, I took the salute at the Yundum Barracks where forty-nine recruits passed into the ranks of the Gambia National Army. I was encouraged by the motivation of the officers and men, as were the confederal parliamentarians, the ministers and training officers who came to witness such an auspicious occasion of collaboration and graduation.

It was a splendid turnout and I told the troops how proud I was to be their commander-in-chief. I paid tribute to the training teams whose officers were there with me to see our first battalion's march past. There was every sign that the future was bright, and that the security of this country seemed to be in professional hands. I pointed out that it was now their turn to answer the call of duty, and they must take it to be their fullest responsibility and pride rising up as they were from the Gambia Branch of the Royal West African Frontier Force that was disbanded in 1959 and renamed the Gambia Field Force and which was now giving way to the Gambia National Army.

I thanked the governments of Britain, France and Senegal for providing assistance in training and equipping our defence forces. I was delighted to have our British partners in a team led by Major Kenneth Wright. Major Wright had come to help us through the Anglo-Gambia Agreement on the British Military Assistance I signed, following talks we held at the Foreign and Commonwealth Office in London in 1983.

To underscore the importance my government attached to the confederation, I recall the enthusiastic manner in which I presented the case for it to parliament in the address in which I made the fine connection between our confederation as a building block towards the realisation of international monetary reform which, if planned realistically, would be an indispensable step to African unity and collective self-reliance. It was one important demonstration of the possibilities within the larger framework of sub-regional integration as enshrined in the objectives of ECOWAS.

We saw the Senegambia confederation as complementary in that light just as all the agreements that were on the table in the sub-regional associations in the Mano River Union, ECOWAS and the OMVG – all complementary to international monetary reform and were always to be seen in their productive role within the worldwide but decentralised monetary system. The case of the Senegambia confederation was even more relevant, reinforced as it was by kinship ties and common culture of the Senegalese and Gambian people.

Senegalo-Gambian cooperation could therefore boast small but important steps gradually being taken as the years went by. By 1985 most of the key protocols had been negotiated and concluded. The experts' groups from the two sides that had been working on the *modus operandi* of establishing an economic and monetary union submitted their final reports on the different approaches to the union. They proposed a Free Trade Area as the first step towards a customs union. They also submitted the various reactions from studies on the choices open to The Gambia for either an independent entry to WAMU or as a confederated unit with Senegal. The final outcome was left to negotiation of the specifics at inter-ministerial level.

My government studied the options for membership of WAMU and we opted for an independent entry, if at all. However, Senegal was not pleased with this decision. They regarded this as foot dragging on our side, which was a misrepresentation. We thought it necessary to be cautious and ensure that proper time and study was given to matters as important as unified customs and tariffs, unified central banking, a common currency, a common market and all the concomitant adjustments – political, social, foreign and domestic.

Anyway, while we set up the confederation, the ministry of finance and economic affairs was busy dealing with the difficulties of the scarcity of foreign exchange, high fuel prices and hoarding by unscrupulous businesspeople who asked ordinary citizens to pay for local goods in CFA francs. British Petroleum (BP) and Texaco fuel importers in Banjul were strapped for foreign exchange to bring in more fuel and that led to serious shortages for the consumer. By the time the fuel arrived, the price had increased considerably but was cheap, compared to Senegal where it was four times that of The Gambia.

In the midst of consolidating the confederation, we were finalising the Structural Adjustment Programme with the IMF. We had to take measures designed to tackle the difficulties we had accessing foreign exchange, by expanding output in critical sectors and removing constraints to growth generally. Those were trying times for the people and the government alike. There was panic buying to beat the erratic price rises as day-to-day items began to disappear from shop shelves. Suppliers began hoarding and soon created an artificial scarcity thus sending prices rocketing. The black market thrived and private money changers were working the sidewalk outside the banks in currency trading already in excess of $50 million every year. The uncontrolled flight of scarce foreign currency from the country exacerbated our predicament.

Tensions simmered among the people and at the marketplaces. We had to put major policies in place to stop the decline. Vice President Bakary B Dabo, also the leader of government business in parliament, made it clear that it was illegal to refuse the country's legal tender and asked the public to report to the security authorities anyone who was refusing to accept the dalasi in the normal course of business. Justice was applied to all across the board.

The year 1989 started with the confirmation of the overtures from North Korea for a normalisation of diplomatic relations. I received the letters of credence of Ambassador Byong Chol thus ending nearly eight years of rupture between us and the government of Kim Il-Sung. We sent a delegation to Pyongyang where they delivered my message that The Gambia would like to consider North Korea a friendly partner, especially in the multilateral financing of our economic development programmes.

I was not just limiting my trumpeting the success of our collaboration in home-based speeches. I cited our Confederation with Senegal as an example of efforts everyone could adopt towards total unity of peoples and the dismantling of borders. I highlighted it as the sample of what might obtain in other areas in West Africa when I took the message with me in my travels in March and April to Thailand, Bangladesh and the Central African Republic. I promoted the greater awareness of the confederation and, in drawing the attention of my hosts to strengthening South-South cooperation, used our small confederation as a microcosm of the economic blocks through which those countries could successfully do business. In my visit to the Central African Republic I exchanged thoughts with President

Andre Kolingba, the Chairman of the Economic Community of Central African States. His encouragement was tremendous; he emphasised that South-South dialogue was the answer to the establishment of an African common market.

For Senegal, 1989 was not an easy year. There were disruptive troubles erupting between it and its northern neighbour, Mauritania. Its southern neighbour, Guinea Bissau, was bitterly disputing a recent arbitration over a piece of maritime zone, where oil deposits were being prospected. As if that was not enough already on President Diouf's plate, rebels loyal to Father Diamacoune Senghor and his MFDC in the Casamance were demanding independence for the southern region. Lives were already being lost in attacks along the ninety-mile border with the Foni districts of The Gambia.

As chairman of both CILSS and ECOWAS at the time, I was concerned about the flashes of unrest that blighted the West African landscape. In April, I received the Mauritanian Minister Mohammed Lamin Ould Ahmed, a special envoy of President Ahmed Ould Taya. He delivered a message from his head of state apprising me of the strained relations between Senegal and his country following recent border incidents and isolated acts of communal violence in the capitals of the two countries.

I phoned Dakar and Nouakchott and expressed to Diouf and Taya my sadness over the state of tension between them. I urged the two leaders to do everything possible to defuse the tension and to seek an early settlement of the dispute. I explained how the sore relations were also touching on Senegalese and Mauritanian communities in The Gambia where the two groups featured prominently in the business and cultural life of Gambians.

I transmitted both leaders' reassurances of restraint and desire for peace to the ECOWAS Secretariat, urging Executive Secretary Abass Bundu to intervene as soon as possible. However, the tensions worsened to such an extent that the Senegalese and Mauritanians began attacking each other in their respective capitals. The results were grave.

One hundred Mauritanian refugees had arrived in The Gambia in the preceding few days. My government was already working closely with the Gambia Red Cross in settling them in various places around the country. I visited the camp where the Red Cross was holding the refugee Mauritanians who had fled over to The Gambia from violence in Senegal. By May the number of refugees arriving had swelled to 3,245. In addition to the holding centre at Kanifing, we had to open up others in Kaur, Farafenni, Bansang and Basse. We sent a Red Cross delegation to Nouakchott for discussions with the government in which we expressed our concern over the development, and explored what could be done immediately to end the attacks and stem the flight of the refugees. I also instructed Bundu to go to Nouakchott as my special envoy.

We worked relentlessly, and soon good sense prevailed. Tensions died down and peace returned. I then set myself special oversight for the early return of the refugees. We put our Gambia Air Shuttle commercial aircraft on the job, airlifting them to Mauritania. Algeria sent military transport planes to join a fleet from Morocco, France and Spain already in action shuttling people back to Nouakchott. We gave priority to the women and children, the sick and the elderly. The Gambia Air Shuttle plane on hire had already evacuated nearly three hundred Mauritanians when it broke down at Nouakchott airport. We then called on the International Red Cross in Geneva which promptly sent a Norwegian Red Cross plane to take over from the crippled Air Shuttle.

We felt a deep sense of utility in playing our part by helping to bring about peace between our neighbours and rising to the occasion to see to the welfare of their citizens who had come to us to seek refuge in our country. As Chairman of ECOWAS, it was my mandate to build peace and it was gratifying indeed when peaceful human and business traffic resumed at Rosso Senegal and Rosso Mauritanie, the important twin crossing points between the two countries on the Senegal River. I received phone calls of gratitude and support for timely concern and action from Dakar and Nouakchott and from many people and international organisations.

It was with equal satisfaction that I served on the mediation team that went to Lomé, Togo, in the heady days of disagreement and trading of sore exchanges between Senegal and Guinea Bissau on one hand and Ivory Coast and Guinea Conakry on the other.

While many initiatives and proposals on our part lent themselves to showing Senegal that The Gambia was serious about its obligations to treaties and protocols, the niggling issues of economic union and monetary integration proved very stubborn hurdles. And Senegal was unable to hide its frustration and impatience over the slow pace in those two directions. In August 1989, I felt it was time, after eight years, to attempt to inject some life into the confederation. It had become quite clear in Dakar and Banjul that while the little things about confederation – a joint parliament, ministerial contacts and others – were working at great cost to both countries, the central objectives had stalled. We felt in Banjul that it was necessary to review the state of the confederation to make it more workable.

I wrote to President Diouf and brought up once again the issue of rotating the presidency. Diouf's reaction became apparent a few days later. He agreed that the view from Dakar also was that things had stalled at an expensive and cosmetic level, and the achievements so far were probably not worth the billions of CFA francs it was costing both our treasuries to run the club. However, my optimism was ever fresh. The confederation was not dead, I assured listeners to a BBC interview I gave after the letter to Dakar, but was a little ill. The two countries needed to start a thorough review to put it on a basis that was entirely satisfactory to both sides.

But apparently, Dakar, while it agreed that there was some stiffness in the patient, did not share my optimism that a rotation of the presidency was part of the answer. On Friday 18 August 1989, I left for work only to discover that I had no bodyguards posted or any other security detail for that matter apart from my orderly and aide-de-camp. The bulk of the Presidential Guard was Senegalese and they had not reported for duty. Strange as it looked, it did not deter me from proceeding to my office and to start my day. I immediately approved the emergency request by Commander Mansour Niang, then Presidential Guard commander to see me. He arrived at 08.45 am and informed me that he had received instructions the night before that all Senegalese troops in the Confederal Gendarmerie including the Presidential Guard were to leave immediately. He had no answers for the fact that I had received no official notification of this major action.

I phoned President Diouf and asked for an explanation. There was not much he had to say but would leave it to Confederal Defence Minister Medoun Fall who, he said, would come to explain. At midday, I summoned an extraordinary cabinet meeting and followed it up with rapid consultations with members of my government and others over the sudden and unceremonious withdrawal of Senegalese troops. I sought wide opinion on the best way to handle the emergency.

On Tuesday 22 August, as soon as I got to the office I put a call through to the US to my daughter, Nema, and wished her a happy birthday. We are a large family and birthdays come by thick and fast. Many times it had struck me to think whether I would have been able to remember all the names and dates of the even larger numbers we had in my father's household in Barajaly. It was a good thing we did not mark birthdays in the *musu bungo*; otherwise the list on the wall would have been very long indeed.

It promised to be a busy day. At 10.30, Senegal's Defence Minister Medoun Fall arrived in my office. He explained that his country had been facing situations of emergency with insurgency on its southern borders with Guinea Bissau, on its northern borders with Mauritania and inside Casamance as well. He tried to explain the situation which demanded that all its troops be recalled to attend to those national emergencies.

I was blunt in expressing my disappointment at such a unilateral and certainly hasty decision on the part of Dakar. In all honesty, I was flabbergasted by the abrupt manner of the withdrawal from an organisation that had attracted the focus of the African and international communities and over which both countries had worked so hard. However, before we parted it had become clear to us that the confederation had been ill for some time and it did not seem it would ever get any better. A new and simpler arrangement had to be sought.

At 12.00 noon, Mauritanian Minister of Foreign Affairs, Cheikh Sidi Ahmed Ould Baba, came to State House. The special envoy of President Ould Taya discussed with me the ongoing strain in relations with Senegal and the mounting refugee situation that was possible if measures towards a solution were not taken immediately. I offered what tangible advice I could give.

On Wednesday 23 August 1989, President Diouf went on national television and told his people that the confederation was not working. He said the meetings of the Council of Ministers, the Confederal Parliament and other formal meetings were a waste of time if no real progress was being made in ironing out the real issues that hampered the integration of the two states. He called for the two governments to muster the necessary courage to freeze the functioning of the confederation since the primary objective of economic integration seemed premature. Diouf promised his people that Senegal had decided it would begin sound and frank talks with The Gambia to set up instead a simpler and less expensive structure which would reflect a consensus on this privileged cooperation. Therefore the confederal treaty was being suspended and Senegalese troops were being withdrawn.

At dawn after the *fajr* prayers on Thursday 31 August, I wished Njaimeh a happy birthday before leaving for my office. I sat down with the Minister of the Interior, his Permanent Secretary and the Inspector General of Police and we prepared the ground for the bigger and tougher meeting the following day.

On Friday 1 November, we met with the Defence and Security Council and laid down the official policy on ways of limiting the fallout from of the sudden pullout of the Senegalese forces from the confederal army and its effect on the general security situation in the country. We put in place our instruments for the final wrapping up of the confederation.

I was now fully armed with views from other high-level consultations. At 11.45 am, I received Cheikh Sylla, the outgoing Secretary General of the Senegambia Confederation, who had arrived as a special envoy of President Diouf's. We began official discussions on the unwinding of the confederal arrangements. We set a timetable which was later officially confirmed by both countries' executives to bring the treaty to a close in September 1989.

After his departure, I continued consultations with our own senior officials such as Acting Commander of the National Gendarmerie Pa Sallah Jagne. We went back to the drawing board with the military technicians from Britain, Nigeria and Turkey and studied the new arrangements for a unified armed forces system.

We were adjusting well and taking the immediate post-confederation problems in our stride. It was not easy working out the repatriation of the administrative instruments and hardware. It was a less formidable task for the finance officers of the confederation who would simply carry on until the intricate issues of gratuities, back pay, leave arrears and the settling of all other money matters were sorted out.

With a hot and sticky last two weeks of August gone, I left for the meeting of the Non-Aligned Movement taking place in Belgrade, Yugoslavia, from 3 to 6 September. I managed to catch the forty odd winks of thorough rest during what was supposed to be my time away on a short leave.

On 13 September 1989, I sat down with the BBC African Service's Veronique Edwards who asked for updates on and my reactions to the breakdown of the confederation and the way forward. My message was a simple one: close economic and social collaboration between Senegal and The Gambia was unavoidable and from the experience of the Senegambia confederation a simpler and more workable method was the answer.

Back in Banjul, I went straight to the list of agencies and groups to be consulted further on the closure of the confederation. The PPP Central Committee met on 15 September. Things had moved rapidly, in fact precipitously, over the previous four weeks and the Committee provided rather insightfully on the arguments that helped to strengthen and adequately inform our positions on the main issues. The Committee's view was for the two countries to replace the confederation with a more equitable and less expensive association.

In a bitter twist, the Senegalese immediately ordered border closures and slammed down traffic and transport restrictions. Trans-border trade even at the petty trading level of women carrying roasted peanuts or cashew nuts on their heads was restricted. Customs and police checks at the borders truly amounted to harassment. Goods were stopped in transit and the GPTC bus shuttles between Dakar and Banjul were stopped. No Gambian taxis were allowed through. There were frequent seizures of goods and the institution of a law that allowed only CFA20,000 francs[15] per traveller – a pittance and a gross inconvenience by any standards.

In early November, we sent a diplomatic note to Dakar protesting against the harassment of Gambian travellers to and from Senegal and against the imposition of sanctions and embargoes on trade with us: "The Government of The Gambia is of the considered opinion that the deliberate harassment of Gambians is in contravention of international agreements and conventions and is not conducive to the maintenance of the friendly and indeed privileged relations that exist between The Gambia and Senegal."

I went to Dakar on 14 December on a one-day working visit in an attempt to break the ice and defuse the tension building up between us. I proposed a Treaty of Friendship to President Diouf and urged that both sides begin to work immediately on it so that we could get back on a proper footing as partners and neighbours.

I told Diouf that to jaw-jaw was better than to war-war. I put on the table the evidence that The Gambia had honoured all the obligations as stipulated in the protocols of the confederation and had not flinched from fulfilling its responsibilities. I drew the president's attention to his own words at the last ministerial meeting in Banjul on the setting up of the Preferential Trade Area in which he attested to the fact that the ball was in Senegal's court. It was a complete surprise that when Senegal played a hand it was the unilateral decision we saw that called the troops home. We relayed the reports that External Affairs Minister Omar Sey had laid before cabinet on investigated complaints he had received over the two months since my letter to Diouf for a re-study of the confederal protocols. The details were indeed descriptive of a great deal of unfriendly treatment of Gambians by Senegalese border authorities.

Diouf and I exchanged hugs and handshakes and I returned to Banjul with assurances from him that something would be done to ease the bottlenecks at the borders.

That dangerous and undesirable lacuna persisted until late 1990 when the two governments resumed contacts since my ice-breaking visit to Dakar. Omar Sey and his Senegalese counterpart Foreign Minister Moustapha Niass met and the two countries signed a Treaty of Friendship.

---

[15] Equivalent to D500 at the time.

In my Christmas message to the nation, I enjoined Gambians to forgo personal and sectional compulsions and to work as brothers and sisters. I wished everyone the peace and joy of the festive season and blessings in the New Year. Later that evening, in a black tie, I joined the men of the Banjul Dinner Club for their 500th regular monthly dinner since the Club's inception in 1947.

To close the year, I received the Pakistani envoy, High Commissioner A J Naim, on Friday 29 December. He was the last of the nearly two dozen foreign dignitaries who had presented letters of credence or of commission or had come on courtesy calls over the course of the year. I emphasised to Naim the importance of peace if our Third World communities must develop. I urged for peace and understanding among all peoples and between India and Pakistan, especially over the protracted dispute over Kashmir.

After work, I drove to the Dippakunda Mosque for Friday prayers to honour the invitation to perform the *aljumaat* prayers there that day. I had gladly accepted when the Mosque Committee led by their chairman, B O Semega-Janneh, extended an invitation to me to pray with them, when they paid me a courtesy visit during the week. The following day, 30 December was Nacesay's birthday. Baby Chilel's was on 11 December.

27

The early 1990s

For the better part of the 1980s, we had been prudent under the structural adjustment programme. We had come through with great plusses on our side for turning the economy around. The Gambia's efforts were lauded by the Director for West Africa of the World Bank, Mr Michael Gillette, who, while visiting with us, had declared us to be ahead in West Africa in the adjustment of our economy. We were such a leading light in structural adjustment that the Sierra Leonean Minister of Finance, Tommy Taylor Morgan, and researchers came to study the implementation of adjustments Sierra Leone had been trying since 1983 without success.

Playing by the rules of restructuring had already brought us worthy mention as before in October 1989 at the IMF and World Bank meeting in Washington. We were there to sign the letter of intent for the Policy Framework Paper under the extended Structural Adjustment Facility with the IMF. The Fund's Managing Director, Michel Camdessus, congratulated The Gambia on its steady and good performance under the programme.

Many leaders in the sub-region asked me on several occasions what made our recovery and restructuring so successful. Ours was a simple answer. The country had taken on the whole programme as a package and did not cherry pick which of its aspects were *convenient* to apply. We went the whole hog, whether it was administrative reform, retrenchment, reduction of subsidies to farmers or any of the measures on a tough list we had to introduce. But because we knew it was a massive load to demand of the people, I went on a countrywide tour to explain the ERP. I told the people what it meant, and shared with them the purposeful outcomes if they came through with us. Through four years of commitment and understanding it worked. The foreign exchange problems eased; and shop stalls filled up again.

Just as individuals looked forward to new and exciting things when a new year rolled in, so it was also for governments and countries. On the domestic front, the Programme for Sustained Development (PSD) was the thing of the 1990s. When I addressed parliament in December 1990 I said the new programme was introduced to strengthen the successes of the ERP which had seen a four percent growth in the economy in the previous four years. I reported that despite the setback in the groundnut harvest in the 1988-89 year, coupled with adverse trade conditions in the sub-region, the volume of domestic product had risen 20% higher than it had at the start of the ERP in 1985. This meant that The Gambia, by its performance, became qualified under the Enhanced Structural Adjustment Facility (ESAF) programme of the World Bank and the IMF, one of the first African countries to do so.

As part of the desired improvement in the performance of parastatal companies, I proposed that they sign performance contracts with government. Drastic disciplinary attitudes had to be adopted if the PSD was to remain meaningful.

In the field of foreign policy, the way forward for Africa and other developing countries was collaboration, compelling African governments to push for more South-South dialogue and trade. The European Economic Community – African, Caribbean and Pacific (EEC-ACP) arrangement was the leading light in North-South cooperation. Under the EEC-ACP programmes billions of dollars had been transferred as economic intervention as well as the enhancement of capacity to the mutual benefit of countries in the North and the South. The Gambia had benefited a lot from vital development assistance under the Lomé Convention programmes.

With regard to South-South collaboration, my government always stressed the importance of the Brandt Commission Report of 1980 for a reorganisation of the world economic order and the rearrangement of the pattern of economic relationships between the industrialised nations and developing countries. We thought it most unfortunate that the reaction to the Brandt Report by some developed countries ranged from detached scepticism to plain indifference and outright rejection. The developed world must assist the weak and vulnerable if communities were to be stable and the world to live in peace.

For such reforms to come about, the South must engage the North in serious dialogue towards a just and equitable resolution of key issues in development such as international trade, external debt, protectionism and official development assistance.

Dr Manmohan Singh, the South-South Commission's Secretary General, stated in a memorandum to the UN secretary general that most indebted countries were trapped in a vicious circle of stagnation, macroeconomic instability and high resource transfers abroad, and they needed to break out from this to enter a virtuous circle of economic growth. Debt relief could contribute to this in three ways: by reducing the burden on public finances, thus facilitating macroeconomic stability; freeing resources for investment and imports, thereby promoting economic recovery; and by encouraging the repatriation of capital, thus contributing indirectly to the reversal of resource transfer.

Foreign policy standards must be balanced with those on the domestic front; otherwise there is little gained if the most vulnerable in our own societies go without the attention to make them full participants in national development. Women, youth, children (especially girls) and the aged are groups long identified among us as needing special attention.

Democracy therefore would hardly be workable if women and children continue as the most disadvantaged groups in society. Women form slightly more than 50% of our population and no economy can afford to marginalise half its potential workforce and expect to succeed in bringing development to the nation. We had long recognised the need for the greater participation of women and with the help of non-governmental organisations, a wide range of projects at divisional level were in various stages of implementation under the management of village committees. I assented to a National Women's Council Act in 1980 which created the Women's Bureau to implement the decisions of the council. Parliament ratified the UN Convention on the Elimination of All Forms of Discrimination Against Women (CEDAW) in 1992.

In recognition of our commitment to women's development, in 1990 the World Bank identified The Gambia as a pilot location for the Women in Development (WID) programme, with funding from the Norwegian government and the African Development Bank. WID developed programmes of intervention that cut across all sectors of women's activities, all geared towards developing a national policy for women. Then we instituted the Ministry of Women's Affairs but kept it under my purview until it was moved to the Office of the Vice President in 1992.

The PPP government had always endeavoured to break the mould of gender discrimination by involving women in national development. In 1962 we put up Augusta Jawara as a candidate in national elections. I later nominated Mrs Lucretia St Claire Joof to the House of Representatives, the first woman to be so honoured in The Gambia. We regularly exhorted the Bathurst (Banjul) City Council to engage the wisdom of women and get them involved in leadership in the municipality. Mrs Lilly Mama Buxton Wright became active in council's affairs. It was encouraging to see my former teacher, Ms Lilian Johnson, stand in BCC elections. We left a proud legacy of opportunities we had given to women in the political and legislative arena, not to speak of responsibility in the civil service.

After our re-election to government in 1982, I appointed Louise Antoinette Njie as a minister in my cabinet. She served from 1985 to 1992. In the 1982 parliamentary elections PPP's Nyimasata Sanneh-Bojang, the only female candidate, won the Kombo North District. She was later made parliamentary secretary for Education. Elizabeth Renner, Mary Mboge, Fatou Ceesay, Agnes Jawo and others were all nominated to serve in parliament. As the political parties contested to win the trust of the people, I was glad to take note that opposition parties fielded women candidates. Amie Sillah of PDOIS (Banjul South), Anna Francess Thomas, Independent (Banjul Central), and Fatou Sanneh Colley of the GPP (Kombo Central) were nominated to contest the 1992 parliamentary elections.

The Gambia National Army had its first Trooping the Colours in February 1990. The addition of 84 soldiers passing out was a milestone towards achieving our recommended force strength of 700. I addressed the men at the passing-out parade at Yundum Barracks, urging them to uphold the discipline and dedication to their call to duty. I pointed to the tremendous improvements in place with twelve quarters for forty-eight junior NCOs having been completed under the first phase of the Yundum Barracks Project. Also, Chinese technicians had constructed two moveable armouries and a moveable magazine for the storage of ammunition and light weapons, a gift from the People's Republic of China to the GNA.

The barracks now had dining and recreational halls and a standard soldiers' kitchen. I thanked Britain, the USA, Morocco, France, Pakistan and Senegal for the great work done. I announced that technical teams from the People's Republic of China were expected to arrive to train GNA personnel in the handling of special types of light and heavy weapons and to update the maintenance standards and skills of two patrol vessels of the Marine Unit. The newly trained soldiers joined the rifles company at Yundum, Kartong, Farafenni and Kudang.

At the end of the ceremony, they had their own flag which I urged should be a source of inspiration under which they must serve.

The year 1990 will always be remembered for one important event - Nelson Mandela was freed on Sunday 11 February 1990. It was a cause which many people and organisations who had respect for human rights and democracy had championed for almost three decades. It was of great significance that shortly after he walked out of prison, Mandela agreed to the suspension of the armed struggle.

We expressed The Gambia's hope that the release of Mandela would now herald a new era in the process that would lead to the establishment of a free, multiracial and democratic South Africa. I commended President

F W de Klerk for his boldness against a hostile environment that we knew South Africa to be. Our message was unequivocal. While it was recognised that the South African authorities had taken the right step by releasing Mandela, the government of The Gambia would still urge them to lift the state of emergency and release all other political prisoners. Those two measures were crucial as a prelude to the holding of the meaningful negotiations for the peaceful resolution of the conflict in South Africa.

At the same time, we called on the international community to maintain the sanctions and the pressures on South Africa, which would hopefully lead to the total eradication of apartheid. I followed that with a personal message to Oliver Tambo, president of the ANC, congratulating him and reassuring him of our unequivocal support for the ANC and our unwavering solidarity with the oppressed people of South Africa in their legitimate struggle for freedom and justice.

On 18 February 1990 we celebrated 25 years of our country's independence. The Silver Jubilee celebrations were marked by many activities including cultural shows, the commissioning of projects and exhibitions. Among the distinguished guests present were President Ibrahim Babangida of Nigeria, Her Royal Highness Princess Anne, the Princess Royal and George W Bush, Governor of the state of Texas, USA.

In April 1990 I travelled with Chilel to Dallas, Texas, at the invitation of Texas Governor George W Bush and his wife, Laura.

During their short visit earlier in February, the Bushes had taken a keen note of our efforts in conservation and environmental protection. In the more relaxed circumstances of my visit to Dallas, I gave them firsthand information on what we were doing in that vital area and why the programmes under CILSS were so important to us.

During the visit I played a round of golf with Bush. However the highlight of the visit took place on 6 April when I opened a city zoo called *The Wilds of Africa*, reputed to be the largest zoo in the world. More importantly my fullest acquiescence in the honour was in my support of the zoo's enviable efforts at the preservation of wildlife, some already on the endangered list. At a gathering on the same day of about three hundred guests including the mayor, councillors and invited dignitaries, I read out the Banjul Declaration and explained the desperate situation of environmental degradation and how forest depletion and drought were affecting even the cultural balance and expression of the people in the Sahel. I also highlighted the policies and programmes we were engaged in to stem the advance of desertification. I took the opportunity to open the lines for any fruitful partnerships.

The theme of the environment and perhaps the recognition of my personal commitment to defend and protect our wildlife were also shared by the Board of Education of Dallas Independent School who invited me to speak to them and receive a citation. I reiterated The Gambia's concern that "in a relatively short period of our history most of our larger wildlife species had disappeared together with much of the original forest cover. The concern was a duty we owed to ourselves, to our great African heritage and to the world." The Board of Education commended us for the foresight and outstanding leadership that went into the preparation and propagation of standards contained in the Declaration.

From Dallas we flew to New Orleans where Mayor Sidney Barthelmy welcomed us with a tumultuous carnival atmosphere. We had a wonderful stay in the city popularly nicknamed *The Big Easy*. Built around the Vieux Carre French quarter, the city lay below sea level just like parts of Banjul and also laid claim to the annual world renowned fiesta of the Mardi Gras, which drew hundreds of thousands of revellers annually to New Orleans.

Mayor Barthelmy presented me with an award of the Order of Merit and a key to the city. This way the mayor tied me spiritually and emotionally to New Orleans with a citation during the award ceremony that highlighted The Gambia's contribution to international understanding among peoples of the world.

The year 1990 saw me serve as chairman of ECOWAS for the second time, after serving my first term from 1988 to 1989. Of all the member countries, The Gambia was one of the few not bogged down with civil war or other turmoil. One journalist put it that West Africa needed a role model which The Gambia was proving to be.

In February 1990, some people questioned how we could so soon after celebrating our silver jubilee host the ECOWAS Heads of State and Government summit in May 1990. A veteran civil servant answering the press on the same issue replied, "Give us an impossible situation, limited time, scant resources and we'll do the job. It's the crisis management ethic we thrive on. Look at the Structural Adjustment Programme; everyone thought we had one foot in the grave but look, how we managed to tighten our belts!"

We were hosting ECOWAS at one of the most turbulent times in the sub-region. Of course, President Samuel Doe was absent from the meeting in Banjul as he was struggling with the civil war in his country. With his country under great threat from that civil war, President Joseph Saidu Momoh of Sierra Leone said in his speech at the meeting: "None of us is immune to the whims of political upheaval."

As it happened, he was out of office a short while later in a military coup that characterised the arrival in office of some of the other heads of state in attendance at the ECOWAS summit – Captain Blaise Compaoré of Burkina Faso, General Ibrahim Babangida of Nigeria, and General Joao Bernardo Vieira of Guinea Bissau.

The civil war had started in December 1989 and it greatly tested our cohesion and effectiveness as a sub-regional authority. ECOWAS had to seriously review the crisis and set tangible plans for action to bring peace to the country. There were three players in the fight for power - President Samuel Doe, Charles Taylor the leader of the National Patriotic Front of Liberia (NPFL), and Prince Johnson, a defector of the NPFL. At the end of the 13th session on 30 May 1990, we signed a communiqué that many considered the strongest yet on the unification and integration of the economies of the sixteen member countries.

We also formed the Standing Mediation Committee comprising The Gambia, Togo, Nigeria, Ghana and Benin. It was crucial that the committee went to work immediately. For want of a venue, I offered Banjul again for a follow-up meeting and in August 1990 all the parties in the Liberian conflict arrived for the mediation summit. I was quite pleased with the turnout of leaders at a meeting on such a major issue of peace in the sub-region. The meeting on 6 and 7 August 1990 was attended by Ghana's Chairman, Flight Lt Jerry Rawlings, Nigeria's President, Ibrahim Babangida, Mali's Foreign Minister, Niolo Traoré, and Togo's Justice Minister, Bitokotipou Yagninim. In attendance were key observers such as OAU Secretary General Salim Ahmed Salim and Chairman of the Liberian Inter-Faith Mediation Committee, the Rev Burghess Carr, as did the leaders of Liberia's two neighbouring states badly affected by the conflict, Sierra Leone's President Joseph Saidu Momoh and Guinea's President Lansana Conté.

A major outcome of the meeting was the setting up of the ECOWAS Monitoring Group (ECOMOG), a force that would go to Liberia essentially to keep the peace, restore law and order, and prepare Liberia for a return to a democratically and freely elected government. ECOMOG comprised 800 Ghanaians, 700 Nigerians, 550 Guineans, 350 Sierra Leoneans and 105 Gambians. Ghana's Lieutenant General Arnold Quainoo was selected to head the mission.

We also agreed there should be an interim government and proposed elections in Liberia. For the Election Observer Group and ECOMOG to work, we set up the Special Emergency Fund to take care of all ECOWAS operations in Liberia. We needed $50 million for a start; contributions were to come from member states, the OAU and the international donor community.

However shortly after the troops arrived in Liberia, they were caught up in intense fighting. Charles Taylor's NPFL was carrying out the threat their representative, Tom Woewiyu, had issued at the Banjul meeting, that NPFL forces would shoot at ECOMOG forces. Many of the military minds on the ground wanted to engage the rebel troops and were therefore irked by my approach against their desired all-out involvement in the fighting. I was of the strong opinion that ECOMOG forces were in Liberia primarily to keep the peace. I insisted that the capture of Taylor was not our mandate. I would therefore not let our soldiers take the law into their own hands in Liberia's domestic affairs.

I was accused of being too cautious. But when the NPFL continuously attacked ECOMOG positions, they were left with no choice but to exercise their right to self-defence. Nonetheless, we continued to try to end the crisis as quickly and as peacefully as possible.

Back in the Middle East, tensions rose again when Iraq under Saddam Hussein invaded Kuwait on 2 August 1990. We took the strongest position against the Iraqi aggression and sent External Affairs Minister Omar Sey to address the meeting of the OIC and unequivocally condemn the invasion. We supported resolutions of the OIC and other international voices that called on Saddam Hussein and his forces to withdraw to the pre-war frontiers and for talks to begin. Our position was drawing deeply from my experience years before as chairman of the Ninth Session of the Islamic Peace Committee on the Iran-Iraq War.

It was with great sadness that we received news that President Doe had been captured by Prince Johnson and killed on 9 September 1990. His gruesome torture was captured on video and aired worldwide.

In October 1990, I decorated Retired Sergeant Major Ousman A Jallow with the insignia of Commander of the National Order of the Republic of The Gambia (CRG). Jallow, a WWII veteran mentioned in despatches for retrieving his wounded European superior officer, Major Lynch, under a blistering barrage of enemy fire in the Burma campaign, was a veritable role model for the young soldiers. An ace marksman, he had come out of retirement to stand by loyal forces that held out against the rebel attack on the police headquarters in Banjul during the coup attempt of 1981.

At the end of 1990, we hosted the West African Parliamentary Workshop on Children in Banjul. Members of the House of Representatives joined the Global Committee of Parliamentarians on Population and Development and UNICEF to take stock of the legal status of children in the sub-region and exchanged ideas on ways of implementing the UN Convention on the Rights and Welfare of the Child and the role of parliamentarians in the actual implementation of those protocols.

The declaration of the 1990s as *The African Decade for Child Survival* and the designation of 16 June as *The Day of the African Child* followed our adoption at the OAU of the African Charter on the Rights and Welfare of the Child.

The year 1991 started with the Gulf War. On 17 January 1991 the Coalition Force from 34 nations attacked key positions in Iraq. UN Security Council Resolution 678 was the legal authorisation for the Gulf War and was passed on 29 November 1990. It authorised "all necessary means to uphold and implement Resolution 660" which authorised the use of force. On 28 February 1991 the Iraqi forces were defeated.

During the 26 independence anniversary celebrations on 18 February 1991 I granted amnesty to 35 more prisoners involved in the 1981 abortive coup. If nothing, it was to demonstrate, among other things, that my government recognised its duty to allowing convicted felons a second chance at a decent living and a more positive contribution to national development.

Ending the Liberian civil war looked promising in February 1991. At a meeting in Lomé, Togo, the three sides agreed to disarm and form an interim government. It was refreshing to see all the parties agreeing a national conference on Liberia that was finally held in Monrovia in March 1991. There they elected the Interim Government of Liberia with Dr Amos Sawyer as president. It was my pleasure and honour to be chairman of that conference. I was grateful for the assistance and support of President Gnassingbe Eyadema of Togo, President Moussa Traore of Mali, President Blaise Compaoré of Burkina Faso, all members of the ECOWAS Standing Mediation Committee and representatives of the leaders of Ghana and Nigeria.

On 16 April, I left for Abidjan, Ivory Coast, where I attended the two-day sessions of the first African African-American Summit. Organised and co-chaired by the Reverend Leon Sullivan, the summit was attended by 320 African Americans, African heads of state including Quett Masire of Botswana, Blaise Compaoré of Burkina Faso and Gen Joao Bernardo Vieira of Guinea-Bissau. The professions and faith-based organisations were fully represented by educators, politicians, business, civil rights and religious leaders. Sullivan expounded on the chief object of the summit, ie to strengthen the bonds of heritage and history between Africans and African-Americans.

The guests, nearly a thousand strong, chanted "Africa! Africa!" as the Rev Sullivan spoke in the auditorium of Abidjan's Hotel Ivoire on the opening day of the summit. The workshops proper focused on education, economic development, agriculture, health care and other concerns vital to capitalising on the untapped potential in many African nations. The summit came out with a declaration of principles and actions calling for, among other things, an end to price-fixing measures which have denied African nations a fair return for their produce, the cancellation of the $100 billion in official debt which was a burden to many African countries, stifling their development, and affirmed support for the concept of dual citizenship that would enable African-Americans to also hold citizenship of selected African countries.

I led a delegation on a visit to the People's Republic of China from 2 to 20 May 1991. The visit was a successful one and consolidated our relations. I reiterated the gratitude of the Gambian people as I had done earlier in the year when I accepted the letters of credence of Chinese Ambassador Lin Tinghai.

An OAU Summit took place from 2 to 5 June 1991. Liberia continued to be a key subject at meetings I attended in Yamoussoukro presided over by President Houphouet Boigny. The NPFL leader, Charles Taylor, who always managed to sit next to the Ivorian leader addressing him as "My father" throughout the deliberations, seemed indeed in good company.

The PPP Central Committee met on 2 August 1991 and approved the ad hoc committee that would organise the party's 5th Congress.

I went on the annual Meet the Farmers Tour from Monday 23 September 1991 to Wednesday 2 October 1991. We heard from the farming communities that reported their problems and their successes. We shared with them our expectations and aspirations in our common push towards the objectives of national development. We noted their concerns and went back to the drawing board and worked out policies that would address poverty, the effects of low rainfall and unfavourable world market prices.

We let the people, especially those in our party, know of the forthcoming congress that would review the progress of our party and plan for the future. The district party representatives were advised to bring their proposals to the congress for deliberations.

From 14 to 18 October 1991 in Harare, Zimbabwe, at the Commonwealth Heads of Government Meeting (CHOGM), we laid down the Harare Principles mainly dealing with good governance and human rights in member countries. From Harare our delegation flew to London where I addressed the Joint Meeting of the Commonwealth Human Rights Initiative and the Commonwealth Human Rights Trust.

On 1 December 1991, we opened the 5th PPP National Congress at Mansokonko. In my keynote address on 4 December 1991, I thanked the members of parliament, chairman and the constituency party of Western Jarra, the Lower River Division area party organisation and in general all the people of Jarra and Kiang for the generous way in which they opened their doors to us as hosts of the Congress. I extended my thanks to the members of the Central Committee, to all constituency delegates, representatives of the party's Women's Wing and Youth Movement, all party militants, supporters and well-wishers.

I reminded them that the PPP was not merely a party that happened to be in power; as a movement we had a mission. We had since the party's inception in 1959 espoused a cause, a national cause; we had opted for a body of beliefs, ideas and principles by which we had always stood. The congress was not only to take stock of our policies and our activities in the light of those guiding principles and beliefs but also to chart the future direction of the party, a future direction that would be consistent with our fundamental options while at the same time reflecting the prevailing realities and trends of our times. And the times were indeed exciting, characterised by sweeping changes in ideas, institutions and international relations. I urged the congress therefore to evaluate our party's principles and policies in the light of the situation and thereby help determine the best way forward.

At the end of my stocktaking, I presented my view on the way forward for the party. I announced that I would not like to be put forward as a candidate in the 1992 presidential election. With this timely gesture, I was expecting that 1991 would end with me quietly taking my first steps into retirement. But immediately after my announcement, it seemed all hell had broken loose. Speakers after me demanded that I withdraw the statement. Thereafter appeals began pouring in from many quarters asking me not to refuse to stand in the elections in 1992. I was taken aback by the reaction. I was shocked by the outpouring. Apparently people had not been paying attention to my wish to retire from the leadership of the PPP, a point I had made known to the party Central Committee in March 1991.

We went away from Mansakonko with obviously a lot of soul-searching to do. Many appeals were made that four months' notice for the leadership transition was not enough for the consultation required at all levels of the party. There was very little time to spare in deciding concretely which would have sway – my decision to step down or the people's call for me to remain for at least one more term.

The party settled in again to do the task of preparing the electorate to ask them for their votes for the party's seventh term in office in thirty years. There was a distinct need for the resolution of the apparent rivalries that had emerged by then among the top hierarchy. Senior party members were polarised along different lines with some wanting me to step down, sharpening divisions within the party.

Over the next couple of months mass rallies were held across the country, all calling for me to rescind my decision. In the end I thought of the Party's Motto: "Vox Populi Vox Dei – The Voice of the People is the Voice of God" and bowed down to popular pressure and rescinded my decision not to seek a further term as president.

In March 1992, the PPP Selection Committee met to choose the party's candidates for the presidential and general elections. I was the sole presidential candidate. We went out and explained the confusion to the people and also presented our choices of parliamentary candidates to them. The issue at that time was for them to help us pinpoint how we could better serve their cause in the future.

At a mass rally in Baddibu, Salikene, the home village of the NCP leader, Sheriff Mustapha Dibba, I was confronted with rumours that I had been holding secret meetings with Dibba and was negotiating to step down after the elections and to hand power over to him. I described those rumours as a mere dream and explained the truth of the matter: the NCP leadership had approached me several times on the subject of our two parties coming together in a coalition. I made it clear in a meeting I had at State House on 29 August 1990 with Lamin K Jabang, Yaya Ceesay, Kelepha Samba, Aji Fatou Sallah, Matarr Jah, Sheriff Dibba, Kemeseng Jammeh, Gibou Jagne and Solo Dabo that the PPP had an overwhelming majority in parliament, hence there was no need for a coalition. I said that any member of the opposition who wished to join the PPP would be welcomed.

By the close of the rally, Alhaji Kemba Kassama, a former NCP supporter, joined the PPP and donated D72,000 towards the construction of a bridge and causeway in the local rice fields. We presented our PPP candidate for Central Badibbu, Dr Lamin Saho, who was confident that the PPP would win and retain the seat for the third time in a row and keep Dibba out of parliament.

For our 27 independence anniversary celebrations in February 1992 we invited President Vieira of Guinea Bissau as guest of honour. The celebrations were relatively low key in recognition of the difficult times the country was going through.

On 29 April 1992, the nation went to the polls. After the close of polling, Chief Justice Emmanuel Olayinka Ayoola, the returning officer for the presidential election, announced that out of 220,017 votes cast for all the five presidential candidates, my closest rival, Dibba, polled 44,639 (22%) of the votes. Assan Musa Camara got 16,287 (8%), Dr Lamin Bojang, 11,999 (6%), and Sidia Jatta, 10,543 (5%) of the votes. I polled 117,549 (58%). The Chief Justice declared me the winner.

The PPP took 25 out of the 36 constituency seats in the general elections. The NCP won six seats including Central Baddibu where Dibba won back his seat after two consecutive losses in 1982 and 1987. The GPP won two seats. Assan Musa Camara lost in his Kantora stronghold against the PPP candidate. Three independent candidates won in Tumana, Niamina and Niani constituencies. The PDP and PDOIS parties failed to win a single seat.

The press thronged State House the following day. I told the journalists that the results had both refreshed and strengthened me in my fervent conviction that this country realised that its future and prosperity lay with the PPP. On that joyous occasion, I thanked all those who by voting for me and my party had given us a great victory.

I was sworn in as president on Monday, 11 May 1992 at MacCarthy Square. On that solemn day, I granted amnesty to all the perpetrators involved in the 1981 coup attempt except those who had had their death sentences commuted to life imprisonment. I also invited all those at large to return home. I called them back to their country, so they could play their part in the noble task of nation-building. I prayed that the message would reach Kukoi Samba Sanyang who was said to be in Ouagadougou, Burkina Faso.

I sponsored the President's Trophy Golf Tournament over the weekend of my swearing-in. After a pleasant first day out on the course at the Fajara Golf Club, I gave an interview to Radio Gambia's magazine programme, *Weekend Forum*. The reporter asked me the question he asserted was on everybody's mind. He wanted to know if at 68 I would be able to go the full length of my new mandate. My first reaction to the question was a fallback on my ancient spur: why not? Yes, I answered; otherwise I would have been honest enough not to stand for election. He asked if the appointment of Saihou Sabally as vice president with extended powers was an indication of a successor. I explained that the powers of the vice president had not been increased in any way; if anything, they had been reduced. The devolution from my office of the Defence and Women's Affairs to the new vice presidency did not necessarily make the position more powerful than the previous one which had responsibility for large ministries such as Education, Youth, Sports and Culture and the entire civil service. The bitter aftertaste of rancour in Mansakonko was apparently still the topic of discussion, according to the radio reporter.

Perhaps like some of the people whose views he claimed to represent, the reporter was reading wrongly into the appointment of Saihou Sabally as vice president and Bakary Dabo to minister of finance and economic affairs as an indication of upgrading and demotion respectively. Far from it. Appointments to Cabinet were made with deep appreciation of what the conditions at hand demanded for cohesion and firm holding of the fabric of government and party together through the mandate. The characters were appointed to fit the play, not the other way around. The play was naturally bigger than the individual actors who needed to trust the counsel of the principal who appointed them to the team to tackle the objectives. I emphasised that under our constitution it was not for the president to choose a successor. "That would be unconstitutional," I said. "It would not be democratic. The process of choosing someone to replace the president is spelt out in the constitution. Appointing someone vice president does not mean you are choosing him to be a president in the future. There is a wide choice as it should be in a democratic country and it will be a matter for the electorate to decide."

Admittedly, Mansakonko brought to the fore the underlying rivalries in the PPP. But the party found its way back on the platform of the principles of consensus and common counsel. We fought against the temptations of short cuts and ad hoc solutions and went to the people to ask for their confidence. Contrary to the criticism that the party swayed to my whims and caprices, my ideas were tabled and torn apart and I was lucky if they were finally accepted and endorsed. My leadership of the PPP was never a ritual with diktats swallowed lock, stock and barrel. People sometimes disagreed with me. Some of my proposals were often trimmed to size or simply thrown out. That is democracy.

In July 1992, my daughter Fatoumata graduated from Reading University with a Bachelor of Science degree in Agriculture. Upon graduating, she came back home and joined the Ministry of Agriculture.

The Gambia National Gendarmerie (GNG) was disbanded in 1992 and its officers and men redeployed into the Gambia Police Force (GPF)[16] and the Gambia National Army (GNA).

In 1993, the Central Committee of the PPP finally endorsed my proposal to have the minister of justice put a bill before parliament to abolish the death penalty. If there was one act comparable in meaning for me to the lowering of the Union Jack and the raising of our national colours on 18 February 1965, it would have to be the lifting of the death penalty. The abrogation law was a sign of my country's ultimate show of respect for the sanctity and dignity of human life.

---

[16] The members of the GNG redployed into the Gambia Police Force formed the Tactical Support Group (TSG), a paramilitary force.

If diplomatic activity were anything to go by, 1994 opened with a clean bill of health for The Gambia with ambassadors from Italy, the People's Democratic Republic of Korea, Syria, Pakistan, Indonesia, Malaysia, Mali, Saudi Arabia and the UK renewing our relationships through letters of commission and credence that their envoys presented to me in January. Two visits of ministerial delegations to Mauritania and Guinea reinforced our sub-regional contacts and in the case of the latter we made our presence felt at the inauguration ceremony of President Lansana Conté in Conakry.

The Nigerian Army Training and Advisory Group (NATAG) had taken over the training of the Gambia National Army from BATT. The Turkish Gendarmerie Training Team (TGTT) was responsible for training the Tactical Support Group. NATAG was headed by Colonel Abubakar Dada.

On 11 February 1994 we celebrated Army Day. I endorsed the soldiers' expressions of gratitude for the work being carried out by the Chinese on the new barracks at Yundum and shared with them my government's plans to provide other ancillary facilities such as more vehicles to make their work easier and more efficient. It was great to see the army present its first ever Flag March with the troops divided according to the four flags of the army – First Battalion, Second Battalion, Marine Company and the Army Headquarters. It was for me a great sign of their efforts towards self-motivation and professionalism.

There was much to celebrate of the similar fine turnout of our men in uniform demonstrated on 18 February 1994 when the country celebrated twenty-nine years of sovereignty at the Independence Stadium in Bakau. We celebrated with the GPF when I officially opened their new headquarters at Buckle Street on 17 February 1994. I thanked the People's Republic of China for giving us yet another splendid edifice adding to the Independence Stadium and several other vital health centres they had constructed in the provinces.

In mid-April 1994, we received with great sadness the news of the passing away of my father-in-law Momodou Mboge (Njaimeh's father). He had served with the Royal West African Frontier Force in Burma during the Second World War, later joining the Gambia Police Force. I despatched a strong family delegation to express my condolences with the people of Dankunku in particular and Niamina district in general. A heavy schedule ranging from cabinet meetings to consultations on the sitting of the House of Representatives and on the CILSS summit in Cape Verde prevented my attendance at the funeral.

In the last week of April 1994, I proceeded on an official visit to Addis Ababa. Prime Minister Meles Zenawi and senior officials of the Ethiopian

Transition Government received me. I addressed the 29th session of the Economic Commission for Africa, which also coincided with the marking of its thirty-fifth anniversary. The 20 Conference of African Ministers of Economic and Social Development and Planning was also taking place there.

I highlighted the alarming deterioration of the economies of African states as a result of the global economic recession, mounting external debt and the collapse of commodity prices as well as the decline of official development assistance. I told the gathering that the success we achieved with the SAP, ERP and PSD was due to the prudent economic management in place in The Gambia. Africa must develop the leadership and credibility to efficiently express the concern of African states at the highest level.

I was asked to preside over a thought-provoking debate that followed my address in which prominent personalities took part. The UN Under-Secretary General, Layahsi Yaker, OAU Secretary General, Salim Ahmed Salim, President of the African Development Bank, Babacarr Ndiaye, UNDP Assistant Administrator Ellen Johnson-Sirleaf, and UN Under-Secretary General in Charge of the Economic Policy Analysis Unit, Jean Claude Millerson, contributed immensely to the discussions.

I was back in my professional elements when I visited the International Livestock Centre for Africa (ILCA), headquartered in Addis Ababa and heard presentations made by ILCA officials on various livestock production and research projects. I seized the opportunity to listen to a well-thought-out delivery given by my old friend, Dr Leon Sullivan, Chairman and Convener of the African/African-American Summit. He spoke eloquently on the theme, "The Emergence of the New Africa".

I could not for the world miss to be there in person in Pretoria on 10 May 1994 for the swearing-in of Nelson Mandela as President of the Republic of South Africa. Under the invigorating autumn sunshine in Pretoria, I witnessed the once-in-a-lifetime event.

Mandela took the oath of office and mesmerised his audience and millions of viewers around the world watching on international TV networks with a riveting inaugural address. He left printed indelibly on my mind the concluding statements in his speech: "Never, never, and never again shall it be that this beautiful land will again experience the oppression of one over another and suffer the indignity of being the skunk of the world. Let freedom reign. The sun shall never set on so glorious a human achievement. God bless Africa!" Emotive, compelling, uplifting!

The common struggle of a united voice of Africa came to bear fruit at last. The protracted years of the fallacy of apartheid had ended. What grace, equipoise and dignity with which Mandela with open arms had invited all the colours of the rainbow republic to work as one, united under the single banner of our common humanity!

Back home we opened the Annual Livestock Show in mid-May 1994. The National Youth Conference and Festival opened the same time at Soma. I used the occasion to spread the love and goodwill to the youth of the country by spending some time with them at Soma where the events were organised to coincide with my birthday. Thousands of young people converged on the town that along with Farafenni on the North Bank were twin growth centres on the trans-Gambia highway.

It was a wise decision on the part of the ministry of youth and sports to take that year's youth festival to Soma and in that manner to stimulate that sense of inclusion in an up-country setting, from where a good number of the young and active population hailed. The Youth Festival was one bold attempt to throw people's minds back to the importance of farming and making life in the provinces more liveable.

Mrs Catherine Marshall, Director of the World Bank Sahel Department, came to the festival. She was in Banjul with her team to finalise the Gateway Project. She saw the energy of the youth in action and understood more clearly why the project would be so important to us in job creation and human resource development. A letter she sent to me on her return to Washington shared her favourable impressions of what she saw during the festival and the standards we had laid down for the young people as expressed in my speech to them.

I drew the attention of the youth to their relevance to national development. The importance of youth to development in this country could never be over-emphasised. I highlighted my government's concern for the youth in the adoption of a National Youth Policy in 1990, which culminated in the creation of a fully-fledged Ministry of Youth, Sports and Culture in 1992.

Jobs were and will always be the hottest issue for the youth after they leave school. It was important to know how many of them were entering the job market annually and how the system could cater for them. All of that was linked to the population and the rate of population growth. We needed to better manage our numbers to advantage, hence our establishment of the National Population Commission.

We had to take drastic action to slow down the rate of population growth, which was putting so much pressure on the land for settlement, agriculture and recreation. Although our population was less than one million people, we were growing at an alarming rate of 3.4% annually.

Despite all those efforts however there was still the challenge to ensure that young people were brought fully into the mainstream of development by having them understand and appreciate their roles and responsibilities. I warned them against the indolence that went with *ataya* drinking at the *vous* – hours of idleness brewing and drinking China green tea and waiting for a passage to Europe. There were many other more productive enterprises young people could engage in to accelerate the achievement of their dreams. The future was in their hands but unless we built it together, with government and the private sector creating the opportunities and the youth seizing them, development would come to a halt and we, each and everyone in society, would pay dearly for it.

On 9 June 1994, I left for Tunisia to attend the 30th OAU summit in the company of Njaimeh. I was taking with me very disturbing reports of the great difficulties ECOMOG and the UN troops were encountering on the ground in Liberia with the disarmament process. By the end of the month matters would deteriorate badly when armed members of ULIMO abducted six UN military observers in the ongoing conflict in that war-torn country. According to UN Secretary General Boutros Boutros-Ghali this was a serious threat to the continued support the UN and ECOMOG forces were giving to monitor the disarmament of the rival factions and to pave the way towards elections on 7 September that year.

My delegation used the stop-over in London to put the finishing touches to our dossiers to strengthen the bid for The Gambia in the person of Dr Ebrima M Samba to head the WHO Africa regional office. We walked the corridors of the OAU Heads of States and Government meeting in Tunis with an intensified campaign strategy.

The House of Representatives met for the 1994/95 budget on 22 June. Even though I was out of the country, I followed the four-day sitting with the keenest interest. The MPs ratified the budget of D1 billion, a historic peak for a budget in The Gambia and laid out a projected expenditure ceiling of D958 million, a D858 million revenue forecast that left a budget deficit of about D100 million in our current account amounting to 2.7% of GDP. Finance Minister Dabo informed parliament however that with D172 million expected in grants, including project grants in the new financial year, the budget was expected to rise to a surplus of nearly D72 million.

A Gambia government delegation was on its way to Washington to attend the signing of the Gateway Project. This project was an elaborate initiative developed by the Gambia government, the World Bank and other donors to start some small-scale manufacturing.

On 30 June 1994 there was a banquet at Westminster Palace, London, to mark the 150th anniversary of the Royal College of Veterinary Surgeons. I had the honour of sharing the limelight with Her Royal Highness,

Princess Anne the Princess Royal, Britain's Secretary of Agriculture, Gillian Shephard MP, the college's president, Dr Barry Johnson and some of Britain's most prominent scientists.

The Princess Royal gave a toast to the College. In her speech she still found warm thoughts of her visit to Banjul in February 1990 and paid tribute to our efforts in setting up the International Trypanotolerance Centre (ITC) in The Gambia. She pointed out the importance of the research being carried out to improve animal stocks and to raise their resistance to disease. It was indeed a flattering tribute in the presence of the head of the ITC, Professor Ian McIntyre.

On 1 July 1994, we took the train up north to Scotland. We arrived in Glasgow where Prof Jimmy Armour received us. I deeply appreciated the dinner given that weekend in my honour by the veterinary faculty of the University of Glasgow. Prof Armour was one of my contemporaries at the Royal Dick in Edinburgh and he presided over the dinner.

He and his team had arranged first-rate hospitality that included a visit to the Memorial Centre set up in honour of our Director of Studies, the late Prof William L Weipers.[17] To close a busy day, I received in my hotel suite a group of thirteen Gambians who lived and worked in Glasgow. I told them of the Gateway Project which, I said, was poised to transform The Gambia to the level of Mauritius by 2010. I told them it was an ambitious programme but with the World Bank and the IMF believing it was feasible on account of the country's location and its prudent macroeconomic policies, there were great things that the Chinese-backed small industries package under the Gateway Project would bring to the ordinary Gambian. I said whatever we would put on the ground for the project must find people ready and able to implement the programme. That meant the level of education among boys and girls must of necessity be accelerated. The government must provide universal primary education and expand secondary education, in which case it might be necessary to make primary education compulsory.

On 4 July we drove to Stoneleigh in Warwickshire. I had the privilege to officially open the Royal Show, the first foreign head of state to do so in the history of the 155-year-old agricultural event. Some prominent British personalities in modern times to have opened the Show have been Prince

---

[17] I remembered a favourite quip that ran beneath his photo in our final year dinner brochure in 1953 quoting the US poet, essayist and transcendentalist, Waldo Emerson: "If you must rule the world quietly then you must keep it amused". Weipers did both and well; he ruled the world of veterinary science quietly and he kept that world amused with wit, directness and scholarship.

Philip, the Duke of Edinburgh, former British Prime Minister, Margaret Thatcher, and former Chancellor of the Exchequer, Sir Leon Brittan.

It had become the world's biggest farm exhibition and which in 1994 had attracted 220,000 people to the showground where The Gambia had a stand among the 1,500 exhibits displaying the latest products and technologies in various fields of crop production, animal husbandry, food processing and preservation and motor manufacturing. The Gambia's display of various agricultural and small manufacturing items was impressive just as had been showcased in Banjul during the annual National Horticultural Show on 19 March 1994.

On 15 July 1994, Njaimeh and I were proud guests at the graduation of our son, Foday Sheriffo, at the University of Nottingham, where he was awarded a Bachelor of Science degree in civil engineering. Later that year two of Foday's elder brothers would be awarded Bachelor of science degrees by the University of Aberdeen – Momodou in science and Kawsu in computer science.

Nottingham University would in fact attract another Jawara sibling when Fatoumata took a short course there in October 1994 before going on to take a master's degree at Cornell University in New York State. She co-authored a book entitled *Behind the Scenes at the WTO*, published by Zed Books, London, in 2003.

On 19 July we visited the German Siemens Plessey Systems headquarters in Chessington, Surrey. Earlier in April I had received Mr D D Raltson and Ms Grace Quartey of Siemens in Banjul, where they had expressed their company's interest for a development project they envisaged in connection with Banjul International Airport. I was highly impressed by the plans I saw at Chessington. As our airport had always been an important beacon for our international contacts I left with feelings of taking the Siemens proposals forward upon my return to Banjul.

On Thursday 21 July 1994, I left for Gatwick Airport with Foday and boarded the Gambia Airways flight at 12.30 pm. Njaimeh decided to stay in London for another week or so. I spent some time during the flight jotting down some thoughts on the final draft of my reply to the letters of credence the Chinese Ambassador-designate Wang Jiaji was scheduled to present to me. Part of my discussions with the ambassador would have covered the date for the important visit by the Chinese foreign minister to Banjul. We landed at Banjul International Airport at about 7 pm.

28

Democracy overturned

On our arrival at Banjul on 21 July 1994 I caught myself having to piece together a chain of strange events unfolding right before my eyes. To begin with Vice President and Minister of Defence Saihou Sabally was not there to receive me. Instead I was being received at the foot of the aircraft by Attorney General and Minister of Justice, Hassan Jallow. Sabally, I was informed in due course, had accompanied the corpse of his brother, Kebba Ngansu Sabally, to their home village in Kataba in Sabach-Sanjal for burial. Under the shrill notes of the bugles Hassan walked me to the waiting guard of honour. In all my years of arrival and departure I had never seen a more excited honour guard commander in action - Captain Sonko clearly appeared nervous. Odd! Considering he was not inexperienced, he must have been under some influence, I thought. In spite of the guard of honour commander's faltering, I accepted his invitation and inspected the guard.

We breezed through the formalities of handshakes with the party of ministers, senior government officials and members of the diplomatic corps waiting to receive us. We were soon boarded and rolling out of the airport in a motorcade. I learnt much later that there had been some tension at the airport before our flight landed when the Nigerian Army officers had given instructions to disarm a group of junior officers of the Gambia National Army, because it was unusual for the men to be armed on official airport welcoming duties.

Among those men disarmed was the 29-year-old lieutenant in charge of the Military Police named Yahya A J J Jammeh. The order to disarm them had come from the senior officer of NATAG holding the fort for Colonel Lawan Gwadabe, the new commander head of NATAG and commander of the GNA. Colonel Gwadabe was away for consultations in Abuja at the time. It was odd that Dada whom he came to replace was still in The Gambia and had refused to hand over to his successor.

There was nothing unusual about our drive to Banjul. Upon alighting from our vehicles at State House, I discovered that Hassan Jallow who had just received me officially at the airport was not there. I learnt that he had broken off from the motorcade and gone home. The traditional debriefing session after foreign visits had to be scrapped because the Attorney General who had deputised for the Vice President at the airport was absent. Tired as I was, the question that kept me awake for a while before I could sleep was the absence of the Vice President and the failure of the Attorney General to come for the debriefing at State House.

The following day, Friday 22 July 1994, National Security Service Director General Kebba S Ceesay and the National Security Adviser arrived in my private quarters at 9.15 am to brief me about rumours of a coup which, they said, started circulating some three weeks earlier. They had come to inform me that they had checked out all the sources and found the reports to be just rumours. They handed me a report entitled *INTERIM REPORT: REPORTED PLAN TO OVERTHROW THE GOVERNMNET OF THE GAMBIA,* dated 21 July 1994. I thanked them for their diligence and watched them leave.

At about 9.40 am my Aide de Camp (ADC), Captain Momodu Kassama, burst in upstairs looking agitated. He urged me to leave for the US warship. It was the first time I heard anything of a warship in our port. Captain Kassama was beside himself and was insisting with near hysteria that I must leave immediately. He kept insisting that there was a coup taking place and that soldiers were approaching Banjul. He said that the US Ambassador Andrew Winter who was at State House at the time had just given him reliable information that there was, indeed, a coup under way.

Kassama pointed out that State House was too big for the less than 30 Presidential Guards (PG) on duty at the time to defend against the company[18] of GNA soldiers who were advancing. The GNA soldiers were heavily armed with pistols, AK 47 assault rifles, grenades, light machine guns, heavy machine guns, and rocket propelled grenades (RPGs). The PG at State House had only pistols, AK 47s with an average of two magazines each, and a couple of light machine guns. There was also the lack of a defendable fallback position at State House. The PG was clearly outnumbered and outgunned. It would have been suicide not to surrender or relocate.

In the case of security emergencies, the contingency measure was for the cabinet to converge on the Marine Unit in Banjul, where they would board one of the boats that would then sail out to sea. It was envisaged that the government could be run securely from the boat.

In this instance there was a strong possibility (later proven) that the Marine Unit was part of the coup plot. Hence Kassama advised that we go to the *USS La Moure County* instead, until the situation was properly assessed. I thought it sounded plausible that the ship could be a tactical

---

[18] Company is a military unit comprising between 75 and 200 men.

location from which to consider further action, especially after the Americans had already offered to evacuate us to the ship. It was at this point that Chilel suddenly came to my room, looking very agitated, to confirm what I had just been told – that all the children and some domestic staff were already seated in the cars and ready to go!

I walked with Chilel and Kassama securing the prepared copy of my intended reply to the ambassador-designate of the People's Republic of China whom I was expecting to receive at midday. Out in the forecourt a convoy of cars stood with engines revving and inside already seated were some of my children, grandchildren and a few domestic staff. Also present was the US Ambassador, Andrew Winter, and his compatriots, the military attaché from the US Embassy in Dakar and the captain of the US Navy ship, *USS La Moure County* and Saihou Sabally. Sabally must have travelled all night to be able to make it back to his office that early the next morning and in a fit state to coordinate the evacuation of my household.

We rolled out of the State House grounds past the Six-Gun Battery overlooking the beach where Brig Charles MacCarthy had put it 169 years before. We drove past MacCarthy Square named after the brigadier and which ironically would assume the new name – July 22nd Square – to celebrate the events unfolding right at that moment. We made our way through the shopping crowds down Russell Street past the Albert Market and on down Wellington Street on a straight drive to the Admiralty Wharf at Half Die, a stone's throw from my boyhood home, 37 Wellington Street. American navy guards let us through some barricades. There, for the first time, I set eyes on the American Navy ship, the *USS La Moure County*.

It was strange that in all the official messages I had received daily from Banjul, my Vice President and Minister of Defence had not mentioned to me that he and our security chiefs had given permission for anything as massive as a joint GNA and US Navy training exercise, complete with a warship. I thought if the armed forces of another sovereign nation were going to engage with our national forces in any kind of bilateral military exercise, it would have been important enough for the head of state and commander-in-chief of the armed forces of the host country, at home or abroad, to be informed of such a major engagement. Those who knew timelines and clearance procedures to get the US State Department and the Department of Defence machinery in Washington to conceive, approve and fund a public diplomacy engagement of such diplomatic complexity and magnitude would wonder at the speed and secrecy of this operation.

Before we boarded the *La Moure County*, Bakary B Dabo appeared. He said he and Attorney General Hassan Jallow and Minister of Tourism Alkali James Gaye had been on their way to report to the Marine Unit as was the procedure in that kind of situation. His driver, he said, made a wrong turning and ended up driving to the ship, missing the Marine Unit entrance, a few metres away. The other two and several other ministers who had already reported to the Marine Unit were immediately detained. Bakary B Dabo joined us and we sailed away.

Pa Sallah Jagne, the Inspector General of Police and Captain Kaba Bajo, Commander of the PG, also made it to the ship with a few members of the PG. At some point I wondered who was coordinating and commanding loyal forces on the ground.[19]

Members of my family on board the ship included my wife Chilel, seven of my children - Housainou, Ramatoulie, Chilel, Njaimeh, Mariam, Foday and Fatoumata, and three of my grandchildren. Incidentally Ebrima, Almami and Dawda were still in the country. Dawda and Almami who both lived in Bakau, a stone's throw away from the Bakau Barracks, could not make it to Banjul in time to join us and found it safer to stay put.

Ebrima had left early that morning for Radville Farm where he was working. However the US Embassy sent him a driver and vehicle[20] to stay with him. He and the driver could not make it back to Banjul, so they spent the night at the farm in Nemakunku. The next day they drove to the US Embassy on Kairaba Avenue, where Ebrima was told by a US diplomat that the AFPRC had made it clear that they were not concerned with the former president's family and that he was free to go about his business as any other citizen. He was reassured that he really was in no danger from the new regime.[21]

Things moved fast, and before midday on 22 July 1994, it appeared the coup had succeeded. The US troops could not intervene without the green light from Washington. Unfortunately Washington was reluctant to get involved beyond granting me and my party safe passage to Senegal who had agreed to grant me asylum.

On the morning of 23 July the Armed Forces Provisional Ruling Council led by Lieutenant Yahya A J J Jammeh as its Chairman, Lieutenant Sana B

---

[19] I later learnt that Major Ebrima Chongan, then Deputy Inspector General of Police, had tried to stop the advancing soldiers at the Denton Bridge, on his own and with only a pistol.

[20] White Chevrolet van with registration No US136.

[21] Different from the coup attempt of 1981, when innocent civilians including some of my children were used as bargaining chips by Kukoi.

Sabally as Vice Chairman, Lieutenant Edward Singhatey and Lieutenant Sadibou Hydara as members was effectively in charge of the country.

Later that day, while still on board the ship I had a telephone conversation with Lieutenant Edward Singhatey, arranged by the Defence Attaché of the US Embassy in Dakar, who was in Banjul during the takeover. The young lieutenant, speaking on behalf of the new regime, asked me to return as a senior citizen, perhaps even as an adviser to the regime. He described me as a president to whom they owed the respectable image The Gambia had in the international community. They had no intention of harming or humiliating me; they wanted to treat me as an elder statesman. My instinct however was not to return to Banjul at that time. I told him that they should return to barracks and that I would only return as President and Commander-in-Chief of the Armed Forces and take note of any grievances they had. This he flatly rejected.

After a couple more days we arrived in Dakar, and my household and I were driven to the Residence de Medina[22], the now famous mansion that had hosted presidential exiles such as Hissein Habré and Ghoukouni Oueddei.

Meanwhile, the world was just waking up to the fall of democracy in Banjul. On 28 July 1994 (just 6 days after the coup) Taiwan recognised the military regime and flew its ambassador to present his letters of credence to the Chairman of the AFPRC – the first country to do so. That same day Almami and Ebrima joined us, having arrived via Casamance.

The military junta had in detention former ministers including Landing Jallow Sonko, Yaya Ceesay, Alieu E W F Badjie, Omar Sey, Hassan Jallow, Omar Jallow, Sarjo Touray, Bubacarr Baldeh, Mathew Yaya Baldeh and Alkali James Gaye. Managing Directors of parastatals arrested and detained included Pa O B Cham (Gambia Ports Authority), Sankung Fatty (Social Security and Housing Finance Corporation), Alieu Mboge (National Trading Corporation) and Abdoulie M Touray (National Investment Board). There were also over 20 officers detained.

On 29 July President Diouf made a public declaration assuring the Chairman of the AFPRC of Senegal's total resolve to stay out of the events in The Gambia, avowing that he would "not tolerate anybody attempting subversive and hostile actions directed against the Government of The Gambia". Perish the thought that I would ever want to engage in subversive or hostile actions against my own country, even if I had the power to do so. All fears in Banjul of my invoking again the 1965 Defence Agreement with Senegal as a counter measure were allayed. Diouf also confirmed that he had granted me and my family political asylum purely on humanitarian grounds.

---

[22] It is now a cultural centre.

There were many overtures from Banjul for some members of my cabinet to be reinstated if they were only willing to collaborate with the junta. Lamin Kiti Jabang, Minister of the Interior, had left Banjul just before the coup for Dakar, via Casamance. Senegalese Foreign Minister Moustapha Niasse, boasted to me that Lamin would soon be going back to Banjul to a red carpet treatment by the AFPRC. But perhaps the biggest surprise was Bakary B Dabo, who, within ten days of our arrival in Dakar, was back in Banjul serving the new military junta. In my last meeting with him before he left for Banjul, he told me that he was going back "in the interest of the nation." He emphasised that he was "working for the Gambia and not for one man." I told him that if he felt it was safe for him to return then I had no objection to him doing so. Indeed there was nothing I could do about it.

Other members of my party who returned were Ebou Ndure (my Chief of Protocol), Pa Sallah Jagne and Kaba Bajo. I also asked them if they were assured of their safety back home; they weren't sure, but they were determined to return for various reasons.

Bakary Dabo was back at his desk in early August at his old job as Minister of Finance and Economic Affairs. He was soon boldly assuring the general public that there was, among other things, enough foreign exchange available in the banking system to hold up the country. He called a special press conference of local and international journalists to dispel rumours of scarcity. He said there would be a continuation of the economic policies of the ousted government. At a meeting with businessmen and senior officials of the Gambia Chamber of Commerce, he revealed that there were adequate reserves to cover the country's import bill and that there was enough supply of basic commodities including rice and fuel to keep the country going. He signed a letter on 13 August 1994 and circulated it to all on the list of the country's development partners assuring everyone that there would be a timetable for the restoration of civilian rule in forty-five days.

I could not help but ask myself the question: What kind of plunder of the economy had we been guilty of then to warrant our overthrow? It was unlikely that a corrupt and vile government would have left a buoyant Central Bank reserve, a functioning chamber of commerce and shops filled with basic commodities. That rosy picture of a stable and vibrant business and consumer environment presided over by my government might begin to lend credence to the suspicion that the reasons for the overthrow of my government were probably far removed from the impression the sing-song "rampant corruption and flamboyant lifestyle" of my government was meant to convey.

Power will always be prone to the allure of abuse. In government the baits for graft are everywhere. Friends, lobbyists, family members, public relations and business agents are ready with suggestions every step of the way. The slippery slopes are full of people willing to compromise power with the strangest overtures – anything that would promote their own personal ambitions. What they offer government officials and politicians is really not for them but what they can do to further the ambitions of the giver.

While visitors could come and see me at Residence de Medina, the telephones were restricted to local calls. I was essentially denied access to making international calls. Among important visitors I received were diplomats of European and other foreign missions who came to chat or simply to commiserate with me. One of them from the US Embassy in Dakar suggested that it might ease my sense of isolation and restriction if I were moved to some place more spacious. He asked whether I would be interested in moving to the luxurious palace in Dakar, owned by President Mobutu Sese Seko of Zaire. It would have been ridiculous for me to have accepted such an offer.

I was more inclined to listen to the British Ambassador to Senegal, Alan Furness, who paid me a courtesy visit on 5 August for a heart-to-heart talk. It was not the only time he would come to see how I was doing. I asked him what Britain's attitude was to the situation in The Gambia, where the military had overthrown a democratically elected government. He explained the UK's official stand as being in line with that of the Commonwealth and the European Union and others that called for the retraction of aid and support, if not complete withdrawal. I told him it was very important that Britain did not withdraw completely from The Gambia. Rather, it should show disagreement with the takeover and take action for the immediate return of the country to democratic government.

At the end of our discussions Furness relayed the gratitude of the British government for taking them in my confidence. Britain, he said, was going to leave the door open to me with the offer of asylum. I shared the outcome of my deliberations with everyone in my party and gave each some time to think over what they might wish to do and where they might choose to go. I accepted the offer to move to the UK where the fact of my owning a home there made it even more attractive. There were those in the party who preferred to go to the United States. Others considered Canada. I left it to the Americans and the UNHCR to work things out with those who opted in those directions, as a handful of them finally did.

On 4 August the leader of the main opposition party, Parti Democratique Senegalais (PDS), Abdoulaye Wade, who had only just come out of detention, declared his total support for the coup. Press reports in Banjul quoted him as saying that "The PPP was just like a barracuda, surrounded by small fish. So I support the change of leadership in The Gambia, as it allows democracy to take its proper course." He had already sent a telegram to congratulate Jammeh on his actions.

On the same day five of my children - Ramatoulie, Chilel, Njaimeh, Foday and Fatoumata – left Dakar for Banjul under Senegalese protection. Chairman Jammeh was gracious enough to allow them back into State House in order to retrieve personal items. Most of our personal belongings were taken to my private residence at 40 Atlantic Boulevard. Chairman Jammeh sent a message through my son Dawda for me to return as an elder statesman.

We flew out of Dakar on 27 August and made a stop-over at Paris Charles de Gaulle Airport. Senegalese Ambassador to France, Masamba Sarre, came with his Chief of Protocol, Ndiouga Ndiaye, to see how we were faring and to update us on details of our planned reception. The Senegalese government was kind enough to extend the courteous gesture of procuring the plane tickets for everyone in my entourage. I thanked Ambassador Sarre and asked him to extend the same again on my behalf to Dakar. It was a short flight over the English Channel and we touched down at London's Heathrow Airport at 6.00 pm. A representative of the Foreign and Commonwealth Office, Jeremy Jesper, an assistant standing in for Baroness Lynda Chalker, was waiting to receive us. Our high commissioner to the UK, Momodou Bobb, was there and with him, the Senegalese Ambassador to the UK, Gabriel Alexandre Sar.

Baroness Chalker[23] rang me up from the airport. She apologised that she could not have met me in person as she was on her way out on a mission to Rwanda, Burundi and Egypt. She welcomed me to the UK and expressed sympathy with my situation. She suggested a gentleman in her office named Anthony Goodenough would be at my service and would be able to make settling in as comfortable as possible for me. I found Anthony a worthy and efficient man. In the course of my settling down, I consulted closely with him and we developed a great rapport. He was instrumental in setting up meetings with my international contacts and I briefed him on the outcomes. Not long after our acquaintance, I was glad when the Foreign Office appointed him high commissioner to Canada.

It was an easy passage through the Heathrow Airport routine into a waiting motorcade. The Foreign Office saw to the papers and the luggage. Despite all the pleasurable influences of an English summer night there

---

[23] Baroness Chalker was then Minister of State for Overseas Development

was a touch of disheartening apprehension in the air in my car. For long moments of the ride the gentle hum of the engines was its only contradiction. As soon as we alighted, the quietness in the house suddenly evaporated into the chatter and noise of a dozen or so people lugging goods and looking for a patch to bed down. I went to bed long before the rest of the household quietened down for the night.

I began to work with solicitors writing affidavits in support of political asylum claims for a long list of people. My phone kept ringing continuously from Gambians in Canada, the Caribbean, Germany, Russia, Scandinavia, France and the USA – all seeking my help in support of their applications for asylum .

My small office became a clinic, as it were, with the visitors that came. I sought from each of them reasons for their fear for them or their families. I then wrote affidavits explaining why each person qualified for consideration, and I took those to solicitors in Haywards Heath to be notarised. I was so busy helping others that I nearly forgot that I probably needed help more than most. Only a few weeks before, I earned a salary as president. Now I was faced with asking a friendly government to shelter and support me and a host of people who were in exile with me. I still felt it was my duty and service to ensure that all were taken care of. After all, they were journeying with me and had become part of my life story. This was no time to abandon any one of them. The asylum process was not all plain sailing. I will always remember two wonderful solicitors, Kipling Waistel and Peter Benner, who argued most of the cases I supported. Our success rate was quite high. We were very careful with the cases we supported because we were working within a system that was already generous in providing asylum tribunals to hear appeals.

I gave my first public interview on 25 September 1994 to the British Broadcasting Corporation (BBC). While we sorted out tough immigration as well as domestic issues, it was also my responsibility to make known to the world the political and human rights situation in The Gambia.

Our country was now in the hands of soldiers who marked their arrival to power with decrees curtailing the human, civic and media rights that had hitherto become a way of life for Gambians. I had cause to plead with the world to save one little island of democracy in Africa, a continent torn apart by political upheaval, human rights violations and social strife.

I did not wait to be in government or out of it to believe in democracy. In every dealing with my fellows the first line of engagement had to be the understanding of the sanctity of life, the inviolability of the rights of the individual as well as of those of groups and cultures and for the individual's adherence to the rule of law. These were the *sine qua non* of a happy, stable and well-run society. It was the way I learnt it from my father, reinforced by my mother, who on a daily basis in her every interaction with family, friend or even foe drilled values into me just as did others in my adolescence. Such were men like Sering Habib and M D Salla at Mohammedan School, Sering Modou Sillah at our Qur'anic school and my high school principal, J J Baker.

In September 1994, I was asked to come back and face a commission of inquiry or risk the loss of all my assets, under Decree No 11. And indeed, by decree, the AFPRC regime seized Bakamon (21 Leman Street) even though the property is owned by a political party, the PPP.[24] All my properties were also seized and transferred to Central Government. My private residence, 40 Atlantic Road, was reserved for visiting dignitaries. My farm at Banjulinding was occupied by the GNA and then AMRC; 7 Louvel Street in Banjul was occupied by the Gambia Navy and 34 Wellington Street was occupied by the State Guards. Four other properties were sold to a Lebanese businessman by the AMRC.

On 3 October 1994, about a week after my interview, Foday, who was staying at 40 Atlantic Boulevard, was given a couple of hours by the soldiers to grab what he could and leave. With the help of friends he packed as much as he could into a car and handed over the property.

On the night of 11 November 1994, gunfire was heard coming from the Bakau army barracks. The next day there were reports of a failed coup attempt, in which there was some loss of life.

Bakary Dabo left the country for Senegal on 16 November, where he stayed for a day before proceeding to London.

---

[24] The building is still occupied by the Ministry of the Interior.

29

Campaign for the restoration of democracy

The Gambia under military rule and the news of the decrees being promulgated by the AFPRC government left me with no choice but to seek an effective platform to speak.

After they took over, the AFPRC was faced with the testing issue of a transition programme back to democratic governance. On 24 July 1994, the British High Commissioner to The Gambia, Michael J Hardie, sent Chairman Jammeh a note. It conveyed a message from the Presidency of the European Union stating the EU's position that called for the junta to return to barracks immediately and to give full allegiance to the legitimate government of The Gambia, with which the EU enjoyed excellent relations. The note reaffirmed the EU's attachment to the principles of responsible democracy and the rule of law. It also drew attention to the implications of the reported coup for the economy of the country if EU member states were obliged to review their aid programmes.

There was a review of development assistance from the UK government just as there was an immediate disengagement by USAID and limited participation of the European Union to governance and humanitarian portfolios only. It was a wait-and-see situation for democrats and human rights watchers. As a follow-up action, the three major donor countries represented by High Commissioner Hardie, the EU Delegate to The Gambia, Mr Robert Collingwood, and the German Ambassador to The Gambia, Tomas Fischer-Dieskan, went to see Chairman Jammeh to hear what his plans were to return the country to civilian rule.

The pledge from Chairman Jammeh was the same as he had made in his first interview with the *Daily Observer*. He would not tell when they would hand over to civilian rule. He said it depended on answers the people would give. Although they did not threaten to cut aid to The Gambia, it was the kind of pressure that the situation called for. It pressed the council to set in motion a programme of transition and, it appeared, assistance would only be cut if the junta failed to test its legitimacy by a plebiscite.

The AFPRC established the National Consultative Commission (NCC) on 13 December 1994. This was set up to sound out the opinion of the Gambian public on several issues including the date for the soldiers' return to barracks. The NCC drew much credibility from its composition and was chaired by the poet and surgeon, Lenrie Peters. It submitted its report on 27 January 1995.

We were physically too far removed in exile to play a direct role; and those of our militants on the ground were neutralised. The PPP was languishing under a ban and with its headquarters and all other assets seized, it had no effective platform for action. The junta would not announce a timetable until September 1995.

Statements from Chairman Jammeh and Interior Minister Sadibou Hydara, who was also the regime's official spokesman, were all indicative of a mindset that the soldiers would indeed hand over to a proposed interim government. After June, the successor spokesman to Sadibou Hydara, Captain Ebou Jallow, loudly denied all accusations that the AFPRC was secretly campaigning to remain in office. He told the press that the council had been mandated by the people in the NCC report to remain a transition government for two years at the end of which they would return to barracks.

As far as my campaign for the restoration of democracy was concerned, the NCC report had turned on the heat after its submission in January 1995. It had become the central issue on the table for the transition period. Although it took the council and government a long while in disclosing key elements of the report, it was obvious they were working in the background on the document. The fact was that their envisaged four years of transition had now been tailored by public expression to two years; and in our opinion that was one big step in the right direction. The US, UK and EU position calling for one year or less was ignored by the government.

The call for a constitutional review was crucial among the components that underscored the transition of the registration of voters, the setting up of commissions of inquiry, the review of the electoral lists and constituency boundaries. The junta was working on a draft constitution to replace the 1970 Constitution, which it had suspended. A draft constitution finally emerged that the NCC took round the country for the people to give an opinion.

The PPP did not waste time in pitching in on perhaps the most important piece of democratic weaponry – the Constitution! It was certainly the most authoritative instrument of governance at society's disposal. I wished many more individuals and organisations on the ground had taken the pains to come up with suggestions to improve the regime's draft constitution. We promptly addressed our views in a document we called *The Declaration of* *the People's Progressive Party (PPP) on the Transition Back to Democracy in The Gambia (*See Appendix II*).*

Meanwhile, we were fully alive to two counter currents flowing overall in the campaign. While it seemed international pressure was moving the regime towards the desired solution of their departure, the continued relief of recognition by foreign governments was reinforcing the inevitability of their staying in power. Chairman Jammeh visited Dakar on 22 September 1994, his first foreign trip since taking power two months before.

The restoration so soon of diplomatic relations with Libya in January 1995 was not unexpected. We had broken off relations with Tripoli in 1980 for meddling in our internal affairs.

I was greatly encouraged to take the messages of democratisation even further out to the rest of Europe and the United States. To that end, I contracted the services of a firm of international consultants, Szlavik, Hogan & Miller, Inc in the US and, in London I engaged communications and government affairs expert, Anthony McCall-Judson. This way, from both sides of the Atlantic we began programming the campaign for the most effective publicity. Gambians in the UK and elsewhere needed to know what was really happening so that they could arrive at educated and well-informed decisions about their country.

The few voluntary aides I had – Sara Janha, Momodou Ndow Njie, Momodou N Bobb, Phoday Jarjussey and Momodou Lamin Kassama – dealt with all the official and other matters from typing affidavits for asylum seekers to enquiries and schedules for interviews and travel.

In London I set out plans for some speaking events to give impetus to the campaign and to take the message to the Foreign and Commonwealth Office and to the US and even back home in Africa. The world had to be told of the human rights conditions in my country. Consequently, I had a Sunday briefing with the Nigerian High Commissioner, Alhaji Abubakar Alhaji, one of the first on our contacts list outside the British government. Through him we kept the Nigerian government abreast of our programmes. I spoke to the American and French embassies in London. There was condemnation in principle all round against military takeovers of democratic governments.

I was able to reach many sympathisers and contacts in the international family. I had an invitation from His Highness the Emir of Kuwait and visited him on 25 January 1995. He had been chairman of the OIC when I was chairman of its Peace Committee on the Iran- Iraq War a few years before. The emir thanked me for my work and for my outspokenness on the Palestinian cause and expressed gratitude for my stand generally in the cause of world peace.

I went about sensitising British and European audiences, bringing to their attention evidence of violations of human rights occurring in Banjul, as gathered from victims on the ground and those reported in the local and international media. I utilised reports that were from reliable sources, avoiding anything that could not be corroborated.

On 16 February 1995, I travelled to Washington, USA with Sara Janha and my nephew Musa Basadi Jawara. We met with George Moose, the Assistant Secretary of State for Africa. It was good to see Arlene Render, the former US Ambassador to The Gambia, who sat in at that meeting. We exchanged frank opinions on developments back home in The Gambia. I impressed upon them that The Gambia since independence had flourished as a multi-party democracy until the takeover. To say the least, the reaction of the US government was at best lukewarm. I was not surprised by their well-rehearsed diplomatic lines deploring the breach of democratic governance in The Gambia.

I went to New York for similar frank and open meetings with UN Secretary General Boutros Boutros-Ghali. I told him of the serious situation my country was in and suggested possible measures the UN could adopt to keep the pressure for democratisation on the AFPRC. Whether with the US or the UN, mine was the duty to put the case of The Gambia forward and theirs it was to respond whichever way their specific agendas dictated.

During my visit to the US Assistant Secretary of State, a group of Gambians led a peaceful demonstration outside the State Department to draw attention to the importance of our mission. The public relations firm I had engaged in the US was able to bring our friends together at a reception thrown in our honour. I explained the situation and why it was important for pressure on the government back home for democratic standards to be maintained. It was evident though that the cream of the Gambian community of intellectuals and technocrats were missing from my venues for the simple reason that a group of them were associated in what they called a pro-democracy movement. They had already been in advanced talks with the AFPRC government, proposing to assist it "in speedily mobilizing the human resources which the government might identify as critical to the effective completion of specific activities".

The movement could provide such assistance by supporting the council's approaches to the country's development partners or helping to identify and encourage suitably qualified Gambians abroad to undertake temporary assignments. A mission including Ebou Jallow, spokesman for the AFPRC and Ousman Koro Ceesay, Permanent Secretary at the Office of the Chairman, was in Washington from 4 to 9 March 1995, during which they arrived at key agreements with the Pro-Democracy Movement for the promotion of effective implementation of the AFPRC's programmes.

Apart from recruitment possibilities which had whetted the appetites of some of the group who were eyeing ambassadorial and other portfolios in London, Paris, New York, Washington and elsewhere, the movement undertook to assist in reopening the channels of communication recently strained with the World Bank and other leading development partners. In fact, the movement was able to arrange at least one meeting between the council and the bank's director of the West African Department, Jean Louis Sarbib, and his core Gambia Country Team for an exchange of views, key among them the credibility of the transition programme and the need for the government to refrain from any action that would be prejudicial to the country's prospects for growth and economic stability.

However, a great deal of the movement's plans with the regime backfired. The outcome was sufficient proof that theirs was a grave underestimation of the soldiers who came to power in Banjul. Thoughts that the soldiers would hand over government to them on a silver platter was a political miscalculation. The movement must have been stunned when State House announced the appointment of Tombong Saidy as Ambassador to Washington. He ended his short tour of duty in Washington by being declared *persona non grata* by the US government.

In all my discussions during my tour, my aim was to apprise my interlocutors of the realities in The Gambia. That was the theme when we spent a couple of days with the Gambian community in Atlanta, Georgia. The talk of 'restoration' was not about me but about democracy. My involvement in the government in any way after I had gone into exile, would have been limited to my returning to Banjul, addressing the grievances of the soldiers, dissolving Parliament and preparing the country for fresh general elections. Then I would have gracefully retired - exactly what I had planned and, in fact, announced for May 1992.

I was back in Haywards Heath after ten days. It was the end of fasting and the family drove to Brighton for the *Id-ul-fitr* prayers.

I briefed Goodenough on my visit to Washington and expressed my true reactions to Jim Young of the US Embassy who also wanted a briefing. I told the Americans that I felt very strongly that the system we had left behind in Banjul was worth protecting. We had made impressive strides in the economic field. The country had successfully come through nine years of managing a structural adjustment programme and was about to embark on a bold and far-reaching initiative which would have propelled the country on a sustainable and accelerated development path when the military struck - The Gateway Project. All that hard work was dashed by the military takeover on 22 July 1994.

Chief Emeka Anyaoku raised the issue of The Gambia during his speech to the Commonwealth Trust on 10 May 1995 in preparation for the November Commonwealth Heads of Government Meeting (CHOGM)[25] in Auckland, New Zealand. The secretary general was discussing The Gambia in light of the stock-taking exercise on how the Commonwealth had fared since they last met in October 1993 in Limassol , and how the association as a whole, and the respective governments, severally, had lived up to the standards which they had adopted in the Harare Principles, two years before. Those principles had given the Commonwealth its agenda for democratisation and good governance for the 1990s and beyond.

The case of a military regime in Banjul was set against strides made since the 1991 Harare Principles which Anyaoku detailed by citing Ghana and Lesotho, formerly under military rule, and Kenya, Malawi, Seychelles and Zambia, formerly with one-party systems, as having made the transition to multi-party democracy. It was a fact that at the time, there were only three countries in the Commonwealth with military regimes and it was sad that The Gambia was among them. In the process of his making a valid case for more attention for political work to be properly underpinned and integrated with members' economic and social development, I was consoled to hear the secretary general underscore my call always to place the little issues against the bigger picture. He concluded by saying that development sustains democracy and democracy sustains development.

I left Heathrow on 11 June 1995 and spent the next sixteen days in Dakar before flying out to Lagos. A special flight lifted me from there to Abuja where Head of State Sani Abacha received me despite his heavy schedule, especially with the report from the Constitutional Commission due to be delivered to him that same day. I made it quite clear that pressure must be put at the level of ECOWAS and the OAU to have democracy restored.

In July, I went to France and at Quai d'Orsay I met with French officials, Director Jean-Marc de Sablière and his deputy, Amaurac du Chauffant, of La Direction des Affaires Africaines et Malagaches. The situation in Africa in general featured highly in our discussions especially in light of the planned visit that month of President Jacques Chirac to Africa. I was back in Paris in October 1996 on my way to Dakar.

---

[25] Every two years Commonwealth leaders meet to discuss Commonwealth and global issues. There are formal and informal meetings of the heads of government.

I flew on Ghana Airways to Dakar where I met with President Diouf on 18 October 1996. He extended excellent formal courtesies to me and I handed two letters for him to deliver on my behalf – one addressed to President Lansana Conté of Guinea Conakry and the other to President Joao Bernardo "Nino" Vieira of Guinea Bissau.

I proceeded to Accra, where I was received by President Jerry John Rawlings and Dr Mohamed Ibn Chambas, his deputy minister of foreign affairs. In our talks, I put forward The Gambia's case. Democracy had been reversed in my country and we must do all we could to restore it. The former military chairman understood what I meant but clearly had his hands tied. It was indeed a difficult hand he was playing especially when, while welcoming me, he also had to meet a visiting delegation of the AFPRC. The meeting with the AFPRC delegates was scheduled and held in Akosombo, away from the publicity that might have arisen with my own presence there as a guest of the same government.

I flew on to Nigeria where I passed the same message to the government in Abuja. On my way back from the Nigerian capital I stopped over in Accra again and Ibn Chambas was kind enough to spend the two-hour stop-over with me. We discussed many points on developments in Banjul. I was informed that the Ghanaian government had already agreed with the Gambia government to send lawyers and judges as bilateral assistance.

During the transition (1994-1996), the military regime brought in foreign judges to sit in the commissions of inquiry that it had put together. We had done similarly when we tried hundreds of suspects in connection with the coup attempt in 1981. While the regime waited for the long-awaited bench of judges to arrive it preached 'accountability, transparency and probity' and condemned what it said characterised my government – "rampant corruption and flamboyant lifestyles." This seemed to be an attempt to win public sympathy for the young soldiers wanting to correct the wrongs they said I had condoned in thirty-two years of government and which, they alleged, had made the coup justifiable.

I found it the usual story in every African coup d'état. Corruption had always been the justification in Africa for the military to seize power from civilian or even other military governments. In February 1995, I used the opportunity of a BBC *Focus on Africa* interview to deny the charge. Corruption was never rampant in my government. However, I did not say there was no wrongdoing in ministries and departments in my government. Indeed, while admitting there were problems, I always highlighted the moral demand for probity and honesty in all who serve the people.

It was our thinking that the UK and the US were being quite lenient with the regime and that there ought to be tougher measures against the AFPRC. However, the events of 11 November 1994 at the Bakau Barracks and the assassination attempt against Chairman Jammeh by two of his fellow council members – Sana Sabally and Sadibou Hydara – on 27 January 1995 pointed to a great deal of instability in the country. They were both jailed.[26] The UK government put out a Travel Advice in which the Home Office warned tourists against travelling to The Gambia. For me, any measures that would hurt the income and livelihoods of thousands of ordinary Gambians pained me, even though it was meant to put pressure on the regime to speed up the return to democratic civilian rule.

It was becoming quite clear to us that the soldiers were gaining recognition. There were growing numbers of converts – governments, organisations and individual Gambians traditionally opposed to the former PPP government – who were steadily offering support to the regime.

At home, some religious leaders prayed for long life for the regime and said that it was God who placed people in power. The song in many quarters was rapidly changing by the day. Foreign embassies and consulates were opening up in Banjul, thus further recognising the regime. This growing recognition was of grave concern to us. More worrisome however was the attempted departure from democratic principles which soon emerged in a highly vocal *No Elections* campaign that supporters of the regime ran during the constitutional consultations and the preparations for the presidential election.

While I kept an eye on Banjul, I addressed chains of letters to prominent people in British political, business and civil society. I wrote to many members of the House of Lords and the House of Commons. Some of them acted upon my petitions and relayed my concerns to Baroness Chalker. Lord Judd, Lord Howe of Aberavon, Lord Tomson of Monifieth, Prime Minister John Major and others wrote back to me with some very encouraging suggestions. Edward V K Jaycox, Africa Region Vice President at the World Bank, wrote back assuring me that the Bank was maintaining an open dialogue with the military government in Banjul in the hope that the transition programme would be successfully achieved and that the gains in economic reforms that had been achieved over the previous few years were not lost.

As planned and sealed in the pledges made to the US government and the UNDP and the World Bank in May 1995, the AFPRC Rectification

---

[26] Hydara died in prison in early June 1995, while Sabally was tried, found guilty and convicted. He served his sentence and moved to Senegal upon his release.

Programme was on course for the return of the country to democracy later in 1996. Then Minister of Finance Bala Garba Jahumpa and the junta's spokesman, Capt Ebou Jallow[27], went to Washington where they gave pledges for good governance, the transition and the financial auditing of public enterprises. The AFPRC was able to convince the US government and the major donor partners that they could keep pace with the desired transition in a few months. The EU also promised it would continue its assistance in response to the Poverty Alleviation Programme. The UN accepted to perform its traditional role of bringing together the roundtable of donors in Banjul in May 1995.

It was a significant signal to the AFPRC that the world was ready to work with it if it kept to the programme of democratic transition. What was still unclear was what ideas the regime was harbouring about its continued stay in politics. That was why we quickly took issues with the suspected foot-dragging in the implementation of the transition programme. We kept an eye on that and followed closely the developments in the political and economic scene on the ground in Banjul.

In August 1995, the military government restored the death penalty. The world reacted with speed in condemning the decision. Dr Nigel Ashford, the UK Vice President of the International Society for Human Rights, described the restoration of the death penalty as a step backwards for human rights and dignity in the country. It was a good thing that the world was paying attention to my message to restore democracy in The Gambia. Many people and organisations criticised the reinstatement of the death penalty.

On 22 April 1996, I was at the Commonwealth Secretariat with Commonwealth Secretary General Chief Emeka Anyaoku at Marlborough House. Central to my visit was for a more heightened campaign to get the AFPRC to lift the ban on political parties. The indications were there that 1996 was going to be an election year. But the PPP and most of the other old political parties remained under a ban, a situation that played into the hands of the military regime even before a single vote was cast. It was clear that for democracy to prevail, the ban on selected political parties had to be lifted.

Baroness Chalker announced the lifting of the Travel Advice in March 1996. It had lasted from November 1995 to March 1996 and had made that year's tourist season the worst ever. The travel ban was a bitter-sweet pill

---

[27] In October 1995, Radio Gambia announced that AFPRC spokesman Captain Ebou Jallow had absconded with $3m. He settled in the United States.

the campaign had to endure, just to see our countrymen and women get back to democracy.

Meanwhile several commissions of inquiry had opened into the assets and acquisitions of members of my government. There was the Alghali Commission, the Macauley Commission among others, one of which, the Akoto-Bamfo Commission, was adjudicating my affairs.

The chairperson of the commission, Judge Vida Akoto-Bamfo, left The Gambia under a cloud immediately after the submission of her report. The cool reception of her report from the regime did not match the media fanfare that surrounded the Alghali and Macauley submissions.

Although the Akoto-Bamfo report was never made public, we were finally able to have access to the White Paper the government eventually published. The major areas of concern, it appeared, were my properties, foreign travels, taxes and foreign exchange money transactions. But because I am eager for closure on this issue and, at the same time, to enjoy the final right of response, I pronounced again that I had bought all my properties on the market and those that I had acquired through bank mortgages were paid for by proper monthly loan deductions from my bona fide emoluments.

In July 1996 I was privileged to receive the Ambassador of Kuwait in London who dropped in to see me at Birchen Lane. I informed him of the political situation in The Gambia and was much energised by his support. I followed that quickly with visits to London where I kept Anyaoku abreast of things. I also attended a meeting in the House of Commons with Lord Avebury, Chairman of the Joint-Party Parliamentary Human Rights Committee.

On 7 August 1996, the people of The Gambia voted in the referendum on the draft constitution and the timetable. It was a great step forward that put to the test the regime's reaction to the findings of the consultation that Dr Lenrie Peters and his NCC had conducted.

On 14 August 1996, the regime announced the lifting of the ban on political parties but re-imposed it two days later. The ban would not be lifted again until 2001. Chairman Jammeh announced that he would be a candidate in the presidential election, a firm date for which had been set for 26 September 1996. The PPP had been waiting for the ban to be lifted at any point for them to be able to exercise their democratic rights and had always stood poised to squeeze in a campaign. But despite all the pressure from the international community, the AFPRC stuck to their guns and maintained the ban on the PPP.

Four political parties registered and fanned out into the country to make their bid. Many seats went unopposed to the incumbent AFPRC/

APRC. Campaign time was short and it was a challenge getting party faces and symbols understood by the electorate. The United Democratic Party (UDP) was led by well-known lawyer, Ousainou Darboe, a newcomer to politics. He absorbed a great deal of Sheriff Mustapha Dibba's following in the banned NCP and earned the sympathies of a great many former adherents of the UP and the PPP.

The National Reconciliation Party (NRP) was led by Hamat Bah, another newcomer who quit his hotel job to run for president. He launched the NRP in September at Gunjur, saying he had come up with a party to develop a new way of thinking for the people of the country. He challenged the people who, he said, might be thinking he was not a serious candidate; he said those people would know whether or not he was serious, when he got into State House.

The People's Democratic Organisation for Independence and Socialism (PDOIS), the only pre-1994 party not banned, put up Sidia Jatta as its candidate. The incumbent in government, Yahya A J J Jammeh, now retired from the army, led the Alliance for Patriotic Re-orientation and Construction (APRC). Chairman Jammeh launched his party on Monday 26 August 1996 at the July 22nd Square, claiming that the only reason he was running was that leaders in the community had urged him to do so.

The pressures on the military government continued from London. The Commonwealth Ministerial Action Group (CMAG), formed in November 1995 at the CHOGM in New Zealand, appealed to Chairman Jammeh to rescind the ban on the old parties. Vested with the mandate to deal with serious and persistent violations of the basic principles of the Commonwealth, the chairman of CMAG, Zimbabwean Foreign Minister Stan Mudenge, added his voice that the banning of the parties that were there from 1965 to 1994 was of grave concern and would create an uneven playing field. He said the rules of the election were flawed and would result in the country's military leaders strengthening their grip on power. CMAG declared it remained ready to continue to assist the transition but it clearly could not be expected to endorse a process which was obviously flawed and which was likely to result in the consolidation of military rule in The Gambia.

Following a meeting of CMAG in London, Mohamed Ibn Chambas, Ghana's deputy foreign minister, told the BBC on Wednesday 28 August 1996 that although it was clear and universally accepted that there existed specific laws to punish those found to have committed specific crimes including abuse of office, the 'blanket ban' on political organisations and personalities rightly caused deep-seated reactions and concern from some organisations, notably the Commonwealth body. Chambas said while The Gambia had responded positively to the latent concern of the Commonwealth on issues of democratisation in the recent past, it was necessary to recognise the critical messages embedded in their decision.

Meanwhile, the Provisional Independent Electoral Commission (PIEC) was reaching out to the international community and was asking for help for pre-election assessment teams to come to the country and for organisations to register to observe the elections. PIEC Chairman Gabriel John Roberts wrote to the OAU, the Commonwealth, the UNDP and many other inter-governmental, non-governmental, human rights and watchdog agencies, advising them to contact the nearest Gambian embassy or to call the Ministry of Foreign Affairs in Banjul.

The PIEC announced a voters' roll of nearly 500,000 Gambians and on 26 September 1996, 394,537 of that number went out to cast their votes countrywide. In keeping with the thirty-two-year-old democratic tradition laid down for elections in The Gambia, in the evening of the same day, the chairman of the PIEC announced the results. The APRC polled 220,011 votes or nearly 56% of the votes. The UDP had 36%; the NRP, 5% and PDOIS, 3%.

On Friday 18 October 1996, Yahya A J J Jammeh was sworn in as President of the Republic of The Gambia.

Sadly at least five GNA soldiers lost their lives when the Farafenni army barracks was attacked on 8 November 1996. Government forces were able to overcome and capture the insurgents. Incidentally there were allegations that the men were acting on the orders of Kukoi Samba Sanyang.

It was with great joy that we received news that 12 detainees who had been arrested for planning a peaceful demonstration outside the US Embassy on Kairaba Avenue were released that same month. They had been held by the regime for thirteen months. They included former PPP minister of agriculture, Omar Jallow; my brother-in-law, Housainou Njie; my nephew, Ismaila Jawara; and my niece, Mama Jawara.

After the APRC's victory, the only action left for the PPP was to continue the call for the lifting of the ban on the old parties, for the international community to increase the pressure for good governance and for the rescinding of the decrees that limited individual political participation. Meanwhile the campaign for the restoration would have to turn to special advocates within the House of Commons to keep The Gambia on the front burner of the British parliamentary agenda. Fortunately, the campaign attracted a wider audience that was reaching prominent members of the House of Commons.

The lobby was however fruitful. Members of the British Parliament, mainly from the Labour Party, took up The Gambia as a subject for regular probing in the House of Commons. Phoday Jarjussey was instrumental in laying our cause to the MP in the Borough of Hillingdon where he was elected on a Labour ticket to the local council in 2002. As a constituent in Hayes and Harlington, he worked with Member of Parliament John McDonnell.[28] John was a rising voice in the Labour Party and Phoday had gathered experience over seven years of living in Hillingdon organising local leafleting, community meetings, seminars, conferences and canvassing as well as dealing with individual cases and assisting the local MP.

The participation and contribution of John McDonnell was invaluable to our campaign. In June 1999, he questioned the Secretary of State for Foreign and Commonwealth Affairs on his assessment of the human rights record of the Gambia government. The Hon Tony Lloyd in his response said that the British government reviewed the Gambian human rights record on a bilateral basis, and through CMAG, which had a standing unit to monitor the situation in The Gambia. Lloyd pointed out that the British government had consistently made it clear that developments in the bilateral relationship, not the least the UK's development assistance programme, depended on Gambian observance of human rights and commitment to good governance. All of that sounded great to me except that the UK government, to my mind, needed to be better informed on the day-to-day situation in Banjul.

Lloyd went on to report improvements in recent months in which he said the harassment of the independent media had declined and the UDP opposition party had managed to hold regular rallies without interference. Nonetheless, Lloyd also offered information in his response that the UK government was continuing to press for repeal of the decrees which proscribed certain politicians and which placed heavy burdens on the independent media. However, John McDonnell questioned that against the report that a UDP member, Shyngle Nyassi, had gone missing in Banjul. The high commissioner, he reported, had pursued the matter again with the Foreign Ministry in Banjul on 11 June and, along with other diplomatic colleagues, went to meet with President Jammeh on 18 June. Nyassi was released on 21 June.

---

[28] Labour MP for Hayes and Harlington

McDonnell became very active in the campaign. Diane Abbott[29] came on board as well as many other sympathisers from the Labour Party. Diane's dynamic voice within the British parliamentary community was a great boost to our mission. The issues were also soon taken up by the African Civil Society Forum (ACSF) and other democratically minded individuals. McDonnell soon brought them together with his parliamentary group under the more formal Movement for the Restoration of Democracy in The Gambia – UK (MRDG-UK).

The MRDG-UK developed the Strategic Political Alliance (SPA) which aimed at seeking effective solutions to civil society problems and providing moral and political support to project implementation as part of the strategic approach of sustained structural reform, civic education and awareness and civil society advocacy in The Gambia. The movement had a great momentum, and with the help of the British parliamentarians we were able to raise the profile of The Gambia and keep the democracy issue alive in the debates in the British House of Commons.

Our work of sensitising the British government and helping to shape their engagement with the APRC government was rewarded in significant ways. Through McDonnell any withdrawal of basic civil liberties and democratic freedoms within The Gambia which would otherwise have largely gone unreported in the British media would be placed in statements before the House. The MP prepared statements any time there was an imprisonment and harassment of opposition party supporters.

The unfolding events in Banjul were of great concern to the international community. In October 1999, the UK government declared its satisfaction with the improvements in Banjul and resumed military contacts with the government. British High Commissioner Tony Millson announced the resumption of the contacts between the British and Gambian armed forces after a gap of several years. More importantly, the high commissioner seized the occasion of the Queen's birthday reception at his residence at Fajara to announce to his guests that British development assistance had started back in July 1998 with D36 million assigned to fund three major projects and with D136 million earmarked over the following three years. It was gratifying to note that the money was to be used in the areas of health, education and the independent media which are vital pillars in a democracy.

The resumption of British cooperation with the regime more or less put paid to our campaign. But we understood that life would not just stand still

---

[29] Dianne Abbott is Labour Party MP for Hackney North and Stoke Newington. She was the first black woman to be elected to the House of Commons.

for the APRC government. It was fully engaged with the rest of the world and things were bound to grow out of the country's international relations.

There was a little break in this weather of gloom in February 1999 with the news that reached me of the release of Imam Karamo Touray of the Brikama mosque, along with Waa Juwara and nine others. I felt justice had been well served when the courts found the cleric had no case to answer over charges brought against him and some of his followers over the demolition of a part of the mosque complex in Brikama.

I had a special interest in the case which dragged on for several months. I had been personally connected to the development of the mosque in the constituency of which I was an MP for a decade. I called Mariam Denton and Ousainou Darboe, the defence team, to congratulate them on the brilliant work in getting the magistrate to dismiss the case. Imam Touray had suffered greatly while his case was on. We shared the good news with the members of the MRDG-UK stressing that we were glad to see the law take its course.

I received an invitation from Miami University, Oxford, Ohio, USA, to be the speaker at the 1999 - 2000 Grayson Kirk Distinguished Lecture Series at the university. Professor Abdoulaye Saine, a Gambian on the staff of the Department of Political Science, had been in England a few months before to interview me for a research document he was co-authoring with Paula Boxie[30] called *Dawda Kairaba Jawara: The Man, His Politics and Legacy*. Saine then talked about the possibility of arranging to have me deliver a lecture at the university.

I shared the information of the invitation with my team and we decided Sara Janha would travel with me. I set down a few ideas around the subject - *Promotion of Sustainable Democracy in Africa*. We travelled to the US to a wonderful welcome Saine and the university authorities had arranged. Generally, the lecture went down well and many Gambians travelled from far and wide to hear it. However, there was an unfortunate disturbance by a couple of them, a Malafi Jarju[31] and one Bajo[32] who tried to disrupt the lecture but failed abysmally. In fact, Jarju and Bajo came in from Atlanta, Georgia, where the former was apparently the coordinator of the APRC support group in Atlanta.

When the minor disturbance died down, I addressed the issue relevant to my lecture and put forward in brief reasons why Africa was in greater

---

[30] Paula Boxie was in Miami University's Department of Teacher Education.

[31] Malafi Jarju would later return to Banjul where he would be made a Secretary of State briefly.

[32] He is a relative of Kaba Bajo who was then an APRC Secretary of State.

danger when the democratic machinery in governance was suspended as was the case in Banjul at that moment. I pointed to milestones Africa had achieved such as the African Charter on Human and Peoples' Rights and the African Commission as evidence that Africa can and must democratise.

I further analysed the state of affairs in The Gambia and the tradition of human rights and the rule of law. I explained the motives of the MRDG-UK and highlighted the campaign to ensure that the APRC government played by the international community's demands for the rescinding of Decree 89[33] in preparation for free and fair elections in 2001.

Later in Atlanta, we met many Gambians who came out to see us at our hotel. They were the PPP support base there and included Kebba Jallow who was Chairman of the Kanifing Municipal Council at the time of the coup. Our meetings were orderly and we shared information with each other. I updated everyone on the work of the MRDG-UK and how they could use their own leverage to increase the pressure for democratisation in The Gambia.

Sara had decided just before we were due to leave for the airport that he would not be travelling with me back to England. Although his sudden decision caught me by surprise, I wished him well. He and Kebba Jallow saw me off at the airport.

I arrived at Gatwick unaccompanied – for the first time since 1962 – and followed the disembarking passengers through immigration and out to the luggage carousel. I kept a sharp eye out for my luggage – four large pieces that I heaved off the rolling ramp on to a trolley. I started pushing only to realise that it was the first time in over forty years that I was handling luggage, and my own for that matter. It was also clear that I had well passed my years to handle such heavy luggage dexterously. In my lonely struggle to keep the trolley straight along the long corridors of the sprawling airport buildings, I was slowing down to catch my breath when I ran into Dr Ulric Jones and his wife, Doreen.[34] My medical chart was firmly printed in his mind, and I was sure he could tell the ordeal in which I found myself travelling alone and pushing a trolley full of bags.

She and Ulric were great ballroom dancers and many times we all enjoyed around the dance floor either at fundraising occasions for health or the ceremonial galas for the West African College of Surgeons. I could feel their yearning to help but they too had a flight to catch. In my brief

---

[33] Decree 89 banned all parties pre-July 1994, except PDOIS.

[34] The Sierra Leonean surgeon was once my personal physician when I was president.

chat with them I did not hide the fact that I was touched by their kindness in wishing they could offer help.

Life was teaching me that there would be times when there would be luggage trolleys to push on my own. I managed to look at the brighter side of life. I was particularly encouraged by the generally positive reception of my call in the Kirk lecture espousing the case of democracy and the rule of law to prevail in Africa in general and The Gambia in particular. The main concern was not to allow the standard of human rights observance, as people knew it during my presidency, to become a thing of the past in The Gambia.

30

15 Birchen Lane

My residence 15 Birchen Lane in Haywards Heath, West Sussex, is a five-bedroom house I bought in 1980. It had served me wonderfully for nearly twenty-five years. It began to serve its original objective as a home away from home after the military overthrew my government. Birchen Lane served me well whether I was on holiday or just passing through England; it was also my resting place during medical check-ups with my doctors.

Such regular visits to England had been made imperative since my brain surgery in 1973 following an accident in which a swaying boom in a dinghy in which I was sailing hit me on the back of the head, leaving me unconscious with sub-dural haematoma.[35] President Senghor's personal physician, who was flown in from Dakar to carry out an emergency check-up on me, recommended my immediate evacuation to London. He had told Vice President Assan Musa Camara and Secretary General Eric Christensen that if I did not get to London within forty-eight hours, I would probably die.

I was flown to Freetown on President Senghor's official aeroplane, where a British Caledonian Airways flight was awaiting departure from Lungi Airport for a direct flight to London. At Lungi I must have drifted in and out of consciousness however briefly, because I remember seeing and hearing, however faintly, faces and voices of a host of people, definitely among them President Siaka Stevens, talking around my stretcher as I was being taken on board the British Caledonian flight. I was taken to The Maudsley Hospital in DeCrespigny Park in London's South East, where the Director of the Neurological Unit, Mr Murray A Falconer, went to work with his team and in a one-and-a-half-hour operation relieved my haematoma.

He said it was a miracle that I had lived and part of that miracle, he underlined, was aided by what he said was a fascinating will on my part to live. I convalesced for a while at the Royal Gardens Hotel in Central London before moving to the country where our High Commissioner to the UK, Mr B O Semega-Janneh, had arranged with a friend of his, a gentleman named Fred Keil, who kindly offered his mansion to me and Chilel, the high commissioner himself and my staff for the period of my convalescence. The nurses, medics and physiotherapists were remarkable

---

[35] I bled under the lining of my brain.

as they helped me regain rudimentary functions such as recognising colour or little objects like pencils or butterflies until I could read newspapers on my own again.

The few visitors I was allowed included Assan Musa Camara and Eric Christensen who flew out to see me. I gave my best wishes and official blessing to the Vice President continuing his headship of the government as was constitutionally transferred to him at my State House bedside during the emergency. From that point on, the emergency use of someone else's country home for my convalescence had set me thinking of the absolute need for a place of my own if only to reduce the costs of accommodation in such emergencies and at the same time to eliminate the inconvenience of the head of government and leader of an independent country having to depend on friends to provide facilities for him and his retinue.

Those thoughts and, of course, the objective of a home in England where I could relax after the hectic round of politics, led to my discussions with my golfing partner, Sir Adam Thomson[36], who then kept his eyes glued to the real estate columns in the British papers. He came up with the suggestion of 15 Birchen Lane in 1980 when the owners had put it up for sale. I had nothing even close to the £98,000 they were asking for at the time. So I approached my bankers, Standard Chartered Bank, London, who were willing to accept a 10% deposit (£9,800), the title deeds of my freehold property at 34 Wellington Street, Banjul, and of course the title deeds of 15 Birchen Lane as security for the mortgage. I had fifteen years in which to pay off the balance through monthly instalments which began almost immediately.

Some time in the 1980s while on a short break away at Birchen Lane, I suffered an emergency. My General Practitioner Dr H T Davies referred me for admission to the Hurstwood Park Neurological Centre in Haywards Heath. The consultant neurologist, Dr J E Rees, described it as a transient ischaemic episode, a slight stroke. I came through it quickly and rested in bed at home, where I was mildly amused to read Dr Rees's report back to Dr Davies that I was a fit man who played golf and that I was in no danger whatsoever of any damage from the episode.

In 1995 I purchased a used Ford to get me around. It was sturdy and functional with 501 on its number plate, opportunely so as if in celebration of the giant score of '501 Not Out' that Brian Lara had scored for Warwickshire against Durham in June 1994. The young West Indian cricketer continued to warm the hearts of millions around the world with

---

[36] Sir Adam Thomson was one of the four founders and a major shareholder of British Caledonian Airways. He was also its Chairman and Chief Executive.

the batting finesse that finally won me over to the art in the game. It was a far cry from 1940 when cricket to me was no more than an insane and dangerous game that proved my point when the hard red ball left a dent on my forehead.

A car of my own was useful in reducing the strain of the enormous taxi bills. It drove the household out shopping, on our regular trips to the golf course and to Brighton on the special occasions of the *Eid* prayers. The mosque in Brighton was the closest to us and although it was a converted residence it adequately served the congregation of a few hundred of us mainly from Pakistan and Bangladesh, plus a sprinkling from Saudi Arabia and Africa.

In March 1995, we were thrown into a medical emergency that had us scurrying to hospital with little Musa Kassama, the toddler son of my former ADC, Momodou Lamin Kasama. The child had been diagnosed with heart trouble and had been scheduled for a surgical operation. The five-hour-long operation which took place on 22 March at the Royal Brompton, London, under the National Health Service, was successful beyond our wildest expectations. The surgeons discharged the infant after only three days in intensive care to the relief of all of us. We also kept in touch with Barajaly where the family was gathering for the annual *gamo,* which took place at the mosque on Friday 24 March 1995. We made phone calls to show our support for the tradition of the annual vigil and prayers. We also asked them to pray for young Musa who was recovering from his operation.

Chilel and I went to Cambridge where we visited Trevor and Mary Blackburn. We were conducted on a tour of the Vet School in the company of Professor Leo Cott, the Dean. In June, I joined the members and officers of the British Veterinary Association at a reception in the Marquee Terrace of the House of Commons. The African-European Community celebrated Africa Day on 25 May 1995 with a luncheon. It was a wonderful gathering and one other opportunity for me to link up with people concerned with politics and development in The Gambia.

On 7 April 1996, the extended family gathered for the wedding of my son, Kawsu, and Amie Saine[37], a former Miss Gambia. Amie was crowned Miss Gambia in January 1994 and won the bigger sub-regional Miss ECOWAS crown in August in Benin that same year. The drama of her visit to Benin was that she was seen off in July in grand style by the Minister of Youth and Sports in my government, Bubacar Baldeh, but was welcomed back home on her return in August by Minister of Youth and

---

[37] Kawsu and Amie have since given me two lovely granddaugthers, Ramzia and Mariam.

Sports, Amina Faal-Sonko, of the AFPRC regime. Things do move quickly at times, don't they?

That kind of swiftness of things in politics, I suppose, was not unlike Prime Minister Margaret Thatcher extending a warm invitation to me in 1990 for a state visit to Britain only for me to make the visit in the middle of winter that year and to be welcomed at 10 Downing Street by Prime Minister John Major. The Conservative Party had in the interim dispensed with the services of the Iron Lady. No wonder another British Prime Minister Harold Wilson said: "A week is a long time in politics".

Fatma Denton, the daughter of former accountant general, Abou Denton, interviewed me for material towards writing up her doctoral thesis at the University of Birmingham. In February 1998, she produced a well-researched thesis, which she titled *Foreign Policy Formation in The Gambia 1965 to 1994: Weak Developing States and Their Foreign Policy Choices*. This work on important events, especially of the period 1981 to 1994, made for a remarkably knowledgeable account of the political history of the country.

The Gambian novelist, the late Ebou Dibba, also visited. Arnold Hughes, a lecturer at the University of Birmingham, came to Birchen Lane for a lengthy discussion about material for a book he was working on. I dug into my archives and bookcases and gave him enough of what I knew and remembered. In November 2006, he published a book entitled *A History of The Gambia: 1816 to 1994*. Arnold had even toyed with the idea of doing a biography of me.

My frustrations about The Gambia were all the while compounded by the desperate realities of more military interventions in politics taking place in the rest of Africa. The coup in Sierra Leone in May 1997 mounted by Johnny Paul Koroma against President Ahmed Tejan Kabbah was a disturbing development.

On 3 July 1997 I attended Ebrima's graduation ceremony at Reading University, where he had attained a Bachelor of Science degree in agricultural economics. I was accompanied by Njaimeh and Momodou Bobb.

In July, the Commonwealth Office invited me to a conference entitled "Preventing Future Wars – Action or Inertia?" that was organised under its Commonwealth Strategies for Peace Programme. The conference was held at the Cumberland Lodge, the palatial 17th century retreat run by the King George VI and Queen Elizabeth Foundation of St Catherine's in the heart of Windsor Great Park, a few miles outside London.

Everything to prevent war was an important subject for me. I listened to some impassioned deliveries on hopeful ways of ensuring a peaceful and dignified world. Some delegates proposed dynamic new strategies of engaging societies and cultures away from the choice of warfare as a solution to a divergence of views. The conference examined the balance of power and also examined strategies that could contribute to the reduction of international misunderstanding, eg through inclusion and more intercultural exchange and exposure. The importance of peace for the realisation of human worth and growth in society was paramount in all the arguments, even among those who sometimes found value in *pax para bellum* – the attainment of peace through warfare.

Her Majesty the Queen, the patron of the Cumberland Lodge, attended the Sunday service on 20 July in the Royal Chapel on the grounds of the Royal Lodge next door. An emissary came to us with an invitation from Her Majesty asking if delegates would like to join her at the service and to meet her for a chat afterwards. It was a short service inside the captivating splendour of Victorian Gothic architecture.

After the service, the Queen met the delegates on the grounds of the Royal Lodge together with the Duke of Edinburgh and their son, Prince Edward. It was early summer and the morning was great outdoors. Her Majesty remembered me from CHOGM in Cyprus in 1993, when for the first time ever she spoke at a CHOGM dinner. It was at Limasol that the Queen broke tradition and gave a short speech after the dinner to which I was invited to reply. She shared her ideas with us for stronger partnerships within the Commonwealth family and for broader channels that would enhance cultural inclusion for peace and understanding in the world.

Back at Birchen Lane, we kept our ears to the ground on issues from back home. Kipling Waistel, one of the solicitors handling the affidavits, got even busier with transactions because the political developments on the ground in Banjul were beginning to make it more and more difficult to argue that the regime was a danger to the lives and liberty of the applicants.

August 1997 closed with the tragic death of Diana, Princess of Wales, in a car crash in a Paris underpass. September saw the death of another remarkable woman, Mother Teresa, who passed away the same day Diana, was being buried. The deaths of a princess and a saint overshadowed the death on 8 September of President Mobutu Sese Seko of the former Zaire.

I was most touched by the procession of William and Harry in step with their father behind the cortege. Memories flooded back of a similar walk I took with my own children, Dawda, Nema, Nacesay, Almami and Kawsu, behind their mother's casket at her burial at the Wesley Methodist Church in Banjul on 4 February 1981.

Christmas 1997 and the end-of-year celebrations began early in England as was usual for the festive season. The shop windows in London and the suburbs were already glittering to overflowing with colourful lights and gifts. We had a couple of outings to make, all the same, to dinner and dance dates in December. We attended the first one in the company of Saihou Sabally and his wife, Fatma Alami. Saihou had flown in from Dakar where he had lived since July 1994. Ndow Njie and his wife, Kumba, were with us at the gala given by the Body Circuit gym of which I was a member. I could not tell how the sumptuous menu worked out in terms of calories but the dinner was quite good.

The second engagement was at the invitation of the President of the British Veterinary Association to a dinner at its headquarters, 7 Mansfield Street, London. It was another grand occasion to meet with the old boys and to catch up on developments at the Royal Dick at Edinburgh and the old school at Glasgow.

A great occasion that we found most enjoyable and relaxing was our time away on 17 December 1997 in Tenerife where we celebrated with the Kieslings the twenty-fifth anniversary of Loro Parque.

On 6 February 1998, I presented a paper on "Democracy and Human Rights: The Gambian Experience" at University College London. Professor Murray Last had invited me to speak to a group of students and some professionals who wanted to hear from me on the state of democracy and human rights on the continent. The audience was made up mostly of African students who at the end of the presentation discussed at length and agreed that Africa had to do a whole lot more to improve on its democracy and human rights record.

Our independence day, 18 February 1998, was obviously a good day to focus on The Gambia. I was happy to accept the invitation of the students at the University of Buckingham where I spoke on the topic, "Aspects of Multi-Party Democracy and Human Rights: The Gambian Experience". They were a good group and had a great deal to contribute. Needless to say - they asked me questions about The Gambia's political situation. That was my own outreach to students and faculty, who needed to hear about The Gambia and, through that, to create an informed platform for them to assess what we had laid down in thirty-two years of my government. With the AFPRC/APRC government having been in power for four years already, there was an opportunity to compare and contrast policies and laws, thereby identifying any improvement or decline in terms of the observance of human rights and the rule of law in The Gambia.

I was happy to chart the history of the country from the pre-colonial to the colonial era, through the formative years of the post-war period, the transformation of the nascent political landscape to self-government, independence and finally to republican status. I told them that for us in The Gambia the promotion and upholding of civil and political rights, both at home and abroad, was a *sine qua non* for the formulation and implementation of the appropriate socio-economic measures in health, education, transport and communications, the provision of clean potable water and a host of other essential services designed to improve the quality of life of the population.

It was a well-known fact that Commonwealth African countries achieved independence with democratic institutions based on the British parliamentary system. I pointed out however that continued multi-party democracy in most parts of Africa quickly became the exception rather than the rule in the wake of the emergence of strong presidential rule, the one-party state and, in far too many cases, military rule. At one stage in the history of Commonwealth Africa, for example, only The Gambia, Botswana and Mauritius consistently adhered to multi-party democracy. The Gambia steadfastly maintained this practice and created an enabling political environment which facilitated socio-economic activity without restrictions.

In July 1998, Baby Njaimeh graduated from the University of Southampton. Chilel and I attended the colourful ceremony in which our twenty-five-year-old became the first paediatrician in the Jawara clan. I sent word all around the *kabilo* back home in The Gambia in Banjul, Brikama, Barajaly and Bansang. Dr Jawara received many telephone messages of felicitations from home and the family feted her to a barbecue in the garden at 15 Birchen Lane. The joy of seeing the children succeed in their education was always a morale booster.

It was a great pleasure for us to see her take up contract work in a local hospital until she decided to join a private practice in Chertsey, Surrey. Baby Njaimeh and her fiancé, Richard Asamoah-Owusu, a Ghanaian, soon got married and settled down to raising a family. Richard, an affable young man, worked in the municipal council. It was my joy that the children were bringing us happy occasions for celebration in our lives.

Throughout the year there was a steady flow of visitors who came in by appointment. But two visitors stand out who came to me with voluntary confessions of things they said they had done amiss and asked for my forgiveness. In August 1998, Boima Fahnbulleh, a Liberian national and former foreign minister and founder of MOJA, arrived at my house accompanied by Phoday Jarjussey. I frankly spared him the litany of woes his organisation had put us through in West Africa, including The Gambia. But Fahnbulleh insisted on confessing his role and wishing the past to be the past. In the end, he offered his voluntary services to me, should I need him for errands. I never took him up on his offer.

The family soon got together again at Birchen Lane for the naming of Fatou Kess's baby boy who was born on 28 September 1998. My old schoolmate in Banjul, ET, phoned to ask Fatou and Momodou Lamin Kassama for the favour of giving him the honour to name his grandson after me. He wanted it that way to show his appreciation of our lifetime of friendship and for my giving home, love and care to his daughter and her family. I was touched by ET's wonderful gesture and felt honoured that Fatou and Momodou accepted to name their child after me – Dawda Kairaba.

Chilel and I flew to Tenerife for the wedding of Wolfgang Kiessling's daughter - Isabel, to her fiancé, Paco Buerbaum, in 1998, and we were most thrilled for them to return the favour when Wolfgang and Brigitte came to Haywards Heath as our guests at the wedding of our daughter, Baby Njaimeh.

On 12 December 1998, I was once again at Reading University for Ebrima's graduation, where he had been awarded a Master of Science degree in agricultural economics. I was accompanied by Njaimeh, Mariam and her daughter Nadua and a friend of Ebrima's.

My bank accounts lay frozen in Banjul and rents from my properties in The Gambia were not forthcoming. Without a pension or a salary to my name, I started to feel the pinch in spite of the support I received from friends like Wolfgang Kiessling[38] and Rolf Becker[39] among others. Much of the support I had received from 1994 had run dry. Some of it had gone into the campaign to restore democracy in The Gambia. The rest went to the housekeeping at 15 Birchen Lane.

Meanwhile the Gambian press carried on with the vilification that was coming out of the regime that I was loaded with money stashed in coded Swiss bank accounts and that I had villas and hotels in exotic resort islands. On the contrary, I had no such assets and I had to appeal to my friends for help.

By the end of 1998, I was broke. Eventually I faced reality and decided to put 15 Birchen Lane up for sale. I reckoned that with the proceeds of the sale, I could buy a smaller house that was cheaper to run, and use the difference to live on. I invited Connells, an estate agency, to put it on the

---

[38] Wolfgang Kiessling, founder of Loro Parque in Tenerife, was Gambia's Honorary Consul General to Tenerife, Canary Islands.

[39] Rolf Becker was the Honorary Consul General for The Gambia in the German city of Frechen.

market. After the first prospective buyers came and left, I felt a great surge of ease that I had taken a good decision.

I was almost clinching a deal when M C Cham came to my home with two Englishmen, Michael Hart and Nigel Gladstein. They came with a proposal that would ease my financial situation.

It seemed a simple enough proposal. I was told that Michael Hart and Nigel Gladstein were managing a fund on behalf of Cerino Holdings that would pay investors the principal invested plus a generous interest on a monthly basis, ie the principal invested plus the interest would be paid back in 12 monthly instalments. I pointed out to them that if I had the funds available to invest in their fund, I would not have found it necessary to sell the house.

M C Cham said I could take out a mortgage with a finance company (Fast Track) owned by another friend of his, Michael Villiers. I pointed out that I had already approached several mortgage lenders who all turned me down on account of my age (I was then 74) and also that I had no regular income that could repay the mortgage. He assured me my mortgage application with Fast Track would be successful.

The monthly amounts I was guaranteed would have been enough to settle the monthly mortgage payments and also meet my living expenses. I rue the day when I accepted that as a great proposal. I should have known that it was too good to be true. I should have sold my property as planned, put my money in the bank and keep Cham and his friends out of my private business transactions altogether.

On 10 December 2001, I took an early train out of Haywards Heath to Victoria Station where I found M C Cham waiting for me, as arranged. He was with a chauffeur driven limousine that drove us to the offices of Hobson and Ardity, the lawyers Cham and Michael Villiers had chosen to handle my mortgage agreement. They placed a file before me, which was the legal charge containing the terms and conditions of the loan that I could hardly digest, even if I were given days to read through it. Without having sought any legal advice to help me look carefully through the thick jungle of legal language in a folder I signed the documents. Little did I realise that by so doing, I had signed away 15 Birchen Lane into the hands of sharks.

I also signed a contract with Michael Hart (drafted by Hart) and which was witnessed by M C Cham, which spelt out the terms and conditions of the fund. It was only one page. With hindsight I should have sought independent legal advice before signing. Later I realised that there were no covenants protecting me if the fund failed. I handed over most of the principal I received from Fast Track to them.

Things started well and I received 2 instalments as promised. The third instalment never came, and I never saw Hart or Gladstein again – they had simply disappeared. M C Cham had also returned to Banjul. Meanwhile I still had to service the mortgage with Fast Track. Obviously with no payments from the fund and with no other source of income Fast Track took me to court when I defaulted on the mortgage repayments.

It was with deep grief and pain that I surrendered 15 Birchen Lane to Fast Track after a few years battling it out in court. This was when I was able to convince myself that property, like most material things in life, after all, is all but vanity. I shed the grief of its loss and learnt more from the experience of what human nature truly is. I was amazed at my own gullibility – that I would open myself to such a scam at the hands of some people close to me. I could easily blame age for my slip-ups but frankly it had more to do with my relationship with M C Cham. He was a minister in my cabinet for many years, and someone with very close connections to my wife Chilel's family, hence I trusted him and his friends.

I celebrated the New Year 1999 with the purchase on 1 January 1999 of a new Hewlett-Packard desktop personal computer. There was good reason for opening the year with thoughts of electronics and cyberspace. Technology was moving so fast that I did not want to be left out in this age of communication and information technology. It seemed electronic gadgetry had created a new form of illiteracy for those who would not move up with the times and learn to use the computer. No less important was the HP software I found fascinating as the new millennium approached, with fears of disaster which the Y2K bug would bring, leaving the world in chaos and disorder.

I was 74 years old but I was not too old to learn, I told myself. I updated myself by taking day classes in Information Technology (IT) for the National Vocational Qualification (NVQ). I found those the most beneficial way to spend my spare time away from the relatively more expensive golf course while I enjoyed the added value of catching up with the latest forms of communication my contacts around the world were using to reach me. I also registered for a course given by the BBC at Haywards Heath College. After a whole day's work, I graduated and earned the Web Wise certificate. It meant that I could turn my PC on and off. I learnt that the plural of *mouse* in computer grammar was not *mice* but *mouses*. I could send emails and get on with operating a full desk-top facility at home. My daughter Chilel was also doing the same course. It was kind of funny being in the same class with my daughter.

I began to enjoy a new lease of life and was able to view my internet bill online. All I needed to do was to simply log on to the company homepage, click on 'Account' and then on 'Your e-Bill' and enter my username and password. Just as it said in the brochure, an itemised bill showed up after I clicked on the statement number I required further information on. That information was updated every two hours to show as up-to-date a figure as possible and allowed me to pro-actively budget my usage of it. I felt very educated, useful and modern – in step with the world every time I 'clicked'. By mid-year I got brave enough to buy myself a CellNet mobile phone.

I picked up some intriguing tips on computer operations by mid-February 1999 and I enjoyed the pleasure of explaining my new-found skills to Winton Lane and his wife, Delia, who invited Chilel and me to lunch at a place called the *Travellers* on 106, Pall Mall. We talked about the old times in the colonial service in The Gambia. We had a relaxing afternoon and I was glad to hear him talk about the time he was on the board of the International Planned Parenthood Federation (IPPF). I took the opportunity to express my gratitude to him for the work he had rendered to The Gambia since his arrival there in 1957 as an administrative officer, and diligently made his way up in the colonial service to Acting Colonial Secretary in a space of only three years. He recalled fondly his time as Chairman of the Bathurst Town Council and how, when I became premier in 1962, he had to take on two positions in my office as Secretary to the Prime Minister and Secretary to the Cabinet.

As head of the civil service when we gained independence, Winton was instrumental in setting up the guidelines for refreshed and forward-looking engagements of the few new talents that were available to us. Although he retired only a year later, he returned to The Gambia as the UN adviser on relations with Senegal. I considered it a personal great loss when he had to leave in October just after the mechanics of a republic had been put in place; he had had to go away to Nairobi, Kenya, where he was appointed the resident representative of the IPPF for East, Central and Southern Africa.

He was sympathetic to my campaign schedule which continued busily among the members of parliament even though my preoccupation with affidavits was slowly winding down. The longer the APRC government continued in power and the international community by and large was fully engaging with it, the more difficult the qualification for asylum applicants became. However, my sustained opinion was that with the PPP still under a ban and unable to contest the election, the APRC had still gone largely unchallenged.

On 5 March 1999 I went to Sir John Moore Barracks in Winchester for Foday's passing-out parade. It was a cold day but the parade was impressive. I was there with Njaimeh, Mariam, Ebrima, Momodou Ndow Njie and Momodou Lamin Kassama. Foday had joined in 1998, at the age of 27. Even though he was a graduate, he had passed the cut-off age of 26 for officer training and could only join as an enlisted man. He would reach the rank of sergeant by 2008. He has served in Argentina, Germany, Belize, Kosovo and Iraq.

On 16 October 1999, the family gathered again when they came to celebrate with Foday and Kathleen Simms at their wedding at a civic ceremony at Sussex University. There was a wonderful reception afterwards and it was an opportunity to catch up with close friends and relatives. As would be expected, some of the guests had plenty of gossip to pass around about home. However, no one missed the essence of the evening – to celebrate the new life Foday was entering with his new bride.

On 2 December 1999 Koro Sallah, a leading member of MOJA-G, the Banjul chapter of the parent MOJA, fulfilled his wish, as he put it, to come by and see me. Phoday Jarjussey and I listened to Sallah confess that he orchestrated the arson attacks in the 1980s on the official government launch, the *Mansa Kila Kuta* and my personal sailing boat, *The Barajaly*. In 1981, after the coup attempt, he slipped through the police dragnet and went to Sweden where he has been living since then.

Sallah came along on the visit with another Gambian, Abdoulie Jobe, and expressed his regret for all the harm he had done to me and my government. He asked me to understand that he was young at the time and had not fully realised what damage he was doing to his own country by burning the boats. My reaction was one of indifference at first. I guess the years since the arson attacks and graffiti and clandestine leafleting in the 1980s had dulled the sharpness of the crimes.

31

The new millennium

It was a frosty morning on 1 January 2000. All day I had been expecting the bang as everyone had anticipated would happen with the bombshell of the Y2K bug otherwise known as the millennium bug. Fortunately 2000 rolled in without any incident related to the Y2K bug.

I kept an eye on the television set and the newspapers and I noted in my diary the quite dramatic developments of a different kind that were unfolding in Senegal. Maitre Abdoulaye Wade of the main opposition PDS had performed well enough in the first round of voting with 31% of the votes denying President Diouf a first round majority, leading to a second round of voting. Wade won the second leg with 58.49% of the vote. His victory changed the Senegalese political landscape that for nearly fifty years had seen the Parti Socialiste (PS) in power. The outgoing president, Abdou Diouf, handed over peacefully to Wade, thus giving the democratic process a great boost in Africa and setting it on a firmer footing in Senegal.

In February 2000 I would not allow myself to be left out when the Fit For Life gym invited its old and new members to a dance party at a local discotheque. I showed them what I could do on my feet and left the instructors to decide for themselves whether I was a fit 76-year-old or not. They cheered me on, and it was good fun.

I also attended perhaps my first and only annual meeting of the Birchen Lane Residents Association at Saxbre House. It was agreeably relaxing and, it turned out to be a way of spending a couple of hours discussing how to make the necessary repairs on the Lane and to take decisions on what to do about noise, lighting, policing and recreation issues.

On April 10 2000 we received news of civil unrest in Banjul. Initial reports were of riots taking place. It all started on 7 April 2000 when the Gambia Students Union (GAMSU) decided to organize what they called a peaceful march on 10 April 2000. It was in protest of the death of student Ebrima Barry, allegedly at the hands of fire service personnel and the alleged rape of a young girl by a soldier. Apparently the students applied for a permit to demonstrate but were refused one. They still went ahead with the march.

The events that took place on that day and the following heralded one of the darkest periods in our history – at least 13 students and a Red Cross volunteer would die and many more injured when security personnel stepped in to stop the march. Outraged students and youths went on the rampage destroying vehicles and damaging public buildings.

The Gambia government set up a Coroner's Inquest to ascertain the cause of deaths, and the findings were that the killings resulted from gunshot wounds.

The National Assembly passed a backdated bill amending the Indemnity Act, thus indemnifying the security personnel that were involved. When it eventually became law, the Supreme Court declared it null and void and of no effect.

I wrote a letter that was published in *The Point* newspaper of 14 April 2000, extending my condolences to the bereaved families and to those who sustained injuries and called on the APRC government to bring those responsible to justice.

Omar Jallow had called me on the phone on 9 June 2000 giving me details of meetings he had had with some former ministers, Landing Jallow Sonko and Alkali James Gaye and others on the plans to revive and reorganise the PPP. He told me he had brought together Assan Musa Camara and Sheriff Mustapha Dibba at several meetings at the Francisco Bar & Restaurant in Fajara with the intention of bringing the parties back together in a coalition. It was understandably necessary to begin working from the grassroots up; and the opportunity to launch out again into the political arena, which for many had become a thing of the past, was welcome news. It was a particularly great boost for the democratisation campaign.

I gave my unreserved support to the idea of resurgence. I urged them to press on and to get as many of the old guard as possible involved. There were a handful of them on the ground who were waiting for the ban to be lifted, giving them the opportunity to scour the countryside again and rouse the people into action. It was important to keep in mind that it would not be an easy campaign.

Meanwhile Professor Abdoulaye Saine at the University of Miami delivered messages of apologies from one Mr Bayo, who had tried to disrupt my Kirk lecture back in November 1999 in Oxford, Ohio.

At this point, an old friend paid me a visit - the Nigerian High Commissioner to the UK, Prince Bola Ajibola. He had come on a courtesy call and also to personally pass on greetings from President Olusegun Obasanjo. It was good to see Prince Ajibola again after the many visits he had paid me at State House in Banjul, when he was the Attorney General and Minister of Justice of Nigeria. He had been especially helpful to the government in selecting Nigerian judges to join our badly understaffed judiciary.

I sent greetings through him back to Abuja with expressions of deepest appreciation to President Obasanjo, whom I commended for having been a military person who organised elections and handed government over to a civilian administration in 1979. I reminded him of my happiness that it was The Gambia that Obasanjo had chosen for his well-earned rest during which he began writing *My Command*, his telling memoirs.

The resurgence of the old political cadres of the PPP to join the struggling opposition gave a great boost to my hopes. On 28 February 2001, I went to the House of Commons for a special briefing session on The Gambia attended by Gambian opposition leaders who had come to London to participate in it. It was convened by the MRDG-UK and John McDonnell. Femi Peters represented the leader of the Gambia People's Party, Assan Musa Camara. Hamat Bah, leader of the National Reconciliation Party (NRP) also came, as did Omar Jallow, the convener of the PPP, even though it was still banned. His home at Kanifing had become the party's office. The briefing session was well attended by members of the British political establishment, including MPs as well as members of international organisations who came to discuss the political situation in The Gambia.

Assan Musa and Femi had called me earlier from Banjul before Femi set off for London and we laid down some basics. They explained their own stance on the proposed coalition to challenge the APRC.

Two sections of the 1997 Constitution automatically barred me from running for president in the 2001 elections. These are Section 62 subsection (1) (b) and subsection (1) (c). The former disqualifies anyone under the age of 30 and anyone above the age of 65, and the latter anyone who was not ordinarily resident in The Gambia for the five years immediately preceding the election from running for president. I would have been 77 and over seven years not ordinarily resident in The Gambia.

They wanted to know what my role would be if the opposition came together in a coalition and put forward a common standard-bearer for the elections expected in 2001. I suggested a few ideas for them to discuss among themselves in Banjul, and kept my doors open for further discussions. Basically my role was limited to that of a father-figure.

The meeting was successful in the main for capturing the three central themes: first, the need for all opposition parties to come together in a united front, second, to make sure the elections were conducted freely and fairly and, third, to work for the repeal of Decree 89 that would allow the old parties to participate again in national politics. It was a loud appeal to the international community to come along with Gambians to create a partnership for democratic freedom in our country.

I called for all the pro-democracy movements and their allies to campaign actively for the early repeal of Decree 89 as it was incompatible with democracy and trampled on the basic rights of Gambians. Decrees such as Newspaper Decrees No 70[40] and 71[41] also had to be got rid of. Every effort, I said, should be made to ensure that presidential and parliamentary elections when held were closely monitored by international observers and representatives of the opposition parties.

Diane Abbott and Jeremy Corbyn[42], Femi Peters, Hamat Bah and Omar Jallow underscored the call for action not only from Gambians but also from friends of The Gambia. I congratulated MacDonnell and his parliamentary colleagues on the interest they had shown in trying to restore the democratic process in The Gambia to what it was before the 1994 coup.

We all left that meeting hoping that 2001 would be crucial if, as we expected, there would be presidential and parliamentary elections. Therefore, no effort should be spared to salvage the country and, towards that end, the repeal of Decree 89 was crucial to free and popular expression.

Former politicians and civil servants were still barred from contesting in elections. John McDonnell followed up with submissions to the British Minister for Africa, Baroness Valerie Amos, and to the House of Commons, clearly pointing out that that and several other inconsistencies constituted the lack of a level playing field in the run-up to the 2001 elections.

On 16 June 2000, we celebrated the wedding of Housainou Camara, Chilel's nephew and my niece, Fatou Jawara, at 15 Birchen Lane.

On 28 June 2000, Nema arrived with her children – Hannah, Abigail, Sterling and Michaela. They had come from Arizona in the USA to spend their holidays with us. It was good to have some cheer through the restful month they spent with us.

In February 2001 Gregory Larkin, an African-American, arrived in Haywards Heath, West Sussex. On an earlier visit of his he had come with a proposal to write my biography. We had started the process with draft agreements and a couple of interviews. On 18 February 2001 he married my daughter Mariam according to Muslim and local Gambian rites and tradition. He had converted to Islam and took the name Mohammad-ul-Mustapha. Momodou N Bobb deputised for Gregory to ask for the hand

---

[40] Decree 70 required any new privately-owned newspapers to pay a registration fee of D100,000
[41] Decree 71 was an extension of Decree 70 and required all privately-owned newspapers to pay a registration bond of D100,000 and also provide property as collateral or face closure.
[42] Britsh Labour Party MP for Islington North

of my daughter while Alhaji Tayib Cham officiated. At the ceremony, I deferred my right to give away the bride to Hamadi Ibrahim Njie, an uncle of Mariam's, an honour which the gentleman carried out with Momodou Ndow Njie, Mustapha Ngum, Ebrima and Ebrima Charles Jarra as witnesses.

My eyes were causing me some discomfort so I went in for an eye test at Bateman's on South Road. My personal GP, Dr William Fulford, sent me to see a surgeon at the Princess Royal Hospital. In February 2001, my appointment came through to see Mr McLeod, an eye specialist. I had been waiting a whole year in the queue under the National Health Service before I was called in for the first operation in the right eye. Although the waiting was long, the fact that my name was on the list assured me that something would get done to help me with my sight that was worsening each day. I regained a great deal of corrected sight and when months later he finished off the job on the left eye, I was even more thrilled with the sharpness of the primary colours that I had missed for so long.

While I was enjoying the euphoria of a successful eye operation one shock announcement ripped through my stomach and left me helpless with perplexity. That came on 12 March 2001 when, while examining me after an attack of flu, Dr Lambert who was on duty at the Newton's Surgery discovered that I was also suffering from diabetes, Type 2. I just sat and stared blankly with the test results in my hand. Dr Lambert there and then prescribed tablets that I was to take several times daily. He said even though diabetes was not yet curable, it could be controlled to some extent. After a couple of months, Dr Fulford advised that I stop taking the tablets and instead try to control the disease on a strict diet regime and regular exercise. I had to immediately adopt a new lifestyle that entailed dieting and an increased frequency at the Fit for Life gym. I did not know how I would succeed being 'fit for life' when my food intake and my feeding times had become so drastically regulated. I watched many of my favourite items disappear from my shopping list and dinner menu. I withdrew a little more from the routine of politics and concentrated on the challenge posed by this devastating disease. I responded to a circular invitation from the Haywards Heath branch of Diabetes UK and I attended an introductory meeting. It was an encouraging session with senior citizens and a few younger people all sharing experiences and encouraging each other.

When I resigned myself to the diet regime, the disease became less of a worry for me, especially when in retrospect there had been occurrences of diabetes in some relatives of mine. One of the most difficult things for me was that I had to stop taking sugar in food and drinks. I discovered fortunately that this aspect of it could be mitigated by the use of sweeteners in powder, tablet or even liquid form. I immediately got on brand name sugar substitutes that soon featured prominently on my kitchen table – *Canderel, Splenda, Sweet'n'low, Equal* and others. These made the management of my diabetes much easier.

I went back over the Commonwealth Secretariat news release after the 15 CMAG meeting on the Harare Declaration held from 19 to 20 March 2001, at Marlborough House, London. I refreshed my memory on its concluding statements requesting the Commonwealth Secretary General to remain engaged with the government of The Gambia and to provide appropriate assistance to widen the process of democratisation in the country. The action group decided also that The Gambia should remain on its agenda subject to the imminent repeal of the Schedule to Decree 89 and the creation of an environment in which all political parties and individuals could freely take part.

I also paid keen attention to the concluding statements on Sierra Leone. That country had seen the horror of fratricide and war with a people left to pick up the pieces aided at great financial and human cost by the UN and international and regional organisations, to strengthen the country's capacity, to enforce peace and to advance the momentum in its reconstruction and rehabilitation drive.

On the ground at home, PPP militants had long set to work quietly waiting for an announcement of a date for the elections. By all indications, President Jammeh was preparing to run for a second term. The Independent Electoral Commission (IEC), now graduated from its former provisional status, seemed ready for an announcement. We too had been at work. The build-up in Banjul kept the country as a forefront issue on the agenda of both John McDonnell in the House of Commons and of CMAG.

On 22 July 2001, during the celebration of the seventh anniversary of the coup, President Jammeh announced the lifting of Decree 89, at last opening the way for the participation of political parties and certain personalities. It was, as it were, a breath of fresh air in the democratisation of the political space for everyone in The Gambia, but there was a lot of work to do.

The mantle of interim party leader and spokesman had fallen on Omar Jallow. After much ordeal in being and keeping faith with the PPP, Omar Jallow would proudly recall when the former AFPRC Vice Chairman, Sanna Saballly, ripped my portrait off the wall of his home when he went to arrest him. It was a small act but a loud statement of resistance to threat and intimidation. Omar Jallow put the photograph back up as soon as he was released from detention. On four or five more occasions when he had come to arrest him, Capt Sabally would remove the portrait and every time after his release, Omar Jallow would put it back up. Today in much calmer times the same portrait hangs in his living room over the archway leading to his dining room at his home – a defiant symbol now of the freedom of expression.

In retrospect, Omar Jallow joined the PPP in 1968 and had shown a presence that made the party choose him in 1969 to lead a delegation of PPP youths on an exchange visit with youths of the PS party in Senegal. Three years later, in 1972, he stood for election and although he lost, the experience braced him for a comeback and a life in politics. He won his bid in 1977 and I appointed him parliamentary secretary. At the time of the 1994 coup, he was minister of agriculture, well after he had launched the Ministry of Water Resources that first brought him to the cabinet in 1982. He was a popular figure in his Serekunda East constituency and, with the advantage of his location in the Greater Banjul Area, was of great advantage in keeping our party alive in the hearts of the people there, even under the ban. This high level of tenacity and open espousal of the party was bound to contribute greatly to the reorganisation of the party and to his choice initially as a convenor of the re-born party and thereafter, on my recommendation, as deputy leader.

Meanwhile, the now un-banned political parties were working diligently on a *modus operandi* of a united front of opposition parties. They would select by consensus from their ranks a leader who would be the standard-bearer in the 2001 presidential election.

I revisited my diary where I jotted down some important thoughts which went through my mind on Thursday 26 July 2001 during my phone conversation with Landing Jallow Sonko. I congratulated him and the others who, after much brainstorming, had arrived at the idea of reviving the PPP. I advised that the party rise up again on the basic principles of MULTI-PARTY DEMOCRACY, respect for HUMAN RIGHTS and the RULE OF LAW. I wrote these words in capital letters. I do so here as well to highlight their importance.

I recommended the immediate take-off with basic groundwork for the re-establishment of the party. They were to work on a revised and updated party constitution and they were to elect a bureau and an executive committee immediately. I urged Landing to see to it that the branches got immediate attention. I reminded him of the wisdom of the Mandinka saying: *Samata kotoo juluding kesiyaa ti je*. I told Landing that the PPP had championed the democratic process and been through enough elections in the past that the 2001 elections shouldn't be more difficult than lacing an old shoe.

The reorganisation of the PPP and its participation in the coalition of opposition political parties was a big step towards the restoration of democracy and the rule of law. The National Executive Committee of the PPP met on Thursday 26 July 2001 and elected me to lead the party once again as secretary general and elected Omar Jallow as interim leader.

Unity was the watchword. A united front was our best bet. These social preparations were indicative of our will as PPP to join forces with well-meaning opposition parties to fulfil the democratisation of The Gambia. I prayed with Landing during that very important phone call that our coalition would win both the 2001 presidential and 2002 parliamentary elections. I was certain that if the coalition played its part well, democracy would be re-established. Of course, the success of this demanding programme would, to a large extent, lie in the coalition's ability to raise funds and more importantly remain united.

On Monday 13 August 2001, the opposition political parties met under the chairmanship of Assan Musa Camara and issued a press release reporting on the Inter-Party meeting of the PPP, UDP, GPP, NCP and the PDP held in the conference hall of the YMCA in Kanifing. I received a copy of the release a day after the meeting. It was unanimously agreed that a coalition of the political parties be formed to contest the forthcoming presidential and parliamentary elections. The majority of the parties at the meeting further agreed that Ousainou Darboe of the UDP should be the presidential candidate of the coalition. But that decision rubbed uncomfortably on the PDP leader, Dr Lamin Bojang, who said he could not make the commitment. The NCP representatives declared that they preferred Sheriff Mustapha Dibba as the presidential candidate. When that idea was not endorsed by the majority of those present and voting, the NCP opted out of the coalition. The PPP, GPP and UDP then went ahead and formed a working committee to look into the modalities of what remained of the coalition and to plan a way forward.

When campaigning started, the coalition was narrowed down to only three parties – the UDP, PPP and GPP. The others, the NCP and the GDP, opted out, thereby cutting down the potential votes of the coalition. I was not happy with the fact that old scores got in the way and fractured what could have been a formidable platform. Anyway, there was a coalition and a standard-bearer and the stage was set for the elections.

CMAG welcomed the repeal of Decree 89 but noted the need to take further measures to create the environment in which all political parties and individuals could freely take part in the political process. Nonetheless it concluded that The Gambia be removed from its remit from the time that the repeal of Decree 89 came into force. It also requested the secretary general to continue to monitor the situation and to provide technical assistance to strengthen the democratic process and institutions in the country.

I was received by Diane Abbott at the House of Commons and shared with her updates on the follow-up actions in Banjul, taken by the leaders of the Gambian opposition groups who visited London in February 2001. I was glad she was on our side and acting as a willing and conscientious conduit of our troubles to the British political establishment.

Baroness Amos, the Parliamentary Under-Secretary of State for Foreign and Commonwealth Affairs, highlighted the support the British High Commission in Banjul had been giving to the IEC throughout the pre-election period and said that the Department for International Development had also been working with the IEC on various projects including voter registration. The Commonwealth also provided the IEC with advisers.

John wrote to Baroness Amos expressing concerns with portions of the 1997 Constitution that unfairly barred some former civil servants from contesting. Section 62 subsection (3) (a) states: "A person who, while holding public office in The Gambia has been compulsorily retired, terminated or dismissed from such office shall not be qualified for election as President." And Section 62 subsection (3) (c) states: "A person who, while holding public office in The Gambia has been found liable for misconduct, negligence, corruption or improper behaviour by any commission or committee of inquiry established by law shall not be qualified for election as President."

John reminded Baroness Amos that on 29 March 1995 the military regime promulgated Decree 30 with retrospective effect from 22 July 1994, the day of the coup. Section 5 of that Decree therefore dismissed forthwith all those who then held office as President, Vice President, Minister, Parliamentary Secretary etc. That effectively banned all members of the pre-coup government from contesting the forthcoming elections irrespective of whether they had been found guilty of any of the categories of offences laid down. In addition, John argued that scores of professional civil servants who had similarly been arbitrarily dismissed in the wake of the coup were therefore banned under Section 62. Section 90 also disqualified from membership of the National Assembly any person found by the report of a commission of inquiry to be incompetent to hold public office. The constitution contained further similar political restrictions. Therefore, a combination of the constitution and military decrees undermined the potential for free and fair elections.

In an early day motion in the House of Commons, John McDonnell made a presentation to the House on good governance in The Gambia, in which he urged strong condemnation of the continuing human rights and civil rights abuses in the country as reported by the US State Department and Amnesty International.

We had been apprised of his intention to address the House on those themes in a package he sent inviting me to a meeting at the House of Commons on Tuesday 11 September 2001. The meeting was scheduled for 4.30 pm. The meeting never took place because right about that same time television screens were relaying the shocking horror unfolding in the skyline of New York City. Two aeroplanes had just flown, one after the other, into the Twin Towers of the World Trade Center (WTC). We heard that two other passenger jets had also crashed, one into an open field in the Pennsylvania countryside and the other into a wing of the Pentagon, the headquarters of the United States national defence establishment.

The sight of the billowing smoke and the crumbling buildings of the WTC were unreal. It took some time for me to fully comprehend what I was watching. It was a terrible sight. It horrified me that human beings could be so heartless as to fly planes full of people into public buildings to make a political point.

The events that we all now know as 9/11 would overshadow every speech, every debate and every strategy in international relations. The world immediately took on the containment of terrorism as one of its most important preoccupations.

During the normal proceedings in the House of Commons following the attacks on the World Trade Center, John informed the House that the UN Security Council had placed a travel ban under Resolution 1343 on one of the senior members of the APRC government, the Majority Leader, Baba Jobe, for his alleged involvement in arms and diamond smuggling in the war-afflicted countries of Liberia and Sierra Leone. He also commended and encouraged the opposition parties in The Gambia for their brave and determined effort to form a democratic alliance and try to bring about change in the country.

On 18 October 2001, Gambians went to the polls to elect a president. The elections were observed by representatives of many governmental and international agencies including the EU and the Commonwealth Parliamentary Association (CPA). At the end of the voting, the Chairman of the IEC, being the chief returning officer, announced the results. The incumbent, President Yahya Jammeh, was elected president for a second time. The election observers declared the elections free and fair, and Ousainou Darboe, leader of the opposition coalition, called and congratulated President Jammeh on his victory.

32

Reconciliation and homecoming

On Thursday 29 August 2001, my niece Mina Alami-Njie arrived at 15 Birchen Lane in the company of two of her elder sisters, Mariam and Fatma. It was certainly a happy family reunion and, naturally, I was eager to know why the sisters had come to see me and why one of them had to fly over five thousands miles to do so.

Mariam opened the conversation and said the visitor from Banjul had something to say. Mina explained that she had come to London with a message from President Jammeh. The president had asked her to consult with Mariam and Fatma to see if they could convince me to come home. She said the main point President Jammeh wanted to emphasise in the message was that he did not think it proper or of any advantage to the image of The Gambia that I should continue to live in exile. The president was therefore asking me to consider returning home as an elder statesman, in dignified retirement befitting a former head of state.

I was sincerely touched. But how could such a simple message be so loaded with implications? I had to try to adjust myself to it. I was not saying as much under the circumstances that I was *au fait* with hints of the president's desire for reconciliation. I could see my nieces were clearly overwhelmed by the gesture. They seemed rather disappointed in my initial reaction that I was not rushing for my travelling bag and passport.

I understood their excitement but they were not seeing the red light blinking in the political darkness and which needed more robust thinking for an answer. In their enthusiasm, I thought they did appreciate the complexity of the situation. I can't recall every detail Mina gave in explaining the initiation of the contacts with government but, to cut a long story short, she and Deputy Director General of the National Intelligence Agency (NIA), Abdoulie Kujabi, got into a conversation about me ending my exile and returning home. Soon after that conversation, Kujabi called Mina inviting her to a meeting with the president at Kanilai. President Jammeh told Mina that he had been thinking about the matter for some time and would be pleased if Mina, Mariam and Fatma were able to convince me to return home. At the end of the conversation, the president asked Mina to travel immediately to Haywards Heath and that while she was there a phone call from State House would confirm all of it.

Early in the morning of 31 August 2001, the phone rang. I answered and it was Abdoulie Kujabi at the other end of the line. He greeted me in elaborate style in Mandinka, full of jovial respect and witticism. I immediately pressed the broadcast button on the telephone set so that everyone in the room could follow the discussion. When he finished the copious pleasantries, Kujabi asked me to stay on the line – President Jammeh wanted to speak with me. The president was obviously in high spirits and broke immediately into a casual conversation asking after my health and family and paying all the customary courtesies. He said I was his father and continued to refer to me in those endearing terms for the rest of the conversation.

There was a writing pad on the telephone table and I instinctively began scribbling notes from what he was saying. I wish it were possible to get everything down exactly as he put them but the president took his time chit-chatting at times and philosophising at other times. In the end, he stated the essential reason for his call, which was to make a formal request for me to end my exile and come home to my people. He told me the government was ready to give me back all my properties, which, he said, would have long been sold off had he not considered that they belonged to his father, a man who had worked for many years for his country. He assured me that the properties were still there in spite of the number of people who had offered to buy them. Because he had protected the properties, he said, many people had thought that he and I were regularly in touch since I left Banjul, which, of course, had not been the case. He said he always told them the truth - that it was simply a matter of consideration for an elder statesman such as me, who, he said, ought to be treated properly and differently.

As he spoke and I scribbled, I was observing my nieces' reactions, especially when he repeated that he had nothing against me or anyone else in my family. He reminded me that my nephew, Kaba Jawara, was working in the government without hindrance after the coup and that he had once asked Mariam why she had left the country without telling him. Mariam, he said, had answered that she was scared and he had asked her: "Scared of what?" At the point of such a delicate disclosure, I saw quite a range of emotions on the girls' faces. The president said that he had spoken with my son Dawda before he left the country and had told him clearly that he held nothing against me.

He said he was asking for a cordial way out of this unfortunate situation in which his own father was living in exile because he knew what

I personally stood for. That was why he had seized the opportunity when the matter came up to consult with Mina and to send her to England to see me. In consideration of my enormous contribution to my country and the fact that the country did not belong to him or anyone else, he said he would advise that I take his offer. He asked that I should forget the past; what had happened had happened and he concluded by saying that Allah was a witness to the truth that he was speaking from the bottom of his heart. He said he had made it clear to Mina that all he wanted was a clear conscience concerning my affairs.

I did not throw caution to the wind. I reminded the president that there had been hints that a government delegation was about to see me on this matter. But he said that he had long shelved that idea of formality and had decided not to talk to anyone outside the family about my affairs. He would rather thrash matters out between the two of us as was happening on the phone at that very moment.

When we returned to the main subject of his phone call, the president referred to our ethnic connections pointing to the fact, which I confirmed, that my maternal grandmother Sona Sambou was a Jola from Karoni. He recalled that as a young man he was in the crowd which gathered when I came to Kanilai during an election campaign and that I had given a gift of a handsome walking stick to his uncle, Jejew, the renowned bone healer.

We were nearly an hour and a half into the conversation when the president asked to make certain expectations of his clear. He said reconciliation between us did not mean that I was compelled to make any statements in support of him or his party. He was not asking for my support – just that I return as an elder statesman.

It was quite a telling silence when he stopped talking. And even though we were miles apart on either end of a telephone line, the moment left its charged impression.

Before the drama of the silence ended, President Jammeh assured me that he would make an announcement any time before the 18th about my return home. He asked me to send someone I trusted to come and take an inventory of my properties before making a formal announcement.

I interpreted the 18 to mean 18 September 2001, barely a month away. After a brief pause, I told him that I observed he was now an accomplished diplomat. President Jammeh broke into a hearty laugh and we carried on a short flurry of quite friendly exchanges. He then mentioned that Mariam had once asked him if it would be possible for his government to provide a pension for me once I came home. He informed me that he told Mariam that a pension would be my entitlement, and that it should not be a problem.

Indeed, the government tabled the issue before the National Assembly that passed the bill in June 2006 establishing the Office of Former Presidents (See Appendix 2).

Anyway, President Jammeh drew the conversation to a close with jovial small talk that we continued to exchange. We laughed together and we were bidding each other goodbye when he asked me to hold the line. During the brief wait, I could see the mist lift off the faces of my nieces. There were dramatic changes in their looks, even in the way they sat. The phone rang again and Kujabi came back on. He opened with a barrage of clichés and aphorisms in Mandinka. There was excitement in his voice and he was unreservedly assertive: *"A fa ye i bi na i dingho le kang; ite le ya wuluu,"* he said. *"A song ta, a mang song, ite le ya wuluu. Meng mang song wo la – a kungho kang!"* His words were to reassure me that I was coming home to my own son; whether anybody liked it or not he was my son. Anyone else who is unhappy about that relationship would just have to live with it!

Kujabi said that at last he would sleep well when he went to bed. He said he considered his role in the matter typical of the old saying that it was always one person that had to do the spade work for the many to benefit just as is to be found in the wisdom of the words of the old people: *Ning moo ye silo teh, a dammaa te taama no la kang!* A man might struggle and sweat alone in clearing a road through the bush but it was certain that he will not be the only one to use it! Kujabi said the president was undertaking an important step alone and was doing so with a good heart and spirit. He advised that all I had to do was to accept, and everything would be resolved. He said that hundreds, if not thousands of people were waiting to benefit from this historic reconciliation between a father and his own son. Kujabi repeated the promise to make a public statement of the president's intentions and I asked that he send me a copy of the statement before it was broadcast. He promised that he would do so.

President Jammeh came on again and we briefly recapped in the process of his saying a final goodbye. He mentioned that I would be free to do whatever I wanted when I came back. I assured him that I would think over the matter and consult my family and friends. He closed in English, expressing again the deep sense in him of a son wanting his father to come back home.

I replaced the receiver. All eyes were on me. Mariam broke the silence. She said I must accept the offer. Naturally, the girls were paying attention to superficial issues and perhaps misunderstanding the concept of political neutrality the president and I had just agreed on.

It was 2 am, so I asked my nieces to go to bed and get some well-deserved sleep. I spent the coming days thinking deeply over those dramatic two hours on the phone with President Jammeh. Mariam and Fatma could not see why I had to think long on this matter. I explained to them that the issue was a complex one, and every detail had to be thought out properly. Mina went back to Banjul, her message delivered successfully. In the weeks following, Mariam and Fatma waited for news back in London.

Incidentally, there had been individuals who tried to mediate on the subject of my homecoming. For example, Jaipaul Thakur, a Gambian legal practitioner had on his own initiative made a trip to The Gambia and had gone as far as speaking with people, including the Roman Catholic Bishop of Banjul, the Rt Rev Michael Cleary, and other dignitaries in search of ways to meet President Jammeh to discuss possible reconciliation between us.

The next day, 1 September 2001, I discussed the offer from President Jammeh with my sons Dawda, Kawsu, Foday and Ebrima. In the discussions they pointed out that I had spent over seven years and almost all of the meagre resources I had trying to restore democracy and the rule of law in The Gambia without breaking the law and through peaceful means[43]. I was also not getting any younger at 77. They pointed out that the APRC regime was each day gaining more recognition and respectability in the international scene. They advised that I should accept the offer, but to wait until after the elections were held and things had quietened down before returning home.

Some time passed and nothing happened. It was not clear to me why there was a lull since Kujabi and the president phoned me. I had still not received the promised draft I asked for of any statement the president intended to make so that we would all be on the same wavelength, as it were, on the matter. However, it also struck me that there had not been an inauguration ceremony for the president since his election in October. I assumed the two things were connected. I was right. President Jammeh finally took the oath of office on Friday 21 December 2001 and, in his inaugural address, announced he had granted me unconditional amnesty.

In a phone call I had with Omar Jallow I pointed out to him that I thought the word *amnesty* was rather inappropriate. He and I analysed the mood of the moment and he advised strongly that we ignore technicalities and semantics and concentrate on the spirit of the language rather than the text. He urged me to accept the offer. He had heard reactions already from some quarters urging me not to accept but he advised that I should

---

[43] I had dismissed offers from soldiers of fortune who claimed they could return me to power.

never be swayed by those opinions. He said my peace of mind and my homecoming from a long exile were more important.

As the days went by, I seriously thought of unplugging my telephone. It had never rung like that for many months since the heat of the affidavits for asylum had died down. The calls were the usual opinions from self-appointed gurus, doomsayers or simply callers with some good intentions or prayer. Others feared for my personal safety; yet others averred that my return would mean an endorsement of the regime.

I would discuss cautiously with some callers but many among them were simply sniffing for gossip. Nonetheless, I was learning a great deal in the process how to use the spectrum of views to focus on taking advantage of the offer while minimising all the possible risks. Omar Jallow was one of the more trustworthy contacts I still had on the ground in Banjul. I found no reason to doubt his reading of the situation.

The festive season passed quietly and the New Year 2002 opened for me with a medical appointment on 2 January at the Queen Victoria Hospital in East Grinstead. I needed to secure a booking for a pre-assessment operation which was set for 16 January. The flurry of e-mail and telephone contacts continued on the issue of reconciliation. The word had gone round, and former army officers, ex-civil servants, highly placed people in the government and exiles in the UK called or sent e-mails.

I also called Alhaji Sir Alieu Sulayman Jack. I briefed him on the situation and we talked about the announcement in the inaugural address. He offered his candid views and at the end of our conversation he left me with one rather magisterial instruction: "Do not forget your aides". From the things he said he obviously sounded as one with whom some of my chief aides had been in touch. All the reservations I heard were those I knew were from inside my team in London who were jittery over my possible predisposition to accept President Jammeh's offer and return home. I noted however there was one major thread of misunderstanding running through most observations and opinions I had obtained both within and outside the UK. It was the fear most of my aides had as did a few others that the British government might rescind their asylum status and take away their benefits as soon I was reconciled with the government and went back home.

I cleared that grave misreading of the asylum regulations when I quickly invited my aides to Birchen Lane on 14 January 2002 for deliberations on the subject of my return to The Gambia. Sara Janha came; so did Phoday Jarjussey, Momodou Lamin Kassama, Modou Njie, Alpha Jallow, Sarjo Jammeh, Momodou Ndow Njie, Momodou Bobb, Tijan Touray and a few others. I was frank on the issue and listened to the reservations or endorsements they had to offer. They were anxious to know how the contacts with President Jammeh had come about. I gave them details of Mina's visit. They asked what my response was to the offer. I told them I would request the government of The Gambia for the extension of the same privileges to everyone who wanted to return, which was all I could do.

They listened but with each playing the usual cards very close to their chest. Some pleaded with me not to leave unless I was able to negotiate the return of all their properties to them. Others suggested that my return must be guaranteed in writing by President Jammeh. Frankly, some of the conditions they put forward I simply did not consider feasible. The shift of emphasis from the goodwill and informality of the family level negotiations between President Jammeh and me could easily hamper the reconciliation process by bringing in formality and third parties.

It was clear to me that some of my aides were not readily grasping that the discussion between the UK government and me was also working around recommendations I forwarded that, by extension, anyone who asked to come with me would be covered by the same privileges that would be granted me and members of my immediate family. Letters between McDonnell and Baroness Amos in February and May 2002 finally confirmed that my refugee status in the UK would not be jeopardised in the medium term by my return to The Gambia. The baroness pointed out that any return, though voluntary, would be, to some extent, an exercise to test the water and in those circumstances re-assessment of my refugee status would not be made until two years after my return. Within that time, I would retain indefinite leave to remain in the UK. That, by any stretch of the imagination, was mightily generous already considering that, ordinarily, a refugee who went back to their own country for any reason automatically lost their refugee status. These privileges were extended to all my aides but, in the end, only three of them took the offer and submitted their names to travel with me.

On 16 January 2002, I caught the seven o'clock train out of Haywards Heath to East Grinstead and went to the Queen Victoria Hospital where I had an operation for cataract in my right eye. It was a successful one. The job on my cataract complaints would be finally completed later in July after the operation on the left eye. Then I gave thanks to medical science that I received my full sight again. Over the next couple of weeks, I refrained from reading and, miraculously, very soon, I began enjoying my full and brilliant view of colours again.

The news of the reconciliation spread fast and aroused interest at the level of the OAU and among Gambians in the Diaspora. On 19 February, I honoured an invitation from the Ghanaian High Commissioner to the UK, Isaac Osei, to visit him in his office. Osei, a fellow *Akora*[44], discussed with me the details of my proposed return. Chilel, Alex da Costa and I met Osei and his deputy and we went over the major details of the offer from Banjul. I briefed him on how to keep the international focus on the issue in light of its importance. I apologised again that I had been away in Tenerife during President John Kufuor's visit to London in December. President Kufuor met my son Dawda.[45]

Kufuor had wanted to meet me for a discussion over the developments. Osei promised to relay my greetings to Accra and to let Kufuor know of my deep appreciation of his kind gesture of calling me on the phone while I was in Tenerife and asking that I keep him updated. Osei briefed us further that President Kufuor was in touch with regional leaders who were keenly following the situation. They wished to see me return safely.

Meanwhile, arrangements were on course for Dawda and Kawsu to visit The Gambia and take an inventory of the properties as President Jammeh had promised. They left on 8 January 2002, and I called Omar Jallow to let him know my two sons were on their way to Banjul.

On 11 January 2002, Kawsu and Dawda were invited to meet the president at Kanilai. He reassured them that the properties were safe and that arrangements would be made for them to be inspected. They found my farm at Banjulinding run down and much of the equipment if not stolen in a poor state of repair. My son Ebrima today manages the farm after extensive repairs were carried out on it. Dawda, a civil engineer, observed that the property at Brikama was structurally unsound and recommended its demolition.[46] 34 Wellington Street was also in a poor state of repair. The Gambia Navy would vacate 7 Louvel Street, leaving it in pretty good shape. My residence on 40 Atlantic Boulevard was also in good shape, but needed some repairs. Renovations on 40 Atlantic by Gamsen took several weeks to complete, which delayed my return home. President Jammeh had insisted that the house be renovated before my homecoming.

Even though President Jammeh had instructed that *all* my properties be returned to me, 66 Dobson Street and three other smaller undeveloped properties of mine that were sold by AMRC were never returned.

---

[44] Term used to describe ex-pupils of Achimota College.

[45] Kufuor told Dawda something like: "Tell your father there is only one president in The Gambia and that is Jammeh. He should remember not to steal the sunshine from him".

[46] It was demolished in 2006 and replaced by stores.

On 28 March 2002, Chilel and I went out for a dinner. It was our thirty-fourth wedding anniversary and we asked Ndow Njie and his wife, Kumba, to join us. I told them that I would definitely accept the offer to return home and that I had made that known to Abdoulie Kujabi and Amadou Samba in an earlier telephone conversation. Subsequently Kujabi and Samba came to Birchen Lane in April. The three of us looked more closely at the details of the reconciliation offer. Kujabi further stressed President Jammeh's desire to see me return and settle down as soon as possible while Amadou suggested the travel plans.

I asked that the Gambia government consider extending reconciliation to each exile and for each to retrieve any properties that had been seized and to unfreeze their bank accounts.

Kujabi and Samba returned to 15 Birchen Lane on 31 May 2001. They accompanied me back to The Gambia on Red Air.[47] On board were Chilel, Baby Njaimeh and her husband Richard, Kawsu, Nacesay, Mariam Alami, Fatma Alami, Tijan Touray, Tayib Cham and a few others. Incidentally, Tayib Cham was not a refugee and officially not one of the returnees.

There were a lot of empty seats on the flight that any Gambian who wished to return could have taken. It was an uneventful flight. There was more snoring and dozing through the night flight than anything else. It was also the maiden return journey for Red Air. The airline had recently been set up and granted landing rights in the UK. After a six-hour flight we landed at Banjul International Airport. A great deal went through my mind as we touched down at 4.20 am. A new terminal building shone in the darkness. It looked quite impressive.

A convoy of cars were waiting and we drove straight to 40 Atlantic Boulevard in Fajara. I learnt later that some members of my family and friends had gathered at the VIP lounge waiting for us. They must have been disappointed to miss us.

On Monday 24 June 2002, at 2.30 pm, I walked up the steps to my former office after nearly eight years away. President Jammeh was in a white gown and neck scarf and hat. I immediately sensed a genuine welcome in our embrace before we sat down to a warm and open conversation. He seemed to fit well into his surroundings and to command a presence within it.

Alone in that closed-door meeting we went over the territory we had covered during the telephone conversation and in the end assured each other that we had arrived at perhaps the best thing for the government, for me, for him and, best of all, for the image of the country. President Jammeh

---

[47] Red Air is a Gambian registered airline company, and Amadou Samba was its Chairman.

reiterated that it did not do The Gambia any good for me to continue to live in exile. He said it was important to recognise someone who had worked all his life for his country.

I told the press in a short interview after that historic meeting that the president's gesture and my return should contribute greatly to national reconciliation and harmony.

I returned to the UK on 4 July and went for the yag laser treatment at the Queen Victoria Hospital in East Grinstead. Ophthalmic technology had now gone beyond scalpels and tweezers. With my left eye under treatment I used the right eye to read the calendar that told me I had missed the annual reception of the British Veterinary Association held on 2 July. I enjoyed BVA meetings whenever I could attend them. My recovery was quick and steady.

33

40 Atlantic Boulevard: Retirement

I wrote a letter on 29 August 2001 to Yaya Ceesay, the national president of the PPP. I reminded him that in various statements I had made following the 2001 presidential election, I had announced my decision for personal reasons to retire from active party politics. In light of that decision, the party might wish to elect a secretary general and in order to facilitate that essential process in the evolution of the party, I was tendering my resignation. I wished my successor and the party in general every success in the service of the nation.

Yaya Ceesay replied to me accepting my decision to resign. He also saw my new role as a public figure fostering unity and true national reconciliation. In that way, he concluded, The Gambia would make greater scores on the international scene. I had decided to resign from the leadership of the PPP forty-three years after it was offered me in March 1959. When I was writing forty-three years ago to accept the leadership of the PPP, I was doing so in an official bungalow that I was about to vacate because I had entered politics. When I wrote forty-three years later resigning from the leadership of the PPP, it was in a house that I was about to lose to sharks.

It was of great help to me that my accounts at Standard Chartered Bank in Banjul had been un-frozen. There was not much in the current account but dividends paid out over the years on my Standard Chartered Bank Gambia Ltd shares had accumulated to a tidy sum. That gave me something to live on.

It was with sadness that we received news of the death on 5 September 2002 of Housainou Njie, Chilel's brother. Chilel flew home to Banjul the following day to attend the funeral. The family in London organised a memorial service with recitations from the Holy Qu'ran.

On 12 October 2002, I received more sad news - the passing away of Mamanding Dampha, one of my faithful trio of PPP supporters. I would like to pay tribute here to him and two other party stalwarts Sambunanding Touray and Kunta Mamburay, men I was able to depend on for loyalty. I gave them the nickname *Active*! Sambunanding sadly passed away on 8 September 2007 and I joined mourners in Banjul at his funeral. Old friends gathered there and recalled with fondness the man's dedication to the PPP. Mamanding, Sambunanding and Kunta had no formal schooling but they were men of experience and enthusiasm, who put their wisdom to the service of the PPP.

On 2 February 2003, I went on the pilgrimage to Mecca on the invitation of an Islamic organisation, the World Assembly of Muslim Youth (WAMY). Considering how tough the pilgrimage could be for a person of my age, they gave me all the assistance I needed.

I read of the passing away on 19 April 2003 of Edward Frank Brewer, a man who worked with dedication at Abuko. I was a veterinary officer when Eddie arrived in 1957 to work in forestry. I got to know his wife, Lillian, and their daughters, Lorna, Stella and Heather. Brewer built the Abuko Nature Reserve and developed it into a major wildlife sanctuary before he retired in 1992. He helped with the formation of our laws on conservation and, more importantly, changed our attitudes towards the protection of flora and fauna and the enhancement of our environment.

Sir John Paul, the governor who always emphasised the importance of making haste slowly, died on 31 March 2004. His wife, Lady Audrey, sent me a handwritten note on her bereavement and gave me news of their children, Dilly, Louise and Harriet. It was touching when Lady Audrey wrote that time had finally caught up with them. She asked that we should try to get together again soon. I cast my mind back to the 1960s and thought of the energy and courageous presence with which Lady Audrey supported the work of Sir John in Bathurst.

At 40 Atlantic Boulevard, I never cease to wonder as I look out over its terraces back to the time when, like any ordinary customer of the bank, I applied to the GCDB for a loan to build it. A young man named Bakary B Dabo was the bank's loans officer. I accepted plans made by a Jamaican architect, Vincent Saunders, and contracted the building of it to a local firm - Papa Njie & Sons. They put their creative talents together and produced this beautiful Caribbean-style villa to which I have retired.

I was still in England in May 2004 when I turned eighty. I celebrated but, with the strictest diet. Since I had been diagnosed I had never thrown caution to the wind. Diabetes, they say, is a disease of lifestyle and I think I could safely say that I have got the hang of it, as the Americans would say. My family threw a luncheon party on my behalf.

I began putting together my domestic staff at 40 Atlantic Boulevard. I appointed Santigie Bangura, a former employee of Sailor's Restaurant, as my cook. Some State House domestic staff (retired and current) came to visit me. I engaged a few of them at 40 Atlantic Boulevard. I retained Hoja

Sanneh, a former nanny as assistant cook and appointed Kebba Camara, a retired chief driver as one of my drivers and Therese Senghore, a former lady-in-waiting and nanny as my protocol officer.

Kebba Camara gave his very best until he passed away in 2005. He simply wanted the pleasure of working for me again and I am so glad that I granted him his wish. He drove a second-hand Mercedes Benz that I bought in 2004.

When Red Coat Express called to inform me that my personal effects had arrived in Banjul, I felt I had at last completed my return home to The Gambia, ten years to the day since I left on board the US Navy warship, the *USS La Moure County*.

On 1 July 2004 we celebrated the wedding of Ebrima to Yagou Cham. She is the daughter of Sainey Cham who was once managing director of the GUC. They have two beautiful daughters, Njaimeh and Marie.

Out in the garden I had noticed a stray kitten struggling on her feet. It must have been only a few days old and looked as if it could do with some milk and a home. I had her cleaned up and spayed; and named her *Frisky Mark II*. At last I had found the time again to keep house pets.

We kept a dog named Boxer, a beautiful local breed in the early 1960s at No 1 Marina and later at State House. The children adored him but I became concerned when it bit one of the policemen guarding the prime minister's residence. Well before that in 1957, I was the proud owner of the first Frisky. I had given it that name because that was exactly what she was – frisky and being all over the bungalow at Abuko mostly in places where she was not supposed to be. She was great fun though and a lovely playful animal with great black patches on her furry white coat. Other pet dogs came: Haiko a great dane that was a gift from my friend Horst Sommers, Sprite (we had her the year Sprite was first sold in The Gambia) and the last dog was Boxer whom we sadly left behind in 1994. There was also a cockatoo called Kairaba, a gift from the Kiesslings in December 1990. He was also left behind in 1994.

One evening, I left for a walk and did not realise that Frisky had followed me out of the house. I went across the main road and as Frisky was running across to follow me a speeding car hit her. I only heard the screeching breaks and a squelching cry from behind me. As the driver sped off, I went to inspect the bleeding, immobile animal on the side of he road; it was Frisky. I did not know what came over me. I could hardly continue my walk. I had the sad and very bitter task of digging a hole under the trees to bury my pet. I returned to the bungalow and when I told Augusta and the children what had just happened she too was very sad. The children were simply devastated.

I had always thought of keeping a pet cat again. At last I did – after forty-seven years. Frisky Mark II is right at this moment out on the ledge of my study intermittently chasing pigeons she can never catch. She is a spoilt cat, provided with a flea collar, a cushion bed, well-balanced meals and regular visits by a paid veterinarian. She is my good friend and, thank God, the house at Fajara is a long way from the road. I take regular evening walks to the beach and back, but gladly Frisky is too sleepy or too lazy to follow me. Thanks to a now priceless photograph Augusta and I had taken in our garden with the first Frisky, Mark II can always take a look at her namesake from nearly half a century ago.

In June 2005, I responded to an invitation from the National Democratic Institute (NDI)[48], an international organisation based in Washington, to attend a meeting of former African leaders held in Bamako. On 5 June 2005, we assembled in the historic and sun-drenched Malian capital – Bamako. The symposium called the African Statesmen Initiative (ASI) discussed leadership and democratisation efforts across Africa. Ken Wollack, President of the NDI, in his opening address at the launch of the ASI, said the idea was borne out of the simple fact that there existed a significant number of elder statesmen who had contributed to development in their respective countries and could continue to seek solutions to African development challenges. He said it was therefore necessary to bring them together to harness their energy towards addressing daunting political, economic and social challenges.

It was a grand challenge which affirmed that former heads of state could certainly continue to make positive contributions to society. The subjects the symposium covered were varied but pertinent to our existing conditions on the continent – leadership, security, conflict management, health and education, civil society and development. We looked at the relationship with the G8 and the international financial institutions and considered the Millennium Development Goals. It was important in our cause to look at issues such as 'leading after leaving' and 'leadership and partnership in life after office'.

---

[48] The National Democratic Institute (NDI) is a nonprofit, nonpartisan, nongovernmental organization that responds to the worldwide quest for popular civic participation, open and competitive political systems, and representative and accountable government. Since its founding in 1983, NDI and its local partners have worked to establish and strengthen democratic institutions and practices by building political and civic organisations, safeguarding elections, and promoting citizen participation, openness and accountability in government. *(Taken from NDI website)*

During the third part of the sessions on 7 June, I was privileged to share the rostrum with former heads of state Yakubu Gowon of Nigeria and Sam Nujoma of Namibia. The discussion was on the public health challenges to democratic transitions in Africa, with particular reference to malaria, tuberculosis and HIV/AIDS. We were ably supported on the panel by Dr Gail Andrews, Director of Social Aspects of HIV/AIDS at the Research Alliance of South Africa and Dr Awa Coll-Seck, Executive Secretary of the Roll Back Malaria Partnership Secretariat, hosted by the WHO.

In a brief introduction, I touched on the political, social, financial and medical import of the three killer diseases that present challenges to us all in Africa. Approximately six million people die each year with more than 16,000 deaths recorded every day. In sub-Saharan Africa alone, malaria kills one million people every year, that is, 3,000 a day and the bulk of that number are children.

Against that background, I briefly identified the public health challenges that we face in Africa and suggested a few ways in which the ASI could respond to those challenges. There is a need to improve advocacy by a concerted national and international approach. This we should do to translate awareness of interventions into sustained behavioural change. For example, insecticide treated nets have proved very effective against mosquitoes and in the prevention of malaria. However, its acceptance is low and therefore there has to be a behavioural change to bring about the use of bed nets as a matter of course.

At the end of the symposium, we produced the *Bamako Declaration of the African Statesmen Initiative* in which we reinforced our commitment to be lead advocates for presidential leadership and good governance in Africa. The African former heads of state and government participating in the symposium expressed their commitment to continue using their good offices to foster dialogue and the peaceful resolution of the continent's conflicts and to promote human security and democratic models of government. They would continue to play a constructive role in democratisation initiatives across the continent.

The leaders agreed that the symposium had opened new vistas for our continued usefulness. The fact of that statement would soon be seen when invitations began circulating for former African leaders to meet again in 2006, this time under their own aegis to see how the idea of the Africa

Forum (AF)[49] would serve to help Africa's former leaders take the lead based on the issues raised at the ASI symposium. Back home, I pondered on the importance of that initiative I read in a letter sent me by former President Joachim Chissano.

By the end of 2005, people were used to seeing me out on my walks or at the supermarket. People were generally nice and respectful. They would often have the courtesy to cede their places to me at the till.

In January 2006, my niece Mariam Alami came to Fajara to see me in the company of Amadou Samba. The two had brought me greetings from President Jammeh who, according to them, wondered why I had never honoured his invitations to official and public functions. That was a complete surprise to me because I could not remember ever receiving an invitation from State House. I told them that I had never received an invitation from State House and that I would attend and if not I would at least be courteous enough to decline. That information turned out to be a surprise too to the president who said invitations had been prepared for me on every national event since my return home.

Mariam Alami and Amadou Samba returned on a subsequent visit and said the confusion had been located in the protocol office. In February, an official invitation arrived at Fajara. I was being invited to attend the ceremonies to be held at the July 22nd Square to mark the 41st anniversary of our country's independence.

On the morning of 18 February 2006, dressed in traditional attire, I joined thousands of people thronging the July 22nd Square in Banjul for the independence anniversary celebrations. When President Jammeh arrived, he came to shake hands with people sitting on the presidential dais where government officials and special guests were waiting. We shook hands and embraced each other. Then we posed for photographs. It was the one moment everyone was waiting for. Tumultuous cheers rang from the crowds and camera shutters clicked profusely.

The ceremony was grand and colourful, and it was a view to which I had long been accustomed. It was nostalgic to hear the president begin his speech with 'Boys and Girls', the traditional salutation at independence celebration speeches which I enjoyed using to greet the children on such occasions. The march past was splendid.

---

[49] The Africa Forum constitutes an informal network of former African Heads of State and Government and other African leaders designed to support the implementation of the broad objectives of the African Union (AU) and its initiative, the New Partnership for Africa's Development (NEPAD), at national, sub-regional and regional levels. *(Taken from Africa Forum Website).*

In March 2006, Njaimeh had to travel to New York to evacuate her sister, Marie Mboge, who had fallen very ill and wanted to come home.

On 26 March 2006 I attended the graduation ceremony of the Bilal Boarding School at Yundum. It was a wonderful day's treat, with students displaying scholarship with Qu'ranic recitations. The Mayor of Banjul, Samba Faal, graced the occasion as did the secretary general of the Gambia Supreme Islamic Council. The school was doing very well under its founder and principal, Alhaji Essa Jawara.

At the end of the ceremony, the secretary general of the Gambia Supreme Islamic Council, Muhammed Sarr, introduced himself, reminding me that he was the young student at Muslim High School who was asked to recite a verse from the Holy Qu'ran when I attended the school's first speech day in 1974. He was surprised when I reminded him that he had chosen the *surat Fatah*. It is one that has always fascinated me.

On 7 April 2006 I attended the annual gathering of the Barajaly Gamo. On our way home a couple of days later, the vehicle heading the convoy drove into a herd of bush pigs outside Panchang, a village in Upper Saloum. The driver lost control and the vehicle somersaulted. Sadly Jang Korka Jallow and Omar Fadera, two members of the Police Intervention Unit who were sent to augment my security detail for the trip to Barajaly, died on the spot. A few of the passengers sustained injuries. Ismaila Jawara, my nephew who was thrown out of the vehicle sustained the most serious injuries. He was admitted at the Royal Victoria Teaching Hospital and later evacuated to Dakar for further treatment. Mba Jawara, wife of my nephew, Kaba Jawara, also sustained major injuries and was sent to Dakar. It was a deeply distressing moment for me. I had looked forward so much to the *gamo* which I had followed with particular interest every year while I was away in the UK. Thankfully they all recovered from their injuries.

On 25 June 2006, I accepted to chair a workshop ECOWAS was holding in Banjul on the subject *Towards the ECOWAS Framework for Conflict Prevention*. This was a subject very close to my heart.

The ECOWAS Commission had asked Professor Amadu Sesay to interview me on the history and development of ECOWAS, background information that would be useful to him in his research. Sesay was on the staff of Obafemi Awolowo University in Nigeria and I went with him through time, back to 16 December 1978, when the institution, then known as the University of Ife, awarded me the degree of Doctor of Laws *honoris causa*.[50] I remember the Nigerian president, Olusegun Obasanjo, was there

---

[50] In 1986, I received an honorary Doctor of Science Degree from Colorado State University, USA

at that ceremony as was Wole Soyinka, now a renowned Nobel laureate. It was indeed a great honour for me, and reliving those moments with Professor Sesay was quite refreshing,

On 30 June 2006 I attended the gala dinner in honour of heads of state that had come to attend the Seventh Session of the General Assembly of African Union Heads of State and Government meeting in Banjul. I also attended the opening ceremonies on 1 July 2006.

Just before the gala, the skies opened with heavy rain but not heavy enough to stop me attending my first AU gathering, after the many OAU summits that I had attended in my time as head of state. I considered the rain to be showers of blessing and, even with the thunder and terrific lightning which came with it on the day of the closure of the summit on 22nd July, the rain did not dampen the spirit of the meeting in the least. The Gambia had done a splendid job in its organisation.

During the meetings I chatted with some old faces and met many new ones. It was good to chit-chat with Kenyan President Mwai Kibaki. He is a keen golfer and we recalled the rounds we played on some of the immaculate courses around Nairobi when he was foreign minister. I also reminisced with President Robert Mugabe amongst others.

Life is an admixture of the bitter and the sweet. There was a death in the family. Marie Mboge passed away on 23 June at their family home in Sirimang, in the Fatick region of Senegal, where Njaimeh had taken her to convalesce. My brother, Wandifa, my nephew Kaba, Dr Manneh's wife, Joko and Yagou my son Ebrima's wife accompanied Njaimeh to the village for the funeral.

On 13 July 2006, my grandson Dawda graduated in law from the University of Warwick. It was pleasant to see the *kabilo* boasting their third generation member with a university education.

The good news came right after we had come out of two weeks of Wimbledon fever. I followed the world class tennis extravaganza on the radio. England's Tim Henman fell in the second round to Switzerland's Roger Federer who went on to win the men's singles.

Dr Sammy Palmer constantly challenges me to come on the weekly friendly rounds of golf he plays with the retired Bishop Michael Cleary; but I have yet to oblige him. However, for recreation in general, I do wish I still had the means and the physical strength to sail again over the deep blue waters that I see every day through the trees outside my back veranda. The sparkling Atlantic Ocean is always enticing and I must admit that many times I wish I was out there in a 30-footer Camper Nicholson cutting across the waves and enshrined in those golden sunsets.

On 27 July 2006, I received a letter from the former President of Mozambique, Joachim Chissano, inviting me to the third meeting of the general assembly of the Africa Forum to be held in South Africa, in October.

In September 2006, I received a token sum of money from my grandson Dawda. He had taken it out of his first pay, on his first job with a firm of solicitors. He insisted on keeping the tradition of the newly employed giving 'kola nut' money from their first pay packet to the elders around. It is a deeply rooted Gambian custom. I received it and prayed for success and prosperity in his work. It was a sign that the young man was now a breadwinner and he was thanking the elders for everything they had done to help him that far. I remember how a good bit of my first salary I drew at the end of January 1954 was portioned out to elders at Wellington Street, Barajaly and Walikunda.

On 23 October 2006, my brother, Alhaji Saikounding Jawara passed away. We gave him a fitting funeral in Brikama where Imam Sankung Touray in his tribute praised him for his many years of leadership of the family. He reminded the community of how the Jawara family settled and blended in so well. During his periodic visits to Brikama, my father made good friends of the prominent families who had welcomed him in. Speaking through a man who hollered to the audience at Brikama, the Imam traced history in which he said that Brikama had responded to the warmth, love and high regard of the Jawaras.

The Imam said the grave sites of my mother, two of my sisters and many other relatives were there in the town to prove it. The cleric recalled the days when Kombo Central was carved out as a constituency from the larger Kombo constituency, and the people had given me their support by which I won my contest for political office. I had first won elections there in 1960 when there was only the Kombo constituency. It was later broken up into 4 constituencies – Kombo Central, Kombo North, Kombo South and Kombo East.

Imam Sankung Touray was right that Brikama was indeed our home. My father had long established himself in Brikama from regular visits there in his heyday. He built strong bonds with Seyfo Landing Barabally Bojang. Sanjally Bojang, our first PPP party president, hailed from that family. My father made friends with Saikou Dandanba Sanneh, the renowned head of the Sanneh house of the *falifoo*. Imam Lang Touray was among his circle of friends. We grew up knowing them all very well and sharing family matters with them.

My sister Nacesay moved there with her husband Sidi Faal and their children, when they gave up their old shop in Bwiam in Foni Kansala. She had now assumed the full traditional rights and privileges of 'the Mother' of the Jawara *kabilo*. Our sister, Jarai, also came to live there with her husband, Abdoulai Alami, and their children. Unfortunately, she died and was buried there in August after my election in 1962. After my father died in 1961, my mother moved into the bungalow I built there for her.

With the death of Saikounding, I assumed the mantle of head of the Jawara *kabilo* in The Gambia and abroad.

My Personal Assistant Alex Dacosta and I were in Johannesburg from 31 October to 1 November 2006 to attend the third meeting of the general assembly of the Africa Forum. I was ready to share my experience again with my colleagues and to get first-hand updates of developments since Bamako. The secretariat gave a brief rundown of the history of the AF since its inauguration at a meeting the general assembly held in Maputo, Mozambique, on 11 January 2006. These were the rich fruits of discussions on the sidelines of the ASI symposium in Bamako. It was gratifying to note that the NDI was pointing the way for Africa to make use of its retired leaders.

The setting at the Westcliff Hotel was splendid. President Thabo Mbeki delivered an inspiring note of welcome and emphasised our sense of utility and relevance. AF Chairman Joachim Chissano reflected deeply on the socio-economic and political situation of the continent and underscored the rationale of the forum to help build and sustain democratic governance and the rule of law, which are critical to the implementation of the development and integration agenda of the AU and its initiative, the New Partnership for Africa's Development (NEPAD).

Nineteen former heads of state attended with fifteen other leaders, partners and collaborators. We went through tough working sessions looking at the books of the forum according to the rules and regulations and also the operational and strategic issues related to the mandate and objectives of the forum among other important in-house reports.

We appointed six committees to carry out various tasks. I was elected Chairman of the Committee on Post-Conflict Reconstruction and Development. I opted out of the mission with the Committee to the Democratic Republic of Congo (DRC) when they went there on 3 November, to further highlight the AF's focus on events in that country. Alex Dacosta went with them instead.

On 15 December 2006 Yahya A J J Jammeh was sworn in as president at the Independence Stadium in Bakau. I was there with Njaimeh and President Jammeh introduced us to his mother, Aja Asombi Bojang. We posed for photos, which made front page news. For me the occasion was significant in many ways. It was another public manifestation of the pledged harmony and reconciliation between the forty-one-year-old president and the eighty-two-year-old former president.

In December 2006, the National Assembly passed the Former Presidents (Office, Allowances and Other Benefits) Act 2006.[51] When I received news of the Act, I wrote to the government expressing my sincere belief that the passing of the Act demonstrated that The Gambia government was committed to projecting the respect Gambians have always had for their elders. The provision in the Act of security for former presidents, I said, would enable any former holder of such a high office to live in dignity and to be able to continue to contribute their quota to the service of The Gambia in particular and humanity in general.

My staff now comprise a private secretary, protocol officer, 2 gardeners, 2 drivers, and 4 housekeepers.

Over Christmas, groups of singers called to render carols and to share the season's tidings with my family. I must say that I relished every warm gesture of sharing without religious distinction exactly as we knew it in Bathurst in our youthful days. That set off the festive mood in which we welcomed the New Year 2007 which rolled in as well with the usual cultural fanfare across faiths. From my room I could hear the *kankurang*[52] and the hunting society masquerades that went past and occasionally stopped outside the gate for a display. A popular social club, the Group Boka Halaat, had sent me a letter a month or so before that they were going to name their *fanal* (lantern, in the form of a boat) after me. After they had taken the fanal and showcased it around the neighbourhood, they would present it to me in a ceremony called *jaybaleh,* as was the tradition. I had greatly missed the fun of it during my years in exile and looked forward to the *jaybaleh* on 3 January 2007. The fanal was placed in the front of the house for all to see and admire.

I received the group and its leader, my namesake, Dawda Kairaba Samba. I let them know how happy I was to see them continuing such a rich tradition. I enjoined them to keep the culture going and to look for ways of handing it down to the younger generation who today pay attention mainly to things that pose a threat to our customs and traditions. We set the beautiful lantern boat out in the front yard for everyone to see and admire. It was a good ten-footer at least, and exquisite in its colourful paper art decoration.

---

[51] See Appendix III.
[52] A masquerade that is common among the Mandinkas.

That was an invigorating start to the year for me and it became even more so when Dawda, his wife Ndey Mengeh and their daughter Augusta arrived for a holiday on 9 January 2007.

In January a letter of invitation arrived from the President of the ECOWAS Commission Dr Mohamed Ibn Chambas, asking me to lead a team of experts on a fact-finding mission to Nigeria. The Commission wanted the team to evaluate the state of readiness of the Nigerian people and political organs in connection with the 14 and 21 April elections for legislators, state governors and president. I was off again with Alex Dacosta to Abuja on 31 January. We stayed on through to 26 February, when we returned to Banjul and I gave a press conference. I told the press that it was gratifying to see ECOWAS making such strident marks on the political and social landscape of West Africa; and that it was my privilege and honour to be able to continue to serve the organisation.

In Nigeria, I was given a wonderful team to work with. The Hon Elizabeth Alpha-Lavalie, deputy speaker of the Sierra Leone Parliament and General Seth Obeng, former chief of defence staff of the Ghana Armed Forces who were members of the ECOWAS Council of the Wise were on the team. We also had Dr Kwadwo Afari-Gyan, chairman of the Electoral Commission of Ghana, Dr Abdel-Fatau Musah, ECOWAS Conflict Prevention adviser and Francis Gabriel Oke, the programme officer, Electoral Assistance Unit at the ECOWAS Commission.

We spent the period 5-23 February meeting with media representatives, civil society and development partners. Through interviews and consultations we were able to evaluate the political and security situation and collect and identify the various factors which could influence the election. We studied the legal framework, the mood of the people in the country, the mechanisms in place at the Independent National Electoral Commission (INEC), gauged the conduct of the political parties, the media and civil society. A full picture of Nigeria's state of preparedness was important in also determining any additional or probable ECOWAS contribution to the election preparation, as spelt out in our terms of reference.

The mission was reasonably satisfied with the overall state of preparedness of Nigeria for the elections. Our technical report was definite in this description despite the persistence of uncertainties regarding security, interpersonal feuds and legal challenges. We recommended that ECOWAS proceed with its plans to field a full observer mission to cover the elections. Along with that we made recommendations on the awareness programme INEC was conducting in partnership with the UNDP and the EU.

In our report we emphasised the need to guard against the activities of thugs operating in official uniform during elections. Only authorised security personnel were to be deployed in the vicinity of polling stations and, to help ensure this, severe penalties ought to be imposed on impostors and their paymasters. It was crucial to put all of these in place because it must be said that the Mission was convinced that the elections were best summed up in four words: Anticipation, Suspicion, Fear - but Determination.

In the end, we were able to address some serious issues that had threatened not only the elections specifically but cohesion in the general political structure and future of Nigeria. Prime among those I have already highlighted was the feud that erupted between President Olusegun Obasanjo and Vice President Alhaji Atiku Abubakar. It was important to closely address this particular issue in the technical report my team submitted, considering that the frosty relationship between the two most powerful figures in the Nigerian polity had come to a head and cast a dark shadow over the whole electoral process. The feud, we agreed, had impacted negatively on the electoral process.

I reminded President Obasanjo that he was about to make history repeat itself, this time as an elected civilian president handing over to a successor civilian. I drew his attention to our concern for the preservation of his enviable legacy.

After submitting my report on the fact-finding mission I was invited again to head the ECOWAS election monitoring team in Nigeria. It was a hectic job considering the technological and attitudinal difficulties still on the ground. However, a great deal of logistics was put at our disposal to attain the objective. The governorship and national assembly polls took place on 14 April 2007.

After the state elections, I issued statements on the palpable sense of apprehension and frustration of a number of voters who had problems locating their polling stations, and this was only one of the minor flaws.

In our Fact-finding Report, we enjoined INEC to ensure the mobilisation and security of all available resources to eliminate those shortcomings so that the presidential and national assembly elections would not suffer similar setbacks. On 21 April 2007, nearly sixty million Nigerians went to the polls and the winner of the presidential race was Umaru Musa Yar'Adua.

Nema left for Arizona on 26 July 2007 after six weeks of holidays she had spent with us in Banjul. She reminded me of her nickname Nemadada her mother and I called her, a coinage from Nema's Daddy her live-in cousins Fatma and Mariam Alami had given her for being Daddy's girl. She remembered the nursemaid Aunty Rose who took care of her and her siblings. She also remembered the gardener Ansu Jammeh who taught her the names of the flowers and plants around the garden. We talked about our Sunday picnics and swimming on the beach at Brufut where we had a hut for relaxation. She recalled how senior students Karanta Kalley and Momodou Lamin Sedat Jobe from Gambia High School came to give Dawda, Nacesay, Almami and herself private lessons at No 1 Marina.

A couple of weeks after Nema left, there was an outbreak of foot and mouth disease in England. I could have overlooked the announcement but not when it was about animal disease. The British authorities were not going to take any chances considering the financial loss they suffered from the 2001 outbreak. The authorities finally traced the outbreak to the Animal Research Laboratory in Pirbright, Surrey. The old vet in me could not help straining to keep updated on the development of the outbreak.

On 8 August 2007, I arrived in Lagos with Njaimeh for the celebration of the African Telecom Awards. What started off a few years before as a privately-sponsored Nigeria Telecom Awards initiative to celebrate the Nigerian media industry had soon broadened to include the rest of Africa. My invitation was to preside over the joint telecommunications and media extravaganza in modern electronic gadgetry that was taking the continent by storm. It was an electrifying occasion and a gathering geared towards healthy competition. The industry showed great promise for Africa in terms of growth in the media and electronic service delivery and technical development. I played my modest role of also giving out some of the prestigious awards. I felt especially grateful that the organisers wished to honour me in such grand style. Everything about it bespoke the continued utility of former leaders. While we were in Nigeria, I paid a courtesy call on former president Olusegun Obasanjo at his farm in Ota. He was thrilled when I told him that I had started working on my autobiography. He reminded me that when he retired in 1979 he spent a month's holiday in The Gambia, where he began writing his own autobiography entitled *My Command*.

In August 2008 I was accompanied to Denver, Colorado, USA, by Njaimeh, where I was invited to attend the NDI's International Leaders Forum which was held concurrently with the Democratic National Convention from 24 to 29 August 2008.

We woke up on our first morning in Denver to a wonderful surprise. Nema and all her children, Hannah, Abigail, Michaela and Stirling, plus Hannah's husband Jeremy, and their two children had checked into our hotel on the night of our arrival. They had rooms next to ours. They had driven over 12 hours from Miami, Arizona. We had a most memorable weekend together.

On 25 August we attended a breakfast meeting on behalf of the Global Leadership for Climate Action. It was hosted jointly by Ted Turner (Chairman, United Nations Foundation), Richard Lagos (President, Club of Madrid and Co-Chair, Global Leadership for Climate Action) and Timothy E Wirth (President, United Nations Foundation and Co-Chair Global Leadership for Climate Action).

On 26 August we attended a reception held in honour of the diplomatic corps and international political leaders hosted jointly by Madeleine Korbel Albright (Chairman, NDI), Thomas A Daschle (Director, NDI), Tom Farer (of the Josef Korbel School of International Studies, University of Denver), Richard N Haass (member of the Council on Foreign Relations) and Robert E Rubin (member of the Council on Foreign Relations).

On 29 August 2008 we witnessed Barack Hussein Obama accept his nomination as the US Democratic Party's candidate for the 2008 US presidential elections at the Invesco Field at Mile High. The 76,125 seater stadium was filled to capacity. I can only summarise his acceptance speech as inspirational, visionary and transformational.

In November 2008, I saw democracy the way it should be practised, when Barack Obama, an African-American, swept the polls to become President of the United States of America - the most powerful nation in the world.

My retirement is peculiar in the sense that it emanated from a coup. But, naturally, other things being equal, a servant looks forward to retirement. The human frame is not built to go on forever. Besides, it is a way of allowing fresh thoughts and ideas to flow through the system, from and around the position the faithful worker had occupied. In this way, the necessary ingredients of new perspectives are served.

Of course, retirement from being a leader of a nation is not an everyday occurrence. If anything, it has its own peculiarities. One is for instance bound to be concerned that the legacy of good governance, the seeds of law and order and social and political stability for the people and the nation continue to be guaranteed in succeeding dispensations.

In the twilight of my life, I have re-examined the whole concept of power and dwelt deeply on what it meant to me when I served as a veterinary officer, headed a government department, held a ministerial portfolio or actually led a nation as prime minister and then as executive head of state. I have always seen power as a tool for service. In 1959 when

I was invited to lead the newly formed PPP, we prepared a constitution that said essentially that we wanted to express the will of the people - to be their voice. Thus the choice of *Vox Populi, Vox Dei* as the party motto was descriptive of our understanding of the concept of power – where it derives, what weight it should have and what objectives it should fulfil in its execution.

I have always been a proud father to my children – Dawda, Nema, Nacesay, Almami, Kawsu, Momodou, Fatoumata, Foday, Mariam, Njaimeh, Ebrima, Mustapha, Chilel, Ramatoulie and Housainou. I love and cherish all of them.

I want them to know how sorry I am for any time I may have fallen short of their expectations of me as a good and caring father, a provider and a shoulder they could lean on. I give each and all of them my sincerest apology and ask for their forgiveness. They do not need to thank me where I have been helpful; I probably did what every loving father would have done. For everything they have done amiss that might have displeased me as their father, I give my unconditional forgiveness.

In my shortcomings, I have been but only flesh and blood and a victim within the trappings of my time and place in the perilous arena of politics and public life. If pressed for what I might bequeath to all Gambians, young and old, male and female, it will be the thoughts in my address to the parade of our precious schoolchildren celebrating our fifth independence anniversary at MacCarthy Square in Bathurst in February 1970. If any of those schoolchildren will mark my memory for any reason whatsoever, I would wish that they remember that I leave to all Gambians now and of the future these words of encouragement:

> *Renew your dedication and redouble your efforts in your task of nation building so that coming generations of Gambians would look back with pride to what we their forefathers have bequeathed to them and especially so that it may continue to be said of us: 'Their ways are ways of gentleness; and all their paths are peace.'*

APPENDICES

Appendix I

The Independence Manifesto of the People's Progressive Party

A Blueprint for the Achievement of Self-Determination by the Gambian People

The Gambia cannot afford to remain much longer in the back waters of African political advance. While the whole continent moves to its destiny of freedom and self-determination, the right place for The Gambia, is the mainstream of that movement side by side with Senegal, Mauritania, Sudan, Sierra Leone, Somaliland, Ghana, Gabon, Guinea, Nigeria, Madagascar, etc, etc, etc.

In the political field Gambia has had a steady and sturdy development from the pre-1947 period of complete colonial paternalism through the 1947 Constitution which introduced for the first time an unofficial majority in the Legislature. Then came the 1951 Constitution with the elective element increased and the ministerial system introduced by the appointment of elected Gambians as members of the Government. The 1954 Constitution developed the ministerial system and the present 1960 Constitution introduced universal adult suffrage but stops short of conceding the right of self-determination to the Gambian people.

The People's Progressive Party is pledged to the achievement by the Gambia of Self-Government by 1961 and means to fulfil that pledge by constitutional means if possible.

We, the people of the Gambia, have an indisputable right to freedom and self-determination. We should be free to negotiate in freedom and equality with Britain, Senegal, or any other country matters which affect the economic, social, cultural, military and political destiny of our country.

It is sometimes argued that because of its small size and its lack of rich resources the Gambia dare not claim its freedom. This argument is not valid as all peoples rich or poor are equally entitled to freedom. No right-minded person in this mid-20th Century will deny the claim of the Gambian People to this fundamental human right.

Appendix

We should remember that though small in size, the Gambia is part and parcel of the huge, solid landmass of Africa and will, with the rest of Africa move inevitably to its destiny of freedom and self-determination. The Mandinkas, Jollofs, Jolas, Fulas, Akus, and Sarahules in the Gambia cannot be denied the freedom enjoyed by their brethren across the border in Senegal. It is unnatural, it is unjust, and sooner rather than later it will be resisted.

The People's Progressive Party considers it urgent that Gambia should talk with neighbouring African States in a spirit of brotherhood and equality to determine their common future. It is imperative therefore that attainment of Independence by the Gambia should not be delayed any longer than the time required to prepare for the physical transfer of power to the Gambian people.

The Gambia should have internal Self-Government based on the Party system by May 1961. This should be followed in 1962 by the fulfilment of our destiny as a people and as a nation – INDEPENDENCE.

Apart from the attainment of our birthright of Freedom the most urgent task facing the Gambia today is economic, and the task of raising the living standards of the people. In a recurrent budget which does not exceed £2 million, there is at present a deficit of £500,000 and this deficit is definitely on the increase as our revenue decreases from year to year and our expenditure increases. At the same time the living standards, the productivity and purchasing power of the mass of the people – the farmers and manual workers – are abysmally low. Thus our economic problem needs a drastic remedy. Not only do we need to make good the deficit in our recurrent budget, but also to stimulate the basis of our economy, namely, groundnut farming and rice and palm kernel production.

To help raise the low living standards of the farmers and to enable them to purchase better farming implements and fertilisers and to adopt more advanced methods, the producer price of groundnuts and palm kernels should be guaranteed at a level comparable to that of the price in Senegal. It is significant that even though Senegal is a fully independent state, France will continue to guarantee the Senegal price of groundnuts at a comparatively high level just as they have done in the past. The British Government has promised the Gambia a grant-in-aid of administration. We strongly feel that Her Majesty's Government should go further and guarantee the price of our groundnuts and palm kernels at a level sufficient not only to raise the living standards of the Gambian people but also to stimulate our economy so that in a few years' time the chronic deficit in our recurrent budget will disappear.

The People's Progressive Party will:

Urge the extension of cooperative societies to all parts of the country as soon as possible to help the farmers to help themselves and to protect them against extortion.

Make the fullest use of our human resources by promoting a vigorous, dynamic, and imaginative educational policy for the whole country.

Urge the development of our roads and our river services and of communications in general.

Promote the social and political organisation of all sections of the community including women and youth.

Seek to eliminate bribery and corruption from politics.

You are invited to join the People's Progressive Party in carrying out this patriotic, exciting and important programme and thus share fully in shaping the destiny of your country.

D K JAWARA
Leader, People's Progressive Party
1/10/60

Appendix II

DECLARATION OF THE PEOPLE'S PROGRESSIVE PARTY (PPP) ON THE TRANSITION BACK TO DEMOCRACY IN THE GAMBIA

Today, our nation stands at a very important crossroads. As we embark on the implementation of the governance component of the transition programme we have a unique opportunity to restore and consolidate the genuine democratic tradition and good governance that this country has enjoyed for decades after independence. 1996 will be a decisive year for us. If we are to rise successfully to the challenge of restoring power and sovereignty to the people, we must face the transition in an atmosphere of peace, patience, courage, honesty, dialogue and tolerance. Above all, we must strive relentlessly to establish secure foundations for the future rather than be swayed by short-term political or other gains into sowing the seeds for future instability within the nation.

THE GOVERNANCE ENVIRONMENT

1. The environment within which the transition has been taking place has undoubtedly been a very difficult and trying one for the party, for the nation and indeed for our traditional friends and neighbours. At a time when the necessity for an open national dialogue to decide on our future could not have been more important, a genuine national debate has been all but impossible. The PPP has been banned and with it the voices of thousands of its militants have been silenced. While other political parties such as the NCP and the GPP have likewise been banned, the brunt of the government's harsh measures has been reserved for and directed at the PPP. We commend our militants for their courage and patience during these difficult times and the fortitude with which they have borne their trials. The leadership of the party and of its government have been individually and by name banned by decree not only from engaging in any political activity but from expressing any opinion in public. They have been banned even from travelling beyond certain areas of the country and all their travel documents seized. Little could one foresee that a system akin to apartheid in its worst dimensions could be replicated in what had hitherto been a peace and justice loving country. The party has been dispossessed by the state of its headquarters in Banjul; files and documents have removed from the bureau by agents of the state and taken to an unknown destination; all the vehicles of the party numbering 10 pick-up vans have been seized by

the state and are being used by state agents; other party offices outside the city of Banjul have also been seized by the state and in some cases allocated by it to the 22nd July Movement and others. It is an endless catalogue. All of it is done for no justifiable reason and without any regard to due process of law. We do not recount this catalogue of injustice with any sense of bitterness but more with concern for the blatant disregard of standards of justice and fair play which have traditionally been the norm in our society.

2. Wider afield the whole country has been subjected to measures which have only had the effect of stifling dissent and an open genuine dialogue, instilling fear in the minds and hearts of ordinary Gambians. The Political Activities (Suspension) Decree 1994, The National Goals and Objectives Decree 1995, the AFPRC (Establishment) Decree 1995 with particular reference to its suspension of the human rights provision of the 1970 Constitution, the State Security (Detention of Armed Forces and Police Personnel) Decree 1994, the National Intelligence Decree 1995, the Death Penalty (Restoration) Decree 1995, the National Security (Detention of Persons) Decree 1995 to name but a few have no place in any genuine process of transition to democratic government and should be repealed.

3. At a time when the demand for free and open discourse is absolutely necessary the nation is faced with a complete ban on political activity, even while the officially launched and supported 22nd July Movement, a thinly disguised political movement, has been organising political activities countrywide in support of the establishment.

4. The intelligence and security establishment have been given wide, draconian powers of arrest and detention which continue to be abused and which now have instilled fear and suspicion within the population. Several PPP militants and even security personnel continue to be detained beyond ninety days in blatant contravention of the decrees authorising detention without charge. There is the case of disappearance of a prominent former politician in the person of Lamin Wa Juwara and of a youth leader, Ousman Sillah, on which the authorities have failed to shed any light.

5. It is a sad indictment of what obtains today in our society when The Gambia Court of Appeal was constrained to state that "there are no human right laws in The Gambia any longer" as the Chapter securing to each and every Gambian the fundamental rights and freedoms we have enjoyed, and which are now acknowledged to be universal, has now been repealed by Decree. At one fell swoop our entire citizenry were deprived of rights and freedoms, which is a culmination of centuries of struggle worldwide by people for equality and justice and which today are acknowledged to be universally inherent in the dignity of the human being. It is an unprecedented and unjustifiable action. The National Goals and Objectives Decree which pays lip service to human

rights, without providing any means for their enforcement, is a poor and inadequate substitute for the effective machinery of the 1970 Constitution.

6. A systematic harassment of journalists through arrests, detentions, prosecution and intimidation has been pursued, whose motive appears to be to stifle the independent private press and all open debate of the crucial issues we face today.

7. It is quite clear that an all-pervading atmosphere of enforced silence engendered by the ban on politics, fear and suspicion bred by draconian decrees, indiscriminate detention and blatant official disregard for human rights cannot provide a proper environment for the effective implementation of a transition programme which can put in place a genuine, secure and lasting democratic system of government.

8. As a first measure therefore and in order to improve the governance environment **we demand as follows:**

    i) that in keeping with the transition programme, the ban on political activity should be lifted completely by 1 July 1996;

    ii) that any lifting of such a ban must be general and non- discriminatory; there should be no attempts to ban certain groups or individuals while leaving others free to pursue political activities;

    iii) the restriction on free movement within and outside The Gambia imposed on former politicians for almost two years now should be lifted;

    iv) all political detainees should be released forthwith;

    v) the activities of the security agencies with particular reference to arrests and harassment of political dissidents must cease;

    vi) property sized from the PPP - its office, records, equipment, vehicles etc - must be restored to it; and

    vii) chapter 3 of the 1970 Constitution dealing with fundamental rights and freedoms should be restored.

B. THE ELECTIONS

1. The transition programme envisages a referendum scheduled for 7 August 1996; presidential election scheduled for 11 September 1996 and Parliamentary elections scheduled for 11 December 1996. It is not yet clear when the local and municipal elections, which at one time had been a component of the transition timetable, will be held.

2. We share the apprehension of many in this country – individuals, professional bodies etc – regarding the integrity and organisation of these elections.

3. Elections are not the alpha and omega of a democratic system of government but they are an indispensable element of such a system. Government must rest on the express consent of the people freely given. Elections – free and fair – are the only acceptable means of ascertaining, gauging such consent. Calls

by some for no elections are dangerously misguided and can only be a recipe for disaster. We welcome therefore the decision of the PIEC, in consultation with the government, to fix dates for the elections. We believe this is a firm rejection of the demands of the 'no-election' campaign and hope that under no circumstances would any consideration be given to this bizarre anti-democratic campaign.

4. We do not believe that the **presidential and parliamentary elections** should be held on separate days. This only leads to unnecessary expense – for the government, the political parties, the PIEC, indeed for all those who have any role to play in the elections. At the same time by spacing out three elections over a five-month period, the country is going to be subjected to an extended period of political campaign stretching over five months, with all the necessary interruptions to life and with all the tensions that go with politicking. We do not believe this would be healthy. The presidential and parliamentary elections should be combined and held on 11 December 1996, the date originally set by the PIEC for the parliamentary elections. Since 1982 when the President became popularly elected both these elections have been held simultaneously, without any difficulty.

5. Even more fundamental is the **freeness and fairness of the process.** The maintenance of a level-playing field for all contestants is an indispensable element of the election game. It is clear to all and sundry that the playing field is far from level. The 22nd July Movement, the political party of the AFPRC, has with official blessing been preparing for elections since it was launched on 15 July 1995. It has been the only player in the field.

6. There is widespread apprehension that attempts to tilt the field much further may still be forthcoming through an arbitrary and selective ban of specific individuals, political parties and other groups from contesting any elections to public office. Any attempt to manipulate the elections in such a manner will be fraught with serious danger for our nation and we warn against it seriously. The people must be left to choose whosoever they wish to see at the helm of affairs of this nation. Manipulation of this kind will in our view mar irrevocably the integrity of the electoral process.

7. The process is primarily the concern of Gambians but it is also that of the international community which has in diverse ways sought to assist us as a people to meet the challenge of resources for the implementation of the transition programme. The international community has another important role to play in **monitoring the elections** to ensure they are free and fair. We therefore demand that the Organisation of African Unity, the United Nations, the Commonwealth Secretariat, the African Commission on Human and Peoples' Rights, the African Centre of Democracy and Human Rights Studies, the Carter Center, the National Democratic Institute for International Affairs and all other international organisations which are concerned with democracy

and good government be permitted, indeed invited to observe and monitor all the forthcoming elections with a view to determining their freeness and fairness and indeed by their effective presence in the country to contribute to the attainment of free and fair elections. We the militants of the PPP for our party extend a warm welcome to all such organisations and pledge our fullest cooperation with them.

8. While we welcome the recently concluded nationwide **registration of voters,** subject to certain reservations we cannot fail to point out that it has been carried out in contravention nationwide of the provisions of Sections 17 and 18 of the Elections Decree 1996. These provisions require every person who wishes to be registered to fill a form of claim prescribed in Form 2 of Schedule III to the Decree providing particulars of himself and to present such a claim before a registering officer for his consideration and decision. As far as we are aware, not a single registered voter anywhere in the country has been presented with a claim form or has filled and presented such a form to a registering officer. It is important that electoral laws are complied with fully in all respects, especially by those who made the law or are charged with its administration.

9. We are extremely concerned at **comments attributed to the PIEC** to the effect that it would be very difficult for it to keep to the elections timetable unless extra resources are made available to them. Resource constraints should under no circumstances be used as a cloak for further delays to the timetable. While we welcome with gratitude the support that the international community has provided for the electoral programme and would appeal to them to continue such support, it is important to stress that the primary responsibility for funding the elections rests, as it always has since independence, on the government. No elections have had to be postponed or rescheduled or in any way been adversely affected by resource constraints. A more judicious use of available local resources would, we are certain, together with what is already available from the international community, enable us to meet the challenge of resources.

10. Above all else the elections must be free and fair. The standards of fair play that this country has established and maintained over a period of thirty years and more than 10 elections must not be diluted. The secret ballot; the use of marble tokens; freedom from harassment and intimidation; free access to the official media for all political parties; the independence and impartiality of electoral officers; the transparency of the voting and counting process; the rights of the political parties to monitor the process at all levels; all these and more must be observed if the results of the elections are to be accepted and respected by all and sundry.

11. **The PIEC** must itself not only be fair and impartial. It must be seen to be so. Unfortunately recent pronouncements of some members of the Commission

have only served to reinforce the suspicion of many that the criteria used in the selection of the Commission members were largely their hostility to the previous government which puts a question mark over their impartiality. It is important that the PIEC strives actively to dispel such perception.

12. **Constituencies** are a very important component of the parliamentary system of government as they are the basis on which the composition of the legislature is determined. Manipulation of constituency boundaries or gerrymandering strikes at the very heart of the people's right to representation.

13. Whilst it is impossible to ensure that all constituencies contain an equal number of people, it is necessary that as far as possible there should not be wide and unjustifiable disparities in population size. Several factors no doubt go into the drawing of constituency boundaries but the paramount consideration is demographic. That is why the law requires that there must be a review of the constituency boundaries following every census in order to ensure that the delineation of such boundaries takes into account significant changes in the demographic pattern.

14. We must say at once that we condemn in no uncertain terms the constituency boundaries which have been incorporated in the draft constitution and published by the PIEC, increasing the number of constituencies from 36 to 41. It is clear all the criteria, including demography, which are required to be taken into account, have been ignored by the PIEC and the constituencies drawn solely on the basis of chieftaincy districts. The result is wide and unjustifiable disparities in the population size of the constituencies and a serious blow to the principle of equality of representation. A few examples will suffice to buttress this point. The new constituency of Fulladu West (merging what had hitherto been two constituencies) with a population of 56,952 returns the same number of MPs as Janjangbureh with a population of 2,758! Foni Bondali with a population of 4,602 returns one MP whereas in the KMC area the ratio is one MP to 70,000 people! The whole of the FONIS with a population of 37,580 returns 5 MPs whereas Fulladu West with a population of 56,952 returns one! Fulladu East with a population more than double the 5 Foni constituencies put together has its representation reduced from 3 to 1! And so on and so forth – the pattern is the same – In the MID, the URD and North Bank there has been a reduction in the number of constituencies even though demographic considerations point to an increase. What has been presented to the nation as the electoral constituencies is a complete travesty and mockery of the principles of democracy. Any election conducted on this basis will in effect be disenfranchising thousands of Gambians and providing us with the most unrepresentative legislature in our history.

15. We demand that the forthcoming parliamentary elections should not be based on the PIEC constituencies; that these constituencies should be cancelled and the elections conducted on the basis of the constituencies existing before

22nd July 1994 until such a time as a proper review of the boundaries of such constituencies can be carried out properly.

C THE DRAFT CONSTITUTION

1. An important plank of the transition programme has been the drafting of a new Constitution to replace the 1970 Constitution. To this end Decree 33 of 31 March 1995 established a Constitution Review Commission charged with the task of formulating proposals for a new draft constitution.

2. To some extent the proposals which emanated were a foregone conclusion as by section 6 of the above decree, the draft was required to contain certain matters set out in some detail in the decree, irrespective of the outcome of the Commission's consultations with the people.

3. **The environment** within which the process of constitution making was and continues to be carried out is far from satisfactory. With all political parties and political activity banned, specific individuals banned from speaking, the private media under immense pressure, it is inevitable that the great national debate which should normally have vigorously accompanied such a process would be markedly absent. This factor, we strongly believe, has had a negative impact on the quality of the draft itself.

4. **The constitution making process,** we submit, has been seriously flawed in another respect. Any constitution should reflect the values and aspirations of the people it is supposed to govern. This requires the full and effective participation of the people both at the consultation stage and at the approval stage. The normal practice has been to submit a draft constitution to **an elected constituent assembly** which, with the full authority as representative of the people, is empowered to discuss the draft in detail and modify it where appropriate before it is submitted to the people for approval at a referendum. It should be recalled here that the 1970 Constitution was, before being submitted to a referendum, laid before the House of Representatives performing the function of a constituent assembly. Despite persistent and widespread demands by individuals and professional organisations this key element has tragically been missing from the transition programme. As a result the Gambian people have been denied an opportunity to mould and shape the draft in line with their wishes, values and aspirations. Instead the only option now available to the country is to approve or reject the draft constitution **in toto.** The alternative of collating comments on the draft and forwarding them to the Ministry of Justice for its consideration is a very poor substitute for a constituent assembly. The decisions that now have to be made are not legal ones or matters of drafting. What is involved is the making of political choices by the people. No government or government department or public officer is competent to make these political choices for the people. In any case the disclosure by the PIEC that in certain respects the draft constitution has

failed to reflect the views of the majority of Gambians on particular issues arising during the consultation process entitles us to assume that whatever second draft emanates now from the Ministry of Justice will also not reflect the expressed concerns of the majority of people.

5. We find the draft constitution unsatisfactory in several respects as a basis for the future government of this country. Some of our areas of concern are highlighted below:

i) the **acquisition of Gambian citizenship** by birth by persons born here of foreign parents ordinarily resident in The Gambia (Section 9(1)(b)) is a major and unnecessary departure from the criteria for granting citizenship and does not take into account the space and resource constraints of The Gambia and the probable negative impact of such a provision on our demography.

ii) the Ruling Council when it seized power made much of the fact that the 1970 Constitution has no limits on the **tenure of office of the President** as a result of which the previous government, it was said, had over-stayed. It was clear from the consultation process that the majority of Gambians – and this has been confirmed by the PIEC – favoured a two-term limit on the tenure of office of the President. Notwithstanding this, the draft is silent on the issue. Related to this is also the issue of the 1970 Constitution pegging the minimum age at 30. However in the light of our political experience since July 1994 the vast majority of the population, with the endorsement of professional groups such as The Gambia Bar Association, have opted for a minimum age of 40. Again notwithstanding this popular demand, the draft has retained the original age of 30 years.

iii) to provide for the **disqualification from the presidency** of all persons who have been "compulsorily retired, terminated or dismissed" from public office or have been found liable by a commission of inquiry for misconduct, negligence, corruption or something as vague as "improper behaviour" (Section 62(2)) is to open the door to serious abuse of power. It is an open secret that dozens of public officers have recently been dismissed or retired from the public service without any due inquiry or even been provided with the reason for their dismissal or retirement. All such officers become ineligible as a result of the arbitrary decision of one authority. What of the future? Such a provision can also be used as a tool for eliminating from the political arena all public officers who may be or are feared to have political ambitions. The same concerns of abuse and arbitrariness apply as well to the case of the Commissions of Inquiry, in addition to the unacceptable vagueness of the reasons for disqualification. Surely negligence is not a relevant factor? Surely merely improper behaviour should not be a disqualifying factor? Corruption of course cannot be condoned and should be fought everywhere. The only tenable ground for disqualification should be a conviction by a Competent Court, following due process, for an offence such as corruption which would make a person unsuitable for public office.

iv) in certain respects we believe some of the provisions of the draft do not encourage the **development and strengthening of a sense of national unity** in the Gambia people, cutting across ethnic or sectional lines. Section 12 (1) of the Election Decree which enables a person to register in the constituency in which he resides or in which he was **born** and Section 89(c) which requires an aspiring parliamentary candidate to be resident in the constituency at least one year before the elections are a case in point. Suddenly the issue of where in The Gambia one was born has unfortunately been given constitutional significance and inevitably people become very conscious of their place of origin. Surely a simple residence requirement for registration would have been more appropriate.

The immediate effect of Section 89 is to disqualify from Parliament all those persons who have had to leave their 'roots' in the rural areas and take up residence in the urban areas for various reasons. A Gambian is no longer free to contest an election in whichever part of The Gambia he wishes. The electorate in a constituency are also deprived of the right to select any person they consider suitable irrespective of where they reside. For a small place such as The Gambia, place of residence and place of birth have now unfortunately acquired an unhealthy political significance which may not auger well for national unity.

One curious anomaly which is a result of those two provisions is that a person may be qualified to register and vote in a particular constituency yet, by reason of his non-residence there, be disqualified from contesting an election in that constituency!

v) It is not unusual for most political systems to provide for rules which seek to discourage the frivolous from putting up candidatures which lack all seriousness. But we believe a combination of the following:

a. Section 42 of the Election Decree, which requires a presidential candidate to be nominated by not less then five thousand voters (compared to 100 in the past) with at least 200 from each administrative area. Parliamentary candidates are to be nominated by not less than 300 voters (compared to 3 in the old Elections Act)

b. Section 43 of the Elections Decree requires a deposit of D10, 000 for a presidential candidate and D5, 000 for a parliamentary candidate compared to D2, 500 under the Presidential Elections Act 1982 and D200 under the Elections Act respectively.

c. With regard to forfeiture of deposits, the Electoral Decree provides for forfeiture by a presidential candidate who obtains less than 40% of the votes cast and in the case of the parliamentary candidate less than 20% of the votes cast. This compares with the Election Act where the losing candidate recovers his deposit unless he fails to secure less than one-fifth of the votes cast for the elected candidate.

The same condition is provided in the case of the Presidential Elections Act 1982. These high levels of nomination, deposit and forfeiture of deposit, we believe, will only have the effect of making it extremely difficult for all but incumbent candidates to put forward a candidature. The logistics involved, for instance, in identifying not less than 5,000 registered voters, transporting then to Banjul or the various administrative centres and ensuring that they are all present on the nomination day is a daunting challenge for all but an incumbent candidate.

vi) We reject totally the provisions of **Sections 49 and 55 of the draft constitution** which empower only registered political parties to challenge the result of a presidential election and political parties and candidates only to challenge the results of a parliamentary election. Not only is the draft silent on the situation where there are independent candidates but it ignores the fact that elections to those two offices are not by the political parties but by the registered voters. It is the registered voters who have a right to choose or reject a candidate and therefore the right to challenge an election result. Every registered voter who is aggrieved at an election result should have the right to challenge that result.

We wish to point out furthermore that in fact the proposals in the draft constitution are in conflict with Section 98 of the Elections Decree 1996, which grants the right to challenge an election result to all registered persons, persons who lost at such elections and all those who allege they were candidates at the elections concerned. These provisions of the Decree are to be preferred over those in the draft Constitution.

vii) With the exception of the President, and in a major departure from the established constitutional tradition of this country, none of the members of **the_Cabinet** is drawn from the legislature. They are all appointed directly by the President. Nor is their appointment subject to any vetting process by the legislature. We firmly believe that the entire membership of the executive should be drawn from the legislature, thereby ensuring that those appointed genuinely represent the people of this country. The draft constitution proposal suffers from an additional defect, which makes it possible, given the fact that the vice-president is un-elected, in the event of a vacancy in the office of the President, for him to be succeeded to the office of President by an un-elected vice-president assisted by an entirely un-elected cabinet! To compound matters further in the event of a vacancy occurring in the office of President when there is no vice-president, the functions of President are performed by the Speaker, who is a **nominated,** not elected, member of the legislature! The provisions can thus lead to the absurd situation where the entire executive comprises un-elected persons! The merits of retaining the system of the 1970 Constitution from the legislature and the vice-president appointed from among the **elected** members of the legislature appear to us quite obvious.

viii) Three aspects of the draft constitution and the Elections Decree 1996 relating to the legislature are of immense concern to us:

a. We have stated elsewhere our reservations concerning the wide and unjustifiable disparities in size of the constituencies presented by the PIEC. The PIEC is by Section 50 of the draft constitution mandated to demarcate the constituencies for the purpose of elections to the National Assembly taking into account factors of population etc which are essentially no different from those provided under the 1970 Constitution. Section 88 however provides that each chieftaincy district should constitute a constituency which shall be entitled to elect a member to the legislature. Whereas the PIEC is empowered under Section 192(2) in accordance with an Act of Parliament yet to be enacted, to determine the boundaries of local government authorities (defined in the Constitution to comprise "city councils, municipalities and area councils"), the PIEC has no responsibility for determining the boundaries of chieftaincy districts. Those boundaries are determined by the executive arm of government. In effect the responsibility for the delimitation of constituency boundaries rests not on the PIEC but on the executive which determines the chieftaincy districts and thus the parliamentary constituencies.

Thus the whole scheme of free and fair elections based on constituencies delimited by an independent and impartial body has been subverted. The only solution is to keep constituency boundaries separate from chieftaincy district boundaries as in the past. Not only would revision of the draft be required but the constituencies as announced by the PIEC should be scrapped and those in existence as of 22 July 1994 retained until such a time that a proper demarcation, taking all relevant factors into account, can be effected as we recommended elsewhere.

b. Another area of concern is the requirement for the **registration of political parties.** Section 60 of the draft constitution and part viii of the Elections Decree require all political parties to be registered with the IEC and for them to satisfy certain conditions prior to registration. We have no difficulty whatsoever with the conditions laid down. No party should be formed on ethnic, religious or other division of discrimination criterion.

What we cannot accept is the requirement for registration itself which carries with it a power of rejection and a power of deregistration of an existing political party. The potential for abuse of this power and its implications are too serious for this system to be retained. Already the Criminal Code empowers the Courts to prohibit societies whose objects or activities are prejudicial to public safety, security order etc. We consider those provisions adequate. The acceptability or otherwise of a political party is best left to the decision of the electorate, rather than entrusted to a handful of men in whose hands it can become an instrument for denying people their right freely to associate for political purposes. The old system whereby there was no requirement for the registration of political parties should be retained. It has not caused any difficulties. There is no reason to change it.

c. Thirdly we are concerned about the provision of part vi (Sections 85-89) of the Elections Decree 1996. These provisions empower the IEC to determine the **period for election campaign,** during which political parties may carry out political activities. Section 88 provides that when the campaign period as declared by the IEC comes to an end, all election campaign activity shall cease. We do not accept these proposals, whatever their rationale, if any. Party politics requires constant political activity. Attempts to artificially determine when political activity may or may not be carried out are not only unnecessary and cumbersome, introducing an unnecessary complexity into the political process, but affect the fundamental right of political parties and individuals at all times to propagate their policies and seek to attract new members.

ix) An independent and impartial **judiciary** is the linchpin of any democratic system of government. An important element for securing the independence of judges is by providing them with security of tenure whereby their removal or the termination of their services is for cause and after due inquiry and on the decision of the legislature. While such security is provided in the draft we fully condemn the additional power that the draft gives to the President to terminate the services of a judge in consultation with the Judicial Service Commission.

This provision is a recipe for executive interference and undermining of the judiciary and will subvert the independence of judges as their tenure of office will be at the pleasure and the whims and caprices of the President. Such a provision should not feature in the Constitution.

x) There is little point in drawing up an elaborate bill of rights and fundamental freedoms without any effective machinery for its enforcement. The draft suffers this deficiency in the matter of the enforcement of the rights and freedoms that are guaranteed to every person. It is proposed that responsibility for the enforcement of the human rights chapter as well as for interpretation of the constitution be entrusted to the new Supreme Court, which, unlike the existing Court, sits at the apex of the judiciary above the Court of Appeal, the High Court, the Magistrate's Courts and the District Tribunals and Cadi's Courts. To vest the final court with such a jurisdiction would be to take the enforcement of human rights beyond the reach of the average citizen. Few have the resources to make use of such a court. It is better and indeed the normal thing to vest courts much lower in the hierarchy e.g the proposed High Court, with such a mandate.

xi) For a country which is overwhelmingly Muslim and the majority of whose personal law is **the Sharia,** the draft shows a surprising and unwelcome insensitivity. Until now the Sharia constitutes an important element of our substantive law, regulating for most people issues of marriage and divorce, inheritance, ownership of property etc. Islamic banking law now forms part of our commercial law. The Sharia is applied by all the courts, initially by the Cadis and District Tribunals and subsequently on appeal to the highest courts of the land which deal with questions of Islamic law/Sharia. It is now proposed to abolish the system of appeals from the Cadis' Courts on matters of Sharia with result that questions of Islamic law will no longer be dealt with by the superior courts but only by the Cadis. We believe this is an unjustifiable and unacceptable lowering of the status of the Sharia in this country. The appeals system for the Cadis' Courts should be retained to give an opportunity to parties to bring their grievances before a Superior Court which also has the capacity to expound on and clarify issues of Islamic law to the benefit of both the legal profession and the community at large.

xii) We endorse the inclusion of **the office of Ombudsman** within the draft constitution. It will be recalled that the PPP government had already issued a policy statement declaring its intention to proceed with the creation of the office of the Ombudsman with the mandate of investigating allegations of abuse of office, maladministration, corruption and violations of human rights. Indeed at the time of the military seizure of power the draft legislation was ready for introduction to the legislature. Like the judiciary, an Ombudsman is effective only when it is independent and impartial and is seen to be so. The mode of appointment must not leave room for partisanship. Nor must the mode of removal constitute a sword of Damocles hanging over the Ombudsman. In this respect while we welcome the provisions relating to removal, we are of the view that the power of appointment of the Ombudsman should be exercisable by the President only with the approval or in accordance with the recommendation of another authority such as the legislature. This, in our view, would ensure that such an important office does not become the object of partisan politics.

xiii) The **transitional provisions** of the draft constitution have been of great concern to our party. Firstly we believe it is wrong for the Constitution to come into force only after the election of the President. Once the Constitution is approved at a referendum, it should come into force and thereafter all the elections scheduled should be conducted in accordance with its provisions rather than be regulated by Decree.

A more difficult question relates to the immunity proposed to be granted to all members of the AFPRC, including anybody appointed by them, from any liability or inquiry relating to the performance of their official duties during the period 1994 to the end of the transition. The courts are, it is proposed in the draft, prohibited by law from inquiring into the events of 22 July 1994, the suspension of the 1970 Constitution, the establishment of the AFPRC and the establishment of the new Constitution. No action taken by the AFPRC in the exercise or purported exercise of the executive, legislative or judicial power is to be questioned in any judicial proceedings nor can any court grant a relief or remedy in respect of such act. Confiscation of property or penalties imposed by the AFPRC shall not be questioned or reversed by any law, including the Constitution nor can the courts inquire into alleged violations or contravention of the law by the AFPRC or any person appointed by it. The legislature is prohibited from passing any legislation to alter these provisions. They are not just entrenched and subject to a strict amendment or repeal procedure. They just cannot be changed at all!

We find these provisions - which immunise the AFPRC against any inquiry into their actions and those of their appointees, even those acts which are illegal, prohibit the review and reversal of all the decisions of the AFPRC and its agents whether they are lawful or not and permanently fetter the sovereign right of the people of this country to make such laws as they consider conducive to peace, tranquillity and good government - totally unacceptable. It is ironic and a double standard that the AFPRC should throughout its entire period in office have preoccupied itself and devoted substantial time and resources to probing the past 30 years of government preceding the take-over. That it should also through the draft constitution seek to put in place a system for accountability through Commissions of Inquiry and assets declaration to take effect after the departure of the AFPRC from the political scene. But the AFPRC themselves are to be immune from such accountability and transparency! We reject this proposal in its totality. Accountability and transparency cannot be temporary or selective. The actions of the AFPRC in government are as deserving of accountability as are those of the previous government and the one succeeding it. If the watchword, indeed the whole justification for the AFPRC seizing power, has been the need for accountability and transparency, with what justification can they be exempt from the requirement? Accountability and transparency are good things but we hope they do not end with the previous government.

We understand of course the rationale for provisions such as these in the draft constitution. The terms however on which the AFPRC is to relinquish power is a matter for negotiation and not unilateral imposition by the AFPRC on the nation.

xiv) Finally we believe the draft constitution is overloaded. A Constitution by nature is a framework document, setting out the broad outlines and philosophy on which government is to be based. Ordinary Acts of Parliament, judicial decisions and Constitutional Convention fill out its gaps. It is not a document for setting out the entire machinery of government or dealing with any matter which may be a subject of government concern or interest. In this respect we find that provisions relating to the Central Bank, the National Youth Service, the Parastatals, Local Government including chieftaincy and alkaloship are out of place in the Constitution. These are best regulated by separate legislation. To retain them in the draft constitution would be to elevate relatively routine matters to the level of constitutional issues and thereby open the constitution to a frequency of amendments which is totally undesirable of that kind of instrument. For all these reasons and for many others expressed by the media, private individuals, professional organisations and other political figures, we the PPP have reached the conclusion that the draft constitution is unsatisfactory and cannot provide a sound and secure basis for democracy and good governance. It would have been possible to modify the draft to conform with the wishes of the majority of Gambians. But alas the only mechanism for doing so, ie the elected Constituent Assembly has been denied the people. While it is not every clause of the draft that is being objected to, those which are, are so fundamental that they affect the quality of the entire draft. We are therefore left with no option but to reject the draft constitution. We accordingly call on all Gambians to vote with a resounding 'NO' at the forthcoming referendum.

D. WHAT NEXT?

1. The rejection of the draft constitution at a referendum should under no circumstances be used as a pretext for extension of the transition timetable. The date for handing over to an elected civilian government must remain irrevocable. In the event of the people rejecting the draft, we must revert to the 1970 Constitution. The matter of preparing a new draft constitution must then be left in the hands of a democratically elected civilian government.

2. Any rejection of the draft constitution will necessarily have an impact on the legitimacy of the Elections Decree 1996 as many of the proposals in the draft eg the requirement for the registration of political parties, the number of registered voters required for the nomination of Presidential and Parliamentary candidates, the number and boundaries of the constituencies etc are also contained in the Elections Decree 1996 promulgated by the AFPRC. Proposals rejected in the draft constitution would be robbed of all legitimacy if they are allowed to remain in a decree promulgated without the consent of the people. An inevitable conclusion that has to be drawn from the rejection of the draft constitution therefore is that the forthcoming elections would have to be conducted on the basis of the Elections Act, and not the Elections Decree 1996, and also on the basis of the constituencies existing prior to 22 July 1994.

3. Whatever the outcome of the referendum we believe that the Armed Forces should disengage from politics immediately and hand over to an **interim civilian government of National Unity** to oversee the handing over to civilian rule within the framework of the transition programme. Several factors make such disengagement imperative: the end of the two-year term brokered by the NCC for the AFPRC at end of July 1996; the need to ensure that the elections are not only fair but are also seen to be fair in the light of the long ban on political activity despite the political activities of the 22nd July Movement; the speculation as to whether the leadership of the AFPRC harbour political ambitions, the negative impact both on the country's Armed Forces as well as on the nation at large of the continued involvement of the military in politics. We accordingly call for the AFPRC to hand over power to an interim civilian government of National Unity whose composition would be a matter for consultation between all the political groups in the country.

4. We the militants of PPP are confident that the proposals we have presented in this declaration will enable our nation to move forward in peace and tranquillity and with the spirit of national reconciliation towards the restoration and strengthening of a democratic society based on the rule of law and social justice.

LONG LIVE THE REPUBLIC OF THE GAMBIA!

LONG LIVE THE PEOPLE'S PROGRESSIVE PARTY!

Dawda Kairaba Jawara
Leader, People's Progressive Party (PPP)
10 July 1996

Appendix III

FORMER PRESIDENTS (OFFICE, ALLOWANCES AND OTHER BENEFITS) ACT, 2006

ARRANGEMENT OF SECTIONS

Section
8. Short title
9. Interpretation
10. Establishment of office of Former President
11. Allowances and other benefits
12. Duration of allowances and benefits
13. Budget allocation

SCHEDULE - BENEFITS FOR FORMER PRESIDENTS

Appendix

Interpretation	2. In this Act, unless the context otherwise Requires-
	"Former President" means a person who has held the office of President of the Republic of The Gambia for not less than two terms.
Establishment of office of Former President	3. There is hereby established an office of Former President
Allowances and other benefits	4. (1) Subject to subsection (2), a Former President shall-
	(c) be paid a monthly allowance of fifty thousand dalasis; and
	(d) enjoy the other benefits set out in the schedule
	(2) A President who ceased to hold office under Section 67 of the Constitution of the Republic of The Gambia, 1997 is not entitled to the allowances and benefits provided for a former President under this Act.
Duration of allowances and benefits	5. The allowances and other benefits provided for a Former President under this Act shall be paid for by The Government of The Gambia during the lifetime of the Former President, from the date of his or her leaving the office of President.
Budget Allocation	6. The funds required to meet the expenditure of the Government under this Act shall be provided for in the annual budget.

Medical Services and Vacation

5. (1) Free medical treatment for the former President and his or her spouse within and, where necessary, outside The Gambia, on the recommendation of the Director of Medical Services in the Department of State for Health and Social Welfare

(2) Thirty working days annual vacation for the Former President and his or her spouse, within and outside The Gambia at a location to be selected by the Former President

(3) Where vacation is to be taken outside The Gambia, the Government shall be responsible for the air tickets and payment of the appropriate *per diem* allowances for the former President and his or her spouse.

Office Accommodation

6. (1) A well-furnished and equipped office and

(a) not more than four staff, including the Personal Assistant and Personal Secretary

(b) a motor vehicle, to be maintained and fuelled; and

(c) a motor cycle, to be maintained and fuelled

Appendix

Maintenance of Residential Accommodation

7. The residential accommodation of the former President shall be maintained and provided with telephone, internet and other facilities and the
Following-

(a) two cooks;

(b) four housekeepers; and

(c) two gardeners

PASSED in the National Assembly this Eleventh day of December in the year of Our Lord Two Thousand and Six.

D C M Kebbeh
Clerk of the National Assembly

THIS PRINTED IMPRESSION has been carefully compared by me with the Bill which has passed in the National Assembly, and found by me to be a true and correct copy of the said Bill.

D.C.M. Kebbeh
Clerk of the National Assembly

Appendix

SCHEDULE (section 4)
BENEFITS FOR FORMER PRESIDENTS

A former president shall enjoy the benefits set out in this Schedule.

Personal Staff

1. (1) A Personal Assistant to be selected by the former President.

    (2) A Personal Secretary to be selected by the Former President.

Security

2. Twenty-four hour security service.

Vehicles

3. (1) Three motor vehicles, to be maintained and fuelled.

    (2) The drivers shall be selected by the former President.

Protocol

4. (1) Diplomatic Passport for life.

    (2) Protocol within and outside The Gambia.

    (3) A former President shall take first place after the Vice-President in order of precedence at public functions.

Appendix

<u>Supplement "C" to The Gambia Gazette No. 4 of 8th February, 2007</u>
Former Presidents (Office, Allowances and Other Benefits) Act, 2006
THE GAMBIA
NO. 16 OF 2006
Assented to by The President,
this 5th day of February, 2007

L S

YAHYA A.J.J. JAMMEH
President

AN ACT to establish an office and provide for allowances and other benefits for former Presidents and for matters connected therewith.

[5th February, 2007]

ENACTED by the President and the National Assembly.

Short title 1. This Act may be cited as the Former Presidents (Office, Allowances and Other Benefits) Act, 2006.

Index

1

1959 Constitution · 234, 251
1960 Constitution · 246
1961 Lagos Conference · 347
1964-1966 Development Plan · 271
1970 Constitution · 441

A

Abacha, Sani · 394
Abbott, Diane · 402, 421, 426
Able-Thomas, A S C· 204,290
Abubakar, Alhaji Atiku · 451
Abuja · 379, 394, 395, 420, 449
Abuko · 121, 126, 169, 171, 184, 191, 195, 198, 288, 440, 441
Accra · 103, 141, 150, 151, 152, 153, 157, 194, 229, 230, 395, 436
Achimota · 53, 110, 115, 117, 122, 143, 145, 148, 149, 150, 153, 155, 163, 180, 181, 191, 192, 194, 229, 436
Addis Ababa · 229, 268, 279, 373, 374
Admiralty Wharf · 104, 118, 140, 289, 314, 381
Afienya Gliding School · 230
AFPRC · 269, 297, 382, 384, 388, 389, 390, 393, 395, 396, 399, 409, 411, 424, 459, 461, 470, 472
Africa Day · 408
Africa Forum · 443, 446, 447
African African-American Summit · 367
African and Eastern Trading Co Ltd · 9
African Centre for Democracy and Human Rights Studies · 250
African Charter on Human and Peoples' Rights · 308
African Charter on the Rights and Welfare of the Child · 367
African Civil Society Forum · 402

African Commission on Human and Peoples' Rights (ACHPR) · 250
African common market · 330, 352
African Development Bank · 292, 327, 361, 374,
African Groundnut Council · 229
African Highway network · 303
African Human Rights Day · 309
African self-determination · 150, 162
African self-reliance · 194
African Telecom Awards · 452
agricultural extension services · 295
agricultural stations · 291
Akoto-Bamfo commission of inquiry · 269
Akoto-Bamfo, Judge Vida · 398
Aku · 108, 112, 119, 144, 154, 180,
Alami, Abdoulai · 447
Alami, Fatma · 411, 437
Alami-Njie, Mina · 429, 431, 433, 435
Alami, Mariam · 97, 311, 382, 403, 408, 417, 422, 431, 437, 451, 453
Albert Market · 214, 381
Albion Place · 199, 203, 208, 211
Albright, Madeleine Korbel · 453
Algeria · 268, 353
Alghali Commission · 398
Alhaji, Alhaji Abubakar · 391
Almamy Leh · 11, 12, 37, 39, 40, 43, 44, 45, 62, 91, 95
Alkali of Kunting · 13
All Party Committee · 199, 201
Allen, Sergeant Major Stan · 347
Alpha-Lavalie, Elizabeth · 450
Amaurac du Chauffant · 394
Amos, Baroness Valerie · 421
AMRC · 297, 388, 436
ANC · 363
Andrews, Albert · 103
Andrews, Dr Gail · 442
Andrews, Reuel · 103
Angola · 249
Animal Research Laboratory · 451
Anyaoku, Chief Emeka · 394, 397
apartheid · 254, 266, 268, 308, 374, 458
Arab-Israeli conflict · 265
Armistice Day · 133

481

Armitage School · 52, 76, 116, 127, 128, 217
Armitage, Sir Cecil · 78
Armour, Prof Jimmy · 377
army, confederal · 344, 355
Arona Paa · 80
Asamoah-Owusu, Richard · 412
Ashetton, N M · 59
Ashford, Dr Nigel · 397
ASI · 442, 443, 448
Atlanta · 393, 403, 404
Atlantic Boulevard, 40 · 123, 386, 388, 436, 437, 439, 440
Atlantic Hotel · 240, 263, 323, 331
Auckland · 394
Aureol · 157, 165
Austin, J A · 164
Australia · 78, 99, 252, 258
Ayoola, Olayinka · 331, 370

B

Ba, Saidou Nourou · 312
Babangida, Ibrahim · 363, 365
Baddibu Nokunda · 174
Baddibus · 271
BADEA · 292
Badjan, Amie · 143, 155
Badjie, Alieu E W F · 383
Bah, Eliman · 78, 83, 84
Bah, Hamat · 399, 420, 421
Bah, Imam Waka · 85
Bah, Sait Matty · 85
Bajo, Kaba · 382, 384, 403
Bakamon · 55, 104, 388
Bakau · 85, 205, 207, 209, 310, 311, 315, 333, 341, 373, 382, 388, 396, 448
Baker, J J · 103, 107, 115, 118, 121, 142, 144, 145, 388
Baker, Mrs Ethel · 106
Baldeh, Alhaji Fallai · 12
Baldeh, Bubacarr · 383, 408
Baldeh, Mathew Yaya · 383
Baldeh, Michael · 207
Baldeh, Paul · 221
Balewa, Abubakar Tafawa · 229

Ballanghar · 8, 25
Ballingho · 337
Bamako · 442, 443, 448
Bamako Declaration of the African Statesmen Initiative · 443
Bamba Saho, A S · 200
Bangladesh · 211, 351, 408
Bangura, Santigie · 440
Banjul Charter, the · 309, 328
Banjul Declaration, The · 42, 363
Banjul Dinner Club · 358
Banjul International Airport · 378, 437
Banjul Polyclinic · 47, 339
Banjul power station · 338
Banjul Sewerage and Drainage Project · 338
Banjulinding · 195, 388, 436
Banksian Medal · 170
Bansang · 8, 47, 115, 122, 145, 147, 149, 180, 287, 339, 352, 412
Bansang Hospital · 47, 115, 180, 339
Banta Sunkutu Kafo · 205
Barajaly · 1, 2, 13, 16, 50, 62, 82, 99, 104, 108, 112, 122, 134, 141, 161, 184, 195, 341, 354, 417, 445, 447
Barajaly Tenda · 4, 37
Barra · 84, 98, 156, 206, 298
Barrokunda · 228
Barthelmy, Sidney · 364
Barthes · 23, 28, 94, 105
Basse · 105, 151, 158, 169, 173, 178, 179, 180, 181, 182, 186, 188, 197, 198, 199, 215, 287, 298, 352
Batchilly, Amara 78
Basse Health Centre · 180
Bathurst Club · 66, 67
Bathurst Golf Course · 66
Bathurst Harbour · 285
Bathurst Reform Club · 231
Bathurst Technical School · 125
Bathurst Town Council · 185, 416
Bathurst Trading Co Ltd · 8
Battle of the Atlantic, the · 106
Bay of Biscay · 61, 156
Bayo, Mr · 419
Bayzid, Nadua · 133, 413
BBC · 101, 123, 311, 354, 387, 415

Index

Becker, Rolf · 413
Bedfordshire · 332
Beijing · 266
Belgian Congo · 191, 216
Belgium · 259
Belgrade · 254, 356
Bello, Sir Ahmadu · 229
Benner, Peter · 387
Berchtesgaden · 131
Berlin · 1, 101, 129, 133, 174, 299
Berlin Conference · 174
Besançon · 262
Biafra War · 261
Bidwell, Ernest · 103, 112, 114, 115, 154, 190
Bilal Boarding School · 444
Bintang Bolong · 63, 197
black market · 351
Black Star Square · 153
Blackburn, Mary · 408
Blain, Anton · 9, 10, 12
Blain, Rene A · 203
Blood, Sir Hilary Rupert · 106, 108, 116, 117, 121
Blue March · 206, 209
BOAC · 104
Bobb, Momodou · 386, 391, 421, 434
Bojang, Aja Asombi · 448
Bojang, Jombo · 188, 197, 202
Bojang, Sanjally · 185, 186, 189, 197, 205, 206, 209, 213, 214, 215, 216, 274, 312, 447
Bojang, Seyfo Landing Barabally · 447
Boka Halaat, Group · 449
Bordeaux · 8, 268
border closures · 356
Boutros-Ghali, Boutros · 376, 392
bovine pleuro-pneumonia · 126, 170, 174, 178, 181
Boxie, Paula · 403
Boye, Njai · 80
Brandt Commission Report · 360
Braun, Eva · 131, 132
Bray, John Patrick · 67, 200
Bread and Butter Demonstrations · 200
Brewer, Edward Frank · 440
Brewer, Heather · 440

Brewer, Stella · 440
Bridge Convention, the · 303
Bridges, Philip · 225, 274
Bright, John Bidwell · 127
Brighton · 393, 408
Brikama conference · 186
Brikamaba · 36, 39, 57, 59
Brikamanding · 325
Bristol University · 145
British Army Training Team · 347, 349
British colonies and dependencies · 139, 250
British dependency · 219
British Empire · 252
British Petroleum · 195, 351
British Veterinary Association · 408, 411, 438
Brittan, Sir Leon · 378
Brown Card insurance system · 260
Brufut · 341, 451
Brumen · 287, 301
Brussels · 255, 291
Buckingham Palace · 250
Buckle Street · 12, 14, 40, 75, 80, 96, 101, 121, 124, 150, 310, 373
Bulock · 63
Bundu, Abass · 352
Burkina Faso · 321, 329, 365, 367, 371
Burma · 125, 130, 131, 133, 136, 366
Burundi · 386
Bush, George H W · 261
Bush, George Walker · 262
Bush, Laura · 262, 363
Busumbala · 291
Busy Bees · 118
Butut Scandal · 306
Bwiam · 64, 87, 180, 447

C

Cable & Wireless · 286
Cadamosto, Alvise · 2
Caisse Central · 263
Camara, Andrew David · 207, 209, 225, 254, 274, 290, 306

Camara, Assan Musa, see also Camara, Andrew · 306, 309, 370, 371, 406, 407, 419, 420, 425
Camara, Kebba · 440, 441
Cambodia · 255
Cambridge · 117, 130, 131, 137, 408
Cambridge Certificate, Junior · 107, 110
Camdessus, Michel · 359
Canada · 252, 280, 385, 387
Cape Verde · 104, 249, 267, 373
Carr, Burghess · 365
Carrol, Delphine · 204
Carrol, Dr Arthur E · 120, 138
Carrol, Dr Reynold · 204
Carrol, Henry Richmond · 8
Carrol, Wilfred Davidson · 120
Carter, Jimmy · 328
Carter, Mrs Lillian · 328
Casamance · 63, 314, 352, 355, 383, 384, 456
Castro, Fidel · 223
Catholic Relief Services · 322
Ceesay, Alieu · 93
Ceesay, Fa Kemo · 19
Ceesay, Fanta · 3
Ceesay, Fatou · 362
Ceesay, Hassum · 248
Ceesay, Kebba S · 380
Ceesay, Ousman Koro · 393
Ceesay, Sompo · 182
Ceesay, Yaya · 290, 370, 383, 439
Central African Republic · 351
Central Bank · 290, 296, 335, 337, 384, 471
Central River Province · 25
Ceylon · 194, 223
CFAO · 8, 17, 36, 149, 155, 204
Chalker, Baroness Lynda · 386, 396
Cham Joof, A E · 200
Cham, Alhaji Braima · 341
Cham, Alhaji Tayib · 422
Cham, M C · 274, 329, 414, 415
Cham, Sainey · 441
Cham, Salieu M · 236
Chambas, Mohamed Ibn · 395, 450
Chamber of Commerce · 24, 29, 67, 206, 240, 284, 345, 384

Chamberlain, Neville · 101
Chambers of Commerce and Industry, Association of Senegambia · 345
Chery, Louis · 204
Chessington · 378
chiefs' conference, annual · 188, 198
China, People's Republic of · 266, 399
China, Republic of · 292, 322, 333, 362, 368, 373, 381
Chirac, Jacques · 395
Chissano, Joachim · 444, 446, 448
CHOGM · 368, 394, 399, 410
Chol, Byong · 351
Christensen, Eric · 236, 254, 326, 406, 407
Christianity · 18, 181
Churchill, Winston · 106, 131, 132, 133
CILSS · 267, 327, 328, 352, 363, 373
circumcision · 80, 193
civic education panel · 332
civic expression · 152
Civil Servants' Association, Junior · 220
Civil Service Resettlement Programme · 335
civil service staff audit · 335
Cleary, Bishop Michael · 433, 446
Clerical School · 125
Clifton Road · 16, 68, 104, 129, 182, 206
Clinton, William Jefferson · 262
closed scholarship · 148
Clucas, Mr · 160
CMAG · 399, 401, 423, 426
Coalition Forces · 367
coalition government · 61, 210
Cold War struggles, the · 281
Cold War · 270
Cole, Joseph Francis · 204
Cole, Mrs Cecilia M R · 110
Cole, Mrs Mary · 110
Colin, Jean · 304, 306
Colley, Fatou Sanneh · 362
Collier, Mrs Catherine · 204
Collingwood, Mr Robert · 389
Coll-Seck, Dr Awa · 443
Colonial Boundaries Commission · 7, 299

Index

Colonial Development and Welfare Grant · 171
Colonial Development Scheme · 107
Colonial Development Welfare Fund · 166
Colonial Secretary Circular · 192
colonialism · 298, 303, 308, 344
colony/protectorate gap · 287
Commercialisation Enterprise, Limes · 292
commissions of inquiry · 390, 395, 398
Committee of Gentlemen · 185
Committee of Islamic Solidarity · 257
Committee of Supply · 269
Committee of the Red Cross · 322
Committee on Post-Conflict Reconstruction and Development · 448
Commonwealth Development Corporation · 285
Commonwealth Human Rights Initiative and the Commonwealth Human Rights Trust, Joint Meeting of the · 368
Commonwealth Medical Conference · 253
Commonwealth Parliamentary Association · 427
Commonwealth Prime Ministers' Conference · 250
Commonwealth Secretariat · 253, 397, 423, 461
communism · 206
community development experts · 258
community development strategies · 293
Compaoré, Blaise · 365, 367
Confederation of Japanese Industries · 254
Conference of West African Heads of State · 278
Congo · 136, 217, 249, 448
Congo Kinshasa · 217
Congolese · 136
Connells · 414
conscription · 103, 118, 141
Conservative Party · 409
constituency boundaries · 243, 390, 462, 463, 468
Constitutional Commission · 394
Constitutional Conference · 202
constitutional development · 186, 210, 219
constitutional instruments · 245
constitutional monarchy · 276
Constitutional Talks · 218, 225, 231, 298
Consumer Price Index · 339
Conté, Lansana · 321, 365, 373, 395
Contemporary Review · 250
Convention People's Party · 152
Cooper, Richard · 105, 106, 182
cooperative societies · 206, 235, 240, 284
Cooperative Union (GCU) · 297
Corbyn, Jeremy · 421
Coronation Day · 162
Cott, Professor Leo · 408
Crab Island School hall · 240
criminal justice system · 317
Crooke, Ian · 312
Cuba · 223, 315
customs union · 350
Cyprus · 223, 410

D

da Costa, Alex · 226, 227, 436, 447, 450
daara · 14, 52, 72, 73, 74, 75, 76, 80, 83, 140
Dabo, Bakary B · 262, 313, 351, 372, 382, 384, 388, 440
Dabo, Solo · 370
Dada, Abubakar · 373
Daffeh, J L B · 225
Daily Observer · 389
Dakar · 66, 103, 109, 118, 204, 216, 255, 287, 300, 311, 321, 348, 391
Dallas · 363, 364
Daly, John Sydney · 120
Dampha, Mamanding · 21, 439
Danish International Development Agency · 338
Dankunku · 5, 19, 53, 62, 87, 228
Danquah, J B · 150
Danso, Mustapha · 316, 317

485

Danzig · 96, 101
Darbo, Sainey · 332
Darboe, Bakari · 8
Darboe, Ousainou · 399, 403, 425, 428
Darsilami · 206
Daschle, Thomas A · 453
Davies, Christian · 102, 159
Davies, Dr H T · 407
Davies, V E · 172
de Almeida, Ralphina · 111
de Gaulle, General Charles · 104
de Sablière, Jean-Marc · 394
Declaration of Human Rights · 165, 308
declaration of independence · 153
decolonisation · 249, 308
Decree 30 · 426
Decree 89 · 404, 420, 421, 423, 426
Defence Agreement, Mutual · 310, 311, 313, 316, 383
Defence and Security Council · 355
Democratic Congress Alliance · 185, 205, 240, 285
Democratic National Convention · 452
Democratic Party · 200, 453
demonetisation · 10, 31
Denton Bridge · 26, 65, 67, 286, 382
Denton, Abou · 409
Denton, Fatma · 409
Denton, Mariam · 403
Department for International Development · 426
deputy speaker · 203, 450
Desertification · 329
devaluation · 334, 339
development expenditure · 241
Development Programme in Education for The Gambia 1965-1975 · 279
Dia, Mamadou · 225, 299, 300, 301
Diagne, Blaise · 210
Diallo, Ibou · 225, 300
Diana, Princess of Wales · 410
Dibba, Kutubo · 306
Dibba, Sheriff Mustapha · 225, 243, 255, 265, 289, 290, 291, 306, 312, 318, 371, 399, 419, 425
Dickens, Charles · 114, 118, 121, 127
Dionewar · 70

Diouf, Abdou · 43, 307, 310, 318, 324, 342, 348, 354, 356, 383, 395, 418
Diouf, Harr N'dofen · 241
Dippakunda Mosque · 358
Dixon, C G · 235
Dobson Street · 99, 116, 120, 139, 316, 436
Doe, Samuel · 364, 365
Doon de River · 161
Drameh, A M · 187
Drammeh, Yugo Kasseh · 203
Drammeh, Yusupha · 326
drought · 3, 257, 267, 291, 322, 324, 327, 328, 334, 363
Dumbuya, Foday Kabba · 5
Durham University · 143, 154

E

Earl of Perth · 301
ECOMOG · 365, 366, 376
Economic Commission for Africa · 373
conomic Recovery Programme · 334
eco-tourism · 264
ECOWAS Council of the Wise · 450
ECOWAS election monitoring team · 451
ECOWAS fact-finding mission 449, 451
ECOWAS Lagos Summit · 282
Edina House · 120
Edinburgh · 79, 117, 148, 152, 162, 167, 253, 411
Edinburgh University · 166
Education of Dallas Independent School · 364
Edwards, Veronique · 356
EEC · 255, 297, 338, 360
Education For All · 149
Egypt · 170, 265, 321, 386
Eichner, Engelbert · 263
Election Observer Group · 365
Electoral Ordinance · 201
Emergency Food Aid Programme · 257
Emergency Regulations · 314
Emir of Kuwait, the · 391
Empire Day · 143

English Channel · 157, 386
Enhanced Structural Adjustment Facility · 360
Enter Gambia – The Birth of an Improbable Nation · 246
eradication of apartheid · 363
ERP · 334, 336, 338, 340, 359, 374
Essau · 47
ET, see also Touray, Ebrima M · 74, 77, 79, 80, 144, 413
Ethiopia · 174, 229
Ethiopian Transition Government · 373
EU · 259, 345, 347, 389, 397, 427, 450
European traders · 8
Expo 70 · 254
External Aid Commission · 322
External Aid Fund · 322
Eyadema, Gnassingbe · 367

F

Faal, Samba · 444
Faal, Sidi · 87, 447
Faal-Sonko, Amina · 409
Fadera, Omar · 445
Fahnbulleh, Boima · 413
Fajikunda · 47
Falconer, Murray A · 406
Fall, Idrissa · 347
Fall, Medoun · 347, 354
Fall, Momar · 312
Fang Bondi · 42
FAO · 173, 175, 194, 253, 256, 322
Farafenni · 206, 287, 303, 310, 313
Farah, A A · 330
Fast Track · 414, 415
Fatoto · 69, 105, 143
Fatou Kess · 77, 413
Fatou Sarr Aret · 93
Fatty *kabilo* · 5, 62, 228
Fatty Kunda · 87
Fatty, Bambo · 5
Fatty, Farba · 185
Fatty, Mama · 5, 6, 11, 18, 21, 30, 33, 34, 39, 52, 54, 62, 72, 89, 151, 255
Fatty, Sankung · 383

Faye, Rev J C · 127, 185, 191, 200, 203, 205, 207, 214, 222, 237, 243
Federal Republic of Germany · 118, 126, 292, 338
Federer, Roger · 446
Field Force · 305, 310, 316, 347, 349
Fifth Pan-African Congress · 152
Finden, Harry · 137
First Five Year Development Plan · 327
Firth of Lorne · 163
Fischer-Dieskan, Tomas · 389
Fit For Life gym · 418
Flag March · 373
Foday Burang · 3
Fofana, Bukari · 189
Foni Bintang Karanai · 224
Foni Sintet · 87
food aid rations · 130
food self-sufficiency · 257
Foon, Kebba W · 127, 199, 203, 243
foot and mouth disease · 451
Foot, Sir Hugh · 240
Forbes, Burnham · 162
Formalised Spleen Vaccine (FSV) · 175
Forster, Hettie · 154
Forster, Sam John · 137, 331
Fort James · 299
Forward Group · 165
Forward, Miss Helen · 115
Fourah Bay College · 79, 81, 154
Fowlis, Marion · 103, 154, 164
Fowlis, Master · 102, 129
Fr Grainge, see also Grainge, Fr Alan Herbert · 181, 182, 183
France · 101, 118, 133, 137, 174, 211
Frank, A Lumley · 183
Frankfurt · 264
Frazer, Master Robert A · 76
Frederich Ebert Foundation, the · 263
Free Trade Agreement · 302
Freetown · 8, 29, 51, 80, 117, 154, 229
French Sudan · 3
Fulladu · 4, 5, 39, 44, 45, 98, 169, 463
Furness, Alan · 385
Futa Jallon · 39
Faye, Mustapha 100
Fye, Sheikh Omar · 130, 139, 202

G

Gabon · 212, 330, 455
Gambia, A History of The· 409
Gambia Air Shuttle · 353
Gambia College · 81
Gambia Commercial and Development Bank · 293, 296, 297, 335, 338, 440
Gambia Congress Party · 274
Gambia Court of Appeal · 331, 333, 459
Gambia Cricket Association · 115
Gambia Democratic Party · 127, 187, 200
Gambia Echo · 183, 207
Gambia Government Development Programme 1964 – 1967, The · 227
Gambia Independence Act 1964, The · 244
Gambia Independence Constitution, The · 243
Gambia Minerals Ltd · 285
Gambia Muslim Congress · 127, 203, 205, 243
Gambia National Army · 346, 347, 349, 362, 372, 373, 379, 381, 388, 400
Gambia National Gendarmerie · 347, 372
Gambia National Insurance Corporation · 292, 293
Gambia National Party · 97, 127, 187, 200, 203, 207
Gambia Oilseeds Marketing Board · 26, 171, 206, 240, 284, 292
Gambia People's Party · 362, 425, 458
Gambia Ports Authority · 336, 383
Gambia Public Transport Corporation · 263, 292, 357
Gambia Red Cross · 352
Gambia River Basin Project (OMVG) · 126, 268, 337
Gambia River Transport Company · 293
Gambia Solidarity Party · 213
Gambia Students Union · 418
Gambia Technical Training Institute · 339
Gambia Telecommunications Company (Gamtel) · 262

Gambia Women's Contemporary Society · 204, 205
Gambia Workers' Union · 217, 220
Gambianisation · 219, 233, 234
Gamsen · 436
Gandhi, Mahatma · 72
Garnet, C B · 170
Garscube · 163
Gateway Project · 375, 376, 377, 394
Gaye, Alh Bun · 316
Gaye, Alkali James · 382, 383, 419
Gaye, Sulayman Beran · 203
Gaza · 265
Gendarmerie, Confederal · 354
gender discrimination · 361
Geneva · 115, 122, 353
George, J A · 164
George, Sam H A · 103, 221
Georgetown · 1, 8, 30, 46, 52, 53, 76
German Kaiser · 6
German U-boats · 104
GFCMA · 25
Ghana · 53, 115, 116, 122, 152, 153, 172, 191, 194, 211, 212, 223, 226
Ghana Veterinary Assistants School · 227
Gibb, James A · 163
Gillette, Michael · 359
Gladstein, Nigel · 414
Glasgow · 53, 126, 148, 149, 152, 153
Global Committee of Parliamentarians · 366
Global Leadership for Climate Action · 453
Goddard, Sam Daniel · 220
Goebbels · 132
Golan Heights · 265
Gold Coast · 76, 81, 136, 139, 141
Gold Coasters · 136, 152
Golf Club · 66, 309, 371
Gomez, Diego · 2
Gooch, G P · 250
Goodenough, Anthony · 386
Gore, Paul · 224, 238
Gorée-Ndiaye, Galandou · 249
Gougou, Ebrima · 136
Government House · 78, 156, 199, 200, 224, 245

Government Wharf · 155, 165, 239, 289
GPMB · 204, 292, 297, 335, 336, 337
Grainge, Fr Alan Herbert · 181
Grant Street, 48 · 209
Grante, Frederick E · 235
grants-in-aid · 223, 227, 246, 291, 292
Great Expectations · 119, 123
Greater Banjul Area · 286, 338, 424
Grenoble · 262
Grey-Johnson, Crispin · 200, 203
griots · 7, 10, 41
GSP · 213, 214, 215
GUC · 293, 297, 336, 338, 441
Guinea · 17, 191, 211, 249, 255, 267, 315, 321, 348, 365, 370, 395, 455
Guinea Bissau · 17, 249, 268, 315, 321, 348, 352, 353, 355, 365, 370, 395
Gunjur · 399
Guys Hospital · 180
Gwadabe, Colonel Lawan · 379

H

Haass, Richard N · 453
Habré, Hissein · 383
Hagan Street, 15 · 18, 147
Haley, Alex · 264
Half Die · 12, 32, 50, 75, 98, 104, 113, 138, 157, 184, 193, 206, 381
Hall, Kelvin · 159
Hamlyn, W T · 76
Hammarskjold Dag · 216
Handel, George Frideric · 159
Harare Declaration · 423
Harare Principles · 368, 394
Hardie, Michael J · 389
Harding, Bertil · 264
Harriman, W Averell · 261
Hart, Michael · 414, 415
Haythornwaite, Mr W · 183
Haywards Heath · 176, 309, 311, 387, 393, 406, 407, 413, 414, 415, 421
Health Week · 106
Henman, Tim · 446
Hennemeyer, Robert T · 298
Hetherington, Sir Hector · 163

Hindustan Oil Corporation · 336
Hitler, Adolf · 96, 100, 129, 135, 230
HMCS Mansa Kila Kuta · 228
HMS Gambia · 118
Hogan & Miller · 391
Holmes, Major Robert · 299
Holt, Harold · 250
Honolulu · 254
Honorary Procurator for Afro-European Dialogue · 263
Houphouet-Boigny, Felix · 210, 267, 328, 368
House of Commons · 396, 398, 400, 401, 402, 408, 420, 421, 423, 426, 427
House of Lords · 396
House of Representatives · 121, 201, 203, 209, 222, 225, 231, 234, 235
Howe, J · 183
HRH the Duke of Kent · 245
Hughes, Arnold · 409
Hughes, B A · 164
human rights fundamental · 212, 272
Humphrey-Smith, G · 170
Hydara, Lt Sadibou · 382

I

IDA · 288, 289, 337
IFAD · 332
IMF · 261, 280, 296, 320, 333, 334, 336, 340, 351, 359, 360, 377
import substitution · 331
Indemnity Act · 419
Independence Manifesto, The · 35, 171, 211, 216, 455
Independence Stadium · 333, 373, 448
Independent Electoral Commission · 400, 423
India · 72, 170, 194, 208, 223, 253, 358
indigenisation · 236, 247
Indigenous Business Advisory Service · 335
industrialisation · 285
INEC · 450, 451
insect infestation · 334

Institute of Higher Islamic Studies in Nouakchott · 255
Instruments of Ratification of the Protocols of the Senegambia · 344
Integrated Energy Project · 337
Interim Government, Liberian · 367
internal self-government · 212, 231, 237, 238, 239, 320, 456
International Commission of Jurists · 308
International Labour Office · 125
International Livestock Centre for Africa · 374
International Monetary Fund · 333
International Planned Parenthood Federation · 416
International Red Cross · 353
International Society for Human Rights · 397
international trade · 174, 255, 278, 281, 282, 360
inter-state ministerial meetings · 299, 346
inviolability · 256, 388
Iran- Iraq War · 392
Iran-Iraq Peace Committee · 343
Islam · 6, 42, 74, 181, 256, 257, 422
Islamic Development Bank · 292
Islamic education · 123
Islamic Party · 322
Islamic Peace Committee · 256, 366
Islamic Solidarity Fund · 292
Isle of Arran, · 161, 162
Isle of Mull · 163
Israel · 264, 265, 280, 281
Italy · 47, 254, 259, 328, 373
Ivory Coast · 210, 248, 267, 328, 353, 367

J

Jabang, Lamin K · 370
Jack, Alhaji Sir A S · 434
Jagan, Cheddi · 162
Jagne, C I · 103, 154, 155
Jagne, Gibou · 370
Jagne, Siga Fatma · 111

Jah, Matarr · 370
Jahally · 59, 332, 337
Jahally/Pacharr · 332, 337
Jahumpa, I M Garba · 81, 96, 127, 152, 185, 191, 203, 205, 207, 210, 214
Jaiteh, Alhaji Bakary · 341
Jakarlo · 332
Jallow, Hassan · 379, 382, 383
Jallow, Abdoulie · 143
Jallow, Alpha · 434
Jallow, Arona · 93, 150
Jallow, Ebou · 390, 392, 397
Jallow, Ebrima (Pa Yoma) · 11, 13, 16, 28, 29, 32, 34, 38, 50, 54, 56, 58, 61, 69, 72, 74, 88, 90, 94, 99, 104, 106, 109, 112, 116, 119, 134, 139, 141, 147, 150, 155, 158, 165
Jallow, Korka · 445
Jallow, M E · 217, 220, 221, 222
Jallow, Momodou C · 274
Jallow, Njiin · 79
Jallow, Omar (OJ) · 341, 383, 400, 419, 420, 421, 423, 424, 425, 433, 434, 436
Jallow, Sgt Major Ousman · 134
Jambur · 311
James Island · 298, 299
Jammeh, Ansu · 451
Jammeh, Ebrima · 321
Jammeh, Ismaila · 314
Jammeh, Kemeseng · 370
Jammeh, Sarjo · 434
Jammeh, Seyfo Tamba · 176, 186
Jammeh, Tamba · 203
Jammeh, Yahya A J J · 262, 379, 382, 399, 400, 423, 428, 430, 432, 434, 436, 437, 444, 448
Janha, Abdou Sara · 236, 391, 392, 403, 404, 434
Janneh, Landing Kotoring · 190
Janneh, Madiba · 189
Jarju, Malafi · 403
Jarjussey, Phoday · 391, 401, 413, 417, 434
Jarra, M Mass · 325
Jarra, Tamassa · 76, 81
Jarret, Mr · 115

Index

Jatta, Aja Fatounding · 341
Jatta, Sidia · 370, 399
Jawara Jawara · 295
Jawara, Alfousaine · 5
Jawara, Alhaji Essa · 444
Jawara, Alhaji Saikounding · 447
Jawara, Almami · 382, 383, 410, 452, 453
Jawara, Almamy · 4, 6, 10, 13, 16, 32, 35, 39, 43, 45, 46, 48, 51, 62, 68, 78, 91, 95
Jawara, Augusta · 101, 108, 112, 117, 122, 151, 162, 167, 179, 181, 184, 189, 195, 204, 207, 228, 361, 441, 449
Jawara, Basadi · 3, 6, 7, 13, 15, 19, 34, 53, 124, 145, 146, 392
Jawara, Barrsa · 3, 27
Jawara, Bouba · 6, 7, 19, 33, 39, 48, 53, 55, 57, 63, 65, 68, 74, 89, 92, 112
Jawara, Chilel · 255, 308, 311, 315, 326, 358, 363, 381, 386, 406, 412, 413, 416, 421, 436, 439, 453
Jawara, David Kwesi, see also Jawara Dawda Kairaba · 16, 182
Jawara, Dawda Kairaba · 15, 403, 413, 449, 473
Jawara, Dawda, see also Jawara, Dawda Kairaba · 15, 322, 382, 386, 403, 410, 413, 430, 433, 436, 446, 449, 452, 453, 473
Jawara, Ebrima · 291, 311, 382, 383, 409, 413, 417, 422, 433, 436, 441
Jawara, Fatoumata · 255, 311, 372, 378, 382, 386, 453
Jawara, Foday Sheriffo · 3, 7, 93, 343, 378, 417
Jawara, Fura · 12, 38, 54
Jawara, Ismaila · 400, 445
Jawara, Jarai · 6, 7, 18, 21, 39, 48, 53, 89, 447
Jawara, Kaba · 430, 445
Jawara, Kawsu · 5, 45, 145, 378, 408, 410, 433, 436, 437, 453
Jawara, Kawsukebba · 146
Jawara, Kawsunding · 147, 192
Jawara, Mama · 400

Jawara, Mawdo, see also Jawara, Almamy · 34, 45, 89, 91, 92, 94, 123, 138, 146, 322
Jawara, Mba · 3, 34, 78, 88, 445
Jawara, Nacesay · 219, 303, 452
Jawara, Ndey Mengeh · 449
Jawara, Nema · 121, 354, 410, 421, 452, 452, 453
Jawara, Njaimeh · 43, 255, 291, 302, 308, 311, 333, 355, 373, 378, 382, 409, 413, 417, 441, 444, 446, 452
Jawara, Baby Njaimeh · 412, 413, 437
Jawara, Ramatoulie · 204, 308, 311, 382, 386, 453
Jawara, Saihou Almamy · 13, 16, 77, 78, 80, 98, 124, 297, 310, 371, 379, 381, 411
Jawara, Saikounding · 45, 448
Jawara, Wandifa · 446
Jawara, Yagou Cham· 441
Jawneh, Neneh · 5
Jawo, Agnes · 362
Jaycox, Edward V K · 396
Jaye, Abdoulie · 72, 73
Jeddah · 255
Jejew · 431
Jeng, Sheikh M · 325
Jeshwang · 285, 286
Jesper, Jeremy · 386
Jienna, Mamanding · 21
Jobarteh, Alexander · 97, 123, 127
Jobarteh, Saikou · 97
Jobe, Abdoulie · 417
Jobe, Dodou · 140
Jobe, Imam Ratib Abdoulie · 85, 319
Jobe, Mam Malick · 78
Jobe, Momodou Lamin Sedat · 452
Jobe, Sering Habib · 72, 83, 84, 85, 93, 134, 193, 388
Joe Loss Orchestra · 159
Johannesburg · 447
John, Ibrahim A S Burang · 273, 274
John, Sering Matarr · 69, 72, 73, 74, 83, 93, 121, 134, 142
Johnson, Dr Barry · 377
Johnson, Lilian · 361
Joiner, Thomas Hamilton · 66

Joint Industrial Council, the · 220
Jokadu · 187
Jola · 31, 431
Jones, Doreen · 404, 405
Jones, Dr Sam H O · 145
Jones, Dr Ulric · 404, 405
Jones, Melville Senami Benoni ·127, 200, 207
Jones, Melville E · 316
Jones, Sam H M · 103, 105, 120, 123
Joof, Kaliba · 93
Joof, Mariatou · 78
Joof, Modou · 102
Joof, Lucretia St Claire · 361
Joof, Ousman Kaliba · 77
Jordan · 248
Judicial Service Commission · 272, 469
Juff, Providence · 137
Juffureh · 264
Junges, Rudolf · 258
Juwara, Lamin Waa · 403

K

Kabbah, Ahmed Tejan · 409
Kaduna · 229
Kafo · 185
Kah, Cherno Mass · 85
Kaiaf · 190
Kairaba Avenue · 382, 400
Kairabe · 124
Kaladan · 125, 133
Kaladan valley · 125
Kalagi · 63, 64
Kalley, Karanta · 452
Kambeng Kafo · 185
Kanifing · 352, 404, 420, 425
Kanikunda · 176
Kanilai · 429, 431, 436
Kantora · 39, 42, 133, 197, 206, 371
Kanuteh, Fabala · 326
Kanyi, Amang · 225, 243
Kaolack · 98, 303, 306
Karamo, Seyfo · 190, 198
Karantaba · 2
Karoni · 5, 6, 431

Kartong · 311, 315, 362
Kashmir · 358
Kassama, Kemba · 370
Kassama, Momodu · 380
Katamina · 228
Katchikali · 209
Kaunda, Kenneth · 254, 268
Kaur · 3, 4, 25, 46, 47, 55, 105, 206, 287, 343, 345, 352
Kaur Declaration, the · 341, 343, 344
Kayes · 4, 98
Kebba Dinding · 5
Keil, Fred · 406
Keita, Musa · 185
Kembuje · 215
Kemoto · 228
Keneba · 228
Kent Street Vous, the · 305
Kenya · 170, 175, 176, 191, 259, 276, 308, 317, 394, 416
Kenyatta, Jomo · 198
Kerewan · 206
Kettler, Jacob · 298
Khan, Mam Sulay · 78
Khan, Seyfo Abu · 274
Kiang · 6, 63, 141, 178, 187, 190, 368
Kibaki, Mwai · 446
Kiesslings · 411
Kiessling, Wolfgang · 413
Kijera, Kaddy · 78
Kijera, Lamin · 28
Kijera, Neneh · 5
Kijerah, Jarai · 21
Kijerah, Mustapha · 78
Kim Il-Sung · 351
King George VI · 409
King Abdul Aziz · 256
King sisters · 154
King, Tom · 102, 118
Kinshasa · 216, 249
Kinteh, Kunta · 264
Kirkley Hall Farm Institute · 117
Kirsch, J M · 243
Klerk, F W de · 363
Kohl, Chancellor Helmut · 263
Kolingba, Andre · 352
Kombo Beach Novotel · 264

Index

Kombo Niumi Lillahi Wa Rasuli Society · 185
Kombo St Mary · 191, 201, 211, 322
Koro Wuleng · 59, 61
Koroma, Johnny Paul · 409
Kotu · 338
Koungheul · 97
Kristi Kunda · 182
Krubally, Moriba · 203
Krubally, Muhammadou · 203
Krubally, Nfally · 116
Krubally, Seyfo Jewru · 186
Krubally, Seyfo Moriba · 116
Kudang · 61, 88, 116, 362
Kufuor, John · 436
Kujabi, Abdoulie · 429, 430, 437
Kunta Mamburay · 439
Kuntaur · 8, 30, 45, 78, 88, 97, 105, 140, 153, 206, 220, 287
Kuntaya · 274
Kuru Boy Secka · 16
Kuwait · 366, 398

L

Labour Party · 165, 210, 401, 402, 421
Lady Chilel · 343
Lady Denham · 105
Lady Mahoney · 121
Lady Singhateh, 209
Lady Windley · 170, 216
Lady Wyn-Harris · 170
Lagos, Richard · 452
Lahtharyiou · 83
Lamb, P F C · 183
Lambert, Dr · 422
Lamin, Momodou · 11, 85, 272, 290, 310, 391, 408, 413, 417, 434, 451
Laminkoto · 287
Lane, Delia · 416
Lane, K J W · 225, 235, 243, 416
Langley, Dr Jabez Ayo · 236, 325
Lara, Brian · 407
Larkin, Gregory · 421
LCA · 11, 23, 36
Le Foe, Dominic · 250

Lebanon · 253, 265
Lederles Wingweb Newscastle disease · 176
Lee, Mr Clive · 313
Leeds · 159
Legislative Council · 121, 127, 139, 186, 199, 201, 202, 209, 219, 224
Leigh, Koba · 203
Lellie · 38, 54, 55
Lennox-Boyd, Allan · 199, 200
liberalism · 165
liberation movements · 230, 249
Libya · 255, 257, 268, 292, 315, 317, 321, 322, 391
Lille · 262
Limann, Hilla · 309, 330
Limassol · 394
Linge, Heinz · 131
lingua franca · 13, 252
Lister, J V · 164
livestock development · 288
Livestock Marketing Board · 330, 332
Livestock Show, Annual · 375
Lloyd, Tony · 401
Lloyd-Evans, Marion · 164
Local government administration · 231
Lomé Convention programmes · 360
London Independence Conference · 137
Longfellow, Henry Wadsworth · 147
Louvel Square · 101, 436
Louvel Street · 102, 388
Lowe, Badou · 130
LRV · 173, 175
Lucas, Mr · 183
Luce, Richard · 309, 312
Lumumba, Patrice · 216
Lungi Airport · 406
Lusack, Mr Mungo · 183
Lusaka · 254
Luther, Martin King · 72
Lyon · 174

M

Macauley Commission, the · 398
Macauley QC, Berthan · 226

Index

Macauley, Patricia · 297
MacCarthy Island · 1, 2, 3, 8, 35, 42, 45, 47, 93, 188, 217
MacCarthy Island Province · 1, 2, 3, 8, 35, 42, 45, 47, 93
MacCarthy Square · 103, 114, 130, 245, 274, 288, 324, 371, 381, 454
MacCarthy, Brigadier Gen Charles · 78
Macmillan, Harold · 198
Madalo · 3
Madi, Bobby · 9
Madi, Henry · 9, 12, 23, 66, 67, 186, 198, 199, 203, 221, 222
Maghreb · 268
Magna Carta · 165
Mahoney, Eku · 316
Mahoney, Fergusson · 192, 198
Mahoney, Florence · 2, 122
Mahoney, G W Fergusson · 188
Mahoney, Hannah · 162, 182, 204, 421
Mahoney, J E · 203
Mahoney, James L · 122, 198, 203
Mahoney, Sir John · 119
Mahoney, John Andrew · 162
Mahoney, Louise · 103, 154
Major, John · 396, 409
Malaria · 46, 443
Malaysia · 236, 248, 373
Mali · 3, 93, 191, 267, 343, 365, 373
Malta Solution · 210
Mam Laity · 16, 93
Management Development Inst · 339
Management Services Gambia · 293
Mandela, Nelson · 72, 362, 374
Mandinaba – Selety road · 302
Manjago · 31, 140
Manneh, Bakary · 185
Manneh, Dr Momodou · 18
Manneh, Foday · 74, 78, 79
Manneh, Jikiba · 17
Mano River Union · 350
Mansa Kila Kuta III · 258
Mansakonko · 287, 369, 371, 372
Mansfield Street, London · 411
Maputo · 448
marble system · 203
Marché Mussanté · 70, 140
Mardi Gras · 364
Marenah, Lamin · 61, 116, 143, 185, 190, 279
Margai, Albert · 229
Marine Dockyard · 285
Marine Unit · 362, 380, 382
Marketing · 25, 292
Marlborough House · 137, 242, 397, 423
Marriage of Figaro · 160
Marseille · 8
Marshall, Catherine · 375
Martin, Sir John · 243
Maryhill · 160
Masire, Quett · 367
Massawa · 174
maternal and child health delivery · 47
Mau Mau · 191, 198
Maudsley Hospital, The · 406
Maurel & Prom · 8, 23, 122
Maurel Frères · 8
Mauritania · 83, 212, 255, 321, 455
Mbakeh, Seyfo Omar · 209, 222, 243
Mbeh · 143, 166
Mbeki, Thabo · 448
Mboge, Alieu · 383
Mboge, Lamin Bora · 274, 291
Mboge, Mary · 362
Mboge, Momodou · 373
Mboge, Saja · 188
Mboge, Seyfo Bora · 62
Mboge, Seyfo Saja · 302
Mboob, Abdoulie · 310, 325, 330
Mbye, Abdou Wally · 150
Mbye, Demba · 193
Mbye, Joanna · 81
McCall-Judson, Anthony · 391
McDonnell, John · 401, 402, 420, 421, 423
McGregor Laird · 156, 164
McIntyre, Professor Ian · 259, 377
McLeod, Iain · 218, 221, 422
Mecca Declaration · 256
Medical Research Council · 48, 259, 315
medicine, human · 74, 145, 148, 149
Medina · 59
Meet the Farmers Tour · 178, 338, 368
Meeting of Foreign Ministers · 249

Index

Mein Kampf · 134
Mendy, Bissenti · 31, 54
Mer, Kebbeh · 32
Messrs Cable & Wireless Co Ltd · 225
Messrs L Vezia & Co Ltd · 8
Messrs S Horton Jones & Co Ltd · 8
Methodist Boys' High School · 59, 74, 79, 97, 100, 105, 111, 117, 120, 128, 131, 138, 143, 150, 183
Methodist Girls' High School · 106, 109, 111, 115, 119, 127, 154, 164
MFDC · 352
Miami University · 403
Middle East · 265, 281, 366
Mile 2 · 310
millennium bug · 418
Millennium Development Goals · 442
Millerson, Jean Claude · 374
Millson, Tony · 402
Ministry of Economic Planning and Industrial Development · 264, 291
Ministry of Finance · 296
Ministry of Women's Affairs · 361
Ministry of Youth and Sports · 304
Miss ECOWAS · 408
Mitterrand, François · 262
mobilisation of personnel · 103
Mobutu Sese Seko · 249, 385, 410
Mohammad-ul-Mustapha · 421
Mohammedan School · 13, 14, 52, 72, 77, 81, 85, 91, 95, 98, 117, 182, 193, 388
MOJA · 316, 317, 413, 417
Momoh, Joseph Saidu · 321, 364, 365
monarchical constitution · 234
Monday, H R · 238
Monday, Horace R Jr · 289, 293
monetary integration · 343, 346, 353
monetary union · 344, 346, 347, 350
Monrovia · 267, 278, 282, 308, 367
Moose, George · 392
Morgan, Tommy Taylor · 359
Morocco · 268, 348, 353, 362
Mother Teresa · 410
Mount Holyoke College · 298
Movement for the Restoration of Democracy · 402
Mozambique · 249, 446, 448

Mozart · 160
Mpolo, Maurice · 216
MRDG-UK · 402, 403, 404, 420
Mudenge, Stan · 399
Mugabe, Robert · 268, 446
Muguga · 175, 176
Mules, S G · 79, 115
multi-party democracy · 392, 394, 412
Mungo Park · 2
Munich · 101, 131, 263
Musa Molloh · 4, 5
Muslim Congress · 200
Muslim High School · 444
Muslim *Ummah* · 256
Mussolini · 132
Mutual, Defence Pact · 307
MV Aureol · 164
MV Sekondi · 167
My Command · 420, 452

N

Naim, A J · 358
Nairobi · 198, 249, 308, 317, 416, 446
Najum · 140
Namibia · 268, 282, 442
Nancy · 55, 120
nassarano · 8, 36, 184
Nasser · 265
National Agricultural Research Institute (NARI), the · 259
National Consultative Commission · 389
national currency · 211, 289
National Democratic Institute · 442, 461
National Development Programme · 284, 285, 290, 292, 327
National Health Development Project · 339
National Health Service · 168, 408, 422
National Horticultural Show · 378
national identity · 111
National Investment Board · 293, 336, 383
National Museum · 105
National Order of the Republic of The Gambia · 290, 302, 366

National Party · 200, 210
National Population Commission · 375
national press corps · 269
National Reconciliation Party · 399, 420
national sovereignty · 211, 214
National Trading Corporation · 292, 335, 383
National Union of Senegalese Chambers of Commerce and Industry · 345
National Women's Council Act · 361
National Youth Conference and Festival · 375
National Youth Policy · 375
nationwide examinations · 82
NCP · 291, 314, 320, 345, 371, 399, 425, 458
Ndey Kendak Sarr · 140, 141
Ndey Kumba · 57, 58, 62, 63, 68, 69, 88, 98, 158
NDI · 442, 448, 452
Ndiaye, Ababacar · 275
Ndiaye, Waldiodio · 299
Ndiouga, Ndiaye · 386
Ndour, Youssou · 303
Ndow, Demba A · 236
Ndow, Harriet · 110
Ndow, Seyfo Dodou · 78
Ndure, Ebou · 384
Nemakunku · 382
Nene Wally · 79, 150
Netherlands, Kindgom of the · 47, 258, 328, 332, 337
New Orleans · 364
New Partnership for Africa's Development · 448
New York · 226, 248, 255, 265, 278, 378, 392, 393, 427, 444
*New York Time*s · 226
New Zealand · 252, 394, 399
Newcastle · 117, 149, 176
News Bulletin, Daily · 130
Newspaper Decrees · 421
Ngum, Mustapha · 422
Niamina · 5, 35, 37, 61, 62, 87, 98, 228, 302, 371, 373
Niang, Mansour · 354
Niani · 1, 5, 8, 21, 35, 78, 187, 371

Niass, Cheikh Ahmed · 322
Niasse, Moustapha · 345, 384
NIB · 293, 296, 335
Niger · 22, 267, 329
Nigeria · 76, 81, 139, 168, 172, 176, 198, 211, 223, 236, 255, 261, 276, 292, 330, 356, 363, 365, 395, 419, 442, 449, 455
Nigerian Army Training and Advisory Group · 373, 379
Nigerian Trust Fund · 332
Niodior · 70
Niumi Samba · 78, 88
Nja Kunda · 206
Njie, Alieu Badara · 187, 207, 209, 217, 225, 226, 243, 250, 325, 342
Njie, Andrew · 103
Njie, Bakary · 263
Njie, E D · 226, 238, 239
Njie, Ebrima · 185
Njie, Harriet · 111
Njie, Housainou · 400, 439
Njie, Ibrahim · 422
Njie, Isatou · 111
Njie, Louise Antoinette · 110, 323, 362
Njie, M D · 235
Njie, Master Abdoulie · 81
Njie, Momodou Musa · 274, 312
Njie, Momodou Ndow · 391, 411, 417, 422, 434, 437
Njie, Awa · 81
Njie, P S · 185, 191, 200, 209, 214, 217, 222, 226, 238, 243, 273, 300
Nkrumah, Kwame · 116, 150, 151, 152, 153, 162, 191, 194, 216, 226, 229
Nna, Isatou 34
Nna Jarai · 11, 21, 34, 39, 40, 89
No Elections campaign · 396
Non-Aligned Movement · 254, 270, 356
non-formal and adult functional education · 339
Norodom Sihanouk, Prince · 255
North Atlantic Treaty Organisation (NATO) · 254, 281
North Korea · 254, 255, 351
North-South cooperation · 360
North-South trade · 289

496

NPFL · 365, 366, 368
Nujoma, Sam · 442
Nyabally, Alhaji Yusupha · 133
Nyassi, Shyngle · 402
Nyerere, Mwalimu Julius · 268

O

OAU · 229, 249, 253, 260, 265, 268, 270, 275, 277, 281, 307, 308, 317, 365, 368, 374, 394, 435, 446
Obafemi Awolowo University · 445
Obama, Barack Hussein · 453
Obasanjo, Olusegun · 419, 445, 450, 452
OECD · 292
Office of Former Presidents · 432
OIC · 256, 257, 270, 343, 348, 366, 391
Okito, Joseph · 216
OMVG · 303, 337, 350
one-party system of governance · 319
open scholarship · 145, 148, 155, 160
Operation Foday Kabba · 316
Operation Tesito · 293
Osaka · 254
Osei, Isaac · 436
Othman, Shariff · 159, 161, 162
Ouagadougou · 267, 321, 371
Oueddei, Ghoukouni · 383
Ould Ahmed, Mohammed Lamin · 352
Ould Baba, Cheikh Sidi Ahmed · 355
Ould Daddah, Mouktar · 255
Ould Taya, Ahmed · 352
Owens, Mary · 110
Oyster Creek Bridge · 337

P

Pa Abdou Karim · 11, 46, 50, 91
Pa Arthur Johnson · 113, 120
Pa Cecil Richards · 102, 129
Pa Horton Jones · 106
Pa Jones · 50
Pa Miguel · 18
Pa O B Cham · 383
Pa Omar Jallow · 143
Pa Ousman Semega Janneh · 18
Pa Puye Njie · 248
Pa Sallah Jagne · 356, 382, 384
Paco Buerbaum · 413
Pakau · 5
Pakistan · 170, 223, 358, 362, 373, 408
Palestine and Jerusalem Session · 256
Pall Mall gentleman · 154
Palmer, Arnold · 332
Palmer, Dr Sammy · 103, 194, 446
Palmer, J · 145, 316
Palmer, Rachel · 221, 222, 290
Palmine Ltd · 8
pan-Africanism · 194
Panchang · 445
Panda Lewis Commission · 220
Papa Njie & Sons · 440
Paradise Lost · 234
parastatals · 292, 293, 296, 330, 336, 383
Paris · 1, 101, 137, 210, 262, 263, 299, 386, 393, 395, 410
Parliament, Confederal · 345, 346, 355
parliamentary democracy · 319
Parti Democratique Senegalais · 385
Parti Socialiste · 240, 418
partitioning · 1
passaging · 173
Paton, Sergeant Major Tim · 347
Paul, Lady Audrey · 440
Paul, Sir John Warburton · 224, 440
pax para bellum · 410
PDOIS · 362, 371, 399, 400, 404
Peace Committee · 256, 348, 391
Peace Corps volunteers · 279
Percival, D A · 235
performance contracts · 336, 360
peripheral and dependent status · 257
Perth · 162
Peters, Asi, see also Mahoney, Florence · 122
Peters, Capt George · 103, 130
Peters, Femi · 420, 421
Peters, Lenrie · 390, 398
Petersen, V Q · 66, 67, 286
Pettitt, R G · 243
Peutinger Collegium, the · 132, 263
Phan Buoy Hak · 255

Photo, the · 78, 99, 120
Pignard, Charles · 137
Pinai · 6
pioneer church missions · 76
Pisania · 2
Plan of Action · 282
Plowright, Dr Walter · 174, 175
Poland · 95, 96, 101, 102
Port of Banjul · 288
Poverty Alleviation Programme · 397
Powell, Clifford · 79
PPP · 17, 58, 59, 61, 77, 78, 104, 187, 188, 190, 197, 198, 204, 206, 208, 287, 404, 447, 453, 458, 460, 470
PPP Bureau · 319
PPP Central Committee · 218, 356, 368, 369, 372
PPP, Third National Congress of the · 323
PPS · 126, 128, 185, 188, 202, 209
pre-colonial heritage · 303
pre-election assessment teams · 400
prefect of the class · 83
Preferential Trade Area · 357
Pretoria · 374
price control · 332
price stabilisation · 240
Primary Health Care · 47
Prince Charles, Prince of Wales · 309
Prince Johnson · 365, 366
Prince Philip, the Duke of Edinburgh · 378
Princess Anne · 363, 377
Princess Royal Hospital · 422
principles of democracy · 134, 263, 282, 319, 463
principles of natural justice · 135
principles of responsible democracy · 389
privatisation · 284, 292
Pro-Democracy Movement · 393
Programme for Sustained Development, the · 359
programme of democratic transition · 397
programme of transition · 389
Protectionism · 289

Protectorate People's Society · 173
provincial chiefs · 127
PSD · 359, 360, 374
Public Records Section · 229
Public Service Commission · 172, 233, 237, 243, 272
Public Utilities Department · 129
Public Works Department · 221, 286, 287
Pyongyang · 351

Q

Quainoo, Arnold · 365
Quartey, Grace · 378
Quartey, Sidney · 194, 227
Queen Elizabeth II · 121, 162, 164, 244, 245, 250, 291, 410
Queen of Tonga · 162

R

Rabat · 348
Radio Syd · 315
Radville Farm · 382
Raltson, D D · 378
Rawlings, Flight Lt Jerry · 330, 365
Rebellion · 205
reconstruction · 285, 293, 302, 342, 423
recovery and restructuring · 359
Rectification Programme · 397
recurrent and development expenditure · 246
Rees, Dr J E · 407
Reffles, Joseph Fox · 137
Reffles, William · 137
reforestation · 328
rehabilitation and reconstruction programme · 330
Reitsch, Hanna · 230
religion · 6, 76, 82, 85, 93, 94, 108, 109, 123, 181, 182, 259, 281, 348
Rendall, Cecilia · 110
Render, Arlene · 392
Renner, Elizabeth · 362

498

Republican Constitution · 271, 276
republicanism · 244, 271, 273
Research Alliance of South Africa · 442
Research and Diversification Project · 337
Residence de Medina · 383, 385
residency clauses · 203
resigning my appointment · 173, 192
retrenchment · 335, 359
Rhodesia · 249, 251, 252, 253, 268, 282
Rice, Berkeley · 246
rights of the individual · 278, 388
Riley, Mrs · 15, 77
Riley, Petersen · 102
rinderpest · 86, 126, 169, 170, 173, 174, 175, 176, 178, 186, 216, 329
Rio Pongas · 39, 120
rites of passage · 42
Ritz Cinema · 198
River Clyde · 161
River Niger · 2
Road infrastructure · 228
Robben Island · 72
Robert R Nathan Associates Inc · 296
Roberts, Gabriel John · 400
Roman Catholic Mission · 76
Roosevelt, Franklin · 133
Roots · 264
Rosso Mauritanie · 353
Royal Air Force · 66, 129, 136
Royal College of Veterinary Surgeons · 163, 164, 376
Royal Dick School of Veterinary · 166, 377
Royal Infirmary · 162
Royal Navy · 104
Royal Norwegian Society Emergency AID · 297
Royal Scottish National Orchestra · 159, 160
Royal Show, the · 377
Royal Victoria Hospital · 47, 74, 115, 255, 325, 339
Royal West Africa Frontier Force · 129, 373
Rubin, Robert E · 453
rural vocational schools · 279

Rural Water Resources Division · 338
Rural water supply · 126
Rusk, Dean · 223, 261
Russell · 102, 129, 161, 381
Russian Red Army · 131
Rwanda · 386

S

Saba · 271
Sabally, Kebba Ngansu · 379
Sabally, Lt Sana B · 383, 396, 423
Sabally, Saihou · 310, 371, 379, 381, 411
Sadat, Anwar · 265
Saddam Hussein · 366
Sagnia, Mamadi · 186
Sahel Development Programme · 328
Sahel, the · 257, 282, 327, 328, 329, 363
Saho, Lang · 185
Saho, Mohammadou Lamin · 220, 272, 289, 290, 310, 316
Saidy, Foday · 164
Saidy, Jay · 325, 329
Saidy, Jikiba · 164
Saidy, Tombong · 393
Saine, Amie · 408
Salikene · 370
Salim, Ahmed Salim · 365, 374
Salisbury · 251
Salla, Master M D · 81, 82, 86, 94, 95, 99, 121, 191
Sallah, Aji Fatou · 370
Sallah, Koro · 417
Salmond, Alex Elliot · 210
Saloum · 39, 207, 445
Sam Jack Terrace · 208
Samba Dawda Kairaba · 449
Samba, Amadou · 437, 444
Samba, Kelepha · 370
Samba, Rohey · 81
Samba, Yusupha · 225, 227
Sambou, Kumba · 6
Sambou, Sona · 5, 6, 431
Sandu · 5, 39, 178
Sandys, Rt Hon Duncan · 137, 242, 243, 244

Index

Sanger-Davies, Vidal Joseph · 120, 121, 149
Sanneh, Hoja · 440
Sanneh, Jallow · 12, 13, 69, 83, 92, 96, 134, 220, 291, 322, 326, 366, 404, 424
Sanneh, Kaba · 198
Sanneh, Karamo · 203
Sanneh, Saikou Dandanba · 447
Sanneh-Bojang, Nyimasata · 362
Sanoh, Alhaji Kalifa · 341
Sanyang, Fabakary · 203
Sanyang, Kukoi Samba · 134, 258, 310, 311, 314, 321, 371, 400
SAP · 374
Sar, Gabriel Alexandre · 386
Sarahule · 28, 59, 77, 108, 295
Sarbib, Jean Louis · 393
Sare Ngai · 12, 44
Sarkis Madi · 8, 9, 90
Sarr, Marie · 5, 150, 155
Sarr, Muhammed · 445
Sarr, Sam J O · 103
Sarre, Ambassador Masamba · 386
Saudi Arabia, Kingdom of · 126, 256, 322, 373, 408
Saudi Sahel Rural Water Supply Programme · 339
Savage, Francis A J · 167, 235
Sawyer, Dr Amos · 367
Scandinavia · 264, 387
scarecrows · 50
Schmidt, Chancellor Helmut · 263
scholarship committee · 138, 145, 148, 149
science of the telephone · 77
Science School · 116, 121, 149
Scotland · 153, 158, 163, 165, 166, 377
Scottish Academy of Music · 160
Scottish country dances · 111
Scottish National Party · 210
secco · 2, 10, 23, 25, 35, 45, 91, 112, 161
Second Agricultural Development Project · 337
Second Education Policy · 339
Second Five Year Development Plan · 327, 329

Second World War · 102, 131, 223, 373
Security Council · 248, 266, 282, 305, 427
Sekou, Karang · 13
selective mandatory sanctions · 266
Selety · 311
self-determination · 137, 212, 220, 228, 239, 242, 256, 300, 455, 456
self-government · 152, 201, 212, 216, 221, 233, 234, 237, 239, 271, 412
self-help basis · 294
self-reliance · 110, 206, 226, 228, 239, 240, 293, 339
self-reliance, collective · 257, 350
Seligson, Eva · 298
Semega-Janneh, B O · 358, 406
Semega-Janneh, Hatib B · 235
Semega-Janneh, Howsoon · 187
Senegal River · 353
Senegalese High Commission · 305, 310, 312, 314, 315
Senegalo-Gambia cooperation · 300, 301, 302, 305, 312, 350
Senegalo-Gambian Secretariat · 302, 305, 312
Senghor, Diamacoune · 352
Senghor, Leopold Sedar · 116, 210, 225, 241, 259, 267, 300, 301, 302, 303, 305, 306, 307, 343, 344, 406
Senghore, Abdoulie · 193
Senghore, T G G · 235
Senghore, Therese · 440
Senior Civil Servants, the · 220
Senior, Norah · 109, 111
separation of powers · 272, 294
Serekunda · 209, 311, 338, 341, 424
Sesay, Amadu · 445
Sey, Omar · 321, 357, 366, 383
Shakespeare, William · 111, 191
Shephard, Gillian · 377
Sierra Leone · 29, 51, 76, 122, 154, 199, 212, 219, 226, 255, 276, 282, 307, 328, 359, 404, 423, 450, 455
Sikko Gambia · 209
Sikko music · 209
Sillah, Amie · 362
Sillah, Bajen Awa · 184

500

Index

Sillah, Sering Modou · 74, 80, 193, 388
Simms, Kathleen · 417
Sine, Kingdom of · 85
Singh, Manmohan · 360
Singhateh, Saffiatou · 111
Singhateh, Sir Farimang · 209, 244
Singhatey, Lt Edward · 382
Sir John Moore Barracks · 417
Sirleaf, Ellen Johnson · 374
Sisay, Seyfo Sekouba · 61, 88
Sisay, Sheriff Sekouba · 61, 128, 186, 209, 217, 221, 243, 269, 274, 345
Sise, Seyfo Matarr · 203
Sissoho, S M · 235
Six Day War, the · 265, 281
Sleight, Dr D F · 279
slogan, the national · 294
Small, Edward Francis · 25, 152
Smiling Coast · 264
Smith, Ian · 253, 268
Smith, Kenneth G · 212, 220
SOBEA · 338
socialism · 206
Sokone · 98
Soma · 375
Somono tribesmen · 41
Sonko, Captain · 379
Sonko, Landing · 203
Sonko, Landing Jallow · 383, 419, 424
Sonko, Seyfo Landing Sali · 198
Sorbonne · 262
SOS Kinderdorf · 333
South Africa · 252, 254, 263, 266, 268, 278, 282, 308, 363, 374, 446
South West Africa · 266
Southern, Sir Thomas · 105
South-South cooperation · 257, 351
South-South dialogue · 352, 360
Soviet imperialism · 223
Sowe, Imam Omar · 97
Soyinka, Wole · 445
Spain · 353
Special Air Service (SAS) troopers · 312
Special Criminal Court · 331
Spencer, Lady Diana · 309
Spooner, A C · 167, 168
St Cuthbert's Church · 182, 183

Staff Site, No 3 · 170
Standard Chartered Bank · 407, 439
Standby Arrangement · 333
Standing Mediation Committee · 365
State Department and Amnesty International · 427
State House · 133, 269, 310, 325, 329, 355, 370, 379, 381, 393, 430, 444
state of emergency · 323, 363
status in the Organisation of the Senegal River Basin States · 302
Steel, H · 243
Stevens, Siaka · 406
Stoneleigh · 377
Stradivarius · 160
strange farmers · 39, 46, 47, 125, 161
Strategic Political Alliance · 402
Strategies for Peace Programme · 409
Structural Adjustment Credit · 335
structural adjustment programme · 261, 280, 359, 393
sub-regional cooperation · 226
subsistence credit · 327
Sudan · 22, 174, 212, 455
Sukoh, Sira · 11, 21
Sukur · 59
Sukuta · 21, 79, 338, 341
Sullivan, Dr Leon · 374
summit of wisdom · 249
Sunderland flying boats · 133, 289
Super Eagles Band · 303
superpower politics · 282
Supreme Islamic Council · 444
Surprise Symphony · 161
survival techniques · 75
Sussex · 77, 309, 406, 417, 421
Swanzy, Kaw · 226, 227
Sweden · 322, 417
Switzerland · 254, 259, 446
Sy, Seydina · 302
Sylla, Cheikh · 356

T

Taal, Ebou M · 236
Tafsir · 193

Taif · 256
Taiwan · 255, 266, 277, 383
Taiwan rice growing programme · 277
Taiwanese rice mission · 279
talking films · 108, 109
Tambacounda · 98
Tambo, Oliver · 363
Tanzania · 223, 268
Taylor, Charles · 366, 368
TCRV · 175, 176
Telegraph, The · 158
Tendaba · 141, 228
Tenerife · 291, 411, 413, 436
tenets of democratic governance · 263
terms of world · 252
Tesito · 80, 110, 206, 293, 294, 295
Tesito Farms · 80
Texaco · 350
Thailand · 130, 351
Thakur, Jaipaul · 433
Thatcher, Margaret · 312, 378, 409
Thiam, Doudou · 225
Thomas, Anna Francess · 362
Thomson, Sir Adam · 161, 407
Timbuktu · 4
Tinghai, Lin · 368
Tokyo · 254
Touray, Abdoulie M · 383
Touray, Baba · 187
Touray, Ebou · 74
Touray, Ebrima M, see also ET · 77
Touray, Famara Wassa · 197, 202, 243, 290
Touray, Imam Sankung · 447
Touray, Lang · 447
Touray, Sambunanding · 439
Touray, Sarjo · 383
Touray, Tijan · 434, 437
Touré, Sekou · 211, 256, 268
tourism industry · 240, 246, 337
Towards the ECOWAS Framework for Conflict Prevention · 445
trading posts · 1, 8, 55
training and empowerment of women · 111
Transatlantic Slave Trade · 298
Trans-border trade · 356

transfer of technology · 289
Trans-Gambia Highway · 301
Traore, Moussa · 367
Traoré, Niolo · 365
Travel Advice · 396, 398
travel ban · 398, 427
travelling commissioners · 7
treachery · 58, 214, 215
Treaty of, Association, 1967 · 302
Treaty of Friendship · 304, 357
Treaty of Mutual Defence · 304
Treaty on the Non-Proliferation of Nuclear Weapons · 254
tree planting · 43, 328
treks · 126, 174
Treleaven, Mrs · 115
Trinidad · 117
Tripoli · 256, 321, 391
Trophée Lancome International Pro-am · 332
trypanosomiasis · 259
Tsitsiwu, William · 161
Tumana · 274, 371
Tunisia · 268, 376
Turkish Gendarmerie Training Team (TGTT) · 373
Turner, Ted · 453
Twelfth Night · 111
Twin Towers · 427
two-China policy · 266

U

U Thant · 301, 305
UAC · 23, 94
UDI regime · 268
UGCC · 150, 152
ULIMO · 376
ultra-democratic system · 272
UN Charter · 165
UN Convention on the Elimination of All Forms of Discrimination Against Women · 361
UN Convention on the Rights and Welfare of the Child · 366
UNCD · 126

UNCDF/UNDP · 338
unconditional amnesty · 433
UNDP · 126, 194, 374, 397, 400, 450
UNESCO · 125, 205, 279
UNHCR · 385
UNICEF · 366
Unilateral Declaration of Independence · 253
United Democratic Party · 399
United Gold Coast Convention · 150
United Kingdom · 47, 157, 228, 236, 239, 241, 243, 248
universal adult suffrage · 127, 203, 205
universal primary education · 279, 377
University of East Africa · 259
University of Glasgow · 122, 163, 377
University of Ibadan · 262
University of Liverpool · 115, 120
University of Newcastle · 117, 154, 190
United Party · 185, 200, 203, 207, 210, 214, 217, 224, 227, 272, 399
Upper Baddibu · 176, 187
US Navy training exercise · 381
USA · 228, 255, 261, 265, 279, 328, 348, 362, 387, 403, 421, 445, 452
USAID · 302, 389
USS La Moure County · 380, 381, 382, 441
Utilities Holding Company · 293

V

V Q Petersen Co Ltd · 66
Van Mook, Hubertus · 301
VE Day · 129
Versailles · 332
Veterinary School · 159, 163, 174
Vezia · 23
VHF Radio · 199
Vichy forces · 103, 109
Vichy Government · 66
Vieira, Joao Bernardo · 315, 321, 365, 367, 395
Vietnam · 130, 266
Viggio Quistgaard Petersen Company · 286

village credit systems · 293
village development committees · 48, 293
Villiers, Michael · 414
VISACA · 304
vocational education · 124, 339
vocational training · 304
Vocational Training Centre, The · 125
Volta River · 45
Vom · 175, 176
VSO scheme · 280

W

Wadda, Mustapha B · 106
Wade, Abdoulaye · 348, 385, 418
Wadner Beach · 263
Waistel, Kipling · 387, 410
Wales · 78, 99, 117, 154, 158
Walikunda · 2, 5, 9, 21, 26, 29, 34, 46, 51, 56, 58, 62, 67, 75, 89, 99, 107, 138, 142, 147, 161, 195, 286, 447
Wally, Dodou · 79, 150
Walshe, Sam L H · 166, 169, 170, 172
Walter Suskind · 160
WAMU · 347, 350
Wang Jiaji · 378
War Office · 129, 141
Warsaw · 101
Washington · 34, 248, 256, 261, 288, 359, 375, 381, 392, 393, 397, 442
Water Supply Project · 338
Weipers, Prof William L · 377
Weismann Institute of Science at Rehoboth · 264
Welfare Grants · 286
Wellington Street · 14, 32, 61, 66, 74, 79, 93, 109, 138, 143, 155, 165, 190, 195, 239, 289, 388, 436, 447
West Cliff Hotel · 448
Wesleyan Mission · 25
West Africa Air Corps · 136
West African College of Surgeons · 405
West African Currency Board · 146, 290
West African Parliamentary Workshop on Children · 366

Index

West Bank · 265
West Germany · 228, 254, 332
Western Allies · 101
White, R K M · 235
WHO · 115, 122, 322, 376, 443
Wilds of Africa · 363
William the Conqueror · 81
Williams, F D C · 243
Williams, Julia · 204
Williams, Master J E · 76, 80, 81, 93, 95, 96, 98, 100, 156
Wilson, Harold · 165, 251, 409
Wilson, Master J D O · 76, 81
Windley, Governor Edward · 81, 188, 189, 198, 200, 201, 203, 207, 209, 210, 224
Winter, Andrew · 380, 381
Wirth, Timothy E · 453
Wisehart, Prof G M · 164
Woewiyu, Tom · 366
Wolfe, Mrs · 120
Wollof · 13, 24, 57, 69, 108, 129, 345
Women in Development · 361
World Assembly of Muslim Youth · 440
World Bank · 47, 261, 335, 338, 340, 359, 361, 375, 377, 393, 397
world economic order · 360
World Festival of Negro Arts in Dakar · 259
World Food Programme · 256, 322, 329
world recession · 278, 291
World Trade Center · 427
World Veterinary Association · 258
World War I · 114, 131, 133, 230
Wright, Governor Andrew · 67
Wright, Kenneth · 347, 349
Wright, Lilly Mama Buxton · 361
Wuli · 178
Wyn-Harris Constitution, the · 127, 185, 202
Wyn-Harris, Governor Percy · 170, 192

Y

Y2K · 415, 418
Ya Amie Gaye · 69, 75, 90, 143, 147, 166
Ya Awa Sillah · 74, 75
Ya Fatou Jobarteh · 13, 15, 17, 27, 36, 54, 55, 56, 57, 59, 63, 69, 75, 130, 155, 156, 190
Ya Fatou Kess · 27
Ya Mariam Jallow · 97
Ya Njaimeh Mboge · 302
Ya Sai Njie · 155
Yafa, Momodou Lamin · 12
Yagninim, Bitokotipou · 365
Yaker, Layahsi · 374
Yakubu Gowon · 442
Yar'Adua, Umaru Musa · 451
Yerroberikunda · 169, 178, 190

Yidda · 88
Yoff · 302
Young, Mr and Mrs Arthur · 162
Yugoslavia · 356
Yundum Airport · 241, 285, 286, 288, 311, 314, 332
Yundum Barracks · 349, 362
Yundum College · 81
Yundum Teacher Training College · 285

Z

Zanzibar · 159, 162
Zenawi, Meles · 373
Ziguinchor · 303, 305, 306
Zimbabwe · 249, 268, 282, 368
Zimbabwe African National Union · 268